AN ESSAY CONCERNING

HUMAN UNDERSTANDING

BY

JOHN LOCKE

COLLATED AND ANNOTATED, WITH

PROLEGOMENA, BIOGRAPHICAL, CRITICAL, AND HISTORICAL

BY

ALEXANDER CAMPBELL FRASER

IN TWO VOLUMES

VOL. II

DOVER PUBLICATIONS, INC.
NEW YORK • NEW YORK

Published in Canada by General Publishing Company, Ltd., 30 Lesmill Road, Don Mills, Toronto, Ontario.

Published in the United Kingdom by Constable and Company, Ltd., 10 Orange Street, London WC 2.

This new Dover edition first published in 1959 is an unabridged and unaltered republication of the First Edition. It is published through special arrangement with Oxford University Press.

International Standard Book Number: 0-486-20531-2
Library of Congress Catalog Card Number: 59-3771

Manufactured in the United States of America

Dover Publications, Inc.
180 Varick Street
New York 14, New York

CONTENTS

OF

THE SECOND VOLUME

————•◆•————

AN ESSAY CONCERNING HUMAN UNDERSTANDING.

BOOK III.

OF WORDS.

BOOK IV.

OF KNOWLEDGE AND PROBABILITY.

BOOK III

OF WORDS

SYNOPSIS OF THE THIRD BOOK.

AFTER teaching in the Second Book that the only ideas to which a human mind can attain are composed of simple ideas or phenomena, presented in 'sensation' and 'reflection,' as attributes of substances; and that even our loftiest thoughts are concerned only with the modes of those phenomena, the substances in which they appear, and their relations—Locke, in the Third Book, supplements this teaching, by unfolding the connexion between ideas of each sort and verbal signs, on which ideas depend, words being means for enabling men to regard ideas, in themselves particular, as general or universal (ch. iii). The names of simple ideas and of their simple modes; the names of mixed modes and of relations; and the names of the different sorts of substances, have each something peculiar, regarded as signs of ideas (chh. iv, v, vi). All names of simple ideas and of ideas of substances 'intimate real existence'; but the common names of simple ideas signify the real essence, as well as the nominal, of the qualities that the names stand for, while the common names of substances can express only the nominal essence of the species within which men place the substance. Names of mixed modes, again, and of all ideas of relation, signify only the essences that men have annexed to the names. Simple ideas, moreover, are undefinable, and their names are of all others the least liable to ambiguity. Mixed modes, on the other hand, being formed arbitrarily by men, and sometimes very complex, their names are apt to be used ambiguously, on account of this complexity, and also because they have no absolute standard. The common names of substances, the most important of all, are determined by our limited experience of qualities, and can signify therefore only the connotation we have annexed to the names, not the real essence of the particular substances denoted. On the whole, words are naturally imperfect signs of ideas (ch. ix), especially of mixed modes, and above all of substances; and this natural imperfection of words is aggravated by 'wilful faults and neglects' of which men are guilty when they employ them, some of which are illustrated in detail (ch. x). The Book closes (ch. xi) with an account of five 'remedies' for the 'inconveniences' caused by the natural and acquired imperfection of language.

ESSAY

CONCERNING

HUMAN UNDERSTANDING

————

BOOK III.

————

CHAPTER I.

OF WORDS OR LANGUAGE IN GENERAL.

1. GOD, having designed man for a sociable creature, made him not only with an inclination, and under a necessity to have fellowship with those of his own kind, but furnished him also with language, which was to be the great instrument and common tie of society. Man, therefore, had by nature his organs so fashioned, as to be fit to frame articulate sounds, which we call words. But this was not enough to produce language; for parrots, and several other birds, will be taught to make articulate sounds distinct enough, which yet by no means are capable of language.

2. Besides articulate sounds, therefore, it was further necessary that he should be able to use these sounds as signs of internal conceptions; and to make them stand as marks for the ideas within his own mind [1], whereby they might be made known to others, and the thoughts of men's minds be conveyed from one to another [2].

---

[1] That words immediately signify only his ideas who uses them, is more fully set forth in ch. ii. § 2.

[2] But words are needed not only for conveying thought from one man to another; they also enable each man to exercise his higher faculties, the development and exercise of

BOOK III.

CHAP. I.

To make them general Signs.

3. But neither was this sufficient to make words so useful as they ought to be. It is not enough for the perfection of language, that sounds can be made signs of ideas, unless those signs can be so made use of as to comprehend several particular things : for the multiplication of words would have perplexed their use, had every particular thing need of a distinct name to be signified by. [[1] To remedy this inconvenience, language had yet a further improvement in the use of *general terms*, whereby one word was made to mark a multitude of particular existences : which advantageous use of sounds was obtained only by the difference of the ideas they were made signs of : those names becoming general, which are made to stand for *general ideas*[2], and those remaining particular, where the *ideas* they are used for are *particular.*]

To make them signify the absence of positive Ideas.

4. [3] Besides these names which stand for ideas, there be other words which men make use of, not to signify any idea, but the want or absence of some ideas, simple or complex, or all ideas together ; such as are *nihil* in Latin, and in English, *ignorance* and *barrenness*. All which negative or privative words cannot be said properly to belong to, or signify no ideas : for then they would be perfectly insignificant sounds ; but they relate to positive ideas, and signify their absence[4].

Words ultimately

5. It may also lead us a little towards the original[5] of all

which depends upon the use of signs that can be perceived by the senses. Yet thought is not constituted by, nor identical with, language, which on the contrary is originated and formed by thought.

[1] Added in the second edition.

[2] 'Les termes généraux ne servent pas seulement à la perfection des langues, mais même ils sont nécessaires pour leur constitution essentielle. Car, si par les *choses particulières* on entend les individuelles, il serait impossibles de parler, s'il n'y avait que des noms *propres*, et point d'*appellatifs* ; c'est-à-dire, s'il n'y avait des mots que pour les individus.' (*Nouveaux Essais.*)

[3] In the first edition, this section commenced thus :—'Words then are made to be signs of our ideas, and are general or particular as the ideas they stand for are general or particular.' The sentence was omitted in the following editions.

[4] Cf. Bk. II. ch. viii. §§ 1-6. Negative terms are not necessarily meaningless. Some of the most important philosophical meanings are conveyed by them, e. g. 'infinite.'

[5] 'original,' i. e. origin, meaning *exordium*, — origin in the order of succession, which may be discovered in the 'historical plain' method, overlooking the logically implied conditions of percipient intelligence in the abstract.

our notions and knowledge, if we remark how great a dependence our words have on common sensible ideas; and
how those which are made use of to stand for actions and
notions quite removed from sense, have their rise from thence,
and from obvious sensible ideas are transferred to more
abstruse significations, and made to stand for ideas that come
not under the cognizance of our senses; v. g. to *imagine,
apprehend, comprehend, adhere, conceive, instil, disgust, disturbance, tranquillity,* &c., are all words taken from the operations
of sensible things, and applied to certain modes of thinking.
Spirit, in its primary signification, is breath; *angel,* a
messenger: and I doubt not but, if we could trace them to
their sources, we should find, in all languages, the names
which stand for things that fall not under our senses to have
had their first rise from sensible ideas [1]. By which we may
give some kind of guess what kind of notions they were, and
whence derived, which filled their minds who were the first
beginners of languages [2], and how nature, even in the naming
of things, unawares suggested to men the originals and
principles of all their knowledge: whilst, to give names that
might make known to others any operations they felt in
themselves, or any other ideas that came not under their
senses, they were fain to borrow words from ordinary known
ideas of sensation [3], by that means to make others the more
easily to conceive those operations they experimented in
themselves, which made no outward sensible appearances;
and then, when they had got known and agreed names to
signify those internal operations of their own minds, they
were sufficiently furnished to make known by words all their

BOOK III.
—•◦•—
CHAP. 1.
derived
from such
as signify
sensible
Ideas.

[1] This is only what might be expected, if the external ' senses precede
reflection ' in the development of a
human mind. Moreover there are
apparent exceptions. Maine de Biran
notes, that in what relates to the idea
of *power* and *causality,* the language
originally applied to the mental operations has been transferred by analogy
to the world of sense.

[2] Locke sometimes (as here) speaks
of language, and always of civil
government, as the artificial result of
contract or agreement—which became
the favourite theory in the eighteenth
century, rather than as phenomena
that have been unconsciously evolved
under natural law. See Condillac,
*Essai sur l'Origine des Connoissances
Humaines,* Second Partie, sect. pre-
mière.

[3] ' ideas of sensation,' i. e. phenomena presented to the senses by
material substances.

BOOK III.
CHAP. I.

other ideas; since they could consist of nothing but either of outward[1] sensible perceptions, or of the inward[1] operations of their minds about them; we having, as has been proved, no ideas at all, but what originally come either from sensible objects without, or what we feel within ourselves, from the inward workings of our own spirits, of which we are conscious to ourselves within.

Distribution of subjects to be treated of.

6. But to understand better the use and force of Language [2], as subservient to instruction and knowledge, it will be convenient to consider:

First, *To what it is that names, in the use of language, are immediately applied.*

Secondly, Since all (except proper) names are general, and so stand not particularly for this or that single thing, but for sorts and ranks of things, it will be necessary to consider, in the next place, what the sorts and kinds, or, if you rather like the Latin names, *what the Species and Genera of things are, wherein they consist, and how they come to be made* [3]. These being (as they ought) well looked into, we shall the better come to find the right use of words; the natural advantages and defects of language ; and the remedies that ought to be used, to avoid the inconveniences of obscurity or uncertainty in the signification of words : without which it is impossible to discourse with any clearness or order concerning knowledge : which, being conversant about propositions [4], and

---

[1] Locke throughout presupposes the distinction of ' outward ' and ' inward,' as given from the first,—the qualities and powers of extended things presented in the simple ideas of the five senses, in contrast to the operations of the ' thinking substance,' presented in our ideas of reflection. His ' simple ideas ' are virtually the recognised ' qualities ' of individual substances.

[2] Words, Coleridge says, are ' living —the wheels of the intellect; such as Ezekiel beheld in the visions of God. Whithersoever the Spirit was to go the wheels went, and thither was their Spirit to go ; for the Spirit of the living creature was in the wheels also.' (*Aids to Reflection.* Preface.)

[3] ' Abstract (general) ideas,' and their relation to words, form the chief subject of the third Book.

[4] Mental ' propositions,' or judgments, are the units of ' knowledge,' as distinguished from mere ' ideas,' which must enter into them, with which the second Book was concerned, in preparation for the theory of knowledge in the fourth Book.

those most commonly universal ones [1], has greater connexion BOOK III.
with words than perhaps is suspected.

CHAP. I.

These considerations, therefore, shall be the matter of the
following chapters [2].

---

[1] The attainment of new and true *universal* propositions, affirmative and negative, is the chief end of all purely intellectual activity; but, as the condition of its attainment, capacity for being universalised is presupposed, on the part of the things about which men reason.

[2] 'Some parts of that third Book, concerning Words, though the thoughts were easy and clear enough, yet cost me more pains to express than all the rest of my *Essay*. And therefore I shall not much wonder, if there be in some places of it obscurity and doubtfulness.' (Locke to Molyneux, Jan. 20, 1693.)

CHAPTER II.

OF THE SIGNIFICATION OF WORDS.

BOOK III.

—•◆•—

CHAP. II.

Words are
sensible
Signs,
necessary
for Com-
munication
of Ideas.

1. MAN, though he have great variety of thoughts, and such from which others as well as himself might receive profit and delight ; yet they are all within his own breast, invisible and hidden from others, nor can of themselves be made to appear. The comfort and advantage of society not being to be had without communication of thoughts, it was necessary that man should find out some external sensible signs, whereof those invisible ideas, which his thoughts are made up of, might be made known to others[1]. For this purpose nothing was so fit, either for plenty or quickness, as those articulate sounds, which with so much ease and variety he found himself able to make. Thus we may conceive how *words*, which were by nature so well adapted to that purpose, came to be made use of by men as the signs of their ideas ; not by any natural connexion that there is between particular articulate sounds and certain ideas, for then there would be but one language amongst all men ; but by a voluntary imposition, whereby such a word is made arbitrarily[2] the mark of such an idea.

[1] Leibniz (*Nouveaux Essais*) dwells on the illustration the peculiar genius of a people receives from the qualities which they select, as the basis of their classifications of things. Topographical nomenclatures are largely determined by this consideration. See Prof. Veitch's *Border History and Poetry*, pp. 16–18.

[2] Locke's tendency to see in language the issue of *arbitrary contract* (*ex instituto*) rather than of spontaneous evolution, determined under natural laws, does not necessarily imply that the connexion of an idea with a particular sign is other than arbitrary. This is proved by the fact of a plurality of languages. Locke's emphatic recognition of 'arbitrariness' in this connexion probably suggested Berkeley's metaphor of a divine visual language, and his favourite conception of the 'arbitrariness' of all natural laws.

The use, then, of words, is to be sensible marks of ideas ; and the ideas they stand for are their proper and immediate signification.

2. The use men have of these marks being either to record their own thoughts, for the assistance of their own memory [1]; or, as it were, to bring out their ideas [2], and lay them before the view of others : words, in their primary or immediate signification, stand for nothing but *the ideas in the mind of him that uses them*, how imperfectly soever or carelessly those ideas are collected from the things which they are supposed to represent [3]. When a man speaks to another, it is that he may be understood : and the end of speech is, that those sounds, as marks, may make known his ideas to the hearer. That then which words are the marks of are the ideas of the speaker : nor can any one apply them as marks, immediately, to anything else but the ideas that he himself hath : for this would be to make them signs of his own conceptions, and yet apply them to other ideas ; which would be to make them signs and not signs of his ideas at the same time ; and so in effect to have no signification at all. Words being voluntary signs, they cannot be voluntary signs imposed by him on things he knows not. That would be to make them signs of nothing, sounds without signification. A man cannot make

[1] Not only, nor chiefly, ' memory,' —indispensable to the activity of discursive reason. ' The concept formed by an abstraction of the re-sembling from the non-resembling qualities of objects, would again fall back into the confusion and infinitude from which it has been called out, were it not rendered permanent for consciousness by being fixed and rati-fied in a verbal sign.' (Hamilton.) But Locke is apt to disparage generalisation as no more than a means for relieving memory; and to suspect ' generalities,' as a hindrance to observation of the properties and powers of individual things.

[2] ' bring out their ideas,' i. e. com-municate them to other men—' assist-ance of their own memory,' and communication of ideas to others, being thus the two uses of language here noted.

[3] In representing words as, ' in their *primary* or *immediate* significa-tion,' signs of ' his *ideas* who uses them,' Locke does not exclude the beliefs and knowledge of him who uses them—belief and knowledge presup-posing ideas. Each man's words represent things, as they are regarded by his individual mind. Cf. Hobbes, *Computation or Logic*, ch. ii. § 5; also Mill's *Logic*, Bk. I. ch. ii. § 1. When Locke speaks of words as signs of ideas, it must be remembered that his ' ideas' include perceived pheno-mena (' simple ideas ') presented by substances, in external and internal sense.

his words the signs either of qualities in things, or of conceptions in the mind of another, whereof he has none in his own.
Till he has some ideas of his own, he cannot suppose them to
correspond with the conceptions of another man ; nor can he
use any signs for them : for thus they would be the signs of
he knows not what, which is in truth to be the signs of nothing.
But when he represents to himself other men's ideas by some
of his own, if he consent to give them the same names that
other men do, it is still to his own ideas ; to ideas that he has,
and not to ideas that he has not.

Examples
of this.
3. This is so necessary in the use of language, that in this
respect the knowing and the ignorant, the learned and the
unlearned, use the words they speak (with any meaning) all
alike. They, in every man's mouth, stand for the ideas he
has, and which he would express by them. A child having
taken notice of nothing in the metal he hears called *gold*,
but the bright shining yellow colour, he applies the word
gold only to his own idea of that colour, and nothing else ;
and therefore calls the same colour in a peacock's tail gold.
Another that hath better observed, adds to shining yellow
great weight : and then the sound gold, when he uses it,
stands for a complex idea of a shining yellow and a very
weighty substance. Another adds to those qualities fusibility :
and then the word gold signifies to him a body, bright,
yellow, fusible, and very heavy. Another adds malleability.
Each of these uses equally the word gold, when they have
occasion to express the idea which they have applied it to :
but it is evident that each can apply it only to his own idea ;
nor can he make it stand as a sign of such a complex idea as
he has not.

Words are
often
secretly
referred,
First to
the Ideas
supposed
to be in
other
men's
minds.
4. But though words, as they are used by men, can
properly and immediately signify nothing but the ideas that
are in the mind of the speaker ; yet they in their thoughts
give them a secret reference to two other things.

First, *They suppose their words to be marks of the ideas
in the minds also of other men, with whom they communicate* : for else they should talk in vain, and could not be
understood, if the sounds they applied to one idea were such
as by the hearer were applied to another, which is to speak

two languages. But in this men stand not usually to ex-amine, whether the idea they, and those they discourse with have in their minds be the same : but think it enough that they use the word, as they imagine, in the common accepta-tion of that language ; in which they suppose that the idea they make it a sign of is precisely the same to which the understanding men of that country apply that name.

5. Secondly, Because men would not be thought to talk barely of their own imagination [1], but of things as really they are ; therefore they often suppose the *words to stand also for the reality of things* [2]. But this relating more particularly to substances and their names, as perhaps the former does to simple ideas and modes, we shall speak of these two different ways of applying words more at large, when we come to treat of the names of mixed modes and substances in particular : though give me leave here to say, that it is a perverting the use of words, and brings unavoidable obscurity and confusion into their signification, whenever we make them stand for anything but those ideas we have in our own minds.

6. Concerning words, also, it is further to be considered : First, that they being immediately the signs of men's ideas, and by that means the instruments whereby men com-municate their conceptions, and express to one another those thoughts and imaginations they have within their own breasts; there comes, by constant use, to be such a connexion between certain sounds and the ideas they stand for, that the names heard, almost as readily excite certain ideas as if the objects themselves, which are apt to produce them, did actually affect the senses. Which is manifestly so in all obvious sensible qualities, and in all substances that frequently and familiarly occur to us.

7. Secondly, That though the proper and immediate signi-fication of words are ideas in the mind of the speaker, yet,

[1] Locke's 'simple ideas'—always assumed by him to be other than 'bare imaginations,' or subjective fancies.

[2] Which Hobbes denies. It is manifest, he says, that words 'are not the signs of the things themselves;

for that the sound of the word *stone* should be the sign of a stone, cannot be understood in any sense but this— that he that hears it collects that he that pronounces it thinks of a stone.' (*Logic*, ch. ii. § 5.)

BOOK III.

CHAP. II.

Significa-
tion, and
why.

because by familiar use from our cradles, we come to learn certain articulate sounds very perfectly, and have them readily on our tongues, and always at hand in our memories, but yet are not always careful to examine or settle their significations perfectly[1]; it often happens that men, even when they would apply themselves to an attentive consider-ation, do set their thoughts more on words than things. Nay, because words are many of them learned before the ideas are known for which they stand: therefore some, not only children but men, speak several words no otherwise than parrots do, only because they have learned them, and have been accustomed to those sounds. But so far as words are of use and signification, so far is there a constant connexion between the sound and the idea, and a designation that the one stands for the other; without which application of them, they are nothing but so much insignificant noise.

Their
Significa-
tion
perfectly
arbitrary,
not the
conse-
quence of
a natural
connexion.

8. Words, by long and familiar use, as has been said, come to excite in men certain ideas so constantly and readily, that they are apt to suppose a natural connexion between them. But that they signify only men's peculiar ideas, and that *by a perfect arbitrary imposition*[2], is evident, in that they often fail to excite in others (even that use the same language) the same ideas we take them to be signs of : and every man has so inviolable a liberty to make words stand for what ideas he pleases, that no one hath the power to make others have the same ideas in their minds that he has, when they use the same words that he does. And therefore the great Augustus himself, in the possession of that power which ruled the world, acknowledged he could not make a new Latin word: which was as much as to say, that he could not arbitrarily appoint what idea any sound should be a sign of,

[1] This is what Leibniz called 'sym-bolical,' in contrast to 'intuitive' thought; in which the verbal symbol is substituted for the sensuous image. Cf. Hume's *Treatise*, pt. i. sect. 7; Stewart's *Elements*, ch. iv. sect. 2, on the analogy of ordinary language, so substituted, to signs in Algebra.

[2] Hence by analogy Bacon's *naturae*

interpretatio ; and Berkeley's metaphor of a 'language' of sense, in virtue of which nature is *interpretable* — the orderliness of its sequences being an expression of the supreme rational Will, which the terms of the sequence signify as words signify their mean-ings by the arbitrary appointment of men.

in the mouths and common language of his subjects.   It is
true, common use, by a tacit consent, appropriates certain
sounds to certain ideas in all languages, which so far limits
the signification of that sound, that unless a man applies it
to the same idea, he does not speak properly : and let me
add, that unless a man's words excite the same ideas in the
hearer which he makes them stand for in speaking, he does
not speak intelligibly.   But whatever be the consequence of
any man's using of words differently, either from their general
meaning, or the particular sense of the person to whom he
addresses them ; this is certain, their signification, in his use
of them, is limited to his ideas, and they can be signs of
nothing else [1].

[1] ' Let us consider the false appearances that are imposed upon us by words, which are framed and applied according to the conceit and capacities of the vulgar sort : and although we think we govern our words, and prescribe it well, *Loquendum ut vulgus, sentiendum ut sapientes*; yet certain it is that words, as a Tartar's bow, do shoot back upon the understanding of the wisest, and mightily entangle and pervert the judgment.   So that it is almost necessary, in all controversies and disputations, to imitate the wisdom of the mathematicians, in setting down in the very beginning the definitions of our words and terms, that others may know how *we* accept and understand them, and whether they concur with us or no.   For it cometh to pass, for want of this, that we are sure to end there where we ought to have begun, which is—in questions and differences about words.'   (Bacon, *Advancement of Learning*, Bk. II.)

CHAPTER III.

OF GENERAL TERMS.

BOOK III.

Chap. III.
The greatest Part of Words are general terms.
1. ALL things that exist being particulars, it may perhaps be thought reasonable that words, which ought to be conformed to things, should be so too,—I mean in their signification : but yet we find quite the contrary. The far greatest part of words that make all languages are general terms : which has not been the effect of neglect or chance, but of reason and necessity.

2. First, It is impossible that every particular thing should have a distinct peculiar name. For, the signification and use of words depending on that connexion which the mind makes between its ideas and the sounds it uses as signs of them, it is necessary, in the application of names to things, that the mind should have distinct ideas of the things, and retain also the particular name that belongs to every one, with its peculiar appropriation to that idea. But it is beyond the power of human capacity to frame and retain distinct ideas of all the particular things we meet with : every bird and beast men saw ; every tree and plant that affected the senses, could not find a place in the most capacious understanding. If it be looked on as an instance of a prodigious memory, that some generals have been able to call every soldier in their army by his proper name, we may easily find a reason why men have never attempted to give names to each sheep in their flock, or crow that flies over their heads ; much less to call every leaf of plants, or grain of sand that came in their way, by a peculiar name [1].

---

[1] Locke, here and elsewhere, speaks of 'general terms' as needed only to save excessive multiplication of proper names. ' Now it is so far from being

3. Secondly, If it were possible, it would yet be useless ; because it would not serve to the chief end of language. Men would in vain heap up names of particular things, that would not serve them to communicate their thoughts. Men learn names, and use them in talk with others, only that they may be understood : which is then only done when, by use or consent, the sound I make by the organs of speech, excites in another man's mind who hears it, the idea I apply it to in mine, when I speak it. This cannot be done by names applied to particular things ; whereof I alone having the ideas in my mind, the names of them could not be significant or intelligible to another, who was not acquainted with all those very particular things which had fallen under my notice [1].

4. Thirdly, But yet, granting this also feasible, (which I think is not,) yet a distinct name for every particular thing would not be of any great use for the improvement of know- ledge : which, though founded in particular things, enlarges itself by general views [2] ; to which things reduced into sorts, under general names, are properly subservient. These, with the names belonging to them, come within some compass,

true that general names are only make- shifts for an infinite number of proper names, that even the possession of an infinite store of such names would not enable us to think one jot, or to frame a single sentence. Each object being a mere particular, no occasion for predication could arise. . . . The in- finite number of proper names would be like so many *unmeaning* numerical marks put upon absolutely non-resem- bling objects. We cannot say of five that it is six, or of any one number that it is another number.' (Prof. Seth's *Scottish Philosophy,* p. 169.) Thus, as Plato shows in his Theætetus, philo- sophical nominalism refutes itself. From the moment of its first imposition for a reason upon any one object, a name is *potentially* the name of a class. It is from the first a general term, a universal, though it may chance to be applied to only one individual.

It is from the beginning capable of extension to other individuals found to possess the like qualities.

[1] The unintelligibility, for the pur- pose of conveying meaning from one mind into another, of a language which contained only proper names, is an obvious, but not the most significant, explanation of the fact, that, while the things that actually exist are par- ticular, most of our words are general, and the chief function of language is connected with generality.

[2] That generality, and ultimately universality, is of the essence of knowledge, explains why most terms are general ; not the impossibility of sufficient economy of language if proper names exclusively were used. Moreover capacity for being thus subjects of predication is implied in *things* being even perceivable in sense.

and do not multiply every moment, beyond what either the mind can contain, or use requires.   And therefore, in these[1], men have for the most part stopped : but yet not so as to hinder themselves from distinguishing particular things by appropriated[2] names, where convenience demands it.   And therefore in their own species, which they have most to do with, and wherein they have often occasion to mention particular persons, they make use of proper names; and there distinct individuals have distinct denominations.

What things have proper Names, and why.

5. Besides persons, countries also, cities, rivers, mountains, and other the like distinctions of place have usually found peculiar names, and that for the same reason ; they being such as men have often an occasion to mark particularly, and, as it were, set before others in their discourses with them.   And I doubt not but, if we had reason to mention particular horses as often as we have to mention particular men, we should have proper names for the one, as familiar as for the other, and Bucephalus would be a word as much in use as Alexander. And therefore we see that, amongst jockeys, horses have their proper names to be known and distinguished by, as commonly as their servants : because, amongst them, there is often occasion to mention this or that particular horse when he is out of sight.

How general Words are made.

6. The next thing to be considered is,—How general words come to be made.   For, since all things that exist are only particulars[3], how come we by general terms ; or where find we those general natures they are supposed to stand for[4]? Words become general by being made the signs of general ideas : and ideas[5] become general, by separating from them

---

[1] 'these,' i. e. in general names.

[2] ' appropriated,' i. e. proper names.

[3] The unreality of universals, and the reality of individual substances *only,* is one of Locke's reiterated assumptions.   In this and in the sixth chapter, we have some of his chief statements about 'abstract ideas.' (See also Bk. II. ch. xi. §§ 10, 11 ; Bk. IV. ch. vii. § 9.

[4] By so-called Realists, who hold to the substantial reality of universal natures, existing either *ante res* or *in rebus* ; not, as Locke held, only in the ideas of individual men, i. e. *post res.*

[5] All ideas, according to Locke, are particular : knowledge is perception, of relations among particular ideas ; generality or universality being accidental to it—when the particular ideas happen in fact to represent more than one thing.

the circumstances of time and place, and any other ideas that may determine them to this or that particular existence[1]. By this way of abstraction they are made capable of representing more individuals than one; each of which having in it a conformity to that abstract idea[2], is (as we call it) of that sort.

7. But, to deduce this a little more distinctly, it will not perhaps be amiss to trace our notions and names from their beginning, and observe by what degrees we proceed, and by what steps we enlarge our ideas from our first infancy. There is nothing more evident, than that the ideas of the persons children converse with (to instance in them alone) are, like the persons themselves, only particular[3]. The ideas of the nurse and the mother are well framed in their minds; and, like pictures of them there, represent only those individuals. The names they first gave to them are confined to these individuals; and the names of *nurse* and *mamma*, the child uses, determine themselves to those persons. Afterwards, when time and a larger acquaintance have made them observe that there are a great many other things in the world, that in some common agreements of shape, and several other qualities, resemble their father and mother, and those persons they have been used to, they frame an idea, which they find those many particulars do partake in; and to that they give, with others, the name *man*, for example. And thus they come to have

---

[1] In annexing words to abstract ideas or notions, intelligence transcends sense and sensuous imagination, which is limited to what is concrete or particular, presented or represented as placed and dated. Man's power to do this is one of the most obtrusive illustrations of the fact, that sense is inadequate to intellect,—the merely animal to the spiritual.

[2] What Locke calls an 'abstract idea' is called by some logicians a *concept*, in contrast to a concrete image. The limitation of the term *idea* to what is imaginable, is at the root of Berkeley's rejection of Locke's 'abstract ideas'; which, however, he accepts under another name, after clearly demonstrating that they cannot be formed in the sensuous imagination. (See *Principles of Human Knowledge*, Introd. § 16.) Locke calls all 'general' ideas ('concepts') *abstract*, because they all presuppose abstraction, or withdrawal of attention, from the qualities in which things differ, in order to concentrate attention upon those in which they agree, and which constitute the concept. Abstraction is one of the functions of Locke's 'discerning faculty.' Cf. Bk. II. ch. xi. §§ 9, 10.

[3] They are complex ideas of this or that particular substance.

BOOK III.
Chap. III.

a general name, and a general idea. Wherein they make nothing new; but only leave out of the complex idea they had of Peter and James, Mary and Jane, that which is peculiar to each, and retain only what is common to them all[1].

And further enlarge our complex ideas, by still leaving out properties contained in them.

8. By the same way that they come by the general name and idea of *man*, they easily advance to more general names and notions. For, observing that several things that differ from their idea of man, and cannot therefore be comprehended under that name, have yet certain qualities wherein they agree with man, by retaining only those qualities, and uniting them into one idea, they have again another and more general idea; to which having given a name they make a term of a more comprehensive extension[2]: which new idea is made, not by any new addition, but only as before, by leaving out the shape, and some other properties signified by the name man, and retaining only a body, with life, sense, and spontaneous motion, comprehended under the name animal[3].

General natures are nothing but abstract and partial ideas of more complex ones.

9. That this is the way whereby men first formed general ideas, and general names to them, I think is so evident, that there needs no other proof of it but the considering of a man's self, or others, and the ordinary proceedings of their minds in knowledge. And he that thinks *general natures* or *notions* are anything else but such abstract and partial ideas of more complex ones, taken at first from particular existences, will, I fear, be at a loss where to find them. For let any one

[1] Condillac comments on this passage, in his *Essai sur l' Origine des Connoissances Humaines*, Section cinquième, in the spirit of his analysis of knowledge, even in its highest generality, into *sensations transformees*, and his interpretation of Locke in correspondence with this.

[2] 'Extension.' The *extensive* quantity of an abstract or general idea is measured by the number of less extensive ideas which can enter into it, in contrast to its (so-called, but not by Locke) *comprehensive* quantity, which is measured by the number of attributes it contains, forming the connotation of its name. This now familiar logical antithesis Locke may have taken from his favourite *Port Royal Logic*, Pt. I. ch. vi.

[3] Our inability to *imagine* what we are able, in these processes, to have an *abstract notion* of, was afterwards shown conclusively by Berkeley, who did not thereby prove that we cannot form what Locke means by an abstract idea. He only proves that abstract ideas are not sensuous imaginations, and that our power of forming them implies possession of higher faculties than the one of sense.

effect, and then tell me, wherein does his idea of *man* differ
from that of *Peter* and *Paul,* or his idea of *horse* from that of
Bucephalus, but in the leaving out something that is peculiar
to each individual, and retaining so much of those particular
complex ideas of several particular existences as they are
found to agree in[1]? Of the complex ideas signified by the
names *man* and *horse,* leaving out but those particulars
wherein they differ, and retaining only those wherein they
agree, and of those making a new distinct complex idea, and
giving the name *animal* to it, one has a more general term,
that comprehends with man several other creatures. Leave
out of the idea of *animal,* sense and spontaneous motion, and
the remaining complex idea, made up of the remaining simple
ones of body, life, and nourishment, becomes a more general
one, under the more comprehensive term, *vivens.* And, not to
dwell longer upon this particular, so evident in itself; by the
same way the mind proceeds to *body, substance,* and at last to
being, thing, and such universal terms, which stand for any of
our ideas whatsoever. To conclude: this whole mystery of
genera and species, which make such a noise in the schools,
and are with justice so little regarded out of them, is nothing
else but *abstract ideas,* more or less comprehensive, with names
annexed to them. In all which this is constant and unvariable,
That every more general term stands for such an idea, and is
but a part of any of those contained under it [2].

10. This may show us the reason why, in the defining of
words, which is nothing but declaring their signification, we
make use of the *genus,* or next general word that comprehends
it. Which is not out of necessity, but only to save the labour
of enumerating the several simple ideas which the next general
word or *genus* stands for; or, perhaps, sometimes the shame
of not being able to do it. But though defining by *genus* and

---

[1] Are *all* universals generalisations
from 'particular existences'? Must
there not be 'abstract ideas' that are
necessarily implied in our having an
experience that can be rationally interpreted, and which are thus latent in
the experience, not gradually formed

by tentative comparison of particulars?

[2] That is to say, the 'more general
term' includes in its connotation only
a part of the connotation of the terms
of less denotation that are contained
under it, as species of which it is the
genus.

differentia[1] (I crave leave to use these terms of art, though originally Latin, since they most properly suit those notions they are applied to), I say, though defining by the *genus* be the shortest way, yet I think it may be doubted whether it be the best. This I am sure, it is not the only, and so not absolutely necessary. For, definition being nothing but making another [2] understand by words what idea the term defined stands for, a definition is best made by enumerating those simple ideas that are combined in the signification of the term defined : and if, instead of such an enumeration, men have accustomed themselves to use the next general term, it has not been out of necessity, or for greater clearness, but for quickness and dispatch sake. For I think that, to one who desired to know what idea the word *man* stood for ; if it should be said, that man was a solid extended substance, having life, sense, spontaneous motion, and the faculty of reasoning, I doubt not but the meaning of the term man would be as well understood, and the idea it stands for be at least as clearly made known, as when it is defined to be a rational animal : which, by the several definitions of *animal, vivens,* and *corpus,* resolves itself into those enumerated ideas. I have, in explaining the term *man,* followed here the ordinary definition of the schools ; which, though perhaps not the most exact, yet serves well enough to my present purpose. And one may, in this instance, see what gave occasion to the rule, that a definition must consist of *genus* and *differentia* ; and it suffices to show us the little necessity there is of such a rule, or advantage in the strict observing of it. For, definitions, as has been said, being only the explaining of one word by

---

[1] A definition, according to ordinary logical rule, should consist of the *nearest genus* and the *lowest difference.* Its purpose is to present an exhaustive analysis of the connotation of the term defined, on the assumption that *its* genus has been previously defined, and in like manner the genus in the preceding definition, backwards to an indefinable term, by which a stop is put to the regress. On this assumption, in order to save trouble, the already defined *genus* is substituted for the exhaustive analysis of its connotation in detail which would otherwise be required. But, as Locke implies, languages are not always so made according to the rules of logic that the detailed analysis can be thus dispensed with, and the name of the genus substituted for it.

[2] Or the author of the definition himself.

several others, so that the meaning or idea it stands for may
be certainly known; languages are not always so made
according to the rules of logic, that every term can have its
signification exactly and clearly expressed by two others.
Experience sufficiently satisfies us to the contrary; or else
those who have made this rule have done ill, that they have
given us so few definitions conformable to it. But of definitions more in the next chapter.

11. To return to general words: it is plain, by what has General
been said, that *general* and *universal* belong not to the real and Universal are
existence of things; but are the inventions and creatures of Creatures
of the
the understanding, made by it for its own use, and concern Under-
only signs, whether words or ideas[1]. Words are general, as standing,
and
has been said, when used for signs of general ideas, and so belong not
are applicable indifferently to many particular things; and to the Real
Existence
ideas are general when they are set up as the representatives of things.
of many particular things: but universality belongs not to
things themselves, which are all of them particular in their
existence[2], even those words and ideas which in their signification are general. When therefore we quit particulars, the

---

[1] Locke often speaks not only of
words but of ideas as 'signs,' on the
supposition that *our knowledge* of
things is measured by *our ideas* of
them; also because ' the scene of ideas
which makes up one man's thoughts
cannot be laid open to the *immediate*
view of another.' Cf. Bk. IV. ch. xxi.
§ 4.

[2] Nature, that is to say, makes individual things alike *in various respects*
to other individual things, so that each
thing may be placed in *any one of
many classes*, according to the resembling qualities which one arbitrarily
selects. In this way species are ' inventions and creatures of the understanding.' Our modes of conceiving
and classifying things are influenced,
in each case, by the end we have in
view. ' In different sciences and arts
different attributes are fixed on, as
essentially characterising each species,

according as this or that is most important in reference to the matter we
are engaged in. In navigation, for
instance, the *polarity* of the magnet is
the essential quality, but to manu-
facturers the *attracting* power is the
essential point.' (Whately.) But with
all this the existence of science and
philosophy presupposes that some
generalisations of things are more
natural—more rational—more nearly
accordant with the universal reason,
according to which things exist, than
others that might have been formed are.
Such species are the ideals to which
science and philosophy approximate,
although the ideal is unattainable by
man. Even Locke's 'real essences'
and J. S. Mill's ' natural classes' recognise this. They presuppose a reality
that exists in the (by man) undiscoverable ultimate constitution of particular
substances. Cf. § 13.

BOOK III.
CHAP. III.

generals that rest are only creatures of our own making; their general nature being nothing but the capacity they are put into, by the understanding, of signifying or representing many particulars. For the signification they have is nothing but a relation that, by the mind of man, is added to them [1].

Abstract Ideas are the Essences of Genera and Species.

12. The next thing therefore to be considered is, What kind of signification it is that general words have. For, as it is evident that they do not signify barely one particular thing; for then they would not be general terms, but proper names, so, on the other side, it is as evident they do not signify a plurality; for *man* and *men* would then signify the same; and the distinction of numbers (as the grammarians call them) would be superfluous and useless. That then which general words signify is a *sort* of things [2]; and each of them does that, by being a sign of an abstract idea [3] in the mind; to which idea, as things existing are found to agree, so they come to be ranked under that name, or, which is all one, be of that sort. Whereby it is evident that the *essences* of the sorts, or, if the Latin word pleases better, *species* of things, are nothing else but these abstract ideas. For the having the essence of any species, being that which makes anything to be of that species; and the conformity to the idea to which the name is annexed being that which gives a right to that name; the having the essence, and the having that conformity, must needs be the same thing: since to be of any species, and to have a right to the name of that species, is all one. As, for example, to be a *man*, or of the *species* man, and to

---

[1] To say, as Locke here does, that 'only particulars are real,' logically means, according to Green, that only *the feeling of each moment* is real; that is, that the really existent is the un-meaning, and that any *judgment* about it is impossible. While it is only by being judged that it acquires generality, so that all generality, according to the *Essay*, must be 'fictitious,' and cannot be in things. But, as we have seen, the 'particular' is, with Locke, an *individual substance manifested in its simple ideas*, i. e. qualified, or related in

as far as qualities mean relations. Locke's *minimum intelligibile* is not an isolated sense-feeling, of which nothing can be predicated: it is the individual substance.

[2] A 'sort'—a lot, according to which things are allotted to a class.

[3] 'An abstract idea'—unimaginable, but containing a plurality of attri-butes, and so capable of being defined, although it cannot be represented in a mental image, which must be indi-vidual or concrete.

have right to the *name* man, is the same thing. Again, to be
a man, or of the species man, and have the *essence* of a
man, is the same thing. Now, since nothing can be a man, or
have a right to the name man, but what has a conformity to
the abstract idea the name man stands for [1], nor anything be
a man, or have a right to the species man, but what has the
essence of that species ; it follows, that the abstract idea for
which the name stands, and the essence of the species, is one
and the same. From whence it is easy to observe, that the
essences of the sorts of things, and, consequently, the sorting
of things, is the workmanship of the understanding that
abstracts and makes those general ideas.

13. I would not here be thought to forget, much less to
deny, that Nature, in the production of things, makes several
of them alike : there is nothing more obvious, especially in
the races of animals, and all things propagated by seed [2].
But yet I think we may say, *the sorting of them under names
is the workmanship of the understanding, taking occasion, from
the similitude it observes amongst them, to make abstract
general ideas*, and set them up in the mind, with names
annexed to them, as patterns or forms, (for, in that sense, the
word *form* has a very proper signification,) to which as particular things existing are found to agree [3], so they come to be
of that species, have that denomination, or are put into that

They are the Workman-ship of the Under-standing, but have their Founda-tion in the Similitude of Things.

---

[1] That is, has the attributes which
have been chosen by us to make the
connotation of the name 'man.' But the
fact that the choice of the classifying
attributes may be more or less reasonable — more truly scientific — shows
that there *is* an objective criterion ;
and this criterion at last resolves itself
into what in Platonic language might
be called 'Ideas,' according to which
the universe changes its forms of existing, in the experience of man, and
according to which also things exist
in their natural kinds.

[2] See Bk. III. ch. vi. ; also *Third
Letter* to Stillingfleet, p. 357, in which
Locke refers to this passage, and to 'Bk.

III. ch. vi,' as evidence that he has not
neglected to 'consider beings as God
had ordered them in their several sorts
and ranks.'

[3] This implies that the resemblances
according to which men bring things
under classes correspond at least to
something superficially presented to
observation by the things that are
classified, which is (so far) a real
foundation for the classes formed.
'Agreement,' as Green remarks, 'implies some content *in the things agreeing*' (p. 37), a consideration which
might have modified his interpretation
of the 'nominal and real essences' of
Locke.

classis. For when we say this is a man, that a horse; this justice, that cruelty; this a watch, that a jack; what do we else but rank things under different specific names, as agreeing to those abstract ideas, of which we have made those names the signs? And what are the essences of those species set out and marked by names, but those abstract ideas in the mind; which are, as it were, the bonds between particular things that exist, and the names they are to be ranked under? And when general names have any connexion with particular beings, these abstract ideas are the medium that unites them: so that the essences of species, as distinguished and denominated by us, neither are nor can be anything but those precise abstract ideas we have in our minds [1]. And therefore the supposed real essences of substances, if different from our abstract ideas, cannot be the essences of the species *we* rank things into. For two species may be one, as rationally as two different essences be the essence of one species: and I demand what are the alterations [which] may, or may not be made in a *horse* or *lead*, without making either of them to be of another species? In determining the species of things by *our* abstract ideas, this is easy to resolve [2]: but if any one will regulate himself herein by supposed *real* essences, he will, I suppose, be at a loss: and he will never be able to know when anything precisely ceases to be of the species of a *horse* or *lead* [3].

Each distinct abstract Idea is a distinct Essence.
14. Nor will any one wonder that I say these essences, or abstract ideas (which are the measures of name, and the boundaries of species) are the workmanship of the understanding, who considers that at least the complex ones are often, in several men, different collections of simple ideas; and therefore that is *covetousness* to one man, which is not so

---

[1] That is, they are the deepest and truest modes of classifying *things* which *men* can arrive at.

[2] Because we have only to see that the individual things we apply the names 'horse' or 'lead' actually possess those qualities, however superficial the qualities may be, which we have resolved to make the connotation of those names.

[3] Inasmuch as the 'real essence' is determined by the *Divine* or ultimate scheme of thought that is immanent in the universe, according to which the universe is viewed as it were from the centre, while *our* empirical generalisations are all formed from side-views of things.

to another [1]. Nay, even in substances, where their abstract
ideas seem to be taken from the things themselves, they are
not constantly the same; no, not in that species which is most
familiar to us, and with which we have the most intimate
acquaintance: it having been more than once doubted, whether
the *foetus* born of a woman were a *man*, even so far as that it
hath been debated, whether it were or were not to be nourished
and baptized : which could not be, if the abstract idea or
essence to which the name man belonged were of nature's
making ; and were not the uncertain and various collection of
simple ideas [2], which the understanding put together, and then,
abstracting it, affixed a name to it. So that, in truth, every
distinct abstract idea is a distinct essence ; and the names that
stand for such distinct ideas are the names of things essentially
different. Thus a circle is as essentially different from an
oval as a sheep from a goat; and rain is as essentially different
from snow as water from earth : that abstract idea which is
the essence of one being impossible to be communicated to
the other. And thus any two abstract ideas, that in any part
vary one from another, with two distinct names annexed to
them, constitute two distinct sorts, or, if you please, *species*, as
essentially different as any two of the most remote or opposite
in the world.

15. But since the essences of things are thought by some Several
(and not without reason) to be wholly unknown, it may significa-
not be amiss to consider the several significations of the word the word
essence. Essence.

---

[1] Cf. ch. xxii. § 6.

[2] That the human understanding has
only imperfect insight into the ultimate
'natures' of things proves, Locke
argues, that the Realistic theory of
universals cannot be worked out and
applied by human faculties. The only
'universal characters' that *man* can
discover are those derived empirically
from his insufficient observations of
things, and therefore *post res.* Cf.
First Letter to Stillingfleet, pp. 172-
213. 'The real constitutions or essences of particular things existing do
not depend on the ideas of men but on
the will of the Creator ; but their being
ranked into sorts, under such and such
names, does depend, and wholly depend, upon the ideas of men' (i. e.
upon the partial and superficial manifestations of themselves which things
make to the senses and understanding
of men, and upon the manifestations
which men select for forming them
into classes.) *First Letter* to Stillingfleet, pp. 212, 213 ; also p. 172.

BOOK III.

—+—

CHAP. III.
Real
Essences.

First, Essence may be taken for the very being of anything, whereby it is what it is[1]. And thus the real internal, but generally (in substances) unknown constitution of things, whereon their discoverable qualities depend, may be called their essence. This is the proper original signification of the word, as is evident from the formation of it; *essentia*, in its primary notation, signifying properly, being. And in this sense it is still used, when we speak of the essence of *particular* things, without giving them any name.

Nominal
Essences.

Secondly, The learning and disputes of the schools having been much busied about *genus* and *species*, the word *essence* has almost lost its primary signification: and, instead of the real constitution of things, has been almost wholly applied to the artificial constitution of *genus* and *species*[2]. It is true, there is ordinarily supposed a real constitution of the sorts of things ; and it is past doubt there must be some real constitution[3], on which any collection of simple ideas co-existing[4] must depend. But, it being evident that things are ranked under names into sorts or species, only as they agree to certain abstract ideas, to which we have annexed those

---

[1] The *whatness* of things was said to constitute their *essence* or *nature* (Arist. *Met.* iv. c. 4). It is that in them which so makes them the real things they are, that, according to the universal system, the thing occupies its real place, or discharges its real function, and which thus affords the philosophic answer to the question—*What is it?*

'He knows *what's what*, and that's as high,

As metaphysic wit can fly.'

It is that in things themselves which constitutes their *true* kind, though to discover this may transcend the range of human faculty. It is Aristotle's 'substantial form' (εἶδος).

[2] The term *essence*, thus confined to the superficial appearances that are within the cognisance of man, has come to signify the *contents* of our concepts of things ; fully cognizable by those who have formed the concepts, but being due to what is given in the

limited sphere of human observation, this content falls far short of that ' essence' by which things are what they are, according to their ultimate constitution. Our deepest abstract ideas of things are far short of their *ultimate* reality, or *real* essences.

[3] Locke's conception of the (undiscoverable) real essence is that in material substances it is something *physical* —texture of the primary particles, on which their secondary qualities and other powers depend, and from which, if discovered, those qualities and powers might be deduced *a priori*; and in man, that unknown natural constitution, on which his spiritual powers and character depend. This physical conception of ' real essences' thus differs from the Aristotelian hyperphysical *form*.

[4] ' any collection of simple ideas coexisting,' i. e. any complex idea of a particular sort of substance.

names, the essence of each *genus*, or sort, comes to be nothing but that abstract idea which the general, or sortal (if I may have leave so to call it from sort, as I do general from genus,) name stands for. And this we shall find to be that which the word essence imports in its most familiar use.

These two sorts of essences, I suppose, may not unfitly be termed, the one the *real*[1], the other *nominal*[2] essence.

16. Between the *nominal essence* and the *name* there is so near a connexion, that the name of any sort of things cannot[3] be attributed to any particular being but what has this essence, whereby it answers that abstract idea whereof that name is the sign.

17. Concerning the *real essences* of corporeal substances (to mention these only) there are, if I mistake not, two opinions. The one is of those who, using the word essence for they know not what[4], suppose a certain number of those essences, according to which all natural things are made, and wherein they do exactly every one of them partake, and so become of this or that species. The other and more rational opinion is of those who look on all natural things to have a real, but unknown, constitution of their insensible[5] parts; from which flow those sensible qualities which serve us to distinguish them one from another[6], according as we have occasion to rank them into sorts, under common

---

[1] 'real,' i. e. physically real essence with Locke.

[2] 'nominal,' called also the *logical* essence.

[3] 'cannot,'—unless the attributes which make the connotation of the term by which this 'essence' is signified are found, by observation, to be actually possessed by the individual things to which it is proposed to apply the term.

[4] That is, for a supposed, but incognisable, hyperphysical or non-material *form*, transcending sensuous imagination, and which seemed to Locke a meaningless supposition; unlike his own physically real essence, concealed in individual material substances, because composed of particles of matter too small for our organs to perceive.

[5] 'insensible' for *our* organs, but not in themselves hyperphysical.

[6] But although the *observed* qualities, according to which *our* classifications are made, so depend on this (by us) *undiscoverable* physical constitution (in each individual thing), that we cannot deduce the qualities we observe from a knowledge of this constitution, that defective knowledge of ours does not disprove the supposition of the objective constitution itself. Given finer senses and a more subtle intelligence, we might then construct physical science *a priori*, and with demonstrable conclusions.

denominations.   The former of these opinions, which supposes these essences as a certain number of forms or moulds, wherein all natural things that exist are cast, and do equally partake, has, I imagine, very much perplexed the knowledge of natural things.   The frequent productions of monsters, in all the species of animals, and of changelings, and other strange issues of human birth, carry with them difficulties, not possible to consist with this hypothesis; since it is as impossible that two things partaking exactly of the same real essence should have different properties, as that two figures partaking of the same real essence of a circle should have different properties [1].   But were there no other reason against it, yet the supposition of essences that cannot be known; and the making of them, nevertheless, to be that which distinguishes the species of things, is so wholly useless and unserviceable to any part of our knowledge, that that alone were sufficient to make us lay it by, and content ourselves with such essences of the sorts or species of things as come within the reach of our knowledge: which, when seriously considered, will be found, as I have said, to be nothing else but, those *abstract* complex ideas to which we have annexed distinct general names.

Real and nominal Essence

18. Essences being thus distinguished into nominal and real [2], we may further observe, that, in the species of simple

---

[1] Locke's ' real essence ' belongs to the *individual.* The immaterial essence, or substantial form, against which he argues, was supposed to belong to the *species,* as that in which all the individuals participate; and a definite, if unknown, number of such species was supposed to exist, the universe being created according to them—after ' its kinds.'

[2] What Locke calls ' nominal ' is more commonly called ' logical ' essence; in contrast to the ' real' essence, or (by us) incognisable (physical?) constitution of individuals which makes them the sorts of things they are, in the ultimate ideal of the universe. A knowledge of the real essences of

created things, which might enable us to deduce all their attributes from those real essences or natures, seems, says Reid, ' to be quite beyond the human faculties.   We know the essence of a triangle, and from that essence can deduce its properties.   [Here the real essence is only the nominal essence fully expressed in its definition.]   It is an universal, and might have been conceived and reasoned about though no individual triangle [with *its* real essence that is *not* the nominal one] had ever actually existed.   But every individual thing that exists actually has a real essence, which is above our comprehension; and therefore we cannot deduce its properties or attri-

BOOK III.
—◆—
CHAP. III.
the same
in simple
Ideas and
Modes,
different
in Sub-
stances.

ideas and modes, they are always the same ; but in substances always quite different. Thus, a figure including a
space between three lines, is the real as well as nominal
essence of a triangle ; it being not only the abstract idea to
which the general name is annexed, but the very *essentia*
or being of the thing itself ; that foundation from which
all its properties flow, and to which they are all inseparably
annexed. But it is far otherwise concerning that parcel of
matter which makes the ring on my finger ; wherein these
two essences are apparently different. For, it is the real
constitution of its insensible parts [1], on which depend all
those properties of colour, weight, fusibility, fixedness [2], &c.,
which are to be found in it [3] ; which constitution we know
not, and so, having no particular idea of, having no name
that is the sign of it. But yet it is its colour, weight, fusibility, fixedness, &c., which makes it to be gold, or gives it
a right to that name, which is therefore its nominal essence.
Since nothing can be called gold but what has a conformity
of qualities to that abstract complex idea to which that name
is annexed. But this distinction of essences, belonging particularly to substances, we shall, when we come to consider
their names, have an occasion to treat of more fully [4].

19. That such abstract ideas, with names to them, as we
have been speaking of are essences, may further appéar by
what we are told concerning essences, viz. that they are
all ingenerable and incorruptible [5]. Which cannot be true

---

butes from its nature, as we do in
the triangle. We must take a contrary road [to that of *a priori* deduction
from real essences] in the knowledge of
God's works, and satisfy ourselves
with their attributes as [observed]
facts, and with the general conviction
that there *is* a subject [substance with
its real essence] to which these attributes belong' [by which the substance
is only inadequately manifested to us].
See Hamilton's Reid, p. 392; also
p. 404. This of Reid is not inconsistent
with Locke.

[1] The physically, or chemically, real

essence, which Locke recognises and
accepts, while insisting that it is undiscoverable by man.

[2] 'fixedness.' See Boyle's *Works*,
vol. i. pp. 454, 634 ; iii. p. 78.

[3] That is, which are observable by
us—unlike the physical essence, which
escapes our rude senses.

[4] In ch. vi.

[5] The Peripatetics held that form or
essence cannot be generated, or regarded as an effect, and that it must be
combined with matter. (Arist. *Met.*
Bk. VI.)

of the real constitutions of things [1], which begin and perish with them. All things that exist, besides their Author, are all liable to change ; especially those things we are acquainted with, and have ranked into bands under distinct names or ensigns. Thus, that which was grass to-day is to-morrow the flesh of a sheep ; and, within a few days after, becomes part of a man: in all which and the like changes, it is evident their real essence—i. e. that constitution whereon the properties of these several things depended—is destroyed, and perishes with them. But essences being taken for ideas established in the mind, with names annexed to them, they are supposed to remain steadily the same, whatever mutations the particular substances are liable to. For, whatever becomes of *Alexander* and *Bucephalus*, the ideas to which *man* and *horse* are annexed, are supposed nevertheless to remain the same ; and so the essences of those species are preserved whole and undestroyed, whatever changes happen to any or all of the individuals of those species. By this means the essence of a species rests safe and entire, without the existence of so much as one individual of that kind. For, were there now no circle existing anywhere in the world, (as perhaps that figure exists not anywhere exactly marked out [2],) yet the idea annexed to that name would not cease to be what it is ; nor cease to be as a pattern to determine which of the particular figures we meet with have or have not a right to the *name* circle, and so to show which of them, by having that essence, was of that species. And though there neither were nor had been in nature such a beast as an *unicorn,* or such a fish as a *mermaid* ; yet, supposing those names to stand for complex abstract ideas that contained no inconsistency in them, the essence of a mermaid is as intelligible as that of a man ; and the idea of an unicorn as certain, steady, and permanent as that of a horse.

---

[1] The 'real essences' which Locke presupposed would be created and annihilated with the creation and dissolution of the individual things which they constituted. His 'nominal essences,' on the contrary, are independent of individuals, and thus remain true as long as the same name continues to carry the same signification.

[2] Pure geometry, not perfectly realised in our sensuous perceptions of things.

From what has been said, it is evident, that the doctrine of
the immutability of essences proves them to be only abstract
ideas; and is founded on the relation established between
them and certain sounds as signs of them ; and will always
be true, as long as the same name can have the same signification [1].

20. To conclude. This is that which in short I would
say, viz. that all the great business of *genera* and *species*, and
their *essences*, amounts to no more but this :—That men
making abstract ideas, and settling them in their minds
with names annexed to them, do thereby enable themselves to consider things, and discourse of them, as it were in
bundles, for the easier and readier improvement and communication of their knowledge, which would advance but
slowly were their words and thoughts confined only to
particulars [2].

[1] Lotze's contrast between the changeless world of abstract ideas, and the ever-changing world of real things and events is in analogy with this section. See *Logic*, Bk. III. ch. 2.

[2] Our concepts of individual things, which are their 'nominal essences,' help our progress towards those unattainable 'real essences' which, as ideals, are the springs of our intellectual advance, but in which the scientific secrets of the physical universe lie hid. The *inadequacy* of all *human* 'abstract ideas' to the actual reality, is the lesson of this chapter. But the inadequate is not the contradictory; and even our conceptions may be real as far as they go; and are gradually approaching adequacy, so far as there is real progress in a knowledge which, as finite, must always be charged with enigmas at the last.

CHAPTER IV.

OF THE NAMES OF SIMPLE IDEAS.

BOOK III.

Chap. IV.
Names of
simple
Ideas,
Modes,
and Sub-
stances,
have each
something
peculiar.

First,
Names of
simple
Ideas, and
of Sub-
stances
intimate
real
Existence.

Secondly,
Names of
simple
Ideas and
Modes
signify
always
both real
and
nominal
Essences.

Thirdly,
Names of

1. THOUGH all words, as I have shown, signify nothing immediately but the ideas in the mind of the speaker ; yet, upon a nearer survey, we shall find the names of *simple ideas*, *mixed modes* (under which I comprise *relations* too), and *natural substances*, have each of them something peculiar and different from the other. For example :—

2. First, the names of *simple ideas* and *substances*, with the abstract ideas [1] in the mind which they immediately signify, intimate also some real existence, from which was derived their original pattern. But the names of *mixed modes* terminate in the idea that is in the mind, and lead not the thoughts any further ; as we shall see more at large in the following chapter [2].

3. Secondly, The names of simple ideas and modes signify always the real as well as nominal essence of their species. But the names of natural substances signify rarely, if ever, anything but barely the nominal essences of those species ; as we shall show in the chapter that treats of the names of substances in particular.

4. Thirdly, The names of simple ideas are not capable of any definition ; the names of all complex ideas are. It has

---

[1] That is, *general* ideas, or generalisations, which involve abstraction.

[2] Our 'simple ideas,' or the phenomena actually presented by the things of sense, or in the operations of our own mind ; and our (imperfect) ideas of particular substances, are thus the only ideas that are concerned with reality, as distinguished from arbitrary combinations elaborated by the minds of men.

not, that I know, been yet observed by anybody what words BOOK III.
are, and what are not, capable of being defined [1] ; the want
whereof is (as I am apt to think) not seldom the occasion CHAP. IV.
of great wrangling and obscurity in men's discourses, whilst simple
some demand definitions of terms that cannot be defined ; Ideas
and others think they ought not to rest satisfied in an are undefinable.
explication made by a more general word, and its restriction,
(or to speak in terms of art, by a genus and difference,) when,
even after such definition, made according to rule, those who
hear it have often no more a clear conception of the meaning
of the word than they had before. This at least I think,
that the showing what words are, and what are not, capable
of definitions, and wherein consists a good definition, is not
wholly besides our present purpose ; and perhaps will afford
so much light to the nature of these signs and our ideas,
as to deserve a more particular consideration.

5. I will not here trouble myself to prove that all terms are If all
not definable, from that progress *in infinitum*, which it will names
were
visibly lead us into, if we should allow that all names could definable,
be defined. For, if the terms of one definition were still to be a
be defined by another, where at last should we stop [2] ? But I Process
in in-
shall, from the nature of our ideas, and the signification of *finitum.*
our words, show *why some names can, and others cannot be
defined* ; and *which they are.*

6. I think it is agreed, that a *definition* is nothing else but What a
the showing the meaning of one word by several other not Definition
is.
synonymous terms [3]. The meaning of words being only the

---

[1] The impossibility of defining all
words, with a reason for this, is stated
in the *Port Royal Logic*, especially
Part i. ch. xii, which anticipates some
of Locke's remarks. 'To say that
simple ideas are indefinable means,'
according to Green (p. 42), 'that
nothing can be said of such ideas'—
that they are meaningless till brought
into relations. Locke means that a
man born blind cannot be made to
picture mentally a red or white colour,
merely by naming it and defining the
name, nor indeed by any other way

than by presenting a red or a white
thing to his awakened sense of sight.

[2] 'Il faut nécessairement s'arrêter
à des termes primitifs qu'on ne dé-
finisse point ; et ce serait un aussi
grand défaut de vouloir trop définir,
que de ne pas assez définir.' (*La
Logique de Port Royal.*)

[3] Verbal or nominal definition, which
Locke has here in view, is merely
explicative—an exhaustive exhibition
of the plurality of attributes which
men have chosen to include in the
connotation of the term defined. By

BOOK III.
CHAP. IV.

ideas they are made to stand for by him that uses them, the meaning of any term is then showed, or the word is defined, when, by other words, the idea it is made the sign of, and annexed to, in the mind of the speaker, is as it were represented, or set before the view of another ; and thus its signification ascertained. This is the only use and end of definitions ; and therefore the only measure of what is, or is not a good definition.

Simple Ideas, why undefinable.

7. This being premised, I say that the *names of simple ideas, and those only, are incapable of being defined.* The reason whereof is this, That the several[1] terms of a definition, signifying several ideas, they can all together by no means represent an idea which has no composition at all : and therefore a definition, which is properly nothing but the showing the meaning of one word by several others not signifying each the same thing, can in the names of simple ideas have no place[2].

Instances : Scholastic definitions of Motion.

8. The not observing this difference in our ideas, and their names, has produced that eminent trifling in the schools, which is so easy to be observed in the definitions they give us of some few of these simple ideas. For, as to the greatest part of them, even those masters of definitions were fain to leave them untouched, merely by the impossibility they found in it. What more exquisite jargon could the wit of man invent, than this definition :—' The act of a being in power, as far forth as in power[3] ;' which would puzzle any rational man,

spreading out those which entitle an 'abstract idea' to its name, the idea is *defined*, i. e. made perfectly clear and distinct, so that it can be absolutely distinguished from every other abstract idea.

[1] 'several,' i. e. different.

[2] There is nothing new in this statement, already made by Descartes and others. Simple ideas, as containing only a single attribute, of course, cannot be defined ; because a definition presupposes a plurality of attributes. They may be exemplified, however, in a sensuous image. See also *Port Royal Logic*, Pt. I. ch. xiii, where reason is

given why ' it is impossible to define all words.'

[3] Arist. *Metaph.* xi. 9. This Aristotelian definition of *motion* had been already discarded in the *Port Royal Logic*. ' Is not our natural idea of motion a hundred times clearer than that given through this definition ; and who could ever learn from it any of the properties of motion ? ' (Pt. II. ch. xvi.) This is the modern spirit of reaction against definitions of the schools, expressed in abstract language, and professedly related to ultimate principles, and the universal scheme of things. The Aristotelian

to whom it was not already known by its famous absurdity, to guess what word it could ever be supposed to be the explication of. If Tully, asking a Dutchman what *beweeginge* [1] was, should have received this explication in his own language, that it was 'actus entis in potentia quatenus in potentia;' I ask whether any one can imagine he could thereby have understood what the word *beweeginge* signified, or have guessed what idea a Dutchman ordinarily had in his mind, and would signify to another, when he used that sound?

9. Nor have the modern philosophers, who have endeavoured to throw off the jargon of the schools, and speak intelligibly, much better succeeded in defining simple ideas, whether by explaining their causes [2], or any otherwise. The atomists [3], who define motion to be 'a passage from one place to another,' what do they more than put one synonymous word for another? For what is *passage* other than *motion*? And if they were asked what passage was, how would they better define it than by motion? For is it not at least as proper and significant to say, Passage is a motion from one place to another, as to say, Motion is a passage, &c.? This is to translate, and not to define, when we change two words of the same signification one for another; which, when one is better understood than the other, may serve to discover what idea the unknown stands for; but is very far from a definition, unless we will say every English word in the dictionary is the definition of the Latin word it answers, and that motion is

definition turns upon the difference between the actual (ἐνέργεια) and the potential (δύναμις) in the nature of things. Locke condemns it, as if it pretended to explicate the simple sensation which motion occasions in us. This was foreign to its purpose, which was to exhibit motion as the *actualisation* of what before existed only *potentially*.

[1] *Beweeginge* is the Dutch for movement (so German *Bewegung*). Locke's residence in Holland, when he was finishing the *Essay*, suggested this and similar local illustrations.

[2] 'Simple ideas of sense' are not defined by stating physical occasions or conditions of their manifestations; because the occasion bears no likeness to the sensation occasioned. An explication of the physical causes of our having a sensation of colour could not convey an image of the colour to one born blind.

[3] 'atomists'—Democritus and the Epicureans, also the Gassendists in the seventeenth century, sought in indivisible atoms and their motions for the ultimate constituents of whatever exists.

BOOK III. a definition of *motus.* Nor will 'the successive application of
CHAP. IV. the parts of the superficies of one body to those of another[1],'
which the Cartesians give us, prove a much better definition
of motion, when well examined.

Definitions   10. 'The act of perspicuous, as far forth as perspicuous,' is
of Light.   another Peripatetic definition of a simple idea; which, though
not more absurd than the former of motion, yet betrays its
uselessness and insignificancy more plainly ; because experience will easily convince any one that it cannot make the
meaning of the word *light* (which it pretends to define) at all
understood by a blind man[2], but the definition of motion
appears not at first sight so useless, because it escapes this
way of trial.   For this simple idea, entering by the touch as
well as sight[3], it is impossible to show an example of any one
who has no other way to get the idea of motion, but barely
by the definition of that name.   Those who tell us that light
is a great number of little globules, striking briskly on the
bottom of the eye, speak more intelligibly than the Schools :
but yet these words never so well understood would make the
idea the word light stands for no more known to a man that
understands it not before, than if one should tell him that
light was nothing but a company of little tennis-balls, which
fairies all day long struck with rackets against some men's
foreheads, whilst they passed by others.   For granting this
explication of the thing to be true, yet the idea of the cause
of light, if we had it never so exact, would no more give us the
idea of light itself, as it is such a particular perception in us,
than the idea of the figure and motion of a sharp piece of
steel would give us the idea of that pain which it is able to
cause in us.   For the cause of any sensation, and the sensation

---

[1] Cf. Descartes, *Princip.* Pt. II. § 25 ;
also Berkeley's *C. P. B.,Works,* vol. iv.
p. 424.

[2] This is Aristotle's definition of
light—φῶς δέ ἐστιν ἡ τούτου ἐνέργεια τοῦ
διαφανοῦς ἤ διαφανές (*De Anim.* II. iii),
i. e. the essence or common nature
which enables things to transmit light
—their diaphanous, or, as Locke has
it, 'perspicuous' constitution, in which

is latent the physical cause of the
sensation (simple idea) of light.   The
definition is not meant to make the
sensation of light imaginable by one
born blind, but only to express its
physical cause, regarded as an energy
and not as a potentiality only.   It
might be understood by one who never
had the sensation.

[3] Cf. Bk. II. ch. v.

itself, in all the simple ideas of one sense, are two ideas ; and BOOK III.
two ideas so different and distant one from another, that no CHAP. IV.
two can be more so[1]. And therefore, should Des Cartes's
globules strike never so long on the retina of a man who was
blind by a *gutta serena,* he would thereby never have any idea
of light, or anything approaching it, though he understood
never so well what little globules were, and what striking on
another body was. And therefore the Cartesians[2] very well
distinguish between that light which is the cause of that
sensation in us, and the idea which is produced in us by it,
and is that which is properly light[3].

11. Simple ideas, as has been shown, are only to be got by Simple
those impressions objects themselves make on our minds, by Ideas,
the proper inlets appointed to each sort. If they are not definable,
received this way, all the words in the world, made use of to explained.
explain or define any of their names, will never be able to
produce in us the idea it stands for. For, words being
sounds, can produce in us no other simple ideas than of those
very sounds ; nor excite any in us, but by that voluntary
connexion which is known to be between them and those
simple ideas which common use has made them the signs of.
He that thinks otherwise, let him try if any words can give
him the taste of a pine apple, and make him have the true
idea of the relish of that celebrated delicious fruit[4]. So far as
he is told it has a resemblance with any tastes whereof he has
the ideas already in his memory, imprinted there by sensible

---

[1] The idea of a sensuous feeling is
here contrasted with the idea (formed
after physiological research) of the
organic conditions on which the sensuous feeling naturally depends ; although we are not necessarily aware
of the conditions in being conscious of
the sensuous feeling.

[2] The definitions referred to do not
pretend to be substitutes for an experience of the sensation of light, in
which alone we can receive an idea
of the sensation. They only pretend
to determine its physical cause, and
their inadequacy in this respect is a

fault different from the absurdity which
Locke alleges against them.

[3] This and the preceding section are
among Locke's few express references
to Descartes or to the Cartesians. Yet
Stewart says that he does not recollect
that Locke has anywhere in his *Essay*
mentioned the name of either Hobbes,
Gassendi, Bacon, Montaigne, or Descartes.

[4] So Hume—' We cannot form to
ourselves a just idea of the taste of a
pine apple, without having actually
tasted it.' (*Treatise,* I. i. 1.)

BOOK III. objects, not strangers to his palate, so far may he approach
CHAP. IV. that resemblance in his mind.   But this is not giving us that
idea by a definition, but exciting in us other simple ideas by
their known names ; which will be still very different from the
true taste of that fruit itself.   In light and colours, and all
other simple ideas, it is the same thing : for the signification of
sounds is not natural, but only imposed and arbitrary.   And
no *definition* of light or redness is more fitted or able to
produce either of those ideas in us, than the *sound* light or red,
by itself.   For, to hope to produce an idea of light or colour [1]
by a sound, however formed, is to expect that sounds should
be visible, or colours audible ; and to make the ears do the
office of all the other senses.   Which is all one as to say, that
we might taste, smell, and see by the ears: a sort of philosophy
worthy only of Sancho Pança, who had the faculty to see
Dulcinea by hearsay [2].   And therefore he that has not before
received into his mind, by the proper inlet, the simple idea
which any word stands for, can never come to know the
signification of that word by any other words or sounds
whatsoever, put together according to any rules of definition.
The only way is, by applying to his senses the proper object ;
and so producing that idea in him, for which he has learned
the name already.   A studious blind man, who had mightily
beat his head about visible objects, and made use of the
explication of his books and friends, to understand those
names of light and colours which often came in his way,
bragged one day, That he now understood what *scarlet* signified.   Upon which, his friend demanding what scarlet was?
The blind man answered, It was like the sound of a trumpet.
Just such an understanding of the name of any other simple
idea will he have, who hopes to get it only from a definition,
or other words made use of to explain it [3].

[1] I. e. an idea of the sensation of
light or colour, as distinguished from
an idea of its ultimate physical cause,
or ' real essence,' as Locke calls it.

[2] ' How can that be ?' cried Don
Quixote ; ' didst thou not tell me that
thou *sawest* her winnowing wheat ? '
' Take no heed of that, sir,' replied

the squire; 'for the fact is, her message, and the sight of her too, were
both by *hearsay,* and I can no more
tell who the lady Dulcinea is than I
can buffet the moon.' (*Don Quixote,*
Second Part, Bk. I. ch. ix.)

[3] Intelligible definitions always presuppose a relative experience, sen-

12. The case is quite otherwise in *complex ideas*; which, BOOK III.
consisting of several simple ones, it is in the power of words, standing for the several ideas that make that composition, to imprint complex ideas in the mind which were never there before, and so make their names be understood[1]. In such collections of ideas, passing under one name, definition, or the teaching the signification of one word by several others, has place, and may make us understand the names of things which never came within the reach of our senses[2]; and frame ideas suitable to those in other men's minds, when they use those names : provided that none of the terms of the definition stand for any such simple ideas, which he to whom the explication is made has never yet had in his thought. Thus the word *statue* may be explained to a blind man by other words, when *picture* cannot; his senses having given him the idea of figure[3], but not of colours, which therefore words cannot excite in him. This gained the prize to the painter against the statuary : each of which contending for the excellency of his art, and the statuary bragging that his was to be preferred, because it reached further, and even those who had lost their eyes could yet perceive the excellency of it. The painter agreed to refer himself to the judgment of a blind man ; who being brought where there was a statue made by the one, and a picture drawn

CHAP. IV. The contrary shown in complex ideas, by instances of a Statue and Rainbow.

---

suous or spiritual. A simple idea, either of sensation or reflection, must be realised in consciousness before the name which signifies it can be understood. Hence Locke sends men to their senses, external and internal, if they want to have ideas of this sort. They can be got only by being actually presented, being absolutely dependent upon their manifestation in a concrete experience. They are 'given' to us, not formed by us.

[1] There must, of course, in that case, have been an immediate presentation in sense of the 'several ideas' that make up that 'composition,' to make the definition intelligible.

[2] In what he says of the 'names of simple ideas,' Locke has those of 'sen-

sation,' rather than those of 'reflection,' in his view. He says nothing about the overwhelming tendency of simple ideas of *reflection* to separate from their signs, and to become ambiguous.

[3] That is, of *tangible* figure, or figure as presented in the sense of touch. Whether the idea of figure, thus given by touch, could *at once* be identified with the idea of figure given by sight, when a born-blind man is made to see, is the problem proposed by Molyneux to Locke (Bk. II. ch. ix. § 8), and further developed by Berkeley, in his *New Theory of Vision*. See also Condillac, *Essai sur l'Origine des Connoissances Humaines*—section sixième, on this problem.

by the other; he was first led to the statue, in which he traced with his hands all the lineaments of the face and body, and with great admiration applauded the skill of the workman. But being led to the picture, and having his hands laid upon it, was told, that now he touched the head, and then the forehead, eyes, nose, &c., as his hand moved over the parts of the picture on the cloth, without finding any the least distinction: whereupon he cried out, that certainly that must needs be a very admirable and divine piece of workmanship, which could represent to them all those parts, where he could neither feel nor perceive anything.

Colours indefinable to the born-blind. 13. He that should use the word *rainbow* to one who knew all those colours, but yet had never seen that phenomenon, would, by enumerating the figure, largeness, position, and order of the colours, so well define that word that it might be perfectly understood. But yet that definition, how exact and perfect soever, would never make a blind man understand it; because several of the simple ideas that make that complex one, being such as he never received by sensation and experience, no words are able to excite them in his mind.

Complex Ideas definable only when the simple ideas of which they consist have been got from experience. 14. Simple ideas, as has been shown, can only be got by experience from those objects which are proper to produce in us those perceptions. When, by this means, we have our minds stored with them, and know the names for them, then we are in a condition to define, and by definition to understand, the names of complex ideas that are made up of them. But when any term stands for a simple idea that a man has never yet had in his mind, it is impossible by any words to make known its meaning to him. When any term stands for an idea a man is acquainted with, but is ignorant that that term is the sign of it, then another name of the same idea, which he has been accustomed to, may make him understand its meaning. But in no case whatsoever is any name of any simple idea capable of a definition.

Fourthly, Names of simple Ideas of less doubtful mean- 15. Fourthly, But though the names of simple ideas have not the help of definition to determine their signification, yet that hinders not but that they are generally less doubtful and uncertain than those of mixed modes and substances; because they, standing only for one simple perception, men for the

most part easily and perfectly agree in their signification ; and
there is little room for mistake and wrangling about their
meaning. He that knows once that whiteness is the name of
that colour he has observed in snow or milk, will not be apt to
misapply that word, as long as he retains that idea; which
when he has quite lost, he is not apt to mistake the meaning
of it, but perceives he understands it not. There is neither
a multiplicity of simple ideas to be put together, which makes
the doubtfulness in the names of mixed modes; nor a supposed,
but an unknown, real essence, with properties depending thereon, the precise number whereof is also unknown, which makes
the difficulty in the names of substances. But, on the contrary,
in simple ideas the whole signification of the name is known at
once, and consists not of parts, whereof more or less being put
in, the idea may be varied, and so the signification of name be
obscure, or uncertain[1].

16. Fifthly, This further may be observed concerning simple
ideas and their names, that they have but few ascents *in lineâ
prædicamentali*[2], (as they call it,) from the lowest species to the
summum genus. The reason whereof is, that the lowest species
being but one simple idea, nothing can be left out of it, that
so the difference being taken away, it may agree with some
other thing in one idea common to them both ; which, having
one name, is the genus of the other two : v.g. there is nothing
that can be left out of the idea of white and red to make them
agree in one common appearance, and so have one general
name ; as *rationality* being left out of the complex idea of
man, makes it agree with brute in the more general idea and
name of animal. And therefore when, to avoid unpleasant
enumerations, men would comprehend both white and red,
and several other such simple ideas, under one general name,

---

[1] As remarked in a former note,
this applies to 'simple ideas of sense,'
but not equally to 'simple ideas of reflection.' The meaning of *perception*
or *volition* is more uncertain than the
meaning of *white* or *hard*. On the

sorts of words liable to ambiguity, cf.
Novum Organum, I. aph. 59, 60.

[2] 'The predicamental line,' i. e.
formed by the intermediate genera and
species which connect a lowest species
with its highest genus.

they have been fain to do it by a word which denotes only the way they get into the mind. For when white, red, and yellow are all comprehended under the genus or name colour, it signifies no more but such ideas as are produced in the mind only by the sight, and have entrance only through the eyes. And when they would frame yet a more general term to comprehend both colours and sounds, and the like simple ideas, they do it by a word that signifies all such as come into the mind only by one sense. And so the general term *quality*, in its ordinary acceptation, comprehends colours, sounds, tastes, smells, and tangible qualities, with distinction from extension, number, motion, pleasure, and pain, which make impressions on the mind and introduce their ideas by more senses than one.

Sixthly, Names of simple Ideas not arbitrary, but perfectly taken from the existence of things.

17. Sixthly, The names of simple ideas, substances, and mixed modes have also this difference: that those of *mixed modes* stand for ideas perfectly arbitrary ; those of *substances* are not perfectly so, but refer to a pattern, though with some latitude ; and those of *simple ideas* are perfectly taken from the existence of things, and are not arbitrary at all[1]. Which, what difference it makes in the significations of their names, we shall see in the following chapters.

Simple modes.

The names of *simple modes* differ little from those of simple ideas[2].

[1] Regarded, that is to say, as sensations, and without respect to their physical causes.

[2] 'Simple modes' of simple ideas, in contrast to 'mixed modes,' are thus treated as phenomena of substances that are presented in the senses or in reflection, like the simple ideas of which they are the modes. But *immensity, eternity*, and *infinity* (names of simple modes, according to Locke) are not so presented, and are surely more apt to be obscure and ambiguous than *white* or *red*. While, in Locke's view, our simple ideas and their simple modes are, in themselves and at first, particular and concrete, their *names* are for the most part general, and not proper names. *Yellow, hot, soft, sweet*, and other simple ideas, or qualities, of sensible things ; *remembering, judging, believing*, and other simple ideas of which we are conscious when we reflect,—are all individual phenomena in our living experience ; but when we speak about them, the terms we use are general.

CHAPTER V.

OF THE NAMES OF MIXED MODES AND RELATIONS.

1. THE names of *mixed modes*[1], being general, they stand, as has been shewed, for sorts or species of things, each of which has its peculiar essence. The essences of these species also, as has been shewed[1], are nothing but the abstract ideas in the mind, to which the name is annexed[2]. Thus far the names and essences of mixed modes have nothing but what is common to them with other ideas: but if we take a little nearer survey of them, we shall find that they have something peculiar, which perhaps may deserve our attention.

2. The first particularity I shall observe in them, is, that the abstract ideas, or, if you please, the essences, of the several species of mixed modes, are *made by the understanding*, wherein they differ from those of simple ideas : in which sort the mind has no power to make any one, but only receives such as are presented to it by the real existence of things operating upon it[3].

3. In the next place, these essences of the species of mixed modes are not only made by the mind, but *made very arbi-*

---

[1] Ch. xxii. Names of mixed modes and of relations, abstracted by the understanding from particular substances, are more apt to be of ambiguous and uncertain meaning than the names of the simple ideas that compose them.

[2] They are ' nominal ' and not ' real '

essences, constituted by the connotation annexed by men to the words which stand for and sustain them in men's minds.

[3] Cf. Bk. II. ch. ii. § 2; ix. § 1. ' Simple ideas' are here spoken of as ' presented'—either by external things, or by our own mind when we reflect.

BOOK III.

CHAP. V.

and without Patterns.

trarily[1], *made without patterns, or reference to any real existence.* Wherein they differ from those of substances, which carry with them the supposition of some real being, from which they are taken, and to which they are conformable. But, in its complex ideas of mixed modes, the mind takes a liberty not to follow the existence of things exactly. It unites and retains certain collections, as so many distinct specific ideas; whilst others, that as often occur in nature, and are as plainly suggested by outward things, pass neglected, without particular names or specifications. Nor does the mind, in these of mixed modes, as in the complex idea of substances, examine them by the real existence of things; or verify them by patterns containing such peculiar compositions in nature. To know whether his idea of *adultery* or *incest* be right, will a man seek it anywhere amongst things existing? Or is it true because any one has been witness to such an action? No: but it suffices here, that men have put together such a collection into one complex idea, that makes the archetype and specific idea[2]; whether ever any such action were committed *in rerum naturâ* or no.

How this is done.

4. To understand this right, we must consider wherein this making of these complex ideas consists; and that is not in the making any new idea, but putting together those which the mind had before. Wherein the mind does these three things: First, It chooses a certain number; Secondly, It gives them connexion, and makes them into one idea; Thirdly, It ties them together by a name. If we examine how the mind proceeds in these, and what liberty it takes in them, we shall easily observe how these essences of the species of mixed modes are the workmanship of the mind;

[1] The arbitrariness in the constitution of *mixed* modes, on which Locke insists so much, is not independent of considerations of utility; and thus the mixed modes required, for purposes of convenience, in one age or country, differ from those which men are led, for like purposes, to form in other times and places. Cf. Bk. II. ch. xxii. §§ 5–8. Moreover, mixed modes, like all other complex ideas, cannot consist of contradictory attributes. The 'arbitrariness' is therefore limited by the formal laws of thought, as well as by convenience; and in some cases, as already noted, by the ultimate constitution of reason.

[2] Which 'idea' is the test for determining to what 'real existences' (if any) the name may be applied.

and, consequently, that the species themselves are of men's
making.

5. Nobody can doubt but that these ideas of mixed modes
are made by a voluntary collection of ideas, put together in
the mind, independent from any original patterns in nature,
who will but reflect that this sort of complex ideas may be
made, abstracted, and have names given them, and so a species
be constituted, before any one individual of that species ever
existed. Who can doubt but the ideas of *sacrilege* or *adultery*
might be framed in the minds of men, and have names given
them, and so these species of mixed modes be constituted,
before either of them was ever committed ; and might be as
well discoursed of and reasoned about, and as certain truths
discovered of them[1], whilst yet they had no being but in the
understanding, as well as now, that they have but too frequently a real existence? Whereby it is plain how much the
sorts of mixed modes are the creatures of the understanding,
where they have a being as subservient to all the ends of real
truth and knowledge, as when they really exist[2]. And we
cannot doubt but law-makers have often made laws about
species of actions which were only the creatures of their own
understandings ; beings that had no other existence but in
their own minds. And I think nobody can deny but that the
resurrection was a species of mixed modes in the mind, before
it really existed[3].

6. To see how arbitrarily these essences of mixed modes
are made by the mind, we need but take a view of almost any
of them. A little looking into them will satisfy us, that it is
the mind that combines several scattered independent ideas
into one complex one ; and, by the common name it gives
them, makes them the essence of a certain species, without
regulating itself by any connexion they have in nature[4]. For

The marginal notes read: Evidently arbitrary, in that the Idea is often before the Existence.

Instances: Murder, Incest, Stabbing.

---

[1] Accordingly Locke holds that abstract 'morality' is a pure science,
which may be developed by demonstration, like pure mathematics, in a
series of what he seems to regard as
analytical judgments.

[2] This suggests a consideration of
the connexion between the relations involved in abstract notions of the under-

standing and empirical facts—between
contingent data and the notions that
must be embodied in the data.

[3] That is, before any one had actually
risen from the dead.

[4] Connexions of convenience, he
means to say, not scientific relations,
determine the mixed modes which
men choose to make.

what greater connexion in nature has the idea of a man than the idea of a sheep with killing, that this is made a particular species of action, signified by the word *murder*, and the other not? Or what union is there in nature between the idea of the relation of a father with killing than that of a son or neighbour, that those are combined into one complex idea, and thereby made the essence of the distinct species *parricide*, whilst the other makes no distinct species at all? But, though they have made killing a man's father or mother a distinct species from killing his son or daughter, yet, in some other cases, son and daughter are taken in too, as well as father and mother: and they are all equally comprehended in the same species, as in that of *incest*. Thus the mind in mixed modes arbitrarily unites into complex ideas such as it finds convenient; whilst others that have altogether as much union in nature are left loose, and never combined into one idea, because they have no need of one name. It is evident then that the mind, by its free choice, gives a connexion to a certain number of ideas, which in nature have no more union with one another than others that it leaves out: why else is the part of the weapon the beginning of the wound is made with taken notice of, to make the distinct species called *stabbing*, and the figure and matter of the weapon left out? I do not say this is done without reason[1], as we shall see more by and by; but this I say, that it is done by the free choice of the mind, pursuing its own ends; and that, therefore, these species of mixed modes are the workmanship of the understanding. And there is nothing more evident than that, for the most part, in the framing these ideas, the mind searches not its patterns in nature, nor refers the ideas it makes to the real existence of things, but puts such together as may best serve its own purposes, without tying itself to a precise imitation of anything that really exists.

But still subservient to the End of Language, and not made at random.

7. But, though these complex ideas or essences of mixed modes depend on the mind, and are made by it with great liberty, yet they are not made at random, and jumbled together without any reason at all. Though these complex

---

[1] Therefore it cannot in all cases be entirely capricious. Cf. § 7.

ideas be not always copied from nature, yet they are always suited to the end for which abstract ideas are made : and though they be combinations made of ideas that are loose enough, and have as little union in themselves as several other to which the mind never gives a connexion that combines them into one idea ; yet they are always made for the convenience of communication, which is the chief end of language[1]. The use of language is, by short sounds, to signify with ease and dispatch general conceptions ; wherein not only abundance of particulars may be contained[2], but also a great variety of independent ideas collected into one complex one. In the making therefore of the species of mixed modes, men have had regard only to such combinations as they had occasion to mention one to another. Those they have combined into distinct complex ideas, and given names to ; whilst others, that in nature have as near a union, are left loose and unregarded. For, to go no further than human actions themselves, if they would make distinct abstract ideas of all the varieties which might be observed in them, the number must be infinite, and the memory confounded with the plenty, as well as overcharged to little purpose. It suffices that men make and name so many complex ideas of these mixed modes as they find they have occasion to have names for, in the ordinary occurrence of their affairs. If they join to the idea of killing the idea of father or mother, and so make a distinct species from killing a man's son or neighbour, it is because of the different heinousness of the crime, and the distinct punishment is due to the murdering a man's father and mother, different to what ought to be inflicted on the murder of a son or neighbour ; and therefore they find it necessary to mention it by a distinct name, which is the end of making that distinct combination. But though the ideas of mother and daughter are so differently treated, in reference to the idea of killing, that the one is joined with it to make a distinct abstract idea with a name, and so

---

[1] Cf. § 10, in which it appears that language exists not merely for conveying ideas from one mind into another, but also for saving *complex* ideas from dissolution in the mind that has formed or received them.

[2] Cf. ch. iii. § 2.

a distinct species, and the other not ; yet, in respect of carnal knowledge, they are both taken in under *incest* : and that still for the same convenience of expressing under one name, and reckoning of one species, such unclean mixtures as have a peculiar turpitude beyond others; and this to avoid circumlocutions and tedious descriptions.

Whereof the intranslatable Words of divers Languages are a Proof.

8. A moderate skill in different languages will easily satisfy one of the truth of this, it being so obvious to observe great store of words in one language which have not any that answer them in another.   Which plainly shows that those of one country, by their customs and manner of life, have found occasion to make several complex ideas, and given names to them, which others never collected into specific ideas.   This could not have happened if these species were the steady workmanship of nature, and not collections made and abstracted by the mind, in order to naming, and for the convenience of communication.   The terms of our law, which are not empty sounds, will hardly find words that answer them in the Spanish or Italian, no scanty languages ; much less, I think, could any one translate them into the Caribbee or Westoe tongues: and the *versura*[1] of the Romans, or *corban*[2] of the Jews, have no words in other languages to answer them ; the reason whereof is plain, from what has been said.   Nay, if we look a little more nearly into this matter, and exactly compare different languages, we shall find that, though they have words which in translations and dictionaries are supposed to answer one another, yet there is scarce one of ten amongst the names of complex ideas, especially of mixed modes, that stands for the same precise idea which the word does that in dictionaries it is rendered by.   There are no ideas more common and less compounded than the measures of time, extension, and weight ; and the Latin names, *hora, pes, libra,* are without difficulty rendered by the English names, *hour, foot,* and *pound* : but yet there is nothing more evident than that the ideas a Roman annexed to these Latin names, were

---

[1] *Versura*—payment by borrowing —a 'mixed mode,' due to a Roman custom.

[2] A 'mixed mode,' occasioned by the custom, peculiar to Jews, of reserving from common use what has been consecrated.

very far different from those which an Englishman expresses
by those English ones[1]. And if either of these should make
use of the measures that those of the other language designed
by their names, he would be quite out in his account. These
are too sensible proofs to be doubted; and we shall find this
much more so in the names of more abstract and compounded
ideas, such as are the greatest part of those which make up
moral discourses: whose names, when men come curiously to
compare with those they are translated into, in other languages,
they will find very few of them exactly to correspond in the
whole extent of their significations.

9. The reason why I take so particular notice of this is, that This
we may not be mistaken about *genera* and *species*, and their shows
Species
essences[2], as if they were things regularly and constantly made to be
by nature, and had a real existence in things; when they made for
Communi-
appear, upon a more wary survey, to be nothing else but an cation.
artifice of the understanding, for the easier signifying such
collections of ideas as it should often have occasion to communicate by one general term; under which divers particulars,
as far forth as they agreed to that abstract idea, might be
comprehended. And if the doubtful signification of the word
species may make it sound harsh to some, that I say the species
of mixed modes are 'made by the understanding'; yet, I
think, it can by nobody be denied that it is the mind makes
those abstract complex ideas to which specific names are given.
And if it be true, as it is, that the mind makes the patterns for
sorting and naming of things, I leave it to be considered who
makes the boundaries of the sort or species; since with me
species and *sort* have no other difference than that of a Latin
and English idiom.

10. The near relation that there is between *species*, *essences*, In mixed
and their *general name*, at least in mixed modes, will further Modes it is
the Name
appear when we consider, that it is the name that seems to that ties
preserve those essences, and give them their lasting duration. the Combination of
For, the connexion between the loose parts of those complex simple

[1] The mixed modes, so named in
Latin, differ in connotation from the
mixed modes for which the analogous
English terms stand.

[2] This must be limited in its application to the essences of mixed modes,
and is not equally applicable to the
genera and *species* of substances.

BOOK III.

CHAP. V.
ideas to-
gether,
and makes
it a
Species.
ideas being made by the mind, this union, which has no particular foundation in nature, would cease again, were there not
something that did, as it were, hold it together, and keep the
parts from scattering.   Though therefore it be the mind that
makes the collection, it is the name which is as it were the
knot that ties them fast together[1].   What a vast variety of
different ideas does the word *triumphus* hold together, and
deliver to us as one species! Had this name been never made,
or quite lost, we might, no doubt, have had descriptions of
what passed in that solemnity : but yet, I think, that which
holds those different parts together, in the unity of one complex
idea, is that very word annexed to it; without which the
several parts of that would no more be thought to make one
thing, than any other show, which having never been made
but once, had never been united into one complex idea, under
one denomination.   How much, therefore, in mixed modes,
the unity necessary to any essence depends on the mind ; and
how much the continuation and fixing of that unity depends
on the name in common use annexed to it, I leave to be
considered by those who look upon essences and species as
real established things in nature.

11. Suitable to this, we find that men speaking of mixed
modes, seldom imagine or take any other for species of them,
but such as are set out by name : because they, being of man's
making only, in order to naming, no such species are taken
notice of, or supposed to be, unless a name be joined to it, as
the sign of man's having combined into one idea several loose
ones ; and by that name giving a lasting union to the parts
which would otherwise cease to have any, as soon as the mind
laid by that abstract idea, and ceased actually to think on it.

---

[1] 'The concept, formed by an abstraction of the resembling from the
non-resembling qualities of objects,
would fall back into the confusion and
infinitude from which it has been called
forth, were it not rendered permanent
for consciousness by being fixed and
ratified in a verbal sign.   Considered
in general, thought and language are
reciprocally dependent ; each bears
all the perfections and imperfections
of the other; but without language
there could be no knowledge realised
of the essential properties of things
and of the connexion of their accidental states.'   (Sir W. Hamilton,
Logic, vol. i. p. 137.)   But we are
not therefore to identify words and
thoughts ; for without ideas words are
empty sounds.

But when a name is once annexed to it, wherein the parts of that complex idea have a settled and permanent union, then is the essence, as it were, established, and the species looked on as complete. For to what purpose should the memory charge itself with such compositions, unless it were by abstraction to make them general? And to what purpose make them general, unless it were that they might have general names for the convenience of discourse and communication? Thus we see, that killing a man with a sword or a hatchet are looked on as no distinct species of action; but if the point of the sword first enter the body, it passes for a distinct species, where it has a distinct name, as in England, in whose language it is called *stabbing*: but in another country, where it has not happened to be specified under a peculiar name, it passes not for a distinct species. But in the species of corporeal substances[1], though it be the mind that makes the nominal essence, yet, since those ideas which are combined in it are supposed to have an union in nature whether the mind joins them or not, therefore those are looked on as distinct species, without any operation of the mind, either abstracting, or giving a name to that complex idea.

12. Conformable also to what has been said concerning the essences of the species of mixed modes, that they are the creatures of the understanding rather than the works of nature; conformable, I say, to this, we find that their names lead our thoughts to the mind, and no further. When we speak of *justice*, or *gratitude*, we frame to ourselves no imagination of anything existing[2], which we would conceive; but our thoughts terminate in the abstract ideas of those virtues, and look not further; as they do when we speak of a *horse*, or *iron*, whose specific ideas we consider not as barely in the mind, but as in things themselves, which afford the original patterns of those ideas. But in mixed modes, at least the most considerable parts of them, which are moral beings, we consider the original patterns as being in the mind, and to those we refer for the distinguishing of particular beings under

For the Originals of our mixed Modes, we look no further than the Mind; which also shows them to be the Workman-ship of the Understanding.

---

[1] As distinguished from the species of mixed modes.

[2] 'existing,' independently of the contingent existence of the abstract idea itself, in a mind that is conscious of it.

BOOK III.

—◆◆—

CHAP. V.

names.   And hence I think it is that these essences of the species of mixed modes are by a more particular name called *notions*[1]; as, by a peculiar right, appertaining to the understanding.

Their being made by the Under-standing without Patterns, shows the Reason why they are so com-pounded.

13. Hence, likewise, we may learn why the complex ideas of mixed modes are commonly more compounded and de-compounded than those of natural substances.   Because they being the workmanship of the understanding, pursuing only its own ends, and the conveniency of expressing in short those ideas it would make known to another, it does with great liberty unite often into one abstract idea things that, in their nature, have no coherence ; and so under one term bundle together a great variety of compounded and decompounded ideas.   Thus the name of *procession* : what a great mixture of independent ideas of persons, habits, tapers, orders, motions, sounds, does it contain in that complex one, which the mind of man has arbitrarily put together, to express by that one name ?   Whereas the complex ideas of the sorts of substances are usually made up of only a small number of simple ones ; and in the species of animals, these two, viz. shape and voice, commonly make the whole nominal essence.

Names of mixed Modes stand alway for their

14. Another thing we may observe from what has been said is, That the names of mixed modes always signify (when they have any determined signification) the *real* essences of their species.   For, these abstract ideas being the workman-

---

[1] ' That *notion* will not stand for every immediate object of the mind in thinking, as *idea* does, I have, as I guess, somewhere given a reason in my book, by showing that the term notion is more peculiarly appropri-ated to a certain sort of those objects which I call *mixed modes* ; and I think it would not sound altogether so well to say the *notion* of red and the *notion* of a horse, as the *idea* of red and the *idea* of a horse.   But if any one thinks it will, I contend not ; for I have no fondness for, no antipathy to, any par-ticular articulate sounds.' (Locke's Second *Letter* to Stillingfleet.) ' No-tions' are thus distinguished from the presentations or ideas of sense ($\alpha i \sigma \theta \acute{\eta}$-$\mu \alpha \tau \alpha$), and from the concrete repre-sentations of the sensuous imagination ($\phi \alpha \nu \tau \acute{\alpha} \sigma \mu \alpha \tau \alpha$),—as products of elabora-tive intelligence ($\delta \iota \alpha \nu o \acute{\eta} \mu \alpha \tau \alpha$ or $\nu o \acute{\eta}$-$\mu \alpha \tau \alpha$). ' Besides the sensations, or phantasms, the sensible ideas of cor-poreal things, passing impressed upon us from without, there must be also *conceptions* [concepts or notions] or intelligible ideas of them, actually exerted from the mind itself; or other-wise they could never be understood.' (Cudworth, *Morality*, p. 192.) Berkeley reserves ' notion,' as a term to desig-nate mind and its operations, and the abstract relations of things.

ship of the mind, and not referred to the real existence of BOOK III. things, there is no supposition of anything more signified by that name, but barely that complex idea the mind itself has CHAP. V. formed; which is all it would have expressed by it; and is real Essences, that on which all the properties of the species depend, and which are the work- from which alone they all flow: and so in these the real and manship of nominal essence is the same; which, of what concernment it our minds. is to the certain knowledge of general truth, we shall see hereafter[1].

15. This also may show us the reason why for the most Why their part the names of mixed modes are got before the ideas they Names are usually stand for are perfectly known. Because there being no species got before of these ordinarily taken notice of but what have names, and their Ideas. those species, or rather their essences, being abstract complex ideas, made arbitrarily by the mind, it is convenient, if not necessary, to know the names, before one endeavour to frame these complex ideas: unless a man will fill his head with a company of abstract complex ideas, which, others having no names for, he has nothing to do with, but to lay by and forget again. I confess that, in the beginning of languages, it was necessary to have the idea before one gave it the name: and so it is still, where, making a new complex idea, one also, by giving it a new name, makes a new word[2]. But this concerns not languages made, which have generally pretty well provided for ideas which men have frequent occasion to have and communicate; and in such, I ask whether it be not the ordinary method, that children learn the names of mixed modes before they have their ideas? What one of a thousand ever frames the abstract ideas of *glory* and *ambition*, before he has heard the names of them? In simple ideas and sub- stances I grant it is otherwise; which, being such ideas as have a real existence and union in nature, the ideas and names are got one before the other, as it happens.

16. What has been said here of *mixed modes* is, with very Reason little difference, applicable also to *relations*; which, since every of my being so

---

[1] See Bk. IV. ch. ii. §9; iv. §§5–10; vi.
[2] Inasmuch as words are not iden- tical with, but presuppose ideas, which make them significant.

BOOK III.
CHAP. V.
large on
this
Subject.

man himself may observe, I may spare myself the pains to enlarge on : especially, since what I have here said concerning Words in this third Book, will possibly be thought by some to be much more than what so slight a subject required. I allow it might be brought into a narrower compass ; but I was willing to stay my reader on an argument[1] that appears to me new and a little out of the way, (I am sure it is one I thought not of when I began to write,) that, by searching it to the bottom, and turning it on every side, some part or other might meet with every one's thoughts, and give occasion to the most averse or negligent to reflect on a general miscarriage, which, though of great consequence, is little taken notice of. When it is considered what a pudder[2] is made about *essences*, and how much all sorts of knowledge, discourse, and conversation are pestered and disordered by the careless and confused use and application of words, it will perhaps be thought worth while thoroughly to lay it open. And I shall be pardoned if I have dwelt long on an argument which I think, therefore, needs to be inculcated, because the faults men are usually guilty of in this kind, are not only the greatest hindrances of true knowledge, but are so well thought of as to pass for it. Men would often see what a small pittance of reason and truth, or possibly none at all, is mixed with those huffing[3] opinions they are swelled with ; if they would but look beyond fashionable sounds, and observe what *ideas* are or are not comprehended under those words with which they are so armed at all points, and with which they so confidently lay about them. I shall imagine I have done some service to truth, peace, and learning, if, by any enlargement

[1] The 'argument' is chiefly intended to show that the *essences* of mixed modes are not determined by the objective 'natures' of things, but by the will of man, influenced by motives of convenience and utility. It is not so new as Locke supposes. The argument in this chapter gives evidence of his disposition to empirical conceptualism or nominalism. It overlooks the rational constitution of the *ultimate* mixed modes—those concerned with morality for example.

[2] 'pudder,' pother, or bother, i. e. to raise a dust, or cause confusion. Cf. *Conduct of Understanding*, § 13.

[3] 'huffing.' To *huff* is to swell or bluster. According to Horne Tooke from *hove*, the past tense of *heave*—not uncommon in the literature of the seventeenth century.

on this subject, I can make men reflect on their own use of BOOK III.
language; and give them reason to suspect, that, since it is
frequent for others, it may also be possible for them, to have CHAP. V.
sometimes very good and approved words in their mouths
and writings, with very uncertain, little, or no signification.
And therefore it is not unreasonable for them to be wary
herein themselves, and not to be unwilling to have them
examined by others[1]. With this design, therefore, I shall go
on with what I have further to say concerning this matter[2].

[1] To deliver men from the bondage of empty words, and the *idola fori*, was a chief motive with Locke in the preparation of the *Essay*, and in all his intellectual work.

[2] Names of simple ideas, along with those of their simple modes; and names of complex ideas of particular substances, are not 'arbitrary,' being determined by 'the existence of things.' On the other hand, names of mixed modes and abstract relations, dealt with in this chapter, comprehending all our remaining ideas, are made (or left unmade) by individual minds, 'without reference to any real existence,' according to Locke, and thus depend wholly upon individual caprice or convenience. But if knowledge and morality ultimately involve relations that are immutable and eternal, grounded in reason, as Locke

seems also to allow, in what he says, for instance, about the relations of cause and effect (Vol. I. p. 433, note), and of morality (p. 477, note), it follows that *some* ideas of relation are endowed with the character of intellectual necessity, and are thus raised above individual caprice and mere convenience.

With Locke the *mixed modes* of our simple ideas, and our *ideas of relation*, are abstracted from the simple ideas in which particular substances are presented in the senses and in reflection; and thus, unlike simple ideas, in themselves and from the first involve generality, their names of course being abstract and general terms. Thus *government* and *obligation*, and the relations of *causality* and *morality*, are abstractions from particular ideas, and universality belongs to the names.

CHAPTER VI.

OF THE NAMES OF SUBSTANCES.

BOOK III.

⸺✦⸺

CHAP. VI.
The
common
Names of
Sub-
stances
stand for
Sorts.

1. THE common names of substances, as well as other general terms, stand for *sorts*: which is nothing else but the being made signs of such complex ideas wherein several particular substances do or might agree, by virtue of which they are capable of being comprehended in one common conception, and signified by one name[1]. I say do or might agree: for though there be but one sun existing in the world, yet the idea of it being abstracted, so that more substances (if there were several) might each agree in it, it is as much a sort as if there were as many suns as there are stars[2]. They want not their reasons who think there are, and that each fixed star would answer the idea the name sun stands for, to one who was placed in a due distance: which, by the way, may show us how much[3] the sorts, or, if you please, *genera*

---

[1] Cf. ch. iii. § 11, according to which *particular substances*, and *their simple ideas* or *qualities* are the only real beings; generality or universality being the elaboration of the human understanding, accidental to real beings.

Our ideas of substances are thus originally of this, that, or the other concrete substance, dimly and imperfectly presented in its simple ideas; generality issues when we discover that it may represent other substances that resemble it. The names of substances are for the most part general, but almost all the proper names in language are names of substances, conceived as this or that individual substance.

[2] 'Abstract ideas' may thus be potentially, not actually, general; they do not depend upon the actual existence of a plurality of individual things corresponding to them.

[3] 'how much.' He does not deny that the 'sorts' which men make may be founded on something in the nature of 'particular beings'; nor that generalisations, made by man, may also be demanded by something in the constitution of the 'particular substances' of which the universe consists, and to which some modes of sorting and naming them more nearly correspond than others do.

and *species* of things (for those Latin terms signify to me no
more than the English word sort) depend on such collections
of ideas as men have made, and not on the real nature of
things; since it is not impossible but that, in propriety of
speech, that might be a sun to one[1] which is a star to another.

2. The measure and boundary of each sort or species, The
whereby it is constituted that particular sort, and distinguished Essence
from others, is that we call its *essence*, which is nothing but of each
that abstract idea[2] to which the name is annexed; so that is our
everything contained in that idea is essential to that sort. abstract
This, though it be all the essence of natural substances that which the
we know, or by which we distinguish them into sorts, yet I call name is
it by a peculiar name, the *nominal essence*, to distinguish it annexed.
from the real constitution of substances, upon which depends
this nominal essence, and all the properties of that sort; which,
therefore, as has been said, may be called the *real essence*: v. g.
the nominal essence of gold is that complex idea the word
gold stands for, let it be, for instance, a body yellow, of a
certain weight, malleable, fusible, and fixed. But the real
essence is the constitution of the insensible parts of that body,
on which those qualities and all the other properties of gold
depend. How far these two are different, though they are
both called essence, is obvious at first sight to discover[3].

3. For, though perhaps voluntary motion, with sense and The
reason, joined to a body of a certain shape, be the complex nominal
idea to which I and others annex the name *man*, and so be Essence
the nominal essence of the species so called: yet nobody will different.
say that complex idea is the real essence and source of all
those operations which are to be found in any individual of
that sort[4]. The foundation of all those qualities which are

---

[1] To one who has not conceived that stars are really suns.

[2] Otherwise called 'concept' or 'notion,' which makes the meaning of the general name.

[3] Cf. Bk. II. ch. viii, and the other passages of the *Essay*, in which Locke treats of a supposed relation between the secondary qualities and powers of bodies and those collocations and

motions of their primary particles, in which he would have their 'real essence' to consist—an essence physical, and not metaphysical as with Aristotle. The 'real essence' of *spirits* is referred to in § 3.

[4] Our generalisations, that is to say, are founded upon the superficially manifested, and therefore incompletely revealed, constitution of the things

the ingredients of our complex idea, is something quite different: and had we such a knowledge of that constitution of man, from which his faculties of moving, sensation, and reasoning, and other powers flow, and on which his so regular shape depends, as it is possible angels have, and it is certain his Maker has[1], we should have a quite other idea of his essence than what now is contained in our definition of that species, be it what it will: and our idea of any individual man would be as far different from what it is now, as is his who knows all the springs and wheels and other contrivances within of the famous clock at Strasburg, from that which a gazing countryman has of it, who barely sees the motion of the hand, and hears the clock strike, and observes only some of the outward appearances[2].

Nothing essential to Individuals.

4. That *essence*, in the ordinary use of the word, relates to sorts, and that it is considered in particular beings no further than as they are ranked into sorts, appears from hence: that, take but away the abstract ideas by which we sort individuals, and rank them under common names, and then the thought of anything essential[3] to any of them instantly vanishes: we have no notion of the one without the other, which plainly shows their relation. It is necessary for me to be as I am; God and nature has made me so: but there is nothing I have is essential to me. An accident or disease may very much alter my colour or shape; a fever or fall may take away my reason or memory, or both; and an apoplexy leave neither sense, nor understanding, no, nor life. Other creatures of my shape may be

classed. Hence the connotation of their class-names does not represent the deepest and truest conception of particular substances, as in the Divine Ideas, but only so far as they are cognisable at our one-sided point of view.

[1] It is here implied that the 'real essences,' incognisable at the side point of view of a finite intelligence, are fully known only at the Divine centre, or in Platonic language in the Divine Ideas.

[2] The illustration found in this famed astronomical clock may suit the real essence of *bodies*, but not of self-con-

sciousness, unless its essence is to be found in the organic conditions on which it now depends in man.

[3] 'essential,' i. e. there is nothing of which we have any idea that is essential to the existence of a particular thing, except the simple ideas or qualities needed to entitle it to receive a name that has been charged by us with a certain connotation, which thus forms its 'nominal' essence, or the essence of the name we apply to it. For meanings of the word *essence*, see ch. iii. § 15.

made with more and better, or fewer and worse faculties than
I have; and others may have reason and sense in a shape and
body very different from mine. None of these are essential to
the one or the other, or to any individual whatever, till the
mind refers it to some sort or species of things[1]; and then
presently, according to the abstract idea of that sort, something is found essential. Let any one examine his own
thoughts, and he will find that as soon as he supposes or
speaks of essential, the consideration of some species, or the
complex idea signified by some general name, comes into his
mind; and it is in reference to that that this or that quality is
said to be essential. So that if it be asked, whether it be
essential to me or any other particular corporeal being, to
have reason? I say, no; no more than it is essential to this
white thing I write on to have words in it. But if that
particular being be to be counted of the sort *man*, and to have
the name *man* given it, then reason is essential to it; supposing reason to be a part of the complex idea the name man
stands for: as it is essential to this thing I write on to contain
words, if I will give it the name *treatise*, and rank it under
that species[2]. So that essential and not essential relate only

---

[1] Hence ' proper names' are not, as such, charged with any connotation, and not until the 'individual' is brought under a class name do we regard any set of qualities as *nominally essential to it*, i.e. conditions we have agreed to regard as indispensable to its being entitled to receive the name. It is only when an individual is regarded as a member of a class, that we can specify certain of its attributes as 'essential,' i.e. all those which we have chosen to include in the meaning of its common name. But this *essentiality* originates in *us*, and not in *it*.

[2] In 'nominal essences,' the *meaning of the name* is thus the criterion and archetype; and particular things are regarded only so far as they are found to agree with this archetype made by man, and thus to be entitled to have the names the connotation of which is the archetype, applied to them. And as he afterwards says (Bk. IV. ch. iv. § 5), all our knowledge, when confined to the meanings of abstract words (analytical judgments), is 'in-fallibly certain; because, in the concepts and reasonings of which it consists,' we 'intend things no further than as they are conformable to our ideas,' i.e. to the connotations we have an-nexed to the names applied to them. If any other 'conformity' is errone-ously assumed, the 'particular things' are irrelevant to the name; just as an arithmetical calculation may be ab-stractly accurate, and yet misapplied. In this sense he tells Molyneux (Aug. 23, 1693) that he 'finds upon examina-tion that *all* general truths are eternal verities; though by mistake some men have selected some, as if they alone were eternal verities.'

to our abstract ideas, and the names annexed to them ; which amounts to no more than this, That whatever particular thing has not in it those qualities which are contained in the abstract idea which any general term stands for, cannot be ranked under that species, nor be called by that name ; since that abstract idea is the very essence of that species [1].

The only essences perceived by us in individual substances are those qualities which entitle them to receive their names.

5. Thus, if the idea of *body* with some people [2] be bare extension or space, then solidity is not essential to body : if others make the idea to which they give the name *body* to be solidity and extension, then solidity is essential to body [3]. That therefore, and that alone, is considered as essential, which makes a part of the complex idea the name of a sort stands for ; without which no particular thing can be reckoned of that sort, nor be entitled to that name.   Should there be found a parcel of matter that had all the other qualities that are in iron, but wanted obedience to the loadstone, and would neither be drawn by it nor receive direction from it, would any one question whether it wanted anything essential ?   It would be absurd to ask, Whether a thing really existing wanted anything essential to it.   Or could it be demanded, Whether this made an essential or specific difference or no, since *we* have no other measure of essential or specific but our abstract ideas ?   And to talk of specific differences in *nature*, without reference to general ideas in names, is to talk unintelligibly.   For I would ask any one, What is sufficient to make an essential difference in nature between any two particular beings, without any regard had to some

---

[1] That common names are applicable to things *only so far as the things possess the (superficial) attributes which we have arbitrarily chosen to connote by the names*, and which are thus ' essential ' to their having the names, does not prove that there is no deeper and truer conception of them, in accordance with which their common names might have received a different connotation, if only we could see things as God sees them.   It does not even show that the notions which a human understanding of things is able to annex to its scientific and philosophic terms may not approximate indefinitely towards that ideal, in the progress of man's knowledge of the universe ; so that Locke's empirical conceptualism exaggerates the inevitable imperfection of finite concepts of particular substances.

[2] Descartes and the Cartesians.

[3] But one of these conceptions of *body* is more accordant with the reason that is immanent in things than the other ; and another, attainable by man, may be still more rational than either.

abstract idea, which is looked upon as the essence and
standard of a species [1]? All such patterns and standards
being quite laid aside, particular beings, considered barely in
themselves, will be found to have all their qualities equally
essential ; and everything in each individual will be essential
to it ; or, which is more, nothing at all [2]. For, though it may
be reasonable to ask, Whether obeying the magnet be essential to iron? yet I think it is very improper and insignificant to ask, whether it be essential to the particular
parcel of matter I cut my pen with ; without considering it
under the name *iron*, or as being of a certain species [3]. And
if, as has been said, our abstract ideas, which have names
annexed to them, are the boundaries of species, nothing can
be essential but what is contained in those ideas.

6. It is true, I have often mentioned a *real essence*, distinct   Even
in substances from those abstract ideas of them, which I call   the real
their nominal essence. By this real essence I mean, that real   essences
constitution of anything, which is the foundation of all those   of individual sub-
properties that are combined in, and are constantly found to   stances
co-exist with the nominal essence ; that particular constitu-   imply
potential
tion which everything has within itself, without any relation   sorts.
to anything without it. But essence, even in this sense,
relates to a sort, and supposes a species. For, being that real
constitution on which the properties depend, it necessarily
supposes a sort of things, properties belonging only to species,
and not to individuals : v. g. supposing the nominal essence
of gold to be a body of such a peculiar colour and weight,
with malleability and fusibility, the real essence is that constitution of the parts of matter on which these qualities and

---

[1] May we not refer to the perfect idea of them, at the (by us unattainable) divine point of view, as an ideal 'standard,' from which human science, valid it may be as far as it goes, necessarily falls short, in respect of depth and completeness?

[2] Are 'particular beings' ever 'considered barely in themselves,' when they are considered and conceived at all? May not some of their relations be deeper and truer than others, and hence too the correlative concepts ? Cf. Spinoza, *Ethices*, Pt. II, xi. Schol. 1, in analogy with §§ 4, 5.

[3] Green, in commenting on this passage (Introduction, parag. 94, 95), supposes that by a 'particular being' Locke means the *abstract individual* stripped of all qualities, not the particular being, presenting to us only a few of the qualities, and these on the surface, as it were, for us to make our abstract or general ideas of it.

BOOK III.
⟶
CHAP. VI.

their union depend ; and is also the foundation of its solubility in *aqua regia* and other properties, accompanying that
complex idea [1]. Here are essences and properties, but all upon
supposition of a sort or general abstract idea, which is considered as immutable; but there is no individual parcel of
matter to which any of these qualities are so annexed as to
be essential to it or inseparable from it [2]. That which is essential belongs to it as a condition whereby it is of this or that
sort : but take away the consideration of its being ranked
under the name of some abstract idea, and then there is
nothing necessary to it, nothing inseparable from it.   Indeed, as to the real essences of substances, we only suppose
their being, without precisely knowing what they are ; but
that which annexes them still to the species is the nominal
essence, of which they are the supposed foundation and
cause [3].

[1] The 'real essences,' even if brought within our reach, would still be species and not individuals—species formed of deeper and truer qualities of the things whose nominal essences they might still be—their ultimate constitution, in short, i. e. the things as they appear in the divine ideas of them. The atomic 'texture' of material substances, however, is Locke's example of 'real essence,' out of reach of human senses and understanding, but the source of those superficial and mutable phenomena that alone come within human observation.

[2] So that 'all general truths are eternal verities,' being in themselves abstract, or independent of all 'individual parcels of matter.'

[3] The *nominal essences* of Locke are *the meanings of terms*: his *real essences* are *the ultimate (physical) constitution of particular things*. We may have a demonstrably necessary knowledge of nominal essences and their relations ; for the 'meanings' are formed by, and therefore fully intelligible to, the mind that forms them ; but it is only a *verbal* knowledge that is thus demon-

strated.   The knowledge of the real essences of things, with all their implicates, is omniscience, and thus transcends human intelligence.   Man's knowledge of the universe, unconsciously involved in the phenomena given by his senses and reflection, is intermediate between the notional science that alone is demonstrable, and the omniscience of Divine knowledge. Ours is the sphere of probable presumption, by which human life has to be determined, as it regulates all the judgments of man that are dependent on what the future may bring forth, and depends on the unknown forces which may modify the laws of things, as things can be known by us. To explain man's intellectual office and duty, in this his *intermediate* position—capable of something deeper and more real than a merely verbal science, yet incapable of knowledge of 'real essences'—is, on a liberal interpretation, the drift of the *Essay*—more apparent in its fourth Book, for which this, on 'nominal and real essences,' prepares the way.   It there leads to the conclusion, that demonstrable science

7. The next thing to be considered is, by which of those essences it is that substances are determined[1] into sorts or species; and that, it is evident, is by the nominal essence. For it is that alone that the name, which is the mark of the sort, signifies. It is impossible, therefore, that anything should determine the sorts of things, which *we* rank under general names, but that idea which that name is designed as a mark for; which is that, as has been shown, which we call nominal essence. Why do we say this is a horse, and that a mule ; this is an animal, that an herb? How comes any particular thing to be of this or that sort, but because it has that nominal essence ; or, which is all one, agrees to that abstract idea, that name is annexed to? And I desire any one but to reflect on his own thoughts, when he hears or speaks any of those or other names of substances, to know what sort of essences they stand for.

8. And that the species of things to us are nothing but the ranking them under distinct names, according to the complex ideas in *us*, and not according to precise, distinct, real essences in *them*[2], is plain from hence :—That we find many of the individuals that are ranked into one sort, called by one common name, and so received as being of one species, have yet qualities, depending on their real constitutions, as far different one from another as from others from which they are accounted to differ specifically. This, as it is easy to be observed by all who have to do with natural bodies, so chemists especially are often, by sad experience, convinced of it, when they, sometimes in vain, seek for the same qualities in one parcel of sulphur, antimony, or vitriol, which they have found in others. For, though they are bodies of the same species, having the same nominal essence, under the

of 'particular substances' is unattainable by man, who cannot form universally necessary propositions about finite things. Cf. Bk. IV. ch. xii. §§ 9, 10.

[1] 'determined,' i. e. by *men*, with their limited faculties and experience.

[2] Yet not, as in mixed modes, without any relation at all to things; but related only to certain observable qualities in the substances, selected for this purpose by the generalising mind, and not to their *real* essences, of which we can have no ideas, because they are unperceivable, either by our limited senses or in self-consciousness.

same name, yet do they often, upon severe ways of examination, betray qualities so different one from another, as to frustrate the expectation and labour of very wary chemists. But if things were distinguished into species, according to their real essences, it would be as impossible to find different properties in any two individual substances of the same species, as it is to find different properties in two circles, or two equilateral triangles. That is properly the essence to *us*, which determines every particular to this or that *classis*; or, which is the same thing, to this or that general name: and what can that be else, but that abstract idea to which that name is annexed[1]; and so has, in truth, a reference, not so much to the being of particular things, as to their general denominations?

Not the real Essence, or texture of parts, which we know not.

9. Nor indeed can we rank and sort things, and consequently (which is the end of sorting) denominate them, by their real essences; because we know them not. Our faculties carry us no further towards the knowledge and distinction of substances, than a collection of *those sensible ideas which we observe in them*; which, however made with the greatest diligence and exactness we are capable of, yet is more remote from the true internal constitution from which those qualities flow, than, as I said, a countryman's idea is from the inward contrivance of that famous clock at Strasburg, whereof he only sees the outward figure and motions. There is not so contemptible a plant or animal, that does not confound the most enlarged understanding. Though the familiar use of things about us take off our wonder, yet it cures not our ignorance. When we come to examine the stones we tread on, or the iron we daily handle, we presently find we know not their make; and can give no reason of the different qualities we find in them. It is evident the internal constitution, whereon their properties depend[2], is unknown to us: for to go no

---

[1] That connotation, in other words, which we have chosen to introduce into the name, in virtue of their *apparent* qualities, constitutes the title of things to have a general name applied to them. The species formed by human understanding are thus relative, superficial, and arbitrary, not absolute; they depend on such 'collection' of their simple ideas as we have made out of the many simple ideas which 'we can observe in them.'

[2] I. e. their 'real essences.'

further than the grossest and most obvious we can imagine
amongst them, What is that texture of parts, that real essence[1],
that makes lead and antimony fusible, wood and stones not?
What makes lead and iron malleable, antimony and stones
not? And yet how infinitely these come short of the fine
contrivances and inconceivable real essences of plants or
animals, every one knows. The workmanship of the all-wise
and powerful God in the great fabric of the universe, and
every part thereof, further exceeds the capacity and comprehension of the most inquisitive and intelligent man, than the
best contrivance of the most ingenious man doth the conceptions of the most ignorant of rational creatures. Therefore
we in vain pretend to range things into sorts, and dispose
them into certain classes under names, by their real essences,
that are so far from our discovery or comprehension. A blind
man may as soon sort things by their colours, and he that
has lost his smell as well distinguish a lily and a rose by
their odours, as by those internal constitutions which he
knows not. He that thinks he can distinguish sheep and
goats by their real essences, that are unknown to him, may
be pleased to try his skill in those species called *cassiowary* [2]
and *querechinchio* [3]; and by their internal real essences determine the boundaries of those species, without knowing the
complex idea of sensible qualities that each of those names
stand for, in the countries where those animals are to be
found.

10. Those, therefore, who have been taught that the several
species of substances had their distinct internal *substantial*
forms [4], and that it was those *forms* which made the distinction

---

[1] He here supposes that the 'real
essence' of things is physical, not
metaphysical — a 'texture of parts,'
which might be patent to sense, if we
had more acute senses, able to see or
feel this *essential* 'texture' of things.

[2] This bird is said by Buffon to have
been brought to Europe by the Dutch
from Java, about a hundred years
before Locke's *Essay* appeared. It is
referred to more than once. Cf. § 34.

[3] A species of hare found in Chili.

[4] The 'form' of a thing, in Peripatetic philosophy, is *that which makes
it the sort of real thing that it is*,—thus
discharging the function which Locke
assigns to the supposed 'real essences'; hyperphysically, however,
with Aristotle, not, as with Locke, the
natural issue of a physical 'texture' of
particles; and so necessarily unperceivable by the senses, which it cannot

BOOK III.
CHAP. VI.

of substances into their true species and genera, were led yet further out of the way by having their minds set upon fruitless inquiries after 'substantial forms'; wholly unintelligible, and whereof we have scarce so much as any obscure or confused conception in general.

That the Nominal Essence is that only whereby we distinguish Species of Substances, further evident, from our ideas of finite Spirits and of God.

11. That our ranking and distinguishing natural substances into species consists in the nominal essences the mind makes, and not in the real essences to be found in the things themselves, is further evident from our ideas of spirits. For the mind getting, only by reflecting on its own operations, those simple ideas which it attributes to spirits, it hath or can have no other notion of spirit but by attributing all those operations it finds in itself to a sort of beings; without consideration of matter. And even the most advanced notion we have of GOD [1] is but attributing the same simple ideas which we have got from reflection on what we find in ourselves, and which we conceive to have more perfection in them than would be in their absence; attributing, I say, those simple ideas to Him in an unlimited degree. Thus, having got from reflecting on ourselves the idea of existence, knowledge, power and pleasure —each of which we find it better to have than to want; and the more we have of each the better—joining all these together, with infinity to each of them, we have the complex idea of an eternal, omniscient, omnipotent, infinitely wise and happy being. And though we are told that there are different species of angels [2]; yet we know not how to frame

come into relation with. For the individual unity of whatever is, was supposed to be constituted by its transcendental 'substantial form,' the *unum per se*, in contrast to the *unum per accidens*. Form (εἶδος) and matter (ὕλη) are correlative, in the constitution of things, each necessarily dependent on the other, according to Aristotle. See *Metaph.* Bk. vi.

[1] On the 'notions we have of God,' cf. Bk. II. ch. xxiii. §§ 33-35, and afterwards in Bk. IV. ch. x. Locke always leans to the deistical conception, which regards God as one person among other persons, capable of being

classed among them under categories of finite thought. In truth neither *He* nor *It* are adequate pronouns for the God in whom we live and have our being—thus presupposed in all our thought and active faith concerning the universe. The difference is well put in Professor Schurman's Winkley Lectures, on *Belief in God.*

[2] So St. Thomas Aquinas, *Summa Theologiæ*, Pt. I. qu. cviii, where the continuous gradations of angels—'ordines angelorum'—are signalised. Locke makes many references to angels, in the essay and elsewhere.

distinct specific ideas of them: not out of any conceit[1] that the existence of more species than one of spirits is impossible; but because having no more simple ideas (nor being able to frame more) applicable to such beings, but only those few taken from ourselves, and from the actions of our own minds in thinking, and being delighted, and moving several parts of our bodies; we can no otherwise distinguish in our conceptions the several species of spirits, one from another, but by attributing those operations and powers we find in ourselves to them in a higher or lower degree; and so have no very distinct specific ideas of spirits[2], except only of GOD, to whom we attribute both duration and all those other ideas with infinity; to the other spirits, with limitation: nor, as I humbly conceive, do we, between GOD and them in our ideas, put any difference, by any number of simple ideas which we have of one and not of the other, but only that of infinity. All the particular ideas of existence, knowledge, will, power, and motion, &c., being ideas derived from the operations of our minds, we attribute all of them to all sorts of spirits, with the difference only of degrees; to the utmost we can imagine, even infinity, when we would frame as well as we can an idea of the First Being; who yet, it is certain, is infinitely more remote, in the real excellency of his nature, from the highest and perfectest of all created beings, than the greatest man, nay, purest seraph, is from the most contemptible part of matter; and consequently must infinitely exceed what our narrow understandings can conceive of Him.

12. It is not impossible to conceive, nor repugnant to reason, that there may be many species of spirits, as much separated and diversified one from another by distinct properties whereof we have no ideas, as the species of sensible things are distinguished one from another by qualities which we know and observe in them. That there should be more species of intelligent creatures above us, than there are of sensible and material below us, is probable to me from hence: that in all the visible corporeal world, we see no chasms or gaps[3]. All

Of finite Spirits there are probably numberless Species, in a continuous series or gradation.

---

[1] 'conceit'—fancy. So concept, in use with Bacon and Shakespeare.

[2] 'spirits,' i. e. unembodied spirits.

[3] What follows is a recognition of the principle of Continuity, which since, in development and application,

quite down from us the descent is by easy steps, and a continued series of things, that in each remove differ very little one from the other. There are fishes that have wings, and are not strangers to the airy region : and there are some birds that are inhabitants of the water, whose blood is cold as fishes, and their flesh so like in taste that the scrupulous are allowed them on fish-days. There are animals so near of kin both to birds and beasts that they are in the middle between both : amphibious animals link the terrestrial and aquatic together ; seals live at land and sea, and porpoises have the warm blood and entrails of a hog ; not to mention what is confidently reported of mermaids, or sea-men[1]. There are some brutes that seem to have as much knowledge and reason as some that are called men : and the animal and vegetable kingdoms are so nearly joined, that, if you will take the lowest of one and the highest of the other, there will scarce be perceived any great difference between them : and so on, till we come to the lowest and the most inorganical parts of matter, we shall find everywhere that the several species are linked together, and differ but in almost insensible degrees. And when we consider the infinite power and wisdom of the Maker, we have reason to think that it is suitable to the magnificent harmony of the universe, and the great design and infinite goodness of the Architect, that the species of creatures should also, by gentle degrees, ascend upward from us toward his infinite perfection, as we see they gradually descend from us downwards : which if it be probable, we have reason then to be persuaded that there are far more species of creatures above us than there are beneath ; we being, in degrees of perfection, much more remote from the infinite being of GOD than we are from the lowest state of being, and that which approaches nearest to nothing.

has played so great a part in modern science and its methods. Leibniz made much of it, in insisting that there must be throughout the universe a continuous progressive ascent (*non per saltum*) towards perfection from the lowest to the highest dependent monad, all culminating in the supreme Monad (*monas monadum*) or God. So too Aristotle in the *De Anima*, for there are curiously analogous suggestions in Aristotle.

[1] Did Locke believe the reports, or is this sarcasm ?

And yet of all those distinct species, for the reasons abovesaid,
we have no clear distinct ideas.

13. But to return to the species of corporeal substances. If The
I should ask any one whether ice and water were two distinct Nominal
species of things, I doubt not but I should be answered in the Essence
that of the
affirmative: and it cannot be denied but he that says they are Species, as
two distinct species is in the right. But if an Englishman conceived
by us,
bred in Jamaica, who perhaps had never seen nor heard of ice, proved
from
coming into England in the winter, find the water he put in Water
his basin at night in a great part frozen in the morning, and, and Ice.
not knowing any peculiar name it had, should call it hardened water; I ask whether this would be a new species to
him, different from water?   And I think it would be answered
here, It would not be to him a new species, no more than
congealed jelly[1], when it is cold, is a distinct species from the
same jelly[1] fluid and warm ; or than liquid gold in the furnace
is a distinct species from hard gold in the hands of a workman.
And if this be so, it is plain that *our distinct species* are *nothing
but distinct complex ideas, with distinct names annexed to them.*
It is true every substance that exists has its peculiar constitution, whereon depend those sensible qualities and powers we
observe in it ; but the ranking of things into species (which is
nothing but sorting them under several titles) is done by us
according to the ideas that *we* have of them : which, though
sufficient to distinguish them by names, so that we may be
able to discourse of them when we have them not present
before us ; yet if we suppose it to be done by their real internal constitutions, and that things existing are distinguished
by nature into species, by real essences, according as we distinguish them into species by names, we shall be liable to
great mistakes[2].

14. To distinguish substantial beings[3] into species, accord- Difficulties
ing to the usual supposition, that there are certain precise in the supposition of
a certain

---

[1] 'jelly'—'gelly,' in the early editions.

[2] The profoundest of our scientific
classifications, or ' natural classes,' as
J. S. Mill calls them, fail to reach the
ultimate physical constitution, and so

cannot give an exhaustive conception
of the sum of conditions on which
the general changes in the things
classified depend.

[3] ' substantial beings '—individual
substances.

BOOK III.
CHAP. VI.

number of real Essences. A crude supposition.

essences or forms of things, whereby all the individuals existing are, by nature distinguished into species, these things are necessary :—

15. First, To be assured that nature, in the production of things, always designs them to partake of certain regulated established essences, which are to be the models of all things to be produced. This, in that crude sense it is usually proposed [1], would need some better explication, before it can fully be assented to.

Monstrous births.

16. Secondly, It would be necessary to know whether nature always attains that essence it designs in the production of things. The irregular and monstrous births [2], that in divers sorts of animals have been observed, will always give us reason to doubt of one or both of these.

Are monsters really a distinct species?

17. Thirdly, It ought to be determined whether those we call monsters [2] be really a distinct species, according to the scholastic notion of the word species ; since it is certain that everything that exists has its particular constitution. And yet we find that some of these monstrous productions have few or none of those qualities which are supposed to result from, and accompany, the essence of that species from whence they derive their originals, and to which, by their descent, they seem to belong.

Men can have no ideas of Real Essences.

18. Fourthly, The real essences of those things which we distinguish into species, and as so distinguished we name, ought to be known ; i. e. we ought to have ideas of them. But since we are ignorant in these four points, the supposed real essences of things stand *us* not in stead for the distinguishing substances into species.

Our Nominal Essences of Substances not perfect collections of the properties

19. Fifthly, The only imaginable help in this case would be, that, having framed perfect complex ideas of the properties of things flowing from their different real essences, we should thereby distinguish them into species. But neither can this be done. For, being ignorant of the real essence itself, it is impossible to know all those properties that flow from it, and

---

[1] He refers to the hypothesis of a definite number of Lowest Species, according to which, or by participation in which, it was supposed that all individual things continued to exist.

[2] Locke repeatedly refers to ‘monsters’ in this connection.

are so annexed to it, that any one of them being away, we may certainly conclude that that essence is not there, and so the thing is not of that species[1]. We can never know what is the precise number of properties depending on the real essence of gold[2], any one of which failing, the real essence of gold, and consequently gold, would not be there, unless we knew the real essence of gold itself, and by that determined that species. By the word *gold* here, I must be understood to design a particular piece of matter; v. g. the last guinea that was coined[3]. For, if it should stand here, in its ordinary signification, for that complex idea which I or any one else calls gold, i. e. for the nominal essence of gold, it would be jargon[4]. So hard is it to show the various meaning and imperfection of words, when we have nothing else but words to do it by

20. By all which it is clear, that our distinguishing substances into species by names, is not at all founded on their real essences; nor can we pretend to range and determine them exactly into species, according to internal essential differences[5].

21. But since, as has been remarked, we have need of *general* words, though we know not the real essences of things; all we can do is, to collect such a number of simple ideas[6] as,

---

[1] Cf. Bk. II. ch. viii, on the (hypothetical) relation between the secondary qualities and powers of matter, on the one hand, and its primary qualities and constitution; also, on our inability, on account of inadequate experience, to predict the former, by means of our necessarily deficient knowledge of the latter.

[2] But we *can* know 'the precise number of properties' which constitute the *nominal* essence of gold; for they consist of those simple ideas or qualities which men have themselves introduced into the meaning of the name *gold*, entitling any particular substance which presents those qualities to have that name applied to it.

[3] Which one calls 'gold' hypothetically, while ignorant what qualities

being absent would imply a different real essence.

[4] It would be 'jargon' to say that all the properties of a particular 'parcel of matter,' to which the name 'gold' is applied, could be deduced from the nominal essence of the term applied to it; and it would be a contradiction to say, that we do not know what qualities being absent the nominal essence 'gold' would cease to be gold; for 'gold' means to each of us what we have resolved that it shall mean.

[5] Our highest discoveries in physical science fall short of the *axiomata prima*, and always lie within the sphere of the *axiomata media* of Bacon—the sphere within which Locke believes that human life mainly turns.

[6] 'Simple ideas,' i. e. the qualities

BOOK III.

CHAP. VI.

ideas
as we
have made
the Name
stand for.

by examination, we find to be united together in things existing, and thereof to make one complex idea. Which, though it be not the real essence of any substance that exists, is yet the specific essence to which our name belongs, and is convertible with it; by which we may at least try the truth of these nominal essences [1]. For example: there be that say [2] that the essence of body is *extension*; if it be so, we can never mistake in putting the essence [3] of anything for the thing itself. Let us then in discourse put extension for body, and when we would say that body moves, let us say that extension moves, and see how ill it will look. He that should say that one extension by impulse moves another extension, would, by the bare expression, sufficiently show the absurdity of such a notion. The essence of anything in respect of us, is the whole complex idea comprehended and marked by that name; and in substances, besides the several distinct simple ideas that make them up, the confused one of substance, or of an unknown support and cause of their union [4], is always a part: and therefore the essence of body is not bare extension, but an extended solid thing; and so to say, an extended solid thing moves, or impels another, is all one, and as intelligible, as to say, *body* moves or impels [5]. Likewise, to say that a rational animal is capable of conversation, is all one as to say a man; but no one will say that rationality is capable of conversation, because it makes not the whole essence to which we give the name man.

of things, and the attributes of our minds, as actually presented in the senses, and in reflection; so that, in this respect, the *nominal* essences that men form are arbitrary, and independent of things.

[1] There is here, too, a virtual recognition of 'natural,' as distinguished from merely arbitrary or capricious generalisations. The nominal essence of the term 'man' involves a classification that is *more* 'natural' than that formed by the term 'red.' It goes deeper into the 'nature' of the individuals classed.

[2] Descartes and the Cartesians, who

held that there cannot be pure extension, so that a vacuum is impossible. (Descartes, *Principia*, Pt. II. §§ 11, 12, 16, 18.)

[3] 'Essence,' i. e. the nominal essence—the simple ideas which constitute our meaning of the name 'body,' which may of course be substituted for the name itself.

[4] That is, the abstract idea of 'substance in general, stripped of all the qualities which make up *our* complex ideas of particular substances. Cf. Bk. II. ch. xxiii. § 2.

[5] Cf. Bk. II. ch. iv. and ch. xiii. § 11, where it is held that solidity or im-

22. There are creatures in the world that have shapes like ours, but are hairy, and want language and reason. There are naturals amongst us that have perfectly our shape, but want reason, and some of them language too. There are creatures, as it is said, (*sit fides penes authorem*, but there appears no contradiction that there should be such,) that, with language and reason and a shape in other things agreeing with ours, have hairy tails; others where the males have no beards, and others where the females have. If it be asked whether these be all *men* or no, all of human species? it is plain, the question refers only to the nominal essence: for those of them to whom the definition of the word man, or the complex idea signified by that name [1], agrees, are men, and the other not. But if the inquiry be made concerning the supposed real essence; and whether the internal constitution and frame of these several creatures be specifically different, it is wholly impossible for us to answer, no part of that going into our specific idea: only we have reason to think, that where the faculties or outward frame so much differs, the internal constitution is not exactly the same. But what difference in the real internal constitution makes a specific difference it is in vain to inquire; whilst our measures of species be, as they are, only our abstract ideas, which we know; and not that internal constitution, which makes no part of them [2]. Shall the difference of hair only on the skin be a mark of a different internal specific constitution between a changeling [3] and a drill [4], when they agree in shape, and

BOOK III.

CHAP. VI.

Our Abstract Ideas are to us the Measures of the Species we make: instance in that of Man.

---

penetrability is the essence of our idea of body, and so included in the connotation which makes the name 'body' applicable to solids presented in space.

[1] I. e. those living beings that present the qualities which we have chosen to include in the connotation of the name 'man,' which arbitrary connotation of ours is the standard for determining whether any actual individual is, or is not, entitled to receive the name 'man.'

[2] Inasmuch as the discovery of it transcends our resources of sense and intelligence. We must therefore be satisfied with an empirical science of nature, in our inability to attain the demonstrably necessary science that is nevertheless latent in the sum of the physical conditions on which the changes in the object ultimately depend.

[3] An idiot. 'Such men do chaungelings call, so chaunged by faries' theft.' Spenser, *Faerie Queen*, Bk. I. c. x; also Shakespeare, *Midsummer Night's Dream*, ii. 1. 21.

[4] An ape or baboon.

want of reason and speech? And shall not the want of reason and speech be a sign to us of different real constitutions and species between a changeling and a reasonable man? And so of the rest, if we pretend that distinction of species or sorts[1] is fixedly established by the real frame and secret constitutions of things.

Species in Animals not distinguished by Generation.
23. Nor let any one say, that the power of propagation in animals by the mixture of male and female, and in plants by seeds, keeps the supposed *real* species distinct and entire. For, granting this to be true, it would help us in the distinction of the species of things no further than the tribes of animals and vegetables. What must we do for the rest? But in those too it is not sufficient: for if history lie not, women have conceived by drills; and what real species, by that measure, such a production will be in nature will be a new question: and we have reason to think this is not impossible, since mules and jumarts, the one from the mixture of an ass and a mare, the other from the mixture of a bull and a mare, are so frequent in the world. I once saw a creature that was the issue of a cat and a rat, and had the plain marks of both about it; wherein nature appeared to have followed the pattern of neither sort alone, but to have jumbled them both together. [2 To which he that shall add the monstrous productions that are so frequently to be met with in nature, will find it hard, even in the race of animals, to determine by the pedigree of what species every animal's issue is; and be at a loss about the real essence, which he thinks certainly conveyed by generation, and has alone a right to the specific name. But further, if the species of animals and plants are to be distinguished only by propagation, must I go to the Indies to see the sire and dam of the one, and the plant from which the seed was gathered that produced the other, to know whether this be a tiger or that tea?]

Not by substantial Forms.
24. Upon the whole matter, it is evident that it is their own collections of sensible qualities that men make the essences of *their* several sorts of substances; and that their real internal

---

[1] I. e. the 'species or sorts' that issue from the observed qualities which men happen to choose, for generalising the particular beings in which the selected qualities appear.

[2] Added in second edition.

structures are not considered by the greatest part of men in the sorting them [1]. Much less were any *substantial forms* ever thought on by any but those who have in this one part of the world learned the language of the schools : and yet those ignorant men, who pretend not any insight into the real essences, nor trouble themselves about substantial forms, but are content with knowing things one from another by their sensible qualities, are often better acquainted with their differences ; can more nicely distinguish them from their uses ; and better know what they expect from each, than those learned quick-sighted men, who look so deep into them, and talk so confidently of something more hidden and essential.

25. But supposing that the *real* essences of substances were discoverable by those that would severely apply themselves to that inquiry, yet we could not reasonably think that the ranking of things under general names was regulated by those internal real constitutions, or anything else but their *obvious* appearances ; since languages, in all countries, have been established long before sciences. So that they have not been philosophers or logicians, or such who have troubled themselves about forms and essences, that have made the general names that are in use amongst the several nations of men : but those more or less comprehensive terms have, for the most part, in all languages, received their birth and signification from ignorant and illiterate people, who sorted and denominated things by those sensible qualities they found in them ; thereby to signify them, when absent, to others, whether they had an occasion to mention a sort or a particular thing [2].

26. Since then it is evident that we sort and name substances by their nominal and not by their real essences, the next thing to be considered is how, and by whom these essences come to be made. As to the latter, it is evident

The specific Essences that are commonly made by Men.

Therefore very various and uncertain in the ideas of

---

[1] Accordingly our *nominal essences* are neither applied by us, nor formed by us, according to the essences that would be recognised by perfect intelligence.

[2] The want of adaptation between the nomenclature and nominal essences of ordinary knowledge, and the nomenclature and nominal essences needed to represent even the imperfect sciences and philosophy attained by intellectual men, is an old, and is likely to be an endless complaint.

they are made by the mind, and not by nature [1]: for were they Nature's workmanship, they could not be so various and different in several men as experience tells us they are.   For if we will examine it, we shall not find the nominal essence of any one species of substances in all men the same : no, not of that which of all others we are the most intimately acquainted with.   It could not possibly be that the abstract idea to which the name *man* is given should be different in several men, if it were of Nature's making ; and that to one it should be *animal rationale* [2], and to another, *animal implume bipes latis unguibus* [3].   He that annexes the name man to a complex idea, made up of sense and spontaneous motion, joined to a body of such a shape, has thereby one essence of the species man ; and he that, upon further examination, adds rationality, has another essence of the species he calls man : by which means the same individual will be a true man to the one which is not so to the other.   I think there is scarce any one will allow this upright figure, so well known, to be the essential difference of the species man ; and yet how far men determine of the sorts of animals rather by their shape than descent, is very visible ; since it has been more than once debated, whether several human fœtuses should be preserved or received to baptism or no, only because of the difference of their outward configuration from the ordinary make of children, without knowing whether they were not as capable of reason as infants cast in another mould : some whereof, though of an approved shape, are never capable of as much appearance of reason all their lives as is to be found in an ape, or an elephant, and never give any signs of being acted by a rational soul.   Whereby it is evident, that the outward figure, which only was found wanting, and not the faculty of reason, which nobody could know would be wanting in its due season, was made essential to the human species.   The learned divine and lawyer must, on such occasions, renounce his sacred definition of *animal rationale*, and substitute some other essence of the human species.   [[4] Monsieur Menage furnishes us with an

---

[1] I. e. by the mind of man, and not by, nor fully according to, the reason that is immanent in nature.

[2] The Peripatetic definition.
[3] That attributed to Plato.
[4] Added in fourth edition.

example worth the taking notice of on this occasion : 'When the abbot of Saint Martin,' says he, 'was born, he had so little of the figure of a man, that it bespake him rather a monster. It was for some time under deliberation, whether he should be baptized or no. However, he was baptized, and declared a man provisionally [till time should show what he would prove]. Nature had moulded him so untowardly, that he was called all his life the Abbot Malotru ; i. e. ill-shaped. He was of Caen [1].' (*Menagiana*, 278, 430.) This child, we see, was very near being excluded out of the species of man, barely by his shape. He escaped very narrowly as he was ; and it is certain, a figure a little more oddly turned had cast him, and he had been executed, as a thing not to be allowed to pass for a man. And yet there can be no reason given why, if the lineaments of his face had been a little altered, a rational soul could not have been lodged in him ; why a visage somewhat longer, or a nose flatter, or a wider mouth, could not have consisted, as well as the rest of his ill figure, with such a soul, such parts, as made him, disfigured as he was, capable to be a dignitary in the church [2].]

27. Wherein, then, would I gladly know, consist the precise and unmovable boundaries of that species ? It is plain, if we examine, there is no such thing made by Nature, and established by her amongst men [3]. The real essence of that or any other sort of substances, it is evident, we know not; and therefore are so undetermined in our nominal essences, which we make ourselves, that, if several men were to be asked concerning some oddly-shaped *fœtus*, as soon as born, whether it were a *man* or no, it is past doubt one should meet with different answers. Which could not happen, if the nominal essences, whereby we limit and distinguish the species of substances, were not made by man with some liberty ; but were exactly copied from precise boundaries set by nature, whereby

---

[1] Giles Menage, the French philologist and critic, born 1613, died 1692, whose *Menagiana*, or miscellany of anecdotes and *bons mots*, contains this reference to the 'Abbot Malotru.'

[2] Cf. Bk. IV. ch. iv. §§ 13–17.

[3] He does not deny the potential existence of real species, incognisable in the imperfect intelligence and experience of men, but implied in the immanent reason in accordance with which all things subsist.

it distinguished all substances into certain species. Who would undertake to resolve what species that monster was of which is mentioned by Licetus [1] (lib. i. c. 3), with a man's head and hog's body? Or those other which to the bodies of men had the heads of beasts, as dogs, horses, &c. If any of these creatures had lived, and could have spoke, it would have increased the difficulty. Had the upper part to the middle been of human shape, and all below swine, had it been murder to destroy it? Or must the bishop have been consulted, whether it were man enough to be admitted to the font or no? As I have been told it happened in France some years since, in somewhat a like case. So uncertain are the boundaries of species of animals to us, who have no other measures than the complex ideas of our own collecting : and so far are we from certainly knowing what a *man* is ; though perhaps it will be judged great ignorance to make any doubt about it. And yet I think I may say, that the certain boundaries of that species are so far from being determined, and the precise number of simple ideas which make the nominal essence so far from being settled and perfectly known, that very material doubts may still arise about it. And I imagine none of the definitions of the word *man* which we yet have, nor descriptions of that sort of animal, are so perfect and exact as to satisfy a considerate inquisitive person ; much less to obtain a general consent, and to be that which men would everywhere stick by, in the decision of cases, and determining of life and death, baptism or no baptism, in productions that might happen.

But not so arbitrary as Mixed Modes. 28. But though these nominal essences of substances are made by the mind, they are not yet made so arbitrarily as those of mixed modes. To the making of any nominal essence, it is necessary, First, that the ideas whereof it consists have such a union as to make but one idea [2], how compounded

---

[1] Fortunato Liceto, an Italian physician and Aristotelian student (1577–1657). The reference is to his work *De Monstrorum Causis.* On 'Monsters,' see the article by C. Devaine, in the *Dictionnaire Encyclopédique des Sciences Médicales,* vol. ix. series ii.

[2] The concept, or nominal essence, connoted by the common term, must be *individualisable,* i. e. capable of being exemplified in sense-perception and sensuous imagination. Further,

soever. Secondly, that the particular ideas so united be exactly the same, neither more nor less. For if two abstract complex ideas differ either in number or sorts of their component parts, they make two different, and not one and the same essence. In the first of these, the mind, in making its complex ideas of substances, only follows nature ; and puts none together which are not supposed to have a union in nature. Nobody joins the voice of a sheep with the shape of a horse ; nor the colour of lead with the weight and fixedness of gold, to be the complex ideas of any real substances ; unless he has a mind to fill his head with chimeras, and his discourse with unintelligible words. Men observing certain qualities always joined and existing together, therein copied nature ; and of ideas so united made their complex ones of substances. For, though men may make what complex ideas they please, and give what names to them they will ; yet, if they will be understood *when they speak of things really existing*, they must in some degree conform their ideas to the things they would speak of ; or else men's language will be like that of Babel ; and every man's words, being intelligible only to himself, would no longer serve to[1] conversation and the ordinary affairs of life, if the ideas they stand for be not some way answering the common appearances and agreement of substances as they really exist.

29. Secondly, Though the mind of man, in making its complex ideas of substances, never puts any together that do not really, or are not supposed to, co-exist ; and so it truly borrows that union from nature : yet the number[2] it combines depends upon the various care, industry, or fancy of him that makes it. Men generally content themselves with some few sensible obvious qualities ; and often, if not always, leave out others as material and as firmly united as those that they take. Of sensible substances there are two sorts : one of organized

---

as he goes on to say, the nominal essences must 'in some degree' conform to what exists in nature, and so are not wholly 'arbitrary,' else 'men's language would be like that of Babel.'

[1] 'serve *to*' — serve *for* in later English.

[2] 'number,' i. e. the number of qualities that the mind puts into its connotations, or chooses to make the names it uses stand for.

bodies, which are propagated by seed ; and in these the *shape* is that which to us is the leading quality, and most character- istical part, that determines the species. And therefore in vegetables and animals, an extended solid substance of such a certain figure usually serves the turn. For however some men seem to prize their definition of *animal rationale*, yet should there a creature be found that had language and reason, but partaked not of the usual shape of a man, I believe it would hardly pass for a man, how much soever it were *animal rationale*. And if Balaam's ass had all his life discoursed as rationally as he did once with his master, I doubt yet whether any one would have thought him worthy the name man, or allowed him to be of the same species with himself. As in vegetables and animals it is the shape, so in most other bodies, not propagated by seed, it is the *colour* we most fix on, and are most led by. Thus where we find the colour of gold, we are apt to imagine all the other qualities comprehended in our complex idea to be there also : and we commonly take these two obvious qualities, viz. shape and colour, for so presumptive ideas of several species, that in a good picture, we readily say, this is a lion, and that a rose ; this is a gold, and that a silver goblet, only by the different figures and colours represented to the eye by the pencil[1].

Yet, imperfect as they thus are, they serve for common converse.

30. But though this serves well enough for gross and con- fused conceptions, and inaccurate ways of talking and thinking ; yet *men are far enough from having agreed on the precise number of simple ideas or qualities belonging to any sort of things, signified by its name.* Nor is it a wonder ; since it requires much time, pains, and skill, strict inquiry, and long examination to find out what, and how many, those simple ideas are, which are constantly and inseparably united in nature, and are always to be found together in the same

---

[1] The most familiar acts of sense-perception imply a suggestion of the qualities that are absent from sense at the time, but which are recalled by means of the few qualities of which one is *actually* percipient. When I only perceive what is visible in a tree, and yet recognise that is a thing entitled to be called 'tree,' I imply that the thing seen contains many other quali- ties, proper to the other senses, that are needed to entitle it to that name.

subject[1]. Most men, wanting either time, inclination, or industry enough for this, even to some tolerable degree, content themselves with some few obvious and outward appearances of things, thereby readily to distinguish and sort them for the common affairs of life : and so, without further examination, give them names, or take up the names already in use. Which, though in common conversation they pass well enough for the signs of some few obvious qualities co-existing, are yet far enough from comprehending, in a settled signification, a precise number of simple ideas, much less all those which are united in nature. He that shall consider, after so much stir about genus and species, and such a deal of talk of specific differences, how few words we have yet settled definitions of, may with reason imagine, that those *forms* which there hath been so much noise made about are only chimeras, which give us no light into the specific natures of things. And he that shall consider how far the names of substances are from having significations wherein all who use them do agree, will have reason to conclude that, though the nominal essences of substances are all supposed to be copied from nature, yet they are all, or most of them, very imperfect. Since the composition of those complex ideas are, in several men, very different : and therefore that these boundaries of species are as men, and not as Nature, makes them, if at least there are in nature any such prefixed bounds. It is true that many particular substances are so made by Nature, that they have agreement and likeness one with another, and so afford a foundation of being ranked into sorts. But the sorting of things by us, or the making of determinate species, being in order to naming and comprehending them under general terms, I cannot see how it can be properly said, that Nature sets the boundaries of the species of things : or, if it be so, our boundaries of species are not exactly conformable[2] to those in nature. For we, having need

---

[1] This again implies that even the species of things which men are able to make may be more than merely arbitrary. Though not adequate to the *ultimate constitution* of the things classed, yet the principle of classification is, in the best generalisations of science, a discovery due to 'time, pains, skill, and strict inquiry.' All calculated or scientific induction shows this.

[2] This qualification —'exactly'—

of general names for present use, stay not for a perfect discovery of all those qualities which would *best* show us their most material differences and agreements; but we ourselves divide them, by certain obvious appearances, into species, that we may the easier under general names communicate our thoughts about them. For, having no other knowledge of any substance but of the simple ideas that are united in it; and observing several particular things to agree with others in several of those simple ideas; we make that collection our specific idea, and give it a general name; that in recording our thoughts, and in our discourse with others, we may in one short word designate all the individuals that agree in that complex idea, without enumerating the simple ideas that make it up; and so not waste our time and breath in tedious descriptions: which we see they are fain to do who would discourse of any new sort of things they have not yet a name for.

Essences of Species under the same Name very different in different minds.

31. But however these species of substances pass well enough in ordinary conversation, it is plain that this complex idea, wherein they observe several individuals to agree, is by different men made very differently; by some more, and others less accurately. In some, this complex idea contains a greater, and in others a smaller number of qualities; and so is apparently such as the mind makes it. The yellow shining colour makes gold to children; others add weight, malleableness, and fusibility; and others yet other qualities, which they find joined with that yellow colour, as constantly as its weight and fusibility. For in all these and the like qualities, one has as good a right to be put into the complex idea of that substance wherein they are all joined as another. And therefore different men, leaving out or putting in several simple ideas which others do not, according to their various examination, skill, or observation of that subject, have different essences[1] of gold, which must therefore be of their own and not of nature's making.

should be noted. Our deepest and truest scientific generalisations fall far short of the meanings of things in their Divine or universal reason; but they involve relations that are due to our participation in reason, and not merely to our caprice.

[1] Nominal essences.

32. If the number of simple ideas that make the nominal essence of the lowest species, or first sorting[1], of individuals, depends on the mind of man, variously collecting them, it is much more evident that they do so in the more comprehensive classes, which, by the masters of logic, are called *genera.* These are complex ideas designedly imperfect: and it is visible at first sight, that several of those qualities that are into be found in the things themselves are purposely left out of generical ideas. For, as the mind, to make general ideas comprehending several particulars, leaves out those of time and place, and such other, that make them incommunicable to more than one individual; so to make other yet more general ideas, that may comprehend different sorts, it leaves out those qualities that distinguish them, and puts into its new collection only such ideas as are common to several sorts. The same convenience that made men express several parcels of yellow matter coming from Guinea[2] and Peru under one name, sets them also upon making of one name that may comprehend both gold and silver, and some other bodies of different sorts. This is done by leaving out those qualities, which are peculiar to each sort, and retaining a complex idea made up of those that are common to them all. To which the name *metal* being annexed, there is a genus constituted; the essence whereof being that abstract idea, containing only malleableness and fusibility, with certain degrees of weight and fixedness, wherein some bodies of several kinds agree, leaves out the colour and other qualities peculiar to gold and silver, and the other sorts comprehended under the name metal. Whereby it is plain that men follow not exactly the patterns set them by nature, when they make their general ideas of substances; since there is no body to be found which has barely malleableness and fusibility in it, without other qualities as inseparable as those. But men, in making their

BOOK III.

Chap. VI.

The more general our Ideas of Substances are, the more incomplete and partial they are.

---

[1] A *lowest species*, or species that cannot become a genus, properly presupposes '*universals*' *in nature*, and thus their real existence, as well as that of the individuals. But if the only 'species' man has to do with are those of his own 'creation'—his own 'abstract ideas,' or connotations lodged in words—we cannot arbitrarily arrest, at a so-called lowest species, the descending process of concept-making—unless for purposes of convenience.

[2] 'Guinea'—'Guiny' in the early editions.

general ideas, seeking more the convenience of language, and quick dispatch by short and comprehensive signs, than the true and precise nature of things as they exist, have, in the framing their abstract ideas, chiefly pursued that end; which was to be furnished with store of general and variously comprehensive names. So that in this whole business of genera and species, the genus, or more comprehensive, is but a partial conception of what is in the species; and the species but a partial idea of what is to be found in each individual. If therefore any one will think that a man, and a horse, and an animal, and a plant, &c., are distinguished by real essences made by nature, he must think nature to be very liberal of these real essences, making one for body, another for an animal, and another for a horse; and all these essences liberally bestowed upon Bucephalus. But if we would rightly consider what is done in all these genera and species, or sorts, we should find that there is no new thing made[1]; but only more or less comprehensive signs, whereby we may be enabled to express in a few syllables great numbers of particular things, as they agree in more or less general conceptions, which we have framed to that purpose. In all which we may observe, that the more general term is always the name of a less complex idea; and that each genus is but a partial conception of the species comprehended under it[2]. So that if these abstract general ideas be thought to be complete, it can only be in respect of a certain established relation between them and certain names which are made use of to signify them; and not in respect of anything existing, as made by nature.

This all accommodated to the end of Speech.
33. This is adjusted to the true end of speech, which is to be the easiest and shortest way of communicating our notions. For thus he that would discourse of things, as they agreed in the complex idea of extension and solidity, needed but use the word *body* to denote all such. He that to these would join others, signified by the words life, sense, and spontaneous

---

[1] There is no new *individual thing* 'made,' but there is an already made *relation* (*in rebus*, if not *ante res*), sought for in scientific generalisation.

[2] This is simply an imperfect statement of what logic teaches about the natural relations of *extent* and *content*, in the abstract concepts, or nominal essences, formed by the human understanding.

motion, needed but use the word *animal* to signify all which
partaked of those ideas, and he that had made a complex idea
of a body, with life, sense, and motion, with the faculty of
reasoning, and a certain shape joined to it, needed but use the
short monosyllable *man*, to express all particulars that correspond to that complex idea. This is the proper business of
genus and species: and this men do without any consideration
of real essences, or substantial forms ; which come not within
the reach of our knowledge when we think of those things,
nor within the signification of our words when we discourse
with others.

34. Were I to talk with any one of a sort of birds I lately
saw in St. James's Park [1], about three or four feet high, with a
covering of something between feathers and hair, of a dark
brown colour, without wings, but in the place thereof two or
three little branches coming down like sprigs of Spanish
broom, long great legs, with feet only of three claws, and
without a tail ; I must make this description of it, and so may
make others understand me. But when I am told that the
name of it is *cassuaris*, I may then use that word to stand in
discourse for all my complex idea mentioned in that description ; though by that word, which is now become a specific
name, I know no more of the real essence or constitution of
that sort of animals than I did before ; and knew probably as
much of the nature of that species of birds before I learned
the name, as many Englishmen do of swans or herons, which
are specific names, very well known, of sorts of birds common
in England.

35. From what has been said, it is evident that *men* make
sorts of things. For, it being different essences alone that
make different species, it is plain that they who make those
abstract ideas which are the nominal essences do thereby make
the species, or sort. Should there be a body found, having all
the other qualities of gold except malleableness, it would no
doubt be made a question whether it were gold or not, i.e.
whether it were of that species. This could be determined only

---

[1] Where a collection of animals was then kept, to which there are allusions
in contemporary literature.

by that abstract idea to which every one annexed the name gold : so that it would be true gold to him, and belong to that species, who included not malleableness in his nominal essence, signified by the sound gold ; and on the other side it would not be true gold, or of that species, to him who included malleableness in his specific idea. And who, I pray, is it that makes these diverse species, even under one and the same name, but men that make two different abstract ideas, consisting not exactly of the same collection of qualities? Nor is it a mere supposition to imagine that a body may exist wherein the other obvious qualities of gold may be without malleableness; since it is certain that gold itself will be sometimes so eager, (as artists call it,) that it will as little endure the hammer as glass itself. What we have said of the putting in, or leaving out of malleableness, in the complex idea the name gold is by any one annexed to, may be said of its peculiar weight, fixedness, and several other the like qualities : for whatever is left out, or put in, it is still the complex idea to which that name is annexed that makes the species : and as any particular parcel of matter answers that idea, so the name of the sort belongs truly to it ; and it is of that species. And thus anything is true gold, perfect metal. All which determination of the species, it is plain, depends on the understanding of man, making this or that complex idea.

Nature makes the Similitudes of Substances. 36. This, then, in short, is the case : Nature makes many *particular things*, which do agree one with another in many sensible qualities, and probably too in their internal frame and constitution : but it is not this real essence that distinguishes them into species ; it is men who, taking occasion from the qualities they find united in them, and wherein they observe often several individuals to agree [1], range them into sorts, in order to their naming, for the convenience of comprehensive signs ; under which individuals, according to their conformity to this or that abstract idea, come to be ranked as under ensigns : so that this is of the blue, that the red

---

[1] But the quality thus selected may more or less approximate to those that constitute the true or ultimate nature of the things named, making language not only the vehicle of abstract thought, but the wheels of scientific research.

regiment; this is a man, that a drill: and in this, I think, consists the whole business of genus and species.

37. I do not deny but nature, in the constant production of particular beings, makes them not always new and various, but very much alike and of kin one to another : but I think it nevertheless true, that the boundaries of the species, whereby men sort them, are made by men [1] ; since the essences of the species, distinguished by different names, are, as has been proved, of man's making, and seldom adequate to the internal nature of the things they are taken from [1]. So that we may truly say, such a manner of sorting of things is the workmanship of men [2].

The manner of sorting particular beings the work of fallible men, though nature makes things alike.

38. One thing I doubt not but will seem very strange in

Each abstract

---

[1] But they may be made, on a *scientific* principle or on a *superficial* one ; though doubtless, in few cases, as he adds, 'adequate to the internal nature of the things they are taken from.' The meaning of the name now and then may contain the nature.

[2] This about universals is thus commented on by Molyneux, in one of his letters to Locke (Dec. 22, 1692) :— 'What you say concerning *genera* and *species* is unquestionably true; and yet it seems hard to assert, that there is no such sort of creatures in nature as *birds*; for though we may be ignorant of the particular essence that makes a bird to be a bird, or that determines and distinguishes a bird from a beast ; or the just limits and boundaries between each ; yet we can no more doubt of a sparrow's being a bird, and an horse's being a beast, than we can of this colour being black, and the other white : though by shades they may be made so gradually to vanish into each other that we cannot tell where either determines.' To which Locke replies (Jan. 20, 1693) :—' In the objection you raise about *species*, I fear you are fallen into the same difficulty I often found myself under, when I was writing on that subject, where I was very apt to suppose dis-

tinct species I could talk of without names. For pray, sir, consider what it is you mean when you say, that " we can no more doubt of a sparrow's being a bird, and a horse's being a beast, than we can of this colour being black, and that other white," but this, that the combination of simple ideas [qualities] which the word bird stands for is to be found in that particular thing we call a sparrow. And therefore I hope I have nowhere said, " there is no such sort of creatures in *nature* as birds ; " if I have, it is both contrary to truth and to my opinion. This I dare say : that there are real constitutions in [particular] things, from whence those simple ideas [qualities] flow which we observe in them. And this I further say : that there are real distinctions and differences in those real constitutions, one from another, whereby they are distinguished one from another, *whether we think of them, or name them, or no* ; but that that whereby *we* distinguish and rank particular substances into sorts, is *not those real essences or internal constitutions*, but *such combinations of simple ideas as we observe in them*. This I designed to show, in Lib. III. ch. vi.'

BOOK III.
CHAP. VI.
Idea, with
a name to
it, makes a
nominal
Essence.

this doctrine, which is, that from what has been said it will follow, that each abstract idea, with a name to it, makes a distinct species. But who can help it, if truth will have it so? For so it must remain till somebody can show us the species of things limited and distinguished by something else; and let us see that general terms signify not our abstract ideas, but something different from them. I would fain know why a shock and a hound are not as distinct species as a spaniel and an elephant. We have no other idea of the different essence of an elephant and a spaniel, than we have of the different essence of a shock and a hound; all the essential difference, whereby we know and distinguish them one from another, consisting only in the different collection of simple ideas, to which we have given those different names.

How
Genera
and
Species
are related
to naming.

39. How much the making of species and genera is in order to general names; and how much general names are necessary, if not to the being, yet at least to the completing of a species, and making it pass for such, will appear, besides what has been said above concerning ice and water, in a very familiar example. A silent and a striking watch are but one species to those who have but one name for them: but he that has the name *watch* for one, and *clock* for the other, and distinct complex ideas to which those names belong, to *him* they are different species. It will be said perhaps, that the inward contrivance and constitution is different between these two, which the watchmaker has a clear idea of. And yet it is plain they are but one species to him, when he has but one name for them. For what is sufficient in the inward contrivance to make a new species? There are some watches that are made with four wheels, others with five; is this a specific difference to the workman? Some have strings and physies [1], and others none; some have the balance loose, and others regulated by a spiral spring, and others by hogs' bristles. Are any or all of these enough to make a specific difference to the workman, that knows each of these and several other different contrivances in the internal constitutions of watches? It is certain each of these hath a real difference from the rest; but whether it be an essential, a specific

[1] 'phisies'—fusees, which transmit motion to the wheels.

difference or no, relates only to the complex idea to which the
name watch is given : as long as they all agree in the idea
which that name stands for, and that name does not as a
generical name comprehend different species under it, they
are not essentially nor specifically different. But if any one
will make minuter divisions, from differences that he knows
in the internal frame of watches, and to such precise complex
ideas give names that shall prevail ; they will then be new
species, to them who have those ideas with names to them,
and can by those differences distinguish watches into these
several sorts ; and then *watch* will be a generical name. But
yet they would be no distinct species to men ignorant of
clock-work, and the inward contrivances of watches, who had
no other idea but the outward shape and bulk, with the
marking of the hours by the hand. For to them all those
other names would be but synonymous terms for the same
idea, and signify no more, nor no other thing but a watch.
Just thus I think it is in natural things. Nobody will doubt
that the wheels or springs (if I may so say) within, are
different in a *rational man* and a *changeling* ; no more than
that there is a difference in the frame between a *drill* and
a *changeling*. But whether one or both these differences be
essential or specifical, is only to be known to us by their
agreement or disagreement with the complex idea that the
name man stands for : for by that alone can it be determined
whether one, or both, or neither of those be a man.

40. From what has been before said, we may see the reason Species of
why, in the species of artificial things, there is generally less Artificial
Things
confusion and uncertainty than in natural. Because an arti- less con-
ficial thing being a production of man, which the artificer Natural.
designed, and therefore well knows the idea of, the name of it
is supposed to stand for no other idea, nor to import any
other essence, than what is certainly to be known, and easy
enough to be apprehended. For the idea or essence of the
several sorts of artificial things, consisting for the most part
in nothing but the determinate figure of sensible parts, and
sometimes motion depending thereon, which the artificer
fashions in matter, such as he finds for his turn ; it is not
beyond the reach of our faculties to attain a certain idea

thereof ; and so settle the signification of the names whereby the species of artificial things are distinguished, with less doubt, obscurity, and equivocation than we can in things natural, whose differences and operations depend upon contrivances beyond the reach of our discoveries.

Artificial Things of distinct Species.

41. I must be excused here if I think artificial things are of distinct species as well as natural : since I find they are as plainly and orderly ranked into sorts, by different abstract ideas, with general names annexed to them, as distinct one from another as those of natural substances. For why should we not think a watch and pistol as distinct species one from another, as a horse and a dog ; they being expressed in our minds by distinct ideas, and to others by distinct appellations ?

Substances alone, of all our several sorts of ideas, have proper Names.

42. This is further to be observed concerning substances, that they alone of all our several sorts of ideas have particular or proper names, whereby one only particular thing is signified. Because in simple ideas, modes, and relations, it seldom happens that men have occasion to mention often this or that particular when it is absent. Besides, the greatest part of mixed modes, being actions which perish in their birth, are not capable of a lasting duration, as substances which are the actors ; and wherein the simple ideas that make up the complex ideas designed by the name have a lasting union [1].

Difficult to lead another by words into the thoughts of things stripped of those abstract ideas we give them.

43. I must beg pardon of my reader for having dwelt so long upon this subject, and perhaps with some obscurity. But I desire it may be considered, how difficult it is to lead another by words into the thoughts of things, stripped of those specifical differences we give them : which things, if I name not, I say nothing ; and if I do name them, I thereby rank them into some sort or other, and suggest to the mind the usual abstract idea of that species ; and so cross my purpose. For, to talk of a man, and to lay by, at the same time, the

[1] This contrast between *mixed modes*, which, formed by men, consist of simple ideas or phenomena that 'perish in their birth,' and complex ideas of *substances*, in which the ideas 'designed by the name have a lasting union' in nature, is fundamental in the *Essay*. On it is based the possibility of general propositions about real things, which nevertheless cannot rise above probability into the unconditional certainty that is essential to what Locke means by knowledge.

ordinary signification of the name man, which is our complex idea usually annexed to it ; and bid the reader consider man, as he is in himself, and as he is really distinguished from others in his internal constitution, or real essence, that is, by something he knows not what, looks like trifling : and yet thus one must do who would speak of the supposed real essences and species of things, as thought to be made by nature, if it be but only to make it understood, that there is no such thing signified by the general names which substances are called by. But because it is difficult by known familiar names to do this, give me leave to endeavour by an example to make the different consideration the mind has of specific names and ideas a little more clear ; and to show how the complex ideas of modes are referred sometimes to archetypes in the minds of other intelligent beings, or, which is the same, to the signification annexed by others to their received names ; and sometimes to no archetypes at all. Give me leave also to show how the mind always refers its ideas of substances, either to the substances themselves, or to the signification of their names, as to the archetypes ; and also to make plain the nature of species or sorting of things, as apprehended and made use of by us ; and of the essences belonging to those species : which is perhaps of more moment to discover the extent and certainty of our knowledge than we at first imagine.

44. Let us suppose Adam, in the state of a grown man, with a good understanding, but in a strange country, with all things new and unknown about him ; and no other faculties to attain the knowledge of them but what one of this age has now. He observes Lamech more melancholy than usual, and imagines it to be from a suspicion he has of his wife Adah, (whom he most ardently loved) that she had too much kindness for another man. Adam discourses these his thoughts to Eve, and desires her to take care that Adah commit not folly : and in these discourses with Eve he makes use of these two new words *kinneah* and *niouph*. In time, Adam's mistake appears, for he finds Lamech's trouble proceeded from having killed a man : but yet the two names *kinneah* and *niouph*, (the one standing for suspicion in a husband of his wife's

Instances of mixed Modes named kinneah and niouph.

disloyalty to him; and the other for the act of committing disloyalty,) lost not their distinct significations. It is plain then, that here were two distinct complex ideas of mixed modes, with names to them, two distinct species of actions essentially different; I ask wherein consisted the essences of these two distinct species of actions? And it is plain it consisted in a precise combination of simple ideas, different in one from the other. I ask, whether the complex idea in Adam's mind, which he called *kinneah*, were adequate or not? And it is plain it was; for it being a combination of simple ideas, which he, without any regard to any archetype, without respect to anything as a pattern, voluntarily put together, abstracted, and gave the name *kinneah* to, to express in short to others, by that one sound, all the simple ideas contained and united in that complex one; it must necessarily follow that it was an adequate idea. His own choice having made that combination, it had all in it he intended it should, and so could not but be perfect, could not but be adequate; it being referred to no other archetype which it was supposed to represent.

45. These words, *kinneah* and *niouph*, by degrees grew into common use, and then the case was somewhat altered. Adam's children had the same faculties, and thereby the same power that he had, to make what complex ideas of mixed modes they pleased in their own minds; to abstract them, and make what sounds they pleased the signs of them: but the use of names being to make our ideas within us known to others, that cannot be done, but when the same sign stands for the same idea in two who would communicate their thoughts and discourse together. Those, therefore, of Adam's children, that found these two words, *kinneah* and *niouph*, in familiar use, could not take them for insignificant sounds, but must needs conclude they stood for something; for certain ideas, abstract ideas, they being general names; which abstract ideas were the essences of the species distinguished by those names. If, therefore, they would use these words as names of species already established and agreed on, they were obliged to conform the ideas in their minds, signified by these names, to the ideas that they stood for in other men's minds, as to their

patterns and archetypes; and then indeed their ideas of these complex modes were liable to be inadequate, as being very apt (especially those that consisted of combinations of many simple ideas) not to be exactly conformable to the ideas in other men's minds, using the same names; though for this there be usually a remedy at hand, which is to ask the meaning of any word we understand not of him that uses it: it being as impossible to know certainly what the words jealousy and adultery (which I think answer קנאה and נאוף) stand for in another man's mind, with whom I would discourse about them; as it was impossible, in the beginning of language, to know what *kinneah* and *niouph* stood for in another man's mind, without explication; they being voluntary signs in every one.

46. Let us now also consider, after the same manner, the names of substances in their first application. One of Adam's children, roving in the mountains, lights on a glittering substance which pleases his eye. Home he carries it to Adam, who, upon consideration of it, finds it to be hard, to have a bright yellow colour, and an exceeding great weight. These perhaps, at first, are all the qualities he takes notice of in it; and abstracting this complex idea, consisting of a substance having that peculiar bright yellowness, and a weight very great in proportion to its bulk, he gives the name *zahab*, to denominate and mark all substances that have these sensible qualities in them. It is evident now, that, in this case, Adam acts quite differently from what he did before, in forming those ideas of mixed modes to which he gave the names *kinneah* and *niouph*. For there he put ideas together only by his own imagination, not taken from the existence of anything; and to them he gave names to denominate all things that should happen to agree to those his abstract ideas, without considering whether any such thing did exist or not: the standard there was of his own making. But in the forming his idea of this new substance, he takes the quite contrary course; here he has a standard made by nature; and therefore, being to represent that to himself, by the idea he has of it, even when it is absent, he puts in no simple idea into his complex one, but what he has the perception

of from the thing itself.   He takes care that his idea be conformable to this archetype, and intends the name should stand for an idea so conformable.

47.   This piece of matter, thus denominated *zahab* by Adam, being quite different from any he had seen before, nobody, I think, will deny to be a distinct species, and to have its peculiar essence ; and that the name *zahab* is the mark of the species, and a name belonging to all things partaking in that essence.   But here it is plain the essence Adam made the name *zahab* stand for was nothing but a body hard, shining, yellow, and very heavy.   But the inquisitive mind of man, not content with the knowledge of these, as I may say, superficial qualities, puts Adam upon further examination of this matter.   He therefore knocks, and beats it with flints, to see what was discoverable in the inside : he finds it yield to blows, but not easily separate into pieces : he finds it will bend without breaking.   Is not now ductility to be added to his former idea, and made part of the essence of the species that name *zahab* stands for?   Further trials discover fusibility and fixedness.   Are not they also, by the same reason that any of the others were, to be put into the complex idea signified by the name *zahab*?   If not, what reason will there be shown more for the one than the other?   If these must, then all the other properties, which any further trials shall discover in this matter, ought by the same reason to make a part of the ingredients of the complex idea which the name *zahab* stands for, and so be the essence of the species marked by that name.   Which properties, because they are endless, it is plain that the idea made after this fashion, by this archetype, will be always inadequate [1].

---

[1] This of Adam, and the manner in which he must have formed the *mixed modes* 'jealousy' and 'adultery,' as compared with the process which gave rise to his complex idea of the *substance* 'gold,' is a quaint illustration of what is meant by the identity of the nominal and real essence in mixed modes, and the inevitable inadequacy of the nominal to the real essence in all our ideas of particular substances.   In the former, Adam put simple ideas together solely according to the standard of his own fancy: in the latter he had to take the simple ideas from the standard presented by nature, as discovered by his observation of the qualities actually presented by the particular substance before him.   These, although they do not

48. But this is not all. It would also follow that the names of substances would not only have, as in truth they have, but would also be supposed to have different significations, as used by different men, which would very much cumber the use of language. For if every distinct quality that were discovered in any matter by any one were supposed to make a necessary part of the complex idea signified by the common name given to it, it must follow, that men must suppose the same word to signify different things in different men: since they cannot doubt but different men may have discovered several qualities, in substances of the same denomination, which others know nothing of.

BOOK III.

CHAP. VI.

The Abstract Ideas of Substances always imperfect, and therefore various.

49. To avoid this[1] therefore, they have supposed a real essence belonging to every species, from which these properties all flow, and would have their name of the species stand for that. But they, not having any idea of that real essence in substances, and their words signifying nothing but the ideas they have, that which is done by this attempt is only to put the name or sound in the place and stead of the thing having that real essence, without knowing what the real essence is[2], and this is that which men do when they speak of species of things, as supposing them made by nature, and distinguished by real essences.

50. For, let us consider, when we affirm that 'all gold is fixed,' either it means that fixedness is a part of the definition, i. e., part of the nominal essence the word gold stands for; and so this affirmation, 'all gold is fixed,' contains nothing but the signification of the term gold. Or else it means, that fixedness, not being a part of the definition of the gold, is a property of that substance itself: in which case

embrace its physical essence, i. e. the 'texture' of the atoms of which it consists, and on which its secondary qualities and powers are supposed to depend, may nevertheless form a sufficient basis for *probable* inferences regarding many of its unperceived qualities and powers, and its physical relations to other substances.

[1] 'To avoid this,' i. e. the variation and uncertainty regarding the species to which a particular thing belongs; inasmuch as, in view of its perceived qualities, it may be placed in many different classes, and so have many nominal essences. Hence the craving for the ultimate essence which alone is regarded as 'real.'

[2] Thus leaving the name an empty sound, and therefore of course indefinable.

it is plain that the word gold stands in the place of a substance, having the real essence of a species of things made by nature. In which way of substitution it has so confused and uncertain a signification, that, though this proposition—' gold is fixed '—be in that sense an affirmation of something real ; yet it is a truth will always fail us in its particular application, and so is of no real use or certainty. For let it be ever so true, that all gold, i. e. all that has the real essence of gold, is fixed, what serves this for, whilst we know not, in this sense, *what is or is not gold*? For if we know not the real essence of gold, it is impossible we should know what parcel of matter has that essence, and so whether *it* be true gold or no[1].

51. To conclude : what liberty Adam had at first to make any complex ideas of *mixed modes* by no other pattern but by his own thoughts, the same have all men ever since had. And the same necessity of conforming his ideas of *substances* to things without him, as to archetypes made by nature, that Adam was under, if he would not wilfully impose upon himself, the same are all men ever since under too. The same liberty also that Adam had of affixing any new name to any idea, the same has any one still, (especially the beginners of languages, if we can imagine any such;) but only with this difference, that, in places where men in society have already

---

[1] To make the proposition about gold an intelligible one, the name ' gold ' must signify the presence of the qualities comprehended in our ' abstract idea' in anything which this name stands for ; not the 'real essence' of the particular parcel of matter we call ' gold,' seeing that this real essence is unknown, because not presented in human experience. To make ' gold ' a significant term, it must signify what can be verified by our senses ; not what is always out of their reach, and is perhaps even hyperphysical. Cf. ch. x. § 17.
    We have a complex idea of the sort of substance called gold only so far as anything so named is an aggregate of simple ideas that can be manifested to the senses, not in its unmanifested ultimate constitution. We can conceive and know things only as we have simple ideas of them. Out of those simple ideas, or presented qualities, we can make those complex ideas called ' nominal essences'; and we can determine whether the essence to which we annex the name gold shall include the simple idea of ' fixedness' or not, as well as determine by our senses whether any particular substance answers to this *nominal essence.* But the *real essence* of that particular substance is left undetermined by our nominal essence, which only entitles the thing to the name.

established a language amongst them, the significations of
words are very warily and sparingly to be altered. Because
men being furnished already with names for their ideas, and
common use having appropriated known names to certain
ideas, an affected misapplication of them cannot but be very
ridiculous. He that hath new notions will perhaps venture
sometimes on the coining of new terms to express them : but
men think it a boldness, and it is uncertain whether common
use will ever make them pass for current. But in communication with others, it is necessary that we conform the ideas we
make the vulgar words of any language stand for to their
known proper significations, (which I have explained at large
already,) or else to make known that new signification we
apply them to [1].

[1] The sixth chapter is the most significant in the third Book. Taken apart, it contains passages in which Locke seems to express an extreme nominalism that would resolve physics into purely logical evolution of the implicates of arbitrarily-formed complex ideas of substances, formulated in nominal definitions, thus making it analytical, not synthetical, and so carrying us back by a new way into the verbal scholasticism against which the whole *Essay* is a reaction. The 'essences' with which alone we can deal are only, he insists, essences elaborated by ourselves; for the real essences of the individual substances which make up the universe are hid from the view of man. But this chapter must be compared with the fourth Book, in those parts of it especially which treat of our 'knowledge of relations of coexistence among ideas,' i. e. of the qualities that coexist in substances, the discovery of which is the ideal and end of all experimental science. 'Relations of coexistence,' Locke there teaches, belong to the sphere of probability, not of certainty ; inasmuch as the real essences, which contain the ultimate secrets of nature, are hid from man's senses and intellectual view. Physics therefore cannot rise to absolute certainty of knowledge, and must consist of probabilities, founded on qualities of things that are open to observation, and in virtue of which humanly made nominal essences, or the names which signify them, are applicable to things. Locke thus sees man in a position intermediate between that assigned to him by absolute realism, which pretends to demonstrate all the qualities of substances, from their *real essences,* and the nescient nominalism which reduces it all to an affair of names. A human understanding of the qualities of substances is confined, according to Locke, to the region of probabilities.

CHAPTER VII.

OF PARTICLES [1].

Particles
connect
Parts, or
whole
Sentences
together.

1. Besides words which are names of ideas in the mind, there are a great many others that are made use of to signify the *connexion* that the mind gives to ideas, or to propositions, one with another. The mind, in communicating its thoughts to others, does not only need signs of the ideas it has then before it, but others also, to show or intimate some particular action of its own, at that time, relating to those ideas. This it does several ways ; as *Is*, and *Is not*, are the general marks, of the mind, affirming or denying. But besides affirmation or negation, without which there is in words no truth or falsehood, the mind does, in declaring its sentiments to others, connect not only the parts of propositions, but whole sentences one to another, with their several relations and dependencies, to make a coherent discourse.

In right
use of
Particles
consists
the Art
of Well-
speaking.

2. The words whereby it signifies what connexion it gives to the several affirmations and negations, that it unites in one continued reasoning or narration, are generally called *particles* : and it is in the right use of these that more particularly consists the clearness and beauty of a good style. To think well, it is not enough that a man has ideas clear and distinct in his thoughts, nor that he observes the agreement or disagreement of some of them ; but he must think in train, and observe the dependence of his thoughts and reasonings upon one another. And to express well such methodical and

---

[1] Thus far the third Book has dealt with nouns (substantive and adjective), pronouns, and verbs. This chapter, under the head of ' Particles,' touches the functions of adverbs, prepositions, and conjunctions, or what in logic are called syncategorematic words.

rational thoughts, he must have words to show what con- BOOK III.
nexion, restriction, distinction, opposition, emphasis, &c., he
gives to each respective *part* of his discourse. To mistake CHAP. VII.
in any of these, is to puzzle instead of informing his hearer :
and therefore it is, that those words which are not truly by
themselves the names of any ideas are of such constant and
indispensable use in language, and do much contribute to
men's well expressing themselves.

3. This part of grammar has been perhaps as much They show
neglected as some others over-diligently cultivated. It is what Relation
easy for men to write, one after another, of cases and gen- the Mind
ders, moods and tenses, gerunds and supines : in these and gives to its own
the like there has been great diligence used ; and particles Thoughts.
themselves, in some languages, have been, with great show
of exactness, ranked into their several orders. But though
prepositions and *conjunctions*, &c., are names well known
in grammar, and the particles contained under them carefully ranked into their distinct subdivisions ; yet he who
would show the right use of particles, and what significancy
and force they have, must take a little more pains, enter
into his own thoughts, and observe nicely the several postures of his mind in discoursing [1].

4. Neither is it enough, for the explaining of these words, They are
to render them, as is usual in dictionaries, by words of another all marks of some
tongue which come nearest to their signification : for what action or
is meant by them is commonly as hard to be understood in intimation of the
one as another language. They are all marks of some action mind.
or intimation of the mind ; and therefore to understand them
rightly, the several views, postures, stands, turns, limitations,
and exceptions, and several other thoughts of the mind, for
which we have either none or very deficient names, are dili-
gently to be studied. Of these there is a great variety,
much exceeding the number of particles that most languages
have to express them by: and therefore it is not to be wondered that most of these particles have divers and sometimes
almost opposite significations. In the Hebrew tongue there
is a particle consisting of but one single letter, of which there

---

[1] 'Discoursing'—exercising the discursive or elaborative faculty—reasoning.

are reckoned up, as I remember, seventy, I am sure above fifty, several significations.

5. 'But' is a particle, none more familiar in our language : and he that says it is a discretive [1] conjunction, and that it answers to *sed* Latin, or *mais* in French, thinks he has sufficiently explained it. But yet it seems to me to intimate several relations the mind gives to the several propositions or parts of them which it joins by this monosyllable.

First, 'But to say no more:' here it intimates a stop of the mind in the course it was going, before it came quite to the end of it.

Secondly, 'I saw but two plants ;' here it shows that the mind limits the sense to what is expressed, with a negation of all other.

Thirdly, 'You pray; but it is not that God would bring you to the true religion.'

Fourthly, 'But that he would confirm you in your own.' The first of these *buts* intimates a supposition in the mind of something otherwise than it should be ; the latter shows that the mind makes a direct opposition between that and what goes before it.

Fifthly, 'All animals have sense, but a dog is an animal :' here it signifies little more but that the latter proposition is joined to the former, as the minor of a syllogism.

This
Matter
of the use
of Particles
but lightly
touched
here.
6. To these, I doubt not, might be added a great many other significations of this particle, if it were my business to examine it in its full latitude, and consider it in all the places it is to be found : which if one should do, I doubt whether in all those manners it is made use of, it would deserve the title of *discretive*, which grammarians give to it. But I intend not here a full explication of this sort of signs. The instances I have given in this one may give occasion to reflect on their use and force in language, and lead us into the contemplation of several actions of our minds in discoursing, which it has found a way to intimate to others by these particles, some whereof constantly, and others in certain constructions, have the sense of a whole sentence contained in them.

---

[1] 'discretive'— disjunctive : to discrete, to disjoin.

CHAPTER VIII.

OF ABSTRACT AND CONCRETE TERMS.

1. THE ordinary words of language, and our common use of them, would have given us light into the nature of our ideas, if they had been but considered with attention. The mind, as has been shown, has a power to abstract its ideas, and so they become essences, general essences, whereby the sorts of things are distinguished. Now each abstract idea being distinct, so that of any two the one can never be the other, the mind will, by its intuitive knowledge[1], perceive their difference, and therefore in propositions no two whole ideas can ever be affirmed one of another. This we see in the common use of language, which permits not any two abstract words, or names of abstract ideas, to be affirmed one of another. For how near of kin soever they may seem to be, and how certain soever it is that man is an animal, or rational, or white, yet every one at first hearing perceives the falsehood of these propositions: *humanity is animality*, or *rationality*, or *whiteness*: and this is as evident as any of the most allowed maxims. All our affirmations then are only in concrete[2], which is the affirming, not one abstract idea to be another, but one abstract idea to be joined to another; which abstract ideas, in substances, may be of any sort; in all the rest are little else but of relations; and in substances the most frequent are of powers: v. g. 'a man is white,' signifies that the thing that has the essence of a man has also in it the essence of whiteness, which is

Abstract Terms not predicable one of another, and why.

---

[1] Cf. Bk. IV. ch. ii. § 1.

[2] Locke has everywhere a sober dread of abstractions, and clings to the particular and concrete, with a sense of the risk of losing the real in the emptiness of the universal.

BOOK III. nothing but a power to produce the idea of whiteness in
one whose eyes can discover ordinary objects: or, 'a man is
CHAP. rational,' signifies that the same thing that hath the essence of
VIII. a man hath also in it the essence of rationality, i. e. a power
of reasoning.

They
show the
Difference
of our
Ideas.

2. This distinction of names shows us also the difference
of our ideas: for if we observe them, we shall find that *our
simple ideas have all abstract as well as concrete names*: the
one whereof is (to speak the language of grammarians) a
substantive, the other an adjective; as whiteness, white;
sweetness, sweet [1]. The like also holds in our ideas of modes
and relations; as justice, just; equality, equal: only with
this difference, that some of the concrete names of relations
amongst men chiefly are substantives; as, *paternitas, pater*;
whereof it were easy to render a reason. But as to our ideas
of substances, we have very few or no abstract names at all.
For though the Schools have introduced *animalitas, humanitas,
corporietas*, and some others; yet they hold no proportion
with that infinite number of names of substances, to which
they never were ridiculous enough to attempt the coining of
abstract ones: and those few that the Schools forged, and
put into the mouths of their scholars, could never yet get
admittance into common use, or obtain the license of public
approbation. Which seems to me at least to intimate the
confession of all mankind, that they have no ideas of the real

---

[1] In reference to this sentence, Professor Case remarks that 'Locke forgot to ask in which meaning he should call a simple idea an object of sense. The abstract whiteness is a quality; the concrete white is the qualified. Now nobody ever saw whiteness; the object of vision is the white, the red, &c. An object of sense is never a quality, but always the qualified; and a quality is an abstraction; though we may sometimes speak of perceiving it, we do so only for convenience. But the qualified is a substance; whiteness and sweetness are qualities, but the white and the sweet are substances. The object of sense, therefore, is always a substance.' (*Physical Realism*, p. 150.) I do not suppose that Locke would have dissented from this, or that he would have denied that our 'simple ideas' are the appearances presented to our senses by the particular substances, which with him form the *minima intelligibilia* of reality. But simple ideas may be considered under abstract as well as under concrete terms; and they also form (uncomplex) nominal essences (cf. Bk. II. ch. xxxi. § 12), the simple idea *red* being the essential meaning of a common term applicable to all substances in which that colour is presented to the visual sense.

essences of substances, since they have not names for such
ideas: which no doubt they would have had, had not their
consciousness to themselves of their ignorance of them kept
them from so idle an attempt. And therefore, though they
had ideas enough to distinguish gold from a stone, and metal
from wood; yet they but timorously ventured on such terms,
as *aurietas* and *saxietas*, *metallietas* and *lignietas*, or the like
names, which should pretend to signify the real essences of
those substances whereof they knew they had no ideas. And
indeed it was only the doctrine of *substantial forms*, and the
confidence of mistaken pretenders to a knowledge that they
had not, which first coined and then introduced *animalitas*
and *humanitas*, and the like; which yet went very little
further than their own Schools, and could never get to be
current amongst understanding men. Indeed, *humanitas* was
a word in familiar use amongst the Romans; but in a far
different sense, and stood not for the abstract essence of any
substance; but was the abstracted name of a mode, and its
concrete *humanus*, not *homo*.

CHAPTER IX.

OF THE IMPERFECTION OF WORDS.

BOOK III.

CHAP. IX.
Words
are used
for re-
cording
and com-
municat-
ing our
Thoughts.

1. FROM what has been said in the foregoing chapters, it is easy to perceive what imperfection there is in language, and how the very nature of words makes it almost unavoidable for many of them to be doubtful and uncertain in their significations. To examine the perfection or imperfection of words, it is necessary first to consider their use and end: for as they are more or less fitted to attain that, so they are more or less perfect. We have, in the former part of this discourse often, upon occasion, mentioned a double use of words.

First, One for the recording of our own thoughts.

Secondly, The other for the communicating of our thoughts to others [1].

2. As to the first of these, *for the recording our own thoughts for the help of our own memories*, whereby, as it were, we talk to ourselves, any words will serve the turn. For since sounds are voluntary and indifferent [2] signs of any ideas, a man may use what words he pleases to signify his own ideas to himself: and there will be no imperfection in them, if he constantly use the same sign for the same idea: for then he cannot fail of having his meaning understood, wherein consists the right use and perfection of language.

Communi-
cation by
Words
either for
civil or
philo-
sophical
purposes.

3. Secondly, As to *communication by words*, that too has a double use.

    I. *Civil.*

    II. *Philosophical.*

---

[1] Cf. ch. x. § 23.

[2] 'indifferent,' i.e. there being no abstract reason for preferring one verbal sign to another to signify any idea.

First, By their *civil* use, I mean such a communication of thoughts and ideas by words, as may serve for the upholding common conversation and commerce, about the ordinary affairs and conveniences of civil life, in the societies of men, one amongst another.

Secondly, By the *philosophical* use of words, I mean such a use of them as may serve to convey the precise notions of things, and to express in general propositions certain and undoubted truths, which the mind may rest upon and be satisfied with in its search after true knowledge. These two uses are very distinct; and a great deal less exactness will serve in the one than in the other, as we shall see in what follows.

4. The chief end of language in communication being to be understood, words serve not well for that end, neither in civil nor philosophical discourse, when any word does not excite in the hearer the same idea which it stands for in the mind of the speaker. Now, since sounds have no natural [1] connexion with our ideas, but have all their signification from the arbitrary imposition of men, the doubtfulness and uncertainty of their signification, which is the imperfection we here are speaking of, has its cause more in the ideas they stand for than in any incapacity there is in one sound more than in another to signify any idea : for in that regard they are all equally perfect.

The imperfection of Words is the Doubtfulness or ambiguity of their Signification, which is caused by the sort of ideas they stand for.

That then which makes doubtfulness and uncertainty in the signification of some more than other words, is the difference of ideas they stand for.

5. Words having naturally no signification, the idea which each stands for must be learned and retained, by those who would exchange thoughts, and hold intelligible discourse with

Natural Causes of their Imperfection,

[1] 'natural,' i. e. in the nature of things, and apart from the convention of men, there is no reason why this word rather than some other sign should be connected with the meaning actually annexed to it. Locke's expressions exaggerate the 'arbitrariness' of the imposition of signs, as if the use of a special sign to signify a special idea, in the several languages of men, were so wholly capricious and independent of natural law that an inductive science of language would be impossible.

BOOK III.

CHAP. IX.

especially in those that stand for Mixed Modes, and for our ideas of Substances.

others, in any language.   But this is the hardest to be done where,

First, The ideas they stand for are very complex, and made up of a great number of ideas put together.

Secondly, Where the ideas they stand for have no certain connexion in nature ; and so no settled standard anywhere in nature existing, to rectify and adjust them by.

Thirdly, When the signification of the word is referred to a standard, which standard is not easy to be known.

Fourthly, Where the signification of the word and the real essence of the thing are not exactly the same.

These are difficulties that attend the signification of several words that are intelligible.   Those which are not intelligible at all, such as names standing for any simple ideas which another has not organs or faculties to attain ; as the names of colours to a blind man, or sounds to a deaf man, need not here be mentioned.

In all these cases we shall find an imperfection in words ; which I shall more at large explain, in their particular application to our several sorts of ideas : for if we examine them, we shall find that the *names of Mixed Modes are most liable to doubtfulness and imperfection, for the two first of these reasons* ; and the *names of Substances chiefly for the two latter.*

6. First, The names of *mixed modes* are, many of them, liable to great uncertainty and obscurity in their signification.

I. Because of that *great composition* these complex ideas are often made up of.   To make words serviceable to the end of communication, it is necessary, as has been said, that they excite in the hearer exactly the same idea they stand for in the mind of the speaker.   Without this, men fill one another's heads with noise and sounds ; but convey not thereby their thoughts, and lay not before one another their ideas, which is the end of discourse and language.   But when a word stands for a very complex idea that is compounded and decompounded, it is not easy for men to form and retain that idea so exactly, as to make the name in common use stand for the

same precise idea, without any the least variation. Hence it
comes to pass that men's names of very compound ideas, such
as for the most part are moral words, have seldom in two
different men the same precise signification ; since one man's
complex idea seldom agrees with another's, and often differs
from his own—from that which he had yesterday, or will
have to-morrow.

7. Because the names of mixed modes for the most part Secondly, because they have no Standards in Nature.
want standards in nature, whereby men may rectify and
adjust their significations ; therefore they are very various and
doubtful. They are assemblages of ideas put together at the
pleasure of the mind, pursuing its own ends of discourse, and
suited to its own notions ; whereby it designs not to copy
anything really existing, but to denominate and rank things
as they come to agree with those archetypes or forms it has
made. He that first brought the word *sham*, or *wheedle*, or
banter [1], in use, put together as he thought fit those ideas he
made it stand for ; and as it is with any new names of modes
that are now brought into any language, so it was with the
old ones when they were first made use of. Names, therefore,
that stand for collections of ideas which the mind makes at
pleasure must needs be of doubtful signification, when such
collections are nowhere to be found constantly united in
nature, nor any patterns to be shown whereby men may
adjust them. What the word *murder* [2], or *sacrilege*, &c.,
signifies can never be known from things themselves : there
be many of the parts of those complex ideas which are not
visible in the action itself ; the intention of the mind, or the
relation of holy things, which make a part of murder or
sacrilege, have no necessary connexion with the outward and
visible action of him that commits either : and the pulling the
trigger of the gun with which the murder is committed, and
is all the action that perhaps is visible, has no natural connexion with those other ideas that make up the complex one
named murder. They have their union and combination only
from the understanding which unites them under one name :

---

[1] Words only recently in use when
Locke wrote.

[2] 'murder'—'murther' in the early
editions.

but, uniting them without any rule or pattern, it cannot be but that the signification of the name that stands for such voluntary collections should be often various in the minds of different men, who have scarce any standing rule to regulate themselves and their notions by, in such arbitrary ideas.

Common use, or propriety not a sufficient Remedy.

8. It is true, common use, that is, the rule of propriety may be supposed here to afford some aid, to settle the signification of language ; and it cannot be denied but that in some measure it does. Common use regulates the meaning of words pretty well for common conversation ; but nobody having an authority to establish the precise signification of words, nor determine to what ideas any one shall annex them, common use is not sufficient to adjust them to Philosophical Discourses ; there being scarce any name of any very complex idea (to say nothing of others) which, in common use, has not a great latitude, and which, keeping within the bounds of propriety, may not be made the sign of far different ideas. Besides, the rule and measure of propriety itself being no-where established, it is often matter of dispute, whether this or that way of using a word be propriety of speech or no. From all which it is evident, that the names of such kind of very complex ideas are naturally liable to this imperfection, to be of doubtful and uncertain signification ; and even in men that have a mind to understand one another, do not always stand for the same idea in speaker and hearer. Though the names *glory* and *gratitude* be the same in every man's mouth through a whole country, yet the complex collective idea which every one thinks on or intends by that name, is apparently very different in men using the same language.

The way of learning these Names contributes also to their Doubtfulness.

9. The way also wherein the names of mixed modes are ordinarily learned, does not a little contribute to the doubtfulness of their signification. For if we will observe how children learn languages, we shall find that, to make them understand what the names of simple ideas or substances stand for, people ordinarily show them the thing whereof they would have them have the idea ; and then repeat to them the name that stands for it ; as *white, sweet, milk, sugar, cat, dog.* But as for mixed modes, especially the most material of them, *moral words*, the sounds are usually learned first ; and then, to know

what complex ideas they stand for, they are either beholden to the explication of others, or (which happens for the most part) are left to their own observation and industry; which being little laid out in the search of the true and precise meaning of names, these moral words are in most men's mouths little more than bare sounds; or when they have any, it is for the most part but a very loose and undetermined, and, consequently, obscure and confused signification. And even those themselves who have with more attention settled their notions, do yet hardly avoid the inconvenience to have them stand for complex ideas different from those which other, even intelligent and studious men, make them the signs of. Where shall one find any, either controversial debate, or familiar discourse, concerning honour, faith, grace, religion, church, &c., wherein it is not easy to observe the different notions men have of them? Which is nothing but this, that they are not agreed in the signification of those words, nor have in their minds the same complex ideas which they make them stand for, and so all the contests that follow thereupon are only about the meaning of a sound. And hence we see that, in the interpretation of laws, whether divine or human, there is no end; comments beget comments, and explications make new matter for explications; and of limiting, distinguishing, varying the signification of these moral words there is no end. These ideas of men's making are, by men still having the same power, multiplied *in infinitum.* Many a man who was pretty well satisfied of the meaning of a text of Scripture, or clause in the code, at first reading, has, by consulting commentators, quite lost the sense of it, and by these elucidations given rise or increase to his doubts, and drawn obscurity upon the place. I say not this that I think commentaries needless; but to show how uncertain the names of mixed modes naturally are, even in the mouths of those who had both the intention and the faculty of speaking as clearly as language was capable to express their thoughts[1].

[1] 'The inadequacy of the words of ordinary language for the purposes of Philosophy, is an ancient and frequent complaint; of which the justness will be felt by all who consider the state to which some of the most important arts would be reduced, if the coarse tools of the common labourer were the only

BOOK III.

CHAP. IX.

Hence
unavoid-
able
Obscurity
in ancient
Authors.

10. What obscurity this has unavoidably brought upon the writings of men who have lived in remote ages, and different countries, it will be needless to take notice. Since the numerous volumes of learned men, employing their thoughts that way, are proofs more than enough, to show what attention, study, sagacity, and reasoning are required to find out the true meaning of ancient authors. But, there being no writings we have any great concernment to be very solicitous about the meaning of, but those that contain either truths we are required to believe, or laws we are to obey, and draw inconveniences on us when we mistake or transgress, we may be less anxious about the sense of other authors ; who, writing but their own opinions, we are under no greater necessity to know them, than they to know ours. Our good or evil depending not on their decrees, we may safely be ignorant of their notions : and therefore in the reading of them, if they do not use their words with a due clearness and perspicuity, we may lay them aside, and without any injury done them, resolve thus with ourselves,

Si non vis intelligi, debes negligi [1].

11. If the signification of the names of mixed modes be

instruments to be employed in the more delicate operations of manual expertness. The cultivator of Mental and Moral Philosophy can seldom do more than mend the faults of his words by definition ; a necessary but very inadequate expedient ; in a great measure defeated in practice by the unavoidably more frequent recurrence of the terms in their vague than in their definite acceptation ; in consequence of which the mind, to which the definition is faintly but occasionally present, naturally suffers, in the ordinary state of attention, the scientific meaning to disappear from remembrance, and insensibly ascribes to the word a great part, if not the whole, of that popular sense which is so very much more familiar even to the most veteran speculator. The obstacles which stood in the way of Lucretius and Cicero, when they began to translate the subtle philosophy of Greece into their narrow and barren tongue, are always felt by the philosopher when he struggles to express, with the necessary discrimination, his abstruse reasonings, in words which, though those of his own language, he must take from the mouths of those to whom his distinctions would be without meaning.' (Sir James Mackintosh.) The comments and controversies to which Locke's own *Essay* has given rise abundantly illustrate this.

[1] Locke's inadequate appreciation of the speculative work of his predecessors, and of the connection of the past with the future in the sequence of human thought, appears here as in so many other places.

uncertain, because there be no real standards existing in nature
to which those ideas are referred, and by which they may be
adjusted, the names of *substances* are of a doubtful signification, for a contrary reason, viz. because the ideas they stand
for are supposed conformable to the reality of things, and are
referred to as standards made by Nature. In our ideas of
substances we have not the liberty, as in mixed modes, to
frame what combinations we think fit, to be the characteristical
notes to rank and denominate things by [1]. In these we must
follow Nature, suit our complex ideas to real existences, and
regulate the signification of their names by the things themselves, if we will have our names to be signs of them, and
stand for them. Here, it is true, we have patterns to
follow; but patterns that will make the signification of
their names very uncertain : for names must be of a very
unsteady and various meaning, if the ideas they stand for
be referred to standards without us, that either cannot be
known at all, or can be known but imperfectly and uncertainly.

CHAP. IX.
stances of
doubtful
Significa-
tion,
because
the ideas
they stand
for relate
to the
reality of
things.

12. The names of substances have, as has been shown [2],
a double reference in their ordinary use.

First, Sometimes they are made to stand for, and so their
signification is supposed to agree to, *the real constitution of
things*, from which all their properties flow, and in which
they all centre. But this real constitution, or (as it is apt to
be called) essence, being utterly unknown to us [3], any sound
that is put to stand for it must be very uncertain in its
application; and it will be impossible to know what things
are or ought to be called a *horse*, or *antimony*, when those
words are put for real essences that we have no ideas of at

Names
of Sub-
stances
referred,
1. To real
Essences
that can-
not be
known.

---

[1] This is another acknowledgment
that the species to which we refer particular substances, and their nominal
essences, are not wholly ' arbitrary,'
but accommodated to what we find in
things, by calculated observation and
experiment. Some principles of classification are more ' natural,' more in
harmony with the reason that is in the
things themselves, than others are.

[2] Ch. vi.

[3] In *material* substances Locke supposes that it consists of the (by us)
imperceptible texture and motions
of the atoms into which the individual
thing may be resolved, and on which,
as he conjectures, all its qualities and
powers depend. Cf. Bk. II. ch. viii.
He supposes that this forms its *real
essence.*

all. And therefore in this supposition, the names of sub-stances being referred to standards that cannot be known, their significations can never be adjusted and established by those standards.

Secondly, To co-existing Qualities, which are known but imper-fectly.

13. Secondly, The simple ideas that are *found to co-exist in substances*[1] being that which their names immediately signify, these, as united in the several sorts of things, are the proper standards to which their names are referred, and by which their significations may be best rectified. But neither will these archetypes so well serve to this purpose as to leave these names without very various and uncertain significations. Because these simple ideas that co-exist, and are united in the same subject, being very numerous, and having all an equal right[2] to go into the complex specific idea which the specific name is to stand for, men, though they propose to themselves the very same subject to con-sider, yet frame very different ideas about it; and so the name they use for it unavoidably comes to have, in several men, very different significations. The simple qualities which make up the complex ideas, being most of them powers, in relation to changes which they are apt to make in, or receive from other bodies, are almost infinite. He that shall but observe what a great variety of alterations any one of the baser metals is apt to receive, from the different application only of fire; and how much a greater number of changes any of them will receive in the hands of a chymist, by the application of other bodies, will not think it strange that I count the properties of any sort of bodies not easy to be collected, and completely known, by the ways of inquiry which our faculties are capable of. They being therefore at least so many, that no man can know the precise and definite number, they are differently discovered by different men, according to their various skill, attention, and ways of handling; who therefore

---

[1] In other words the qualities and powers that men find in things, by external observation, or inference founded thereon, and in their own conscious life, by reflection.

[2] Any of the qualities of things may be taken as a basis of classification, but all do not equally constitute a scientific classification, or verified inductive generalisation of science.

cannot choose but have different ideas of the same substance [1], and therefore make the signification of its common name very various and uncertain. For the complex ideas of substances, being made up of such simple ones as are supposed to co-exist in nature, every one has a right to put into his complex idea those qualities he has found to be united together. For, though in the substance of gold one satisfies himself with colour and weight, yet another thinks solubility in *aqua regia* as necessary to be joined with that colour in his idea of gold, as any one does its fusibility; solubility in *aqua regia* being a quality as constantly joined with its colour and weight as fusibility or any other; others put into it ductility or fixedness, &c., as they have been taught by tradition or experience. Who of all these has established the right signification of the word, gold? Or who shall be the judge to determine? Each has his standard in nature, which he appeals to, and with reason thinks he has the same right to put into his complex idea signified by the word gold, those qualities, which, upon trial, he has found united; as another who has not so well examined has to leave them out; or a third, who has made other trials, has to put in others. For the union in nature of these qualities being the true ground of their union in one complex idea, who can say one of them has more reason to be put in or left out than another [2]? From hence it will unavoidably follow, that the complex ideas of substances in men using the same names for them, will be very various, and so the significations of those names very uncertain.

14. Besides, there is scarce any particular thing existing, which, in some of its simple ideas, does not communicate with a greater, and in others a less number of particular beings: who shall determine [3] in this case which are those

Thirdly, To co-existing Qualities which are known

---

[1] 'Different ideas of the same substance.' Different persons may also put the substance in a different class, according to the resembling qualities chosen by each to form the essence of its name.

[2] There may be more reason for choosing one quality than for choosing another; but this does not determine what qualities have actually been chosen by each person who uses the word, so as to constitute his connotation of 'gold.'

[3] There is no infallible authority for determining the connotation of names which signify sorts of substances—

but im-
perfectly.

that are to make up the precise collection that is to be signified by the specific name? or can with any just authority prescribe, which obvious or common qualities are to be left out; or which more secret, or more particular, are to be put into the signification of the name of any substance? All which together, seldom or never fail to produce that various and doubtful signification in the names of substances, which causes such uncertainty, disputes, or mistakes, when we come to a philosophical use of them.

With this im-
perfection, they may serve for civil, but not well for philosophical Use.

15. It is true, as to civil and common conversation, the general names of substances, regulated in their ordinary signification by some obvious qualities, (as by the shape and figure in things of known seminal propagation, and in other substances, for the most part by colour, joined with some other sensible qualities,) do well enough to design the things men would be understood to speak of: and so they usually conceive well enough the substances meant by the word gold or apple, to distinguish the one from the other. But in *philosophical* inquiries and debates, where general truths are to be established, and consequences drawn from positions laid down, there the precise signification of the names of substances will be found not only not to be well established, but also very hard to be so. For example: he that shall make malleability, or a certain degree of fixedness, a part of his complex idea of gold, may make propositions concerning gold, and draw consequences from them, that will truly and clearly follow from gold, taken in such a signification: but yet such as another man can never be forced to admit, nor be convinced of their truth, who makes not malleableness, or the same degree of fixedness, part of that complex idea that the name gold, in his use of it, stands for.

Instance, Liquor.

16. This is a natural and almost unavoidable imperfection in almost all the names of substances, in all languages whatsoever, which men will easily find when, once passing from confused or loose notions, they come to more strict and close inquiries. For then they will be convinced how doubtful and

material or spiritual. It is determined largely by each man, according to his point of view, or purpose in using them, 'Gold' suggests one connotation to the banker, another to the mineralogist, another to the artist.

obscure those words are in their signification, which in
ordinary use appeared very clear and determined. I was
once in a meeting of very learned and ingenious physicians,
where by chance there arose a question, whether any liquor
passed through the filaments of the nerves. The debate
having been managed a good while, by variety of arguments
on both sides, I (who had been used to suspect, that the
greatest part of disputes were more about the signification of
words than a real difference in the conception of things)
desired, that, before they went any further on in this dispute,
they would first examine and establish amongst them, what
the word *liquor* signified. They at first were a little surprised
at the proposal; and had they been persons less ingenious [1],
they might perhaps have taken it for a very frivolous or
extravagant one: since there was no one there that thought
not himself to understand very perfectly what the word
liquor stood for; which I think, too, none of the most
perplexed names of substances. However, they were pleased
to comply with my motion; and upon examination found
that the signification of that word was not so settled or certain
as they had all imagined; but that each of them made it a
sign of a different complex idea. This made them perceive
that the main of their dispute was about the signification of
that term; and that they differed very little in their opinions
concerning *some* fluid and subtle matter, passing through the
conduits of the nerves; though it was not so easy to agree
whether it was to be called *liquor* or no, a thing, which,
when considered, they thought it not worth the contending
about.

17. How much this is the case in the greatest part of disputes that men are engaged so hotly in, I shall perhaps have
an occasion in another place to take notice. Let us only here
consider a little more exactly the fore-mentioned instance
of the word *gold*, and we shall see how hard it is precisely
to determine its signification. I think all agree to make
it stand for a body of a certain yellow shining colour; which
being the idea to which children have annexed that name,

Instance,
Gold.

---

[1] ' ingenious '—acute or clever.

the shining yellow part of a peacock's tail is properly to them gold. Others finding fusibility joined with that yellow colour in certain parcels of matter, make of that combination a complex idea to which they give the name gold, to denote a sort of substances; and so exclude from being gold all such yellow shining bodies as by fire will be reduced to ashes; and admit to be of that species, or to be comprehended under that name gold, only such substances as, having that shining yellow colour, will by fire be reduced to fusion, and not to ashes. Another, by the same reason, adds the weight, which, being a quality as straightly joined with that colour as its fusibility, he thinks has the same reason to be joined in its idea, and to be signified by its name: and therefore the other made up of body, of such a colour and fusibility, to be imperfect; and so on of all the rest: wherein no one can show a reason why some of the inseparable qualities, that are always united in nature, should be put into the nominal essence, and others left out: or why the word gold, signifying that sort of body the ring on his finger is made of, should determine that sort rather by its colour, weight, and fusibility, than by its colour, weight, and solubility in *aqua regia*: since the dissolving it by that liquor is as inseparable from it as the fusion by fire; and they are both of them nothing but the relation which that substance has to two other bodies, which have a power to operate differently upon it. For by what right is it that fusibility comes to be a part of the essence signified by the word gold, and solubility but a property of it? Or why is its colour part of the essence, and its malleableness but a property [1]? That which I mean is this, That these being all but properties, depending on its real constitution, and nothing but powers, either active or passive, in reference to other bodies, no one has authority to determine the signification of the word gold (as referred to such a body existing in nature) more to one collection of ideas to be found in that body than to another: whereby the signification of that name must unavoidably be very uncertain. Since, as has been

---

[1] 'property,' i. e. a quality that forms no part of the nominal essence, and yet is always found in conjunction with it.

said, several people observe several properties in the same
substance; and I think I may say nobody all. And therefore we have but very imperfect descriptions of things, and
words have very uncertain significations.

18. From what has been said, it is easy to observe what has
been before remarked, viz. that the *names of simple ideas* are,
of all others, the least liable to mistakes, and that for these
reasons. First, Because the ideas they stand for, being each
but one single perception, are much easier got, and more
clearly retained, than the more complex ones, and therefore
are not liable to the uncertainty which usually attends those
compounded ones of substances and mixed modes, in which
the precise number of simple ideas that make them up are
not easily agreed, so readily kept in mind. And, Secondly,
Because they are never referred to any other essence, but
barely that perception they immediately signify: which
reference is that which renders the signification of the names
of substances naturally so perplexed, and gives occasion to
so many disputes. Men that do not perversely use their
words, or on purpose set themselves to cavil, seldom mistake,
in any language which they are acquainted with, the use
and signification of the name of simple ideas. *White* and
sweet, yellow and *bitter,* carry a very obvious meaning with
them, which every one precisely comprehends, or easily
perceives he is ignorant of, and seeks to be informed. But
what precise collection of simple ideas *modesty* or *frugality*
stand for, in another's use, is not so certainly known. And
however we are apt to think we well enough know what is
meant by *gold* or *iron*; yet the precise complex idea others
make them the signs of is not so certain : and I believe it is
very seldom that, in speaker and hearer, they stand for
exactly the same collection. Which must needs produce
mistakes and disputes, when they are made use of in discourses, wherein men have to do with universal propositions,
and would settle in their minds universal truths, and consider
the consequences that follow from them[1].

The Names of simple Ideas the least doubtful.

---

[1] Names of simple ideas are un-
ambiguous, according to Locke, and
this because they refer only to 'that
perception they immediately signify,'

BOOK III.
CHAP. IX.
And next
to them,
simple
Modes.

19. By the same rule, the names of *simple modes* are, next to those of simple ideas, least liable to doubt and uncertainty; especially those of figure and number, of which men have so clear and distinct ideas. Who ever that had a mind to understand them mistook the ordinary meaning of *seven,* or a *triangle?* And in general the least compounded ideas in every kind have the least dubious names.

The most
doubtful
are the
Names of
very com-
pounded
mixed
Modes
and Sub-
stances.

20. Mixed modes, therefore, that are made up but of a few and obvious simple ideas, have usually names of no very uncertain signification. But the names of mixed modes which comprehend a great number of simple ideas, are commonly of a very doubtful and undetermined meaning, as has been shown. The names of substances, being annexed to ideas that are neither the real essences, nor exact representations of the patterns they are referred to, are liable to yet greater imperfection and uncertainty, especially when we come to a philosophical use of them.

Why this
Imperfec-
tion
charged
upon
Words.

21. The great disorder that happens in our names of substances, proceeding, for the most part, from our want of knowledge, and inability to penetrate into their real constitutions, it may probably be wondered why I charge this as an imperfection rather upon our words than understandings. This exception has so much appearance of justice, that I think myself obliged to give a reason why I have followed this method. I must confess, then, that, when I first began this Discourse of the Understanding, and a good while after, I had not the least thought that any consideration of words was at all necessary to it. But when, having passed over

—*white, sweet, yellow,* and *bitter* signifying only that sensible quality which forms the nominal essence of their respective names, and nothing beyond. But Locke takes as illustrations, and seems to have in view, only simple ideas of *sensation,* leaning mainly, as he is apt to do, on those materials of thought which are got from external observation, rather than on those provided by reflection. When we turn to his own examples of simple ideas of

reflection (Bk. II. ch. vi. § 2), or of both sensation and reflection (Bk. II. ch. viii) we have, in 'remembrance, discerning, reasoning, judging, knowledge, faith'; and in 'existence, unity, power, and succession,' names of simple ideas that are associated with much verbal controversy. But some of Locke's ideas of reflection are really complex, while some of his complex ideas are simple, ' suggested ' by the mind.

the original and composition of our ideas[1], I began to examine BOOK III.
the extent and certainty of our knowledge[2], I found it had
so near a connexion with words, that, unless their force CHAP. IX.
and manner of signification were first well observed, there
could be very little said clearly and pertinently concerning
knowledge: which being conversant about truth, had constantly to do with propositions. And though it terminated
in things, yet it was for the most part so much by the
intervention of words, that they seemed scarce separable
from our general knowledge[3]. At least they interpose themselves so much between our understandings, and the truth
which it would contemplate and apprehend, that, like the
medium through which visible objects pass, the obscurity
and disorder do not seldom cast a mist before our eyes,
and impose upon our understandings. If we consider, in
the fallacies men put upon themselves, as well as others,
and the mistakes in men's disputes and notions, how great
a part is owing to words, and their uncertain or mistaken
significations[4], we shall have reason to think this no small
obstacle in the way to knowledge; which I conclude we
are the more carefully to be warned of, because it has been
so far from being taken notice of as an inconvenience, that
the arts of improving it have been made the business of
men's study, and obtained the reputation of learning and
subtilty, as we shall see in the following chapter[5]. But I am
apt to imagine, that, were the imperfections of language, as
the instrument of knowledge, more thoroughly weighed, a

[1] In Bk. II.

[2] In Bk. IV.

[3] The *Essay*, as its author tells us in the prefixed 'Epistle' (p. 10), was 'written by incoherent parcels,' with 'long intervals of neglect,' during nearly twenty years, so that it is diffi-cult to determine the order in which it was composed. Probably not only most of the second, but parts of the fourth Book had been thought out, and reduced to writing, before the subject of the third Book was seen to be necessary to the original design of the

'Discourse,' which, 'though it ter-minates in things,' comprehends 'words,' indispensable to the forma-tion of complex and general ideas of things. Of this elsewhere.

[4] 'To expose a sophism, and to detect the equivocal or double meaning of a word, is, in the great majority of cases, one and the same thing.' (Coleridge, *Aids to Reflection.* Preface.)

[5] See especially §§ 6-22, where the arts that encourage verbal disputa-tion, and their consequences, are illus-trated in this connection.

This should teach us Moderation in imposing our own Sense of old Authors.

great many of the controversies that make such a noise in the world, would of themselves cease ; and the way to knowledge, and perhaps peace too, lie a great deal opener than it does.

22. Sure I am that the signification of words in all languages, depending very much on the thoughts, notions, and ideas of him that uses them, must unavoidably be of great uncertainty to men of the same language and country. This is so evident in the Greek authors, that he that shall peruse their writings will find in almost every one of them, a distinct language, though the same words. But when to this natural difficulty in every country, there shall be added different countries and remote ages, wherein the speakers and writers had very different notions, tempers, customs, ornaments, and figures of speech, &c., every one of which influenced the signification of their words then, though to us now they are lost and unknown ; it would become us to be charitable one to another in our interpretations or misunderstandings of those ancient writings ; which, though of great concernment to be understood, are liable to the unavoidable difficulties of speech, which (if we except the names of simple ideas, and some very obvious things) is not capable, without a constant defining the terms, of conveying the sense and intention of the speaker, without any manner of doubt and uncertainty to the hearer. And in discourses of religion, law, and morality, as they are matters of the highest concernment, so there will be the greatest difficulty.

Especially of the Old and New Testament Scriptures.

23. The volumes of interpreters and commentators on the Old and New Testament are but too manifest proofs of this. Though everything said in the text be infallibly true, yet the reader may be, nay, cannot choose but be, very fallible in the understanding of it. Nor is it to be wondered, that the will of God, when clothed in words, should be liable to that doubt and uncertainty which unavoidably attends that sort of conveyance, when even his Son, whilst clothed in flesh, was subject to all the frailties and inconveniences of human nature, sin excepted. And we ought to magnify his goodness, that he hath spread before all the world such legible characters of his works and providence, and given all mankind so sufficient a light of reason, that they to whom this

written word never came, could not (whenever they set themselves to search) either doubt of the being of a God, or of
the obedience due to him. Since then the precepts of Natural
Religion are plain, and very intelligible to all mankind, and
seldom come to be controverted ; and other revealed truths,
which are conveyed to us by books and languages, are liable
to the common and natural obscurities and difficulties in-
cident to words ; methinks it would become us to be more
careful and diligent in observing the former, and less magisterial, positive, and imperious, in imposing our own sense and
interpretations of the latter [1].

---

[1] Locke's remarks in this section, on the insufficiency of language, as an organ for the infallible transmission of divine revelation, and on the superior catholicity of natural religion, show his tendency in later life to depart from inherited Puritanic conceptions.

CHAPTER X.

OF THE ABUSE OF WORDS.

BOOK III.

CHAP. X.
Woeful
abuse of
Words.1. BESIDES the imperfection that is naturally in language, and the obscurity and confusion that is so hard to be avoided in the use of words, there are several *wilful* faults and neglects which men are guilty of in this way of communication, whereby they render these signs less clear and distinct in their signification than naturally they need to be[1].

First,
Words
are often
employed
without
any, or
without
clear
Ideas.
Some
words
introduced
without
clear ideas
annexed
to them,
even in
their first
original.2. *First,* In this kind the first and most palpable abuse is, the using of words without clear and distinct ideas ; or, which is worse, signs without anything signified. Of these there are two sorts :—

I. One may observe, in all languages, certain words that, if they be examined, will be found in their first original, and their appropriated use, not to stand for any clear and distinct ideas. These, for the most part, the several sects of philosophy and religion have introduced. For their authors or promoters, either affecting something singular, and out of the way of common apprehensions, or to support some strange opinions, or cover some weakness of their hypothesis, seldom fail to coin new words, and such as, when they come to be examined, may justly be called *insignificant terms*[2]. For, having either

---

[1] The foregoing chapter treats of the natural imperfection of words, as instruments for conveying into the mind of another the ideas which men desire to communicate. This chapter illustrates aggravations of this natural imperfection, caused by the 'wilful faults and neglects which men are guilty of' when they employ words. Cf. *Novum Organum,* Bk. I. ap. 60, on the *idola fori.*

[2] 'insignificant,' i. e. meaningless. He recognises in the next chapter (§ 12) that, with the advance of philo-

had no determinate[1] collection of ideas annexed to them when BOOK III.
they were first invented ; or at least such as, if well examined, —◆—
will be found inconsistent, it is no wonder, if, afterwards, in CHAP. X.
the vulgar use of the same party, they remain empty sounds,
with little or no signification, amongst those who think it
enough to have them often in their mouths, as the distinguishing characters of their Church or School, without much
troubling their heads to examine what are the precise ideas
they stand for.   I shall not need here to heap up instances ;
every man's reading and conversation will sufficiently furnish
him.   Or if he wants to be better stored, the great mint-
masters of this kind of terms, I mean the Schoolmen and
Metaphysicians (under which I think the disputing natural
and moral philosophers of these latter ages may be comprehended) have wherewithal abundantly to content him [2].

3. II. Others there be who extend this abuse yet further, II. Other
who take so little care to lay by words, which, in their Words,
to which
primary notation have scarce any clear and distinct ideas ideas were
which they are annexed to, that, by an unpardonable neg- annexed
at first,
ligence, they familiarly use words which the propriety of used afterwards
language *has* affixed to very important ideas, without any without
distinct meaning at all. *Wisdom, glory, grace,* &c., are words distinct
meanings.
frequent enough in every man's mouth ; but if a great many
of those who use them should be asked what they mean by
them, they would be at a stand, and not know what to answer :
a plain proof, that, though they have learned those sounds,

sophy, men must ' come to have ideas
different from the vulgar and ordinary
received ones,' and so need, either
a special philosophical nomenclature,
or the employment of old terms for
the conveyance of new meanings, with
the risk of ambiguity to which this
double use exposes them.   But this
necessity does not vindicate those
who offer new terms that are empty
of meaning, not annexed to new and
genuine thought.

[1] 'determinate,' i. e. clear and distinct.   See 'Epistle to the Reader,'
pp. 22, 23.

[2] This abuse by professed disciples
of terms specially formed by the masters
to express subtle philosophical distinctions is not peculiar to mediæval
schoolmen.   It is illustrated in the
history of every great philosophical
system—Locke's own, with its 'ideas,'
' simple and complex,' ' modes, simple
and mixed ' and ' relations,' not excepted.   Philosophers have been dis-
credited by the parrots of their nomenclature, incapable of thinking out the
meanings with which that nomenclature was originally charged by the
genius of discoverers.

BOOK III.

CHAP. X.

and have them ready at their tongues ends, yet there are no determined ideas laid up in their minds, which are to be expressed to others by them [1].

This occasioned by men learning Names before they have the Ideas the names belong to.

4. Men having been accustomed from their cradles to learn words which are easily got and retained, before they knew or had framed [2] the complex ideas to which they were annexed, or which were to be found [3] in the things they were thought to stand for, they usually continue to do so all their lives ; and without taking the pains necessary to settle in their minds determined ideas, they use their words for such unsteady and confused notions as they have, contenting themselves with the same words other people use ; as if their very sound necessarily carried with it constantly the same meaning. This, though men make a shift with in the ordinary occurrences of life, where they find it necessary to be understood, and therefore they make signs till they are so ; yet this insignificancy in their words, when they come to reason concerning either their tenets or interest, manifestly fills their discourse with abundance of empty unintelligible noise and jargon, especially in moral matters, where the words for the most part standing for arbitrary and numerous collections of ideas, not regularly and permanently united in nature, their bare sounds are often only thought on, or at least very obscure and uncertain notions annexed to them. Men take the words they find in use amongst their neighbours ; and that they may not seem ignorant what they stand for, use them confidently, without much troubling their heads about a certain fixed meaning ; whereby, besides the ease of it,

---

[1] The fact that words often circulate among men without any meaning annexed to them is signalised by Locke throughout the *Essay*. Cf. Bk. II. ch. xxii. § 8; xxix. § 9; xxxi. § 8; Bk. III. ch. iv. § 6; *Conduct of the Understanding*, §§ 27, 28, &c. See also Hume's *Treatise on Human Nature*, Part I. sect. vii ; and Campbell's *Philos. of Rhet.* Bk. II. ch. vii, in which he seeks to explain how it happens 'that nonsense so often escapes being detected both by the writer and the reader.'

Campbell and Stewart (*Elements*, ch. iv. sect. iv) credit Hume with originality in the remark, that men often use words without annexing any meaning to them. But this is here anticipated by Locke, and explained by Leibniz, in his account of symbolical thought. See Hamilton's *Logic*, vol. i. pp. 74–79.

[2] As in the wilful abuse of names of mixed modes.

[3] As in the abuse of names of our complex ideas of substances.

they obtain this advantage, That, as in such discourses they
seldom are in the right, so they are as seldom to be convinced that they are in the wrong; it being all one to go
about to draw those men out of their mistakes who have
no settled notions, as to dispossess a vagrant of his habitation
who has no settled abode. This I guess to be so; and
every one may observe in himself and others whether it be
so or not.

5. *Secondly*, Another great abuse of words is *inconstancy* Secondly,
in the use of them [1]. It is hard to find a discourse written Unsteady
on any subject, especially of controversy, wherein one shall Applica-
not observe, if he read with attention, the same words (and tion of
those commonly the most material in the discourse, and them.
upon which the argument turns) used sometimes for one collection of simple ideas, and sometimes for another; which is
a perfect abuse of language. Words being intended for signs
of my ideas, to make them known to others, not by any
natural signification, but by a voluntary imposition, it is plain
cheat and abuse, when I make them stand sometimes for one
thing and sometimes for another; the wilful doing whereof
can be imputed to nothing but great folly, or greater dishonesty [2]. And a man, in his accounts with another may,
with as much fairness make the characters of numbers stand
sometimes for one and sometimes for another collection of
units: v. g. this character 3, stand sometimes for three,
sometimes for four, and sometimes for eight, as in his discourse or reasoning make the same words stand for different
collections of simple ideas. If men should do so in their
reckonings, I wonder who would have to do with them? One
who would speak thus in the affairs and business of the
world, and call 8 sometimes seven, and sometimes nine, as
best served his advantage, would presently have clapped upon

It were to be wished that Locke had supplied fewer examples of this abuse in his own employment of words in the *Essay*, in which he is so vacillating.

[2] With the necessary scanty provision of names in each of the languages of mankind, it is often impossible to avoid annexing several meanings to the same word, and so using it in different senses on different occasions; which need not mislead if writer and readers are accustomed to verify the meaning of words by reflection.

BOOK III.

——*+*——

CHAP. X.

him, one of the two names[1] men are commonly disgusted with. And yet in arguings and learned contests, the same sort of proceedings passes commonly for wit and learning; but to me it appears a greater dishonesty than the misplacing of counters in the casting up a debt; and the cheat the greater, by how much truth is of greater concernment and value than money.

Thirdly, Affected Obscurity, as in the Peripatetic and other sects of Philosophy.

6. *Thirdly.* Another abuse of language is an *affected obscurity*; by either applying old words to new and unusual significations; or introducing new and ambiguous terms, without defining either; or else putting them so together, as may confound their ordinary meaning. Though the Peripatetick philosophy has been most eminent in this way, yet other sects have not been wholly clear of it. There are scarce any of them that are not cumbered with some difficulties (such is the imperfection of human knowledge,) which they have been fain to cover with obscurity of terms, and to confound the signification of words, which, like a mist before people's eyes, might hinder their weak parts from being discovered. That *body* and *extension* in common use, stand for two distinct ideas, is plain to any one that will but reflect a little. For were their signification precisely the same, it would be as proper, and as intelligible to say, 'the body of an extension,' as the 'extension of a body;' and yet there are those[2] who find it necessary to confound their signification. To this abuse, and the mischiefs of confounding the signification of words, logic, and the liberal sciences as they have been handled in the schools, have given reputation; and the admired Art of Disputing[3] hath added much to the natural imperfection of languages, whilst it has been made use of and fitted to perplex the signification of words, more than to discover the knowledge and truth of things: and he that will look into that sort of learned writings, will find the words there much more obscure, uncertain, and

---

[1] 'two names'—knave and fool.

[2] He refers to the Cartesians, who identified body and extension. Cf. Bk. II. ch. xiii. §§ 11, 21-24.

[3] Cf. Bk. IV. ch. vii. § 11, on 'dis-putation,' a favourite exercise in the Schools, as 'a touchstone of men's abilities,' and 'criterion of knowledge.'

undetermined in their meaning, than they are in ordinary
conversation [1].

7. This is unavoidably to be so, where men's parts and
learning are estimated by their skill in disputing. And if
reputation and reward shall attend these conquests, which
depend mostly on the fineness and niceties of words, it is no
wonder if the wit of man so employed, should perplex, involve,
and subtilize the signification of sounds, so as never to want
something to say in opposing or defending any question; the
victory being adjudged not to him who had truth on his side,
but the last word in the dispute.

8. This, though a very useless skill, and that which I think
the direct opposite to the ways of knowledge, hath yet passed
hitherto under the laudable and esteemed names of *subtlety*
and *acuteness*, and has had the applause of the schools, and
encouragement of one part of the learned men of the world.
And no wonder, since the philosophers of old, (the disputing
and wrangling philosophers I mean, such as Lucian wittily
and with reason taxes,) and the Schoolmen since, aiming at

---

[1] Locke elsewhere exhorts 'those who would conduct their understanding right, not to take any term, however authorised by the language of the Schools, to stand for anything, till they have an *idea* of it. A word may be of frequent use and great credit with several authors, and be by them used as if it stood for some real being; but yet if he that reads cannot frame any distinct idea of that being, it is certain to him a mere empty sound without a meaning. . . . It will not perhaps be allowed if I should set down *substantial forms* and *intentional species*, as such that may justly be suspected to be of this kind of insignificant terms. But this I am sure, to one that can form no deter-mined ideas of what they stand for, they signify nothing at all; and all that he thinks he knows about them is to him so much knowledge about nothing, and amounts at most but to a *learned ignorance*. It is not without reason sup-posed there are many such empty terms to be found in some learned writers, to which they had recourse to etch out their systems, where their understand-ings could not furnish them with con-ceptions from things. The supposing of some realities in nature, answering those and the like words, have per-plexed some, and quite misled others in the study of nature. Where men have any conceptions, they can, if they are ever so abstruse or abstracted, explain them, and the terms they use for them. For our conceptions being nothing but [complex] ideas, which are made up of simple ones, if they cannot give us the ideas their *words* stand for, it is plain they have none. . . . To obtrude terms where we have no distinct conceptions, as if they did correspond to, or rather conceal, something, is but an artifice of learned vanity, to cover a defect in a hypothesis, or in our understanding.' (*Conduct of the Understanding*, § 29.)

BOOK III. glory and esteem, for their great and universal knowledge,
CHAP. X. easier a great deal to be pretended to than really acquired, found this a good expedient to cover their ignorance, with a curious and inexplicable web of perplexed words, and procure to themselves the admiration of others, by unintelligible terms, the apter to produce wonder because they could not be understood : whilst it appears in all history, that these profound doctors were no wiser nor more useful than their neighbours, and brought but small advantage to human life or the societies wherein they lived : unless the coining of new words, where they produced no new things to apply them to, or the perplexing or obscuring the signification of old ones, and so bringing all things into question and dispute, were a thing profitable to the life of man, or worthy commendation and reward.

This Learning very little benefits Society.

9. For, notwithstanding these learned disputants, these all-knowing doctors, it was to the unscholastic statesman that the governments of the world owed their peace, defence, and liberties ; and from the illiterate and contemned mechanic (a name of disgrace) that they received the improvements of useful arts. Nevertheless, this artificial ignorance, and learned gibberish, prevailed mightily in these last ages, by the interest and artifice of those who found no easier way to that pitch of authority and dominion they have attained, than by amusing the men of business, and ignorant, with hard words, or employing the ingenious and idle in intricate disputes about unintelligible terms, and holding them perpetually entangled in that endless labyrinth. Besides, there is no such way to gain admittance, or give defence to strange and absurd doctrines, as to guard them round about with legions of obscure, doubtful, and undefined words. Which yet make these retreats more like the dens of robbers, or holes of foxes, than the fortresses of fair warriors : which, if it be hard to get them out of, it is not for the strength that is in them, but the briars and thorns, and the obscurity of the thickets they are beset with. For untruth being unacceptable to the mind of man, there is no other defence left for absurdity but obscurity.

But destroys

10. Thus learned ignorance, and this art of keeping even inquisitive men from true knowledge, hath been propagated

in the world, and hath much perplexed, whilst it pretended to
inform the understanding. For we see that other well-
meaning and wise men, whose education and parts had not
acquired that *acuteness*, could intelligibly express themselves
to one another; and in its plain use make a benefit of language. But though unlearned men well enough understood
the words white and black, &c., and had constant notions
of the ideas signified by those words; yet there were philosophers found who had learning and subtlety enough to prove
that snow was black; i. e. to prove that white was black [1].
Whereby they had the advantage to destroy the instruments
and means of discourse, conversation, instruction, and society;
whilst, with great art and subtlety, they did no more but
perplex and confound the signification of words, and thereby
render language less useful than the real defects of it had
made it; a gift which the illiterate had not attained to.

11. These learned men did equally instruct men's understandings, and profit their lives, as he who should alter the
signification of known characters, and, by a subtle device of
learning, far surpassing the capacity of the illiterate, dull, and
vulgar, should in his writing show that he could put A for B,
and D for E, &c., to the no small admiration and benefit of
his reader. It being as senseless to put *black*, which is a word
agreed on to stand for one sensible idea, to put it, I say, for
another, or the contrary idea; i. e. to call *snow black*, as to put
this mark A, which is a character agreed on to stand for one
modification of sound, made by a certain motion of the organs
of speech, for B, which is agreed on to stand for another
modification of sound, made by another certain mode of the
organs of speech [2].

---

[1] It was argued by ancient philosophers that snow was black, because
water of which it is formed is so, and
thus that in the light of reason it has
one colour, while it has another as
presented in sense.

[2] The following supplement by Locke
to the two preceding sections is preserved in Lord King's *Life,* vol. ii.
pp. 222–25 : ' By this learned Art of
abusing words and shifting their sig-

nifications, the rules left us by the
ancients for conducting our thoughts
in the search, or at least the examination, of truth have been defeated.
The logic of the Schools contains all
the rules of reasoning that are generally taught, and they are believed to
be so sufficient that it will probably be
thought presumption in any to suppose
there needs any other to be sought or
looked after. I grant the method of

BOOK III.

CHAP. X.
This Art
has per-
plexed
Religion

12. Nor hath this mischief stopped in logical niceties, or curious empty speculations; it hath invaded the great concernments of human life and society; obscured and perplexed the material truths of law and divinity; brought confusion, disorder, and uncertainty into the affairs of mankind; and

Syllogism is right as far as it reaches: its proper business is to show the force and coherence of any argumentation; and to that it would have served very well, and one might certainly have depended on the conclusions as necessarily following from the premises, in a rightly ordered Syllogism, if the applauded Art of Disputing had not been taken for knowledge, and the credit of victory in such contests introduced a fallacious use of words, whereby even those forms of arguing have proved rather a snare than a help to the understanding, and so the end lost for which they were invented. For the form of the Syllogism justifying the deduction, the conclusion, though never so false, stood good, and was to be admitted for such. This set men who would make any figure in the Schools to busy their thoughts, not in a search into the nature of *things*, but in studying of *terms*, and varying their signification of words, with all the nicety and, as it was called, the subtlety they could strain their thoughts to, whereby they might entangle the respondent, who if he let slip the observation and detection of the sophistry, whenever any of the terms were used in various significations, he was certainly gone without the help of a like sort of artifice; and therefore, on the other side, was to be well furnished with good store of words, to be used as distinctions—whether they signified anything to the purpose or anything at all, it mattered not; they were to be thrown in an opponent's way, and he was to argue against them: so that whilst one could use his words equivocally, which is nothing but making the same sound stand for different ideas, and the other but use two sounds, as determining the various significations of a thing, whether in truth they had any relation to its signification or no, there could be no end of the dispute, or decision of the question. Or if it happened that either of the disputants, failing in his proper artillery, was brought to a non plus, this indeed placed the laurels on his adversary's head, victory was his; and with it the name of learning, and renown of a scholar: he has his reward and therein his end; but truth gets nothing by it: the question is a question still, and after it has been the matter of many a combat, and by being carried sometimes on the one side and sometimes on the other, has afforded a triumph to many a combatant, is still as far from decision as ever. Truth and knowledge hath nothing to do in all this bustle; nobody thinks them concerned, it is all for victory and triumph: so that this way of contesting for truth often is nothing but the abuse of words for victory;—a trial of skill, without any appearance of a true consideration of the matter in question, or troubling their heads to find out where the truth lies. This not the fault of mode and figure, the rules whereof are of great use in the regulating of argumentation, and trying the coherence and force of man's discourses. But the mischief has been brought in, by placing too high a credit and value on the Art of Disputing, and giving that the reputation and reward of learning and knowledge, which is in truth one of the greatest hindrances of it.' This may be compared with Bk. IV. ch. xvii. §§ 4–8, on Syllogism; also Locke's *Thoughts concerning Education*, §§ 188, 189.

if not destroyed, yet in a great measure rendered useless, these two great rules, religion and justice. What have the greatest part of the comments and disputes upon the laws of God and man served for, but to make the meaning more doubtful, and perplex the sense? What have been the effect of those multiplied curious distinctions, and acute niceties, but obscurity and uncertainty, leaving the words more unintelligible, and the reader more at a loss? How else comes it to pass that princes, speaking or writing to their servants, in their ordinary commands are easily understood; speaking to their people, in their laws, are not so? And, as I remarked before, doth it not often happen that a man of an ordinary capacity very well understands a text, or a law, that he reads, till he consults an expositor, or goes to counsel ; who, by that time he hath done explaining them, makes the words signify either nothing at all, or what he pleases[1].

13. Whether any by-interests of these professions have occasioned this, I will not here examine ; but I leave it to be considered, whether it would not be well for mankind, whose concernment it is to know things as they are, and to do what they ought, and not to spend their lives in talking about them, or tossing words to and fro ;—whether it would not be well, I say, that the use of words were made plain and direct; and that language, which was given us for the improvement of knowledge and bond of society, should not be employed to darken truth and unsettle people's rights; to raise mists, and render unintelligible both morality and religion ? Or that at least, if this will happen, it should not be thought learning or knowledge to do so[2]?

---

[1] Locke's point of view was at the opposite pole to that of the mediaeval schoolmen, and also to that of post-Kantian dialectic.

[2] Locke comments on this section thus, in memoranda preserved in King's *Life*, vii. pp. 225–29 :—'We cannot but think that angels of all kinds much exceed us in knowledge, and possibly we are apt sometimes to envy them that advantage, or at least to repine that we do not partake with them in a greater share of it. Whoever thinks of the elevation of their knowledge above ours, cannot imagine it lies in *a playing with words*, but in the contemplation of things, and having true notions about them; a perception of their habitudes and relations one to another. If this be so, methinks we should be ambitious to come in this part, which is a great deal in our power, as near them as we can. We should cast off all the artifice

BOOK III.

—+•—

CHAP. X.

Fourthly, by taking Words for Things.

14. IV. *Fourthly,* Another great abuse of words is, the *taking them for things.* This, though it in some degree concerns all names in general, yet more particularly affects those of substances. To this abuse those men are most subject who most confine their thoughts to any one system, and give themselves up into a firm belief of the perfection of any received hypothesis: whereby they come to be persuaded that the terms of that sect are so suited to the nature of things, that they perfectly correspond with their real existence. Who is there that has been bred up in the Peripatetick philosophy, who does not think the Ten Names, under which are ranked the Ten Predicaments[1], to be exactly conformable to the nature of things? Who is there of that school that is not

and fallacy of words, which makes so great a part of the business and skill of the disputers of this world, and is contemptible even to rational men, and therefore must needs render us ridiculous to those higher orders of spirits. Whilst we, pretending to the knowledge of things, hinder as much as we can the discovery of truth, by perplexing one another all we can by a perverse use of those signs which we make use of to convey truth to one another, must it not be matter of contempt to them to see us make the studied and improved abuse of those signs have the name and credit of learning? . . . The forms of argumentation should be learned and made use of: but to teach an apprentice to measure well, would you commend and reward him for cheating, by putting off false and sophisticated wares? It is no wonder men never come to seek and to value truth, when they have been entered in sophistry, and questions are proposed and argued, not at all for the resolving of doubts, nor for settling the mind upon good grounds on the right side, but to make a sport of truth, which is only set up to be thrown at, and to be battled as falsehood; and he has most applause who can most effectually do it.' Some account of the legitimate conditions of disputation is then offered. This and the preceding passage from Locke's MSS., along with §§ 6–13, are very characteristic of the spirit in which he wrote, and of the antithesis between the age of Thomas Aquinas and that of which Locke was the intellectual type and representative. The reaction in the nineteenth century towards Aristotle and the Schoolmen is another notable fact.

[1] The Ten Predicaments or Categories of Aristotle, according to which all the judgments that can be made about Being must be either about its Substance (*ens per se*), which is the supreme category; about its matter or its form, under the categories of Quantity and Quality; or about something relative, under the category of Relation in general; or one or other of the subordinate categories of relation in space, i. e. Where; relation in duration, i. e. When; relation of bodies in place, i. e. Posture, relation of possession, i. e. Having; and relation of agent and patient, i. e. Action and Passion—these nine categories being concerned with *ens per accidens*. With different ends in view, analogies may be found between the Aristotelian Categories and Locke's complex ideas of Substances, Modes, and Relations.

persuaded that *substantial forms*[1], *vegetative souls*[2], *abhorrence* BOOK III.
of a vacuum[3], *intentional species*[4], &c., are something real? CHAP. X.
These words men have learned from their very entrance upon
knowledge, and have found their masters and systems lay
great stress upon them : and therefore they cannot quit the
opinion, that they are conformable to nature, and are the
representations of something that really exists. The Platonists
have their *soul of the world*[5], and the Epicureans their
endeavour towards motion in their atoms when at rest[6]. There
is scarce any sect in philosophy has not a distinct set of terms
that others understand not. But yet this gibberish, which, in
the weakness of human understanding, serves so well to
palliate men's ignorance, and cover their errors, comes, by
familiar use amongst those of the same tribe, to seem the
most important part of language, and of all other the terms
the most significant : and should *aërial* and *ætherial vehicles*
come once, by the prevalency of that doctrine[7], to be
generally received anywhere, no doubt those terms would
make impressions on men's minds, so as to establish them in
the persuasion of the reality of such things, as much as Peripatetick *forms* and *intentional species* have heretofore done.

[1] See previous annotations regarding the difference between the 'real essences' of Locke, supposed to be physical and relative to the senses, and the metaphysical 'substantial forms' of Aristotle.

[2] The 'vegetative soul' is the lowest 'form' of the principle of life, according to the Peripatetic philosophy. See *De Anima*, Bk. II.

[3] 'abhorrence of a vacuum'—the metaphor that was put in place of a physical explanation, e. g. of the rise of water in a pump.

[4] 'According to the opinion which generally prevailed among the Peripatetic philosophers of the middle ages, our faculties of knowledge required for their activity a certain *representative medium*, different both from the mind itself and from the external object of thought. These intermediate and vi-

carious objects were called *intentional species*.' See Hamilton's *Reid*, Note M, p. 951, 'On the Doctrine of Species as held by Aristotle and the Aristotelians.'

[5] 'soul of the world'—the idea of the macrocosm of the universe being in analogy with the microcosm in man, belongs to the best philosophical and religious thought.

[6] Lucretius and Gassendi are probably here in Locke's view. (See *De Rerum Natura*, II. 216, 251–93, and Gassendi's *Physica* Lib. II., in which an *ad motum propensio* is attributed to atoms.) While Locke's 'real essences' are supposed to be atomic, they are held to transcend human perception in sense.

[7] A doctrine of the Neo-platonists, vindicated in Henry More's *Immortality of the Soul*, Bk. II. ch. xiv, and referred to by Cudworth.

15. How much names taken for things are apt to mislead the understanding, the attentive reading of philosophical writers would abundantly discover; and that perhaps in words little suspected of any such misuse. I shall instance in one only, and that a very familiar one. How many intricate disputes have there been about *matter*, as if there were some such thing really in nature, distinct from *body*; as it is evident the word matter stands for an idea distinct from the idea of body? For if the ideas these two terms stood for were precisely the same, they might indifferently in all places be put for one another. But we see that though it be proper to say, There is one matter of all bodies, one cannot say, There is one body of all matters : we familiarly say one body is bigger than another; but it sounds harsh (and I think is never used) to say one matter is bigger than another. Whence comes this, then? *Viz.* from hence: that, though matter and body be not really distinct, but wherever there is the one there is the other; yet matter and body stand for two different conceptions, whereof the one is incomplete, and but a part of the other. For body stands for a solid extended figured substance, whereof matter is but a partial and more confused conception; it seeming to me to be used for the substance and solidity of body, without taking in its extension and figure : and therefore it is that, speaking of matter, we speak of it always as one, because in truth it expressly contains nothing but the idea of a solid substance, which is everywhere the same, everywhere uniform. This being our idea of matter, we no more conceive or speak of different *matters* in the world than we do of different solidities; though we both conceive and speak of different bodies, because extension and figure are capable of variation. But, since solidity cannot exist without extension and figure, the taking matter to be the name of something really existing under that precision [1], has no doubt produced those obscure and unintelligible discourses and disputes, which have filled the heads and books of philosophers concerning *materia prima* ; which imperfection or abuse, how far it may concern a great many other general terms I leave to be considered. This, I think,

---

[1] ' prescission '—to prescind or abstract.

I may at least say, that we should have a great many fewer disputes in the world, if words were taken for what they are, the signs of our ideas only; and not for things themselves [1]. For, when we argue about *matter*, or any the like term, we truly argue only about the idea we express by that sound, whether that precise idea agree to anything really existing in nature or no. And if men would tell what ideas they make their words stand for, there could not be half that obscurity or wrangling in the search or support of truth that there is [2].

16. But whatever inconvenience follows from this mistake of words, this I am sure, that, by constant and familiar use, they charm men into notions far remote from the truth of things. It would be a hard matter to persuade any one that the words which his father, or schoolmaster, the parson of the parish, or such a reverend doctor used, signified nothing that really existed in nature: which perhaps is none of the least causes that men are so hardly drawn to quit their mistakes, even in opinions purely philosophical, and where they have no other interest but truth. For the words they have a long time been used to, remaining firm in their minds, it is no wonder that the wrong notions annexed to them should not be removed [3].

This makes Errors lasting.

17. V. *Fifthly,* Another abuse of words is, *the setting them in the place of things which they do or can by no means signify.*

Fifthly, by setting them in

---

[1] Cf. ch. ii. §§ 2, 3.

[2] The Aristotelian *materia prima* (ὕλη πρώτη), or formless matter, referred to throughout this section, is defined in *Phys.* I. 9. See too *Metaph.* VII. 3, and the *De Anima*, III. 4, where he refers to the distinction between actual and potential reality, and the relation of the former to living knowledge. Matter, as given to us in the things of sense, must not be confounded with this formless potential matter of Aristotle—the pre-condition only of the actual things of sense, in which form is united to the matter. The Aristotelian formless matter seems vaguely to haunt Locke, in his account of 'substance in general'; as well as

Berkeley, in his controversy with substance *per se*, and Kant in the *Ding an sich*. The modern scientific conception of 'matter' reduces it to *what is phenomenally given in the senses*, in contrast to the *materia prima* of Aristotle.

[3] After the freshness of their first promulgation, charged with the ideas that filled the minds of their authors, the words and formulas, which originally represented great religious and philosophical systems, become emptied of their meanings, in their ordinary currency, until they recover freshness and significance, when the current of reflective thought re-enters them, and makes the old phrases live again.

BOOK III.

CHAP. X.

the place
of what
they
cannot
signify.

We may observe that, in the general names of substances, whereof the *nominal* essences are only known to us, when we put them into propositions, and affirm or deny anything about them, we do most commonly tacitly suppose or intend, they should stand for the *real* essence of a certain sort of substances. For, when a man says gold is malleable, he means and would insinuate something more than this, That what I call gold[1] is malleable, (though truly it amounts to no more,) but would have this understood, viz. That gold, i.e. what has the real essence of gold[2], is malleable; which amounts to thus much, that malleableness depends on, and is inseparable from the real essence of gold. But a man, not knowing wherein that real essence consists, the connexion in his mind of malleableness is not truly with an essence he knows not, but only with the sound gold[3] he puts for it. Thus, when we say that *animal rationale* is, and *animal implume bipes latis unguibus* is not a good definition of a man; it is plain we suppose the name man in this case to stand for the real essence of a species, and would signify that 'a rational animal' better described that real essence than 'a two-legged animal with broad nails, and without feathers.' For else, why might not Plato as properly make the word ἄνθρωπος, or *man*, stand for his complex idea, made up of the idea of a body, distinguished from others by a certain shape and other outward appearances, as Aristotle make the complex idea to which he gave the name ἄνθρωπος, or *man*, of body and the faculty of reasoning joined together; unless the name ἄνθρωπος, or *man*, were supposed to stand for something else than what it signifies; and to be put in the place of some other thing than the idea a man professes he would express by it[4]?

---

[1] 'what I call gold,' i. e. whatever object I find to be entitled to have the name gold applied to it, inasmuch as it has the qualities (malleableness, &c.) that constitute any connotation of 'gold.'

[2] 'what has the real essence of gold,' i. e. whatever particular substance present to my senses, which is what it is in virtue of the particular texture of atoms that is assumed to be its 'real essence,' must possess 'malleableness.'

[3] Rather with the connotation annexed by us to the 'sound gold,' which forms the 'essence' of that name.

[4] This seems to overlook the fact that some 'nominal essences' may form 'species' that are more in harmony with the reason that is immanent in all that exists than other nominal essences would be. Even in what

18. It is true the names of substances would be much more useful, and propositions made in them much more certain, were the real essences of substances the ideas in our minds which those words signified. And it is for want of those real essences that our words convey so little knowledge or certainty in our discourses about them; and therefore the mind, to remove that imperfection as much as it can, makes them, by a secret supposition, to stand for a thing having that real essence, as if thereby it made some nearer approaches to it. For, though the word *man* or *gold* signify nothing truly but a complex idea of properties united together in one sort of substances; yet there is scarce anybody, in the use of these words, but often supposes each of those names to stand for a thing having the real essence on which these properties depend [1]. Which is so far from diminishing the imperfection

J. S. Mill calls ' real kinds,' or ' natural kinds,' this diversity in reason is in a manner recognised. ' There are some classes the things contained in which differ from others only in certain particulars which may be numbered; while others differ in more than can be numbered, more even than we need ever expect to know. . . . *White things,* for example, are not distinguished by any common properties except whiteness. . . . But a hundred generations have not exhausted the common properties of *animals* or of *plants,* of *sulphur* or of *phosphorus.* . . . Of these two classifications the one answers to a much more radical distinction in the things themselves than the other does. . . . Now these classes, distinguished by unknown multitudes of properties, and not solely by a few determinate ones, are the only classes which, by the Aristotelian logicians, were considered as genera or species.' (*Logic,* Bk. I. ch. vii.)

[1] But although those names do not stand for ideas of the ' real essence,' or ultimate atomic texture and constitution, on which the observed and unobserved properties of the things denoted all depend, Locke grants that they

are more than arbitrary. The things to which common names are applicable must possess those qualities which form the ' essence ' of the names. For example, ' anything will be a true *sun,*' he tells Stillingfleet, ' to which the name sun may be truly and properly applied; and to that substance or thing the name sun may be truly and properly applied *which has united in it* that combination of sensible qualities by which anything else that is called sun is distinguished from other substances, i. e. by the nominal essence. . . . So I humbly conceive, if it had the nominal essence *it would have something besides the name,* viz. that nominal essence [i. e. those simple ideas or qualities] which is sufficient to denominate it truly a sun, or to make it be a true sun; though we know nothing of the real essence whereon that nominal one depends'[i.e. the supposed atomic texture on which the observable secondary qualities and powers depend, or which makes it be what it is.] . . . Again, what makes men ' men '? Locke answers: ' The nominal essence of that species, i. e. the properties answering the complex abstract idea to which the specific name "man" is given, *being actually found*

of our words, that by a plain abuse it adds to it, when we would make them stand for something, which, not being in our complex idea, the name we use can no ways be the sign of.

Hence we think Change of our Complex Ideas of Substances not to change their Species.

19. This shows us the reason why in *mixed modes* any of the ideas that make the composition of the complex one being left out or changed, it is allowed to be another thing, i. e. to be of another species, as is plain in *chance-medley, manslaughter, murder, parricide,* &c. The reason whereof is, because the complex idea signified by that name is the real as well as nominal essence [1]; and there is no secret reference of that name to any other essence but that. But in *substances,* it is not so. For though in that called *gold,* one puts into his complex idea what another leaves out, and vice versâ : yet men do not usually think that therefore the species is changed : because they secretly in their minds refer that name, and suppose it annexed to a real immutable essence of a thing existing, on which those properties depend. He that adds to his complex idea of gold that of fixedness and solubility in *aqua regia,* which he put not in it before, is not thought to have changed the species; but only to have a more perfect idea, by adding another simple idea, which is always in fact joined with those other, of which his former complex idea consisted. But this reference of the name to a thing, whereof we have not the idea, is so far from helping at all, that it only serves the more to involve us in difficulties. For by this tacit reference to the real essence of that species of bodies, the word *gold* (which, by standing for a more or less perfect collection of simple ideas, serves to design that sort of body well enough in civil discourse [2]) comes to have no signification at all, being put for

---

in them, is that which makes them be properly called men, or is the reason why they are called men.' All this is consistent with the fact that some 'nominal essences' refer to something deeper and truer in the things which respond to them than other nominal essences do. When the question is so regarded, Locke's conclusion, that ' things being ranked into sorts, under such and such names, does depend and wholly depend on the ideas of *men*' cannot be taken unconditionally.

[1] Cf. ch. v. § 14.

[2] When the body to which the name is applied is found, or imagined, to present the 'simple ideas' for which the name stands.

somewhat whereof we have no idea at all, and so can signify
nothing at all, when the body itself is away[1]. For however it
may be thought all one, yet, if well considered, it will be
found a quite different thing, to argue about gold in name[2],
and about a parcel in the body itself, v.g. a piece of leaf-gold
laid before us[3]; though in discourse we are fain to substitute
the name for the thing.

20. That which I think very much disposes men to substitute their names for the real essences of species, is the
supposition before mentioned, that nature works regularly in
the production of things, and sets the boundaries to each of
those species, by giving exactly the same real internal constitution to each individual which we rank under one general
name. Whereas any one who observes their different qualities
can hardly doubt, that many of the individuals, called by the
same name, are, in their internal constitution, as different one
from another as several of those which are ranked under
different specific names. This supposition, however, that the
same precise and internal constitution[4] goes always with the
same specific name, makes men forward to take those names
for the representatives of those real essences; though indeed
they signify nothing but the complex ideas they have in their
minds when they use them. So that, if I may so say, signifying one thing, and being supposed for, or put in the place of
another, they cannot but, in such a kind of use, cause a great
deal of uncertainty in men's discourses; especially in those
who have thoroughly imbibed the doctrine of *substantial forms*,

The Cause
of this
Abuse, a
supposi-
tion of
Nature's
working
always
regularly,
in setting
boundaries
to Species.

---

[1] For the 'body' is connected with
the name only by its correspondence
with the nominal essence, which alone
makes the name applicable to it; so
that when the thing called 'gold' is
gone, the name, if it depends on the
idea of the incognisable 'real essence,'
must remain meaningless.

[2] 'gold in name,' i.e. using in our
argument the name to signify the
nominal essence that we have annexed to the name.

[3] 'a parcel .. in a piece of leaf-gold

laid before us,' i.e. a parcel of absolutely imperceptible attributes, supposed to constitute the 'real essence'
of this presented substance.

[4] That is, the same 'real essence.'
Our names and *their* essences are not
necessarily, if ever, in harmony with
the supposed 'real essences' of the
individual things. Things are classed
by us according to the superficial
resemblances that alone come within
our experience.

This Abuse contains two false Supposi- tions.

whereby they firmly imagine the several species of things to be determined and distinguished [1].

21. But however preposterous and absurd it be to make our names stand for ideas we have not, or (which is all one) essences that we know not, it being in effect to make our words the signs of nothing; yet it is evident to any one who ever so little reflects on the use men make of their words, that there is nothing more familiar. When a man asks whether this or that thing he sees, let it be a drill, or a monstrous fœtus, be a *man* or no; it is evident the question is not, Whether that particular thing agree to his complex idea expressed by the name man : but whether it has in it the real essence of a species of things which he supposes his name man to stand for. In which way of using the names of substances, there are these false suppositions contained :—

First, that there are certain precise essences according to which nature makes all particular things, and by which they are distinguished into species. That everything has a real constitution, whereby it is what it is, and on which its sensible qualities depend, is past doubt : but I think it has been proved that this makes not the distinction of species as *we* rank them, nor the boundaries of their names.

Secondly, this tacitly also insinuates, as if we had *ideas* of these proposed essences. For to what purpose else is it, to inquire whether this or that thing have the real essence of the species man, if we did not suppose that there were such a specifick essence known? Which yet is utterly false. And therefore such application of names as would make them stand for ideas which we have not, must needs cause great disorder in discourses and reasonings about them, and be a great inconvenience in our communication by words.

Sixthly, by pro-

22. VI. *Sixthly*, there remains yet another more general,

[1] A human science of things, he means to say, cannot penetrate further than there can be human ideas of the things ; and these are confined to what we can connote in the names we use, which excludes all ideas of their real essences. So that our understanding of the qualities and powers that coexist in the substances of which the universe is made up, except so far as they are actually presented to our senses, must be imperfect ; determined by probabilities, and properly speaking not knowledge or science at all. Cf. Bk. IV. chh. iii. §§ 9–17; xiv, xv.

though perhaps less observed, abuse of words; and that is,
that men having by a long and familiar use annexed to them
certain ideas, they are apt to imagine *so near and necessary*
a connexion between the names and the signification they use
them in, that they forwardly suppose one cannot but understand what their meaning is; and therefore one ought to
acquiesce in the words delivered, as if it were past doubt that,
in the use of those common received sounds, the speaker and
hearer had necessarily the same precise ideas. Whence presuming, that when they have in discourse used any term, they
have thereby, as it were, set before others the very thing they
talked of. And so likewise taking the words of others, as
naturally standing for just what they themselves have been
accustomed to apply them to, they never trouble themselves
to explain their own, or understand clearly others' meaning.
From whence commonly proceeds noise, and wrangling, without improvement or information; whilst men take words to
be the constant regular marks of agreed notions, which in truth
are no more but the voluntary and unsteady signs of their own
ideas. And yet men think it strange, if in discourse, or (where
it is often absolutely necessary) in dispute, one sometimes asks
the meaning of their terms: though the arguings one may
every day observe in conversation make it evident, that there
are few names of complex ideas which any two men use for
the same just precise collection. It is hard to name a word
which will not be a clear instance of this. *Life* is a term,
none more familiar. Any one almost would take it for an
affront to be asked what he meant by it. And yet if it comes
in question, whether a plant that lies ready formed in the seed
have life; whether the embryo in an egg before incubation, or
a man in a swoon without sense or motion, be alive or no; it
is easy to perceive that a clear, distinct, settled idea does not
always accompany the use of so known a word as that of life
is. Some gross and confused conceptions men indeed ordinarily have, to which they apply the common words of their
language; and such a loose use of their words serves them
well enough in their ordinary discourses or affairs. But this
is not sufficient for philosophical inquiries. Knowledge and
reasoning require precise determinate ideas. And though men

CHAP. X.
ceeding
upon the
supposi-
tion that
the Words
we use
have a
certain
and evi-
dent Signi-
fication
which
other men
cannot but
under-
stand.

will not be so importunately dull as not to understand what others say, without demanding an explication of their terms; nor so troublesomely critical as to correct others in the use of the words they receive from them: yet, where truth and knowledge are concerned in the case, I know not what fault it can be, to desire the explication of words whose sense seems dubious; or why a man should be ashamed to own his ignorance in what sense another man uses his words; since he has no other way of certainly knowing it but by being informed. This abuse of taking words upon trust has nowhere spread so far, nor with so ill effects, as amongst men of letters. The multiplication and obstinacy of disputes, which have so laid waste the intellectual world, is owing to nothing more than to this ill use of words. For though it be generally believed that there is great diversity of opinions in the volumes and variety of controversies the world is distracted with; yet the most I can find that the contending learned men of different parties do, in their arguings one with another, is, that they speak different languages. For I am apt to imagine, that when any of them, quitting terms, think upon things, and know what they think, they think all the same: though perhaps what they would have be different.

The Ends of Language: First, To convey our Ideas.

23. To conclude this consideration of the imperfection and abuse of language. The ends of language in our discourse with others being chiefly these three: First, to make known one man's thoughts or ideas to another; Secondly, to do it with as much ease and quickness as possible; and, Thirdly, thereby to convey the knowledge of things: language is either abused or deficient, when it fails of any of these three.

First, Words fail in the first of these ends, and lay not open one man's ideas to another's view: 1. When men have names in their mouths without any determinate ideas in their minds, whereof they are the signs: or, 2. When they apply the common received names of any language to ideas, to which the common use of that language does not apply them: or, 3. When they apply them very unsteadily, making them stand, now for one, and by and by for another idea.

Secondly,

24. Secondly, Men fail of conveying their thoughts with all

the quickness and ease that may be, when they have complex BOOK III.
ideas without having any distinct names for them. This is ⊸⊶
sometimes the fault of the language itself, which has not in it CHAP. X.
a sound yet applied to such a signification ; and sometimes To do it
the fault of the man, who has not yet learned the name for with
that idea he would show another. Quickness.

25. Thirdly, There is no knowledge of things conveyed by Thirdly,
men's words, when their ideas agree not to the reality of There-
things. Though it be a defect that has its original in our ideas, with to
which are not so conformable to the nature of things as atten- the Know-
tion, study, and application might make them, yet it fails not ledge of
to extend itself to our words too, when we use them as signs Things.
of real beings, which yet never had any reality or existence.

26. First, He that hath words of any language, without How
distinct ideas in his mind to which he applies them, does, so Men's
far as he uses them in discourse, only make a noise without in all
any sense or signification ; and how learned soever he may First,
seem, by the use of hard words or learned terms, is not much when used
more advanced thereby in knowledge, than he would be in any ideas.
learning, who had nothing in his study but the bare titles of
books, without possessing the contents of them. For all such
words, however put into discourse, according to the right
construction of grammatical rules, or the harmony of well-
turned periods, do yet amount to nothing but bare sounds,
and nothing else.

27. Secondly, He that has complex ideas, without particular Secondly,
names for them, would be in no better case than a bookseller, when
who had in his warehouse volumes that lay there unbound, ideas are
and without titles, which he could therefore make known to without
others only by showing the loose sheets, and communicate annexed
them only by tale. This man is hindered in his discourse, for to them.
want of words to communicate his complex ideas, which he is
therefore forced to make known by an enumeration of the
simple ones that compose them ; and so is fain often to use
twenty words, to express what another man signifies in one.

28. Thirdly, He that puts not constantly the same sign Thirdly,
for the same idea, but uses the same words sometimes in one when the
and sometimes in another signification, ought to pass in the is not put

BOOK III.
CHAP. X.
for the
same idea.

schools and conversation for as fair a man, as he does in the market and exchange, who sells several things under the same name.

Fourthly,
when
words are
diverted
from their
common
use.

29. Fourthly, He that applies the words of any language to ideas different from those to which the common use of that country applies them[1], however his own understanding may be filled with truth and light, will not by such words be able to convey much of it to others, without defining his terms. For however the sounds are such as are familiarly known, and easily enter the ears of those who are accustomed to them; yet standing for other ideas than those they usually are annexed to, and are wont to excite in the mind of the hearers, they cannot make known the thoughts of him who thus uses them.

Fifthly,
when they
are names
of fantasti-
cal imagin-
ations.

30. Fifthly, He that imagined to himself substances such as never have been, and filled his head with ideas which have not any correspondence with the real nature of things, to which yet he gives settled and defined names, may fill his discourse, and perhaps another man's head, with the fantastical imaginations of his own brain, but will be very far from advancing thereby one jot in real and true knowledge.

Summary.

31. He that hath names without ideas, wants meaning in his words, and speaks only empty sounds. He that hath complex ideas without names for them, wants liberty and dispatch in his expressions, and is necessitated to use periphrases. He that uses his words loosely and unsteadily will either be not minded or not understood. He that applies his names to ideas different from their common use, wants propriety in his language, and speaks gibberish. And he that hath the ideas of substances disagreeing with the real existence of things, so far wants the materials of true knowledge in his understanding, and hath instead thereof chimeras.

How
men's

32. In our notions concerning Substances, we are liable to

[1] 'We ought,' says J. S. Mill, 'when we are restricted to the employment of old words, to endeavour as far as possible that it shall not be necessary to struggle against the old associations with those words. We should, if pos-sible, give the words such a meaning that the propositions in which people are accustomed to use them shall as far as possible still be true.' (*Unsettled Questions*)

all the former inconveniences: v. g. he that uses the word
tarantula, without having any imagination or idea of what
it stands for, pronounces a good word; but so long means
nothing at all by it.   2. He that, in a newly-discovered country,
shall see several sorts of animals and vegetables, unknown to
him before, may have as true ideas of them, as of a horse or
a stag; but can speak of them only by a description, till he
shall either take the names the natives call them by, or give
them names himself.   3. He that uses the word *body* sometimes for pure extension, and sometimes for extension and
solidity together, will talk very fallaciously.   4. He that gives
the name *horse* to that idea which common usage calls *mule*,
talks improperly, and will not be understood.   5. He that
thinks the name *centaur* stands for some real being, imposes
on himself, and mistakes words for things.

33. In Modes and Relations generally, we are liable only
to the four first of these inconveniences; viz. 1. I may have
in my memory the names of modes, as *gratitude* or *charity*,
and yet not have any precise ideas annexed in my thoughts
to those names.   2. I may have ideas, and not know the
names that belong to them: v. g. I may have the idea
of a man's drinking till his colour and humour be altered, till
his tongue trips, and his eyes look red, and his feet fail him;
and yet not know that it is to be called *drunkenness*.   3. I may
have the ideas of virtues or vices, and names also, but apply
them amiss: v. g. when I apply the name *frugality* to that
idea which others call and signify by this sound, *covetousness*.
4. I may use any of those names with inconstancy.   5. But,
in modes and relations, I cannot have ideas disagreeing to
the existence of things: for modes being complex ideas, made
by the mind at pleasure, and relation being but by way of
considering or comparing two things together, and so also an
idea of my own making, these ideas can scarce be found to
disagree with anything existing; since they are not in the
mind as the copies of things regularly made by nature, nor as
properties inseparably flowing from the internal constitution
or essence of any substance; but, as it were, patterns lodged
in my memory, with names annexed to them, to denominate
actions and relations by, as they come to exist.   But the

mistake is commonly in my giving a wrong name to my conceptions; and so using words in a different sense from other people: I am not understood, but am thought to have wrong ideas of them, when I give wrong names to them. Only if I put in my ideas of mixed modes or relations any inconsistent ideas together, I fill my head also with chimeras; since such ideas, if well examined, cannot so much as exist in the mind, much less any real being ever be denominated from them.

Seventhly, Language is often abused by Figurative Speech. 34. Since wit and fancy find easier entertainment in the world than dry truth and real knowledge, figurative speeches and allusion in language will hardly be admitted as an imperfection or abuse of it. I confess, in discourses where we seek rather pleasure and delight than information and improvement, such ornaments as are borrowed from them can scarce pass for faults. But yet if we would speak of things as they are, we must allow that all the art of rhetoric, besides order and clearness; all the artificial and figurative application of words eloquence hath invented, are for nothing else but to insinuate wrong ideas, move the passions, and thereby mislead the judgment; and so indeed are perfect cheats: and therefore, however laudable or allowable oratory may render them in harangues and popular addresses, they are certainly, in all discourses that pretend to inform or instruct, wholly to be avoided; and where truth and knowledge are concerned, cannot but be thought a great fault, either of the language or person that makes use of them. What and how various they are, will be superfluous here to take notice; the books of rhetoric which abound in the world, will instruct those who want to be informed: only I cannot but observe how little the preservation and improvement of truth and knowledge is the care and concern of mankind; since the arts of fallacy are endowed and preferred. It is evident how much men love to deceive and be deceived, since rhetoric, that powerful instrument of error and deceit, has its established professors, is publicly taught, and has always been had in great reputation: and I doubt not but it will be thought great boldness, if not brutality, in me to have said thus much

against it. Eloquence, like the fair sex, has too prevailing
beauties in it to suffer itself ever to be spoken against. And
it is in vain to find fault with those arts of deceiving, wherein
men find pleasure to be deceived [1].

---

[1] Cf. Bk. II. ch. xi. § 2. Descartes repeatedly puts us on our guard against the employment of the sensuous imagination, when we are concerned with self-conscious life and its operations, in the search for spiritual truth. But the comprehensive genius of Bacon is more indulgent than either Descartes or Locke, to those who ' clothe and adorn the obscurity even of philosophy itself with sensible and plausible elocution.'

CHAPTER XI.

OF THE REMEDIES OF THE FOREGOING IMPERFECTIONS
AND ABUSES OF WORDS.

BOOK III.
—✦—
CHAP. XI.
Remedies
are worth
seeking.

1. THE natural and improved[1] imperfections of languages we have seen above at large: and speech being the great bond that holds society together, and the common conduit, whereby the improvements of knowledge are conveyed from one man and one generation to another, it would well deserve our most serious thoughts to consider, what remedies are to be found for the inconveniences above mentioned.

Are not
easy to
find.

2. I am not so vain as to think that any one can pretend to attempt the perfect reforming the languages of the world, no not so much as of his own country, without rendering himself ridiculous. To require that men should use their words constantly in the same sense, and for none but determined[2] and uniform ideas, would be to think that all men should have the same notions, and should talk of nothing but what they have clear and distinct ideas of: which is not to be expected by any one who hath not vanity enough to imagine he can prevail with men to be very knowing or very silent. And he must be very little skilled in the world, who thinks that a voluble tongue shall accompany only a good understanding; or that men's talking much or little should hold proportion only to their knowledge.

But yet
necessary
to those

3. But though the market and exchange must be left to their own ways of talking, and gossipings not be robbed

---

[1] 'improved,' i.e. increased—by wilful abuse. Thus South speaks of a 'universal corruption of manners, caused by the habitual *improvement* of vicious principle.'

[2] 'determined'—clear and distinct.

of their ancient privilege : though the schools, and men of
argument would perhaps take it amiss to have anything
offered, to abate the length or lessen the number of their
disputes ; yet methinks those who pretend seriously to search
after or maintain truth, should think themselves obliged to
study how they might deliver themselves without obscurity,
doubtfulness, or equivocation, to which men's words are
naturally liable, if care be not taken.

BOOK III.

CHAP. XI.
who
search
after
Truth.

4. For he that shall well consider the errors and obscurity,
the mistakes and confusion, that are spread in the world by
an ill use of words, will find some reason to doubt whether
language, as it has been employed, has contributed more to
the improvement or hindrance of knowledge amongst mankind [1]. How many are there, that, when they would think
on things, fix their thoughts only on words, especially when
they would apply their minds to moral matters [2]? And who
then can wonder if the result of such contemplations and
reasonings, about little more than sounds, whilst the ideas
they annex to them are very confused and very unsteady, or
perhaps none at all ; who can wonder, I say, that such
thoughts and reasonings end in nothing but obscurity and
mistake, without any clear judgment or knowledge ?

5. This inconvenience, in an ill use of words, men suffer in
their own private meditations : but much more manifest are
the disorders which follow from it, in conversation, discourse,
and arguings with others. For language being the great
conduit, whereby men convey their discoveries, reasonings, and
knowledge, from one to another, he that makes an ill use of
it, though he does not corrupt the fountains of knowledge,
which are in things themselves, yet he does, as much as in
him lies, break or stop the pipes whereby it is distributed to
the public use and advantage of mankind. He that uses words
without any clear and steady meaning, what does he but lead

---

[1] This is of course a conscious exaggeration, for language (such as it is) is necessary to the exercise of discursive thought. Where would even the present stock of human knowledge have been, if the much abused and naturally imperfect languages of man-kind had never come into existence ?

[2] Many persons are not enough developed, intellectually and morally, all their lives, to be able to introduce adequate meanings into words which stand for moral spiritual truth—as the reflex of their own experience.

BOOK III.
CHAP. XI.

himself and others into errors? And he that designedly does it, ought to be looked on as an enemy to truth and knowledge. And yet who can wonder that all the sciences and parts of knowledge have been so overcharged with obscure and equivocal terms, and insignificant and doubtful expressions, capable to make the most attentive or quick-sighted very little, or not at all, the more knowing or orthodox: since subtlety, in those who make profession to teach or defend truth, hath passed so much for a virtue: a virtue, indeed, which, consisting for the most part in nothing but the fallacious and illusory use of obscure or deceitful terms, is only fit to make men more conceited in their ignorance, and more obstinate in their errors.

Addicted to Wrangling about sounds.

6. Let us look into the books of controversy of any kind, there we shall see that the effect of obscure, unsteady, or equivocal terms is nothing but noise and wrangling about sounds, without convincing or bettering a man's understanding. For if the idea be not agreed on, betwixt the speaker and hearer, for which the words stand, the argument is not about things, but names. As often as such a word whose signification is not ascertained betwixt them, comes in use, their understandings have no other object wherein they agree, but barely the sound; the things that they think on at that time, as expressed by that word, being quite different.

Instance, Bat and Bird.

7. Whether a *bat* be a *bird* or no, is not a question, Whether a bat be another thing than indeed it is, or have other qualities than indeed it has; for that would be extremely absurd to doubt of. But the question is, (1) Either between those that acknowledged themselves to have but imperfect ideas of one or both of this sort of things, for which these names are supposed to stand. And then it is a real inquiry concerning the *nature* of a bird or a bat, to make their yet imperfect ideas of it more complete; by examining whether all the simple ideas to which, combined together, they both give the name bird, be all to be found in a bat[1]: but this is a question

[1] That is, by 'examining,' whether their complex idea of 'this sort of things' corresponds to the observable qualities (simple ideas) presented by the objects to which the name 'bat' is applied by them.

only of inquirers (not disputers) who neither affirm nor deny,
but examine : Or, (2) It is a question between disputants ;
whereof the one affirms, and the other denies that a bat is
a bird. And then the question is barely about the signification of one or both these *words*; in that they not having both
the same complex ideas to which they give these two names,
one holds and the other denies, that these two names may be
affirmed one of another. Were they agreed in the signification
of these two names, it were impossible they should dispute
about them. For they would presently and clearly see (were
that adjusted between them,) whether all the simple ideas of
the more general name bird were found in the complex idea
of a bat or no ; and so there could be no doubt whether
a bat were a bird or no [1]. And here I desire it may be considered, and carefully examined, whether the greatest part
of the disputes in the world are not merely [2] verbal, and
about the signification of words ; and whether, if the terms
they are made in were defined, and reduced in their signification (as they must be where they signify anything) to
determined collections of the simple ideas they do or should
stand for, those disputes would not end of themselves, and
immediately vanish. I leave it then to be considered, what
the learning of disputation is, and how well they are employed for the advantage of themselves or others, whose
business is only the vain ostentation of sounds ; i. e. those
who spend their lives in disputes and controversies. When
I shall see any of those combatants strip all his terms of
ambiguity and obscurity, (which every one may do in the
words he uses himself,) I shall think him a champion for
knowledge, truth, and peace, and not the slave of vain-glory,
ambition, or a party.

8. To remedy the defects of speech before mentioned to Remedies.
some degree, and to prevent the inconveniences that follow
from them, I imagine the observation of these following rules

---

[1] If they were agreed, that is to say, about the connotation of the two terms—'bat' and 'bird'—then they could not fail to agree in their appli-cation of the two terms to particular examples of each.

[2] 'Merely'—'meerly,' here and else-where, in the old editions.

may be of use, till somebody better able shall judge it worth his while to think more maturely on this matter, and oblige the world with his thoughts on it.

First
Remedy :
To use no
Word
without
an Idea
annexed
to it.

First, A man shall take care to use no word without a signification, no name without an idea for which he makes it stand. This rule will not seem altogether needless to any one who shall take the pains to recollect how often he has met with such words as *instinct, sympathy,* and *antipathy,* &c., in the discourse of others, so made use of as he might easily conclude that those that used them had no ideas in their minds to which they applied them, but spoke them only as sounds, which usually served instead of reasons on the like occasions. Not but that these words, and the like, have very proper significations in which they may be used ; but there being no natural connexion between any words and any ideas, these, and any other, may be learned by rote, and pronounced or writ by men who have no ideas in their minds to which they have annexed them, and for which they make them stand ; which is necessary they should, if men would speak intelligibly even to themselves alone.

Second
Remedy :
To have
distinct,
deter-
minate
Ideas
annexed
to Words,
especially
in mixed
Modes.

9. Secondly, It is not enough a man uses his words as signs of some ideas : those he annexes them to, if they be simple, must be clear and distinct ; if complex, must be determinate[1], i. e. the precise collection of simple ideas settled in the mind, with that sound annexed to it, as the sign of that precise determined collection, and no other. This is very necessary in names of modes, and especially moral words ; which, having no settled objects in nature, from whence their ideas are taken, as from their original, are apt to be very confused. *Justice* is a word in every man's mouth, but most commonly with a very undetermined, loose signification ; which will always be so, unless a man has in his mind a distinct compre- hension of the component parts that complex idea consists of : and if it be decompounded, must be able to resolve it still on, till he at last comes to the simple ideas that make it up : and

[1] See ' Epistle to the Reader,' p. 22.

unless this be done, a man makes an ill use of the word, let it
be justice, for example, or any other. I do not say, a man
needs stand to recollect, and make this analysis at large,
every time the word justice comes in his way : but this at
least is necessary, that he have so examined the signification
of that name, and settled the idea of all its parts in his mind,
that he can do it when he pleases. If any one who makes
his complex idea of justice to be, such a treatment of the
person or goods of another as is according to law, hath not
a clear and distinct idea what *law* is, which makes a part of
his complex idea of justice, it is plain his idea of justice itself
will be confused and imperfect. This exactness will, perhaps,
be judged very troublesome ; and therefore most men will
think they may be excused from settling the complex ideas
of mixed modes so precisely in their minds. But yet I must
say, till this be done, it must not be wondered, that they
have a great deal of obscurity and confusion in their own
minds, and a great deal of wrangling in their discourse with
others[1].

10. In the names of substances, for a right use of them, And
something more is required than barely *determined ideas*. In distinct
these the names must also be *conformable to things as they exist*; formable
but of this I shall have occasion to speak more at large ideas in
by and by[2]. This exactness is absolutely necessary in inquiries that stand
after philosophical knowledge, and in controversies about truth. stances.
And though it would be well, too, if it extended itself to
common conversation and the ordinary affairs of life ; yet
I think that is scarce to be expected. Vulgar notions suit
vulgar discourses : and both, though confused enough, yet
serve pretty well the market and the wake. Merchants and
lovers, cooks and tailors, have words wherewithal to dispatch

---

[1] This advice is good, if it could be
put in practice. The obstacles to this
are illustrated in the controversies, in
ancient and modern philosophy, regarding the proper meaning of *justice*,
which cannot be determined by each
individual at his own caprice, nor
merely by the customary definitions
of the word, without reference to

its applications in propositions and
reasonings, and to the presuppositions
on which these ultimately rest. The
famous discussion in the first and
second Books of Plato's *Republic*, of
the 'mixed mode' named justice, is
relevant in this connexion.

[2] Cf. § 24; also Bk. IV. chh. iii. §§
11-17; iv. 11-17.

BOOK III.
━━
CHAP. XI.

their ordinary affairs : and so, I think, might philosophers and disputants too, if they had a mind to understand, and to be clearly understood.

Third Remedy : To apply Words to such ideas as common use has annexed them to.

11. Thirdly, it is not enough that men have ideas, determined ideas, for which they make these signs stand ; but they must also take care to apply their words as near as may be to such ideas as common use has annexed them to[1]. For words, especially of languages already framed, being no man's private possession, but the common measure of commerce and communication, it is not for any one at pleasure to change the stamp they are current in, nor alter the ideas they are affixed to ; or at least, when there is a necessity to do so, he is bound to give notice of it. Men's intentions in speaking are, or at least should be, to be understood ; which cannot be without frequent explanations, demands, and other the like incommodious interruptions, where men do not follow common use. Propriety of speech is that which gives our thoughts entrance into other men's minds with the greatest ease and advantage : and therefore deserves some part of our care and study, especially in the names of moral words. The proper signification and use of terms is best to be learned from those who in their writings and discourses appear to have had the clearest notions, and applied to them their terms with the exactest choice and fitness. This way of using a man's words, according to the propriety of the language, though it have not always the good fortune to be understood ; yet most commonly leaves the blame of it on him who is so unskilful in the language he speaks, as not to understand it when made use of as it ought to be.

Fourth Remedy : To declare

12. Fourthly, But, because common use has not so visibly annexed any signification to words, as to make men know

---

[1] Names already in use have a history, so that the meanings to be annexed to them, while arbitrary *a priori*, may not be shifted capriciously, or without reference to their customary use, which ought not to be changed without evident necessity. That definitions should as far as possible be accommodated to custom, is Locke's own maxim. On the other hand, with the imperfect yet progressive knowledge of things that is characteristic of man, human definitions of the names of substances must be subject to continual change.

always certainly what they precisely stand for: and because
men, in the improvement of their knowledge, come to have ideas
different from the vulgar and ordinary received ones, for which
they must either make new words, (which men seldom venture
to do, for fear of being thought guilty of affectation or novelty,)
or else must use old ones in a new signification: therefore,
after the observation of the foregoing rules, it is sometimes
necessary, for the ascertaining the signification of words, to
declare their meaning; where either common use has left it
uncertain and loose, (as it has in most names of very complex
ideas;) or where the term, being very material in the discourse,
and that upon which it chiefly turns, is liable to any doubtfulness or mistake.

13. As the ideas men's words stand for are of different sorts,
so the way of making known the ideas they stand for, when
there is occasion, is also different. For though *defining* be
thought the proper way to make known the proper signification of words; yet there are some words that will not be
defined[1], as there are others whose precise meaning cannot be
made known but by definition: and perhaps a third, which
partake somewhat of both the other, as we shall see in the
names of simple ideas, modes, and substances.

14. I. First, when a man makes use of the name of any
simple idea, which he perceives is not understood, or is in
danger to be mistaken, he is obliged, by the laws of ingenuity
and the end of speech, to declare his meaning, and make
known what idea he makes it stand for. This, as has been
shown, cannot be done by definition: and therefore, when
a synonymous word fails to do it, there is but one of these
ways left. First, Sometimes the *naming* the subject wherein
that simple idea is to be found, will make its name to be
understood by those who are acquainted with that subject,
and know it by that name[2]. So to make a countryman
understand what *feuillemorte* colour signifies, it may suffice to
tell him, it is the colour of withered leaves falling in autumn.

---

[1] Cf. ch. iii. §§ 4-14.

[2] That is when we substitute a word, or words, the connotation of which happens to be more familiar to the mind of another, than that of the name whose meaning is thereby declared to him.

BOOK III.
CHAP. XI.

Secondly, but the only sure way of making known the signification of the name of any simple idea, is *by presenting to his senses that subject which may produce it in his mind,* and make him actually have the idea[1] that word stands for.

In mixed Modes, by Definition.

15. II. Secondly, Mixed modes, especially those belonging to morality, being most of them such combinations of ideas as the mind puts together of its own choice, and whereof there are not always standing patterns to be found existing, the signification of their names cannot be made known, as those of simple ideas, by any showing : but, in recompense thereof, may be perfectly and exactly defined. For they being combinations of several ideas that the mind of man has arbitrarily put together, without reference to any archetypes, men may, if they please, exactly know the ideas that go to each composition, and so both use these words in a certain and undoubted signification, and perfectly declare, when there is occasion, what they stand for. This, if well considered, would lay great blame on those who make not their discourses about *moral* things very clear and distinct. For since the precise signification of the names of mixed modes, or, which is all one, the real essence of each species is to be known, they being not of nature's, but man's making, it is a great negligence and perverseness to discourse of moral things with uncertainty and obscurity; which is more pardonable in treating of natural substances, where doubtful terms are hardly to be avoided, for a quite contrary reason, as we shall see by and by.

Morality capable of Demonstration.

16. Upon this ground it is that I am bold to think that morality is capable of demonstration[2], as well as mathematics : since the precise real essence of the things moral words stand for may be perfectly known, and so the congruity and incongruity of the things themselves be certainly discovered ; in which consists perfect knowledge. Nor let any one object, that the names of substances are often

---

[1] The 'simple idea' being thus presented to the senses, or represented in sensuous imagination; or presented in a concrete reflex experience, if it is an idea of reflection.

[2] 'Morality,' it is assumed here, is concerned with the abstracted mixed modes of simple ideas. Locke's 'demonstrable morality' is abstracted from consideration of the particular circumstances in which men are actually found. Cf. Bk. IV. chh. iii. §§ 18–20; iv. §§ 7–8; xii. § 8.

to be made use of in morality, as well as those of modes,
from which will arise obscurity. For, as to substances, when
concerned in moral discourses, their divers natures are not
so much inquired into as supposed: v. g. when we say that
man is subject to law, we mean nothing by man but a corporeal rational creature : what the real essence or other
qualities of that creature are in this case is no way considered.
And, therefore, whether a child or changeling be a man, in
a physical sense, may amongst the naturalists be as disputable
as it will, it concerns not at all the moral man, as I may call
him, which is this immovable, unchangeable idea, a corporeal
rational being. For, were there a monkey, or any other
creature, to be found that had the use of reason to such
a degree, as to be able to understand general signs, and to
deduce consequences about general ideas, he would no doubt
be subject to law, and in that sense be a *man*, how much
soever he differed in shape from others of that name. The
names of substances, if they be used in them as they should,
can no more disturb moral than they do mathematical
discourses; where, if the mathematician speaks of a cube
or globe of gold, or of any other body, he has his clear,
settled idea, which varies not, though it may by mistake be
applied to a particular body to which it belongs not.

17. This I have here mentioned, by the by, to show of Defini-
what consequence it is for men, in their names of mixed tions can
modes, and consequently in all their moral discourses, to make
define their words when there is occasion : since thereby moral
Discourses
moral knowledge may be brought to so great clearness and clear.
certainty. And it must be great want of ingenuousness (to
say no worse of it) to refuse to do it : since a definition is the
only way whereby the precise meaning of moral words can
be known ; and yet a way whereby their meaning may be
known certainly, and without leaving any room for any
contest about it. And therefore the negligence or perverseness
of mankind cannot be excused, if their discourses in morality
be not much more clear than those in natural philosophy :
since they are about ideas in the mind, which are none of
them false or disproportionate; they having no external
beings for the archetypes which they are referred to and

BOOK III.
CHAP. XI.

must correspond with. It is far easier for men to frame in their minds an idea, which shall be the standard to which they will give the name justice ; with which pattern so made, all actions that agree shall pass under that denomination, than, having seen Aristides, to frame an idea that shall in all things be exactly like him; who is as he is, let men make what idea they please of him. For the one, they need but know the combination of ideas that are put together in their own minds ; for the other, they must inquire into the whole nature, and abstruse hidden constitution, and various qualities of a thing existing without them.

And is the only way in which the meaning of mixed Modes can be made known.

18. Another reason that makes the defining of mixed modes so necessary, especially of moral words, is what I mentioned a little before, viz. that it is the only way whereby the signification of the most of them can be known with certainty. For the ideas they stand for, being for the most part such whose component parts nowhere exist together, but scattered and mingled with others, it is the mind alone that collects them, and gives them the union of one idea : and it is only by words enumerating the several simple ideas which the mind has united, that we can make known to others what their names stand for; the assistance of the senses in this case not helping us, by the proposal of sensible objects, to show the ideas which our names of this kind stand for, as it does often in the names of sensible simple ideas, and also to some degree in those of substances.

In Substances, both by showing and by defining.

19. III. Thirdly, for the explaining the signification of the names of substances, as they stand for the ideas we have of their distinct species, both the forementioned ways, viz. of showing and defining, are requisite, in many cases, to be made use of. For, there being ordinarily in each sort some leading qualities, to which we suppose the other ideas which make up our complex idea of that species annexed, we forwardly give the specific name to that thing wherein that characteristical mark is found, which we take to be the most distinguishing idea of that species. These leading or characteristical (as I may call them) ideas, in the sorts of animals and vegetables, are (as has been before remarked, ch. vi. § 29,

and ch. ix. § 15) mostly figure; and in inanimate bodies,
colour; and in some, both together. Now,

20. These leading sensible qualities are those which make
the chief ingredients of our specific ideas, and consequently
the most observable and invariable part in the definitions
of our specific names, as attributed to sorts of substances
coming under our knowledge. For though the sound *man,*
in its own nature, be as apt to signify a complex idea made
up of animality and rationality, united in the same subject,
as to signify any other combination; yet, used as a mark
to stand for a sort of creatures we count of our own kind,
perhaps the outward shape is as necessary to be taken into
our complex idea, signified by the word man, as any other
we find in it: and therefore, why Plato's *animal implume
bipes latis unguibus* should not be a good definition of the
name man, standing for that sort of creatures, will not be
easy to show: for it is the shape, as the leading quality, that
seems more to determine that species, than a faculty of
reasoning, which appears not at first, and in some never.
And if this be not allowed to be so, I do not know how they
can be excused from murder who kill monstrous births,
(as we call them,) because of an unordinary shape, without
knowing whether they have a rational soul or no; which can
be no more discerned in a well-formed than ill-shaped infant,
as soon as born. And who is it has informed us that a
rational soul can inhabit no tenement, unless it has just such
a sort of frontispiece; or can join itself to, and inform no sort
of body, but one that is just of such an outward structure?

21. Now these leading qualities are best made known by
showing, and can hardly be made known otherwise. For
the shape of a horse or cassowary[1] will be but rudely and
imperfectly imprinted on the mind by words; the sight of the
animals doth it a thousand times better. And the idea of
the particular colour of gold is not to be got by any description of it, but only by the frequent exercise of the eyes about
it; as is evident in those who are used to this metal, who
will frequently distinguish true from counterfeit, pure from

---

[1] 'Cassuary' in early editions.

adulterate, by the sight, where others (who have as good eyes, but yet by use have not got the precise nice idea of that peculiar yellow) shall not perceive any difference. The like may be said of those other simple ideas, peculiar in their kind to any substance; for which precise ideas there are no peculiar names. The particular ringing sound there is in gold, distinct from the sound of other bodies, has no particular name annexed to it, no more than the particular yellow that belongs to that metal.

The Ideas of the Powers of Substances are best known by Definition.

22. But because many of the simple ideas that make up our specific ideas of substances are powers which lie not obvious to our senses in the things as they ordinarily appear; therefore, in the signification of our names of substances, some part of the signification will be better made known by enumerating those simple ideas, than by showing the substance itself. For, he that to the yellow shining colour of gold, got by sight, shall, from my enumerating them, have the ideas of great ductility, fusibility, fixedness, and solubility, in *aqua regia*, will have a perfecter idea of gold than he can have by seeing a piece of gold, and thereby imprinting in his mind only its obvious qualities. But if the formal constitution[1] of this shining, heavy, ductile thing, (from whence all these its properties flow,) lay open to our senses, as the formal constitution or essence of a triangle does, the signification of the word gold might as easily be ascertained as that of triangle.

A Reflection on the Knowledge of corporeal things possessed by Spirits separate from bodies.

23. Hence we may take notice, how much the foundation of all our knowledge of corporeal things lies in our senses. For how spirits, separate from bodies, (whose knowledge and ideas of these things are certainly much more perfect than ours,) know them, we have no notion, no idea at all. The whole extent of our knowledge or imagination reaches not beyond our own ideas limited to our ways of perception. Though yet it be not to be doubted that spirits of a higher rank than those immersed in flesh may have as clear ideas of the radical constitution of substances as we have of a triangle, and so perceive how all their properties and operations

---

[1] 'formal constitution,' i. e. 'real essence,' or ultimate atomic constitution.

flow from thence : but the manner how they come by that
knowledge exceeds our conceptions.

24. Fourthly, But, though definitions will serve to explain
the names of substances as they stand for our ideas, yet
they leave them not without great imperfection as they stand
for things.   For our names of substances being not put barely
for our ideas, but being made use of ultimately to represent
things, and so are put in their place, their signification must
agree with the truth of things as well as with men's ideas.
And therefore, in substances, we are not always to rest in
the ordinary complex idea commonly received as the signification of that word, but must go a little further, and inquire
into the nature and properties of the things themselves, and
thereby perfect, as much as we can, our ideas of their distinct
species ; or else learn them from such as are used to that
sort of things, and are experienced in them.   For, since it is
intended their names should stand for such collections of
simple ideas as do really exist in things themselves, as well
as for the complex idea in other men's minds, which in their
ordinary acceptation they stand for, therefore, to define their
names right, natural history is to be inquired into, and their
properties are, with care and examination, to be found out.
For it is not enough, for the avoiding inconveniences in
discourse and arguings about natural bodies and substantial
things, to have learned, from the propriety of the language,
the common, but confused, or very imperfect, idea to which
each word is applied, and to keep them to that idea in our
use of them ; but we must, by acquainting ourselves with
the history of that sort of things, rectify and settle our complex idea belonging to each specific name[1] ; and in discourse
with others, (if we find them mistake us,) we ought to tell
what the complex idea is that we make such a name stand
for.   This is the more necessary to be done by all those who
search after knowledge and philosophical verity, in that
children, being taught words, whilst they have but imperfect
notions of things, apply them at random, and without much

BOOK III.
—⧾—
CHAP. XI.
Ideas
of Sub-
stances
must also
be con-
formable
to Things.

---

[1] He allows that our definitions, and
nominal essences, must not be capricious: we must acquaint ourselves with
the 'history' of the things to which we
apply names, in order to rectify their
essences by the standard of experience.

thinking, and seldom frame determined ideas to be signified by them. Which custom (it being easy, and serving well enough for the ordinary affairs of life and conversation) they are apt to continue when they are men: and so begin at the wrong end, learning words first and perfectly, but make the notions to which they apply those words afterwards very overtly. By this means it comes to pass, that men speaking the language of their country, i.e. according to grammar rules of that language, do yet speak very improperly of things themselves; and, by their arguing one with another, make but small progress in the discoveries of useful truths, and the knowledge of things, as they are to be found in themselves, and not in our imaginations; and it matters not much for the improvement of our knowledge how they are called.

25. It were therefore to be wished, That men versed in physical inquiries, and acquainted with the several sorts of natural bodies, would set down those simple ideas wherein they observe the individuals of each sort constantly to agree. This would remedy a great deal of that confusion which comes from several persons applying the same name to a collection of a smaller or greater number of sensible qualities, proportionably as they have been more or less acquainted with, or accurate in examining, the qualities of any sort of things which come under one denomination. But a dictionary of this sort, containing, as it were, a natural history, requires too many hands as well as too much time, cost, pains, and sagacity ever to be hoped for; and till that be done, we must content ourselves with such definitions of the names of substances as explain the sense men use them in. And it would be well, where there is occasion, if they would afford us so much. This yet is not usually done; but men talk to one another, and dispute in words, whose meaning is not agreed between them, out of a mistake that the significations of common words are certainly established, and the precise ideas they stand for perfectly known; and that it is a shame to be ignorant of them. Both which suppositions are false; no names of complex ideas having so settled determined significations, that they are constantly used for the same precise ideas. Nor is it a shame for a man to have a certain

* *insert* not *before* to have

knowledge of anything, but by the necessary ways of attaining
it ; and so it is no discredit not to know what precise idea
any sound stands for in another man's mind, without he
declare it to me by some other way than barely using that
sound, there being no other way, without such a declaration,
certainly to know it.   Indeed the necessity of communication
by language brings men to an agreement in the signification
of common words, within some tolerable latitude, that may
serve for ordinary conversation : and so a man cannot be
supposed wholly ignorant of the ideas which are annexed
to words by common use, in a language familiar to him.   But
common use being but a very uncertain rule, which reduces
itself at last to the ideas of particular men, proves often but
a very variable standard.   But though such a Dictionary as
I have above mentioned will require too much time, cost, and
pains to be hoped for in this age ; yet methinks it is not unreasonable to propose, that words standing for things which
are known and distinguished by their outward shapes should
be expressed by little draughts and prints made of them.   A
vocabulary made after this fashion would perhaps with more
ease, and in less time, teach the true signification of many
terms, especially in languages of remote countries or ages,
and settle truer ideas in men's minds of several things,
whereof we read the names in ancient authors, than all the
large and laborious comments of learned critics.   Naturalists,
that treat of plants and animals, have found the benefit of this
way : and he that has had occasion to consult them will have
reason to confess that he has a clearer idea of *apium* or *ibex*,
from a little print of that herb or beast, than he could have
from a long definition of the names of either of them.   And
so no doubt he would have of *strigil* and *sistrum*, if, instead of
currycomb and *cymbal*, (which are the English names dictionaries render them by,) he could see stamped in the margin
small pictures of these instruments, as they were in use
amongst the ancients.   *Toga, tunica, pallium,* are words easily
translated by *gown, coat,* and *cloak* ; but we have thereby no
more true ideas of the fashion of those habits amongst the
Romans, than we have of the faces of the tailors who made
them.   Such things as these, which the eye distinguishes by

BOOK III.
CHAP. XI.

their shapes, would be best let into the mind by draughts[1] made of them, and more determine the signification of such words, than any other words set for them, or made use of to define them. But this is only by the bye.

Fifth Remedy: To use the same word constantly in the same sense.

26. V. Fifthly, If men will not be at the pains to declare the meaning of their words, and definitions of their terms are not to be had, yet this is the least that can be expected, that, in all discourses wherein one man pretends to instruct or convince another, he should use the same word constantly in the same sense. If this were done, (which nobody can refuse without great disingenuity,) many of the books extant might be spared ; many of the controversies in dispute would be at an end ; several of those great volumes, swollen with ambiguous words, now used in one sense, and by and by in another, would shrink into a very narrow compass ; and many of the philosophers (to mention no other) as well as poets works, might be contained in a nutshell.

When not so used, the Variation is to be explained.

27. But after all, the provision of words is so scanty in respect to that infinite variety of thoughts, that men, wanting terms to suit their precise notions, will, notwithstanding their utmost caution, be forced often to use the same word in somewhat different senses. And though in the continuation of a discourse, or the pursuit of an argument, there can be hardly room to digress into a particular definition, as often as a man varies the signification of any term ; yet the import of the discourse will, for the most part, if there be no designed fallacy, sufficiently lead candid and intelligent readers into the true meaning of it[2] ; but where there is not sufficient to guide the reader, there it concerns the writer to explain his meaning, and show in what sense he there uses that term.

---

[1] 'draughts'—pictures, which exercise the sensuous imagination instead of the abstracting intellect.

[2] This must be remembered in the interpretation of Locke's own *Essay.*

BOOK IV

———

OF KNOWLEDGE AND PROBABILITY

SYNOPSIS OF THE FOURTH BOOK.

————◆◆————

Locke's review of the different sorts of ideas, or appearances of what exists, that can be entertained in a human understanding, and of their relations to words, leads, in the Fourth Book, to an investigation of the extent and validity of the Knowledge that our ideas bring within our reach; and into the nature of faith in Probability, by which assent is extended beyond Knowledge, for the conduct of life. He finds (chh. i, ii) that Knowledge is either an intuitive, a demonstrative, or a sensuous perception of absolute certainty, in regard to one or other of four sorts of agreement or disagreement on the part of ideas:— (1) of each idea with itself, as identical, and different from every other; (2) in their abstract relations to one another; (3) in their necessary connexions, as qualities and powers coexisting in concrete substances; and (4) as revelations to us of the final realities of existence. The unconditional certainty that constitutes Knowledge is perceptible by man only in regard to the first, second, and fourth of these four sorts : in all general propositions only in regard to the first and second; that is to say, in identical propositions, and in those which express abstract relations of simple or mixed modes, in which nominal and real essences coincide, e.g. propositions in pure mathematics and abstract morality (chh. iii, v–viii). The fourth sort, which express certainty as to realities of exist- ence, refer to any of three realities. For every man is able to perceive with absolute certainty that he himself exists, that God must exist, and that finite beings other than himself exist;—the first of these perceptions being awakened by all our ideas, the second as the consequence of perception of the first, and the last in the reception of our simple ideas of sense (chh. i. § 7; ii. § 14; iii. § 21; iv, ix–xi). Agreement of the third sort, or necessary coexistence of simple ideas as qualities and powers in particular substances, with which all physical inquiry is concerned, lies beyond human Knowledge; for here the nominal and real essences are not coincident: general propositions of this sort are determined by analogies of experience, in judgments that are more or less probable : intellectually necessary science of nature presupposes Omniscience; man's interpretations of nature have to turn upon presumptions of Probability (chh. iii. §§ 9–17; iv. §§ 11–17; vi, xiv–xvi). In forming their stock of Cer- tainties and Probabilities men employ the faculty of reason, faith in divine revelation, and enthusiasm (chh. xvii–xix); much misled by the last, as well as by other causes of 'wrong assent' (ch. xx), when they are at work in 'the three great provinces of the intellectual world' (ch. xxi), concerned respectively with (1) 'things as knowable' (*physica*); (2) 'actions as they depend on us in order to happiness' (*practica*); and (3) methods for interpreting the signs of what is, and of what ought to be, that are presented in our ideas and words (*logica*).

CHAPTER I.

OF KNOWLEDGE IN GENERAL.

BOOK IV.

—•+—

CHAP. I.

Our
Know-
ledge con-
versant
about our
Ideas only.

1. SINCE the mind, in all its thoughts and reasonings, hath no other immediate object but its own ideas, which it alone does or can contemplate, it is evident that our knowledge is only conversant about them [1].

2. *Knowledge* then seems to me to be nothing but *the perception of the connexion of and agreement, or disagreement and repugnancy of any of our ideas* [2]. In this alone it consists.

---

[1] In thus limiting *human knowledge* to the simple ideas presented by substances, in the senses and in reflection; their abstracted modes, simple and mixed; our complex ideas of substances, and their abstract relations, Locke does not say that *human faith* is equally confined to what men can have positive ideas of. 'A great many things,' he elsewhere says, 'may be, and are granted to have a being, and be in nature, of which we have no ideas. For example, it cannot be doubted that there are distinct species of separate spirits, of which yet we have no distinct ideas at all: it cannot be questioned but that spirits have ways of communicating their thoughts, and yet we have no idea of it at all.' (First *Letter* to Stillingfleet, p. 83; see also Third *Letter*, pp. 245–47.) The *belief* in the existence of colours in their variations, which a born-blind man can have, though he can have no *ideas* of them, to which Locke elsewhere refers, is a more patent proof that faith is wider than knowledge;

and that belief in the existence of a thing may consist with our having the 'simple idea of its existence' only, without distinct ideas of what the thing is.

[2] Cf. ch. xiv. §§ 3, 4. Locke has been blamed for unduly limiting the application of the terms *knowledge* and *judgment*, by confining the former to 'perceptions,' in which unconditional certainty is intellectually visible, and the latter to the conditional assurance that is naturally caused by presumptions of probability only. To which Reid for example objects, that 'the far greatest part of what all men call human knowledge is in things which neither admit of intuitive nor demonstrative proof. And by judgment I understand that operation of mind by which we determine concerning anything that may be expressed by a proposition, whether it be true or false. A proposition may be simply conceived, without judging of it. But when there is not only a conception of the proposition, but a mental affirmation or

BOOK IV.

—✦—

CHAP. I.

Know-
ledge is
the Per-
ception
of the
Agree-
ment or
Disagree-
ment of
two Ideas.

Where this perception [1] is, there is knowledge, and where it is not, there, though we may fancy, guess, or believe, yet we always come short of knowledge. For when we know that white is not black, what do we else but perceive, that these two ideas do not agree? When we possess ourselves with the utmost security of the demonstration, that the three angles of a triangle are equal to two right ones, what do we more but perceive, that equality to two right ones does necessarily agree [2] to, and is inseparable from, the three angles of a triangle?

This
Agree-
ment or
Disagree-
ment may
be any
of four
sorts.

3. But to understand a little more distinctly wherein this agreement or disagreement consists, I think we may reduce it all to these four sorts:

 I. *Identity*, or *diversity*.

 II. *Relation*.

 III. *Co-existence*, or *necessary connexion*.

 IV. *Real existence* [3].

negation, an assent or dissent of the understanding, whether weak or strong, there is judgment.' (Reid, *Essays*, VI. ch. iii.) Leibniz, too, in the *Nouveaux Essais*, says that taking knowledge in Locke's narrow meaning, i. e. for what is perceived to be unconditionally certain, it must be granted that truth is always founded in agreement or disagreement of ideas, but that what is commonly called ' knowledge' need not amount to the rational perception attained in intuition and demonstration. For we also know truth empirically, he adds, from having experience; and without perceiving necessary connexion of ideas, or necessity of reason latent in what we experience. Locke's definition and examples of knowledge, which he does not himself always follow, show that he requires, in what is so called, this unconditionally certain perception. It is after all a question of names, but, in interpreting Locke, we must never forget that he not only contrasts mere *idea* with *knowledge*, but likewise *knowledge* with *judgment*.

It is also important to note that he makes ' mental proposition' (i. e. *judgment*, in its wider meaning) the unit of *knowledge* and *assent*, as distinguished from mere idea, simple or complex. ' Everything which we either know or believe is some [mental] proposition.' (Third *Letter* to Stillingfleet, p. 245.) And as all propositions imply terms, even belief presupposes at least the idea of ' existence' to be predicable of what is believed to exist, without (it may be) any positive idea of what the existing being is.

[1] ' perception.' Cf. Bk. II. ch. xxi. § 5. Mental *assertion* or *denial* of what is *seen to be unconditionally certain* (rather than simple apprehension of an idea, or of the meaning of a name) is ' perception,' as commonly used in Bk. IV.

[2] ' necessarily agree '—' necessary connexion.' Note how Locke recognises an element of intellectual necessity in the ' agreement' which constitutes ' knowledge.'

[3] This is professedly an exhaustive classification, according to their import,

4. *First,* As to the first sort of agreement or disagreement, viz. *identity* or *diversity.* It is the first act of the mind, when it has any sentiments or ideas at all, to perceive its ideas; and so far as it perceives them, to know each what it is, and thereby also to perceive their difference, and that one is not another. This is so absolutely necessary, that without it there could be no knowledge, no reasoning, no imagination, no distinct thoughts at all [1]. By this the mind clearly and infallibly perceives each idea to agree with itself, and to be what it is; and all distinct ideas to disagree, i. e. the one not to be the other: and this it does without pains, labour, or deduction; but at first view, by its natural power of perception and distinction. And though men of art have reduced this into those general rules, *What is, is,* and *It is impossible for the same thing to be and not to be,* for ready application in all cases, wherein there may be occasion to reflect on it: yet it is certain that the first exercise of this faculty is about particular ideas [2]. A man infallibly knows, as soon as ever he has them in his mind, that the ideas he calls *white* and *round* are the very ideas they are; and that they are not other ideas which he calls *red* or *square.* Nor can any maxim or proposition in the world make him know it clearer or surer than he did before, and without any such general rule [3]. This then is the first agreement or disagree-

BOOK IV.

Chap. I.
First, Of Identity, or Diversity in ideas.

of the sorts of mental propositions, into which our ideas can enter as terms. Locke next wants to determine in which of them the certainty that makes knowledge, and in which only probability, is attainable. The classification itself is crude and hardly logical. 'Agreement or disagreement' is in all cases relation; yet 'relation' is the second member of the division. The analysis and classification may be compared with Kant's analytic and synthetic (*a priori* and *a posteriori*) judgments, and with his dialectical inferences of pure Reason.

[1] Consciousness necessarily implies contrast. *Omnis determinatio est negatio.* We apprehend a circle by a mental negation of every other figure.

[2] Our assertions of identity and diversity in particular cases, with which conscious life begins, when resolved by the abstracting philosopher into their most general form, become the so-called *principles* or *maxims* of Identity and Contradiction, as here enunciated. Although first consciously apprehended by us in concrete examples, these abstract principles are necessary postulates (by implication) in those examples, and become disengaged from them with the development of our power of philosophical abstraction.

[3] Yet the after recognition by the philosopher of the 'general rule,' or

BOOK IV.
Chap. I.

ment which the mind perceives in its ideas; which it always perceives at first sight: and if there ever happen any doubt about it, it will always be found to be about the names [1], and not the ideas themselves, whose identity and diversity will always be perceived, as soon and clearly as the ideas themselves are; nor can it possibly be otherwise.

Secondly, Of abstract Relations between ideas.

5. *Secondly*, the next sort of agreement or disagreement the mind perceives in any of its ideas may, I think, be called *relative* [2], and is nothing but the perception of the *relation* between any two ideas, of what kind soever, whether substances, modes, or any other. For, since all distinct ideas must eternally be known not to be the same, and so be universally and constantly denied one of another, there could be no room for any positive knowledge at all, if we could not perceive any relation between our ideas, and find out the agreement or disagreement they have one with another, in several ways the mind takes of comparing them.

Thirdly, Of their necessary Co-existence in Substances.

6. *Thirdly*, The third sort of agreement or disagreement to be found in our ideas, which the perception of the mind is employed about, is *co-existence* or *non-co-existence* in the *same subject*; and this belongs particularly to substances [3]. Thus when we pronounce concerning gold, that it is fixed, our knowledge of this truth amounts to no more but this, that fixedness, or a power to remain in the fire unconsumed, is

---

abstract principle, makes him aware of the reason of his previous 'perceptions,' or assertions, of identity and difference in particular cases. Cf. chh. vii. viii.

[1] As if we were to call a circle and a square by the same name, e.g. 'figure,' and then deny their difference.

[2] Relation is implied in all 'agreement and disagreement'; but in the last three sorts it is relation between ideas already distinguished from all others *negatively*, in affirmation of their own identity. After that, their *positive* agreements or disagreements, Locke supposes, must be with reference to (*a*) their abstract relations (his relation proper), (*b*) their actual coexistence

in concrete substances, or (*c*) the ultimate realities which they reveal. Cf. Hume's *Treatise*, Pt. I, Sect. v.

[3] Locke's 'relation' (§ 5) means abstract relation (e. g. in pure mathematics), independent of place and time —in other words of change, and of the imperfectly known powers and laws by which changes are determined. It virtually includes the *a priori* synthetic judgments recognised in Kant's more critical analysis. Propositions of 'coexistence' are those which concern concrete substances, constituting physics, and consisting of synthetic judgments—reached *a posteriori*, or by observation and inductive generalisation, according to Locke.

an idea that always accompanies [1] and is joined with that particular sort of yellowness, weight, fusibility, malleableness, and solubility in *aqua regia*, which make our complex idea signified by the word gold,

7. *Fourthly*, The fourth and last sort is that of *actual real existence* agreeing to any idea [2].

Fourthly,
Of real
Existence
agreeing
to any
idea.

Within these four sorts of agreement or disagreement is, I suppose, contained all the knowledge we have, or are capable of. For all the inquiries we can make concerning any of our ideas, all that we know or can affirm concerning any of them, is, That it is, or is not, the same with some other ; that it does or does not always co-exist with some other idea in the same subject ; that it has this or that relation with some other idea ; or that it [3] has a real existence without the mind. Thus, 'blue is not yellow,' is of identity. ' Two triangles upon equal bases between two parallels are equal,' is of relation. 'Iron is susceptible of magnetical impressions,' is of co-existence. 'God is,' is of real existence [4]. Though identity and co-existence are truly nothing but relations, yet they are such peculiar ways of agreement or disagreement of our ideas, that they deserve well to be considered as distinct heads, and not under relation in general ; since they are so different grounds of affirmation and negation, as will easily appear to

---

[1] ' *always* accompanies,' thus forming the orderly coexistences and successions sought for in physics.

[2] While the second sort of ' agreement or disagreement' is found in the relations of simple and mixed modes and other abstract ideas ; and the third in the coexistences and changes in nature; this fourth sort is found in the relation of our other ideas to the ideas of real existence, and of the substances, finite or infinite, of which existence consists, suggesting, but at Locke's very different point of view, the ideas of pure reason and antinomies of Kant.

[3] 'it '—the idea?

[4] 'Lorsqu'on dit qu'une chose existe, ou qu'elle a l'existence réelle, cette existence même est le prédicat, c'est-à-dire, elle a une notion liée avec l'idée dont il s'agit, et il y a connexion entre ces deux notions.' (*Nouveaux Essais.*) If we have no other idea in the predicate when we say that ' I exist,' we at least must have an idea of the actual reality, whatever that means, of ourself. Locke does not say, as Cousin supposes, that in perceiving real existence I first consciously compare an abstract idea of self with an abstract idea of existence, and then find, as the *argued result* of this comparison, that ' I exist.' But Locke's inexact and vacillating language about the mental assertion of real existence opened the way for Hume, and countenanced Reid's suggestion of scepticism being latent in a perception of reality 'by ideas.' Cf. ch. iv.

BOOK IV.
CHAP. I.
any one, who will but reflect on what is said in several places of this *Essay*.

I should now proceed to examine the several degrees of our knowledge, but that it is necessary first, to consider the different acceptations of the word *knowledge*.

Knowledge is either actual or habitual.

8. There are several ways wherein the mind is possessed of truth ; each of which is called knowledge.

I. There is *actual knowledge*, which is the present view the mind has of the agreement or disagreement of any of its ideas, or of the relation they have one to another.

II. A man is said to know any proposition, which having been once laid before his thoughts, he evidently perceived the agreement or disagreement of the ideas whereof it consists ; and so lodged it in his memory, that whenever that proposition comes again to be reflected on, he, without doubt or hesitation, embraces the right side, assents to, and is certain of the truth of it. This, I think, one may call *habitual knowledge*. And thus a man may be said to know all those truths which are lodged in his memory, by a foregoing clear and full perception, whereof the mind is assured past doubt as often as it has occasion to reflect on them. For our finite understandings being able to think clearly and distinctly but on one thing at once, if men had no knowledge of any more than what they actually thought on, they would all be very ignorant : and he that knew most, would know but one truth, that being all he was able to think on at one time [1].

Habitual Knowledge is of two degrees.

9. Of habitual knowledge there are, also, vulgarly speaking, two degrees :

First, The one is of such truths laid up in the memory as, whenever they occur to the mind, it *actually perceives the relation* is between those ideas [2]. And this is in all those truths whereof we have an intuitive knowledge ; where the

---

[1] Cf. Bk. II. chh. x. §§ 8, 9 ; xxvii. § 10.

[2] This can hardly be regarded as an example of knowledge held only through trust in our remembrance of its having been *formerly* known. It is renewed rational perception ; not remembrance instead of the perception. It must also be kept in view that all human knowledge depends upon memory ; for the consciousness implied in living knowledge becomes impossible with the complete extinction of memory. Cf. Bk. II. ch. x. with the annotations.

ideas themselves, by an immediate view, discover their agreement or disagreement one with another

Secondly, The other is of such truths whereof the mind
having been convinced, it *retains the memory of the conviction, without the proofs* [1]. Thus, a man that remembers
certainly that he once perceived the demonstration, that the
three angles of a triangle are equal to two right ones, is
certain that he knows it, because he cannot doubt the truth
of it. In his adherence to a truth, where the demonstration
by which it was at first known is forgot, though a man may
be thought rather to believe his memory than really to know,
and this way of entertaining a truth seemed formerly to me
like something between opinion and knowledge; a sort of
assurance which exceeds bare belief, for that relies on the
testimony of another;—yet upon a due examination I find it
comes not short of perfect certainty, and is in effect true
knowledge. That which is apt to mislead our first thoughts
into a mistake in this matter is, that the agreement or disagreement of the ideas in this case is not perceived, as it was
at first, by an actual view of all the intermediate ideas
whereby the agreement or disagreement of those in the
proposition was at first perceived; but by other intermediate
ideas, that show the agreement or disagreement of the ideas
contained in the proposition whose certainty we remember.
For example: in this proposition, that 'the three angles of
a triangle are equal to two right ones,' one who has seen and
clearly perceived the demonstration of this truth knows it to
be true, when that demonstration is gone out of his mind;
so that at present it is not actually in view, and possibly
cannot be recollected: but he knows it in a different way
from what he did before. The agreement of the two ideas
joined in that proposition is perceived; but it is by the intervention of other ideas than those which at first produced that
perception. He remembers, i. e. he knows (for remembrance
is but the reviving of some past knowledge) that he was
once certain of the truth of this proposition, that the three
angles of a triangle are equal to two right ones. The immu-

[1] Cf. ch. xvi. § 2.

tability of the same relations between the same immutable things[1] is now the idea that shows him, that if the three angles of a triangle were once equal to two right ones, they will always be equal to two right ones. And hence he comes to be certain, that what was once true in the case, is always true; what ideas once agreed will always agree; and consequently what he once knew to be true, he will always know to be true; as long as he can remember that he once knew it[2]. Upon this ground it is, that particular demonstrations in mathematics afford general knowledge. If then the perception, that the same ideas will *eternally* have the same habitudes and relations[3], be not a sufficient ground of knowledge, there could be no knowledge of general propositions in mathematics; for no mathematical demonstration would be any other than particular: and when a man had demonstrated any proposition concerning one triangle or circle, his knowledge would not reach beyond that particular diagram. If he would extend it further, he must renew his demonstration in another instance, before he could know it to be true in another like triangle, and so on: by which means one could never come to the knowledge of any general propositions[4]. Nobody, I think, can deny, that Mr. Newton certainly knows any proposition that he now at any time reads in his book[5] to be true; though he has not in actual

[1] The ground of this assumption of 'immutability' in *mathematical* relations is not considered.

[2] This is the 'revival' through memory of the mental fact that we formerly did perceive the unconditional certainty of the proposition, that 'the three angles of a triangle are equal to two right angles'; but without revival of the perception itself. The two are not equivalent. To remember a conclusion, without an intellectual vision of its proof, is not the same as seeing the conclusion in its proof; it is only seeing it in our memory.

[3] Rational insight of the demonstration of an 'eternally' necessary truth is again insufficiently distinguished from the remembrance that we for-

merly had the rational insight, and now only mechanically remember the result. The difference between direct intuition and demonstration turns partly upon the intervention of memory in the latter, as Locke himself acknowledges in the sequel, when he says that 'demonstrative knowledge is less clear' than intuition.

[4] It is not then by comparison of instances, and tentative generalisation, that we reach what is 'eternally' and unconditionally true, in mathematics or other abstract science.

[5] Newton's *Principia*, which appeared in 1687—three years before the *Essay*. Cf. 'Epistle to the Reader,' p. 14.

view that admirable chain of intermediate ideas whereby he
at first discovered it to be true. Such a memory as that,
able to retain such a train of particulars, may be well
thought beyond the reach of human faculties[1], when the
very discovery, perception, and laying together that wonderful
connexion of ideas, is found to surpass most readers' comprehension. But yet it is evident the author himself knows
the proposition to be true, remembering he once saw the
connexion of those ideas; as certainly as he knows such a
man wounded another, remembering that he saw him run
him through. But because the memory is not always so
clear as actual perception, and does in all men more or less
decay in length of time, this, amongst other differences, is
one which shows that *demonstrative* knowledge is much
more imperfect than *intuitive*, as we shall see in the following
chapter[2].

---

[1] Cf. Bk. II. ch. x. § 9.

[2] Dugald Stewart thus writes of the
Book which opens in this chapter
with an account of the four possible
sorts of mental proposition in which
there can be either certainty of knowledge or assent to probability:—
'It is curious to observe that it is the
Fourth Book of the *Essay* alone which
bears directly on the author's principal
object [as set forth in the "Epistle to
the Reader," and the "Introduction."]
In this Book, it is further remarkable,
there are few, if any, references to
preceding parts of the *Essay* ; so that
it might have been published separately
without being less intelligible than
it is. Hence it seems not unreasonable to conjecture that it was the first
part of the work in the order of composition, and that it contains the
leading and fundamental thoughts
which first offered themselves to the
author's mind, when he began to reflect
on the friendly conversation which
gave rise to his philosophical researches. The inquiries in the First

and Second Books, which are of a much
more abstract, as well as scholastic
nature than the sequel of the work,
probably opened gradually on the
author's mind, in proportion as he
studied his subject with a closer and
more continued attention. They relate chiefly to the origin and technical
classification of our *ideas*, frequently
branching into collateral and somewhat digressive discussions, without
much regard to method and connexion.' (*Dissertation.*) There is
no doubt that the supreme importance of the Fourth Book has been
overlooked by most of Locke's interpreters and critics; and it is likely that,
in the preparation of the *Essay*, 'by
snatches ' and ' at intervals,' portions
of this Book were written when the
preceding parts of the work were incomplete. But if it contains few
express references to what goes before,
its whole texture will be found, after
careful analysis, to be constructed on
the lines of the Second Book, retraced
in the Third.

CHAPTER II.

OF THE DEGREES OF OUR KNOWLEDGE.

BOOK IV.
—◆—
CHAP. II.
Of the
degrees, or
differences
in clear-
ness, of our
Know-
ledge :
I. Intui-
tive.

1. ALL our knowledge consisting, as I have said, in the view the mind has of its own ideas, which is the utmost light and greatest certainty we, with our faculties, and in our way of knowledge, are capable [1] of, it may not be amiss to consider a little the degrees of its evidence [2]. The different clearness of our knowledge seems to me to lie in the different way of perception the mind has of the agreement or disagreement of any of its ideas. For if we will reflect on our own ways of thinking, we will find, that sometimes the mind perceives the agreement or disagreement of two ideas *immediately by themselves*, without the intervention of any other : and this I think we may call *intuitive knowledge* [3]. For in this the mind is at no pains of proving

---

[1] My knowledge, in short, is dependent on, or relative to myself; for I cannot transform myself into another self, with other ideas or phenomena of existence than those presented in my sense-perception and self-consciousness. It is not knowledge in the abstract that Locke is concerned with, but the actual living knowledge for which *man* has opportunity and capacity.

[2] 'the degrees of its evidence.' Locke's 'knowledge,' being an unconditional certainty that is intellectually visible, does not in one sense admit of ' degrees.' But what he means is explained to be, the varied 'clearness' with which this unconditional certainty can become visible in a human under-

standing. It may show itself directly and involuntarily, like the light of day ; or we may have to go in quest of it through demonstrations ; or it may be obscured by the mists of sense. These three ways of perceiving absolute certainty are the subject-matter of this chapter.

[3] Intuition originally meant ocular vision, or visual sense-perception. Locke's 'intuitive knowledge,' or immediate intellectual perception of unconditional certainty in mental propositions, is analogous to this. It must not be confounded with intuitive as opposed to symbolical thought, a use of the term that is foreign to Locke.

or examining, but perceives the truth as the eye doth light,
only by being directed towards it. Thus the mind perceives
that *white* is not *black*, that a *circle* is not a *triangle*, that
three are more than *two* and equal to *one and two*. Such
kinds of truths the mind perceives at the first sight of the
ideas together, by bare intuition; without the intervention of
any other idea: and this kind of knowledge is the clearest
and most certain that human frailty is capable of. This
part of knowledge is irresistible, and, like bright sunshine [1],
forces itself immediately to be perceived, as soon as ever the
mind turns its view that way; and leaves no room for hesitation, doubt, or examination, but the mind is presently filled
with the clear light of it. *It is on this intuition that depends all the certainty and evidence of all our knowledge* [2];
which certainty every one finds to be so great, that he
cannot imagine, and therefore not require a greater: for
a man cannot conceive himself capable of a greater certainty
than to know that any idea in his mind is such as he per-

[1] 'bright sunshine,' and 'the candle of the Lord' (Introd. § 5; Bk. IV. ch. iii. § 20), are metaphors used to signify the 'perception' which gives us knowledge or absolute certainty. The 'candle of the Lord' suggests Locke's favourite preacher, Whichcote, by whom this metaphor was employed with a like purpose; also by Culverwell in his *Light of Nature.*

[2] Locke thus rests human knowledge on intuitive or self-evident perception of agreement or disagreement between the ideas which it interprets. While he rejects innateness (as he understands it), he recognises the need for a direct discernment of what is self-evident, as indispensable to unconditional certainty of every kind. The important statement in the text should be compared with Bk. II. ch. i. § 2, supposed to contradict it,—that a human mind has 'all the materials of reasoning and knowledge from experience, in which all our knowledge is founded, and from which it all ultimately derives

itself.' The ultimate dependence of unconditional certainty upon intuitive intelligence, and the dependence of actual intuitive intelligence itself upon data of experience, in which it is awakened, and on which it can exercise itself, are not contradictory, but mutually complementary propositions. The second is doubtless the more prominent throughout the *Essay*: intuitive intelligence, under the guise of 'common sense,' became afterwards the characteristic of Reid's account of human experience. The two propositions taken together make a text for expounding the relations of Intellect and Sense in the organisation of knowledge. In 'intuitive knowledge' Locke recognises immediate manifestation of truth to intelligence, but without the *a priori* critical analysis afterwards employed by Kant. Locke's 'intuitions' are not *shown* to be necessary postulates of all intelligible experience; they are accepted as facts of common consciousness.

BOOK IV.
—◆—
CHAP. II.

ceives it to be; and that two ideas, wherein he perceives a difference, are different and not precisely the same. He that demands a greater certainty than this, demands he knows not what, and shows only that he has a mind to be a sceptic, without being able to be so. Certainty depends so wholly on this intuition, that, in the next degree of knowledge which I call demonstrative, this intuition is necessary in all the connexions of the intermediate ideas, without which we cannot attain knowledge and certainty.

II. Demon-
strative.

2. The next degree of knowledge is, where the mind perceives the agreement or disagreement of any ideas, but not immediately. Though wherever the mind perceives the agreement or disagreement of any of its ideas, there be certain knowledge; yet it does not always happen, that the mind sees that agreement or disagreement, which there is between them, even where it is discoverable; and in that case remains in ignorance, and at most gets no further than a probable conjecture. The reason why the mind cannot always perceive presently[1] the agreement or disagreement of two ideas, is, because those ideas, concerning whose agreement or disagreement the inquiry is made, cannot by the mind be so put together as to show it. In this case then, when the mind cannot so bring its ideas together as by their immediate comparison, and as it were juxta-position or application one to another, to perceive their agreement or disagreement, it is fain, *by the intervention of other ideas* (one or more, as it happens) to discover the agreement or disagreement which it searches; and this is that which we call *reasoning*[2]. Thus, the mind being willing to know the agreement or disagreement

---

[1] 'presently'—immediately,—'in the bright sunshine of its self-evidence.'

[2] 'reasoning' here means demonstration; and 'demonstration' is, as it were, *indirect intuition*, in which the conclusion is self-evidently contained, either in self-evident, or in already demonstrated truth, from which it is evolved in reasoning. So understood, it is available, according to Locke, only in reasonings about abstract ideas, conceived without regard to any actual beings,—as in abstract mathematics and ethics;—with this exception only, that the real existence of God, or Eternal Mind, is held by him to be 'demonstrable like any abstract conclusion in our mathematical knowledge.'

in bigness between the three angles of a triangle and two
right ones, cannot by an immediate view and comparing
them do it : because the three angles of a triangle cannot be
brought at once, and be compared with any other one, or two,
angles; and so of this the mind has no immediate, no intuitive
knowledge. In this case the mind is fain to find out some
other angles, to which the three angles of a triangle have an
equality; and, finding those equal to two right ones, comes
to know their equality to two right ones.

3. Those intervening ideas, which serve to show the agree- Demon-
ment of any two others, are called *proofs*; and where the stration depends
agreement and disagreement is by this means plainly and on clearly perceived
clearly perceived, it is called *demonstration*[1]; it being *shown* Proofs.
to the understanding, and the mind made to see that it is so.
A quickness in the mind to find out these intermediate ideas,
(that shall discover the agreement or disagreement of any
other,) and to apply them right, is, I suppose, that which is
called *sagacity*.

4. This knowledge, by intervening proofs, though it be As certain,
certain, yet the evidence of it is not altogether so clear and but not so easy and
bright, nor the assent so ready, as in intuitive knowledge. ready as
For, though in demonstration the mind does at last perceive Intuitive Know-
the agreement or disagreement of the ideas it considers; yet ledge.
it is not without pains and attention : there must be more
than one transient view to find it. A steady[2] application and
pursuit are required to this discovery : and there must be
a progression by steps and degrees, before the mind can in
this way arrive at certainty, and come to perceive the agreement or repugnancy between two ideas that need proofs and
the use of reason to show it[3].

[1] 'The term *demonstration* is used in a looser, and in a stricter significa-tion. In the former sense it is equiva-lent to probation or argumentation, in general ; in the latter, to [intel-lectually] necessary probation, or argumentation from *intuitive principles*.' (Hamilton.) It is the stricter meaning that Locke here intends ; and he has pure mathematical reasoning in view

as his ideal of ' demonstration.'

[2] ' steady '—' steddy,' in the early editions.

[3] Locke does not here refer to the part played by memory, in conjunction with intuition, when we discover by demonstration truths that were latent in our narrow intuition of self-evident truth.

BOOK IV.

CHAP. II.

The demonstrated conclusion not without Doubt, precedent to the demonstration.

5. Another difference between intuitive and demonstrative knowledge is, that, though in the latter all doubt be removed when, by the intervention of the intermediate ideas, the agreement or disagreement is perceived, yet before the demonstration there was a doubt ; which in intuitive knowledge cannot happen to the mind that has its faculty of perception left to a degree capable of distinct ideas ; no more than it can be a doubt to the eye (that can distinctly see white and black), Whether this ink and this paper be all of a colour. If there be sight in the eyes, it will, at first glimpse, without hesitation, perceive the words printed on this paper different from the colour of the paper : and so if the mind have the faculty of distinct perception, it will perceive the agreement or disagreement of those ideas that produce intuitive knowledge. If the eyes have lost the faculty of seeing, or the mind of perceiving, we in vain inquire after the quickness of sight in one, or clearness of perception in the other.

Not so clear as Intuitive Knowledge.

6. It is true, the perception produced by demonstration is also very clear ; yet it is often with a great abatement of that evident lustre and full assurance that always accompany that which I call intuitive : like a face reflected by several mirrors one to another, where, as long as it retains the similitude and agreement with the object, it produces a knowledge ; but it is still, in every successive reflection, with a lessening of that perfect clearness and distinctness which is in the first ; till at last, after many removes, it has a great mixture of dimness, and is not at first sight so knowable, especially to weak eyes. Thus it is with knowledge made out by a long train of proof[1].

Each Step in Demonstrated

7. Now, in every step reason makes in demonstrative knowledge[2], there is an intuitive knowledge of that agreement

---

[1] Some of Mr. Herbert Spencer's remarks, in connexion with his ' Universal Postulate,' illustrate and confirm the lesson of this section.

[2] Commenting on the important statement that ' there must be intuitive evidence of *every step* in a demonstration,' Dugald Stewart adds, that ' it is not to be supposed that in every demonstration all the various intuitive judgments leading to the conclusion are actually present to our thoughts. In by far the greater number of instances, we trust entirely to judgments resting on the evidence of memory, by the help of which faculty we are enabled to connect together the most remote truths with the very same confidence as if the one were an immediate consequence of the other.

BOOK IV.
—++—
Chap. II.
Know-
ledge
must have
Intuitive
Evidence.

or disagreement it seeks with the next intermediate idea which it uses as a proof: for if it were not so, that yet would need a proof; since without the perception of such agreement or disagreement, there is no knowledge produced: if it be perceived by itself, it is intuitive knowledge: if it cannot be perceived by itself, there is need of some intervening idea, as a common measure, to show their agreement or disagreement. By which it is plain, that every step in reasoning that produces knowledge[1], has intuitive certainty; which when the mind perceives, there is no more required but to remember it, to make the agreement or disagreement of the ideas concerning which we inquire visible and certain. So that to make anything a demonstration, it is necessary to perceive the immediate agreement of the intervening ideas, whereby the agreement or disagreement of the two ideas under examination (whereof the one is always the first, and the other the last in the account) is found. This intuitive perception of the agreement or disagreement of the intermediate ideas, in each step and progression of the demonstration, must also be carried exactly in the mind, and a man must be sure that no part is left out: which, because in long deductions, and the use of many proofs, the memory does not always so readily

. . . Still, it is true that it is by a continued chain of intuitive judgments that the whole science of geometry *holds together*; inasmuch as the demonstration of any one proposition virtually includes all the previous demonstrations to which it refers. Hence it appears that in mathematical demonstrations we have not, at every step, the *immediate* evidence of intuition, but only the evidence of memory.' (*Collected Works*, Vol. III. pp. 71, 72.) Through the imperfection of memory, as Locke sees, demonstration, i. e. indirect and complex intuition, is less clear evidence than intuition proper. It involves progress of thought in time: intuition is an instantaneous flash. Yet the essential identity of intuition and demonstration is illustrated by the way in which power of intuition supersedes demonstration in exceptional individuals. Mathematical genius is able to dispense with demonstrations in geometry that have to be gone through, bit by bit, to enable less comprehensive minds to reach, in the form of conclusions from premisses, what mathematical genius apprehends in a single intuitive act. The need for reasoning is thus a sign of our intellectual finitude, intermediate between animal sense and Omniscience. We cannot suppose that the Divine Mind is ratiocinative.

[1] 'knowledge,' or unconditional certainty, that is to say, and not merely the probable presumption, in which intuition of reason is so obscured that each step in inductive reasoning looks at first like a leap in the dark.

BOOK IV.

———

CHAP. II.

and exactly retain ; therefore it comes to pass, that this[1] is more imperfect than intuitive knowledge, and men embrace often falsehood for demonstrations.

Hence the Mistake, *ex præcognitis, et præconcessis.*

8. The necessity of this intuitive knowledge, in each step of scientifical or demonstrative reasoning, gave occasion, I imagine, to that mistaken axiom, That all reasoning was *ex præcognitis et præconcessis* : which, how far it is a mistake, I shall have occasion to show more at large, when I come to consider propositions, and particularly those propositions which are called maxims, and to show that it is by a mistake that they are supposed to be the foundations of all our knowledge and reasonings[2].

Demonstration not limited to ideas of mathematical Quantity.

9. [[3] It has been generally taken for granted, that mathematics alone are capable of demonstrative certainty : but to have such an agreement or disagreement as may intuitively be perceived, being, as I imagine, not the privilege of the ideas of number, extension, and figure alone, it may possibly be the

---

[1] 'this,' i. e. demonstration, because it depends on the combination of intuition with memory, in a way that a single act of intuitive intelligence does not.

[2] Although they are not in most cases *consciously* the 'foundation' of our reasonings, 'maxims' are presupposed, in the sense that rejection of them would suspend the 'demonstrated' conclusions. What he calls 'intuitive knowledge' is possible only upon the (conscious or unconscious) *precognition and preconcession* of the trustworthiness of intuition. It is not that the presupposed maxims are more certain in the abstract than when they are embodied in examples, but that, in the former case, the embodied truth takes its ultimate or philosophical expression. Cf. ch. vii. Proof would be impossible, if scepticism were to go so far as to demand proof before accepting the intellectual necessities without which experience and consciousness could not be ; or before accepting proof itself of any sort ; or any answer

to any question.

[3] Instead of this sentence, the first edition reads thus :—'It is not only mathematics, or the ideas alone of number, extension, and figure, that are capable of demonstration, no more than it is these ideas alone, and their modes, that are capable of intuition.' Under each form of expression, he wants here to keep in view his favourite proposition, that *abstract morality*, as well as *abstract mathematics*, is strictly demonstrable. He points to facts in consciousness which refute the assumption that absolute certainty cannot be found outside mathematics ; and then proceeds to explain why men have been apt to make that assumption, not seeing that *all* abstract ideas, determined as they are by nominal essences and definitions, also submit to demonstration. The existence of God, or Eternal Mind, is another of his non-mathematical demonstrable truths ; and not abstract either, but a necessary truth of fact, as Locke puts it.

want of due method and application in us, and not of sufficient
evidence in things, that demonstration has been thought to
have so little to do in other parts of knowledge, and been
scarce so much as aimed at by any but mathematicians.] For
whatever ideas we have wherein the mind can perceive the
immediate agreement or disagreement that is between them,
there the mind is capable of intuitive knowledge ; and where
it can perceive the agreement or disagreement of any two
ideas, by an intuitive perception of the agreement or disagreement they have with any intermediate ideas, there the mind is
capable of demonstration : which is not limited to ideas of
extension, figure, number, and their modes.

10. The reason why it has been generally sought for, and Why it
supposed to be only in those, I imagine has been, not only has been
thought
the general usefulness of those sciences ; but because, in to be so
comparing their equality or excess, the modes of numbers limited.
have every the least difference very clear and perceivable :
and though in extension every the least excess is not so
perceptible, yet the mind has found out ways to examine,
and discover demonstratively, the just equality of two angles,
or extensions, or figures : and both these, i. e. numbers and
figures, can be set down by visible and lasting marks, wherein
the ideas under consideration are perfectly determined ; which
for the most part they are not, where they are marked only
by names and words.

11. But in other simple ideas, whose modes and differences Modes of
are made and counted by degrees, and not quantity, we have Qualities
not
not so nice and accurate a distinction of their differences demon-
as to perceive, or find ways to measure, their just equality, strable
like modes
or the least differences. For those other simple ideas, being of Quan-
appearances of sensations [1] produced in us, by the size, figure, tity.
number, and motion of minute corpuscles singly insensible ;
their different degrees also depend upon the variation of some
or of all those causes : which, since it cannot be observed by
us, in particles of matter whereof each is too subtile to be

---

[1] 'appearances of sensations,' i. e.
those simple ideas of sensation in
which consist the secondary qualities
of things, in distinction from their
modes of quantity, i. e. their primary
or real qualities.

perceived, it is impossible for us to have any exact measures of the different degrees of these simple ideas[1]. For, supposing the sensation or idea we name whiteness be produced in us by a certain number of globules, which, having a verticity about their own centres, strike upon the retina of the eye, with a certain degree of rotation, as well as progressive swiftness; it will hence easily follow, that the more the superficial parts of any body are so ordered as to reflect the greater number of globules of light, and to give them the proper rotation, which is fit to produce this sensation of white in us, the more white will that body appear, that from an equal space sends to the retina the greater number of such corpuscles, with that peculiar sort of motion. I do not say that the nature of light consists in very small round globules; nor of whiteness in such a texture of parts as gives a certain rotation to these globules when it reflects them : for I am not now treating physically of light or colours. But this I think I may say, that I cannot (and I would be glad any one would make intelligible that he did) conceive how bodies without us can any ways affect our senses [2], but by the immediate contact of the sensible bodies themselves, as in tasting and feeling, or the impulse of some sensible particles coming from them, as in seeing, hearing, and smelling; by the different impulse of which parts, caused by their different size, figure, and motion, the variety of sensations is produced in us.

Particles of light and simple ideas of colour.

12. Whether then they be globules or no ; or whether they have a verticity about their own centres that produces the idea of whiteness in us; this is certain, that the more particles of light are reflected from a body, fitted to give them that peculiar motion which produces the sensation of whiteness in us ; and possibly too, the quicker that peculiar motion is,— the whiter does the body appear from which the greatest

---

[1] Therefore we cannot, from its *superficial* primary qualities, in ignorance of the essential texture of its atoms, demonstrate what its secondary qualities must be. We can only reach probability, not science or unconditionally certain knowledge, in all physical inquiries.

[2] 'our senses,' i.e. our organs of sense. Motion consequent upon contact of the extra organic thing with our organism is, he assumes, an indispensable condition of the *organic* affection, but he grants that this leaves the sense-*perception* unexplained.

number are reflected, as is evident in the same piece of paper BOOK IV.
put in the sunbeams, in the shade, and in a dark hole; in each ⎯⎯
of which it will produce in us the idea of whiteness in far CHAP. II.
different degrees.

13. Not knowing, therefore, what number of particles, nor The
what motion of them, is fit to produce any precise degree of secondary
Qualities
whiteness, we cannot *demonstrate* the certain equality of any of things
two degrees of whiteness; because we have no certain not discovered by
standard to measure them by, nor means to distinguish every Demon-
the least real difference, the only help we have being from stration.
our senses, which in this point fail us. But where the
difference is so great as to produce in the mind clearly distinct
ideas, whose differences can be perfectly retained, there these
ideas or colours, as we see in different kinds, as blue and
red, are as capable of demonstration as ideas of number and
extension [1]. What I have here said of whiteness and colours,
I think holds true in all secondary qualities and their modes.

14. These two, viz. intuition and demonstration [2], are the III.
degrees of our *knowledge* ; whatever comes short of one of Sensitive
Know-
these, with what assurance soever embraced, is but *faith* or ledge
of the
opinion, but not knowledge, at least in all general truths [3]. particular
There is, indeed, another perception of the mind, employed Existence
of finite
about *the particular existence of finite beings without us* [4], beings
which, going beyond bare probability, and yet not reaching without
us.
perfectly to either of the foregoing degrees of certainty, passes
under the name of *knowledge.* There can be nothing more
certain than that the idea we receive from an external object

---

[1] As when colours, or other secondary qualities, admit of being expressed in terms of number, or other quantity.

[2] 'Intuition' and 'demonstration' may be regarded as respectively direct or simple, and indirect or complex intuition; or as intuitive and discursive reason. Reason is ultimately and essentially intuitive; but in much it is dependent on demonstration, or intellectually necessitated reasoning—in a finite understanding.

[3] *General* truths, about matters of

fact in the finite universe, are neither given in an intuitive perception, nor perceived through demonstration, according to the *Essay.*

[4] 'without us.' He says nothing here of perception of 'our own existence'—manifested in a self-conscious intuition, according to ch. ix. This is one of Leibniz's intuitive truths of fact, contrasted by him with intuitive truths of reason, or identical truths, denial of which involves contradiction in terms.

BOOK IV.

CHAP. II.

is in our minds [1] : this is intuitive knowledge. But whether there be anything more than barely that idea in our minds ; whether we can thence certainly infer the existence of anything without us, which corresponds to that idea, is that whereof some men think there may be a question made [2] ; because men may have such ideas in their minds, when no such thing exists, no such object affects their senses. But yet here I think we are provided with an evidence that puts us past doubting. For I ask any one, Whether he be not invincibly conscious to himself of a different perception, when he looks on the sun by day, and thinks on it by night ; when he actually tastes wormwood, or smells a rose, or only thinks on that savour or odour? We as plainly find the difference there is between any idea revived in our minds by our own memory, and actually coming into our minds by our senses, as we do between any two distinct ideas [3]. If any one say, a dream may do the same thing, and all these ideas may be produced in us without any external objects [4] ; he may please to dream

[1] 'the idea'—that is to say, when regarded only *per se*, as that of which there is bare consciousness—in abstraction from the presupposition on which Locke has from the first proceeded, viz. that it is also a quality of a material substance. Cf. ch. xi; also Green, Introduction to Hume, § 55.

[2] He may have Descartes and Malebranche here in view. Berkeley is not 'answered by anticipation,' for he did not 'make a question' of there being *something more* than the transitory sense-idea : he only made a question of *what that something more was*; and whether, instead of its presupposing an unmanifested and absolutely unperceivable substance, its objective reality did not mean its physical interpretability, as a unit in a natural and intelligible system that is independent of the volitions and fancies of men.

[3] The difference between (*a*) ideas or phenomena that actually appear in the five senses, and (*b*) their represen-

tative ideas in memory and in imagination, is here recognised, as a unique, undefinable certainty of fact—verified too by an appeal to our consciousness of difference, when we 'actually look on the sun by day,' and only imagine, or 'think on it by night.' But, after this difference in kind (whatever it implies) has been acknowledged, can it still be said that men 'have *such* ideas' as those presented in sense-perception, and yet that *all* their ideas are 'dreams'? There is then something found in the sense-ideas that is wanting in other ideas; even although we may be unable to explain in what the 'reality' of sense-ideas consists, and can only appeal to the *contrast* of the two experiences—that of actually seeing the sun, and only dreaming about the sun, or imagining it when awake.

[4] In case the alleged difference in kind between ideas or phenomena that actually present themselves in sense-perception, and those represented in our fancies, is not regarded

that I make him this answer :—1. That it is no great matter, BOOK IV.
whether I remove his scruple or no : where all is but dream, CHAP. II.

as sufficient to settle that 'whereof
some men [Descartes and others] think
there may be a question made,' Locke
further vindicates the claim of sense-
ideas, to signify more than their own
transitory existence, by suggesting that
they are elements in the natural order
or system by which the pleasures
and pains of life are determined. Our
sense-ideas afford *previsions* of these,
in a calculable way; thus implying that
our pleasures and pains are connected
with a physical system that is sufficiently intelligible for direction of
our actions, beyond which practical
reality, 'we have no concernment
to know.' The immediate sense of
difference between the actually felt,
and the merely imagined ; and the
fact that human conduct, in quest
of happiness and to avoid misery,
is determined by the former, are
Locke's criteria of the absolute certainty of perceptions ' employed about
the particular existence of finite beings
without us ': in which accordingly we
have knowledge, but in a degree of
clearness inferior to pure intellectual
intuition, and even to demonstration.

The certainty of the *connexion* of
all actual sense-phenomena in an
orderly system, on which all men
proceed in their reasonings and
actions, is, with Leibniz, that in which
the ' reality' of sensible things consists, and by which the real material
world is distinguished from what is
commonly meant by a dream. Provided
the calculable connexion of sense-
phenomena be recognised, it seems
of little importance how we *name* the
reality. If it pleases us we may call
the whole a dream ; but our actions all
imply that it is an orderly dream that
lasts all our lives ; and experience
shows that we are not deceived when
we interpret natural phenomena according to principles of reason, thus

postulating that it is a reasonable dream.
In using our senses we may accordingly
proceed on the supposition that we are
face to face with a dream-world that is
regulated according to reason; so that
it can be reasoned about by us, and so
that prudent conduct in relation to its
changes is possible. ' Vous avez raison
de dire,' says Leibniz, 'qu'il y a de la
différence pour l'ordinaire entre les
sentiments et les imaginations ; mais
les sceptiques diront que *le plus et le
moins* ne varie point l'espèce. [So
Hume afterwards, who would resolve
the difference between sense-perception and imagination into their different degrees of intensity.] ... Je
crois que le vrai *critérion*, en matière
des objets des sens, est *la liaison des
phénomenes* ; c'est-à-dire la connexion
de ce qui se passe en différents lieux
et temps, et dans l'expérience de
différents hommes, qui sont eux-mêmes
les uns aux autres des phénomènes
très-importants sur cet article. [There
is a *petitio principii* in this assumption
of the real existence of other men,
while the reality of the external world
in which they are included is in question.] Et la liaison des phénomènes qui
garantit les *vérités de fait* à l'égard des
choses sensibles hors des nous, se
vérifie par le moyen des *vérités de
raison* ; comme les apparences de l'op-
tique s'éclaircissent par la géométrie.
[The ' truths of reason ' of Leibniz are
identical truths, the opposite of which
involves a contradiction in terms ;
truths of fact are immediate experiences of an immediate feeling—' ex-
périences immédiates internes d'une
immédiation de sentiment.'] Cependant il faut avouer que toute cette certitude n'est pas du suprème degré, comme
vous (Locke) l'avez bien reconnu.
Car il n'est point impossible, méta-
physiquement parlant, qu'il y ait *un
songe suivi et durable, comme la vie d'un*

reasoning and arguments are of no use, truth and knowledge nothing. 2. That I believe he will allow a very manifest difference between dreaming of being in the fire, and being actually in it. But yet if he be resolved to appear so sceptical as to maintain, that what I call being actually in the fire is nothing but a dream; and that we cannot thereby certainly know, that any such thing as fire actually exists without us: I answer, That we certainly finding that pleasure or pain follows upon the application of certain objects to us, whose existence we perceive, or dream that we perceive, by our senses; this certainty is as great as our happiness or misery, beyond which we have no concernment to know or to be. So that, I think, we may add to the two former sorts of knowledge this also, of the existence of particular external objects, by that perception and consciousness we have of the actual entrance of ideas from them [1], and allow these three degrees of knowledge, viz. *intuitive, demonstrative,* and *sensitive*: in each of which there are different degrees and ways of evidence and certainty [2].

Knowledge not always clear, where the Ideas that enter into it are clear.

15. But since our knowledge is founded on and employed about our ideas only, will it not follow from thence that it is conformable to our ideas; and that where our ideas are clear and distinct, or obscure and confused, our knowledge will be so too? To which I answer, No: for our knowledge consisting in the perception of the agreement or disagreement of any two ideas, its clearness or obscurity consists in the clearness or obscurity of that perception, and not in the clearness or obscurity of the ideas themselves: v. g. a man that has as clear ideas of the angles of a triangle, and of

homme; mais c'est une chose aussi contraire à la raison que pourrait être la fiction d'un livre qui se formerait par le hasard en jetant pêle-mêle les caractères d'imprimerie. Au reste, il est vrai aussi *que pourvu que les phénomènes soient liés, il n'importe qu'on les appelle songes ou non.*' (*Nouveaux Essais*, Lib. IV. chap. ii.)

[1] That is to say, by our felt perception of actual sense-phenomena, in which alone their practical reality manifests itself.

[2] The three degrees of clearness in which the unconditional certainty of knowledge may be held by man are thus—(1) simple or self-evident perception; (2) complex or demonstrated perception; and (3) sense-perception.

equality to two right ones, as any mathematician in the world, BOOK IV.
may yet have but a very obscure perception of their *agree-*   —••—
ment, and so have but a very obscure knowledge of it.   [¹ But   CHAP. II.
ideas which, by reason of their obscurity or otherwise, are
confused, cannot produce any clear or distinct knowledge ;
because, as far as any ideas are confused, so far the mind
cannot perceive clearly whether they agree or disagree.   Or
to express the same thing in a way less apt to be misunder-
stood : he that hath not determined ideas to the words he
uses, cannot make propositions of them of whose truth he
can be certain.]

¹ Instead of the sentences within brackets the first three editions read :—
' But obscure and confused ideas can never produce clear and distinct know-ledge ; because, as far as any ideas are confused or obscure, so far the mind can never perceive clearly whether they agree or disagree.' This sentence was made part of Stilling-fleet's proof, 'that Locke therefore rejected the mysteries of faith.' To which he replies, that the words them-selves show that ' only so far as' ideas are obscure or indistinct are they in-capable of yielding knowledge, ' our obscure and confused ideas having all of them something in them, whereby they are kept from being wholly im-perceptible and perfectly confounded with all other ideas, and so their agree-ment or disagreement with at least some other ideas may be perceived, and thereby produce certainty.' (*Third Letter,* pp. 71, 72.) This is evident, he says, in the proposition, ' substance does exist' ; for substance (in almost all its *other* relations ob-scure) clearly and distinctly agrees with 'the idea of actual existence.' (Cf. pp. 75–78.)

CHAPTER III.

OF THE EXTENT OF HUMAN KNOWLEDGE.

BOOK IV.

—✦✦—

CHAP. III.

Extent of
our Know-
ledge.

First, it
extends no
further
than we
have
Ideas.

Secondly,
It extends
no further
than we
can per-
ceive their
Agree-
ment or
Disagree-
ment.

Thirdly,
Intuitive
Know-
ledge
extends
itself not
to all the

1. KNOWLEDGE, as has been said, lying in the perception of the agreement or disagreement of any of our ideas, it follows from hence, That,

First, we can have knowledge no further than we have *ideas* [1].

2. Secondly, That we can have no knowledge further than we can have *perception* [2] of that agreement or disagreement. Which perception being: 1. Either by *intuition*, or the immediate comparing any two ideas; or, 2. By *reason*, examining the agreement or disagreement of two ideas, by the intervention of some others; or, 3. By *sensation*, perceiving the existence of particular things: hence it also follows:

3. Thirdly, That we cannot have an *intuitive knowledge* that shall extend itself to all our ideas, and all that we would know about them; because we cannot examine and perceive all the relations they have one to another, by juxta-position, or an immediate comparison one with another. Thus, having the ideas of an obtuse and an acute angled triangle, both drawn from equal bases, and between parallels, I can, by

---

[1] This is only saying that complete certainty about the abstract and concrete relations of our ideas, and about the final realities which they reveal, is impossible, unless we have got positive ideas to deal with. All assertions and denials presuppose intelligible, not empty or *idealess*, terms, and all perceptions need intelligible objects. Without the 'percep-tion,' the ideas or phenomena of existence remain latent; without 'ideas,' there is nothing for us to perceive.

[2] I. e. 'perception,' in any of its three degrees of clearness, as distinguished from the moral presumptions by which probability in all its degrees is determined.

intuitive knowledge, perceive the one not to be the other, but cannot that way know whether they be equal or no ; because their agreement or disagreement in equality can never be perceived by an immediate comparing them : the difference of figure makes their parts incapable of an exact immediate application ; and therefore there is need of some intervening qualities to measure them by, which is demonstration, or rational knowledge.

4. Fourthly, It follows, also, from what is above observed, that our *rational knowledge* [1] cannot reach to the whole extent of our ideas : because between two different ideas we would examine, we cannot always find such mediums as we can connect one to another with an intuitive knowledge in all the parts of the deduction ; and wherever that fails, we come short of knowledge and demonstration.

Fourthly, Nor does Demonstrative Knowledge.

5. Fifthly, *Sensitive knowledge* reaching no further than the existence of things actually present to our senses [2], is yet much narrower than either of the former.

Fifthly, Sensitive Knowledge narrower than either.

6. Sixthly, From all which it is evident, that the *extent of our knowledge* comes not only short of the reality of things [3], but even of the extent of our own ideas [4]. Though our knowledge be limited to our ideas, and cannot exceed them either in extent or perfection ; and though these be very narrow bounds, in respect of the extent of All-being, and far short

Sixthly, Our Knowledge, therefore, narrower

---

[1] ' rational knowledge,' i. e. demonstrative knowledge, or absolute certainty reached through reasoning.

[2] In the sequel he includes in ' sensitive knowledge ' the *past* existence of ' things that have heretofore affected our senses,' the certainty of which is retained in memory; as well as the existence of things actually present to sense. Cf. ch. xi. § 11. By ' things ' he means, ' such *collections* of simple ideas as we have observed by our senses to be united together ' in particular substances. Cf. ch. xi. § 9.

[3] ' short of the reality of things.' This implies that we can and do believe in beings, of which we can have no idea other than that they really exist. It implies that our faith may be wider

than the ideas we can have of the sort of things in the ' real existence ' of which we have faith.

[4] Is this consistent with what is elsewhere said of a *knowledge* of their ' identity ' with themselves and their ' diversity ' from one another being necessary to our having *any* ideas— simple or complex, concrete or abstract? Cf. chh. i. § 4 ; iii. § 8. He perhaps means that this is only *negative* knowledge; and that our *positive* knowledge, or absolute certainty, whether of the relations of our abstract ideas, or of their necessary coexistences as qualities and powers in substances, or of the ultimate realities, is far short of the hypotheses we may form, and our range of imagination.

of what we may justly imagine to be in some even created understandings, not tied down to the dull and narrow information that is to be received from some few, and not very acute, ways of perception, such as are our senses [1]; yet it would be well with us if our knowledge were but as large as our ideas, and there were not many doubts and inquiries *concerning the ideas we have,* whereof we are not, nor I believe ever shall be in this world resolved [2]. Nevertheless, I do not question but that human knowledge, under the present circumstances of our beings and constitutions, may be carried much further than it has hitherto been, if men would sincerely, and with freedom of mind, employ all that industry and labour of thought, in improving the means of discovering truth, which they do for the colouring or support of falsehood, to maintain a system, interest, or party they are once engaged in. But yet after all, I think I may, without injury to human perfection, be confident, that our knowledge would never reach to all we might desire to know concerning those ideas we have ; nor be able to surmount all the difficulties, and resolve all the questions that might arise concerning any of them. We have the ideas of a *square,* a *circle,* and *equality* ; and yet, perhaps, shall never be able to find a circle equal to a square, and certainly know that it is so. We have the ideas of *matter* and *thinking,* but possibly shall never be able to know whether [[3] any mere material being] thinks or no ; it being impossible for us, by the contemplation of our own ideas, without revelation, to discover whether Omnipotency

---

[1] He refers only to the limit to man's knowledge that is imposed by the small number, and few sorts of 'simple ideas' or phenomena actually presented in human experience; not to *a priori* limits to presentation in sense, and representation in thought.

[2] There are innumerable particular and universal propositions as to which, although the meaning of their terms is intelligible to us, which implies that we have ideas embodied in the terms of the assertion, we are nevertheless ignorant, or doubtful, whether their copulas should be affirmative or negative.

[3] 'matter'— in first edition ; for which, on the suggestion of Molyneux (Dec. 29, 1692), 'mere material being' was substituted, in order to guard against the atheistic hypothesis that *mere matter* may be the Supreme Being. But the Eternal Mind (he maintains) may make conscious life an attribute of the human organism, or 'annex' it to our bodies : to deny this would be to limit God's Omnipotence, however improbable it may be that God has actually done so.

has not given to some systems of matter, fitly disposed, a power to perceive and think, or else joined and fixed to matter, so disposed, a thinking immaterial substance : it being, in respect of our notions, not much more remote from our comprehension to conceive that GOD can, if he pleases, superadd to matter *a faculty of thinking*, than that he should superadd to it *another substance with a faculty of thinking* ; since we know not wherein thinking consists, nor to what sort of substances the Almighty has been pleased to give that power, which cannot be in any created being, but merely by the good pleasure and bounty of the Creator[1]. For [2 I see no contradiction in it, that the first Eternal thinking Being, or Omnipotent Spirit, should, if he pleased, give to certain systems of created senseless matter, put together as he thinks fit, some degrees of sense, perception, and thought : though, as I think I have proved, lib. iv. ch. 10, § 14, &c., it is no less than a contradiction to suppose matter (which is evidently in its own nature void of sense and thought[3]) should be that

---

[1] This statement affords one of Stillingfleet's chief articles of indictment against the *Essay*, ' because, upon that supposition, it is possible it may be a material substance that thinks in *us*.' This Locke grants, but adds that 'the general idea of substance being the same everywhere [?] the modification of thinking joined to it makes it a spirit, without considering what other modifications it has [i. e. what other ideas ' coexist ' in it], or whether it has [also] the modification of solidity or no. And therefore, if your lordship means by a spiritual an immaterial substance, I grant I have not proved, nor upon my principles can it be proved, i. e. *demonstratively proved*, that there is an immaterial substance in us that thinks. Though I presume, from what I have said about this supposition of a system of matter thinking (Bk. IV. ch. x. § 16), which there demonstrates that *God* is immaterial, it will prove in the highest degree probable, that the thinking substance in

us is immaterial. But your lordship thinks not probability enough, and seems to conclude it demonstrable from principles of philosophy. That demonstration I would with joy receive from your lordship, or anyone else. For, though all the great ends of morality and religion are well enough secured without it, yet it would be a great advantage of our knowledge of nature.' (*First Letter*, p. 67.)

[2] The bracketed words substituted for the following in the first edition :— ' What assurance of knowledge can anyone have, that certain thoughts, such as e. g. pleasure and pain, should not be in body itself after,' &c. In Bk. II. ch. xxiii. § 5 we have Locke's reason for supposing that the thinking substance in man is not a material substance—' we not apprehending how the operations of mind can belong to body, or be produced by it,' &c.

[3] Hence he argues that, whether or not God has been pleased to delegate the power of thinking to organisms of

Eternal first-thinking Being. What certainty of knowledge can any one have, that some perceptions, such as, v. g., pleasure and pain, should not be in some bodies themselves,] after a certain manner modified and moved, as well as that they should be in an immaterial substance, upon the motion of the parts of body: Body, as far as we can conceive, being able only to strike and affect body, and motion, according to the utmost reach of our ideas, being able to produce nothing but motion ; so that when we allow it to produce pleasure or pain, or the idea of a colour or sound, we are fain to quit our reason, go beyond our ideas, and attribute it wholly to the good pleasure of our Maker. For, since we must allow He has annexed effects to motion which we can no way conceive motion able to produce, what reason have we to conclude that He could not order them as well to be produced in a subject we cannot conceive capable of them, as well as in a subject we cannot conceive the motion of matter can any way operate upon [1]? I say not this, that I would any way lessen the belief

matter or not, matter cannot, at any rate, be the Supreme Being. That the Supreme Being is a Thinking Being is 'as demonstrable as any proposition in pure mathematics,' according to Locke. Cf. ch. x.

[1] 'If God can give no power to any parts of matter but what *men* can account for from the essence of matter in general; if all such [additional] qualities must destroy the [real] essence, or change the essential qualities of matter, which are to *our* conceptions above it, and which *we* cannot conceive to be the natural consequence of that essence —it is plain that the [real] essence of matter is destroyed in most of the sensible parts of this our system. For it is visible that all the planets have revolutions about certain remote centres, which I would have anyone explain by the bare essence of natural powers depending on the essence of matter in general, without something added to that essence which we cannot conceive . . . That Omnipotency

cannot make a substance to be solid and not solid at the same time, I think, with due reverence, we may say; but that a solid substance may not have [coexisting] qualities and powers which have no natural, or visibly necessary, connexion with solidity, is too much for us (who are but of yesterday) to be positive in.' (*Third Letter* to Stillingfleet pp. 398–405.) Cf. the numerous passages in the *Essay* on the relation between the secondary qualities and other powers of matter and its primary or real qualities. Locke here seems to identify *union* of a self-conscious substance with an organism of matter, and endowment of a material substance with self-consciousness as one of its qualities. He grants the *apparent incompatibility* of what is called mind and what is called matter, and the impossibility of adequately expressing the phenomena of the one in terms of the other. Can self-consciousness then be a quality, or an effect, or, in an

of the soul's immateriality: I am not here speaking of
probability, but knowledge; and I think not only that it
becomes the modesty of philosophy not to pronounce
magisterially, where we want that evidence that can produce
knowledge; but also, that it is of use to us to discern how far
our knowledge does reach; for the state we are at present in,
not being that of vision, we must in many things content
ourselves with faith and probability: and in the present
question, about the Immateriality of the Soul, if our faculties
cannot arrive at demonstrative certainty, we need not think it
strange. All the great ends of morality and religion are well
enough secured, without philosophical proofs of the soul's
immateriality [1]; since it is evident, that he who made us at
the beginning to subsist here, sensible intelligent beings, and
for several years continued us in such a state, can and will
restore us to the like state of sensibility in another world, and
make us capable there to receive the retribution he has
designed to men, according to their doings in this life. [[2] And
therefore it is not of such mighty necessity to determine one
way or the other, as some, over-zealous for or against the

intelligible way, a manifestation of what is solid? Are we not more clearly certain of the substantial independence of the self-conscious agent than we are of the substantial independence of solid matter? That in the present life of man, his physical organisation more or less conditions his conscious life, is a matter of fact, quite consistent with the universe being universally grounded in Reason or Spirit.

[1] Locke finds no metaphysical necessity for the immortality of the 'thinking substance' in man. He resolves it into the will of God. In his *Reasonableness of Christianity* he makes man's immortality conditional on faith. Annihilation is represented as the destiny of all who do not retain life after physical death, as the reward of the conduct that issues from faith in Christ. Neither the immateriality nor the immortality of man can be demonstrated, according to the teaching of the *Essay*, and our faith in the immortality is independent of the fact of the immateriality. In both of these positions Kant seems to misunderstand Locke: while Cousin goes so far as to say that if the soul be not immaterial, we ought not to say that its immortality is doubtful; we ought to say that it is impossible. Stillingfleet is more modest when he only says that 'it is not an easy matter to give an account how the soul should be capable of immortality, unless it be an immaterial substance. To suppose that God *gives* bodies accidents which are not modes of being derived from their substance, is, according to Leibniz, to resort to miracles, making God produce their 'thinking,' and be therein the real agent instead of the body.

[2] Added in the fourth edition.

BOOK IV.
CHAP. III.

immateriality of the soul, have been forward to make the world believe. Who, either on the one side, indulging too much their thoughts immersed altogether in matter, can allow no existence to what is not material : or who, on the other side, finding not *cogitation* within the natural powers of matter, examined over and over again by the utmost intention of mind, have the confidence to conclude—That Omnipotency itself cannot give perception and thought to a substance which has the modification of solidity [1]. He that considers how hardly sensation is, in our thoughts, reconcilable to extended matter [2]; or existence to anything that has no extension at all [3], will confess that he is very far from certainly knowing what his soul is. It is a point which seems to me to be put out of the reach of our knowledge [4]: and he who will give himself leave to consider freely, and look into the dark and intricate part of each hypothesis, will scarce find his reason able to determine him fixedly for or against the soul's materiality. Since, on which side soever he views it, either as an *unextended substance*, or as a *thinking extended matter*, the difficulty to conceive either will, whilst either alone is in his thoughts, still drive him to the contrary side. An unfair way which some men take with themselves : who, because of the inconceivableness of something they find in one, throw themselves violently into the contrary hypothesis, though altogether as unintelligible to an unbiassed understanding [5].

[1] Locke's hesitation in recognising certainty of the substantial immateriality of conscious life in man, however probable this may be, is thus hesitation to limit the omnipotence of God.

[2] i. e. it is difficult to imagine that anything solid thinks.

[3] Is this a reasonable difficulty, and not due to popular association of the term *substance* with *solidity*, so that ' unextended substance ' sounds absurd?

[4] But not therefore outside probability and the moral presumptions by which it may be reasonably determined. What gives its deep human interest to the 'point' in question is the conclusion about human destiny which it seems to involve: if a man is only a curiously organised parcel of atoms, what becomes of the man when the curious organism of which substantially he consists is dissolved at death ? Does not self-consciousness disappear in this dissolution of its real essence ?

[5] They are thus guilty of what logicians call the ' fallacy of objections'; which consists in arguing that because a proposition is open to objections it must be rejected as untrue, while the real question is, whether its contradictory does not involve as great or greater difficulties; and of two absolute contradictories one or other must be true. Cf. Bk. II. ch. xxiii. §§ 15-32.

This serves not only to show the weakness and the scantiness of our knowledge, but the insignificant triumph of such sort of ·arguments; which, drawn from our own views, may satisfy us that we can find no certainty on one side of the question : but do not at all thereby help us to truth by running into the opposite opinion; which, on examination, will be found clogged with equal difficulties. For what safety, what advantage to any one is it, for the avoiding the seeming absurdities, and to him unsurmountable rubs, he meets with in one opinion, to take refuge in the contrary, which is built on something altogether as inexplicable, and as far remote from his comprehension? It is past controversy, that we have in us *something* that thinks ; our very doubts about what it is, confirm the certainty of its being, though we must content ourselves in the ignorance of what *kind* of being it is[1]: and it is in vain to go about to be sceptical in this, as it is unreasonable in most other cases to be positive against the being of anything, because we cannot comprehend its nature. For I would fain know what substance exists, that has not something in it which manifestly baffles our understandings. Other spirits, who see and know the nature and inward constitution of things [2], how much must they exceed us in knowledge? To which, if we add larger comprehension, which enables them at one glance to see the connexion and agreement of very many ideas [3], and readily supplies to them the intermediate proofs, which we by single and slow steps, and long poring in the dark, hardly at last find out, and are often ready to forget one before we have hunted out another[4]; we may guess at some part of the happiness of superior ranks

---

[1] We know this much at least, that our conscious life in its successive acts and other states must be the manifestation of a substance that thinks and wills, whether that substance be material or not; and that whatever the self-conscious substance may be, it is the continuous *self* or person guaranteed by memory, and that through all changes is morally identical with itself, that is superior to the death of the organism. So in Bk. II. ch. xxvii.

[2] i. e. the 'real essences' of things, what makes each of them be the sort of substance that by observation we find that it actually is.

[3] Cf. Bk. II. ch. x. § 9.

[4] Cf. ch. ii. §§ 2—13, and annotations.

of spirits, who have a quicker and more penetrating sight [1], as well as a larger field [2] of knowledge [3].]

But to return to the argument in hand : our knowledge, I say, is not only limited to the paucity and imperfections of the ideas we have, and which we employ it about, but even comes short of that too : but how far it reaches, let us now inquire.

How far our Knowledge reaches.
7. The affirmations or negations we make concerning the ideas we have [4], may, as I have before intimated in general, be reduced to these four sorts, viz. identity, co-existence, relation, and real existence. I shall examine how far our knowledge extends in each of these [5] :

[1] ' sight '—including the intellectual vision, or perception of absolute certainty.

[2] 'a larger field,' i. e. a greater number of simple ideas, whether of the senses or of reflection ; and a greater variety in kind of the simple ideas or phenomena in which real substances manifest themselves.

[3] No section in the *Essay* occasioned more contemporary criticism and controversy than this, which refuses to allow that the immateriality of that in man on which his self-conscious life depends is one of our absolute certainties ; and holds that whether man's individual substance is material or not, and also whether men continue in self-conscious life after physical death, are facts that depend upon the will of God, not upon unconditional necessity of reason. This paragraph is the text of a large part of the controversy with Stillingfleet, and also between Clarke and Dodwell, and between Clarke and Collins. It is impossible here to give an abstract of this voluminous argument, as to whether self-consciousness in man necessarily presupposes, in the reason or nature of things, the immateriality and immortality of the substance that is self-conscious ; and as to whether this

is a question of probability, determined by moral, if not by merely physical experience. Leibniz, arguing for the first of these alternatives, thus criticises Locke :—' Lorsqu'on n'a que des idées confuses de la *pensée* et de la *matière*, comme l'on en a ordinairement, il ne faut pas s'étonner si on ne voit pas le moyen de résoudre ces questions. . . . La matière ne saurait subsister sans substances immatérielles, c'est-à-dire sans les unités, après quoi on ne doit plus demander s'il est libre à Dieu de lui en donner ou non ; et si ces substances n'avaient pas en elles la correspondance ou l'harmonie dont je viens de parler, *Dieu n'agirait pas suivant l'ordre naturel*. . . . Vouloir que Dieu agisse autrement, et donne aux choses des accidents qui ne sont pas des *façons d'être*, ou modifications dérivées des substances, c'est recourir aux miracles . . . en quel cas l'on peut même douter si ce serait *le feu* qui agirait, et si *Dieu* ne ferait pas lui-même l'effet, en agissant au lieu du feu.' (*Nouveaux Essais.*)

[4] He thus regards 'the ideas we have' as supplying the *subjects* of the propositions we can make.

[5] He here proposes to inquire how far absolute certainty can be reached as to an idea being the *same* as it is ;

8. *First,* as to *identity* and *diversity.* In this way of agreement or disagreement of our ideas, our intuitive knowledge is as far extended as our ideas themselves: and there can be no idea in the mind, which it does not, presently, by an intuitive knowledge, perceive to be what it is, and to be different from any other[1].

BOOK IV.

CHAP. III.

Firstly, Our Knowledge of Identity and Diversity in ideas extends as far as our Ideas themselves.

9. *Secondly,* as to the second sort, which is the agreement or disagreement of our ideas in *co-existence,* in this our knowledge is very short; though in this consists the greatest and most material part of our knowledge concerning substances[2]. For our ideas of the species of substances[3] being, as I have showed[4], nothing but certain collections of simple ideas united in one subject, and so co-existing together; v.g. our idea of flame is a body hot, luminous, and moving upward; of gold, a body heavy to a certain degree, yellow, malleable, and fusible : for these, or some such complex ideas as these, in men's minds, do these two names of the different substances, flame and gold, stand for. When we would know anything

as to the *necessary coexistence* of simple ideas, as actual qualities and powers in our complex ideas of substances ; as to the *abstract relations* of all other complex ideas than those of substances ; and as to the *agreement with real existence* of the simple ideas which arise in sensation and reflection through which a speculatively inadequate knowledge of ourselves, and of a universe independent of our fancies, is supposed to be given.

[1] That each idea we have is what it is, and is not another idea than it is, we cannot help seeing with the unconditional certainty which finds abstract expression in the principles of identity and non contradiction. Here our knowledge is coextensive with our ideas,— if this negative and formal knowledge, which adds nothing to our positive information about either the abstract or the concrete relations of our ideas, be knowledge, as he seems to say that it is not, when we are told (§ 6) that

' our knowledge comes short of the extent of our own ideas.' On the ideas of ' identity and diversity,' cf. Bk. II. ch. xxvii. § 1 ; also Bk. IV. ch. i. § 4.

[2] All inquiry into matters of fact is really inquiry into the attributes of the substances of which the actual universe consists, and their modes of behaviour to each of us and to one another. Thus all our complex ideas (such as they are) of things and persons belong to this second head; as to which Locke proceeds to argue that here absolute certainty of knowledge cannot be reached by man, or only to a small extent, so that he must be satisfied with presumptions of probability, in lack of a vision of intellectually necessary connexion.

[3] ' the species of substances,' i. e. their nominal, in contrast to their real essences.

[4] Cf. Bk. II. ch. xxiii.; Bk. III. ch. vi.

BOOK IV.
——＋——
CHAP. III.

further concerning these, or any other sort of substances, what do we inquire, but what *other* qualities or powers these substances have or have not? Which is nothing else but to know what *other* simple ideas do, or do not co-exist with those that make up that complex idea[1]?

Because the Connexion between simple Ideas in substances is for the most part unknown.

10. This, how weighty and considerable a part soever of human science, is yet very narrow, and scarce any at all. The reason whereof is, that the simple ideas whereof our complex ideas of substances are made up are, for the most part, such as carry with them, in their own nature, no *visible necessary* connexion or inconsistency[2] with any other simple ideas, whose co-existence with them we would inform ourselves about[3].

Especially of the secondary Qualities of Bodies.

11. The ideas that our complex ones of substances are made up of, and about which our knowledge concerning substances is most employed, are those of their secondary qualities[4]; which depending all (as has been shown) upon the primary qualities of their minute and insensible parts; or, if not upon them, upon something yet more remote from our comprehension[5]; it is impossible we should know which have a *necessary*

[1] See Webb, *Intellectualism*, p. 112. In Kantian language this sort of agreement or disagreement among ideas makes the *a posteriori* synthetic judgment. ' Coexistence ' of ideas in ' that complex idea,' means coexistence of attributes and powers in a particular substance. The argument is, that our knowledge of ' things ' is too narrow and scanty to allow us to conclude *a priori*, that because a substance is seen to be endowed with such and such powers, it *must* therefore be endowed with certain others. What its other powers actually are has to be determined by observation, and inductive presumptions of probability founded thereon. Yet all our practical inquiries are directed to this, so that human life turns upon probabilities.

[2] And ' knowledge ' or absolute certainty, as distinguished from probability, implies, in Locke's meaning, ' a connexion or inconsistency ' that is *seen* to be intellectually ' necessary.'

[3] So that, except in the way of more or less probable presumption, founded on experience, we cannot affirm or deny the coexistence of any *unperceived* simple ideas or qualities in a substance.

[4] He is thus thinking here only of ' *material* substances.'

[5] ' yet more remote from our comprehension.' By this important qualification, which in other passages he omits, Locke guards himself against the dogmatic assumption—that the innumerable secondary qualities and powers with which material substances are endowed, and which give them their chief human interest, *must* be the issue of their primary qualities, i. e. of the variously modified and moved atoms of which each substance consists, and by which it is objectively distinguished from other substances. He allows here that it may depend on ' something yet more remote from our comprehension ' than this. Cf. Bk. II.

union or inconsistency one with another. For, not knowing
the root they spring from, not knowing what size, figure,
and texture of parts they are, on which depend, and from
which result those qualities which make our complex idea
of gold, it is impossible we should know what *other* qualities
result from, or are incompatible with, the same constitution of
the insensible parts of gold ; and so consequently must
always co-exist with that complex idea we have of it, or else
are inconsistent with it.

12. Besides this ignorance of the primary qualities of the Because
insensible parts of bodies, on which depend all their secondary necessary Con-
qualities[1], there is yet another and more incurable part of nexion between
ignorance, which sets us more remote from a certain knowledge any
of the co-existence or *inco-existence* (if I may so say) of secondary and the
different ideas[2] in the same subject ; and that is, that there is primary Qualities
no discoverable connexion between any secondary quality and is undis-
those primary qualities which it depends on[3]. coverable by us.

13. That the size, figure, and motion of one body should We have
cause a change in the size, figure, and motion of another body, no perfect
is not beyond our conception ; the separation of the parts of know-ledge of
one body upon the intrusion of another ; and the change from their
rest to motion upon impulse ; these and the like seem to have Primary Qualities.
some connexion one with another. And if we knew these
primary qualities of bodies, we might have reason to hope we
might be able to know a great deal more of these operations

ch. viii. &c. The hypothetical *atomism* which Locke (here and elsewhere) favours is of course to be distinguished from the mechanical or atheistic atomism which he explicitly rejects. With Locke it is one form of the theistic conception.

[1] The qualification made above is here omitted, and (theistic) atomism is dogmatically asserted.

[2] 'different ideas,' i.e. different qualities and powers.

[3] This is one of the cardinal principles of the *Essay*. Locke referred the 'real essence' of things, on the corpuscularian hypothesis, to the primary qualities of their atoms, not like Aristotle, to 'substantial forms.' There is more analogy between this of Locke and Bacon's doctrine of *forms*. With Bacon the form of any thing is that constitution of its primary qualities on which its nature, manifested in its secondary qualities, depends. The 'forms' of heat and of white, for instance, are referred to invisible motions and arrangements of atoms. But Locke discourages Bacon's sanguine expectation of reducing the sciences of nature to a few universal and necessary truths, by the discovery of the 'forms' of things. Cf. *Nov. Org.* II. 13–16.

BOOK IV.
CHAP. III.

of them one upon another : but our minds not being able to discover any connexion betwixt these primary qualities of bodies and the sensations that are produced in us by them, we can never be able to establish certain and undoubted rules of the *consequence* or *co-existence* of any secondary qualities, though we could discover the size, figure, or motion of those invisible parts which immediately produce them. We are so far from knowing *what* figure, size, or motion of parts produce a yellow colour, a sweet taste, or a sharp sound, that we can by no means conceive how *any* size, figure, or motion of any particles, can possibly produce in us the idea of any colour, taste, or sound whatsoever : there is no conceivable connexion between the one and the other[1].

And seek in vain for certain and universal knowledge of unperceived qualities in substances.

14. In vain, therefore, shall we endeavour to discover by our ideas (the only true way of certain and universal knowledge [2]) what other ideas are to be found constantly joined with that of *our* complex idea of any substance: since we neither know the real constitution of the minute parts on which their qualities do depend ; nor, did we know them, could we discover any necessary connexion between them and any of the secondary qualities: which is necessary to be done before we can certainly know their necessary co-existence[3]. So, that, let

---

[1] That motion should issue in, or be followed by, motion seems to Locke to be intelligible : but why motion, or any other primary quality in the atomic texture of a thing, should be accompanied or followed in that thing by its particular smell, taste, and colour, must remain a mystery to a being whose power of perception is limited as man's is; though we find that they are in fact connected, in the simple ideas of our experience.

[2] 'by our ideas (the only true way of certain and universal knowledge),' i.e. our ideas abstracted from actual substances, and under their abstract relations. With Hume it is only in abstract relations of ideas that we have intuitive or demonstrative certainty. ' Propositions of this sort are discoverable by the mere operation of thought, without dependence on what is anywhere existent in the universe. Though there were never a circle or triangle in nature, the truths demonstrated by Euclid would further retain their certainty and evidence. Matters of fact [Locke's propositions of coexistence] are not ascertained in the same manner. The contrary of every matter of fact is still possible.' (See Hume's *Inquiry concerning Human Understanding*, Sect. iv. ; also Sect. vii.

[3] Note here the criteria by which Locke distinguishes absolute certainty from the probability, which, even in its highest degree, he refuses to recognise as knowledge. ' Necessary connexion '—' necessary coexistence ' —' necessary dependence '—' visibly necessary connexion '—' evident dependence and necessary connexion.'

our complex idea of any species of substances be what it will, BOOK IV.
we can hardly, from the simple ideas contained in it[1], certainly CHAP. III.
determine the necessary co-existence of any other quality[2]
whatsoever. Our knowledge in all these inquiries reaches
very little further than our experience. Indeed some few of
the primary qualities have a necessary dependence and visible
connexion one with another, as figure necessarily supposes
extension ; receiving or communicating motion by impulse,
supposes solidity[3]. But though these, and perhaps some
others of our ideas have : yet there are so few of them that
have a visible connexion one with another, that we can by
intuition or demonstration discover the co-existence of very
few of the qualities that are to be found united in substances :
and we are left only to the assistance of our senses to make
known to us what qualities they contain. For of all the
qualities that are co-existent in any subject, without this
dependence and evident connexion of their ideas one with
another, we cannot know certainly any two to co-exist, any
further than experience, by our senses[4], informs us. Thus,
though we see the yellow colour, and, upon trial, find the
weight, malleableness, fusibility, and fixedness that are united
in a piece of gold ; yet, because no one of these ideas has any
evident dependence or necessary connexion with the other, we
cannot certainly know[5] that where any four of these are, the
fifth will be there also, how highly probable soever it may be ;
because the highest probability amounts not to certainty,
without which there can be no true knowledge. For this
co-existence can be no further known than it is perceived ;

This unconditional connexion he finds
wanting among natural phenomena,
which are all conditioned by powers
only imperfectly comprehensible by
man. He thus suggests the difference
between metaphysical necessity, which
is absolute, and previsive faith, which
is dependent on what man can only
see as through a glass darkly.

[1] The 'simple ideas contained in it,'
i.e. those which constitute its 'nominal
essence.'

[2] 'other quality,' i.e. than those

perceived by our senses.

[3] So that they might give rise to
a priori synthetic judgments at the
root of natural philosophy.

[4] 'by our senses,' i. e. by the ideas
or phenomena of things actually presented in the senses.

[5] 'cannot certainly know,' i. e. we
can only presume, on ground of probability ; because their coexistence in
this piece of 'gold' does not necessarily
guarantee their coexistence in other
pieces, so named.

BOOK IV.
CHAP. III.

Of Repugnancy to co-exist, our knowledge is larger.

and it cannot be perceived but either in particular subjects, by the observation of our senses, or, in general, by the necessary connexion of the ideas themselves[1].

15. As to the incompatibility or repugnancy to co-existence, we may know[2] that any subject may have of each sort of primary qualities but one particular at once: v.g. each particular extension, figure, number of parts, motion, excludes all other of each kind. The like also is certain of all sensible ideas peculiar to each sense; for whatever of each kind is present in any subject, excludes all other of that sort: v.g. no one subject can have two smells or two colours at the same time. To this, perhaps will be said, Has not an opal, or the infusion of *lignum nephriticum*, two colours at the same time[3]? To which I answer, that these bodies, to eyes differently placed, may at the same time afford different colours: but I take liberty also to say, that, to eyes differently placed, it is different parts of the object that reflect the particles of light: and therefore it is not the same part of the object, and so not the very same subject, which at the same time appears both yellow and azure. For, it is as impossible that the very same particle of any body should at the same time differently modify or reflect the rays of light, as that it should have two different figures and textures at the same time.

---

[1] Locke again surrenders as impracticable Bacon's sanguine ideal, in his proposed search for 'forms.' No 'necessary' connexion is perceptible, or can be concluded absolutely. Physical connexion can only be concluded hypothetically, as a probability. To determine the foundation of scientific research, in the absence of perceived connexion in nature, is the aim of Hume's *Inquiry concerning Human Understanding.* 'It may,' he says, 'be a subject worthy of curiosity to inquire, what is the nature of that evidence which assures us of any matter of fact *beyond the present testimony of our senses, or the records of our memory.* This part of philosophy has been little cultivated, either by the ancients or

moderns.' (Sect. iv.) His preliminary assumption is, that ' it is by means of the relation of [customary] cause and effect alone that we can go beyond the evidence of our memory or senses.' The *Inquiry* is virtually directed to the *sort* of connexion on which Locke's affirmations of 'coexistence' turn, with an application of the result to questions of physics and theology.

[2] We may 'know,'—not merely presume to be probable. He asserts the 'knowledge,' without a critical analysis of it.

[3] Opal is celebrated for the variety of colours which it presents according to the point from which it is looked at.

16. But as to the powers of substances to change the sensible qualities of other bodies, which make a great part of our inquiries about them, and is no inconsiderable branch of our knowledge[1]; I doubt as to these, whether our knowledge reaches much further than our experience[2]; or whether we can come to the discovery of most of these powers, and be certain that they are in any subject, by the connexion with any of those ideas which to us[3] make its essence. Because the active and passive powers of bodies[4], and their ways of operating, consisting in a texture and motion of parts which we cannot by any means come to discover; it is but in very few cases we can be able to perceive their dependence on, or repugnance to, any of those ideas which make our complex one of that sort of things. I have here instanced in the corpuscularian hypothesis[5], as that which is thought to go furthest in an intelligible explication of those qualities of bodies; and I fear the weakness of human understanding is scarce able to substitute another, which will afford us a fuller and clearer discovery of the necessary connexion and co-existence of the powers which are to be observed united in several sorts of them. This at least is certain, that, whichever hypothesis be clearest and truest, (for of that it is not my business to determine,) our knowledge concerning corporeal substances

BOOK IV.
CHAP. III.
Our Knowledge of the Co-existence of Powers in Bodies extends but a very little Way.

---

[1] Cf. Bk. II. ch. viii. §§ 23-26. Propositions about 'coexistence' of qualities in substances are virtually propositions about the '[natural] powers of substances,' and are thus determined by the relation of physical cause and effect. The physical and natural sciences are composed of propositions of this kind.

[2] 'our experience,' i. e. the immediate data of sense that are presented in the perception which Locke includes in his 'sensation.'

[3] 'to us,' i. e. in the 'nominal essences,' which we happen to form; in our inability to discover the 'real essences' on which the coexistence of simple ideas, or qualities and powers, in the substance *necessarily* depend.

Cf. Bk. III. ch. xvi.

[4] Cf. Bk. II. ch. xxi. §§ 2-5, where he suggests that '*material* substances may be wholly destitute of active power; yet see next note.

[5] It is to the 'corpuscularian hypothesis' that he appeals in the many passages in the *Essay* which deal with this favourite subject—the *ultimate physical cause* of the secondary qualities and other *powers* of material substances, and the relative subject of their nominal and real essences. Locke, as we have already seen, favours the 'corpuscularian hypothesis,' in subordination to the theistic interpretation of the universe—as a physical explanation, with the Divine Will presupposed as the prime explanation.

BOOK IV.
CHAP. III.

will be very little advanced by any of them, till we are made to see what qualities and powers of bodies have a *necessary* connexion or repugnancy one with another; which in the present state of philosophy I think we know but to a very small degree: and I doubt whether, with those faculties we have, we shall ever be able to carry our general knowledge (I say not particular experience [1]) in this part much further. [[2] Experience is that which in this part we must depend on. And it were to be wished that it were more improved. We find the advantages some men's generous pains have this way brought to the stock of natural knowledge. And if others, especially the philosophers by fire[3], who pretend to it, had been so wary in their observations, and sincere in their reports as those who call themselves philosophers ought to have been, our acquaintance with the bodies here about us, and our insight into their powers and operations had been yet much greater.]

Of the Powers that co-

17. If we are at a loss in respect of the powers and operations of bodies, I think it is easy to conclude we are much

---

[1] We can 'know' by 'particular experience' that a certain quality or power is one of those which should be included in our complex idea of any substance; because, now and here, we are actually receiving from it those simple ideas of sensation which are the manifestations, or the natural effects, of that quality or power. But this knowledge does not give us either intuitive or demonstrative knowledge of the 'necessary connexion' of *other* ideas, i. e. qualities and powers, with those perceived in sense, so that they might be added with unconditional certainty to our previous complex idea of the substance. The addition must be made in faith, because determined by considerations of probability, not by either intuitive or demonstrative 'perception.' Locke does not explain the ground of our assurance, that even those 'qualities and powers' which we refer to the substance because we actually perceive them, must continue to belong to it, after our perception is withdrawn.

[2] Added in second Edition.

[3] Fire played an important part in the cosmological speculations of Greece. The Stoics identified the world-soul with the vital heat. Like Heraclitus, they regarded fire as the universal force by which the mundane system was originated, and by which it is destined to dissolve. See Plutarch, *De Stoic. Rep.* 42 ; Diog. Laert. Lib. vii ; Stob. *Ecl.* Chap. I. The mystery which belonged to fire suggested that it might be the vital spirit of the universe. Berkeley, in *Siris*, conceived all-pervading fire as the original physical cause, or instrument, to which, under the Supreme Mind, all changes in nature may be due. Bacon's speculations on heat were perhaps in Locke's view here.

more in the dark in reference to spirits[1] ; whereof we naturally have no ideas but what we draw from that of our own, by reflecting on the operations of our own souls within us, as far as they can come within our observation. But how inconsiderable a rank the spirits that inhabit our bodies hold amongst those various and possibly innumerable kinds of nobler beings ; and how far short they come of the endowments and perfections of cherubim and seraphim, and infinite sorts of spirits above us, is what by a transient hint in another place[2] I have offered to my reader's consideration.

BOOK IV.

CHAP. III.

exist in Spirits yet narrower.

18. *Thirdly,* As to the third sort of our knowledge, viz. the agreement or disagreement of any of our ideas in any other relation : this, as it is the largest field of our knowledge, so it is hard to determine how far it may extend : because the advances that are made in this part of knowledge, depending on our sagacity in finding intermediate ideas, that may show the relations and habitudes of ideas whose co-existence is not considered[3], it is a hard matter to tell when we are at an end of such discoveries ; and when reason has all the helps it is capable of, for the finding of proofs, or examining the agreement or disagreement of remote ideas. They that are ignorant of Algebra cannot imagine the wonders in this kind are to be done by it : and what further improvements and helps advantageous to other parts of knowledge the sagacious mind of man may yet find out, it is not easy to determine. This at

Thirdly, Of Relations between abstracted ideas it is not easy to say how far our knowledge extends.

---

[1] 'spirits,' i.e. angels or other unembodied spirits—Locke's 'spiritual substances.' The attributes and powers that coexist in them, and that should be included in our complex ideas of any sort of spiritual substance, are less available for human science than those of material substances ; for as to these we have, so far, direct experience, in sense-perception of their primary or real qualities, whereas the only spirit each man actually perceives ideas of is his own. Unlike Locke, Hobbes limits 'substance' to body, asserting that body and substance are two names for the same thing, which is called

body, as it fills place, and substance, as it is subject to accidents and changes. Cf. *Leviathan,* Pt. III. 34.

[2] Cf. Bk. II. chh. x. § 9; xxiii. § 13.

[3] The 'relations' in question are thus those of *abstract* ideas—abstracted from time and place—as in pure mathematics, and also, he argues, in abstract morality. Our affirmations under this third head may be reached by demonstration, because they turn at last on what Kant would call synthetic judgments *a priori* ; but whether Locke means to regard them as more than merely analytic or explicative propositions is not clear.

BOOK IV.
CHAP. III.

least I believe, that the *ideas of quantity*[1] are not those alone that are capable of demonstration and knowledge; and that other, and perhaps more useful, parts of contemplation, would afford us certainty, if vices, passions, and domineering interest did not oppose or menace such endeavours.

Morality capable of Demonstration.

The idea of a supreme Being, infinite in power, goodness, and wisdom, whose workmanship we are, and on whom we depend ; and the idea of ourselves, as understanding, rational creatures, being such as are clear in us, would, I suppose, if duly considered and pursued, afford such foundations of our duty and rules of action as might place *morality* amongst the *sciences capable of demonstration*[2] : wherein I doubt not but from self-evident propositions, by necessary consequences, as incontestible as those in mathematics, the measures of right and wrong might be made out, to any one that will apply himself with the same indifferency and attention to the one as he does to the other of these sciences. The *relation* of other *modes* may certainly be perceived, as well as those of number and extension : and I cannot see why they should not also be capable of demonstration, if due methods were thought on to examine or pursue their agreement or disagreement. ' Where there is no property there is no injustice,' is a proposition[3] as certain as any demonstration in Euclid : for the idea of property being a right to anything, and the idea to which the name 'injustice' is given being the invasion or violation of that right, it is evident that these ideas, being thus established, and these names annexed to them, I can as certainly know this proposition to be true, as that a triangle has three angles equal to two right ones. Again: 'No government allows absolute liberty.' The idea of government being the establishment of society upon certain rules or laws which require

---

[1] I. e. the abstract relations of mathematics.

[2] Cf. Bk. III. ch. xi. § 16. The eternal and immutable nature of the distinctions of abstract morality is maintained by Locke, although he includes prevision of the pleasurable and painful consequences of actions when he explains the motives which influence men to conform to the eternal morality.

Abstract ethics he proposes to evolve by demonstration from relations of abstract ideas ; whatever the particular occasion in experience of the first rise of our ethical ideas may be, and under whatever circumstances of actual life the demonstrated abstract science of morality may have to be applied.

[3] ' a proposition,' i. e. a proposition in abstract morality.

conformity to them; and the idea of absolute liberty being BOOK IV.
for any one to do whatever he pleases; I am as capable of ⟶ CHAP. III.
being certain of the truth of this proposition as of any in the
mathematics.

19. That which in this respect has given the advantage to Two
the ideas of quantity, and made them thought more capable things have made
of certainty and demonstration, is, moral
Ideas to be
First, That they can be set down and represented by sensible thought
marks, which have a greater and nearer correspondence with incapable of Demon-
them than any words or sounds whatsoever. Diagrams drawn stration:
on paper are copies of the ideas in the mind, and not liable to their un-
fitness for
the uncertainty that words carry in their signification. An sensible
represent-
angle, circle, or square, drawn in lines, lies open to the view, ation,
and cannot be mistaken: it remains unchangeable, and may at and their
com-
leisure be considered and examined, and the demonstration be plexed-
revised, and all the parts of it may be gone over more than ness.
once, without any danger of the least change in the ideas.
This cannot be thus done in moral ideas: we have no sensible
marks that resemble them, whereby we can set them down;
we have nothing but words to express them by; which, though
when written they remain the same, yet the ideas they stand
for may change in the same man; and it is very seldom that
they are not different in different persons[1].

Secondly, Another thing that makes the greater difficulty
in ethics is, That moral ideas are commonly more complex
than those of the figures ordinarily considered in mathematics.
From whence these two inconveniences follow:—First, that
their names are of more uncertain signification, the precise
collection of simple ideas they stand for not being so easily
agreed on; and so the sign that is used for them in communication always, and in thinking often, does not steadily carry
with it the same idea[1]. Upon which the same disorder,
confusion, and error follow, as would if a man, going to
demonstrate something of an heptagon, should, in the diagram
he took to do it, leave out one of the angles, or by oversight
make the figure with one angle more than the name ordinarily
imported, or he intended it should when at first he thought of

[1] Cf. Bk. III. chh. v; ix. §§ 6, 7; xi. §§ 15–18.

his demonstration. This often happens, and is hardly avoidable in very complex moral ideas, where the same name being retained, one angle, i.e. one simple idea, is left out, or put in the complex one (still called by the same name) more at one time than another. Secondly, From the complexedness of these moral ideas there follows another inconvenience, viz. that the mind cannot easily retain those precise combinations so exactly and perfectly as is necessary in the examination of the habitudes and correspondences, agreements or disagreements, of several of them one with another; especially where it is to be judged of by long deductions, and the intervention of several other complex ideas to show the agreement or disagreement of two remote ones.

The great help against this which mathematicians find in diagrams and figures, which remain unalterable in their draughts, is very apparent, and the memory would often have great difficulty otherwise to retain them so exactly, whilst the mind went over the parts of them step by step to examine their several correspondences. And though in casting up a long sum either in addition, multiplication, or division, every part be only a progression of the mind taking a view of its own ideas, and considering their agreement or disagreement, and the resolution of the question be nothing but the result of the whole, made up of such particulars, whereof the mind has a clear perception: yet, without setting down the several parts by marks, whose precise significations are known, and by marks that last, and remain in view when the memory had let them go, it would be almost impossible to carry so many different ideas in the mind, without confounding or letting slip some parts of the reckoning, and thereby making all our reasonings about it useless. In which case the cyphers or marks help not the mind at all to perceive the agreement of any two or more numbers, their equalities or proportions; that the mind has only by intuition of its own ideas of the numbers themselves. But the numerical characters are helps to the memory, to record and retain the several ideas about which the demonstration is made, whereby a man may know how far his intuitive knowledge in surveying several of the particulars has proceeded; that so he may without confusion

go on to what is yet unknown; and at last have in one view
before him the result of all his perceptions and reasonings.

20. One part of these disadvantages in moral ideas which
has made them be thought not capable of demonstration, may
in a good measure be remedied by definitions [1], setting down
that collection of simple ideas, which every term shall stand
for; and then using the terms steadily and constantly for that
precise collection. And what methods algebra, or something
of that kind, may hereafter suggest, to remove the other
difficulties, it is not easy to foretel. Confident I am, that,
if men would in the same method, and with the same indifferency, search after moral as they do mathematical truths,
they would find them have a stronger connexion one with
another, and a more necessary consequence from our clear and
distinct ideas, and to come nearer perfect demonstration than
is commonly imagined. But much of this is not to be expected, whilst the desire of esteem, riches, or power makes
men espouse the well-endowed opinions in fashion, and then
seek arguments either to make good their beauty, or varnish
over and cover their deformity. Nothing being so beautiful
to the eye as truth is to the mind; nothing so deformed and
irreconcilable to the understanding as a lie. For though
many a man can with satisfaction enough own a no very
handsome wife in his bosom; yet who is bold enough openly
to avow that he has espoused a falsehood, and received into
his breast so ugly a thing as a lie? Whilst the parties of
men cram their tenets down all men's throats whom they can
get into their power, without permitting them to examine
their truth or falsehood; and will not let truth have fair play
in the world, nor men the liberty to search after it; what
improvements can be expected of this kind? What greater
light can be hoped for in the moral sciences? The subject
part of mankind in most places might, instead thereof, with
Egyptian bondage, expect Egyptian darkness, were not the
candle of the Lord set up by himself in men's minds [2], which

BOOK IV.
—+—
CHAP. III.

Remedies
of our
Difficulties
in dealing
demon-
stratively
with moral
ideas.

---

[1] Cf. Bk. III. ch. xi. §§ 15-18. A
science of morality founded on our
arbitrary definitions of words could be
only a demonstrable science of words.

Locke's examples are all analytical
judgments.

[2] Cf. Introd. § 5; Bk. IV. ch. ii. § 1,
in which he follows Whichcote, in his

BOOK IV.
——◆◆——
CHAP. III.

it is impossible for the breath or power of man wholly to extinguish [1].

Fourthly, Of the three real Existences of which we have certain knowledge.

21. *Fourthly,* As to the fourth sort of our knowledge, viz. of the *real actual existence of things,* we have an intuitive knowledge of *our own existence,* and a demonstrative knowledge of the existence of a *God* : of the existence of *anything else,* we have no other but a sensitive knowledge; which extends not beyond the objects present to our senses [2].

Our Ignorance great.

22. Our knowledge being so narrow, as I have shown, it will perhaps give us some light into the present state of our minds if we look a little into the dark side, and take a view of *our ignorance* ; which, being infinitely larger than our knowledge, may serve much to the quieting of disputes, and improvement of useful knowledge; if, discovering how far we have clear and distinct ideas, we confine our thoughts within the contemplation of those things that are within the reach of our understandings, and launch not out into that abyss of darkness, (where we have not eyes to see, nor faculties to perceive anything), out of a presumption that nothing is

favourite expression, 'the candle of the Lord,' as applied to intuitive and discursive Reason in man.

[1] Cf. Bk. III. ch. xi. §§ 16, 17 ; Bk. IV. ch. xii. § 8. These difficulties, combined with the supreme importance of demonstrating morality, were what led Molyneux to urge Locke (Sept. 1692) to produce a system of demonstrated ethics, as the outcome of these hints. Locke hesitated (Sept. 20, 1692), and in the end declined to make the attempt.

[2] When we remember that almost all the serious doubts and disputes of theologians and philosophers have turned upon the nature and extent of our knowledge of these three 'real existences,' in which the universe, finite or infinite, is for us ultimately consummated, it is strange that in a chapter on the 'extent of human knowledge' Locke should be satisfied with the sentence which constitutes this section. The mysteries which these three ultimate realities of existence involve are the mysteries which, in many subordinate forms, beset human life. They press for consideration more than anything connected with the extent of our knowledge when we reason about the relations of our abstract ideas, or even about the ideas that should be included in our complex ideas of substances, as to which this chapter does little more than repeat preceding statements and arguments in the *Essay.* But the possible 'extent' of a human 'knowledge' of the three realities is touched here and there in the fourth Book—already in ch. ii. § 14 ; afterwards in chh. iv, ix, x, xi, and occasionally, by implication, in chh. v–viii; also in Bk. II. chh. xxiii. and xxvii. § 2.

beyond our comprehension [1]. But to be satisfied of the folly
of such a conceit, we need not go far. He that knows anything, knows this, in the first place, that he need not seek
long for instances of his ignorance. The meanest and most
obvious things that come in our way have dark sides, that
the quickest sight cannot penetrate into. The clearest and
most enlarged understandings of thinking men find themselves
puzzled and at a loss in every particle of matter [2]. We shall
the less wonder to find it so, when we consider the *causes of
our ignorance*; which, from what has been said, I suppose will
be found to be these three :—

First, Want of ideas. Its causes.

Secondly, Want of a discoverable connexion between the
ideas we have.

Thirdly, Want of tracing and examining our ideas.

23. *First,* There are some things, and those not a few, that First, One
Cause of
our
ignorance
Want of
Ideas.
we are ignorant of, for want of ideas.

First, all the simple ideas we have are confined (as I have
shown) to those we receive from corporeal objects by sensation,
and from the operations of our own minds as the objects of I. Want of
simple
ideas that
other
creatures
in other
parts
of the
universe
may have.
reflection. But how much these few and narrow inlets are
disproportionate to the vast whole extent of all beings, will
not be hard to persuade those who are not so foolish as to
think their span the measure of all things. What other simple
ideas it is possible the creatures in other parts of the universe
may have, by the assistance of senses and faculties more or
perfecter than we have, or different from ours, it is not for us
to determine. But to say or think there are no such, because
we conceive nothing of them, is no better an argument than
if a blind man should be positive in it, that there was no such
thing as sight and colours, because he had no manner of idea
of any such thing, nor could by any means frame to himself
any notions about seeing. The ignorance and darkness that

---

[1] Cf. Introd. §§ 5–7.

[2] Ignorance is a necessity in all
conscious intelligence that is short of
Omniscience ; for Omniscience is of
course inconsistent with ignorance,
which cannot be when there can be
nothing more that is knowable. A
sense of ignorance, moreover, presupposes knowledge, or at least probability ; if the second is impossible
the other cannot be without a contradiction. What Locke says in this and
the following sections reminds one of
Glanvill, in his *Scepsis Scientifica.*

is in us no more hinders nor confines the knowledge that is in others, than the blindness of a mole is an argument against the quicksightedness of an eagle. He that will consider the infinite power, wisdom, and goodness of the Creator of all things will find reason to think it was not all laid out upon so inconsiderable, mean, and impotent a creature as he will find man to be; who in all probability is one of the lowest of all intellectual beings. What faculties, therefore, other species of creatures have to penetrate into the nature and inmost constitutions of things; what ideas they may receive of them far different from ours, we know not. This we know and certainly find, that we want several other views of them besides those we have, to make discoveries of them more perfect. And we may be convinced that the ideas we can attain to by our faculties are very disproportionate to things themselves, when a positive, clear, distinct one of substance itself, which is the foundation of all the rest[1], is concealed from us. But want of ideas of this kind, being a part as well as cause of our ignorance, cannot be described. Only this I think I may confidently say of it, That the intellectual and sensible world are in this perfectly alike: that that part which we see of either of them holds no proportion with what we see not; and whatsoever we can reach with our eyes or our thoughts of either of them is but a point, almost nothing in comparison of the rest[2].

---

[1] Cf. Bk. II. ch. xxiii; Bk. III. ch. vi. Locke not only finds 'complex ideas of substances,' but recognises the abstract idea of substance as at the foundation of our ideas of what actually exists; although the idea becomes unimaginable when we try to abstract from all particular substances. But he seems to look for substance otherwise than in its presented qualities,—as a superadded imperceptible *quality*, as Berkeley sarcastically suggests.

[2] The knowledge of things in any human experience must thus be relative to—dependent on—the ideas or appearances which the things happen to present to us. These appearances are, we may infer, indefinitely short of what might be revealed to beings endowed with more powerful senses; or with other sorts of senses than ours. In what qualities would matter appear to a being destitute of *all* the senses which man possesses, but endowed with five (or five hundred) *other sorts* of senses, each presenting phenomena (simple ideas) as inconceivable by man as colour is inconceivable by the born blind? Voltaire supplies a pleasing illustration in his *Micromegas*. Man himself, in another organism, might be thus recipient of ideas that are unpresentable through his present grosser

24. Secondly, Another great cause of ignorance is the want of ideas we are capable of[1]. As the want of ideas which our faculties are not able to give us shuts us wholly from those views of things which it is reasonable to think other beings, perfecter than we, have, of which we know nothing; so the want of ideas I now speak of keeps us in ignorance of things we conceive capable of being known to us. Bulk, figure, and motion we have ideas of. But though we are not without ideas of these primary qualities of bodies in general, yet not knowing what is the particular bulk, figure, and motion, of the greatest part of the bodies of the universe[2], we are ignorant of the several powers, efficacies, and ways of operation, whereby the effects which we daily see are produced. These are hid from us, in some things by being too remote, and in others by being too minute. When we consider the vast distance of the known and visible parts of the world, and the reasons we have to think that what lies within our ken is but a small part of the universe, we shall then discover a huge abyss of ignorance. What are the particular fabrics of the great masses of matter which make up the whole stupendous frame of corporeal beings; how far they are extended; what is their motion, and how continued or communicated; and what influence they have one upon another, are contemplations that at first glimpse our thoughts lose themselves in. If we narrow our contemplations, and confine our thoughts to this little canton—I mean this system of our sun, and the grosser masses of matter that visibly move about it, What several sorts of vegetables, animals, and intellectual corporeal beings, infinitely different from those of our little spot of earth, may there probably be in the other planets, to the knowledge of

---

senses—ideas of matter differing from the present data of sense in kind and not merely in degree—as foreign to his present experience as colour to the born blind; or intensified in the case of his present senses to a degree that is faintly illustrated by the most powerful telescope and microscope.

[1] Our want of what might be called *telescopic* and *microscopic* power, in the senses that we have, is the cause of our ignorance that is illustrated in this and the next section.

[2] Here again we have his favourite atomic hypothesis which runs through all in the *Essay* that is concerned with the qualities and (so-called) 'powers' of material substances, and (akin to this) with their real as distinguished from our nominal essences.

BOOK IV.

CHAP. III.

which, even of their outward figures and parts, we can no way attain whilst we are confined to this earth; there being no natural means, either by sensation or reflection, to convey their certain ideas into our minds? They are out of the reach of those inlets of all our knowledge[1]: and what sorts of furniture and inhabitants those mansions contain in them we cannot so much as guess, much less have clear and distinct ideas of them.

(2) Because of their Minuteness.

25. If a great, nay, far the greatest part of the several ranks of bodies in the universe escape our notice by their remoteness, there are others that are no less concealed from us by their minuteness. These *insensible corpuscles*, being the active parts of matter, and the great instruments of nature, on which depend not only all their secondary qualities, but also most of their natural operations, our want of precise distinct ideas of their primary qualities keeps us in an incurable ignorance of what we desire to know about them. I doubt not but if we could discover the figure, size, texture, and motion of the minute constituent parts of any two bodies, we should know without trial several of their operations one upon another; as we do now the properties of a square or a triangle[2]. Did we know the mechanical affections of the particles of rhubarb, hemlock, opium, and a man, as a watchmaker does those of a watch, whereby it performs its operations; and of a file, which by rubbing on them will alter the figure of any of the wheels; we should be able to tell beforehand that rhubarb will purge, hemlock kill, and opium make a man sleep: as well as a watchmaker can, that a little piece of paper laid on the balance will keep the watch from going till it be removed; or that, some small part of it

---

[1] Because the distance of other planets from this one is a bar to our receiving simple ideas which in other circumstances we might, with our present senses, receive from the things the other planets contain.

[2] Once more the hypothesis of a real atomic essence in material substances, —in this section in a manner, and with illustrations which remind us of Bacon's anticipation of future mastery of things, in a knowledge of their forms, under a reformed method of research. See the opening aphorisms of the Second Book of the *Novum Organum*, with Dr. Fowler's valuable annotations. Locke's conclusion, here and elsewhere, throws cold water on the high ideal and hopes of Bacon.

being rubbed by a file, the machine would quite lose its BOOK IV

motion, and the watch go no more. The dissolving of silver CHAP. III.

in *aqua fortis*, and gold in *aqua regia*, and not *vice versâ*, would be then perhaps no more difficult to know than it is to a smith to understand why the turning of one key will open a lock, and not the turning of another[1]. But whilst we are destitute of senses acute enough to discover the minute particles of bodies, and to give us ideas of their mechanical affections, we must be content to be ignorant of their properties and ways of operation; nor can we be assured about them any further than some few trials we make are able to reach. But whether they will succeed again another time, we cannot be certain[2]. This hinders our certain knowledge of universal truths concerning natural bodies[3] : and our reason carries us herein very little beyond particular matter of fact.

26. And therefore I am apt to doubt that, how far soever Hence no

human industry may advance useful and experimental philo- Science of Bodies

sophy in physical things, *scientifical* will still be out of our within our reach.

---

[1] It is this ideal that Bacon seems to have in view, but without Locke's recognition of man's inability to realise it in human science.

[2] Physical experiments, depending as they all do on identity of conditions, may at any time be disturbed by the operation of (by us) unknown, and therefore incalculable powers. The sudden annihilation of the solar system, against which man has no certain guarantee, would defeat our scientific previsions of particular events, e. g. eclipses of sun and moon, rise and fall of tides, &c., our belief in which wants the unconditional certainty that is essential to knowledge, in Locke's meaning of knowledge.

[3] While he thus disclaims for man, and argues for the impossibility of, physical knowledge, in the sense of absolute certainty and universality in our forecasts of events, he recognises practical probability as often within our reach. He transfers what is now called *science* to the sphere of *probability*.

It is only 'probable' that all men will die, or that the sun will rise to-morrow; although the probability in these cases amounts to proof. In part this is a question about words. 'To conform our language more to common use [than Locke does] we ought to divide arguments into *demonstrations, proofs,* and *probabilities*—by proofs meaning such arguments from experience as leave no room for doubt or opposition.' (Hume.) Physics takes the appearance of a body of absolutely certain conclusions, because our premises assume that the forces with which we are concerned are absolutely constant, and also that the conditions under which they operate are absolutely known to the physical reasoner. Yet the whole fabric is in the end sustained by an act of faith, as much as in any theological or metaphysical conclusion. The main argument in Mr. Balfour's *Defence of Philosophic Doubt* is a subtle vindication of this position.

reach : because we want perfect and adequate ideas of those very bodies which are nearest to us, and most under our command. Those which we have ranked into classes under names, and we think ourselves best acquainted with, we have but very imperfect and incomplete ideas of. Distinct ideas of the several sorts of bodies that fall under the examination of our senses perhaps we may have: but adequate ideas, I suspect, we have not of any one amongst them. And though the former of these will serve us for common use and discourse, yet whilst we want the latter, we are not capable of scientifical knowledge ; nor shall ever be able to discover general, instructive, unquestionable truths concerning them. *Certainty* and *demonstration* are things we must not, in these matters, pretend to. By the colour, figure, taste, and smell, and other sensible qualities, we have as clear and distinct ideas of sage and hemlock, as we have of a circle and a triangle: but having no ideas of the particular primary qualities of the minute parts of either of these plants, nor of other bodies which we would apply them to, we cannot tell what effects they will produce ; nor when we see those effects can we so much as guess, much less know, their manner of production. Thus, having no ideas of the particular mechanical affections of the minute parts of bodies that are within our view and reach, we are ignorant of their constitutions, powers, and operations: and of bodies more remote we are yet more ignorant, not knowing so much as their very outward shapes, or the sensible and grosser parts of their constitutions[1].

Much less a science of unembodied Spirits.

27. This at first will show us how disproportionate our knowledge is to the whole extent even of material beings ; to which if we add the consideration of that infinite number of spirits that may be, and probably are, which are yet more remote from our knowledge, whereof we have no cognizance, nor can frame to ourselves any distinct ideas of their several ranks and sorts, we shall find this cause of ignorance conceal from us, in an impenetrable obscurity, almost the whole

---

[1] An unconditionally demonstrable physical science presupposes Omniscience. Short of this there must always remain that horizon of mysteries, in regard to the powers actually and hereafter at work in the universe, and their collocation, which bar the possibility of demonstration.

intellectual world; a greater certainly, and more beautiful world than the material[1]. For, bating some very few, and those, if I may so call them, superficial ideas of spirit, which by reflection we get of our own[2], and from thence the best we can collect of the Father of all spirits, the eternal independent Author of them, and us, and all things, we have no certain information, so much as of the existence of other spirits[3], but by revelation. Angels of all sorts are naturally beyond our discovery; and all those intelligences, whereof it is likely there are more orders than of corporeal substances, are things whereof our natural faculties give us no certain account at all. That there are minds and thinking beings in other men as well as himself, every man has a reason, from their words and actions, to be satisfied: and the knowledge of his own mind cannot suffer a man that considers, to be ignorant that there is a God[4]. But that there are degrees of spiritual beings between us and the great God, who is there, that, by his own search and ability, can come to know? Much less have we

---

[1] It is impossible, Stillingfleet argues, that we can ever know this, if knowledge implies having ideas of that which is known, as Locke says it does; for he asserts that we 'can have *no* ideas of the world of spirits.' Locke replies that 'if God, instead of showing the very things to St. Paul, only revealed to him that there *were* things in heaven which " neither eye had seen, nor ear heard, nor had it entered into the heart of man to conceive," would he not have *known* the truth of that proposition of whose terms he *had* ideas, viz. of *being* (whereof he had no ideas but barely as something), and the idea of *existence*; though, in the want of any other ideas of them, he could attain no other knowledge of them but barely *that they existed*?'

[2] Locke gives no account in this chapter of the 'extent' of the knowledge each man can get of his own spirit, through his simple ideas of reflection. For he considers exclusively the extent of that knowledge of sub-stances which belongs to ideas of external sensation.

[3] 'other spirits,' i.e. angels or unembodied spirits; for the existence of other *men* is discovered by each man independently of what Locke means by 'revelation,' as he tells us in what follows.

[4] Locke distinguishes the belief we have in the existence of other men, as 'thinking beings,' from our demonstrable knowledge of the existence of the Eternal Mind, which is the express subject of the tenth chapter of this Book. He hardly touches the foundation of the belief, although here he refers it vaguely to analogy. That one may be said to 'see' God in the same way that we are said to see 'thinking beings' in other men, i.e. by signs of which we are visually percipient, was Berkeley's argument for converting his new theory of vision into the theory of a Divine Visual Language presented in the phenomena of sight.

BOOK IV.

CHAP. III.

distinct ideas of their different natures, conditions, states, powers, and several constitutions wherein they agree or differ from one another and from us. And, therefore, in what concerns their different species and properties we are in absolute ignorance.

Secondly, Another cause, Want of a discoverable Connexion between Ideas we have.

28. *Secondly*, What a small part of the substantial beings that are in the universe the want of ideas leaves open to our knowledge, we have seen. In the next place, another cause of ignorance, of no less moment, is a want of a discoverable connection[1] between those ideas we have. For wherever we want that, we are utterly incapable of universal and certain knowledge; and are, in the former case, left only to observation and experiment: which, how narrow and confined it is, how far from general knowledge we need not be told[2]. I shall give some few instances of this cause of our ignorance, and so leave it. It is evident that the bulk, figure, and motion of several bodies about us produce in us several sensations, as of colours, sounds, tastes, smells, pleasure, and pain, &c. These mechanical affections of bodies having no affinity at all with those ideas they produce in us, (there being no conceivable connexion between any impulse of any sort of body and any perception of a colour or smell which we find in our minds,) we can have no distinct knowledge of such operations beyond our experience; and can reason no otherwise about them, than as effects produced by the appointment of an infinitely Wise Agent, which perfectly surpass our comprehensions. As the ideas of sensible secondary qualities which we have in our minds, can by us be no way deduced from bodily causes, nor any correspondence or connexion be found between them and those primary qualities[3] which (experience shows us[4]) produce

---

[1] 'connexion,' i. e. *necessary* connexion, implied in the real essence, or ultimate physical constitution of the things themselves, which 'natural philosophy,' when it pretends to unconditional demonstration, assumes that it has, regarding the powers by which changes in nature are determined.

[2] 'observation and experiment' can compass only 'some': general knowledge, or abstract science, presupposes a necessary and universal judgment regarding 'all.'

[3] Once more we have the favourite doctrine of Locke's cosmological philosophy.

[4] Because they are dependent on the (by us) incalculable contingencies of experience, propositions of this

them in us ; so, on the other side, the operation of our minds BOOK IV.
upon our bodies is as inconceivable. How any thought should ⸺⸺
produce a motion in body is as remote from the nature of our CHAP. III.
ideas, as how any body should produce any thought in the
mind. That it is so, if experience did not convince us[1], the
consideration of the things themselves[2] would never be able
in the least to discover to us. These, and the like, though
they have a constant and regular connexion in the ordinary
course of things ; yet that connexion being not discoverable in
the ideas themselves, which appearing to have no necessary
dependence one on another, we can attribute their connexion
to nothing else but the arbitrary determination of that
All-wise Agent who has made them to be, and to operate
as they do, in a way wholly above our weak understandings to
conceive.

29. In some of our ideas there are certain relations, habitudes, Instances.
and connexions, so visibly included in the nature of the ideas
themselves[3], that we cannot conceive them separable from
them by any power whatsoever. And in these only we are
capable of certain and universal knowledge. Thus the idea of
a right-lined triangle necessarily carries with it an equality of

---

sort must be wanting in that 'intuition'
on which ' rests all the certainty and
evidence of our knowledge.' (Ch. ii.
§ 1.) Till experience can evoke this
intuition, and thus fully reveal its own
rational constitution, it can afford only
a more or less probable presumption,
not absolute knowledge or science.
Because the simple ideas that happen
to arise in our sense-experience are
needed to evoke the intuition of certainty, and thus limit the application of
the intuition, knowledge may be said
to have its ' origin ' in experience ; but
the data of sense fail to awaken an
intuitive knowledge of that on which
the coexistences and sequences of
nature depend, so that here we cannot go beyond the data themselves
except on the path of probability.

[1] 'convince us,' i. e. inasmuch as it
presents the actual fact.

[2] ' the consideration of things,'
a priori, independently of what in
experience we find their coexistences
and sequences to be and to have been.
But we have no intuitive knowledge
of *all* the causes by which changes
are determined. The known or unknown forces at work in the universe
may supersede the subordinate ' laws '
that are alone discoverable by us,
unless finite human experience is itself
superseded by Omniscience.

[3] He finds *necessary* connexions that
are intellectually visible between some
of our ideas, e. g. abstract ideas of
quantity ; while no intellectual necessity is (by us) discernible as immanent
in the coexistences and sequences of
natural phenomena. In them the
necessity that ' knowledge ' requires
lies too deep for us to reach.

its angles to two right ones. Nor can we conceive this relation, this connexion of these two ideas, to be possibly mutable, or to depend on any arbitrary[1] power, which of choice made it thus, or could make it otherwise. But the coherence and continuity of the parts of matter ; the production of sensation in us of colours and sounds, &c., by impulse and motion ; nay, the original rules and communication of motion being such, wherein we can discover no natural connexion with any ideas we have, we cannot but ascribe them to the arbitrary will and good pleasure of the Wise Architect. I need not, I think, here mention the resurrection of the dead, the future state of this globe of earth, and such other things, which are by every one acknowledged to depend wholly on the determination of a free agent. The things that, as far as our observation reaches, we constantly find to proceed regularly, we may conclude do act by a law set them ; but yet by a law that we know not: whereby, though causes work steadily, and effects constantly flow from them, yet their connexions and dependencies being not discoverable in our ideas, we can have but an experimental knowledge of them[2]. From all which it is easy to perceive what a darkness we are involved in, how little it is of Being, and the things that are, that we are capable to know. And therefore we shall do no injury to our knowledge, when we modestly think with ourselves, that we are so far from being able to comprehend the whole nature of the universe, and all the things contained in it, that we are not capable of a philosophical knowledge of the bodies that are about us, and make a part of us: concerning their secondary qualities, powers, and operations, we can have no universal certainty. Several effects come every day within the notice of our senses, of which we have so far sensitive knowledge : but the causes, manner, and certainty of their production, for the two foregoing reasons, we must be content to be very ignorant

[1] This 'arbitrariness' (at the human point of view) of the constitution and laws of nature is Berkeley's favourite ground for recognising the constant supremacy of active Reason in the universe, and for seeing, in all the coexistences and sequences of nature, the language of the Eternal Mind addressed to finite intelligence.

[2] In Locke's strict meaning of 'knowledge,' 'experimental knowledge' is confined to the particular experiment or experiments.

of. In these we can go no further than particular experience informs us of matter of fact, and by analogy to guess[1] what effects the like bodies are, upon other trials, like to produce. But as to a *perfect science* of natural bodies, (not to mention spiritual beings,) we are, I think, so far from being capable of any such thing, that I conclude it lost labour to seek after it[2].

30. *Thirdly*, Where we have adequate ideas, and where there is a certain and discoverable connexion between them, yet we are often ignorant, for want of tracing those ideas which we have or may have; and for want of finding out those intermediate ideas, which may show us what habitude of agreement or disagreement they have one with another. And thus many are ignorant of mathematical truths, not out of any imperfection of their faculties, or uncertainty in the things themselves, but for want of application in acquiring, examining, and by due ways comparing those ideas. That which has most contributed to hinder the due tracing of our ideas, and finding out their relations, and agreements or disagreements, one with another, has been, I suppose, the ill use of words[3]. It is impossible that men should ever truly seek or certainly discover the agreement or disagreement of ideas themselves, whilst their thoughts flutter about, or stick only in sounds of doubtful and uncertain significations. Mathematicians abstracting their thoughts from names, and accustoming themselves to set before their minds the ideas themselves that they would consider, and not sounds instead of them, have avoided thereby a great part of that perplexity, puddering[4], and confusion, which has so much hindered men's progress in other parts of knowledge. For whilst they stick in words of undetermined and uncertain signification, they are unable to distinguish true from false, certain from probable, consistent from inconsistent, in their own opinions. This having been the fate or misfortune of a great part of men of letters, the increase brought

Thirdly,
A third
cause,
Want of
Tracing
our Ideas.

---

[1] Physical science is therefore throughout hypothetical. All *mixed* mathematics is only hypothetically true.

[2] As Bacon nevertheless encouraged men to do, when he invited them to search for the 'forms' of things; and Descartes too, in his attempts to frame a consistent and necessarily connected system of mechanical philosophy.

[3] See Bk. III. chh. ix, x.

[4] 'puddering'—pothering—puzzling.

BOOK IV.
CHAP. III.

into the stock of real knowledge has been very little, in proportion to the schools disputes, and writings, the world has been filled with ; whilst students, being lost in the great wood of words[1], knew not whereabouts they were, how far their discoveries were advanced, or what was wanting in their own, or the general stock of knowledge. Had men, in the discoveries of the material, done as they have in those of the intellectual world, involved all in the obscurity of uncertain and doubtful ways of talking, volumes writ of navigation and voyages, theories and stories of zones and tides, multiplied and disputed ; nay, ships built, and fleets sent out, would never have taught us the way beyond the line ; and the Antipodes would be still as much unknown, as when it was declared heresy to hold there were any. But having spoken sufficiently of words, and the ill or careless use that is commonly made of them[2], I shall not say anything more of it here.

Extent of Human Knowledge in respect to its Universality.

31. Hitherto we have examined the extent of our knowledge, in respect of the several sorts of beings that are. There is another extent of it, in respect of *universality*, which will also deserve to be considered ; and in this regard, our knowledge follows the nature of our ideas. If the ideas are abstract, whose agreement or disagreement we perceive, our knowledge is universal. For what is known of such general ideas, will be true of every particular thing in whom that essence, i. e. that abstract idea, is to be found : and what is once known of such ideas, will be perpetually and for ever true. So that as to all *general knowledge* we must search and find it only in our minds ; and it is only the examining of our own ideas[3] that furnisheth us with that. Truths belonging to essences of things (that is, to abstract ideas) are eternal ; and are to be found out by the contemplation only of those

---

[1] 'The curtain of words'—as Berkeley calls it, in proposing as a remedy, that we should attend to 'the ideas signified, and draw off our attention from the words which signify them,' directing it to concrete examples of their meaning, i. e. that we should 'individualise our concepts,' separating them from their verbal signs. See *Principles*, Introd. §§ 23–25.

[2] In Bk. III.

[3] 'our own ideas'—i. e. our abstract ideas, signified by abstract terms, the meaning or nominal essence of which may be perfectly known.

essences : as the existence of things is to be known only from BOOK IV.
experience [1]. But having more to say of this in the chapters [2]
where I shall speak of general and real knowledge, this CHAP. III.
may here suffice as to the universality of our knowledge in
general [3].

[1] Does this section imply that only (so-called) analytical or explicative judgments can be known by man to be 'necessarily and universally true,'— that all synthetical judgments depend upon probability? Here Kant's question rises—Can synthetical judgments in any instance be necessary and universal, consistently with the limits of human experience, and the conditions of human thought?

[2] Bk. IV. chh. v–viii.

[3] All the knowledge that man can have is thus, according to Locke, of *substances* (material and spiritual); abstract *modes* ; and *relations.* As to particular substances it is limited to their actual manifestations in the senses and in self-consciousness, including memory—except God only, who is demonstrably known; of modes it may be universally true ; of abstract relations, the widest field of all, it is difficult to determine how far it may extend.

CHAPTER IV.

OF THE REALITY OF KNOWLEDGE [1].

BOOK IV.

CHAP. IV.
Objection.
'Know-
ledge
placed in
our Ideas
may be all
unreal or
chimerical.'

1. I DOUBT not but my reader, by this time, may be apt to think that I have been all this while only building a castle in the air ; and be ready to say to me :—

'To what purpose all this stir ? Knowledge, say you, is only the perception of the agreement or disagreement of our own ideas : but who knows what those ideas may be ? Is there anything so extravagant as the imaginations of men's brains ? Where is the head that has no chimeras in it ? Or if there be a sober and a wise man, what difference will there be, by your rules, between his knowledge and that of the most

[1] This chapter above all in the *Essay* was that which Berkeley, in early life, resolved to 'discuss nicely.' (*Commonplace Book*, p. 435.) The philosophical enterprise in which he engaged began in an attempt to determine what we should mean when we predicate 'reality' of the things of sense ; and whether we could in reason suppose actual reality if there were no percipient or self-conscious mind to sustain it. He complains of Locke's lax use of the terms 'existence' and 'reality.' 'Existence,' according to the *Essay*, is 'a simple idea, suggested to the understanding by every object without, and every idea within.' Locke gives no express account of the nature and origin of the idea we should have when we use the word 'reality.' So far this can be gathered, e. g. from Bk. II. ch. xxx ; also ch. viii, where we are told that the simple ideas or qualities in bodies that are otherwise called primary may be also called *real*, because 'they really exist in those bodies'; from the numerous passages about *real* essences ; and from this chapter itself, taken in connection with chh. ix, x, xi which follow —abruptly separated from this one by those which treat of the truth of universal propositions, maxims, and verbal propositions (v, vi, vii, viii). He tells us that in all 'real' knowledge the ideas that are known 'must answer their archetypes,' but that some of our ideas are their own archetypes, being only subjectively real, and made by man, whilst the archetypes of others can by no means be made by men, but exist as things, independently of the will of man, and imperfectly comprehended by the human understanding.

extravagant fancy in the world? They both have their ideas, BOOK IV.
and perceive their agreement and disagreement one with
another. If there be any difference between them, the C<small>HAP.</small> IV.
advantage will be on the warm-headed man's side, as having
the more ideas, and the more lively [1]. And so, by your rules,
he will be the more knowing. If it be true, that all knowledge
lies only in the perception of the agreement or disagreement of
our own ideas, the visions of an enthusiast and the reasonings
of a sober man will be equally certain. It is no matter how
things are : so a man observe but the agreement of his own
imaginations, and talk conformably, it is all truth, all certainty.
Such castles in the air [2] will be as strongholds of truth, as the
demonstrations of Euclid. That an harpy is not a centaur is
by this way as certain knowledge, and as much a truth, as
that a square is not a circle.

' But of what use is all this fine knowledge of *men's own
imaginations,* to a man that inquires after the reality of things?
It matters not what men's fancies are, it is the knowledge of
things that is only to be prized : it is this alone gives a value
to our reasonings, and preference to one man's knowledge
over another's, that it is of things as they really are, and not
of dreams and fancies [3].'

2. To which I answer, That if our knowledge of our ideas Answer.
terminate in them, and reach no further, where there is some-

---

[1] Hume afterwards made their superior 'liveliness' or 'vivacity' the distinguishing character of the impressions of sense, in contrast to our ideas of memory and imagination.

[2] 'castles in the air.' Cf. Bk. I. ch. iii. § 25.

[3] Modern thought, inaugurated by the tentative doubt of Descartes, and re-inaugurated by the criticism of human knowledge shared in, at opposite points of view, by Locke and Kant, is in antithesis to the ages of faith in authority, which preceded, and by reaction produced it. By abstracting ideas from the substances of which they are the appearances, the question of their reality was raised, and the certainty of knowledge seemed to be suspended in doubt, without absolute security that the whole might not be a passing hollow show in which things are only transitory appearances. A more thorough scepticism than in the foregoing sentences soon found expression in Hume, demanding a deeper inquiry into the ultimate constitution of human knowledge and belief than that offered by Locke in this chapter.

Doubt, it must be remembered, is a necessary preliminary to, and accompaniment of, reasonable progressive knowledge; and it is always restrained in the end by forces that unconsciously influence every human mind, and to which in the sequel Locke appeals.

BOOK IV.

CHAP. IV.

Not so, where Ideas agree with Things.

thing further intended [1], our most serious thoughts will be of little more use than the reveries of a crazy brain ; and the truths built thereon of no more weight than the discourses of a man who sees things clearly in a dream, and with great assurance utters them. But I hope, before I have done, to make it evident, that this way of certainty, by the knowledge of our own ideas, goes a little further than bare imagination [2] : and I believe it will appear that all the certainty of general truths a man has lies in nothing else [3].

But what shall be the criterion of this agreement?

3. It is evident the mind knows not things immediately, but only by the intervention of the ideas it has of them [4]. Our knowledge, therefore, is real only so far as there is a *conformity* between our ideas and the reality of things. But what shall be here the criterion? How shall the mind, when it perceives nothing but its own ideas, know that they agree with things themselves? This, though it seems not to want

---

[1] 'something further intended.' As there is, he would say, in the case of all ' simple ideas,' and of ' our complex ideas of substances,' when ideas of either of these two sorts are sought to be known, or truly interpreted; for in neither of these does our knowledge terminate in the ideas themselves regarded *per se.*

[2] It is Locke's ' way of certainty by ideas ' that Stillingfleet, on the ground that scepticism is latent in it, persistently contrasts with ' the way of certainty by reason.' As to which Locke replies, that ' this is nothing against anything I have said ; for I have neither said nor suppose that certainty by reason can be had without ideas ; no more than I say, or suppose, that we can reason without thinking, or think without immediate objects of our minds in thinking, i. e. without ideas. We must have ideas as far as we are certain, and beyond that we have neither certainty nor probability ; everything which we know or believe is some proposition ; and no proposition can be framed wherein two ideas are not joined to, or separated from,

one another.' (Third *Letter,* p. 245.)

[3] Cf. ch. iii. § 31.

[4] This postulate, according to Reid, and in his interpretation of it, is the germ of modern philosophical scepticism. See his *Inquiry,* ' Introduction'; cf. Hume's *Inquiry,* sect. xii, and Hamilton's *Discussions,* II. So-called knowledge that is throughout and ultimately concerned with representative ideas must, it is argued, be radically uncertain, and can never rise into real knowledge, because never face to face with reality. Hence Reid's dogmatic rejection of an ultimately representative perception, and his assumption, in the name of common sense, that we perceive things in the senses without ideas. But Locke's 'simple ideas of sense and reflection ' are the phenomena in which things and our own mind manifest themselves, and without being somehow manifested, things cannot be perceived. But, as already remarked, Locke often uses language which suggests that their simple ideas or phenomena conceal the substances, material and spiritual, which in fact they in part reveal.

difficulty [1], yet, I think, there be two sorts of ideas that we may be assured agree with things.

4. *First,* The first are simple ideas, which since the mind, as has been showed, can by no means make to itself, must necessarily be the product of things operating on the mind, in a natural way, and producing therein those perceptions which by the Wisdom and Will of our Maker they are ordained and adapted to. From whence it follows, that simple ideas are not fictions of our fancies, but the natural and regular productions of things without us, really operating upon us ; and so carry with them all the conformity which is intended ; or which our state requires : for they represent to us things under those appearances which they are fitted to produce in us : whereby we are enabled to distinguish the sorts of particular substances, to discern the states they are in, and so

---

[1] This ' difficulty ' may be expressed in terms of Locke's own definition of knowledge or certainty. (Ch. i. § 2.) How, it is asked, can it be said that knowledge of real existence is perception of the agreement of an *idea* with *a really existing object,* if knowledge must be perception of the agreement of one idea with another idea, unless the ' real object ' is itself an idea, as Berkeley argued that it must be ? Either the real thing is imperceptible, or it must be an idea, since it is impossible ever to get behind ideas, and perceive the things they hypothetically represent : reality cannot consist in the relation of our ideas to that which is not idea, but in the special characteristics and relations of certain of our ideas among themselves. ' Only if real existence were itself an idea,' Green accordingly argues, ' would the consciousness or assurance of the agreement of the idea with it be a case of knowledge ; but to make existence an idea is to make the whole question about the agreement of *ideas as such* with *existence as such* unmeaning. There can be no perception nor assurance of an agreement between an idea and what is not an object of consciousness at all. The question cannot be answered unless existence is, and is given in an object of consciousness, i. e. an idea.' (Introduction to Hume, § 59.) Locke's own interpretation of his definitions of knowledge in general, and of knowledge of real existence, is —that all knowledge is (mental) proposition ; and that no proposition can be formed as the object either of knowledge or assent, in which two ideas are not either united or separated. ' Hence, when I affirm that *something exists whereof I have no idea,* " existence " is affirmed of something, some being ; and I have as clear an idea of *existence* and *something,* the two things joined in that proposition, as I have of them in this proposition, *something exists in the world whereof I have an idea.*' (Third *Letter* to Stillingfleet, p. 246.) When we either know or believe that something really exists, the complex idea of real existence is the predicate, and the idea of which it is predicated is therein judged to be a manifestation of something that really exists. In this Leibniz concurs with Locke.

BOOK IV.

CHAP. IV.

to take them for our necessities, and apply them to our uses. Thus the idea of whiteness, or bitterness, as it is in the mind, exactly answering that power which is in any body to produce it there, has all the real conformity it can or ought to have, with things without us. And this conformity between our simple ideas and the existence of things [1], is sufficient for real knowledge.

Secondly, All Complex Ideas, except ideas of Substances, are their own archetypes.

5. *Secondly*, All our complex ideas, *except those of substances* [2], being archetypes of the mind's own making, not intended to be the copies of anything, nor referred to the existence of anything, as to their originals, cannot want any conformity necessary to real knowledge. For that which is not designed to represent anything but itself, can never be capable of a wrong representation, nor mislead us from the true apprehension of anything, by its dislikeness to it: and such, excepting those of substances [2], are all our complex

---

[1] In this section, as in ch. ii. § 14, we are referred to ground in reason for the assumption made throughout the *Essay* that the reception or presentation of simple ideas in our senses presupposes the real existence of things to which they conform, or which they manifest in the form of living knowledge. The validity of this assumption is more fully considered afterwards in ch. xi, and in regard to self-consciousness and simple ideas of reflection in ch. ix. This perception of the existence of things and of our own existence thus involving a spontaneous judgment of the reality of what is perceived when there is consciousness of receiving simple ideas, involves more than empirical data of sense. ' Notre certitude,' says Leibniz, ' serait petite et plutôt nulle, si elle n'avait point d'autre fondement des idées simples, que celui qui vient des sens. Les idées des qualités sensibles nous viennent des sens, c'est-à-dire, de nos perceptions confuses. Et le fondement de la vérité des choses contingentes et singulaires est *dans le*

succès, qui fait que les phénomènes des sens sont liés *justement comme les vérités intelligibles le demandent*. Voilà la différence qu'on y doit faire ; au lieu que celle que l'auteur fait entre les idées simples et composées et idées composées appartenant aux substances et aux accidents ne me paraît point fondée, puisque toutes les idées intelligibles ont leur archétypes dans la possibilité éternelle des choses.' (*Nouveaux Essais.*) In speaking of 'material things operating on the mind,' Locke loses sight of what he had said (Bk. II. ch. xxi . § 2) about material substances having no active power, and he does not refer to the ' real qualities ' of sensible things.

[2] Locke's inquiry about the reality of knowledge centres in our knowledge of substances — through the simple ideas or phenomena in which they are actually manifested; relations of co-existence and succession with unperceived ideas in the same substance ; and as the three realities in which all our concrete knowledge of what exists is found at last to terminate.

ideas. Which, as I have showed in another place [1], are combinations of ideas, which the mind, by its free choice [2], puts together, without considering any connexion they have in nature. And hence it is, that in all these sorts the ideas themselves are considered as the archetypes, and things no otherwise regarded, but as they are conformable to them. So that we cannot but be infallibly certain, that all the knowledge we attain concerning these ideas is real, and reaches things themselves. Because in all our thoughts, reasonings, and discourses of this kind, we intend things no further than as they are conformable to our ideas. So that in these we cannot miss of a certain and undoubted reality.

6. I doubt not but it will be easily granted, that the knowledge we have of mathematical truths is not only certain, but real knowledge ; and not the bare empty vision of vain, insignificant chimeras of the brain: and yet, if we will consider, we shall find that it is only of our own ideas. The mathematician considers the truth and properties belonging to a rectangle or circle only as they are in idea in his own mind. For it is possible he never found either of them existing mathematically, i. e. precisely true, in his life. But yet the knowledge he has of any truths or properties belonging to a circle, or any other mathematical figure, are nevertheless true and certain, even of real things existing : because real things are no further concerned, nor intended to be meant by any such propositions, than as things really agree to those archetypes in his mind. Is it true of the *idea* of a triangle, that its three angles are equal to two right ones? It is true also of a triangle, wherever it *really exists*. Whatever other figure exists, that it is not exactly answerable to that idea of a triangle in his mind, is not at all concerned in that proposition. And therefore he is certain all his knowledge concerning

---

[1] Cf. Bk. III. ch. v, in which it is argued that all abstract ideas are arbitrarily elaborated by the human understanding, so that in themselves they can be fully known, as creatures of our own understanding, and as, outside themselves, they have no archetypes.

[2] Are there no deeper truths of reason by which even abstract ideas must be ultimately determined, whatever our 'free choice' may be, and still 'without considering any connexion they have in nature?'

BOOK IV.

CHAP. IV.

such ideas is real knowledge : because, intending things no further than they agree with those his ideas, he is sure what he knows concerning those figures, when they have *barely an ideal existence* in his mind, will hold true of them also when they have *a real existence* in matter : his consideration being barely of those figures, which are the same wherever or however they exist [1].

And of Moral.

7. And hence it follows that moral knowledge is as capable of real certainty as mathematics. For certainty being but the perception of the agreement or disagreement of our ideas, and demonstration nothing but the perception of such agreement, by the intervention of other ideas or mediums ; our moral ideas, as well as mathematical, being archetypes themselves, and so adequate and complete ideas [2] ; all the agreement or disagreement which we shall find in them will produce real knowledge, as well as in mathematical figures.

Existence not re-

8. [[3] For the attaining of knowledge and certainty, it is

---

[1] This would resolve pure mathematics into a body of purely analytical knowledge. The recognition of its premises and conclusions as what are now called judgments synthetical and yet *a priori* is foreign to Locke even when he virtually proceeds upon it. General propositions and reasonings are in his view either *a priori* analytical or *a posteriori* synthetical—our certainties consisting of the former and our probabilities of the latter, when in either we pass beyond individual facts.

[2] It is thus only abstract morality, as it is abstract mathematics, in which the archetypes are independent of the contingencies of experience, that Locke asserts to be absolutely certain, and demonstrable *a priori* — like mathematics, too, only a body of analytical knowledge, if we interpret his language and methods strictly, and remember that those of Kant cannot be read into them without an anachronism. But in each he acknowledges a perception of *special* relations, which might imply that neither is a body of merely verbal

reasoning, founded upon arbitrary definitions of words. Cf. § 9, and note.

[3] In first three editions—'That which is requisite to make knowledge certain is the clearness of our ideas.' This is one of the passages produced by Stillingfleet to prove that Locke made 'clear and distinct' ideas necessary to certainty; thus denying by implication that we are certain of any proposition that is obscure or mysterious. In disavowing this meaning, in this and cognate passages, he promised to change the words in which it was expressed, explaining that 'the certainty here spoken of is the certainty of *general* propositions in morality, and not of the particular existence of anything; and therefore tends not at all to any such position as this,—That we cannot be certain of the existence of any particular sort of being, though we have but an obscure and confused idea of it. . . Thus the idea of *substance* is clear and distinct enough to have its agreement with that of *actual existence* perceived ;

requisite that we have determined ideas :] and, to make our BOOK IV.
knowledge real, it is requisite that the ideas answer their
archetypes [1].   Nor let it be wondered, that I place the
certainty of our knowledge in the consideration of our ideas,
with so little care and regard (as it may seem) to the real
existence of things : since most of those discourses which take
up the thoughts and engage the disputes of those who pretend
to make it their business to inquire after truth and certainty,
will, I presume, upon examination, be found to be general
propositions, and notions in which existence is not at all
concerned [2].   All the discourses of the mathematicians about
the squaring of a circle, conic sections, or any other part of
mathematics, concern not the existence of any of those figures :
but their demonstrations, which depend on their ideas, are the
same, whether there be any square or circle existing in the
world or no.   In the same manner, the truth and certainty of
moral discourses abstracts from the lives of men, and the
existence of those virtues in the world whereof they treat :
nor are Tully's Offices less true, because there is nobody in
the world that exactly practises his rules, and lives up to that
pattern of a virtuous man which he has given us, and which
existed nowhere when he writ but in idea.   If it be true in
speculation, i. e. in idea, that murder [3] deserves death, it will
also be true in reality of any action that exists conformable to

CHAP. IV.
quired to
make
Abstract
Know-
ledge real.

but yet it is so far obscure and confused, that there be a great many *other*
ideas with which, by reason of its
obscurity and confusedness, we cannot
compare it, so as to produce such a
perception : and in all those cases we
necessarily come short of certainty.'
(Third *Letter*, pp. 69, 72.) Cf. ch. ii.
§ 15. The point concerns the possibility of certainty in the mysteries of
faith,—whether we can be certain of
the truth of any proposition in which
the ideas compared are in any respect
obscure and incomplete.

[1] This is Locke's account of
' reality ' in knowledge—that the ideas
of which reality is predicated must be
' conformable ' to ' their archetypes.'

And in the case of all complex ideas,
except those of substances, the archetypes, he assumes, are ' made by ourselves.' They are subjective elaborations, which only require to be self-
consistent. Whether they are in all
cases composed of analytical propositions, he does not contemplate.

[2] He takes for granted, as already
proved, that we can name no absolutely certain *general* propositions in
which objective existence is concerned : propositions about real substances must all be particular : when
we make them general, they may rise
to probability, but not to knowledge.

[3] ' murder'—' murther ' in the early
editions.

BOOK IV.

——✦——

CHAP. IV.

Nor will it
be less
true or
certain,
because
Moral
Ideas are
of our own
making
and
naming.

that idea of murder. As for other actions, the truth of that proposition concerns them not. And thus it is of all other species of things, which have no other essences but those ideas which are in the minds of men [1].

9. But it will here be said, that if moral knowledge be placed in the contemplation of our own moral ideas, and those, as other modes, be of our own making, What strange notions will there be of justice and temperance? What confusion of virtues and vices, if every one may make what ideas of them he pleases? No confusion or disorder in the things themselves, nor the reasonings about them; no more than (in mathematics) there would be a disturbance in the demonstration, or a change in the properties of figures, and their relations one to another, if a man should make a triangle with four corners, or a trapezium with four right angles: that is, in plain English, change the names of the figures, and call that by one name, which mathematicians call ordinarily by another. For, let a man make to himself the idea of a figure with three angles, whereof one is a right one, and call it, if he please, *equilaterum* or *trapezium*, or anything else; the properties of, and demonstrations about that idea will be the same as if he called it a rectangular triangle. I confess the change of the name, by the impropriety of speech, will at first disturb him who knows not what idea it stands for: but as soon as the figure is drawn, the consequences and demonstrations are plain and clear. Just the same is it in moral knowledge: let a man have the idea of taking from others, without their consent, what their honest industry has possessed them of, and call this *justice* if he please. He that takes the name here without the idea put to it will be mistaken, by joining another idea of his own to that name: but strip the idea of that name, or take it such as it is in the speaker's mind, and the same things will agree to it, as if you called it *injustice*. Indeed, wrong names in moral discourses breed usually more disorder, because they are not so easily rectified as in mathematics, where the figure, once drawn and seen,

---

[1] So that only in pure mathematics or ethics, and other sciences which deal with abstract ideas, can general conclusions have the rational necessity that is essential to 'knowledge.'

makes the name useless and of no force. For what need of
a sign, when the thing signified is present and in view? But
in moral names, that cannot be so easily and shortly done,
because of the many decompositions that go to the making
up the complex ideas of those modes. But yet for all this,
the miscalling of any of those ideas, contrary to the usual
signification of the words of that language, hinders not but
that we may have certain and demonstrative knowledge of
their several agreements and disagreements, if we will carefully, as in mathematics, keep to the same precise ideas, and
trace *them* in their several relations one to another, without
being led away by their names. If we but separate the idea
under consideration from the sign that stands for it, our
knowledge goes equally on in the discovery of real truth and
certainty, whatever sounds we make use of[1].

10. One thing more we are to take notice of, That where
God or any other law-maker, hath defined any moral names,
there they have made the essence of that species to which
that name belongs; and there it is not safe to apply or use
them otherwise: but in other cases it is bare impropriety of
speech to apply them contrary to the common usage of the
country. But yet even this too disturbs not the certainty of
that knowledge, which is still to be had by a due contemplation and comparing of those even nick-named ideas[2].

11. *Thirdly,* There is another sort of complex ideas, which,
being referred to archetypes without us, may differ from
them, and so our knowledge about them may come short of
being real[3]. Such are our ideas of substances, which, con-

Misnaming
disturbs
not the
Certainty
of the
Know-
ledge.

Thirdly,
Our com-
plex Ideas
of Sub-
stances
have their

---

[1] Locke here virtually recognises
an intellectual necessity that belongs
to the relations of mathematical and
moral ideas, considered apart from
their names, but without pausing to
examine critically its nature and source.
Why is it that, apart from anything in
nature corresponding to them, the abstract truths demonstrated by the
mathematician are recognised to be
eternally and immutably true? He
seems unconscious of what this question implies.

[2] We may name, or even 'nickname,' our abstract notions as we
please. It is the notions and their
perceived relations, not the name
or nickname, that constitute knowledge.

[3] The tug of war is reached, in this
inquiry into the reality of knowledge,
when we inquire into the possibility
of a knowledge of the qualities that
coexist in substances. Here, according
to Locke, the unconditional certainty
of real knowledge fails, leaving us

BOOK IV.

CHAP. IV.

Arche-
types
without
us ; and
here know-
ledge
comes
short.

So far as
our com-
plex ideas
agree
with those
Arche-
types
without us,
so far our
Know-
ledge con-
cerning
Substances
is real.

sisting of a collection of simple ideas, supposed taken from the works of nature, may yet vary from them ; by having more or different ideas united in them than are to be found united in the things themselves. From whence it comes to pass, that they may, and often do, fail of being exactly conformable to things themselves [1].

12. I say, then, that to have ideas of *substances* which, by being conformable to things, may afford us real knowledge, it is not enough, as in *modes*, to put together such ideas as have no inconsistence [2], though they did never before so exist : v. g. the ideas of sacrilege or perjury, &c., were as real and true ideas before, as after the existence of any such fact. But our ideas of substances, being supposed copies, and referred to archetypes without us [3], must still be taken from something that does or has existed : they must not consist of ideas put together at the pleasure of our thoughts, without any real pattern they were taken from, though we can perceive no inconsistence in such a combination. The reason whereof is, because we, knowing not what real constitution it is of substances whereon our simple ideas depend, and which really is the cause of the strict union of some of them one with another, and the exclusion of others ; there are very few of them that we can be sure are or are not inconsistent in nature, any further than experience and sensible observation reach [4].

---

either in ignorance, or trusting to presumptions of probability.

[1] And when they do ' conform,' as he elsewhere argues, it is not because we ' perceive' the conformity to be intellectually *necessary*, but because we ' presume ' that it is *probable.* Cf. Bk. II. ch. xxiii. § 1. *Our* complex ideas of substances, which are their *nominal essences*, are confronted by incognizable *real essences* : propositions about all other sorts of complex ideas are concerned with *nominal essences only.*

[2] 'as have no inconsistence'—the test of merely analytical propositions, which are independent of time and its events, whereas those in which something is asserted of particular sub-

stances, are not thus independent of the phenomenal process of the universe.

[3] Our complex ideas of the substances that exist must conform to, and, in this sense, be 'copies' of, simple ideas or phenomena presentable in the senses, in the case of material substances ; or of reflection, in the case of operations of our own spiritual substance.

[4] He thus makes our knowledge of the substances in the universe depend upon ' experience,' while our knowledge of the mathematical and moral *relations* of abstract ideas is not thus dependent, being perceived to be intellectually necessary ; and yet he has postulated that ' all our knowledge

Herein, therefore, is founded the reality of our knowledge concerning substances—That all our complex ideas of them must be such, and such only, as are made up of such simple ones as have been discovered [1] to co-exist in nature. And our ideas being thus true, though not perhaps very exact copies, are yet the subjects of real (as far as we have any) knowledge of them. Which (as has been already shown) will not be found to reach very far : but so far as it does, it will still be real knowledge. Whatever ideas we have, the agreement we find they have with others will still be knowledge. If those ideas be abstract, it will be general knowledge. But to make it real concerning substances, the ideas must be taken from the real existence of things [2]. Whatever simple ideas have been found [3] to co-exist in any substance, these we may with confidence join together again, and so make abstract ideas of substances. For whatever have once had an union in nature, may be united again.

13. This, if we rightly consider, and confine not our
thoughts and abstract ideas to names, as if there were, or
could be no other *sorts* of things than what known names had
already determined, and, as it were, set out, we should think
of things with greater freedom and less confusion than
perhaps we do [4]. It would possibly be thought a bold
paradox, if not a very dangerous falsehood, if I should say
that some *changelings*, who have lived forty years together,
without any appearance of reason, are something between a
man and a beast : which prejudice is founded upon nothing

In our inquiries about Substances, we must consider Ideas, and not confine our Thoughts to Names, or Species supposed set out by Names.

---

ultimately derives itself from experience.' (Bk. II. ch. i. § 2.)

[1] By our senses, or by reflection upon the operations of our own minds. We have 'taken notice' that they 'go constantly together,' and thus 'presume that they belong to one thing' or substance. Cf. Bk. II. ch. xxiii. § 1.

[2] What is meant by 'ideas' being 'taken from the real existence of things?' Is it not that they must be, or have been, *actually given*, in sense or reflection, as simple ideas or qualities of bodies, or as simple ideas in

which our spiritual operations are manifested.

[3] 'found,' i. e. in and through actual sense-perception, or actual self-consciousness.

[4] We must remember, that is to say, that *our* nominal essences do not provide species adapted to all the real substances that present themselves in our experience. He goes on to illustrate the need for 'other sorts of things than what known names had already determined,' by the need for the names 'changeling,' 'monster,' with their respective nominal essences.

else but a false supposition, that these two names, man and beast, stand for distinct species so set out by real essences, that there can come no other species between them: whereas if we will abstract from those names, and the supposition of such specific essences made by nature, wherein all things of the same denominations did exactly and equally partake; if we would not fancy that there were a certain number of these essences, wherein all things, as in moulds, were cast and formed; we should find that the idea of the shape, motion, and life of a man without reason, is as much a distinct idea, and makes as much a distinct sort of things from man and beast, as the idea of the shape of an ass with reason would be different from either that of man or beast, and be a species of an animal between, or distinct from both.

14. Here everybody will be ready to ask, If changelings may be supposed something between man and beast, pray what are they? I answer, *changelings*; which is as good a word to signify something different from the signification of *man* or *beast*, as the names man and beast are to have significations different one from the other[1]. This, well considered, would resolve this matter, and show my meaning without any more ado. But I am not so unacquainted with the zeal of some men, which enables them to spin consequences, and to see religion threatened, whenever any one ventures to quit their forms of speaking, as not to foresee what names such a proposition as this is like to be charged with: and without doubt it will be asked, If changelings are something between man and beast, what will become of them in the other world? To which I answer, 1. It concerns me not to know or inquire. To their own master they stand or fall. It will make their state neither better nor worse, whether we determine anything of it or no. They are in the hands of a faithful Creator and a bountiful Father, who disposes not of his creatures according to our narrow thoughts or opinions, nor distinguishes them according to names and species of our contrivance. And we that know so little of this present world we are in, may, I think, content ourselves

[1] Cf. Bk. III. ch. vi. § 26.

without being peremptory in defining the different states which creatures shall come into when they go off this stage. It may suffice us, that He hath made known to all those who are capable of instruction, discoursing, and reasoning, that they shall come to an account, and receive according to what they have done in this body.

15. But, Secondly, I answer, The force of these men's question (viz. Will you deprive changelings of a future state?) is founded on one of these two suppositions, which are both false. The first is, That all things that have the outward shape and appearance of a man must necessarily be designed to an immortal future being after this life : or, secondly, That whatever is of human birth must be so. Take away these imaginations, and such questions will be groundless and ridiculous. I desire then those who think there is no more but an accidental difference between themselves and change-lings, the essence in both being exactly the same, to consider, whether they can imagine immortality annexed to any outward shape of the body ; the very proposing it is, I suppose, enough to make them disown it. No one yet, that ever I heard of, how much soever immersed in matter, allowed that excellency to any figure of the gross sensible outward parts, as to affirm eternal life due to it, or a necessary consequence of it ; or that any mass of matter should, after its dissolution here, be again restored hereafter to an ever-lasting state of sense, perception, and knowledge, only because it was moulded into this or that figure, and had such a particular frame of its visible parts. Such an opinion as this, placing immortality in a certain superficial figure, turns out of doors all consideration of soul or spirit ; upon whose account alone some corporeal beings have hitherto been concluded immortal, and others not. This is to attribute more to the outside than inside of things ; and to place the excellency of a man more in the external shape of his body, than internal perfections of his soul : which is but little better than to annex the great and inestimable advantage of immortality and life everlasting, which he has above other material beings, to annex it, I say, to the cut of his beard, or the fashion of his coat. For this or that outward mark of

BOOK IV.
CHAP. IV.

our bodies no more carries with it the hope of an eternal duration, than the fashion of a man's suit gives him reasonable grounds to imagine it will never wear out, or that it will make him immortal. It will perhaps be said, that nobody thinks that the shape makes anything immortal, but it is the shape is the sign of a rational soul within, which is immortal. I wonder who made it the sign of any such thing: for barely saying it, will not make it so. It would require some proofs to persuade one of it. No figure that I know speaks any such language. For it may as rationally be concluded, that the dead body of a man, wherein there is to be found no more appearance or action of life than there is in a statue, has yet nevertheless a living soul in it, because of its shape; as that there is a rational soul in a changeling, because he has the outside of a rational creature, when his actions carry far less marks of reason with them, in the whole course of his life, than what are to be found in many a beast [1].

Monsters.

16. But it is the issue of rational parents, and must therefore be concluded to have a rational soul. I know not by what logic you must so conclude. I am sure this is a conclusion that men nowhere allow of. For if they did, they

---

[1] Cf. ch. iii. § 6. Locke often returns to the question of the natural and necessary *immortality* of men, and its connexion with the *immateriality* of that in man which is self-conscious. He takes for granted that in the ultimate reason of things *matter* is devoid of consciousness ; perhaps of all active power (Bk. II. ch. xxi. § 2) ; and also that it must have been created, or had a beginning of existence. At the same time he objects so to limit the power of God as to deny that God could annex self-conscious activity to a material organism ;—as all their other seemingly active 'powers' are annexed, in like manner, to material substances, which by natural necessity are destitute of them all. The absolute impotence of sensible things *per se*, and the reference of *all* their apparent powers to the Divine Power, seems after all to be involved in this anthro-pological materialism of Locke, which leaves Mind of necessity prior or superior ; so that it is more akin to Berkeley than to Democritus or Hobbes. His disposition is to regard the controversy about the kind of substance on which self-consciousness in man immediately depends, or by which it is conditioned, as of much less moment, in a divinely governed universe, than the rival controversialists supposed. For God can prolong the self-conscious life, in separation from the material substance to which perhaps it is now annexed ; and even if it could be demonstrated to be an independent spiritual substance, God could annihilate the spiritual substance as easily as the material. Locke's tendency to isolate substances from the ideas or attributes in which they manifest themselves here appears again.

would not make bold, as everywhere they do, to destroy ill-formed and mis-shaped productions. Ay, but these are *monsters.* Let them be so: what will your drivelling, un-intelligent, intractable changeling be? Shall a defect in the body make a monster; a defect in the mind (the far more noble, and, in the common phrase, the far more essential part) not? Shall the want of a nose, or a neck, make a monster, and put such issue out of the rank of men; the want of reason and understanding, not? This is to bring all back again to what was exploded just now: this is to place all in the shape, and to take the measure of a man only by his outside. To show that according to the ordinary way of reasoning in this matter, people do lay the whole stress on the figure, and resolve the whole essence of the species of man (as they make it) into the outward shape, how unreason-able soever it be, and how much soever they disown it, we need but trace their thoughts and practice a little further, and then it will plainly appear. The well-shaped changeling is a man, has a rational soul, though it appear not: this is past doubt, say you: make the ears a little longer, and more pointed, and the nose a little flatter than ordinary, and then you begin to boggle: make the face yet narrower, flatter, and longer, and then you are at a stand: add still more and more of the likeness of a brute to it, and let the head be perfectly that of some other animal, then presently it is a monster; and it is demonstration with you that it hath no rational soul, and must be destroyed. Where now (I ask) shall be the just measure; which the utmost bounds of that shape, that carries with it a rational soul? For, since there have been human fœtuses produced, half beast and half man; and others three parts one, and one part the other; and so it is possible they may be in all the variety of approaches to the one or the other shape, and may have several degrees of mixture of the likeness of a man, or a brute;—I would gladly know what are those precise lineaments, which, according to this hypothesis, are or are not capable of a rational soul to be joined to them. What sort of outside is the certain sign that there is or is not such an inhabitant within? For till that be done, we talk at random of *man*: and shall always, I fear, do

BOOK IV.
———
CHAP. IV.

so, as long as we give ourselves up to certain sounds, and the imaginations of settled and fixed species in nature, we know not what. But, after all, I desire it may be considered, that those who think they have answered the difficulty, by telling us, that a mis-shaped fœtus is a *monster*, run into the same fault they are arguing against; by constituting a species between man and beast. For what else, I pray, is their monster in the case, (if the word monster signifies anything at all,) but something neither man nor beast, but partaking somewhat of either? And just so is the *changeling* before mentioned. So necessary is it to quit the common notion of species and essences, if we will truly look into the nature of things, and examine them by what our faculties can discover in them as they exist, and not by groundless fancies that have been taken up about them.

Words and Species.

17. I have mentioned this here, because I think we cannot be too cautious that words and species, in the ordinary notions which we have been used to of them, impose not on us. For I am apt to think therein lies one great obstacle to our clear and distinct knowledge, especially in reference to substances : and from thence has rose a great part of the difficulties about truth and certainty[1]. Would we accustom ourselves to separate our contemplations and reasonings from words, we might in a great measure remedy this inconvenience within our own thoughts : but yet it would still disturb us in our discourse with others, as long as we retained the opinion, that *species* and their *essences*[2] were anything else but our abstract ideas (such as they are) with names annexed to them, to be the signs of them.

Recapitulation.

18. Wherever we perceive the agreement or disagreement of any of our ideas, there is certain knowledge[3]: and wherever

---

[1] The 'perception,' that is to say, in which knowledge consists, and on which unconditional certainty depends, is blurred by confusion in the use of words, and by oversight of the 'arbitrariness' of species and nominal essences.

[2] I. e. so far as they are available in human knowledge.

[3] 'Your lordship says that in my way of " certainty by ideas " we have no criterion of certainty. To *perceive* the agreement or disagreement of two ideas, and *not to perceive* the agree-

we are sure [1] those ideas agree with the reality of things [2], there BOOK IV.
is certain real knowledge. Of which agreement of our ideas CHAP. IV.
with the reality of things, having here given the marks,
I think, I have shown *wherein it is that certainty, real certainty,
consists* [3]. Which, whatever it was to others, was, I confess,
to me heretofore, one of those desiderata which I found great
want of.

---

ment or disagreement of two ideas is,
I think, a criterion to distinguish what
a man is certain of from what he
is not certain of. Has your lordship
any other or better criterion to distinguish certainty from uncertainty?'
(Third *Letter* to Stillingfleet, p. 289.)

[1] ' we are sure.' He rests our objective certainty of the 'reality of things'
on faith or trust ; and this he takes for
granted that we have spontaneously.

[2] As he has assumed they do in
the case of the 'simple ideas' or
qualities that are actually present in
our senses ; or of the 'simple ideas'

of the operations of our own minds,
actually present in 'reflection.' Although our idea of 'reality' is the
most important of all our ideas, Locke
says little about its nature and origin.
What do we predicate of a subject
when we predicate *real existence* of
it ? What is the precise connotation
of the term 'really existing thing'?

[3] Cf. chh. ii. § 14 ; iii. § 21 ; ix ; xi,
and the different places in which actual
sense-perception and self-consciousness are contrasted with fictions of
imagination and of abstraction.

CHAPTER V.

OF TRUTH IN GENERAL.

1. WHAT is truth? was an inquiry many ages since; and it being that which all mankind either do, or pretend to search after[1], it cannot but be worth our while carefully to examine wherein it consists; and so acquaint ourselves with the nature of it, as to observe how the mind distinguishes it from falsehood.

A right
joining or
separating
of signs,
i. e. either
Ideas or
Words.

2. Truth, then, seems to me, in the proper import of the word, to signify nothing but *the joining or separating of Signs, as the Things signified by them do agree or disagree one with another*[2]. The joining or separating of signs here meant, is what by another name we call *proposition*. So that truth properly belongs only to propositions[3]: whereof there are two sorts, viz. mental and verbal; as there are two sorts of signs commonly made use of, viz. ideas and words.

---

[1] 'To love truth for truth's sake is the principal part of human perfection in this world, and the seed plot of all the other virtues.' (Locke to Collins, Oct. 29, 1703—one of many similar expressions of what was really the ruling spirit of his life.) Cf. ch. xix. § 1.

[2] Leibniz complains that this seems to make truth consist in words, so that the same meaning, expressed in different languages, would not be the same truth. *Nouv. Ess.* L. iv. ch. 5. But Locke's 'signs' are primarily our *ideas*; our words only in a secondary and subordinate way, as he suffi-

ciently explains in what follows. Cf. also ch. xxi. § 4.

[3] That truth 'belongs only to propositions' (mental and verbal), and not to isolated ideas, is implied in the construction of the *Essay*, according to which a 'mental proposition' is the unit of human knowledge. Cf. Bk. II. ch. xxii. § 1. Locke does not allow truth to be an attribute of signs *per se*, only of signs (whether ideas or words) in relation to their archetypes. Truth is thus harmony of the individual judgment, with the thought that is latent in the particular data of our experience.

3. To form a clear notion of truth, it is very necessary to consider truth of thought, and truth of words, distinctly one from another : but yet it is very difficult to treat of them asunder. Because it is unavoidable, in treating of mental propositions, to make use of words : and then the instances given of mental propositions cease immediately to be barely mental, and become verbal. For a *mental proposition* being nothing but a bare consideration of the ideas, as they are in our minds, stripped of names, they lose the nature of purely mental propositions as soon as they are put into words.

4. And that which makes it yet harder to treat of mental and verbal propositions separately is, that most men, if not all, in their thinking and reasonings within themselves, make use of words instead of ideas ; at least when the subject of their meditation contains in it complex ideas. Which is a great evidence of the imperfection and uncertainty of our ideas of that kind, and may, if attentively made use of, serve for a mark to show us what are those things we have clear and perfect established ideas of, and what not. For if we will curiously observe the way our mind takes in thinking and reasoning, we shall find, I suppose, that when we make any propositions within our own thoughts about *white* or *black*, *sweet* or *bitter*, a *triangle* or a *circle*, we can and often do frame in our minds the ideas themselves [1], without reflecting on the names. But when we would consider, or make propositions about the more complex ideas, as of a *man*, *vitriol*, *fortitude*, *glory*, we usually put the name for the idea [2] : because the ideas these names stand for, being for the most part imperfect, confused, and undetermined, we reflect on the names themselves, because they are more clear, certain, and distinct, and readier occur to our thoughts than the pure ideas : and so we make use of these words instead of the ideas themselves, even when we would meditate and reason within ourselves, and make tacit mental propositions. In substances, as has been already noticed, this is occasioned by

[1] When we are conscious, that is to say, of mental images, e. g. white or black objects, our thought is intuitive, not symbolical.

[2] Our thought in these instances is symbolical only, not intuitive.

the imperfections of our ideas[1] : we making the name stand for the real essence, of which we have no idea at all. In modes[2], it is occasioned by the great number of simple ideas that go to the making them up. For many of them being compounded, the name occurs much easier than the complex idea itself, which requires time and attention to be recollected, and exactly represented to the mind, even in those men who have formerly been at the pains to do it; and is utterly impossible to be done by those who, though they have ready in their memory the greatest part of the common words of that language, yet perhaps never troubled themselves in all their lives to consider what precise ideas the most of them stood for. Some confused or obscure notions have served their turns ; and many who talk very much of *religion* and *conscience*, of *church* and *faith*, of *power* and *right*, of *obstructions* and *humours*, *melancholy* and *choler*, would perhaps have little left in their thoughts and meditations, if one should desire them to think only of the things themselves, and lay by those words with which they so often confound others, and not seldom themselves also.

Mental and Verbal Propositions contrasted.
5. But to return to the consideration of truth: we must, I say, observe two sorts of propositions that we are capable of making :—

First, *mental*, wherein the ideas in our understandings are without the use of words put together, or separated, by the mind perceiving or judging of their agreement or disagreement.

Secondly, *Verbal* propositions, which are words, the signs of our ideas, put together or separated in affirmative or negative sentences. By which way of affirming or denying, these signs, made by sounds, are, as it were, put together or separated one from another. So that proposition consists in joining or separating signs ; and truth consists in the putting together or separating those signs, according as the things which they stand for agree or disagree.

---

[1] The collection of simple ideas which makes the nominal essence, or complex and imperfect idea, of any actual substance.

[2] Especially in mixed modes.

6. Every one's experience will satisfy him, that the mind, either by perceiving, or supposing, the agreement or disagree- ment of any of its ideas, does tacitly within itself put them into a kind of proposition affirmative or negative; which I have endeavoured to express by the terms putting together and separating. But this action of the mind, which is so familiar to every thinking and reasoning man, is easier to be conceived by reflecting on what passes in us when we affirm or deny, than to be explained by words. When a man has in his head the idea of two lines, viz. the side and diagonal of a square, whereof the diagonal is an inch long, he may have the idea also of the division of that line into a certain number of equal parts; v.g. into five, ten, a hundred, a thousand, or any other number, and may have the idea of that inch line being divisible, or not divisible, into such equal parts, as a certain number of them will be equal to the side-line. Now, whenever he perceives, believes, or supposes such a kind of divisibility to agree or disagree to his idea of that line, he, as it were, joins or separates those two ideas, viz. the idea of that line, and the idea of that kind of divisibility; and so makes a mental proposition, which is true or false, according as such a kind of divisibility, a divisibility into such *aliquot* parts, does really agree to that line or no. When ideas are so put together, or separated in the mind, as they or the things they stand for do agree or not, that is, as I may call it, *mental truth.* But *truth of words* is something more; and that is the affirming or denying of words one of another, as the ideas they stand for agree or disagree: and this again is two-fold; either purely verbal and trifling [1], which I shall speak of, (chap. viii.,) or real and instructive [2]; which is the object of that real knowledge which we have spoken of already.

7. But here again will be apt to occur the same doubt about truth, that did about knowledge: and it will be objected, that if truth be nothing but the joining and separating of words in propositions, as the ideas they stand for agree or

---

[1] Analytical or explicative propositions.

[2] Synthetical or ampliative propositions, *a priori* and *a posteriori.*

disagree in men's minds, the knowledge of truth is not so valuable a thing as it is taken to be, nor worth the pains and time men employ in the search of it: since by this account it amounts to no more than the conformity of words to the chimeras of men's brains.   Who knows not what odd notions many men's heads are filled with, and what strange ideas all men's brains are capable of?   But if we rest here, we know the truth of nothing by this rule, but of the visionary words in our own imaginations; nor have other truth, but what as much concerns harpies and centaurs, as men and horses.   For those, and the like, may be ideas in our heads, and have their agreement or disagreement there, as well as the ideas of real beings, and so have as true propositions made about them.   And it will be altogether as true a proposition to say *all centaurs are animals*, as that *all men are animals*; and the certainty of one as great as the other.   For in both the propositions, the words are put together according to the agreement of the ideas in our minds : and the agreement of the idea of animal with that of centaur is as clear and visible to the mind, as the agreement of the idea of animal with that of man ; and so these two propositions are equally true, equally certain.   But of what use is all such truth to us ?

Answered, Real Truth is about Ideas agreeing to things.
8. Though what has been said in the foregoing chapter to distinguish real from imaginary knowledge might suffice here, in answer to this doubt, to distinguish real truth from chimerical, or (if you please) barely nominal, they depending both on the same foundation ; yet it may not be amiss here again to consider, that though our words signify nothing but our ideas, yet being designed by them to signify things, the truth they contain when put into propositions will be only verbal, when they stand for ideas in the mind that have not an agreement with the reality of things.   And therefore truth as well as knowledge [1] may well come under the distinction of verbal and real; that being only verbal truth, wherein terms are joined according to the agreement or disagreement of the ideas they stand for ; without regarding whether our ideas are such as really have, or are capable of having, an

---

[1] Truth lies in proposition ; knowledge in perception.

existence in nature. But then it is they contain *real truth*, when these signs are joined, as our ideas agree ; and when our ideas are such as we know are capable of having an existence in nature : which in substances we cannot know, but by knowing that such have existed.

9. Truth is the marking down in words the agreement or disagreement of ideas as it is. Falsehood is the marking down in words the agreement or disagreement of ideas otherwise than it is. And so far as these ideas, thus marked by sounds, agree to their archetypes, so far only is the truth real. The knowledge of this truth consists in knowing what ideas the words stand for, and the perception of the agreement or disagreement of those ideas, according as it is marked by those words [1].

10. But because words are looked on as the great conduits of truth and knowledge, and that in conveying and receiving of truth, and commonly in reasoning about it, we make use of words and propositions, I shall more at large inquire wherein the certainty of real truths contained in propositions consists, and where it is to be had ; and endeavour to show in what sort of universal propositions we are capable of being certain of their real truth or falsehood.

I shall begin with *general* propositions [2], as those which most employ our thoughts, and exercise our contemplation. General truths are most looked after by the mind as those that most enlarge our knowledge ; and by their comprehensiveness satisfying us at once of many particulars, enlarge our view, and shorten our way to knowledge.

11. Besides truth taken in the strict sense before mentioned, there are other sorts of truths : As, 1. Moral truth, which is speaking of things according to the persuasion of our own minds, though the proposition we speak agree not to the reality of things [3]; 2. Metaphysical truth, which is nothing

---

[1] ' Truth ' is thus (mental or verbal) proposition that *is* (either consciously or unconsciously) in harmony with the reality to which the proposition relates. ' Knowledge of truth ' is the *perception* self evident or demon-strated) of this real harmony.

[2] Chh. vi, vii, viii.

[3] Propositions may thus be morally true whilst they are intellectually false.

BOOK IV.
—•—
CHAP. V.

but the real existence of things, conformable to the ideas to which we have annexed their names [1]. This, though it seems to consist in the very beings of things, yet, when considered a little nearly, will appear to include a tacit proposition, whereby the mind joins that particular thing to the idea it had before settled with the name to it. But these considerations of truth, either having been before taken notice of, or not being much to our present purpose, it may suffice here only to have mentioned them.

[1] Conformable, that is to say, to their nominal essences. Leibniz thus comments on this section :—' La *vérité morale* est appelée *véracité* par quelques-uns ; et la *vérité métaphysique* est prise vulgairement par les métaphysiciens pour un attribut de l'être ; mais bien inutile, et presque vide de sens. Contentons-nous de chercher la vérité dans la correspondance des *propositions* qui sont dans l'esprit avec les choses dont il s'agit. Il est vrai que j'ai attribué aussi la vérité aux *idées*, en disant qu'elles sont vraies ou fausses ; mais alors je l'entends en effet de la vérité des propositions qui affirment la possibilité de l'objet de l'idée ; et dans ce même sens on peut dire qu'un *être* est *vrai*, c'est-à-dire la proposition qui affirme son existence actuelle ou du moins possible.' (*Nouveaux Essais.*) If we limit the term metaphysical truth to the *ultimate* propositions concerned with real existence, chh. ix, x, xi, which follow, dealing with the three final realities, might be said to refer to *metaphysical* truth ; also ch. vii. On the other hand, ch. vi and others, which insist upon the imperfection of a human knowledge of the qualities and powers that belong to particular substances, are concerned with *physical* truth and probability.

CHAPTER VI.

OF UNIVERSAL PROPOSITIONS: THEIR TRUTH AND CERTAINTY.

1. THOUGH the examining and judging of ideas by them- selves, their names being quite laid aside, be the best and surest way to clear and distinct knowledge: yet, through the prevailing custom of using sounds for ideas, I think it is very seldom practised. Every one may observe how common it is for names to be made use of, instead of the ideas themselves, even when men think and reason within their own breasts; especially if the ideas be very complex, and made up of a great collection of simple ones. This makes the consideration of *words* and *propositions* so necessary a part of the Treatise of Knowledge, that it is very hard to speak intelligibly of the one, without explaining the other[1].

2. All the knowledge we have, being only of particular or general truths, it is evident that whatever may be done in the

---

[1] To carry men out of empty words, and to bring genuine ideas or meanings into words, is in the main the lesson of the *Essay*. Hence 'idea' is its watchword. This lesson is not a new one, though perhaps it was never more persistently enforced. 'The new way, as your lordship calls it, of "ideas," and the old way of speaking intelligibly was always, and will ever be, the same. Herein it consists: (1) That a man use no words but such as he makes the signs of determined objects of his mind in thinking; (2) That he use the same word steadily for the sign of the same immediate object of his mind; (3) That he join the words in propositions according to the grammar of that language he uses; (4) That he unite sentences in a coherent discourse. Thus only one may preserve himself from *jargon*, whether he pleases (with me) to call those immediate objects of his mind, which his words do, or should, stand for, *ideas* or no.' (Third *Letter* to Stillingfleet, pp. 353–54.)

BOOK IV.
—◆—
CHAP. VI.

be understood, but in verbal Propositions.

former of these, the latter, which is that which with reason is most sought after[1], can never be well made known, and is very seldom apprehended, but as conceived and expressed in words. It is not, therefore, out of our way, in the examination of our knowledge, to inquire into the truth and certainty of universal propositions[2].

Certainty twofold—of Truth and of Knowledge.

3. But that we may not be misled in this case by that which is the danger everywhere, I mean by the doubtfulness of terms, it is fit to observe that certainty is twofold : *certainty of truth* and *certainty of knowledge.* Certainty of truth is, when words are so put together in propositions as exactly to express the agreement or disagreement of the ideas they stand for[3], as really it is. Certainty of knowledge is to perceive the agreement or disagreement of ideas, as expressed in any proposition. This we usually call knowing, or being certain of the truth of any proposition[4].

No Proposition can be certainly known to be true, where the real Essence of each Species mentioned is not known.

4. Now, because we cannot be certain of the truth of any general proposition, unless we know the precise bounds and extent of the species its terms stand for, it is necessary we should know the essence of each species, which is that which constitutes and bounds it.

This, in all simple ideas and modes, is not hard to do. For in these the real and nominal essence being the same, or, which is all one, the abstract idea which the general term stands for being the sole essence and boundary that is or can be supposed of the species, there can be no doubt how far the species extends, or what things are comprehended under each term; which, it is evident, are all that have an exact conformity with the idea[5] it stands for, and no other.

---

[1] The goal of the sciences and philosophy is the discovery of general truths.

[2] 'universal propositions,' i. e. propositions in which the *subject* may be the common sign of an indefinite number of individual substances.

[3] 'the ideas they stand for'— whether the ideas are simple, abstract, or complex ideas of substances.

[4] That a certainty which consists only in perception of the agreement or disagreement of *ideas* leads to scepticism was one of the main charges brought against the *Essay* by Stillingfleet. In vindicating himself, Locke says that he means no more than that all mental propositions necessarily presuppose two ideas, even if the proposition affirms bare existence only of its subject, and when the mind may be hardly conscious that a proposition is involved in its percipient act.

[5] 'the idea,' i. e. the abstract idea, or

But in substances, wherein a real essence, distinct from the nominal, is supposed to constitute, determine, and bound the species, the extent of the general word is very uncertain; because, not knowing this real essence, we cannot know what is, or what is not of that species; and, consequently, what may or may not with certainty be affirmed of it. And thus, speaking of a *man*, or *gold*, or any other species of natural substances, as supposed constituted by a precise and real essence which nature regularly imparts to every individual of that kind, whereby it is made to be of that species, we cannot be certain of the truth of any affirmation or negation made of it. For man or gold, taken in this sense, and used for species of things constituted by real essences, different from the complex idea in the mind of the speaker, stand for we know not what; and the extent of these species, with such boundaries, are so unknown and undetermined, that it is impossible with any certainty to affirm, that all men are rational, or that all gold is yellow [1]. But where the nominal essence is kept to, as the boundary of each species, and men extend the application of any general term no further than to the particular things in which the complex idea it stands for is to be found, there they are in no danger to mistake the bounds of each species, nor can be in doubt, on this account, whether any proposition be true or not. I have chosen to explain this uncertainty of propositions in this scholastic way, and have made use of the terms of *essences*, and *species*, on purpose to show the absurdity and inconvenience there is to think of them as of any other sort of realities, than barely abstract ideas with names to them. To suppose that the species of things [2] are anything but the

---

nominal essence, which in this case is itself the archetype, according to the arguments reiterated in Bk. III.

[1] These two propositions, he argues, cannot have for us the certainty which propositions in pure mathematics about abstract triangles and circles have. The connexion, being dependent on what is supplied by experience, in ideas of sense, cannot possess the quality of intellectual necessity, which belongs to knowledge, in contrast with empirical probability.

[2] 'species,' that is to say, formed by us, and therefore knowable by us. For Locke does not deny that 'nature in the production of things makes several of them alike' (Bk. III. ch. iii. § 13), and that, in this sense, they exist objectively, 'according to their kinds'; the properties on which 'natural classes' are based being really in the

sorting of them under general names, according as they agree to several abstract ideas of which we make those names the signs, is to confound truth, and introduce uncertainty into all general propositions that can be made about them. Though therefore these things might, to people not possessed with scholastic learning, be treated of in a better and clearer way ; yet those wrong notions of essences or species having got root in most people's minds who have received any tincture from the learning which has prevailed in this part of the world, are to be discovered and removed, to make way for that use of words which should convey certainty with it.

This more particularly concerns Substances.

5. The names of substances, then, whenever made to stand for species which are supposed to be constituted by real essences which we know not, are not capable to convey certainty to the understanding. Of the truth of general propositions made up of such terms we cannot be sure. [[1] The reason whereof is plain : for how can we be sure that this or that quality is in gold, when we know not what is or is not gold ? Since in this way of speaking, nothing is gold but what partakes of an essence [2], which we, not knowing, cannot know where it is or is not, and so cannot be sure that any parcel of matter in the world is or is not in this sense gold ; being incurably ignorant whether *it* has or has not that

individual things so classed. But the general notion or abstract idea may fail in our application of it. The abstract general idea is really in the mind of him that has it ; and this, he argues, 'will never prove that this general nature (e. g. our abstract idea or nominal essence of *man*) exists in Peter or James. Those properties do not, as your lordship supposes, exist in Peter or in James : they *may* indeed exist in them ; but they are not properties necessarily in either of them, but are properties only of that specific abstract nature which Peter and James, for their supposed conformity to it, are ranked under. For example, rationality, as much a property as it is of

a man, is no property of Peter ; he was rational a good part of his life, could read and write, and was a sharp fellow at a bargain : but about thirty a knock so altered him that for these thirty years past he has been able to do none of these things ; there is to this day not so much appearance of reason in him as in his horse or monkey ; and yet he is Peter still.' (Third *Letter*, p. 358.) Cf. Green's Introduction, §§ 88–96.

[1] Added in second edition.

[2] The assumed, but (by us) incognizable ' real essence,' which Locke elsewhere supposes, in the case of bodies, to lie in the imperceptible atoms of which they consist, and to depend upon motions of those atoms.

which makes anything to be called gold ; i. e. that real essence
of gold whereof we have no idea at all. This being as impossible for us to know as it is for a blind man [1] to tell in
what flower the colour of a pansy is or is not to be found,
whilst he has no idea of the colour of a pansy at all. Or if
we could (which is impossible) certainly know where a real
essence, which we know not, is, v.g. in what parcels of matter
the real essence of gold is, yet could we not be sure that this
or that quality could with truth be affirmed of gold [2] ; since it
is impossible for us to know that this or that quality or idea
has a necessary connexion with a real essence of which we
have no idea at all, whatever species that supposed real essence
may be imagined to constitute.]

6. On the other side, the names of substances, when made The Truth
of few
universal
Proposi-
tions con-
cerning
Sub-
stances
is to be
known.
use of as they should be, for the ideas men have in their
minds, though they carry a clear and determinate signification
with them, will not yet serve us to make many universal
propositions of whose truth we can be certain. Not because
in this use of them we are uncertain what things are signified
by them, but because the complex ideas they stand for are
such combinations of simple ones as carry not with them any
discoverable connexion or repugnancy, but with a very few
other ideas [3].

7. The complex ideas that our names of the species of sub- Because
necessary
Co-exist-
ence of
simple
Ideas in
Sub-
stances
can in few
Cases be
known.
stances properly stand for, are collections of such qualities as
have been observed to co-exist in an unknown substratum,
which we call substance ; but what other qualities necessarily co-exist with such combinations, we cannot certainly
know, unless we can discover their natural dependence ;
which, in their primary qualities, we can go but a very little
way in ; and in all their secondary qualities we can discover

---

[1] One *born* blind.

[2] 'we could not,'—that is to say,
merely in virtue of the supposed knowledge, that this (by us) incognizable
'real essence' is contained in that
parcel of matter to which we apply
the general name 'gold.'

[3] Our abstract ideas, which are their
own archetypes, may be the subjects of
general propositions that are certain.

But the propositions lose their certainty when they assert or deny universally regarding the qualities and
powers that coexist in individual substances, supposed (it may be erro-
neously) to correspond to the predicates
thus misapplied to them. We cannot
be certain, in short, that Peter is
rational merely because we call him
a man.

BOOK IV.
CHAP. VI.

no connexion at all: for the reasons mentioned, chap. iii.[1] Viz. 1. Because we know not the real constitutions of substances, on which each secondary quality particularly depends. 2. Did we know that, it would serve us only for experimental (not universal) knowledge[2]; and reach with certainty no further than that bare instance: because our understandings can discover no conceivable connexion[3] between any secondary quality and any modification whatsoever of any of the primary ones[4]. And therefore there are very few general propositions to be made concerning substances, which can carry with them undoubted certainty.

Instance in Gold.

8. 'All gold is fixed,' is a proposition whose truth we cannot be certain of, how universally soever it be believed. For if, according to the useless imagination of the Schools, any one supposes the term gold to stand for a species of things set out by nature, by a real essence belonging to it, it is evident he knows not what particular substances[5] are of that species; and so cannot with certainty affirm anything universally of gold[6]. But if he makes gold stand for a species determined by its nominal essence, let the nominal

---

[1] Our inability to determine, by means of their primary qualities only, without experience, what the secondary qualities and powers of substances must be, is the chief and often reiterated evidence offered in the *Essay* of the necessarily narrow limits of man's knowledge of the substances that compose the material world. Cf. Bk. II. ch. viii. §§ 7-26.

[2] 'experimental knowledge' is here assumed to be incapable of universality. It cannot transcend the particular instance. Induction cannot become demonstration. When we pass from abstract relations to the concrete relations which are conditioned by the imperfectly known powers and laws that determine the history of the physical universe, we pass from the demonstrably true to the hypothetically true. Because the sun rose this morning and on innumerable past days, we only practically presume, but cannot

demonstrate, that it will rise to-morrow. The solar system may have been broken up by an unexpected collision, or by some other mechanical cause, in the interval.

[3] 'connexion,' i. e. necessary or eternal connexion.

[4] 'C'est que l'auteur suppose toujours que ces qualités sensibles, ou plutôt les idées que nous en avons, ne dépendent point des figures et mouvements *naturellement*, mais seulement du *bon plaisir de Dieu*, qui nous donne ces idées.' (*Nouveaux Essais.*)

[5] What particular 'parcels of matter,' among those that are presented to his senses, are exclusively constituted by this imperceptible 'real essence.'

[6] I. e. of the things to which the name 'gold' is applied—only because he finds in them by his senses the properties which make *his* connotation of the term gold.

essence, for example, be the complex idea of a body of a certain yellow colour, malleable, fusible, and heavier than any other known;—in this proper use of the word gold, there is no difficulty to know what is or is not gold. But yet no other quality can with certainty be universally affirmed or denied of gold, but what hath a *discoverable* connexion or inconsistency with that nominal essence. Fixedness, for example, having no necessary connexion that we can discover, with the colour, weight, or any other simple idea of [1] our complex one, or with the whole combination together; it is impossible that we should certainly know the truth of this proposition, that all gold is fixed [2].

9. As there is no discoverable connexion between fixedness and the colour, weight, and other simple ideas of that nominal essence of gold ; so, if we make our complex idea of gold, a body yellow, fusible, ductile, weighty, and fixed, we shall be at the same uncertainty concerning solubility in *aqua regia*, and for the same reason. Since we can never, from consideration of the ideas themselves, with certainty affirm or deny of a body whose complex idea is made up of yellow, very weighty, ductile, fusible, and fixed, that it is soluble in *aqua regia*: and so on of the rest of its qualities. I would gladly meet with one general affirmation concerning any quality of gold, that any one can certainly know is true. It will, no doubt, be presently objected, Is not this an universal proposition, *All gold is malleable?* To which I answer, It is a very certain proposition, if malleableness be a part of the complex idea the word gold stands for. But then here is nothing affirmed of gold, but that that sound stands for an idea in which malleableness is contained [3]: and such a sort of truth and certainty as this it is, to say a centaur is four-footed. But if malleableness make not a part of the specific essence the name of gold stands for, it is plain, *all gold is*

---

[1] 'of'—i. e. contained in.

[2] Meaning thereby that all 'parcels of matter' which present the above-mentioned properties, included in our complex idea of gold, *must* also possess the property of ' fixedness.'

[3] Nothing is affirmed, that is to say, of the 'parcel of matter' itself, to which we give the name gold. The proposition is only analytic of the connotation which men have attached to its name.

malleable, is not a certain proposition. Because, let the complex idea of gold be made up of whichsoever of its other qualities you please, malleableness will not appear to depend on that complex idea, nor follow from any simple one contained in it : the connexion that malleableness has (if it has any) with those other qualities being only by the intervention of the real constitution of its insensible parts ; which, since we know not, it is impossible we should perceive that connexion, unless we could discover that which ties them together.

As far as any such Co-exist-ence can be known, so far Universal Proposi-tions may be certain. But this will go but a little way.

10. The more, indeed, of these co-existing qualities we unite into one complex idea, under one name, the more precise and determinate we make the signification of that word; but never yet make it thereby more capable of universal certainty, *in respect of other qualities not contained in our complex idea* : since we perceive not their connexion or dependence on one another ; being ignorant both of that real constitution in which they are all founded, and also how they flow from it. For the chief part of our knowledge concerning substances is not, as in other things, barely of the relation of two ideas that may exist separately[1]; but is of the necessary connexion and co-existence of several distinct ideas in the same subject[2], or of their repugnancy so to co-exist. Could we begin at the other end[3], and discover what it was wherein that colour consisted, what made a body lighter or heavier, what texture of parts made it malleable, fusible, and fixed, and fit to be dissolved in this sort of liquor, and not in another ;—if, I say, we had such an idea as this of bodies, and could perceive wherein all sensible qualities originally consist, and how they are produced; we might frame such abstract ideas of them as would furnish us with matter of more general knowledge, and enable us to make universal propositions, that should carry general truth and certainty with them. But whilst our complex ideas of the

---

[1] Of two abstracted ideas to wit.

[2] 'the same subject'—the same concrete subject or substance.

[3] 'at the other end,'—which would be in this case 'the wrong end' referred to, when he warned men against letting their thoughts 'loose into the vast ocean of Being' (Introd. § 7), in *a priori* reasonings about things. The right end for our start is in experience, he argues, and its tentative presumptions of probability.

sorts of substances are so remote from that internal real constitution on which their sensible qualities depend, and are made up of nothing but an imperfect collection of those apparent qualities our senses can discover, there can be few general propositions concerning substances of whose real truth we can be certainly assured; since there are but few simple ideas of whose connexion and necessary co-existence we can have certain and undoubted knowledge. I imagine, amongst all the secondary qualities of substances, and the powers relating to them, there cannot any two be named, whose necessary co-existence, or repugnance to co-exist, can certainly be known; unless in those of the same sense, which necessarily exclude one another, as I have elsewhere showed[1]. No one, I think, by the colour that is in any body, can certainly know[2] what smell, taste, sound, or tangible qualities it has, nor what alterations it is capable to make or receive on or from other bodies. The same may be said of the sound or taste, &c. Our specific[3] names of substances standing for any collections of such ideas, it is not to be wondered that we can with them make very few general propositions of undoubted real certainty. But yet so far as any complex idea of any sort of substances contains in it any simple idea, whose *necessary*[4] co-existence with any other *may* be discovered, so far universal propositions may with certainty be made concerning it: v. g. could any one discover a necessary connexion between malleableness and the colour or weight of gold, or any other part of the complex idea signified by that name, he might make a certain universal proposition concerning gold in this respect; and the real truth of this proposition, that *all gold is malleable*, would be as certain as of this, *the three angles of all right-lined triangles are all equal to two right ones.*

---

[1] Cf. ch. iii. §§ 11–13.

[2] 'certainly know.' But he does not deny that there may be the highest probability, or practical proof, in some cases.

[3] 'specific'—'specifick,' in the early editions here and elsewhere.

[4] I. e. demonstrably or unconditionally 'necessary,' a necessity which he supposes to be undiscoverable by human faculty. Contingency enters into all such propositions, along with the presentations of experience, so that men cannot read them in terms of the real physical essences of the substances which the presentations only superficially reveal.

BOOK IV.
—•—
CHAP. VI.
The
Qualities
which
make our
complex
Ideas of
Sub-
stances
depend
mostly on
external,
remote,
and un-
perceived
Causes.

11. Had we such ideas of substances as to know what real constitutions produce those sensible qualities we find in them, and how those qualities flowed from thence, we could, by the specific ideas of their real essences in our own minds, more certainly find out their properties, and discover what qualities they had or had not, than we can now by our senses: and to know the properties of gold, it would be no more necessary that gold should exist, and that we should make experiments upon it, than it is necessary for the knowing the properties of a triangle, that a triangle should exist in any matter, the idea in our minds would serve for the one as well as the other. But we are so far from being admitted into the secrets of nature, that we scarce so much as ever approach the first entrance towards them. For we are wont to consider the substances we meet with, each of them, as an entire thing by itself, having all its qualities in itself, and independent of other things; overlooking, for the most part, the operations of those invisible fluids they are encompassed with, and upon whose motions and operations depend the greatest part of those qualities which are taken notice of in them, and are made by us the inherent marks of distinction whereby we know and denominate them. Put a piece of gold anywhere by itself, separate from the reach and influence of all other bodies, it will immediately lose all its colour and weight, and perhaps malleableness too; which, for aught I know, would be changed into a perfect friability. Water, in which to us fluidity is an essential quality, left to itself, would cease to be fluid. But if inanimate bodies owe so much of their present state to other bodies without them, that they would not be what they appear to us were those bodies that environ them removed; it is yet more so in vegetables, which are nourished, grow, and produce leaves, flowers, and seeds, in a constant succession. And if we look a little nearer into the state of animals, we shall find that their dependence, as to life, motion, and the most considerable qualities to be observed in them, is so wholly on extrinsical causes and qualities of other bodies that make no part of them, that they cannot subsist a moment without them: though yet those bodies on

which they depend are little taken notice of, and make no
part of the complex ideas we frame of those animals. Take the air but for a minute from the greatest part of living creatures, and they presently lose sense, life, and motion. This the necessity of breathing has forced into our knowledge. But how many other extrinsical and possibly very remote bodies do the springs of these admirable machines depend on, which are not vulgarly observed, or so much as thought on; and how many are there which the severest inquiry can never discover? The inhabitants of this spot of the universe, though removed so many millions of miles from the sun, yet depend so much on the duly tempered motion of particles coming from or agitated by it, that were this earth removed but a small part of the distance out of its present situation, and placed a little further or nearer that source of heat, it is more than probable that the greatest part of the animals in it would immediately perish : since we find them so often destroyed by an excess or defect of the sun's warmth, which an accidental position in some parts of this our little globe exposes them to. The qualities observed in a loadstone must needs have their source far beyond the confines of that body ; and the ravage made often on several sorts of animals by invisible causes, the certain death (as we are told) of some of them, by barely passing the line, or, as it is certain of other, by being removed into a neighbouring country ; evidently show that the concurrence and operations of several bodies, with which they are seldom thought to have anything to do, is absolutely necessary to make them be what they appear to us, and to preserve those qualities by which we know and distinguish them. We are then quite out of the way, when we think that things contain *within themselves* the qualities that appear to us in them ; and we in vain search for that constitution within the body of a fly or an elephant, upon which depend those qualities and powers we observe in them [1]. For which, perhaps, to understand them aright, we ought to look not only beyond this

---

[1] The 'qualities' of things are thus their relations to all other things, so that without knowing all other things, in all their relations, we cannot know any one thing, and must depend on probability.

our earth and atmosphere, but even beyond the sun or remotest star our eyes have yet discovered. For how much the being and operation of particular substances in this our globe depends on causes utterly beyond our view, is impossible for us to determine [1]. We see and perceive some of the motions and grosser operations of things here about us ; but whence the streams come that keep all these curious machines in motion and repair, how conveyed and modified, is beyond our notice and apprehension : and the great parts and wheels, as I may so say, of this stupendous structure of the universe, may, for aught we know, have such a connexion and dependence in their influences and operations one upon another, that perhaps things in this our mansion would put on quite another face, and cease to be what they are, if some one of the stars or great bodies incomprehensibly remote from us, should cease to be or move as it does [2]. This is certain: things, however absolute and entire they seem in themselves, are but retainers to other parts of nature, for that which they are most taken notice of by us. Their observable qualities, actions, and powers are owing to something without them ; and there is not so complete and perfect a part that we know of nature, which does not owe the being it has, and the excellences of it, to its neighbours ; and we must not confine our thoughts within the surface of any body, but look a great deal further, to comprehend perfectly those qualities that are in it [3].

[1] This sentence condenses his whole argument against the possibility of a human knowledge of the attributes and powers of particular substances.

[2] Our general propositions about nature are thus conditioned by unknown and incalculable forces, which at the last convert our physical 'science' into philosophical ignorance.

[3] Thus adequate science of any one thing would be Omniscience, as with the eternal geometer of Leibniz. In our uncritical assumptions, each thing in nature is independent of all other things, for being what it is, and we suppose that its qualities are self-contained, whereas each depends upon an infinite number of other things. A piece of gold, if it were the only existing thing, would lose its qualities ; water would lose its fluidity ; bodies their gravitation; vegetables and animals their motion, life, and sensibility. We are shut out from science of the qualities and powers of bodies, not merely because we cannot perceive their constituent atoms, and the laws which govern these atoms, but because the qualities and powers of each thing depend on its relations to all other things.

12. If this be so, it is not to be wondered that we have very imperfect ideas of substances, and that the real essences, on which depend their properties and operations, are unknown to us. We cannot discover so much as that size, figure, and texture of their minute and active parts, which is really in them; much less the different motions and impulses made in and upon them by bodies from without, upon which depends, and by which is formed the greatest and most remarkable part of those qualities we observe in them, and of which our complex ideas of them are made up. This consideration alone is enough to put an end to all our hopes of ever having the ideas of their real essences; which whilst we want, the nominal essences we make use of instead of them will be able to furnish us but very sparingly with any general knowledge, or universal propositions capable of real certainty.

BOOK IV.

CHAP. VI.

Our nominal essences of Substances furnish few universal propositions about them that are certain.

13. We are not therefore to wonder, if certainty be to be found in very few general propositions made concerning substances: our knowledge of their qualities and properties goes very seldom further than our senses reach and inform us[1]. Possibly inquisitive and observing men may, by strength of judgment[2], penetrate further, and, on probabilities taken from wary observation, and hints well laid together, often guess right at what experience has not yet discovered to them. But this is but guessing[3] still; it amounts only to opinion, and has not that certainty which is requisite to knowledge. For all general knowledge lies only in our own thoughts, and consists barely in the contemplation of our own abstract ideas[4]. Wherever we perceive any agreement or disagreement amongst them, there we have general knowledge; and

Judgment of Probability concerning Substances may reach further : but that is not Knowledge.

---

[1] Can the 'senses' inform us of aught beyond the transitory sense-phenomenon presented at the moment, unless it be taken to include a perception in which intellect is immanent in sense?

[2] In Locke's peculiar meaning of 'judgment,' which limits it to presumptions of probability, in contrast to the 'perception' which constitutes 'knowledge' or 'certainty.' Cf. ch. i. § 2 ; ch. xiv.

[3] The *Essay* is pervaded by the doctrine, that propositions which relate to matters of fact can be only hypothetically true—scientific verification of our inductions itself being a 'guess,' a 'leap in the dark.'

[4] Knowledge or certainty regarding substances, he means to say, is concrete —limited to the particular instance. When 'it becomes general' it inevitably becomes (at most) inductive probability, not knowledge or certainty.

BOOK IV.

CHAP. VI.

by putting the names of those ideas together accordingly in propositions, can with certainty pronounce general truths. But because the abstract ideas of substances, for which their specific names stand, whenever they have any distinct and determinate signification, have a discoverable connexion or inconsistency with but a very few other ideas, the certainty of universal propositions concerning substances is very narrow and scanty, in that part which is our principal inquiry concerning them; and there are scarce any of the names of substances, let the idea it is applied to be what it will, of which we can generally, and with certainty, pronounce, that it has or has not this or that other quality belonging to it[1], and constantly co-existing or inconsistent with that idea, wherever it is to be found.

What is requisite for our Knowledge of Substances.

14. Before we can have any tolerable knowledge of this kind, we must First know what changes the primary qualities of one body do regularly produce in the primary qualities of another, and how. Secondly, We must know what primary qualities of any body produce certain sensations or ideas in us[2]. This is in truth no less than to know *all* the effects of matter[3], under its divers modifications of bulk, figure, cohesion of parts, motion and rest. Which, I think every body will allow, is utterly impossible to be known by us without revelation. Nor if it were revealed to us what sort of figure, bulk, and motion of corpuscles would produce in us the sensation of a yellow colour, and what sort of figure, bulk, and texture of parts in the superficies of any body were fit to give such corpuscles their due motion to produce that colour; would that be enough to make universal propositions with certainty, concerning the several sorts of them; unless we had faculties acute enough to perceive the precise bulk, figure, texture, and motion of bodies, in those minute parts, by which they operate on our senses, so that we might by those frame our abstract ideas of them. I have mentioned here only corporeal substances, whose operations

[1] I. e. necessarily included in its connotation.

[2] Cf. Bk. II. ch. viii.

[3] 'effects of matter.' Does he in this and similar expressions mean to imply that matter is endowed with active power, or that it is more than an impotent subject of changes evolved by supreme active Reason? Cf. Bk. II. ch. xxi. § 2.

seem to lie more level to our understandings. For as to the
operations of spirits, both their thinking and moving of
bodies, we at first sight find ourselves at a loss ; though
perhaps, when we have applied our thoughts a little nearer to
the consideration of bodies and their operations, and examined
how far our notions, even in these, reach with any clearness
beyond sensible matter of fact, we shall be bound to confess
that, even in these too, our discoveries amount to very little
beyond perfect ignorance and incapacity.

15. This is evident, the abstract complex ideas of Whilst our
substances, for which their general names stand, not compre- complex
Ideas of
hending their real constitutions[1], can afford us very little Sub-
universal certainty. Because our ideas of them[2] are not stances
made up of that on which those qualities we observe in them, not ideas
of their
and would inform ourselves about, do depend, or with which real Con-
they have any certain connexion : v. g. let the ideas to which stitutions,
we can
we give the name *man* be, as it commonly is, a body of the make but
ordinary shape, with sense, voluntary motion, and reason few
general
joined to it. This being the abstract idea, and consequently certain
Proposi-
the essence of *our* species, man, we can make but very few tions con-
general certain propositions concerning man, standing for cerning
them.
such an idea. Because, not knowing the real constitution on
which sensation, power of motion, and reasoning, with that
peculiar shape, depend, and whereby they are united together
in the same subject, there are very few other qualities with
which we can perceive them to have a necessary connexion :
and therefore we cannot with certainty affirm : That all men
sleep by intervals ; That no man can be nourished by wood
or stones ; That all men will be poisoned by hemlock :
because these ideas[3] have no connexion nor repugnancy[4]
with this our nominal essence of man, with this abstract idea
that name stands for. We must, in these and the like, appeal
to trial in particular subjects, which can reach but a little

---

[1] Only their *superficial* appearances
patent to our senses, their 'real constitutions,' on which their behaviour
ultimately depends, being (by us) imperceptible.

[2] 'our ideas of them,' i. e. the abstract or general ideas we can form of

them, and which the common names
we apply to them connote as their
nominal essences.

[3] 'ideas'—qualities, when regarded
as in the substances.

[4] I. e. necessary 'connexion or repugnancy.'

way. We must content ourselves with probability in the rest: but can have no general certainty, whilst our specific idea of man contains not that real constitution which is the root wherein all his inseparable qualities are united, and from whence they flow. Whilst our idea the word *man* stands for [1] is only an imperfect collection of some sensible qualities and powers in him, there is no discernible connexion or repugnance between our specific idea, and the operation of either the parts of hemlock or stones upon his constitution. There are animals that safely eat hemlock, and others that are nourished by wood and stones: but as long as we want ideas of those real constitutions of different sorts of animals whereon these and the like qualities and powers depend, we must not hope to reach certainty [2] in universal propositions concerning them. Those few ideas only which have a discernible connexion with our nominal essence, or any part of it, can afford us such propositions. But these are so few, and of so little moment [3], that we may justly look on our certain general knowledge of substances as almost none at all.

16. To conclude : general propositions, of what kind soever, are then only capable of certainty, when the terms used in them stand for such ideas, whose agreement or disagreement, as there expressed, is capable to be discovered by us. And we are then certain of their truth or falsehood, when we perceive the ideas the terms stand for to agree or not agree, according as they are affirmed or denied one of another. Whence we may take notice, that general certainty is never to be found but in our ideas. Whenever we go to seek it elsewhere, in experiment or observations without us, our knowledge goes not beyond particulars. It is the contemplation of our own abstract ideas that alone is able to afford us general knowledge [4].

---

[1] The abstract idea, or concept, which our observation of the individuals we call 'men' induces us to apply to them.

[2] Only probability.

[3] He mentions a few elsewhere. Cf. ch. vii. § 5.

[4] This section, in which empirical propositions, concerned with *our* concrete ideas of substances, are distinguished from truths of reason, discoverable in the relations of abstract ideas, is one of the passages alleged in proof of the extreme nominalism of Locke.

CHAPTER VII.

OF MAXIMS.

1. THERE are a sort of propositions, which, under the name of *maxims* and *axioms* [1], have passed for principles of science :

[1] By *maxims* or *axioms* Locke means supposed *first principles*, or self-evident truths, in their ultimate or most general form of expression. Hence they are called the *maximæ*, or greatest propositions, which by implication contain all other propositions, and determine the articulation of our reasonings; and which are also of chief intellectual worth and dignity (ἄξιος). Locke's application of maxim differs from its common meaning of prudential probable proposition, which may be converted into a rule of conduct ; and from Kant's, whose maxims are principles only of subjective or personal validity. Axiom too is ambiguous, for it is occasionally limited to the self-evident assumptions of the mathematician, and by others extended to propositions generally. Aristotle recognises both of these meanings, and also applies the term to the ultimate presuppositions of knowledge. With Bacon it means propositions formed by generalisation, and he distinguishes *axiomata generalissima* from the *axiomata media* (intermediate between the former and particular facts), to which he is drawn as the sphere of fruitful inquiry. See *Novum Organum*, Dr. Fowler's edition, note 7, pp. 189–90. 'Cette recherche,' says Leibniz, with reference to the opening sentence of

this chapter, ' cette recherche est fort utile et même importante. Mais il ne faut point vous figurer, monsieur, qu'elle ait été entièrement négligée. Vous trouverez en cent lieux que les philosophes de l'École ont dit que ces propositions sont évidentes *ex terminis*, aussitôt qu'on en entend les termes ; de sorte qu'ils étaient persuadés, que la force de la conviction était fondée dans l'intelligence des termes, c'est-à-dire dans la liaison de leurs idées . . . Pour ce qui est des *maximes,* on les prend quelquefois pour des propositions établies, soit qu'elles soient évidentes ou non. Cela pourra être bon pour les commençants ; mais quand il s'agit de l'établissement de la science, c'est autre chose. C'est ainsi qu'on les prend souvent dans la morale, et même chez les logiciens dans leurs *topiques.* . . . Au reste, il y a longtemps que j'ai dit publiquement et en particulier qu'il serait important de démontrer tous nos axiomes secondaires, dont on se sert ordinairement, en les réduisant aux *axiomes primitifs,* ou immédiats et indémonstrables, qui sont ce que j'appelais dernièrement les *identiques.'* (*Nouveaux Essais.*) As related to this chapter, see Note A on the ' Philosophy of Common Sense,' in Hamilton's Reid (pp. 742–803), and Reid's *Essays*, VI. chh. iv–vii.

BOOK IV.

CHAP. VII.

Maxims or Axioms are Self-evident Propositions.

and because they are *self-evident*, have been supposed innate [1], without that anybody (that I know) ever went about to show the reason and foundation of their clearness or cogency. It may, however, be worth while to inquire into the reason of their evidence, and see whether it be peculiar to them alone; and also to examine how far they influence and govern our other knowledge [2].

Wherein that Self-evidence consists.

2. Knowledge, as has been shown, consists in the perception of the agreement or disagreement of ideas. Now, where that agreement or disagreement is perceived immediately by itself, without the intervention or help of any other, there our knowledge is self-evident. This will appear to be so to any who will but consider any of those propositions which, without any proof, he assents to at first sight [3] : for in all of them he will find that the reason of his assent is from that agreement or disagreement which the mind, by an immediate comparing them [4], finds in those ideas answering the affirmation or negation in the proposition.

Self-evidence not peculiar to received Axioms.

3. This being so, in the next place, let us consider whether this self-evidence be peculiar only to those propositions which commonly pass under the name of maxims, and have the dignity of axioms allowed them. And here it is plain, that several other truths, not allowed to be axioms, partake

---

[1] In rejecting 'innate principles,' it has been supposed that Locke intends to reject the claim of any proposition to be self-evident, notwithstanding that in this chapter and in many other parts of the *Essay* he insists upon the fact of self-evident propositions, and the need for them in order to constitute human knowledge. What follows may be compared with the argument in the first Book against 'innate ideas and principles,' and in proof of the dependence of all our ideas and assertions about things upon our experience of their behaviour in their relations to one another. Innateness and self-evidence are contrasted, not identified, by Locke. See third *Letter* to Stillingfleet, pp. 340–44.

[2] Locke recognises self-evidence only in *mental propositions*, not in *ideas*, which can be neither true nor false, unless a proposition regarding the idea is implied. When he is charged by Stillingfleet with holding that 'some of the most obvious ideas are far from being self-evident,' he asks, 'where it is that I once mention any such thing as a self-evident *idea* ? For self-evident is an epithet that I do not remember I ever gave to any idea, or thought belonged at all to ideas.' (Third *Letter*, p. 322.) And as regards propositions, he refuses to limit self-evidence exclusively to 'maxims or axioms.'

[3] In maxims or axioms to wit.

[4] In a direct intuition.

equally with them in this self-evidence [1]. This we shall see,
if we go over these several sorts of agreement or disagreement of ideas which I have above mentioned, viz. identity,
relation, co-existence, and real existence ; which will discover
to us, that not only those few propositions which have had
the credit of maxims are self-evident, but a great many, even
almost an infinite number of other propositions are such.

4. I. For, *First*, The immediate perception of the agree- As to
ment or disagreement of *identity* being founded in the mind's Identity
having distinct ideas, this affords us as many self-evident Diversity,
propositions as we have distinct ideas. Every one that has positions
any knowledge at all, has, as the foundation of it, various and are equally
distinct ideas : and it is the first act of the mind (without evident.
which it can never be capable of any knowledge) to know
every one of its ideas by itself, and distinguish it from others.
Every one finds in himself, that he knows the ideas he has ;
that he knows also, when any one is in his understanding,
and what it is ; and that when more than one are there, he
knows them distinctly and unconfusedly one from another ;
which always being so, (it being impossible but that he should
perceive what he perceives,) he can never be in doubt when
any idea is in his mind, that it is there, and is that idea it is ;
and that two distinct ideas, when they are in his mind, are
there, and are not one and the same idea. So that all such
affirmations and negations are made without any possibility
of doubt, uncertainty, or hesitation, and must necessarily be
assented to as soon as understood ; that is, as soon as we have
in our minds [2 determined ideas,] which the terms in the

---

[1] He does not deny that the maxims
or axioms in question are self-evident.
He only denies that a *perception* of
them, and of their self-evidence, with
the energy of abstract thought which
this perception would imply, is in all
cases necessary to the knowledge in
which they are latent. Their *unconscious presupposition* is a point of
view at which, as we saw in the first
Book, Locke declines to regard them ;
as well as their exclusive claim to self-
evidence, since there are millions of

concrete propositions that are self-
evidently true, as well as those select
propositions of extreme abstraction.
Locke always clings to the concrete.
Yet a chief problem of speculative
philosophy has been, to resolve the
intellectually subordinate truths which
men ordinarily recognise into the
primitive and universal truths which
these presuppose.

[2] In first edition—'the ideas clear
and distinct.'

proposition stand for. [¹ And, therefore, whenever the mind with attention considers any proposition, so as to perceive the two ideas signified by the terms, and affirmed or denied one of the other to be the same or different; it is presently and infallibly certain of the truth of such a proposition; and this equally whether these propositions be in terms standing for more general ideas, or such as are less so: v. g. whether the general idea of Being be affirmed of itself, as in this proposition, 'whatsoever is, is'; or a more particular idea be affirmed of itself, as 'a man is a man'; or, 'whatsoever is white is white'; or whether the idea of being in general be denied of not-Being, which is the only (if I may so call it) idea different from it, as in this other proposition, 'it is impossible for the same thing to be and not to be': or any idea of any particular being be denied of another different from it, as 'a man is not a horse'; 'red is not blue.' The difference of the ideas, as soon as the terms are understood, makes the truth of the proposition presently visible, and that with an equal certainty and easiness in the less as well as the more general propositions; and all for the same reason, viz. because the mind perceives, in any ideas that it has, the same idea to be the same with itself; and two different ideas to be different, and not the same; and this it is equally certain of, whether these ideas be more or less general, abstract, and comprehensive.] It is not, therefore, alone to these two general propositions—'whatsoever is, is'; and 'it is impossible for the same thing to be and not to be'—that this sort of self-evidence belongs by any peculiar right. The perception of being, or not being, belongs no more to these vague ideas, signified by the terms *whatsoever*, and *thing*, than it does to any other ideas. [² These two general maxims, amounting to no more, in short, but this, that *the same is the same,* and *the same is not different,* are truths known in more particular instances, as well as in those general maxims; and known also in particular instances, before these general maxims are ever thought on; and draw all their force from the discernment of the mind employed about particular ideas. There is

---

¹ Added in second edition.   ² Added in second edition.

nothing more visible than that] the mind, without the help of
any proof, [[1] or reflection on either of these general propositions,] perceives so clearly, and knows so certainly, that the
idea of white is the idea of white, and not the idea of blue ;
and that the idea of white, when it is in the mind, is there,
and is not absent ; [[2] that the consideration of these axioms
can add nothing to the evidence or certainty of its knowledge.]
[[3] Just so it is (as every one may experiment in himself) in
all the ideas a man has in his mind : he knows each to be
itself, and not to be another ; and to be in his mind, and not
away when it is there, with a certainty that cannot be greater ;
and, therefore, the truth of no general proposition can be
known with a greater certainty, nor add anything to this.]
So that, in respect of identity, our intuitive knowledge reaches
as far as our ideas. And we are capable of making as many
self-evident propositions, as we have names for distinct ideas.
And I appeal to every one's own mind, whether this proposition, 'a circle is a circle,' be not as self-evident a proposition
as that consisting of more general terms, 'whatsoever is, is' ;
and again, whether this proposition, 'blue is not red,' be not
a proposition that the mind can no more doubt of, as soon as
it understands the words, than it does of that axiom, 'it is
impossible for the same thing to be and not to be?' And so
of all the like [4].

5. II. *Secondly*, as to *co-existence*, or such a necessary
connexion between two ideas that, in the subject where one
of them is supposed, there the other must necessarily be also :
of such agreement or disagreement as this, the mind has an
immediate perception but in very few of them. And therefore in this sort we have but very little intuitive knowledge :

---

[1] Added in second edition.

[2] In first edition—'and so a triangle, a motion, a man, or any other
ideas whatsoever.'

[3] Added in second edition.

[4] In the order of the revelation of
truth to the individual, the embodiment
of the axiom precedes his conscious
recognition of it in its abstract generality (which many never attain to) ;

but in the order of reason in nature
this is reversed. For that has to do
not with the history of the development of intelligence in an individual
mind, which may vary as men vary,
but with the connexion in the reason
of things, which is always the same ;
for we must regard the axiom as
logically latent in the example, being
that which makes an embodied truth.

BOOK IV.

CHAP. VII.

nor are there to be found very many propositions that are self-evident, though some there are : v. g. the idea of filling a place equal to the contents of its superficies, being annexed to our idea of body, I think it is a self-evident proposition, that two bodies cannot be in the same place [1].

In other Relations we may have many.

6. III. *Thirdly*, As to the *relations of modes*, mathematicians have framed many axioms concerning that one relation of equality. As, 'equals taken from equals, the remainder will be equal'; which, with the rest of that kind, however they are received for maxims by the mathematicians, and are unquestionable truths, yet, I think, that any one who considers them will not find that they have a clearer self-evidence than these,—that 'one and one are equal to two'; that 'if you take from the five fingers of one hand two, and from the five fingers of the other hand two, the remaining numbers will be equal.' These and a thousand other such propositions may be found in numbers [2], which, at the very first hearing, force the assent, and carry with them an equal, if not greater clearness, than those mathematical axioms.

Concerning real Existence, we have none.

7. IV. *Fourthly*, as to *real existence*, since that has no connexion [3] with any other of our ideas, but that of ourselves, and of a First Being, we have in that, concerning the real existence of all other beings, not so much as demonstrative, much less a self-evident knowledge : and, therefore, concerning those there are no maxims [4].

---

[1] That 'maxims or axioms' are presupposed in our experience of the coexistences and successions of things is not disproved, by showing that, in physical research, human faculties fail to rise above a contingent or hypothetical apprehension of what actual relations of coexistence and succession are ultimately necessary, at the Divine point of view. Here is the foundation of the distinction between *propositions of fact*, which depend upon the limited experience of man, and *a priori* propositions of reason, which want of Omniscience makes men unable to *apply*, with a like perception of *a priori* necessity, to their experience.

Rational intuition in man is obscured by sense.

[2] Logically implicated in the maxims or axioms of mathematics, which Locke allows to be imposed by a necessity that he fails fully to explain.

[3] 'connexion,' i. e. intellectually necessary connexion.

[4] In this obscurely expressed sentence Locke seems to say, that one's idea of one's self, and one's idea of God, are the only ideas that are perceived to be so connected with the idea of real existence that it is intellectually necessary for us to attribute real existence to ourselves and to God ; whereas the real existence of all finite beings

8. In the next place let us consider, what influence these BOOK IV.
received maxims have upon the other parts of our knowledge.
The rules established in the schools, that all reasonings are ————
Ex præcognitis et præconcessis, seem to lay the foundation CHAP. VII.
of all other knowledge in these maxims, and to suppose them These
to be *præcognita.* Whereby, I think, are meant these two Axioms
things: first, that these axioms are those truths that are first do not
known to the mind; and, secondly, that upon them the other much
parts of our knowledge depend. influence
our other
Know-
ledge.

9. *First,* That they are not the truths first known to the Because
mind is evident to experience, as we have shown in another Maxims or
place. (Book I. chap. i.) Who perceives not that a child Axioms
certainly knows that a stranger is not its mother; that its are not
sucking-bottle is not the rod, long before he knows that ' it is the Truths
we first
impossible for the same thing to be and not to be?' And knew.
how many truths are there about numbers, which it is obvious
to observe that the mind is perfectly acquainted with, and
fully convinced of, before it ever thought on these general
maxims, to which mathematicians, in their arguings, do sometimes refer them? Whereof the reason is very plain: for that
which makes the mind assent to such propositions, being
nothing else but the perception it has of the agreement or
disagreement of its ideas, according as it finds them affirmed
or denied one of another in words it understands; and every
idea being known to be what it is, and every two distinct ideas

other than one's self is neither intuitively nor demonstratively perceived.
Cf. ch. ii. § 14; also ch. iv. § 18,
which makes our certainty of the real
existence of anything that we have
an idea of depend upon our natural
assurance that it really exists. Locke
fails to appreciate the difference
between ' maxims' the intellectual
necessity of which is discerned in the
immediate agreement of abstract ideas,
and propositions of fact determined
by the constitution of the human mind.
The proposition ' I exist' is one of
fact, not an abstract axiom ; and ' demonstrations' that depend upon it are
not pure *a priori* ones. 'Il n'y a

que Dieu,' says Leibniz, ' qui voit
comment ces deux termes *moi* et
l'*existence* sont liés; c'est-à-dire pour-
quoi j'existe. Mais si l'axiome se
prend plus généralement *pour une
vérité immédiate ou non prouvable*, on
peut dire que cette proposition—*je
suis*, est un axiome; et, en tous cas,
on peut assurer que c'est *une vérité
primitive*; c'est-a-dire que c'est une
des énonciations premières connues,
ce qui s'entend dans l'ordre naturel de
nos connaissances; car il se peut
qu'un homme n'ait jamais pensé à
former expressement cette proposition, qui lui est pourtant innée.'
(*Nouveaux Essais.*)

being known not to be the same ; it must necessarily follow, that such self-evident truths must be first known which consist of ideas that are first in the mind. And the ideas first in the mind, it is evident, are those of particular things, from whence, by slow degrees, the understanding proceeds to some few general ones ; which being taken from the ordinary and familiar objects of sense, are settled in the mind, with general names to them. Thus *particular ideas* are first received and distinguished, and so knowledge got about them ; and next to them, the less general or specific, which are next to particular. For abstract ideas are not so obvious or easy to children, or the yet unexercised mind, as particular ones. If they seem so to grown men, it is only because by constant and familiar use they are made so. For, when we nicely reflect upon them, we shall find that *general ideas* are fictions and contrivances of the mind, that carry difficulty with them, and do not so easily offer themselves as we are apt to imagine. For example, does it not require some pains and skill to form the general idea of a triangle, (which is yet none of the most abstract, comprehensive, and difficult,) for it must be neither oblique nor rectangle, neither equilateral, equicrural, nor scalenon ; but all and none of these at once. In effect, it is something imperfect, that cannot exist ; an idea wherein some parts of several different and inconsistent ideas are put together[1].

[1] In this celebrated passage Locke's inexact language suggests that a general idea must include contradictory attributes, and therefore must be logically impossible. Now a general idea or notion consists of attributes that must be found in each of the indefinitely numerous individuals to which the general name is applicable ; but found in them in combination with other attributes peculiar to each individual. This seems to be what Locke really meant ; for he says that a general idea consists of 'some parts' of [complex] ideas which are, as regards their other peculiarly individual attributes, 'inconsistent' with one another. Locke's 'abstract idea' is caricatured by Berkeley, when he says that 'if any man has the faculty of framing in his mind such an idea of a triangle as is here described, it is vain to pretend to dispute him out of it. All I desire is that the reader would fully and certainly inform himself whether he has such an idea or not . . . and try whether he has, or can attain to have, the general idea of a triangle which is neither oblique, nor rectangle, equilateral, equicrural, nor scalenon, *but all and none of these at once.*' (*Principles*—Introd. § 13.) What Locke intends is surely that the idea (nominal essence) is applicable to all these, while it excludes the peculiarities of each ; it contains them under

It is true, the mind, in this imperfect state, has need of such ideas, and makes all the haste to them it can, for the conveniency of communication and enlargement of knowledge; to both which it is naturally very much inclined. But yet one has reason to suspect such ideas are marks of our imperfection[1]; at least, this is enough to show that the most abstract and general ideas are not those that the mind is first and most easily acquainted with, nor such as its earliest knowledge is conversant about[2].

10. Secondly, from what has been said it plainly follows, that these magnified maxims are not the principles and foundations of all our other knowledge. For if there be a great many other truths, which have as much self-evidence as they, and a great many that we know before them, it is impossible they should be the principles from which we deduce all other truths[3]. Is it impossible to know that one and two

BOOK IV.
CHAP. VII.

Because on perception of them the other Parts of our Knowledge do not depend.

---

its *extent*, while it excludes them from its *content*. Berkeley, confounding abstract or general ideas with sensuous images, easily proves that an *image* representing a triangle that is neither obtuse, acute, nor right-angled cannot be formed. This does not prove that ' triangle ' and other common terms are *meaningless*. It only shows that abstract meanings transcend sense and sensuous imagination, and presuppose spiritual intelligence in a human understanding.

[1] While man, in his general ideas, as in his faculty for reasoning, transcends sense and sensuous imagination, he nevertheless shows the inferiority of his understanding to the Omniscience which comprehends all, in all relations, in a single intellectual intuition. Cf. Bk. II. ch. x. § 9, on the limitation of sensuous presentation and representation in man.

[2] Cf. Hume's *Treatise*, Bk. I. pt. i. § 7; Hamilton's *Reid*, pp. 406-10; also Gassendi, in his *Syntagma*, who recognises the difference between sense or sensuous imagination, and intellection proper or discernment of

universality. Locke may have gained any knowledge he had of Gassendi chiefly from the abridgment of the *Syntagma*, by Bernier, the disciple of Gassendi, and the friend of Locke.

[3] But ' maxims ' are presupposed in our deductions, although often the reasoner is unconscious of them. Their *latent* presence in the reason of things is proved by the paralysis of the deductions as soon as the presuppositions are denied. What Locke throughout dreads, and justly, is a dogmatic assumption of our own prejudices, under the guise of maxims or axioms; and also the temptation which propositions of extreme generality afford for confused and fallacious reasoning. Hence his steady endeavour to restrain the flights of abstract speculation, and his warnings against trying to begin our intellectual journey at the centre of the ' ocean of Being.' Hence the indifference to ' first principles ' that is characteristic of Locke, who sees what determines belief and action in experience and expediency rather than in *a priori* principles of pure reason.

are equal to three, but by virtue of this, or some such axiom, viz. 'the whole is equal to all its parts taken together?' Many a one knows that one and two are equal to three, without having heard, or thought on, that or any other axiom by which it might be proved ; and knows it as certainly as any other man knows, that 'the whole is equal to all its parts,' or any other maxim ; and all from the same reason of self-evidence : the equality of those ideas being as visible and certain to him without that or any other axiom as with it, it needing no proof to make it perceived. Nor after the knowledge, that the whole is equal to all its parts, does he know that one and two are equal to three, better or more certainly than he did before. For if there be any odds in those ideas, the whole and parts are more obscure, or at least more difficult to be settled in the mind than those of one, two, and three. And indeed, I think, I may ask these men, who will needs have all knowledge, besides those general principles themselves, to depend on[1] general, innate[2], and self-evident[2] principles. What principle is requisite to prove that one and one are two, that two and two are four, that three times two are six ? Which being known without any proof, do evince, That either all knowledge does not depend on[1] certain *præcognita* or general maxims, called principles ; or else that these are principles : and if these are to be counted principles, a great part of numeration will be so. To which, if we add all the self-evident propositions which may be made about all our distinct ideas, principles will be almost infinite, at least innumerable, which men arrive to the knowledge of, at different ages ; and a great many of these innate principles[2] they never

---

[1] So to ' depend on ' them, he supposes, that without a *conscious* cognition of the *a priori* abstractions one could not see the necessary truth of any one of their concrete exemplifications—a sort of ' dependence ' which no reasonable thinker contends for. Cf. ch. iv. §§ 7, 8.

[2] As already repeatedly shown, Locke distinguishes ' innateness ' of ideas or principles from their ' self-evidence.' He sees in the discovery of ' self-evident ' truth by the individual the reward of intellectual exertion ; but ' innate knowledge ' means with him knowledge that is independent of exertion on the part of its possessor. I find no ground for Hamilton's assertion that Locke ' attempts to show ' that axioms are not only not in this sense innate, but that they are all only ' generalizations from experience.' (Cf. Hamilton's *Reid*, p. 465, *note.*)

come to know all their lives. But whether they come in view
of the mind earlier or later, this is true of them, that they are
all known by their native evidence; are wholly independent;
receive no light, nor are capable of any proof one from another;
much less the more particular from the more general, or the
more simple from the more compounded; the more simple
and less abstract being the most familiar, and the easier and
earlier apprehended [1]. But whichever be the clearest ideas, the
evidence and certainty of all such propositions is in this, That
a man sees the same idea to be the same idea, and infallibly
perceives two different ideas to be different ideas. For when
a man has in his understanding the ideas of one and of two,
the idea of yellow, and the idea of blue, he cannot but
certainly know that the idea of one is the idea of one, and
not the idea of two; and that the idea of yellow is the idea
of yellow, and not the idea of blue. For a man cannot
confound the ideas in his mind, which he has distinct: that
would be to have them confused and distinct at the same
time, which is a contradiction: and to have none distinct,
is to have no use of our faculties, to have no knowledge at all.
And, therefore, what idea soever is affirmed of itself, or whatsoever two entire distinct ideas are denied one of another, the
mind cannot but assent to such a proposition as infallibly true,
as soon as it understands the terms, without hesitation or need
of proof, or regarding those made in more general terms and
called maxims.

11. [[2] What shall we then say? Are these general maxims
of no use? By no means; though perhaps their use is not
that which it is commonly taken to be [3]. But, since doubting

---

[1] We have here some of Locke's
criteria for distinguishing self-evident
propositions from those that are not
self-evident.

[2] The following paragraphs within
brackets (pp. 277–83) were introduced
in the second edition.

[3] Stillingfleet,—in trying to show
the difference between what he calls
Locke's 'method of certainty by *ideas*,'
and his own 'method of certainty by

reason' (between which two methods
Locke himself could find ' no opposition')—charges the *Essay* with treating
' general principles and maxims of
reason' as of little or no use, instead
of being, as this critic held, of ' very
great use, and the only proper foundations of certainty.' ' To which,' says
Locke, ' I crave leave to say, that if
by *principles* and *maxims* your lordship
means all self-evident propositions,

BOOK IV.

CHAP. VII.

Axioms
have.

Of no use
to prove
less gene-
ral propo-
sitions, nor
as founda-
tions on
considera-
tion of
which any
science
has been
built.

in the least of what hath been by some men ascribed to these maxims may be apt to be cried out against, as overturning the foundations of all the sciences; it may be worth while to consider them with respect to other parts of our knowledge, and examine more particularly to what purposes they serve, and to what not.

(1) It is evident from what has been already said, that they are of no use to prove or confirm less general self-evident propositions [1].

(2) It is as plain that they are not, nor have been the foundations whereon any science hath been built [2]. There is, I know, a great deal of talk, propagated from scholastic men, of sciences and the maxims on which they are built: but it has been my ill-luck never to meet with any such sciences; much less any one built upon these two maxims, *what is, is*; and *it is impossible for the same thing to be and not to be.* And I would be glad to be shown where any such science, erected upon these or any other general axioms is to be found: and should be obliged to any one who would lay before me the frame and system of any science so built on these or any such like maxims, that could not be shown to stand as firm without any consideration of them. I ask, Whether these general maxims have not the same use in the study of divinity, and in theological questions, that they

our ways are even in this part the same; for I make self-evident propositions necessary to certainty, and found all certainty only on them. If by *principles* and *maxims* you mean a select number of self-evident propositions, distinguished from the rest by the name "maxims," which is the sense in which I use the term maxims in my *Essay*, it will be necessary to give a list of those maxims, and then to show that a man can be certain of no truth without the help of those maxims.' (*Third Letter*, p. 340; also p. 263.) Locke here, as in the *Essay*, confuses the *conscious* use of an *ulti-mate* principle with *its unconscious presupposition* in the formation of our knowledge.

[1] Cf. ch. ii. § 4.

[2] 'A great part of the chapter on Maxims is levelled against a notion, that all our knowledge is derived from these two maxims. This I take to be a ridiculous notion, justly deserving the treatment which Mr. Locke has given it, if it at all merited his notice. These are identical propositions; they are trifling, and surfeited with truth. No knowledge can be derived from them.' (Reid, *Essay* VI. ch. vii.) It is curious that Locke takes no account of the maxim or principle of causality, on which his own reasonings about God (ch. x) and the whole finite universe external to self (ch. xi) are assumed to depend.

have in other sciences? They serve here, too, to silence BOOK IV.
wranglers, and put an end to dispute. But I think that
nobody will therefore say, that the Christian religion is built CHAP. VII.
upon these maxims, or that the knowledge we have of it is
derived from these principles. It is from revelation we have
received it, and without revelation these maxims had never
been able to help us to it. When we find out an idea by
whose intervention we discover the connexion of two others,
this is a revelation from God to us by the voice of reason:
for we then come to know a truth that we did not know
before. When God declares any truth to us, this is a revelation to us by the voice of his Spirit, and we are advanced
in our knowledge. But in neither of these do we receive our
light or knowledge from maxims. But in the one, the things
themselves afford it: and we see the truth in them by perceiving their agreement or disagreement. In the other, God
himself affords it immediately to us: and we see the truth of
what he says in his unerring veracity [1].

(3) They are not of use to help men forward in the advance- Nor as
ment of sciences, or new discoveries of yet unknown truths. helps in
the dis-
Mr. Newton, in his never enough to be admired book [2], has covery of
demonstrated several propositions, which are so many new yet unknown
truths, before unknown to the world, and are further advances truths.
in mathematical knowledge: but, for the discovery of these,
it was not the general maxims, 'what is, is;' or, 'the whole is
bigger than a part,' or the like, that helped him. These were
not the clues that led him into the discovery of the truth and
certainty of those propositions. Nor was it by them that he
got the knowledge of those demonstrations [3], but by finding

---

[1] The two maxims in question are
those called by logicians the principles
of Identity and Contradiction. In
themselves they are criteria of inconsistency; they can be used to demonstrate an impossibility, not to add to
real knowledge. For this last, as
Locke would say, we must turn to
our sensuous and intellectual perception of things. Now, as in this the
rationality of nature is presupposed,
it follows that all experience of the

real may be regarded as revelation of
God, or the Eternal Reason that is at
the root of all reality; postulated by
implication in all scientific, as well
as expressly in all theological inferences.

[2] The *Principia*, published two years
before the *Essay*.

[3] The author of the *Principia*, in
other words, was not necessarily a
metaphysical philosopher.

out intermediate ideas that showed the agreement or disagreement of the ideas, as expressed in the propositions he demonstrated. This is the greatest exercise and improvement of human understanding in the enlarging of knowledge, and advancing the sciences; wherein they are far enough from receiving any help from the contemplation of these or the like magnified maxims. Would those who have this traditional admiration of these propositions, that they think no step can be made in knowledge without the support of an axiom, no stone laid in the building of the sciences without a general maxim, but distinguish between the method of acquiring knowledge, and of communicating it; between the method of raising any science, and that of teaching it to others, as far as it is advanced—they would see that those general maxims were not the foundations on which the first discoverers raised their admirable structures, nor the keys that unlocked and opened those secrets of knowledge. Though afterwards, when schools were erected, and sciences had their professors to teach what others had found out, they often made use of maxims, i.e. laid down certain propositions which were self-evident, or to be received for true; which being settled in the minds of their scholars as unquestionable verities, they on occasion made use of, to convince them of truths in particular instances, that were not so familiar to their minds as those general axioms which had before been inculcated to them, and carefully settled in their minds. Though these particular instances, when well reflected on, are no less self-evident to the understanding than the general maxims brought to confirm them: and it was in those particular instances that the first discoverer found the truth, without the help of the general maxims: and so may any one else do, who with attention considers them [1].

---

[1] That the 'maxims or axioms' which a human knowledge of the universe necessarily presupposes are appealed to, or evoked into consciousness, when knowledge, reached without their aid consciously, has to be vindicated, and reduced to philosophical order, is a fact which shows that this *recognition* of them is essential to the *ultimate* organisation of human knowledge; but not for forming special sciences, and still less for ordinary knowledge. They are sought in the interest of the speculative philosopher, who tries to see human knowledge as an organic whole. So too men may be good reasoners who are ignorant of abstract logic.

To come, therefore, to the use that is made of maxims.

(1) They are of use, as has been observed, in the ordinary methods of teaching sciences as far as they are advanced: but of little or none in advancing them further.

(2) They are of use in disputes, for the silencing of obstinate wranglers, and bringing those contests to some conclusion [1]. Whether a need of them to that end came not in the manner following, I crave leave to inquire. The Schools having made disputation the touchstone of men's abilities, and the criterion of knowledge, adjudged victory to him that kept the field: and he that had the last word was concluded to have the better of the argument, if not of the cause. But because by this means there was like to be no decision between skilful combatants, whilst one never failed of a *medius terminus* to prove any proposition ; and the other could as constantly, without or with a distinction, deny the major or minor; to prevent, as much as could be, running out of disputes into an endless train of syllogisms, certain general propositions—most of them, indeed, self-evident—were introduced into the Schools : which being such as all men allowed and agreed in, were looked on as general measures of truth, and served instead of principles (where the disputants had not lain down any other between them) beyond which there was no going, and which must not be receded from by either side. And thus these maxims, getting the name of principles, beyond which men in dispute could not retreat, were by mistake taken to be the originals and sources from whence all knowledge began, and the foundations whereon the sciences were built. Because when in their disputes they came to any of these, they stopped

CHAP. VII.

Maxims of use in the exposition of what has been discovered, and in silencing obstinate wranglers.

---

[1] Formal or abstract logic, through its application of the principles of Identity and Contradiction which Locke disparages, has been described as ' the art of terminating wrangling.' Indeed the concrete reasonings which logic formulates all presuppose propositions that have their evidence in themselves, by which alone disputes can be brought to an issue, as Aristotle long ago showed. Otherwise men could not be *logically obliged* to unite in any conclusions on any subject. In common life, and in the special sciences, controversy is commonly kept within the *axiomata media* in its premises. But these virtually depend on preceding premises, and reasoning, properly speaking, becomes philosophical only when it is brought back to *ultimate* premises, i.e. maxims or axioms which are unconditionally true.

BOOK IV.

CHAP. VII.

How
Maxims
came to be
so much in
vogue.

there, and went no further; the matter was determined. But how much this is a mistake, hath been already shown.

This method of the Schools, which have been thought the fountains of knowledge, introduced, as I suppose, the like use of these maxims into a great part of conversation out of the Schools, to stop the mouths of cavillers, whom any one is excused from arguing any longer with, when they deny these general self-evident principles received by all reasonable men who have once thought of them : but yet their use herein is but to put an end to wrangling. They in truth, when urged in such cases, teach nothing : that is already done by the intermediate ideas made use of in the debate, whose connexion may be seen without the help of those maxims, and so the truth known before the maxim is produced, and the argument brought to a first principle. Men would give off a wrong argument before it came to that, if in their disputes they proposed to themselves the finding and embracing of truth, and not a contest for victory [1]. And thus maxims have their use to put a stop to their perverseness, whose ingenuity should have yielded sooner. But the method of the Schools having allowed and encouraged men to oppose and resist evident truth till they are baffled, i. e. till they are reduced to contradict themselves, or some established principles : it is no wonder that they should not in civil conversation be ashamed of that which in the Schools is counted a virtue and a glory, viz. obstinately to maintain that side of the question they have chosen, whether true or false, to the last extremity; even after conviction. A strange way to attain truth and knowledge : and that which I think the rational part of mankind, not corrupted by education, could scarce believe should ever be admitted amongst the lovers of truth, and students of religion or nature, or introduced into the seminaries of those who are to propagate the truths of religion or philosophy amongst the ignorant and unconvinced. How much such a way of learning is like

---

[1] In this the philosopher differs from the mere arguer. The former seeks for propositions which contain their evidence in their meaning, and thus determine questions finally; the mere arguer seeks for victory, on the foundation of dogmatic assumptions which he does not care to criticise.

to turn young men's minds from the sincere search and BOOK IV.
love of truth ; nay, and to make them doubt whether ⎯•⎯
there is any such thing, or, at least, worth the adhering CHAP. VII.
to, I shall not now inquire. This I think, that, bating
those places, which brought the Peripatetic[1] Philosophy into
their schools, where it continued many ages, without teaching the world anything but the art of wrangling, these
maxims were nowhere thought the foundations on which
the sciences were built, nor the great helps to the advancement of knowledge.]

[[2] As to these general maxims, therefore, they are, as I have Of great
said, of great use] in disputes, to stop the mouths of wrang- use to stop
wranglers
lers ; but not of much use to the discovery of unknown in disputes, but
truths, or to help the mind forwards in its search after of little use
knowledge. For who ever began to build his knowledge on to the
discovery
this general proposition, *what is, is* ; or, *it is impossible for* of truths.
the same thing to be and not to be : and from either of
these, as from a principle of science, deduced a system of
useful knowledge[3] ? Wrong opinions often involving contradictions, one of these maxims, as a touchstone, may serve
well to show whither they lead. But yet, however fit to lay
open the absurdity or mistake of a man's reasoning or
opinion, they are of very little use for enlightening the
understanding : and it will not be found that the mind receives much help from them in its progress in knowledge ;
which would be neither less, nor less certain, were these two
general propositions never thought on[4]. It is true, as I have
said, they sometimes serve in argumentation to stop a
wrangler's mouth, by showing the absurdity of what he
saith, [[5] and by exposing him to the shame of contradicting

---

[1] 'Peripatetick,' in the early editions, here and elsewhere.

[2] In first edition—'What shall we
then say? Are these maxims of no
use? Yes, they are of great use,' &c.

[3] Formal or abstract logic evolves
its criteria of verbal consistency on the
foundation of those maxims, the utility
of which is granted in the next sentence.

[4] The two maxims in question, as
developed and applied in logic, do not
directly extend real knowledge; although indirectly they may contribute
to this, by methodising what we have
known in an imperfect manner, and
by purging our beliefs of verbal inconsistencies that may be latent in the
expression.

[5] Added in second edition.

what all the world knows, and he himself cannot but own to be true.] But it is one thing to show a man that he is in an error, and another to put him in possession of truth; and I would fain know what truths these two propositions are able to teach, and by their influence make us know, which we did not know before, or could not know without them. Let us reason from them as well as we can, they are only about identical predications, and influence, if any at all, none but such. Each particular proposition concerning identity or diversity is as clearly and certainly known in itself, if attended to, as either of these general ones: [¹ only these general ones, as serving in all cases, are therefore more inculcated and insisted on.] As to other less general maxims, many of them are no more than bare verbal propositions, and teach us nothing but the respect and import of names one to another. 'The whole is equal to all its parts:' what real truth, I beseech you, does it teach us? What more is contained in that maxim, than what the signification of the word *totum*, or the *whole*, does of itself import? And he that knows that the *word* whole stands for what is made up of all its parts, knows very little less than that the whole is equal to all its parts. And, upon the same ground, I think that this proposition, 'A hill is higher than a valley,' and several the like, may also pass for maxims. But yet [² masters of mathematics, when they would, as teachers of what they know, initiate others in that science do not] without reason place this and some other such maxims [³ at the entrance of their systems]; that their scholars, having in the beginning perfectly acquainted their thoughts with these propositions, made in such general terms, may be used to make such reflections, and have these more general propositions, as formed rules and sayings, ready to apply to all particular cases. Not that if they be equally weighed, they are more clear and evident than the particular instances they are brought to confirm; but that, being more familiar

---

¹ In first edition—'and there is nothing more certain than that by these maxims alone we cannot evidence to ourselves the truth of any one thing really existing.'

² In first edition—'mathematicians do not,' &c.

³ Added in the second edition.

to the mind, the very naming them is enough to satisfy the
understanding. But this, I say, is more from our custom
of using them, and the establishment they have got in our
minds by our often thinking of them, than from the different
evidence of the things. But before custom has settled
methods of thinking and reasoning in our minds, I am apt to
imagine it is quite otherwise ; and that the child, when
a part of his apple is taken away, knows it better in that
particular instance, than by this general proposition, ' The
whole is equal to all its parts ; ' and that, if one of these
have need to be confirmed to him by the other, the general
has more need to be let into his mind by the particular, than
the particular by the general. For in *particulars* our
knowledge begins, and so spreads itself, by degrees, to *generals* [1]. Though afterwards the mind takes the quite contrary
course, and having drawn its knowledge into as general propositions as it can, makes those familiar to its thoughts, and
accustoms itself to have recourse to them, as to the standards
of truth and falsehood [2]. By which familiar use of them, as
rules to measure the truth of other propositions, it comes in
time to be thought, that more particular propositions have
their truth and evidence from their conformity to these
more general ones, which, in discourse and argumentation,
are so frequently urged, and constantly admitted. And
this I think to be the reason why, amongst so many self-
evident propositions, the *most general only* have had the title
of *maxims*.

12. One thing further, I think, it may not be amiss to Maxims,
observe concerning these general maxims, That they are so if care
far from improving or establishing our minds in true know- taken in

---

[1] This is the order in time of the
conscious acquisition of knowledge
that is human. The *Essay* might be
regarded as a commentary on this one
sentence. Our intellectual progress is
from particulars and involuntary recipi-
ency, through reactive doubt and criticism, into what is at last reasoned faith.

[2] This is the philosophic attitude.
Therein one consciously apprehends
the intellectual necessities that were

unconsciously presupposed, in all its
previous intellectual progress. In
philosophy we ' draw our knowledge
into as general propositions as it can '
be made to assume, and thus either
learn to see it as an organic whole in
a speculative unity, or learn that it
cannot be so seen in a finite intelligence, and that even at the last it
must remain ' broken ' and mysterious
in human understanding.

BOOK IV.
CHAP. VII.
the Use of
Words,
may prove
Contradic-
tions.

ledge, that if our notions be wrong, loose, or unsteady, and we resign up our thoughts to the sound of words, rather than [¹ fix them on settled, determined] ideas of things; I say these general maxims will serve to confirm us in mistakes; and in such a way of use of words, which is most common, will serve to prove contradictions ²: v. g. he that with Descartes ³ shall frame in his mind an idea of what he calls body to be nothing but extension, may easily demonstrate that there is no vacuum, i. e. no space void of body, by this maxim, *What is, is.* For the idea to which he annexes the name body, being bare extension, his knowledge that space cannot be without body, is certain. For he knows his own idea of extension clearly and distinctly, and knows that it is what it is, and not another idea, though it be called by these three names,—extension, body, space. Which three words, standing for one and the same idea, may, no doubt, with the same evidence and certainty be affirmed one of another, as each of itself: and it is as certain, that, whilst I use them all to stand for one and the same idea, this predication is as true and identical in its signification, that 'space is body,' as this predication is true and identical, that 'body is body,' both in signification and sound.

Instance
in Vacuum.

13. But if another should come and make to himself another idea, different from Descartes's, of the thing, which yet with Descartes he calls by the same name body, and make his idea, which he expresses by the word body, to be of a thing that hath both extension and solidity together; he will as easily demonstrate, that there may be a vacuum or space without a body, as Descartes demonstrated the contrary. Because the idea to which he gives the name

---

¹ In first edition—' to settled, clear, distinct.'

² It is only through the ambiguity in the words we use that 'contradictions,' which of course cannot be realised in thought, are possible even in expression. Contradiction, which accordingly can exist only in terms, is sustained there by confusion of thought on the part of those who try to make a contradictory use of them.

An inconsiderate application of propositions of extreme abstraction is apt to induce this sort of confusion in thought, due often to the fatigue implied in the endeavour distinctly to realise by reflection what highly abstract words mean. Hence such words are apt to circulate empty of all meaning.

³ Stewart says that Descartes is not named in the *Essay.*

space being barely the simple one of extension, and the BOOK IV.
idea to which he gives the name body being the complex ————
idea of extension and resistibility or solidity, together in the CHAP. VII.
same subject, these two ideas are not exactly one and the
same, but in the understanding as distinct as the ideas of
one and two, white and black, or as of *corporeity* and
humanity, if I may use those barbarous terms : and therefore
the predication of them in our minds, or in words standing
for them, is not identical, but the negation of them one of
another ; [¹ viz. this proposition : ' Extension or space is not
body,' is] as true and evidently certain as this maxim, *It is
impossible for the same thing to be and not to be*, [² can make
any proposition.]

14. But yet, though both these propositions (as you see) But they
may be equally demonstrated, viz. that there may be a vacuum, prove
and that there cannot be a vacuum, by these two certain Existence
principles, viz. *what is, is*, and *the same thing cannot be and* of things
not be : yet neither of these principles will serve to prove to us.
us, that any, or what bodies do exist : for that we are left
to our senses to discover to us as far as they can. Those
universal and self-evident principles ³ being only our constant,
clear, and distinct knowledge of our own ideas, more general
or comprehensive, can assure us of nothing that passes without the mind : their certainty is founded only upon the
knowledge we have of each idea by itself, and of its distinction from others, about which we cannot be mistaken
whilst they are in our minds ; though we may be and
often are mistaken when we retain the names without the
ideas ; or use them confusedly, sometimes for one and sometimes for another idea. In which cases the force of these
axioms, reaching only to the sound, and not the signification
of the words, serves only to lead us into confusion, mistake,
and error. [⁴ It is to show men that these maxims, however

---

¹ Added in second edition.
² Added in second edition. Both,
under these conditions, are merely
verbal or trifling propositions.
³ Locke keeps to the ' maxims ' of
identity and contradiction as his examples, neglecting the axioms of

mathematics, and his own virtual
assumption of the principles of substance and causality, e. g. in his
' demonstration ' of the existence of
God. Aristotle rests philosophy at
last on the principle of contradiction.
⁴ Added in second edition, appa-

BOOK IV.
CHAP. VII.

cried up for the great guards of truth, will not secure them from error in a careless loose use of their words, that I have made this remark. In all that is here suggested concerning their little use for the improvement of knowledge, or dangerous use in undetermined ideas, I have been far enough from saying or intending they should be laid aside; as some have been too forward to charge me. I affirm them to be truths, self-evident truths; and so cannot be laid aside. As far as their influence will reach, it is in vain to endeavour, nor will I attempt, to abridge it. But yet, without any injury to truth or knowledge, I may have reason to think their use is not answerable to the great stress which seems to be laid on them; and I may warn men not to make an ill use of them, for the confirming themselves in errors.]

They cannot add to our knowledge of Substances, and their Application to complex Ideas is dangerous.

15. But let them be of what use they will in verbal propositions, they cannot discover or prove to us the least knowledge of the nature of substances, as they are found and exist without us, any further than grounded on experience[1]. And though the consequence of these two propositions, called principles, be very clear, and their use not dangerous or hurtful, in the probation of such things wherein there is no need at all of them for proof, but such as are clear by themselves without them, viz. where our ideas are [determined] and known by the names that stand for them: yet when these principles, viz. *what is, is*, and *it is impossible for the same thing to be and not to be*, are made use of in the probation of propositions wherein are words standing for complex ideas, v. g. man, horse, gold, virtue; there they are of infinite danger, and most commonly make men receive and retain falsehood for manifest truth, and uncertainty for demonstration: upon which follow error, obstinacy, and all

rently to meet the allegation of critics, that Locke denied the self-evidence of all general propositions, or at least their utility as helps to the improvement of knowledge. It may be noted that in all that Locke says about the self-evidence of these ultimate propositions, he says nothing about their nature—whether analytic or synthetic, or their origin. He simply accepts the fact that we have mental experience of their intuitive necessity.

[1] Unless 'experience' supplies data, there is nothing for the 'maxims' to work upon; but if without their conscious or unconscious presupposition, our real experience cannot be formed intelligibly, there is room for that ulterior inquiry which Locke habitually leaves in the background.

the mischiefs that can happen from wrong reasoning. The
reason whereof is not, that these principles are less true [¹ or
of less force] in proving propositions made of terms standing
for complex ideas, than where the propositions are about
simple ideas. [² But because men mistake generally,—thinking
that where the same terms are preserved, the propositions
are about the same things, though the ideas they stand for
are in truth different, therefore these maxims are made use
of to support those which in sound and appearance are contradictory propositions ; and is clear in the demonstrations
above mentioned about a vacuum. So that whilst men take
words for things, as usually they do, these maxims may and
do commonly serve to prove contradictory propositions; as
shall yet be further made manifest.]

16. For instance : let *man* be that concerning which you Instance
in demon-
strations
about Man,
which can
only be
Verbal.
would by these first principles demonstrate anything, and
we shall see, that so far as demonstration is by these
principles, it is only verbal, and gives us no certain, universal,
true proposition, or knowledge, of any being existing without
us. First, a child having framed the idea of a man, it is
probable that his idea is just like that picture which the
painter makes of the visible appearances joined together ;
and such a complication of ideas together in his understanding
makes up the single complex idea which he calls man, whereof
white or flesh-colour in England being one, the child can
demonstrate to you that a negro is not a man, because white
colour was one of the constant simple ideas of the complex
idea he calls man ; and therefore he can demonstrate, by the
principle, *It is impossible for the same thing to be and not
to be*, that a negro is *not* a man; the foundation of his
certainty being not that universal proposition, which perhaps
he never heard nor thought of, but the clear, distinct perception he hath of his own simple ideas of black and white,

---

¹ Added in second edition.
² Instead of this sentence the first
edition reads thus :—' But because
men mistake generally, thinking such
propositions to be about the reality
of things, and not the bare signification
of words, when indeed they are for
the most part nothing else, as is clear
in the demonstration of *vacuum*, where
the word *body* sometimes stands for
one idea, and sometimes for another:
but shall be yet made more manifest.'

BOOK IV.
CHAP. VII.

which he cannot be persuaded to take, nor can ever mistake one for another, whether he knows that maxim or no. And to this child, or any one who hath such an idea, which he calls man, can you never demonstrate that a man hath a soul, because his idea of man includes no such notion or idea in it. And therefore, to him, the principle of *What is, is,* proves not this matter ; but it depends upon collection and observation, by which he is to make his complex idea called man.

Another instance.

17. Secondly, Another that hath gone further in framing and collecting the idea he calls *man*, and to the outward shape adds laughter and rational discourse, may demonstrate that infants and changelings are no men, by this maxim, *it is impossible for the same thing to be and not to be* ; and I have discoursed with very rational men, who have actually denied that they are men[1].

A third instance.

18. Thirdly, Perhaps another makes up the complex idea which he calls *man*, only out of the ideas of body in general, and the powers of language and reason, and leaves out the shape wholly : this man is able to demonstrate that a man may have no hands, but be *quadrupes*, neither of those being included in his idea of man : and in whatever body or shape he found speech and reason joined, that was a man ; because, having a clear knowledge of such a complex idea, it is certain that *What is, is.*

Little use of these Maxims in Proofs where we have clear and distinct Ideas.

19. So that, if rightly considered, I think we may say, That where our ideas are determined in our minds, and have annexed to them by us known and steady names under those settled determinations, there is little need, or no use at all of these maxims, to prove the agreement or disagreement of any of them. He that cannot discern the truth or falsehood of such propositions, without the help of these and the like maxims, will not be helped by these maxims to do it : since he cannot be supposed to know the truth of these maxims themselves without proof, if he cannot know the truth of others without proof, which are as self-evident as these. Upon this ground it is that intuitive knowledge

---

[1] That is, ' infants and changelings.'

neither requires nor admits any proof, one part of it more
than another[1]. He that will suppose it does, takes away
the foundation of all knowledge and certainty; and he that
needs any proof to make him certain, and give his assent
to this proposition, that two are equal to two, will also
have need of a proof to make him admit, that what is, is.
He that needs a probation to convince him that two are
not three, that white is not black, that a triangle is not
a circle, &c., or any other two [determined] distinct ideas are
not one and the same, will need also a demonstration to
convince him that *It is impossible for the same thing to be
and not to be* [2].

20. And as these maxims are of little use where we have Their Use
determined ideas, so they are, as I have showed, of dangerous dangerous,
use where [[3] our ideas are not determined ; and where] we use where our
words that are not annexed to determined ideas, but such Ideas are not
as are of a loose and wandering signification, sometimes deter-
standing for one, and sometimes for another idea : from mined.
which follow mistake and error, which these maxims (brought
as proofs to establish propositions, wherein the terms stand
for undetermined ideas) do by their authority confirm and rivet[4].

[1] But it admits, and, from the purely intellectual point of view, requires, *analysis* and *criticism*. The problem of speculative philosophy might be described as the conscious elaboration in their most abstract form of the rational implicates that are *latent* in our physical and moral interpretations of the universe—an elaboration adapted not to *prove* the ultimate presuppositions of reason, but simply to exhibit the universe in the greatest possible intellectual light, for the intellectual pleasure of so seeing it.

[2] The concrete example, in which the abstract maxim is embodied, suffices for the purposes of ordinary knowledge and science, but is *per se* inadequate in speculative philosophy.

[3] Introduced in second edition.

[4] This chapter warns against a common abuse of 'maxims,' because (1) although in themselves they are self-

evident, they are not truths of which all men are conscious, but are, on the contrary, the last to arise in our perceptions; (2) all other knowledge may be held without our apprehension of them ; (3) they are apt to involve those who deal much with them in confused and verbally contradictory thinking ; and (4) in their application to complex ideas they are very misleading. But he grants their utility, (1) when they are held in reserve to meet those who are sceptics with regard to less abstract propositions; and (2) to stop the mouths of wranglers—which they could not do if they were not virtually accepted by every man, and virtually embodied in experience, as real and immutable relations between the things or persons therein manifested. And he distinguishes really self-evident propositions from *received* maxims or axioms here included.

CHAPTER VIII.

OF TRIFLING PROPOSITIONS.

Some
Proposi-
tions
bring no
Increase
to our
Know-
ledge.

As, First,
identical
Proposi-
tions.

1. WHETHER the maxims treated of in the foregoing chapter be of that use to real knowledge as is generally supposed, I leave to be considered. This, I think, may confidently be affirmed, That there *are* universal propositions, which, though they be certainly true, yet they add no light to our understanding; bring no increase to our knowledge [1]. Such are—

2. *First*, All purely *identical propositions.* These obviously and at first blush appear to contain no instruction in them; for when we affirm the said term of itself, whether it be barely verbal, or whether it contains any clear and real idea, it shows us nothing but what we must certainly know before, whether such a proposition be either made by, or proposed to us. Indeed, that most general one, *what is, is,* may serve sometimes to show a man the absurdity he is guilty of, when, by circumlocution or equivocal terms, he would in particular instances deny the same thing of itself; because nobody will so openly bid defiance to common sense, as to affirm visible and direct contradictions in plain words; or, if he does, a man is excused if he breaks off any further discourse with him. But yet I think I may say, that neither that received maxim, nor any other identical proposition, teaches us anything; and though in such kind of propositions this great

---

[1] The propositions dealt with in this chapter are purely identical ones, and also all those called analytical or ex-plicative,—the principle of which is expressed in an abstract way in the logical law of identity. The preceding chapter comprehends the maxims or axioms that Kant would regard as judgments synthetic *a priori*.

and magnified maxim, boasted to be the foundation of de- BOOK IV.
monstration, may be and often is made use of to confirm CHAP.
them, yet all it proves amounts to no more than this, That VIII.
the same word may with great certainty be affirmed of itself,
without any doubt of the truth of any such proposition ; and
let me add, also, without any real knowledge.

3. For, at this rate, any very ignorant person, who can but Examples.
make a proposition, and knows what he means when he says
ay or no, may make a million of propositions of whose truth
he may be infallibly certain, and yet not know one thing in the
world thereby ; v. g. 'what is a soul, is a soul;' or, 'a soul is
a soul;' 'a spirit is a spirit ;' 'a fetiche is a fetiche,' &c.
These all being equivalent to this proposition, viz. *what is,
is*[1]; i. e. what hath existence, hath existence ; or, who hath
a soul, hath a soul. What is this more than trifling with
words? It is but like a monkey shifting his oyster from one
hand to the other : and had he but words, might no doubt
have said, ' Oyster in right hand is subject, and oyster in left
hand is predicate:' and so might have made a self-evident
proposition of oyster, i. e. oyster is oyster ; and yet, with all
this, not have been one whit the wiser or more knowing :
and that way of handling the matter would much at one
have satisfied the monkey's hunger, or a man's understanding,
and they would have improved in knowledge and bulk together.

[[2] I know there are some who, because identical propositions How
are self-evident, show a great concern for them, and think Identical
they do great service to philosophy by crying them up ; as if Proposi-
in them was contained all knowledge, and the understanding trifling.
were led into all truth by them only. I grant as forwardly
as any one, that they are all true and self-evident. I grant

---

[1] ' What is, is '—one of the forms in
which the law of Identity is expressed,
being the logical principle of all affirmation and definition, by which each
object or idea is distinguished from all
others. Cf. chh. i. § 4; iii. § 8 ; also
Leibniz, *Nouveaux Essais*, Liv. IV.
ch. ii, who presents it as the fundamental affirmation of reason, or condition of the reality of knowledge, and

makes mathematical proof resolve into
perception of this identity. See too
Aristotle, *Anal. Pr.* I. 32 ; *Metaph.*
Bk. IV. chh. iii, iv, vii. Ambiguity has
been alleged against the law of identity,
and emptiness, as here by Locke.

[2] This and the four following paragraphs were added in the fourth edition,
with reference to criticisms of Stillingfleet and others.

further, that the foundation of all our knowledge lies in the faculty we have of perceiving the same idea to be the same, and of discerning it from those that are different; as I have shown in the foregoing chapter[1]. But how that vindicates the making use of identical propositions, for the improvement of knowledge, from the imputation of trifling, I do not see. Let any one repeat, as often as he pleases, that 'the will is the will,' or lay what stress on it he thinks fit; of what use is this, and an infinite the like propositions, for the enlarging our knowledge? Let a man abound, as much as the plenty of words which he has will permit, in such propositions as these: 'a law is a law,' and 'obligation is obligation;' 'right is right,' and 'wrong is wrong:'—will these and the like ever help him to an acquaintance with ethics, or instruct him or others in the knowledge of morality? Those who know not, nor perhaps ever will know, what is right and what is wrong, nor the measures of them, can with as much assurance make, and infallibly know, the truth of these and all such propositions, as he that is best instructed in morality can do. But what advance do such propositions give in the knowledge of anything necessary or useful for their conduct?

He would be thought to do little less than trifle, who, for the enlightening the understanding in any part of knowledge, should be busy with identical propositions, and insist on such maxims as these: 'substance is substance,' and 'body is body;' 'a vacuum is a vacuum,' and 'a vortex is a vortex;' 'a centaur is a centaur,' and 'a chimera is a chimera,' &c. For these and all such are equally true, equally certain, and equally self-evident. But yet they cannot but be counted trifling, when made use of as principles of instruction, and stress laid on them as helps to knowledge; since they teach nothing but what every one who is capable of discourse knows without being told, viz. that the same term is the same term, and the same idea the same idea. And upon this account it was that I formerly did, and do still think, the offering and inculcating such propositions, in order to give the understanding any new light, or inlet into the knowledge of things, no better than trifling.

[1] See also ch. ii. § 1.

Instruction lies in something very different; and he that would enlarge his own or another's mind to truths he does not yet know, must find out intermediate ideas, and then lay them in such order one by another, that the understanding may see the agreement or disagreement of those in question. Propositions that do this are instructive ; but they are far from such as affirm the same term of itself; which is no way to advance one's self or others in any sort of knowledge. It no more helps to that than it would help any one in his learning to read, to have such propositions as these inculcated to him—'An A is an A,' and 'a B is a B;' which a man may know as well as any schoolmaster, and yet never be able to read a word as long as he lives. Nor do these, or any such identical propositions help him one jot forwards in the skill of reading, let him make what use of them he can.

If those who blame my calling them *trifling propositions* had but read and been at the pains to understand what I have above writ in very plain English, they could not but have seen that by identical propositions I mean only such wherein the same term, importing the same idea, is affirmed of itself : which I take to be the proper signification of identical propositions ; and concerning all such, I think I may continue safely to say, that to propose them as instructive is no better than trifling. For no one who has the use of reason can miss them, where it is necessary they should be taken notice of ; nor doubt of their truth when he does take notice of them.

But if men will call propositions *identical*, wherein the same term is not affirmed of itself, whether they speak more properly than I, others must judge ; this is certain, all that they say of propositions that are not identical in my sense, concerns not me nor what I have said ; all that I have said relating to those propositions wherein the same term is affirmed of itself. And I would fain see an instance wherein any such can be made use of, to the advantage and improvement of any one's knowledge. Instances of other kinds, whatever use may be made of them, concern not me, as not being such as I call identical.]

Secondly, Proposi-
tions in which a part of any complex Idea is predicated of the Whole.

4. II. Another sort of trifling propositions is, *when a part of the complexidea is predicated of the name of the whole*; a part of the definition of the word defined [1]. Such are all propositions wherein the genus is predicated of the species, or more comprehensive of less comprehensive terms. For what information, what knowledge, carries this proposition in it, viz. 'Lead is a metal' to a man who knows the complex idea the name lead stands for? All the simple ideas that go to the complex one signified by the term metal, being nothing but what he before comprehended and signified by the name lead. Indeed, to a man that knows the signification of the word metal, and not of the word lead, it is a shorter way to explain the signification of the word lead, by saying it is a metal, which at once expresses several of its simple ideas, than to enumerate them one by one, telling him it is a body very heavy, fusible, and malleable.

As part of the Definition of the Term defined.

5. Alike trifling it is to predicate any other part of the definition of the term defined, or to affirm any one of the simple ideas of a complex one of the name of the whole complex idea; as, 'All gold is fusible.' For fusibility being one of the simple ideas that goes to the making up the complex one the sound gold stands for, what can it be but playing with sounds, to affirm that of the name gold, which is comprehended in its received signification? It would be thought little better than ridiculous to affirm gravely, as a truth of moment, that gold is yellow; and I see not how it is any jot more material to say it is fusible, unless that quality be left out of the complex idea, of which the sound gold is the mark in ordinary speech. What instruction can it carry with it, to tell one that which he hath been told already, or he is supposed to know before? For I am supposed to know the signification of the word another uses to me, or else he is to tell me. And if I know that the name gold stands for this complex idea of body, yellow, heavy, fusible, malleable, it will not much instruct me to put it solemnly afterwards

---

[1] In a logical definition the simple ideas latent in the subject are exhaustively presented in the predicate, so that the analysis or explication is complete; whereas it is only partial in the 'trifling propositions' dealt with in what follows.

in a proposition, and gravely say, all gold is fusible. Such propositions can only serve to show the disingenuity of one who will go from the definition of his own terms, by reminding him sometimes of it ; but carry no knowledge with them, but of the signification of words, however certain they be [1].

6. 'Every man is an animal, or living body,' is as certain a proposition as can be ; but no more conducing to the knowledge of things than to say, a palfrey is an ambling horse, or a neighing, ambling animal, both being only about the signification of words, and make me know but this— That body, sense, and motion, or power of sensation and moving, are three of those ideas that I always comprehend and signify by the word man : and where they are not to be found together, the *name man* belongs not to that thing : and so of the other—That body, sense, and a certain way of going, with a certain kind of voice, are some of those ideas which I always comprehend and signify by the *word palfrey*; and when they are not to be found together, the name palfrey belongs not to that thing. It is just the same, and to the same purpose, when any term standing for any one or more of the simple ideas, that altogether make up that complex idea which is called man, is affirmed of the term man :—v. g. suppose a Roman signified by the word *homo* all these distinct ideas united in one subject, *corporietas, sensibilitas, potentia se movendi, rationalitas, risibilitas* ; he might, no doubt, with great certainty, universally affirm one, more, or all of these together of the word *homo*, but did no more than say that the word *homo*, in his country, comprehended in its signification all these ideas. Much like a romance knight, who by the word *palfrey* signified these ideas :—body of a certain figure, four-legged, with sense, motion, ambling, neighing, white, used to have a woman on his back—might with the same certainty universally affirm also any or all of these of the *word* palfrey : but did thereby teach no more, but that the word palfrey, in his

[1] He here grants that 'trifling propositions' of this sort, by their explication of the connotation of their subject-terms, may 'carry knowledge of the signification of words' into a mind that had permitted their meanings to become obscure or confused.

BOOK IV.

—*+*—

CHAP.
VIII.

or romance language, stood for all these, and was not to be applied to anything where any of these was wanting. But he that shall tell me, that in whatever thing sense, motion, reason, and laughter, were united, that thing had actually a notion of God, or would be cast into a sleep by opium, made indeed an instructive proposition: because neither having the notion of God, nor being cast into sleep by opium, being contained in the idea signified by the word man, we are by such propositions taught something more than barely what the word *man* stands for: and therefore the knowledge contained in it is more than verbal.

For this teaches but the Signification of Words.

7. Before a man makes any proposition, he is supposed to understand the terms he uses in it, or else he talks like a parrot, only making a noise by imitation, and framing certain sounds, which he has learnt of others; but not as a rational creature, using them for signs of ideas which he has in his mind. The hearer also is supposed to understand the terms as the speaker uses them, or else he talks jargon, and makes an unintelligible noise. And therefore he trifles with words who makes such a proposition, which, when it is made, contains no more than one of the terms does, and which a man was supposed to know before: v. g. a triangle hath three sides, or saffron is yellow. And this is no further tolerable than where a man goes to explain his terms to one who is supposed or declares himself not to understand him ; and then it teaches only the signification of that word, and the use of that sign.

But adds no real Knowledge.

8. We can know then the truth of two sorts of propositions with perfect certainty. The one is, of those trifling propositions[1] which have a certainty in them, but it is only a verbal certainty, but not instructive. And, secondly, we can know the truth, and so may be certain in propositions, which affirm something of another, which is a necessary consequence of its precise complex idea, but not contained in it: as that the external angle of all triangles is bigger than either of the opposite internal angles. Which relation of the outward angle to either of the opposite internal angles, making no

---

[1] Otherwise called analytical or explicative propositions.

part of the complex idea signified by the name triangle, BOOK IV.

this is a real truth, and conveys with it instructive real

knowledge [1].

9. We having little or no knowledge of what combinations
there be of simple ideas existing together in substances, but
by our senses [2], we cannot make any universal certain propositions concerning them, any further than our nominal
essences lead us. Which being to a very few and inconsiderable truths, in respect of those which depend on their real
constitutions [3], the general propositions that are made about
substances, if they are certain, are for the most part but
trifling ; and if they are instructive, are uncertain, and such
as we can have no knowledge [4] of their real truth, how much
soever constant observation and analogy may assist our judgment [5] in guessing. Hence it comes to pass, that one may
often meet with very clear and coherent discourses, that
amount yet to nothing. For it is plain that names of substantial beings, as well as others, as far as they have relative
significations affixed to them, may, with great truth, be
joined negatively and affirmatively in propositions, as their
relative definitions make them fit to be so joined ; and propositions consisting of such terms, may, with the same clearness, be deduced one from another, as those that convey the
most real truths : and all this without any knowledge of the
nature or reality of things existing without us. By this
method one may make demonstrations and undoubted propositions in words, and yet thereby advance not one jot in the
knowledge of the truth of things : v. g. he that having learnt
these following words, with their ordinary mutual relative
acceptations annexed to them ; v. g. *substance, man, animal,
form, soul, vegetative, sensitive, rational,* may make several
undoubted propositions about the soul, without knowing at
all what the soul really is : and of this sort, a man may

BOOK IV.

CHAP.
VIII.

General
Proposi-
tions
concern-
ing Sub-
stances
are often
trifling.

---

[1] The second class corresponds to
Kant's synthetical *a priori* judgments,
which Locke here clearly distinguishes
from analytic, but without recognizing
their peculiarity and importance.

[2] In strictness mere sense only
reveals the coexistence of the moment,
if even this.

[3] Cf. Bk. II. ch. viii.

[4] Knowledge—as contrasted with
presumption of probability.

[5] As 'judgment' is defined in the
Essay, i.e. presumption of what is more
or less probable.

BOOK IV.

CHAP. VIII.

And why.

find an infinite number of propositions, reasonings, and conclusions, in books of metaphysics, school-divinity, and some sort of natural philosophy; and, after all, know as little of God, spirits, or bodies, as he did before he set out[1].

10. He that hath liberty to define, i. e. to determine the signification of his names of substances (as certainly every one does in effect, who makes them stand for his own ideas), and makes their significations at a venture, taking them from his own or other men's fancies, and not from an examination or inquiry into the nature of things themselves; may with little trouble demonstrate them one of another, according to those several respects and mutual relations he has given them one to another; wherein, however things agree or disagree in their own nature, he needs mind nothing but his own notions, with the names he hath bestowed upon them: but thereby no more increases his own knowledge than he does his riches, who, taking a bag of counters, calls one in a certain place a pound, another in another place a shilling, and a third in a third place a penny; and so proceeding, may undoubtedly reckon right, and cast up a great sum, according to his counters so placed, and standing

---

[1] All common names might thus, by verbal definition, as he goes on to show, become terms in a merely verbal system of demonstrated conclusions, after which one would know as little about the actual substances in the universe as he did before. 'It might be possible,' Dugald Stewart remarks, '*by devising a set of arbitrary definitions,* to form a science which, although conversant about moral, political, or physical ideas, should yet be as certain as geometry. It is of no moment whether the definitions assumed correspond with facts or not, provided they do not express impossibilities, and be not inconsistent with each other. From these principles a series of consequences may be deduced by the most unexceptionable reasoning; and the results obtained will be perfectly analogous to mathematical propositions. The terms *true* and *false* cannot be applied to them, at least in the sense in which they are applicable to propositions relative to facts. All that can be said is, that they are, or are not [consistently] connected with the definitions which form the principles of the science; and therefore if we choose to call our conclusions *true* in one case and *false* in the other, these epithets must be understood merely to refer to their connexion with the *data* [arbitrary definitions], and not to their correspondence with things actually existing, or with events which we expect to be realized in future.' (*Collected Works*, vol. iii. p. 115.) This 'science' would be only a demonstrative development of the logical implicates of our own arbitrary nominal essences.

for more or less as he pleases, without being one jot the BOOK IV.
richer, or without even knowing how much a pound, shilling, CHAP.
or penny is, but only that one is contained in the other VIII.
twenty times, and contains the other twelve: which a man
may also do in the signification of words, by making them,
in respect of one another, more or less, or equally comprehensive.

11. Though yet concerning most words used in discourses, Thirdly,
equally argumentative and controversial, there is this more Using
to be complained of, which is the worst sort of trifling, and variously
which sets us yet further from the certainty of knowledge is trifling
we hope to attain by them, or find in them ; viz. that most
writers are so far from instructing us in the nature and
knowledge of things, that they use their words loosely and
uncertainly, and do not, by using them constantly and steadily
in the same significations [1], make plain and clear deductions
of words one from another, and make their discourses coherent
and clear, (how little soever they were instructive); which
were not difficult to do, did they not find it convenient to
shelter their ignorance or obstinacy under the obscurity and
perplexedness of their terms : to which, perhaps, inadvertency
and ill custom do in many men much contribute.

12. To conclude. Barely verbal propositions may be Marks of
known by these following marks : verbal
First, All propositions wherein two abstract terms are tions.
affirmed one of another, are barely about the signification of First,
sounds. For since no abstract idea can be the same with any tion in
other but itself, when its abstract name is affirmed of any Abstract.
other term, it can signify no more but this, that it may, or
ought to be called by that name ; or that these two names
signify the same idea. Thus, should any one say that
parsimony is frugality, that gratitude is justice, that this or
that action is or is not temperate : however specious these
and the like propositions may at first sight seem, yet when

[1] Also when a speaker or writer reasons in words, he may reason with demonstrable verbal consistency, according to his own definitions of the words, but in meanings different from those which his hearers or readers naturally associate with them.

BOOK IV.

Chap.
VIII.

Secondly,
A part
of the
Definition
predicated
of any
Term.

we come to press them, and examine nicely what they contain, we shall find that it all amounts to nothing but the signification of those terms.

13. Secondly, All propositions wherein a part of the complex idea which any term stands for is predicated of that term, are only verbal: v. g. to say that gold is a metal, or heavy. And thus all propositions wherein more comprehensive[1] words, called genera, are affirmed of subordinate or less comprehensive[1], called species, or individuals, are barely verbal.

When by these two rules we have examined the propositions that make up the discourses we ordinarily meet with, both in and out of books, we shall perhaps find that a greater part of them than is usually suspected are purely about the signification of words, and contain nothing in them but the use and application of these signs.

This I think I may lay down for an infallible rule, That, wherever the distinct idea any word stands for is not known and considered, and something not contained in the idea is not affirmed or denied of it[2], there our thoughts stick wholly in sounds, and are able to attain no real truth or falsehood. This, perhaps, if well heeded, might save us a great deal of useless amusement and dispute; and very much shorten our trouble and wandering in the search of real and true knowledge.

[1] 'Comprehensive,' i. e. 'extensive,' according to the best usage, in which a notion is of *comprehensive* quantity according to the greater or smaller of qualities contained in it, and forming the essence of its name, and *extensive* in proportion to the number of species and individuals contained under it, or of which it is the genus. In affirmative propositions the subject is logically subordinate to, i. e. less extensive than, the predicate, when the proposition is interpreted according to the logical extent of its terms.

[2] When the 'distinct idea any word stands for,' according to custom, is 'not known and considered,' and when no other meaning is predicated of it, then of course the word must be empty, and the proposition 'sticks wholly in sounds,' as Locke seems ironically to suggest.

CHAPTER IX.

OF OUR THREEFOLD KNOWLEDGE OF EXISTENCE.

1. HITHERTO [1] we have only considered the essences of things [2]; which being only abstract ideas, and thereby removed in our thoughts from particular existence, (that being the proper operation of the mind, in abstraction, to consider an idea under no other existence but what it has in the understanding [3],) gives us no knowledge of real existence at all. Where, by the way, we may take notice, that universal propositions of whose truth or falsehood we can have certain knowledge concern not existence [4] : and further, that all particular affirmations or negations that would not be certain if they were made general, are only concerning existence ; they declaring only the accidental union or separation of ideas in things existing, which, in their abstract natures, have no known necessary union or repugnancy [5].

BOOK IV.

CHAP. IX.
General Propositions that are certain concern not Existence.

2. But, leaving the nature of propositions, and different

---

[1] 'Hitherto'—especially in chh. v-viii; also Bk. III. chh. v, vi.

[2] 'essences of things,' i. e. the essences of the *names* applied to them, called by Locke nominal essences.

[3] In propositions that concern real existence (as in Locke's fourth sort), and in those concerned with 'coexistence' of qualities and powers in substances (third sort), ideas are considered as manifestations of what exists in individual things, and not as mere subjective work of the individual understanding.

[4] How does this consist with his application, in the following chapter,

of the causal judgment, in its universal form, to demonstrate the existence of God 'with mathematical certainty?'

[5] Thus we do not perceive a 'necessary connexion' between power to think and that animal form which, with some persons, constitutes the nominal essence of *man*, so that the former must be universally predicated of the latter. On the other hand, when something is actually presented to our senses in its simple ideas or phenomena, we are obliged to predicate real existence of that particular thing, in a mental proposition that is somehow latent in sense-perception.

BOOK IV.

CHAP. IX.

A three-fold Knowledge of Existence.

ways of predication to be considered more at large in another place [1], let us proceed now to inquire concerning our knowledge of the *existence of things* [2], and how we come by it. I say, then, that we have the knowledge of *our own* existence by intuition ; of the existence of *God* by demonstration ; and of *other things* by sensation [3].

3. As for *our own existence* [4], we perceive it so plainly and

---

[1] 'in another place.' Was this written before chh. v–viii, which treat of 'propositions' and 'predication'; also before Bk. III, which deals with common terms, and 'abstract ideas'?

[2] 'Existence of things.' It is one of Locke's leading assumptions, that whatever really exists must be particular; so that there can be no known reality in ideas that are abstracted from particular substances in which they present themselves to our senses or reflection. 'Whatever exists,' he says emphatically in his criticism of Norris, 'whether in God or out of God, is singular' (*Remarks*, § 21). Cf. chh. i. § 7 ; ii. § 14 ; iii. § 21 ; iv. §§ 1–4, 11–18.

[3] He thus asserts that men 'come by' an irresistible perception, or absolute certainty, of each of the three final realities, in each of the three degrees of clearness that belong to human knowledge, described in ch. ii. 'Agreement' of all the ideas of which he is conscious with the idea of *his own* actual existence is an intuition, latent if not fully conscious, in the mind of every man who is conscious of any ideas at all, or who uses the personal pronoun 'I': this intuition of his own existence obliges all (who give the needful attention to the question) to perceive with the force of a mathematical demonstration, that the Supreme Mind we call God must exist eternally: and our actual sensations, or ideas of sense, when interpreted in the light of our own existence, and

the existence of God, are perceived to be 'things' that thus make manifestation of their actual existence. Locke proceeds to explain and vindicate all this in the following section, and in the two following chapters.

Human life as well as human knowledge turns on men's relations to these three final realities, and on their mode of thinking about them. While none of the three can be explained away, each may be so exaggerated as to overshadow the other two. Exaggerated or exclusive regard either to the first, the second, or the third, tends to a practically impossible Egoism or Solipsism, Pantheism or Acosmism, or Materialism. An exaggerated sense of the mysteries and seeming contradictions involved in the three distinct yet united, induces the Scepticism or Agnosticism which would discard from human understanding all questions about the ultimate realities by which human life is deepened and dignified, and would confine men to blind guesses about transitory phenomena, abstracted from all permanent realities. The history of religious and philosophical thought is a history of the changing hypotheses under which reflecting men have tried to conceive the three ultimate realities that, in some form, are presupposed in any interpretation of the phenomena of existence which can find response in the human spirit. Cf. Bk. II. chh. xxiii. and xxviii. § 2.

[4] 'our own existence.' What is meant by 'our own existence,' here supposed to be at least tacitly

so certainly, that it neither needs nor is capable of any proof. BOOK IV.
For nothing can be more evident to us than our own existence.
I think, I reason, I feel pleasure and pain : can any of these
be more evident to me than my own existence? If I doubt
of all other things, that very doubt makes me perceive my
own existence, and will not suffer me to doubt of that.   For
if I know I feel pain, it is evident I have as certain perception
of my own existence, as of the existence of the pain I feel :
or if I know I doubt, I have as certain perception of the
existence of the thing doubting, as of that thought which
I *call doubt* [1].   Experience [2] then convinces us, that we have
an *intuitive knowledge* of our own existence, and an internal
infallible perception that we are.   In every act of sensation,
reasoning, or thinking [3], we are conscious to ourselves of our
own being ; and, in this matter, come not short of the highest
degree of certainty.

BOOK IV.

CHAP. IX.
Our Know-
ledge of
our own
Existence
is Intui-
tive.

predicated, in an act of intuitive perception ? Does it include substances
material and spiritual ; or the spiritual
substance only, or the pure personality only, independently of substance, as in the discussion on the
idea of identity of person, in Bk. II.
ch. xxvii ? In the sentences that follow,
this last seems to be in his view ; but
not exclusively in the forensic and
moral aspect in which personality is
presented in the second Book.

[1] All this corresponds with the
cogito ergo sum of Descartes (*Discours
de la Méthode*, iv.), even to the illustrations. Hume treats the whole as
a vulgar error ; the personal pronoun
' I ' signifies only a succession of
isolated impressions and ideas, and is
otherwise a word without meaning,
according to his *Treatise*, Bk. I. pt. iv.
sect. 6.

[2] ' Experience,' i. e. self-conscious
experience, or the simple ideas of our
own mental operations that are presented when we reflect. As we have
seen, Locke sometimes uses expressions which might imply that the

simple ideas of the senses keep us at
a distance from the very ' external '
things or substances of which they are
the actual appearances, as if he forgot
that they were the things themselves,
revealed to us in part and superficially.
Accordingly, he thinks it necessary to
vindicate our perceptions of external
things. Cf. ch. ii. § 14 ; ch. xi. Yet he
does not seem to think it necessary
in like manner to sustain the trustworthiness of the intuition of ' our
own existence ' that is awakened in our
simple ideas of reflection. Moreover,
he does not explain the relation between the ' intuition ' of this chapter
and the ' reflection ' which yields one
of the two classes of our simple ideas.

[3] In every conscious state through
which we pass (he seems here to say)
the idea signified by the personal pronoun ' I ' (of which an insufficient
account was given in Bk. II.) rises up,
in ' agreement ' with the idea of 'real
existence,' so that I am obliged, tacitly
at least, to assert that ' I exist,' whenever I am conscious of ideas of any
sort.

CHAPTER X.

OF OUR KNOWLEDGE OF THE EXISTENCE OF A GOD[1].

BOOK IV.

CHAP. X.
We are
capable of
knowing
certainly
that there
is a God.

1. THOUGH God has given us no innate ideas of himself; though he has stamped no original characters on our minds, wherein we may read his being[2]; yet having furnished us with those faculties our minds are endowed with, he hath not left himself without witness: since we have sense, perception, and reason, and cannot want a clear proof of him, as long as we carry *ourselves* about us. Nor can we justly complain of our ignorance in this great point; since he has so plentifully provided us with the means to discover and know him; so far as is necessary to the end of our being, and the great concernment of our happiness. But, though this be the most obvious truth that reason discovers, and though its evidence be (if I mistake not) equal to mathematical certainty: yet it requires thought and attention; and the mind must apply itself to a regular deduction of it from some part of our intuitive knowledge, or else we shall be as uncertain and ignorant of this as of other propositions, which are in themselves capable of clear demonstration[3]. To show, therefore, that we are

---

[1] 'A God,' instead of 'God,' suggests the inadequacy of Locke's idea of God.

[2] Cf. Bk. I. ch. iii. §§ 8–16, where the innateness of the idea of God, and of the assertion 'God exists' is argued against, whilst here he goes on to show that it is as demonstrable, on self-evident principles, as any truth in mathematics.

[3] The possibility of men remaining ignorant that God exists; the fact that men may remain all their lives without any distinct knowledge of God; and the need for intellectual and spiritual activity on the part of each man, as the condition of its attainment—are marks that distinguish the knowledge of God—demonstrable with 'mathematical certainty,' according to Locke —from any knowledge that could be called 'innate,' in his meaning of innateness.

capable of *knowing*, i.e. *being certain* that there is a God, and how we may come by this certainty, I think we need go no further than *ourselves*, and that undoubted knowledge we have of our own existence.

2. I think it is beyond question, that man has a clear idea of his own being ; he knows certainly he exists, and that he is something. He that can doubt whether he be anything or no, I speak not to ; no more than I would argue with pure nothing, or endeavour to convince nonentity that it were something. If any one pretends to be so sceptical as to deny his own existence, (for really to doubt of it is manifestly impossible,) let him for me enjoy his beloved happiness of being nothing, until hunger or some other pain convince him of the contrary. This, then, I think I may take for a truth, which every one's certain knowledge assures him of, beyond the liberty of doubting, viz. that he is *something that actually exists* [1].

3. In the next place, man knows, by an intuitive certainty, that bare *nothing can no more produce any real being, than it can be equal to two right angles* [2]. If a man knows not that

---

[1] Cf. ch. ix. § 3, which asserts that each man intuitively perceives the ' agreement' of the idea of ' existence' with the idea of ' himself'; so that the former is at least *tacitly* predicated of the latter in every conscious act.

[2] This is an appeal to the ' maxim ' or ' axiom,' that whatever begins to exist must find a concrete cause into which its existence may be refunded— here treated as a universal and necessary principle, ' known by an intuitive certainty.' Yet in Bk. II. ch. xxi. § 1, and ch. xxvi. § 1, which explain the origin of the idea of cause, it is said to arise from our ' observation' of changes. Unless this observation is merely the occasion on which intellect ' suggests' the universal necessity of a cause of change, the use made in this chapter of the causal maxim is not justified by that account of its origin. But in arguing with Stillingfleet, he makes the principle ' that everything that has a beginning must have a cause ' a true principle of reason, or a proposition certainly true ; ' which we come to know by contemplating our ideas, and perceiving that the idea of beginning to be is *necessarily connected* with the idea of some operation ; and the idea of operation with the idea of some substance operating, which we call a cause. And thus it comes to be a certain proposition, and so may be called a *principle of reason* ; as every true proposition is to him that perceives the certainty of it ' (*First Letter*, pp. 135-6). In the text, Locke attempts something like a *proof* of the causal principle. This, as Hume shows, necessarily begs the question, as all attempts to prove what is in itself evident must do. See *Treatise*, Pt. I. bk. i. sect. 10.

BOOK IV.

CHAP. X.

produce a
Being;
therefore
Something
must have
existed
from
Eternity.

nonentity, or the absence of all being, cannot be equal to two right angles, it is impossible he should know any demonstration in Euclid. If, therefore, we know there is some real being, and that nonentity cannot produce any real being, it is an evident demonstration, that *from eternity there has been something*[1]; since what was not from eternity had a beginning; and what had a beginning must be produced by something else.

And that
eternal
Being
must be
most
powerful.

4. Next, it is evident, that what had its being and beginning from another, must also have all that which is in and belongs to its being from another too. All the powers it has must be owing to and received from the same source[2]. This eternal source, then, of all being must also be the source and original of all power; and so *this eternal Being must be also the most powerful*[3].

And most
knowing.

5. Again, a man finds in *himself* perception and knowledge. We have then got one step further; and we are certain now that there is not only some being, but some knowing, intelligent being in the world. There was a time, then, when there was no knowing being, and when knowledge began to be; or

---

[1] This is virtually equivalent to the three first propositions and the fifth of Samuel Clarke's *Demonstration of the Being and Attributes of God*, published in 1704, fourteen years after the first edition of the *Essay*. In these propositions, Clarke claims to demonstrate the eternal existence of Something independent, that exists by a necessity in the rational nature of things—on the ground that '*something* now is'—Locke, on the ground that *I* now am, and that I had a beginning.

[2] That is to say, that every cause must be a *sufficient* cause; so that nothing must be looked for in the actual effects which did not exist potentially in the cause. Thus, if matter consists only of molecules in motion, no motion of the molecules could *per se* become self-conscious mind; or even feel sensation, as in the secondary or imputed qualities. The

causal principle, as interpreted by Locke, implies that effects which can be attributed to any particular cause must be already latent in that cause, and so capable of being *evolved* from it, and *refunded* into it. This differs from the causality recognised by empirical sceptics like Hume; according to whom any particular cause might *à priori* give rise to *any* effects, it being only the accidental custom of our experience that induces us to associate a particular change with anything in particular as its cause.

[3] This (so far) is Samuel Clarke's tenth 'demonstrated' proposition about God; but whilst Locke's conclusion is only that the eternal Being must be '*most* powerful,' Clarke 'demonstrates' that the necessary Being, the supreme Cause of all things, 'must of necessity have *infinite* power.'

else there has been also *a knowing being from eternity.* If it
be said, there was a time when no being had any knowledge,
when that eternal being was void of all understanding; I reply,
that then it was impossible there should ever have been any
knowledge : it being as impossible that things wholly void of
knowledge, and operating blindly, and without any perception,
should produce a knowing being, as it is impossible that
a triangle should make itself three angles bigger than two
right ones. For it is as repugnant to the idea of senseless
matter, that it should put into itself sense, perception, and
knowledge, as it is repugnant to the idea of a triangle, that it
should put into itself greater angles than two right ones [1].

6. Thus, from the consideration of ourselves, and what we
infallibly find in our own constitutions, our reason leads us to
the knowledge of this certain and evident truth,—*That there
is an eternal, most powerful, and most knowing Being*; which
whether any one will please to call God, it matters not. The
thing is evident [2]; and from this idea duly considered, will
easily be deduced all those other attributes, which we ought
to ascribe to this eternal Being. [[3] If, nevertheless, any one
should be found so senselessly arrogant, as to suppose man

---

[1] Locke thus rejects absolute or ultimate materialism, on the ground that it is repugnant to reason, which forbids, by an intellectual necessity, that ' sense, perception, and living knowledge,' should be refunded into blind and meaningless molecular motions ; although reason, he thinks, does not forbid the supposition that, in subordination to the Eternal Mind, the evolution of the human organism may have conscious intelligence annexed to it at some stage of the process. Cf. ch. iv. § 6.

[2] This is not adequate to the ' complex idea' of God, described in Bk. II. ch. xxiii. §§ 33–36, where we are told (§ 35) that ' it is *infinity* which, joined to our ideas of substance, power, and knowledge, makes that complex idea whereby we represent to ourselves, as best we can, the Supreme Being.' But

neither Locke nor Clarke professes to prove, as in a pure mathematical demonstration, that the Eternal Being must be *intelligent* ; although, as Clarke says, ' this is the main question between us and the Atheists.' (Prop. viii.) The infinite cannot be logically concluded from the finite. We are practically obliged to *presuppose* immanent active Reason, in order to conceive the finite and changing, but we cannot, *by logical argument,* sustain the presupposition. Our ' perception' of God is not the conclusion of a syllogism : it is the necessary assumption in all reasoning, whether about our sensuous or our spiritual experience, and the foundation of all certainty. Assume it—rest life upon it—and the universe and life become harmonious.

[3] Added in second edition.

alone knowing and wise, but yet the product of mere ignorance and chance ; and that all the rest of the universe acted only by that blind haphazard ; I shall leave with him that very rational and emphatical rebuke of Tully (l. ii. De Leg.), to be considered at his leisure : ' What can be more sillily arrogant and misbecoming, than for a man to think that he has a mind and understanding in him, but yet in all the universe beside there is no such thing? Or that those things, which with the utmost stretch of his reason he can scarce comprehend, should be moved and managed without any reason at all ?' *Quid est enim verius, quam neminem esse oportere tam stulte arrogantem, ut in se mentem et rationem putet inesse, in cœlo mundoque non putet ? Aut ea quœ vix summa ingenii ratione comprehendat, nulla ratione moveri putet ?*]

From what has been said, it is plain to me we have a more certain knowledge of the existence of a God, than of anything our senses have not immediately discovered to us[1]. Nay, I presume I may say, that we more certainly know that there is a God, than that there is anything else without us[2]. When I say we *know*, I mean there is such a knowledge within our reach which we cannot miss, if we will but apply our minds to that, as we do to several other inquiries[3].

Our idea of a most perfect Being, not 7. How far the *idea* of a most perfect being, which a man may frame in his mind, does or does not prove the *existence* of a God[4], I will not here examine. For in the different

[1] In the simple ideas of which we are percipient as qualities of things of sense.

[2] This seems to imply that we know what is ' within us ' more certainly than we know what is ' without us '; and also that God is ' without us ' in the way that finite beings are.

[3] The origin and progress of religious thought in the individual man only, not its historical growth in the different races of mankind, is chiefly considered by Locke. He contributes little to that natural history of religion which illustrates in its different stages the development of the idea of God in the human mind. Apart from meta-

physical speculation, and as a stage in the history of mankind, monotheism is a comparatively late development of the answer to the question, Whether the evolution of the universe is a succession of blind purposeless changes, or the progressive manifestation of a perfectly reasonable and beneficent purpose.

[4] This has been called the ontological, or pure *à priori*, argument. Anselm and Descartes among others took the mere idea of Perfect Being as proof that Perfect Being actually exists. As the idea of a triangle necessarily contains the idea of three-sidedness, so the idea of the Perfect necessarily contains

make of men's tempers and application of their thoughts,
some arguments prevail more on one, and some on another,
for the confirmation of the same truth. But yet, I think,
this I may say, that it is an ill way of establishing this truth,
and silencing atheists, to lay the whole stress of so important
a point as this upon that sole foundation: and take some
men's having that idea of God in their minds, (for it is evident
some men have none, and some worse than none, and the
most very different,) for the only proof of a Deity ; and out
of an over fondness of that darling invention, cashier, or at
least endeavour to invalidate all other arguments ; and forbid
us to hearken to those proofs, as being weak or fallacious,
which our own existence, and the sensible parts of the
universe [1] offer so clearly and cogently to our thoughts, that
I deem it impossible for a considering man to withstand them.
For I judge it as certain and clear a truth as can anywhere be
delivered, that 'the invisible things of God are clearly seen
from the creation of the world, being understood by the
things that are made, even his eternal power and Godhead [2].'
Though our own being furnishes us, as I have shown, with
an evident and incontestible proof of a Deity ; and I believe
nobody can avoid the cogency of it, who will but as carefully
attend to it, as to any other demonstration of so many parts :
yet this being so fundamental a truth, and of that consequence,

---

the idea of its actual existence. A non-existent God would thus be as impossible as a two-angled triangle. Reid refers to this passage as evidence of Locke's forgetfulness of his own definition of knowledge ; inasmuch as he refuses to recognise knowledge of God in the mere idea of God, and proceeds to demonstrate God's existence from his own existence (Reid, *Essay* VI. ch. iii.), instead of finding it in agreements of ideas. But Locke nowhere deduces knowledge of realities of any sort from abstract ideas, which he tells us can yield nothing but abstractions. Only simple ideas, actually presented in the senses or in consciousness, manifest to him reali-ties of which *they* are attributes ; then, from the reality of 'our own existence' so manifested, he 'demonstrates,' as we have seen, the actual existence of God, as an absolute intellectual necessity.

[1] 'the sensible parts of the universe,' —here added to the fact that 'my own existence' had a beginning, as a contribution to the 'demonstration,' that God must exist eternally.

[2] *Romans* i. 20. Trust in experience is one form of faith in God, and in the absence of this faith, life would be paralysed in universal scepticism. In this sense, the infinite or divine is logically presupposed in all living experience of the particular and finite.

that all religion and genuine morality depend thereon, I doubt not but I shall be forgiven by my reader if I go over some parts of this argument again, and enlarge a little more upon them.

Recapitulation. Something from Eternity.

8. There is no truth more evident than that *something* must be *from eternity.* I never yet heard of any one so unreasonable, or that could suppose so manifest a contradiction[1], as a time wherein there was perfectly nothing. This being of all absurdities the greatest[2], to imagine that pure nothing, the perfect negation and absence of all beings, should ever produce any real existence.

It being, then, unavoidable for all rational creatures to conclude, that *something* has existed from eternity[3]; let us next see *what kind of thing* that must be.

Two Sorts of Beings, cogitative and incogitative.

9. There are but two sorts of beings in the world that man knows or conceives.

First, such as are purely material, without sense, perception, or thought, as the clippings of our beards, and parings of our nails.

Secondly, sensible, thinking, perceiving beings, such as we find ourselves to be. Which, if you please, we will hereafter call *cogitative* and *incogitative* beings; which to our present purpose, if for nothing else, are perhaps better terms than material and immaterial.

---

[1] Not a logical contradiction in terms, but only in contradiction to the assumed maxim, or *à priori* synthetic judgment (as Kant would say), of causality. It would be an express contradiction to say that an *effect* was uncaused; for cause is included in the nominal essence of 'effect,' and this is an explicative proposition. Not so, that a *change* was uncaused, or that there should be an uncaused commencement, in which propositions something is added to the nominal essence of the subject term.

[2] 'of all absurdities the greatest,' because it involves the negation of the principle of causes, whether material, efficient, formal, or final.

[3] But although my existence, which began to be, presupposes something out of which it issued (on the principle of causality), it does not follow that the existence of one Eternal Being is implied in this concrete fact. For it might be said, that I have been produced by something else, and that something else by a predecessor, in an infinite retrogression. And although it is granted that whatever gives existence must give also all the qualities and powers of its issue, it may still be denied that the (sufficient) cause is single, inasmuch as many things may have to concur in the evolution of every change.

10. If, then, there must be something eternal, let us see what sort of being it must be. And to that it is very obvious to reason, that it must necessarily be a cogitative being. For it is as impossible to conceive that ever bare incogitative matter should produce a thinking intelligent being, as that nothing should of itself produce matter [1]. Let us suppose any parcel of matter eternal, great or small, we shall find it, in itself, able to produce nothing [2]. For example : let us suppose the matter of the next pebble we meet with eternal, closely united, and the parts firmly at rest together ; if there were no other being in the world, must it not eternally remain so, a dead inactive lump? Is it possible to conceive it can add motion to itself, being purely matter, or produce anything? Matter, then, by its own strength, cannot produce in itself so much as motion: the motion it has must also be from eternity, or else be produced, and added to matter by some other being more powerful than matter ; matter, as is evident, having not power to produce motion in itself. But let us suppose motion eternal too : yet matter, *incogitative* matter and motion, whatever changes it might produce of figure and bulk, could never produce thought : knowledge will still be as far beyond the power of motion and matter to produce, as matter is beyond the power of nothing or nonentity to produce [3]. And I appeal to every one's own

BOOK IV.

CHAP. X.

Incogitative Being cannot produce a Cogitative Being.

---

[1] On the self-evident principle or 'maxim,' that a cause must contain potentially all the effects which actually issue from it, as opposed to the maxim of the sceptics, that anything may be the cause of anything. 'Je trouve tout ce raisonnement le plus solide du monde,' says Leibniz, ' et non seulement exact, mais encore profond, et digne de son auteur. Je suis parfaitement de son avis, qu'il n'y a point de combinaison et de modification des parties de la matière, quelque petites qu'elles soient, qui puisse produire de la perception ; et que tout est proportionnel dans les petites parties à ce qui peut se passer dans les grandes.' (*Nouveaux Essais.*)

[2] Cf. Bk. II. ch. xxi. § 2, where he suggests that matter *per se* is wholly destitute of active power ; although he elsewhere speaks of secondary qualities and ' powers ' of bodies, in subordination, however, to the power of God.

[3] By ' matter ' is here meant, that which is manifested in its primary or real qualities, as something figured, divisible, and capable of motion. 'But if any man will say that our idea of matter is wrong, and that by matter he will not mean, as other men do, *a solid substance, capable only of division, figure, and motion*, but *an unknown substance, capable of thinking, and of numberless unknown properties besides*; then he trifles only, in putting an ambiguous

thoughts, whether he cannot as easily conceive matter produced by *nothing*, as thought to be produced by pure matter[1], when, before, there was no such thing as thought or an intelligent being existing? Divide matter into as many parts as you will, (which we are apt to imagine a sort of spiritualizing, or making a thinking thing of it,) vary the figure and motion of it as much as you please—a globe, cube, cone, prism, cylinder, &c., whose diameters are but 100,000th part of a *gry*[2], will operate no otherwise upon other bodies of proportionable bulk, than those of an inch or foot diameter; and you may as rationally expect to produce sense, thought, and knowledge, by putting together, in a certain figure and motion, gross particles of matter, as by those that are the very minutest that do anywhere exist. They knock, impel, and resist one another, just as the greater do; and that is all they can do. So that, if we will suppose *nothing* first or eternal, matter can never begin to be: if we suppose bare matter without motion, eternal, motion can never begin to be: if we suppose only matter and motion first, or eternal, thought can never begin to be. [[3] For it is impossible to conceive that

signification upon the word *matter*, making it mean the same as we mean by *substance*.' (Clarke's *Demonstration*, pp. 156–7.)

[1] ' pure matter,' i. e. the substance of which we can predicate only extension and mobility; out of which only new modifications of the extended and movable can be evolved, and which must not, through an ambiguity in the term ' matter,' be confounded with a hypothetical substance possessed of other properties which cannot be refunded into motion.

[2] 'A *gry* is one-tenth of a line, a line one-tenth of an inch, an inch one-tenth of a philosophical foot, a philosophical foot one-third of a pendulum, whose diadroms, in the latitude of forty-five degrees, are each equal to one second of time, or one-sixtieth of a minute. I have affectedly made use of this measure here, and

the parts of it, under a decimal division, with names to them; because I think it would be of general convenience that this should be the common measure in the Commonwealth of Letters.' (Locke.)

[3] Instead of ' Whatsoever therefore is eternal must be a cogitative Being, or Spirit,' in the first edition, what follows within brackets was substituted, in the second edition, to meet a charge of inconsistency with ch. iii. § 6. There, in the first edition, it was asserted, that, without a particular revelation, we have no certainty that matter cannot by God be made to think; here the spirituality of the Supreme Power is argued for, on account of the absurdity of the supposition, that matter should be the supreme or ultimate principle of the universe. In ch. iii. he only indulges the conjecture, that the *Eternal Mind*

matter, either with or without motion, could have, originally, BOOK IV.
in and from itself, sense, perception, and knowledge ; as is CHAP. X.
evident from hence, that then sense, perception, and knowledge, must be a property eternally inseparable from matter
and every particle of it. Not to add, that, though our general
or specific conception of matter makes us speak of it as one
thing, yet really all matter is not one individual thing, neither
is there any such thing existing as *one* material being, or *one*
single body that we know or can conceive. And therefore, if
matter were the eternal first cogitative being, there would
not be one eternal, infinite, cogitative being, but an infinite
number of eternal, finite, cogitative beings, independent one
of another, of limited force, and distinct thoughts[1], which
could never produce that order, harmony, and beauty which
are to be found in nature. Since, therefore, whatsoever is the
first eternal being must necessarily be cogitative ; and] whatsoever is first of all things must necessarily contain in it, and
actually[2] have, at least, all the perfections that can ever after
exist ; nor can it ever give to another any perfection that it
hath not either actually in itself, or, at least, in a higher
degree ; [[3] it necessarily follows, that the first eternal being
cannot be matter.]

11. If, therefore, it be evident, that something necessarily Therefore,
must exist from eternity, it is also as evident, that that there has
been an

---

might have ' annexed some degrees of
sense and thinking' to certain organisa-
tions of matter ; in this chapter he
argues that this *Supreme* Power, at
any rate, cannot be unthinking matter.
See Locke's correspondence with
Molyneux in Dec. 1692 and Jan. 1693,
in which his consistency is vindicated.

[1] ' C'est encore une importante re-
marque sur la matière que celle que
l'auteur fait ici, *qu'on ne la doit point
prendre pour une chose unique en nombre,*
ou (comme j'ai coutume de parler) pour
une vraie et parfaite *monade* ou *unité,*
puis qu'elle n'est qu'un *amas* d'un
nombre infini d'êtres. Il ne fallait ici
qu'un pas à notre excellent auteur
pour parvenir à mon système. Car,

en effet, je donne de la perception
à tous ces êtres infinis.' (*Nouveaux
Essais.*)

[2] ' actually '—rather virtually, since
a cause must be potentially sufficient
for its effects.

[3] Added in second edition. He
seems in this section to have Hobbes
in view, who allows that all matter, as
matter, in each of its atoms, may be
not only capable of motion, but also of
sense-perception. ' Scio fuisse philoso-
phos quosdam,' Hobbes says, ' eosdem-
que viros doctos, qui corpora omnia
sensu predita esse sustinuerunt ; nec
video, si natura sensionis in reactione
sola collocaretur, quo modo refutari
possunt.' (*Physica*, ch. xxv. § 5.)

BOOK IV.

CHAP. X.

Eternal Cogitative Being.

something must necessarily be a cogitative being : for it is as impossible that incogitative matter should produce a cogitative being, as that nothing, or the negation of all being, should produce a positive being or matter [1].

The Attributes of the Eternal Cogitative Being.

12. Though this discovery of the *necessary existence of an eternal Mind* does sufficiently lead us into the knowledge of God ; since it will hence follow, that all other knowing beings that have a beginning must depend on him, and have no other ways of knowledge or extent of power than what he gives them ; and therefore, if he made those, he made also the less excellent pieces of this universe,—all inanimate beings, whereby his omniscience, power, and providence will be established, and all his other attributes necessarily follow : yet, to clear up this a little further, we will see what doubts can be raised against it.

Whether the Eternal Mind may be also material or no.

13. *First*, Perhaps it will be said, that, though it be as clear as demonstration can make it, that there must be an eternal Being, and that Being must also be knowing : yet it does not follow but that thinking Being may also be *material*. Let it be so, it equally still follows that there is a God. For if there be an eternal, omniscient, omnipotent Being, it is certain that there is a God, whether you imagine that Being to be material or no [2]. But herein, I suppose, lies the danger and deceit of that supposition :—there being no way to avoid the demonstration, that there is an eternal knowing Being, men, devoted to matter, would willingly have it granted, that this knowing Being is material ; and then, letting slide out of their minds, or the discourse, the demonstration whereby an eternal *knowing* Being was proved necessarily to exist, would argue

[1] The immanence of God, i. e. supreme Active Reason, is the necessary presupposition of *all* real inferences. It is thus the *basis* of all certainty rather than the *conclusion* of a demonstration.

[2] This passage was made a ground for charging Locke with Spinozism, in a *Dissertation upon the Tenth Chapter of the Fourth Book of Mr. Locke's Essay,* *wherein the author endeavours to establish Spinoza's atheistic hypothesis*, by William Carroll (1706). This 'discovery of Atheism' in the *Essay* is rested by Carroll on Locke's concession of the 'hypothesis of the eternal existence of One *cogitative* and *extended* material Substance, differently modified, to which this author, with Toland and others, gives the holy name of God.'

all to be matter [1], and so deny a God, that is, an eternal cogitative Being : whereby they are so far from establishing, that they destroy their own hypothesis. For, if there can be, in their opinion, eternal matter, without any eternal cogitative Being, they manifestly separate matter and thinking, and suppose no necessary connexion of the one with the other, and so establish the necessity of an eternal Spirit, but not of matter ; since it has been proved already, that an eternal cogitative Being is unavoidably to be granted. Now, if thinking and matter may be separated, the eternal existence of matter will not follow from the eternal existence of a cogitative Being, and they suppose it to no purpose.

14. But now let us see how they can satisfy themselves, or others, that this eternal thinking Being is material.

I. I would ask them, whether they imagine that all matter, *every particle of matter*, thinks ? This, I suppose, they will scarce say ; since then there would be as many eternal think- ing beings as there are particles of matter, and so an infinity of gods. And yet, if they will not allow matter as matter, that is, every particle of matter, to be as well cogitative as extended, they will have as hard a task to make out to their own reasons a cogitative being out of incogitative particles [2],

---

[1] 'matter,' i. e. mere matter, or something that is only solid and immovable, without intelligence. This was an interpretation put upon Hobbes and even Spinoza by some of their contemporaries, and Locke may have had them in view, in this and following sections. (See e. g. Clarke's *Demonstration.*) But Hobbes insists on the absolute incomprehensibility of God— the unknowable of Herbert Spencer, not on the obligation to image a material Supreme Being. 'Forasmuch as God Almighty is incomprehensible, it followeth that we can have no conception or image of the Deity : and consequently all his attributes signify our inability and defect of power to conceive anything concerning his nature, and not any conception of the same, excepting only this, that there is a God. . . . And thus all that will consider may know that God *is*, though not *what* he is.' (*Human Nature*, ch. xi. § 3.) Nor can it be said that Spinoza makes Matter, in its natural order or manner of existence, identical with his *unica substantia* or *natura naturans*. The God of Spinoza is neither body nor mind, on the ground that these are only limited forms of the infinite extension and infinite thought of the universal substance. The sensuous circle is grounded in extension, and the idea of the circle in thought, but neither can be deduced from the other, while both are necessary implicates of Spinoza's God.

[2] He proceeds as usual upon the assumption of the molecular constitution of bodies.

Secondly,
Because
one
Particle
alone of
Matter
cannot be
cogitative.

as an extended being out of unextended parts, if I may so speak.

15. II. If all matter does not think, I next ask, Whether it be *only one atom* that does so? This has as many absurdities as the other; for then this atom of matter must be alone eternal or not. If this alone be eternal, then this alone, by its powerful thought or will, made all the rest of matter. And so we have the creation of matter by a powerful thought, which is that the materialists stick at; for if they suppose one single thinking atom to have produced all the rest of matter, they cannot ascribe that pre-eminency to it upon any other account than that of its thinking, the only supposed difference. But allow it to be by some other way which is above our conception, it must still be creation; and these men must give up their great maxim, *Ex nihilo nil fit.* If it be said, that all the rest of matter is equally eternal as that thinking atom, it will be to say anything at pleasure, though ever so absurd. For to suppose all matter eternal, and yet one small particle in knowledge and power infinitely above all the rest, is without any the least appearance of reason to frame an hypothesis. Every particle of matter, as matter, is capable of all the same figures and motions of any other; and I challenge any one, in his thoughts, to add anything else to one above another.

Thirdly,
Because a
System of
incogita-
tive
Matter
cannot be
cogitative.

16. III. If then neither one peculiar atom alone can be this eternal thinking being; nor all matter, as matter, i. e. every particle of matter, can be it; it only remains, that it is some certain *system* of matter, duly put together [1], that is this thinking eternal Being. This is that which, I imagine, is that notion which men are aptest to have of God; who would have him a material being, as most readily suggested to them by the ordinary conceit they have of themselves and other men, which they take to be material thinking beings. But this imagination, however more natural, is no less absurd than the other: for to suppose the eternal thinking Being to be nothing else but a composition of particles of matter, each whereof is incogitative, is to ascribe all the

---

[1] Specially organised matter, that is to say.

wisdom and knowledge of that eternal Being only to the BOOK IV. juxta-position of parts ; than which nothing can be more —+— absurd. For unthinking particles of matter, however put CHAP. X. together, can have nothing thereby added to them, but a new relation of position, which it is impossible should give thought and knowledge to them.

17. But further : this corporeal system either has all its And that parts at rest, or it is a certain motion of the parts wherein whether this its thinking consists. If it be perfectly at rest, it is but one corporeal lump, and so can have no privileges above one atom. System is in Motion

If it be the motion of its parts on which its thinking or at Rest. depends, all the thoughts there must be unavoidably accidental and limited ; since all the particles that by motion cause thought, being each of them in itself without any thought, cannot regulate its own motions, much less be regulated by the thought of the whole ; since that thought is not the cause of motion, (for then it must be antecedent to it, and so without it,) but the consequence of it ; whereby freedom, power, choice, and all rational and wise thinking or acting, will be quite taken away: so that such a thinking being will be no better nor wiser than pure blind matter; since to resolve all into the accidental unguided motions of blind matter, or into thought depending on unguided motions of blind matter, is the same thing: not to mention the narrowness of such thoughts and knowledge that must depend on the motion of such parts. But there needs no enumeration of any more absurdities and impossibilities in this hypothesis (however full of them it be) than that before mentioned ; since, let this thinking system be all or a part of the matter of the universe, it is impossible that any one particle should either know its own, or the motion of any other particle, or the whole know the motion of every particle ; and so regulate its own thoughts or motions, or indeed have any thought resulting from such motion.

18. *Secondly*, Others would have Matter to be eternal, not- Matter not withstanding that they allow an eternal, cogitative, imma- co-eternal with an terial Being[1]. This, though it take not away the being of a Eternal Mind.

---

[1] Aristotle, for example, held to the eternity of the world, not as opposed to the ultimate supremacy of active Reason, but on the ground that it

God[1], yet, since it denies one and the first great piece of his workmanship, the creation, let us consider it a little. Matter must be allowed eternal: Why? because you cannot conceive how it can be made out of nothing: why do you not also think yourself eternal? You will answer, perhaps, Because, about twenty or forty years since, you began to be. But if I ask you, what that *you* is, which began then to be, you can scarce tell me. The matter whereof you are made began not then to be: for if it did, then it is not eternal: but it began to be put together in such a fashion and frame as makes up your body; but yet that frame of particles is not you, it makes not that thinking thing you are; (for I have now to do with one who allows an eternal, immaterial, thinking Being, but would have unthinking Matter eternal too;) therefore, when did that thinking thing begin to be? If it did never begin to be, then have you always been a thinking thing from eternity; the absurdity whereof I need not confute, till I meet with one who is so void of understanding as to own it. If, therefore, you can allow a thinking thing to be made out of nothing, (as all things that are not eternal must be,) why also can you not allow it possible[2] for a material

must be, in its varying forms, an effect eternally proceeding from the Eternal Mind, yet not existing *per se*.

[1] Because the question in the dispute with atheists and agnostics is not, Whether the material world is eternal, but whether *per se* it can be the Supreme Being? The eternity of matter has been held by ancient and modern philosophers, in consistency with faith in supreme all-governing Mind,—the material world being regarded either as an eternal necessary effect of the Divine energy, or as an eternal voluntary emanation from God. Neither of these opinions excludes the ultimately spiritual constitution and agency of the universe. To hold that the sensible world is an eternal manifestation of active Reason—'an eternal poem of spirit'—is very different from the

hypothesis that resolves all at last into blind atoms, divorced from intelligence. That God should be immanent, and eternally manifested in the sensible universe, or in a succession of waxing and waning sensible worlds, in which every event is regulated by active Reason, implies what is virtually a *constant* creation, instead of creation as a 'singular effect'; and to some minds presents a more impressive idea of the Eternal Mind than the vulgar conception does.

[2] It is not merely a question of abstract possibility, but of actuality or fact. Must we mean by 'creation' in time a beginning in time of the actual existence of the world of sense; or may it mean that, without any such beginning, matter or the material universe exists in eternal dependence upon the active Reason that is

being to be made out of nothing by an equal power, but that BOOK IV.
you have the experience of the one in view, and not of the
other? Though, when well considered, creation [¹of a spirit CHAP. X.
will be found to require no less power than the creation of
matter. Nay, possibly, if we would emancipate ourselves
from vulgar notions, and raise our thoughts, as far as they
would reach, to a closer contemplation of things, we might be
able to aim at some dim and seeming conception how *matter*
might at first be made, and begin to exist, by the power of
that eternal first Being: but to give beginning and being to
a *spirit* would be found a more inconceivable effect of
omnipotent power. But this being what would perhaps lead
us too far from the notions on which the philosophy now
in the world is built, it would not be pardonable to deviate
so far from them; or to inquire, so far as grammar itself
would authorize, if the common settled opinion opposes it² :

throughout Supreme? (See Clarke's *Dem.* p. 548.) An emanation might proceed for ever, like light from an eternal sun, or an impression from an eternally impressing seal.

¹ The first edition reads—' of one, as well as the other, requires an equal power. And we have no more reason to boggle at the effect of that power in one than in the other, because the effect of it in both is equally beyond our comprehension. For,' &c.—instead of the passage within brackets, introduced to strengthen Locke's argument against those who conclude that matter *must* be eternal, because we cannot conceive its creation 'out of nothing.'

² The idea of the creation of matter which Locke had in view in this curious passage has occasioned various conjectures. ' Je regrette,' says Leibniz, ' que la prudence, trop scrupuleuse, de notre habile auteur a empêché de produire tout entière la pensée profonde qu'il l'occupait. Je crois qu'il y a quelque chose de beau et d'important caché sous cette manière d'énigme. . . Je ne sais s'il n'a pas eu en vue les *Platoniciens*, qui

prenaient la matière pour quelque chose de fuyant et de passager.' (*Nouveaux Essais.*) Reid thinks that ' every particular Mr. Locke has hinted with regard to that system which he had in his mind, but thought it prudent to suppress, tallies exactly with the system of Berkeley.' (*Intell. Powers*, Ess. II. 16.) Stewart says that ' when considered in connection with some others in his writings, it would almost tempt one to think that a theory concerning *matter*, somewhat analogous to that of Boscovich, had occasionally passed through his mind.' (*Essay*, II. ch. i. p. 63.) A solution of the difficulty is presented in a note appended to a second edition of Coste's French translation of the *Essay*, to the following effect :—' Here Mr. Locke excites our curiosity, without being inclined to satisfy it. Many persons, imagining that he must have communicated to me this mode of explaining the creation of matter, requested, when my translation first appeared, that I would inform them what it was; but I was obliged to confess that Mr. Locke had not made even me a partner in the

BOOK IV.
Chap. X.

especially in this place, where the received doctrine serves well enough to our present purpose, and leaves this past doubt, that] the creation or beginning of any one [SUBSTANCE[1]] out of nothing being once admitted, the creation of all other but the CREATOR himself, may, with the same ease, be supposed.

Objection:
Creation out of nothing.

19. But you will say, Is it not impossible to admit of the making anything out of nothing, *since we cannot possibly conceive it*? I answer, No[2]. Because it is not reasonable

secret. At length, long after his death, Sir Isaac Newton, to whom I was accidentally speaking of this part of Mr. Locke's book, discovered to me the whole mystery. He told me, smiling, that he himself had suggested to Mr. Locke this way of explaining the creation of matter; and that the thought had struck him one day, when this question chanced to turn up in a conversation between himself, Mr. Locke, and the late Earl of Pembroke. He thus described to them his hypothesis :—We may (he said) have some rude idea of the creation of matter, if we suppose that God by his *power* had (at a certain time) *prevented the entrance of anything into a certain portion of space*,—space being in its own nature penetrable; for henceforward *this portion of space* would be endowed with *impenetrability*, one of the essential qualities of matter; and we have only again to suppose that God communicated the same impenetrability to *another portion of space*, and we should then obtain an idea of the *mobility* of matter, another of its essential qualities.' This 'dim conception,' if it means that the material world may be resolved into a constant manifestation of God's power to man's senses, conditioned by space, so far coincides with Berkeley's account of it; he emphasises the sensuous manifestation of divine power in selected spaces, as well as the ultimate dependence of space on sense. Newton, it seems, suggested that 'creation of matter' means, God causing in sentient beings

the sense-perception of resistance, in an otherwise pure space—a theory akin to Berkeleyism in its recognition of the Supreme Power, and to Boscovich in its conception of the effect.

[1] 'thing'—in first edition.

[2] Locke characteristically seeks to show that 'creation' is not an idealess term, although we are necessarily unable to *image* a *process* of *nothing passing into something*, instead of (as in mechanical causality) *something passing into a new form.* 'Creation out of nothing' is self-contradictory, if it excludes (as a 'something') the power of the creator or emanator. It only excludes pre-existing matter, and the idea that the material world is merely a *transformation* out of pre-existing chaos. Creation out of nothing is not forming Something *out of* pre-existing Nothing; as a physical effect is formed out of its physical cause, in a way that imagination can follow. It is causing something to exist *actually now*, which existed only *potentially before.* This as little involves either a contradiction in terms, or contradiction to reason, as the transformation of chaos into cosmos. What contradicts reason is the absolute beginning of actual existence, without its previous existence in a substance having power. 'Creation *a nihilo* means, only: that the universe, when created, was not merely put into form,—an original chaos, or complement of brute matter having *preceded* a plastic energy of Intelligence; but, that the universe was called into actuality, from potential

to deny the power of an infinite being, because we cannot comprehend its operations. We do not deny other effects upon this ground, because we cannot possibly conceive the manner of their production. We cannot conceive how anything but impulse of body can move body; and yet that is not a reason sufficient to make us deny it possible, against the constant experience we have of it in ourselves, in all our voluntary motions; which are produced in us only by the free action or thought of our own minds, and are not, nor can be, the effects of the impulse or determination of the motion of blind matter in or upon our own bodies; for then it could not be in our power or choice to alter it. For example: my right hand writes, whilst my left hand is still: What causes rest in one, and motion in the other? Nothing but my will,—a thought of my mind; my thought only changing, the right hand rests, and the left hand moves. This is matter of fact, which cannot be denied: explain this and make it intelligible, and then the next step will be to understand creation[1]. [2For the giving a new determination to the motion of the animal spirits (which some make use of to explain voluntary motion) clears not the difficulty one jot. To alter the determination of motion, being in this case no easier nor less, than to give motion itself: since the new determination given to the animal spirits must be either immediately by thought, or by some other body put in their way by thought which was not in their way before, and so must owe *its* motion to thought: either of which leaves *voluntary* motion as unintelligible as it was before.] In the meantime, it is an overvaluing ourselves to reduce all to the narrow measure of our capacities; and to conclude all things impossible to be done, whose manner of doing exceeds our comprehension. This is to make our comprehension infinite,

---

existence, by the Divine fiat. The Divine fiat, therefore, was the proximate cause of the creation; and the Deity, containing the cause, contained *potentially* the effect.' (Sir W. Hamilton.) The reference in the text is to the Cartesians.

[1] The suggested analogy is worked out in a treatise on *Freedom in Willing, or Man a Creative First Cause,* by an American philosopher, Rowland Hazard, LL.D. (Boston, 1883).

[2] Added in second edition.

or God finite, when what He can do is limited to what we can conceive of it. If you do not understand the operations of your own finite mind, that thinking thing within you, do not deem it strange that you cannot comprehend the operations of that eternal infinite Mind, who made and governs all things, and whom the heaven of heavens cannot contain[1].

[1] Another expression of Locke's reverential faith. One ground on which it might be suggested that much in the Fourth Book of the *Essay* was written before the other Books were finished is, that this tenth chapter was referred to by the first Lord Shaftesbury, on his death-bed, in Holland, in Jan. 1683, according to the following in a letter from Thomas Cherry to Thomas Hearne (July 25, 1706):—' The very person in whose arms the late Earl of Shaftesbury expired said that, when he attended him at his last hours, he recommended to him the confession of his faith and the examination of his conscience. The Earl answered him, and talked all clear Arianism and Socinianism, which notions he confessed he imbibed from Mr. Locke and his tenth chapter of *Human Understanding.*' (*Letters to Hearne*, privately printed, 1874.) See Fox Bourne's *Life*, vol. i. p. 469. If this may be trusted, Shaftesbury must have seen this chapter more than seven years before the *Essay* was published.

The demonstration of the existence of the Eternal Mind, offered in this chapter as a truth proved with ' evidence equal to mathematical certainty,' is virtually what is called the *cosmological* argument, or that *a contingentia mundi*. It is not equivalent to pure mathematical reasoning, or ontological proof, because *change*, an idea derived from experience, is mixed up with it, rendering it hypothetical, as thus :—If something now exists, an Eternal Being, sufficient to explain that something, is an eternal necessity of reason ; I myself, a thinking being, began to exist ; the eternal existence of a thinking Being is therefore an ultimate necessity of reason. The paralogisms involved in the argument, and the inadequacy of the legitimate conclusion, are brought out in Kant's transcendental dialectic. It is curious that Locke holds the existence of God to be within the sphere of our unconditionally certain knowledge, and that he excludes from that sphere the phenomena and laws of nature, as to which he says we can rise only to presumptions of probability, and that Kant on the contrary vindicates a pure *à priori* physics, and denies that the existence of God can be known by pure reason.

CHAPTER XI.

OF OUR KNOWLEDGE OF THE EXISTENCE OF OTHER THINGS.

BOOK IV.

CHAP. XI.

Know-
ledge of
the
existence
of other
Finite
Beings is
to be had
only by
actual
Sensation.

1. THE knowledge of our own being we have by intuition. The existence of a God, reason clearly makes known to us, as has been shown.

The knowledge of the existence of *any other thing* we can have only by *sensation*[1]: for there being no necessary connexion of real existence with any *idea* a man hath in his memory[2]; nor of any other existence but that of God with the existence of any particular man[3]: no particular man can know the existence of any other being, but only when, by actual operating upon him, it makes itself perceived by him. For, the having the idea of anything in our mind[4], no more proves the existence[5] of that thing, than the picture of a

---

[1] 'by sensation,' i. e. in and through 'ideas actually coming into our minds by our senses,' and 'actually operating upon him'; either as real or primary qualities of things, or as sensations in us, occasioned by their real qualities, in the case of their imputed or secondary qualities. Cf. ch. ii. § 14; also Bk. II. ch. viii.

[2] 'in his memory,' i. e. 'revived in our minds by our own memory,' and contrasted, in ch. ii. § 14, with 'ideas actually coming into our minds by our senses.'

[3] 'The existence and attributes of the Supreme Being is the only *necessary* truth I know regarding *existence*. All other beings that exist depend for their existence upon the will and power of the First Cause; therefore, neither their existence, nor anything that befals them, is necessary, but contingent. But although the existence of the Deity be necessary, I apprehend we can only deduce it from contingent truths.' (Hamilton's *Reid*, p. 430.) It is an argument, *a contingentia mundi*, he means to say.

[4] 'in our mind,' i. e. in our 'memory,' or in our fancy—as distinguished from 'ideas actually coming into our minds by our senses,' and which we cannot help regarding as appearances presented by what is real.

[5] 'existence,' i. e. its real existence independently of my transitory ideas.

BOOK IV.
CHAP. XI.

Instance:
White-
ness of
this Paper.

man evidences his being in the world, or the visions of a dream make thereby a true history.

2. It is therefore the *actual receiving* of ideas from without[1] that gives us notice of the existence of other things, and makes us know, that something doth exist at that time without us, which causes[2] that idea in us; though perhaps we neither know nor consider how it does it. For it takes not from the certainty of our senses, and the ideas we receive by them, that we know not the manner wherein they are produced[3]: v.g. whilst I write this, I have, by the paper affecting my eyes, that idea produced in my mind, which, whatever object causes, I call *white*; by which I know that that quality or accident (i.e. whose appearance before my eyes always causes that idea) doth really exist, and hath a being without me. And of this, the greatest assurance

---

[1] 'actual receiving ideas from without,'—again distinguished from merely reviving them in memory and fancy.

[2] 'causes,' i.e. occasions. Locke does not attribute active power to matter or bodies. Cf. Bk. II. ch. xxi. § 2.

[3] This is one of Locke's many disavowals of *any theory* of sense-perception. He is satisfied to state the fact, that in sense the real qualities of things become *somehow* manifested to us, as sense ideas in us. Viewed in relation to the *things*, we call those appearances 'qualities'; viewed as *perceptions in us*, we call them 'ideas.' But so to name them is not to explain sense-perception. The only explanation Locke recognises is a physical or physiological explanation of the impressions within the organism, which he regards as motions produced by extra-organic motions. 'The perception we have of bodies at a distance from ours may,' he says, 'be accounted for, as far as we are capable of understanding it, by the motion of particles of matter coming from them, and striking on our organs. But when, by this means, e.g., an image is made on the retina, *how we see it.* . . . *I confess*

I understand not. . . . Impressions made on the retina by rays of light, I think I understand; and motions continued thence to the brain may be conceived; and that these produce ideas *in our minds*, I am persuaded,—but *in a manner to me incomprehensible*. This I can resolve only into the good pleasure of God. The ideas [perceptions] it is certain I have . . . *but the manner how I come by them, how it is that I perceive, I confess I understand not*; though it be plain motion is *appointed* to be the cause [i.e. *physical occasion, or antecedent condition*] of our having them; as appears by the curious and artificial structure of the eye, accommodated to all the rules of refraction and dioptrics, that so visible objects might be exactly and regularly painted on the bottom of the eye.' (*Exam. of Malebranche*, §§ 9, 10 ; see also §§ 15, 16, 18.) The relation between our living perceptions of things and the things themselves is a mystery, and only metaphorically can ideas be said to 'resemble' things: our idea of a tree is not *like* the tree : it cannot be measured as the tree can.

I can possibly have, and to which my faculties can attain, is the testimony of my eyes, which are the proper and sole judges[1] of this thing ; whose testimony I have reason[2] to rely on as so certain, that I can no more doubt, whilst I write this, that I see white and black, and that something really exists that causes that sensation in me, than that I write or move my hand[3] ; which is a certainty as great as human nature is capable of, concerning the existence of anything, but a man's self alone, and of God.

3. The notice we have by our senses of the existing of things without us, though it be not altogether so certain as our intuitive knowledge, or the deductions of our reason employed about the clear abstract ideas of our own minds[4] ; yet it is an assurance that deserves the name of *knowledge*[5]. If we persuade ourselves that our faculties act and inform us right concerning the existence of those objects that affect them, it cannot pass for an ill-grounded confidence : for I think nobody can, in earnest, be so sceptical as to be uncertain of the existence of those things which he sees and feels[6]. At least, he that can doubt so far, (whatever he may have with his own thoughts,) will never have any controversy with me ; since he can never be sure I say anything contrary to his own opinion[7]. As to myself, I think God has given me assurance enough of the existence of things without me :

[1] He here recognises the immanence of 'judgment' in sense-perception, but he does not say whether he is here using judgment in his own narrow meaning of that term.

[2] What is the 'reason' he has in view ?

[3] An odd and inadequate illustration; for ' writing,' and ' moving the hand,' although intraorganic, as much need to have *their* reality vindicated as the sight of black or white does.

[4] As already noted, Locke's 'demonstration of' the existence of God is a deduction which includes more than ' abstract ideas of our own minds.' It is a mixed *à priori* proof, depending upon change, and thus *a contingentia.*

[5] It is an absolute certainty, he means to say,—independent of presumptions of probability.

[6] ' things which he sees and feels,' i. e. in ideas or appearances, which, presented in actual sight or touch, signify the reality of what is thus seen and touched.

[7] The existence of *other men* is revealed to *each man* only through his senses, and presupposes faith in the reason that is immanent in sense. It is therefore a *petitio principii* to produce ' other men,' and ' the consent of mankind,' in evidence of the reality of the sensible world. If the sensible world is an illusion, ' other men ' are included in the illusion.

since, by their different application, I can produce in myself both pleasure and pain, which is one great concernment of my present state. This is certain : the confidence that our faculties do not herein deceive us, is the greatest assurance we are capable of concerning the existence of material beings. For we cannot act anything but by our faculties ; nor talk of knowledge itself, but by the help of those faculties which are fitted to apprehend even what knowledge is[1].

But besides the assurance we have from our senses themselves, that they do not err in the information they give us of the existence of things without us, when they are affected by them[2], we are further confirmed in this assurance by other concurrent reasons[3] :—

Confirmed by concurrent reasons :—
First, Because we cannot have ideas of Sensation but by the Inlet of the Senses.

4. I. It is plain those perceptions are produced in us by exterior causes affecting our senses : because those that want the *organs* of any sense, never can have the ideas belonging to that sense produced in their minds. This is too evident to be doubted : and therefore we cannot but be assured that they come in by the organs of that sense, and no other way[4]. The organs themselves, it is plain, do not produce them : for then the eyes of a man in the dark would produce colours, and his nose smell roses in the winter : but we see nobody gets the relish of a pineapple, till he goes to the Indies, where it is, and tastes it[5].

Secondly, Because

5. II. Because sometimes[6] I find that *I cannot avoid the*

[1] Locke virtually postulates that divine reason is immanent in nature, and in us, in postulating the trustworthiness of the 'judgment' that is inevitably 'suggested' by the data of sense. If in this postulate I am necessarily deceived, I have no other reason or intuition to appeal to.

[2] That is, when ideas, or qualities of things, are being actually presented in sense, and not merely revived in memory or imagination, in the absence of the actual sense-appearances.

[3] This 'confirmation' of faith in sensuous cognition throughout presupposes the trustworthiness of the faith, presenting it however in a variety of lights. It may illustrate, but it does not really prove the validity of sense-perception.

[4] This supposes the existence of other men, and organs of sense. But sceptics doubt the existence of 'organs,' as much as of the extra-organic things, or 'exterior causes,' which the 'organs' are here said to guarantee. My organism is part of that world of which, *ex hypothesi*, the reality is doubted.

[5] He makes no allowance here for the illusions and hallucinations of sense, which arise from abnormal states of the organism.

[6] 'sometimes,' i.e. at those times when ideas are presented to the mind in sense.

having those ideas produced in my mind. For though, when BOOK IV.
my eyes are shut, or windows fast, I can at pleasure recal to
my mind the ideas of light, or the sun, which former sensations had lodged in my memory ; so I can at pleasure lay
by *that* idea, and take into my view that of the smell of a
rose, or taste of sugar. But, if I turn my eyes at noon
towards the sun, I cannot avoid the ideas which the light or
sun then produces in me. So that there is a manifest
difference between the ideas laid up in my memory[1], (over
which, if they were there only, I should have constantly the
same power to dispose of them, and lay them by at pleasure,)
and those which force themselves upon me, and I cannot
avoid having. And therefore it must needs be some exterior
cause, and the brisk acting of some objects without me,
whose efficacy I cannot resist, that produces those ideas in
my mind, whether I will or no[2]. Besides, there is nobody
who doth not perceive the difference in himself between
contemplating the sun, as he hath the idea of it in his memory,
and actually looking upon it : of which two, his perception is
so distinct, that few of his ideas are more distinguishable one
from another. And therefore he hath certain knowledge
that they are not *both* memory, or the actions of his mind,
and fancies only within him ; but that actual seeing hath a
cause without[3].

CHAP. XI.
we find
that an
Idea from
actual
Sensation,
and
another
from
Memory,
are very
distinct
Percep-
tions.

[1] 'ideas laid up in my memory,' elsewhere called 'ideas in our mind' (§ 1),—in contrast to ideas or qualities of things actually present in sensuous perception, and to the ideas of my own mind, of which I am conscious in 'reflection.' The difference here enlarged on is that between percep-tion and self-consciousness, on the one hand, and memory and imagination, on the other hand. The latter are subject to our will ; the former appear involuntarily.

[2] The involuntarily presented ideas or qualities of sense-perception are therefore manifestations to me of *some-thing* that is independent of me, and of the sense-ideas in which it appears.

But if the supposed *matter* is destitute of 'efficacy' or 'active power' (Bk. II. ch. xxi. § 2), how can *it* be the 'some-thing' that 'produces' sense-ideas in us ? Hence Berkeley saw in sense-perception the constant agency of God.

[3] This is an appeal to 'common sense' to support the contrast between actual seeing, and remembering or imagining the unseen—the sense of the contrast being so distinct, when attention is thus directed to it, that all may be challenged to deny, that in actual seeing there is an immediate manifestation of some powerful sub-stance, material or spiritual, that is independent of the percipient person.

BOOK IV.

CHAP. XI.

Thirdly, Because Pleasure or Pain, which accompanies actual Sensation, accompanies not the returning of those Ideas without the external Objects.

6. III. Add to this, that many of those ideas are *produced in us with pain*, which afterwards we remember without the least offence. Thus, the pain of heat or cold, when the idea of it is revived in our minds, gives us no disturbance; which, when felt, was very troublesome; and is again, when actually repeated: which is occasioned by the disorder the external object causes in our bodies when applied to them [1]: and we remember the pains of hunger, thirst, or the headache, without any pain at all; which would either never disturb us, or else constantly do it, as often as we thought of it, were there nothing more but ideas floating in our minds, and appearances entertaining our fancies, without the real existence of things affecting us from abroad [2]. The same may be said of *pleasure*, accompanying several actual sensations. And though mathematical demonstration depends not upon sense [3], yet the examining them by diagrams [4] gives great credit to the ·evidence of our sight, and seems to give it a certainty approaching to that of demonstration itself. For, it would be very strange, that a man should allow it for an undeniable truth, that two angles of a figure, which he measures by lines and angles of a diagram [5], should be bigger one than the other, and yet doubt of the existence of those lines and angles, which by looking on he makes use of to measure that by [6].

Fourthly, Because our Senses assist one

7. IV. Our *senses* in many cases *bear witness to the truth of each other's report*, concerning the existence of sensible things without us. He that *sees* a fire, may, if he doubt whether it

[1] Here again his 'proof' becomes a proof of extra-organic things that rests at last upon impressions on our organism. But the extra-organic occasion, and the intra-organic affection are each equally revealed in sense, and equally dependent on the assumed certainty of the sensuous judgment or perception.

[2] 'from abroad,' i. e. from the space outside our organism; the organism itself with all its impressions being supposed to exist as part of me.

[3] In pure mathematics.

[4] In concrete diagrams of sense and sensuous imagination.

[5] A particular diagram presented to the senses.

[6] This involves what Leibniz calls 'mixed propositions,' drawn partly from premises that contain results of observation—a combination of inductive generalizations and theorems of pure mathematics. As to them, he says, the conclusion follows the weaker of the premises, and cannot have more certainty than it has; so that those mixed propositions have only the degree of probability that belongs to the observations and generalizations. This applies to the cosmological 'demonstration' in ch. x.

be anything more than a bare fancy, *feel* it too ; and be convinced, by putting his hand in it[1]. Which certainly could never be put into such exquisite pain by a bare idea or phantom, unless that the pain be a fancy too : which yet he cannot, when the burn is well, by raising the idea of it, bring upon himself again.

Thus I see, whilst I write this, I can change the appearance of the paper ; and by designing the letters, tell *beforehand*[2] what new idea it shall exhibit the very next moment, by barely drawing my pen over it : which will neither appear (let me fancy as much as I will) if my hands stand still ; or though I move my pen, if my eyes be shut : nor, when those characters are once made on the paper, can I choose afterwards but see them as they are ; that is, have the ideas of such letters as I have made. Whence it is manifest, that they are not barely the sport and play of my own imagination, when I find that the characters that were made at the pleasure of my own thoughts, do not obey them ; nor yet cease to be, whenever I shall fancy it, but continue to affect my senses constantly and regularly, according to the figures I made them. To which if we will add, that the sight of those shall, from another man, draw such sounds as I beforehand design they shall stand for, there will be little reason left to doubt that those words I write do really exist without me, when they cause a long series of regular sounds[3] to affect

BOOK IV.

CHAP. XI.

another's Testimony of the Existence of outward Things, and enable us to predict.

---

[1] One (possibly false) witness cannot thus give credit to another possibly false witness. We have to suppose both trustworthy ; and if we do so there is no need to appeal to the one in support of the other. Unless as an illustration of the rational harmony immanent in nature, this argument, like the three preceding, begs the question ; if indeed one is entitled to make it a question, whether sense-perceived heat, light, and pain are mere fancies, or ideas that are also qualities of things.

[2] 'tell beforehand.' This *prevision* presupposes that reason is immanent in nature, and that the data of sense are not isolated phenomena, but externalised in virtue of their natural order.

'La vérité des choses sensibles,' says Leibniz, 'se justifie par leur liaison, qui dépend des vérités intellectuelles, fondées en raison, et des observations constantes dans les choses sensibles mêmes, lors même que les raisons ne paraissent pas. Et comme ces raisons et observations nous donnent moyen de juger de l'avenir par rapport à notre intérêt, et que le succès répond à notre jugement raisonnable, on ne saurait demander ni avoir même une plus grande certitude sur ces objets.' (*Nouveaux Essais.*)

[3] Their reality is thus implied in that faith in the rational organic unity of all changes in the universe which pervades our sensuous experience.

BOOK IV.

—◆◆—

CHAP. XI.

This
Certainty
is as great
as our
Condition
needs.

my ears, which could not be the effect of my imagination, nor could my memory retain them in that order.

8. But yet, if after all this [1] any one will be so sceptical as to distrust his senses, and to affirm that all we see and hear, feel and taste, think and do, during our whole being, is but the series and deluding appearances of a long dream, whereof there is no reality ; and therefore will question the existence of all things, or our knowledge of anything : I must desire him to consider, that, if all be a dream, then he doth but dream that he makes the question, and so it is not much matter that a waking man should answer him [2]. But yet, if he pleases, he may dream that I make him this answer, That the certainty of things existing in *rerum natura* when we have the testimony of our senses for it is not only as great as our frame can attain to, but as our condition needs. For, our faculties being suited not to the full extent of being, nor to a perfect, clear, comprehensive knowledge of things free from all doubt and scruple ; but to the preservation of us, in whom they are ; and accommodated to the use of life : they serve to our purpose well enough, if they will but give us certain notice of those things, which are convenient or inconvenient to us. For he that sees a candle burning, and hath experi-

---

[1] He who starts with distrust in the judgment that is latent in sense-perception, obscured though it be by the clouds of sense, has no sufficient relief in the four supplementary arguments. Unless we take for granted that sense-ideas are in reason the appearances of real things, no arguments which imply this assumption can prove them to be such.

[2] The reality of sensible things, says Leibniz, consists in a connection of sensuous phenomena that is founded on reason ; and it is *this connection* which distinguishes the realities from dreams. Yet this certainty, it must be granted, is not of the highest, as the author of the *Essay*, he says, has recognised. For it is not metaphysically impossible that there may be a *dream*, continuous and orderly, like the actual sense-life of a man ; but it is a supposition, according to the ordinary meaning of the word ' dream,' as contrary to reason as the supposition of a book formed by throwing type together at random. After all, provided the phenomena be connected in a permanent order, it matters little, as Leibniz remarks, whether they are called *dreams* or not ; since we find that we are not deceived in our actions, when the sensuous data are interpreted on principles of reason. But it cannot be said we discover this order ' by experience,' which only records the past : faith in the Divine order of the universe anticipates the future (of which we can have had no experience), assured that the future cannot put our intelligence to confusion.

mented the force of its flame by putting his finger in it, will little doubt that this is something existing without him, which does him harm, and puts him to great pain : which is assurance enough, when no man requires greater certainty to govern his actions by than what is as certain as his actions themselves [1]. And if our dreamer pleases to try whether the glowing heat of a glass furnace be barely a wandering imagination in a drowsy man's fancy, by putting his hand into it, he may perhaps be wakened into a certainty greater than he could wish, that it is something more than bare imagination [2]. So that this evidence is as great as we can desire, being as certain to us as our pleasure or pain, i. e. happiness or misery ; beyond which we have no concernment, either of knowing or being. Such an assurance of the existence of things without us is sufficient to direct us in the attaining the good and avoiding the evil which is caused by them, which is the important concernment we have of being made acquainted with them [3].

9. In fine, then, when our senses do actually convey into our understandings any idea, we cannot but be satisfied that there doth something *at that time* really exist without us, which doth affect our senses, and by them give notice of itself to our apprehensive faculties, and actually produce that

But reaches no further than actual Sensation.

---

[1] But the reality of 'his actions themselves' cannot, in arguing with sceptics, be thus pre-supposed. This is as much in question as the reality of the 'candle burning.'

[2] If the reality of all sense-perception is in question, the doubt cannot be settled by this appeal to our 'perception' of 'the heat of a glass furnace.'

[3] Leibniz is not content with Locke's practical confutation of the sceptic. He further asks, on what the *connection* of sense-data, in which practical reality consists, is ultimately founded? In the end he seems to resolve it into connection of the universal ideas, that are supreme in the universe, and presuppose the supremacy of Spirit. For these questions lead at last, as the ultimate ground of certainty, to the Supreme and Universal Mind, that cannot but exist, and whose understanding, as Saint Augustine has it, is the region of the eternal truths. To see that we must at last come to this, we must consider that these necessary truths contain the determining reason and regulative principle of all things, including the natural laws of the universe. So that the necessities of reason are anterior in reason to all contingent beings. It is here that Leibniz finds at last the *original* of the ideas and principles which are engraved in our souls, not in the form of propositions, of which we are conscious, but as the latent sources of judgments that rise into consciousness on occasions in experience.

idea[1] which we then perceive: and we cannot so far distrust their testimony, as to doubt that such *collections* of simple ideas as we have observed by our senses to be united together, do really exist together[2]. But this knowledge extends as far as the present testimony of our senses, employed about particular objects that do then affect them, and no further[3]. For if I saw such a collection of simple ideas as is wont to be called *man*, existing together one minute since, and am now alone, I cannot be certain that the same man exists now, since there is no *necessary connexion* of his existence a minute since with his existence now: by a thousand ways he may cease to be, since I had the testimony of my senses for his existence. And if I cannot be certain that the man I saw last to-day is now in being[4], I can less be certain that he is so who hath been longer removed from my senses, and I have not seen since yesterday, or since the last year: and much less can I be certain of the existence of men that I never saw. And, therefore, though it be highly probable that

---

[1] 'produce that idea,' i. e. present that phenomenon or quality.

[2] Accordingly, a real substance is recognised as apprehended in the perception of *aggregated* sense-ideas.

[3] Our sense-perception of the substance is thus coextensive only with the transitory presence of the 'collection' to our senses. We have no unconditional certainty of *its continuance*, after it has been withdrawn from our sense-perception, however great the probability of this may often be. But our ignorance of the forces at work in the universe always makes it possible that, as soon as we cease to see or touch anything, that thing may be disintegrated, or take some new form. It does not follow, however, that although its molecules may thus undergo metamorphoses, they must be annihilated, or that we can ever conceive their annihilation: this question, is not touched by Locke.

[4] There is no perceptible contradiction to pure reason in the supposition, that an actual being, considered to be entitled to the name *man* (because presenting the simple ideas or attributes that constitute my complex idea of the substance named man), seen by me a minute ago, and now no longer seen, may have ceased to exist, *in that form*, e. g. by his death; so that in this view of the matter it may be said that we have no knowledge of particular substances when they are absent from our senses. We cannot indeed demonstrate that henceforward the universe may not be the constant subject of capricious changes; or that we may not be solitary in it as soon as we are alone: but the supposition is inconsistent with the faith on which life rests—that its changes will not put our intelligence to utter confusion; as they would if things and persons might undergo incalculable metamorphoses at every moment, through the mysterious action of unknown causes. Whether this *faith* is to be called *certainty* is a question of names.

millions of men do now exist, yet, whilst I am alone, writing
this, I have not that certainty of it which we strictly call
knowledge; though the great likelihood of it puts me past
doubt, and it be reasonable for me to do several things upon
the confidence that there are men (and men also of my
acquaintance, with whom I have to do) now in the world :
but this is but probability, not knowledge[1].

10. Whereby yet we may observe how foolish and vain Folly to
a thing it is for a man of a narrow knowledge, who having expect
Demon-
reason given him to judge of the different evidence and stration in
every-
probability of things, and to be swayed accordingly; how thing.
vain, I say, it is to expect demonstration and certainty in
things not capable of it ; and refuse assent to very rational
propositions, and act contrary to very plain and clear truths,
because they cannot be made out so evident, as to surmount
every the least (I will not say reason, but) pretence of
doubting. He that, in the ordinary affairs of life, would
admit of nothing but direct plain demonstration, would
be sure of nothing in this world, but of perishing quickly.
The wholesomeness of his meat or drink would not give him

---

[1] The following observations by
Leibniz, in continuation of the passage
quoted on p. 331, n. 2, are weighty :—
' J'ai déjà remarqué que la vérité de
choses sensibles se justifie *par leur
liaison.* . . . . Aussi peut-on rendre
raison des songes mêmes, et de leur
peu de liaison avec d'autres phénomènes. Cependant, je crois qu'on
pourrait entendre l'appellation de la
connaissance et de la *certitude* au delà
des sensations *actuelles,* puisque la
clarté et l'évidence vont au delà, que je
considère comme une espèce de la
certitude : *et ce serait sans doute une
folie de douter sérieusement s'il y a des
hommes au monde, lorsque nous n'en
voyons point.* " Douter sérieusement,"
c'est douter par rapport à la pratique ;
et l'on pourrait prendre la *certitude* pour
une connaissance de la vérité, avec
laquelle on n'en peut point douter, par
rapport à la pratique, sans folie.'
(*Nouveaux Essais.*) This certainty,

where one cannot doubt without mad-
ness, or without supposing that the
universe is mad, Leibniz compares with
the luminous certainty ('certitude lumi-
neuse'), where we cannot doubt on
account of an intellectually necessary
relation actually perceived. The first
sort assures us that Constantinople is
in the world, or that Julius Cæsar
lived, facts which an educated man
could not doubt unless he became
insane ; the other sort is illustrated in
the axioms and demonstrations of pure
mathematics. The former are propositions of fact, founded on the immediate
experience of men ; the latter are
necessary propositions whose necessity
is discerned in the abstract relation
of their terms. God only sees how the
two terms *I* and *existence* are connected,
i. e. why I exist. Yet if a maxim means
an *unproveable* truth, the proposition
' I am ' is an axiom.

reason to venture on it: and I would fain know what it is he could do upon such grounds as are capable of no doubt, no objection[1].

11. As *when our senses are actually employed about any object*, we do know that it does exist; so *by our memory* we may be assured, that heretofore things that affected our senses have existed. And thus we have knowledge of the past existence of several things, whereof our senses having informed us, our memories still retain the ideas; and of this we are past all doubt, so long as we remember well. But this knowledge also reaches no further than our senses have formerly assured us[2]. Thus, seeing water at this instant, it is an unquestionable truth to me that water doth exist: and remembering that I saw it yesterday, it will also be always true, and as long as my memory retains it always an undoubted proposition to me, that water did exist the 10th of July, 1688[3]; as it will also be equally true that a certain number of very fine colours did exist, which at the same time I saw upon a bubble of that water: but, being now quite out of sight both of the water and bubbles too, it is no more certainly known to me that the water doth now exist, than that the bubbles or colours therein do so: it being no more necessary that water should exist to-day, because it existed yesterday, than that the colours or bubbles exist to-day[4], because they existed yesterday, though it be exceedingly much more probable; because water hath been

---

[1] Cf. Introduction, §§ 5-7.

[2] The present testimony of our senses, and the records of our memory are here by Locke, as afterwards by Hume, made the boundary of perfect certainty about finite facts. It remains to inquire into the ultimate nature of our judgments regarding those absent things for which we have *not* the testimony of memory. This inquiry, which comprehends the philosophy of physical induction, and the question of the possibility of *à priori* physics, was afterwards answered in his own critical method, by Kant.

[3] Locke was in Rotterdam at this date—seven months before he returned to England, and eighteen months before the *Essay* appeared. Cf. Bk. II. ch. xiv. § 29.

[4] 'existed,' i.e. in the form it had previously presented. The water might have been transformed in the interval into steam, for example, in the ordinary natural evolution.

observed to continue long in existence, but bubbles, and the BOOK IV.
colours on them, quickly cease to be[1].

CHAP. XI.

12. What ideas we have of spirits, and how we come by The
them, I have already shown[2]. But though we have those Existence
ideas in our minds[3], and know we have them there, the finite
having the ideas of spirits[4] does not make us know that any not know-
such things do exist without us, or that there are any finite able, and
spirits, or any other spiritual beings, but the Eternal God. Faith.
We have ground from revelation, and several other reasons,
to believe with assurance that there are such creatures: but
our senses not being able to discover them, we want the
means of knowing their particular existences. For we can
no more know that there are finite spirits really existing,
by the idea we have of such beings in our minds, than by
the ideas any one has of fairies or centaurs, he can come
to know that things answering those ideas do really exist[5].

And therefore concerning the existence of finite spirits, as
well as several other things, we must content ourselves with
the evidence of faith[6]; but universal, certain propositions

---

[1] Water, that is to say, is less apt to
change the phenomena which its
elements assume in our sense-ideas
than bubbles are. The result of what
Locke here says Green takes to be,—
'That though I may enumerate a multitude of past matters of fact about
water, I cannot gather them up into
any general statement about it as a
real existence.' The future history of
what I now see, and call 'water,'
I cannot be absolutely certain of; but
I may in many cases have sufficient
probable evidence. I cannot be certain
what all its relations to all other bodies
may be, or what is its real essence is,
and so cannot demonstrate its metamorphoses in the future; although I
know *à priori*, according to Kant, that
water must submit to the conditions
of substantiality and causality.

[2] See Bk. II. ch. xxiii. §§ 5, 15,
19-22, 28; Bk. IV. ch. iii. § 27.

[3] 'ideas in our minds,' i.e. either in
memory or in fancy—as distinguished
from the ideas or phenomena presented
by things in our senses, or by our
minds in self-consciousness.

[4] 'spirits,' i.e. of finite, unembodied
spirits.

[5] For, on the principles of the
Essay, it is only the ideas or appearances that are presented by things
in our senses, or by ourselves in the
actual operations of our minds, and not
ideas that are mere fancies, that give
one his absolute assurance of the real
existence either of a thing of sense,
or of his own self.

[6] 'faith' means with Locke either
'probability' (ch. xv. § 3), or 'assent
to a proposition as coming from God
in an extraordinary way' (ch. xviii.
§ 2). Cousin, in his lectures on Locke
(*Vingt-unième Leçon*), curiously mistakes the meaning of this passage; and

concerning this matter are beyond our reach. For however true it may be, v.g., that all the intelligent spirits that God ever created do still exist, yet it can never make a part of our certain knowledge[1]. These and the like propositions we may assent to, as highly probable, but are not, I fear, in this state capable of knowing. We are not, then, to put others upon demonstrating, nor ourselves upon search of universal certainty in all those matters; wherein we are not capable of any other knowledge, but what our senses give us in this or that particular.

Only particular Propositions concerning concrete Existences are knowable.

13. By which it appears that there are two sorts of propositions :—(1) There is one sort of propositions concerning the *existence* of anything answerable to such an idea: as having the idea of an elephant, phoenix, motion, or an angel, in my mind[2], the first and natural inquiry is, Whether such a thing does anywhere exist?   And this knowledge is only of particulars.   No existence of anything without us, but only of God, can certainly be known further than our senses inform us[3].   (2) There is another sort of propositions, wherein

then founds on it a charge of scepticism. ' Sur l'existence de l'esprit,' says Locke, according to Cousin, ' nous devons nous contenter de l'évidence de la foi. . . . . Voilà bien, *ce me semble, le scepticisme absolu.*'   Because Locke makes our assertions about angels and other finite spirits, otherwise foreign to our experience, to depend on faith in what has been supernaturally revealed, he is supposed to ' throw himself into the arms ' of this sort of faith when he affirms *his own existence and that of his own mental operations* ; although he has himself expressly said (ch. ix. § 3), that ' experience convinces us that we have an *intuitive knowledge* of our own existence, and an *infallible perception* that we are.' Yet, according to Cousin, Locke's assumption that we cannot know either bodies or spirits without having ideas of them, ' drives him to abandon his philosophy, and all philosophy,

and to take refuge in Christianity and faith.'   Cousin rightly adds that only through a *petitio principii* is the way into this world of faith here open to him.   The alleged paralogism disappears when we see that Locke is not here speaking of his own existence as a self-conscious spirit, but of the existence of angels and other spirits disclosed in the Christian revelation.

[1] This makes the *present* existence of ' all the intelligent spirits that God ever created,' except our own, a matter of probability, not of the absolute certainty that belongs to knowledge.

[2] ' in my mind,' i.e. in an idea of which there is neither sense-consciousness nor self-consciousness. Cf. p. 337, n. 3.

[3] Locke here tells us that ' our senses,' i. e. ideas or phenomena actually presented in the senses, are our criteria for testing the reality of ideas of which we are conscious in

is expressed the agreement or disagreement of *our abstract*
ideas, and their dependence on one another. Such propositions may be universal and certain. So, having the idea of
God and myself, of fear and obedience, I cannot but be sure
that God is to be feared and obeyed by me : and this proposition will be certain, concerning man in general, if I have
made an abstract idea of such a species, whereof I am one
particular. But yet this proposition, how certain soever,
that ' men ought to fear and obey God ' proves not to me the
existence of *men* in the world ; but will be true of all such
creatures, whenever they do exist[1] : which certainty of such
general propositions depends on the agreement or disagreement to be discovered in those abstract ideas.

14. In the former case, our knowledge is the consequence And all
of the existence of things, producing ideas in our minds by general
our senses[2] : in the latter, knowledge is the consequence of tions that
the ideas (be they what they will) that are in our minds, pro- are known
ducing there general certain propositions[3]. Many of these concern
are called *aeternae veritates*, and all of them indeed are so ; Ideas.
not from being written, all or any of them, in the minds of all
men ; or that they were any of them propositions in any one's
mind, till he, having got the abstract ideas, joined or separated them by affirmation or negation. But wheresoever we
can suppose such a creature as man is, endowed with such
faculties, and thereby furnished with such ideas as we have,

memory or imagination. What we
remember or imagine is tested by
ideas presented in sense ; but these
last must be accepted without any
ulterior criterion, on the ground of
their inherent accordance with the
intelligible order of nature. And this
certainty of sense is confined to particular things now and here present,
excluding general assertions, which
are incapable of being guaranteed by
sense-perception, and involve more or
less a leap in the dark.

[1] If the proposition in question is
meant as an abstract proposition only,
it is absolutely certain, he means to
say, but if as a concrete proposition,

in which the real existence of other
men is implied, then it can only be
hypothetically certain ; for one can
have this absolute certainty only of
the existence of a man who is now and
here present to his senses.

[2] So that the ideas or phenomena
are not merely ' in our minds,' but are
manifestations of something that is
independent of our individual minds.

[3] The contingent element that is
introduced in sense-data, presented in
time, and determined by ultimately unknown powers, and under imperfectly
known conditions, being here elimi-
nated, so that the propositions are no
longer only hypothetically true.

we must conclude, he must needs, when he applies his thoughts to the consideration of his ideas, know the truth of certain propositions that will arise from the agreement or disagreement which he will perceive in his own ideas. Such propositions are therefore called *eternal truths*, not because they are eternal propositions actually formed, and antecedent to the understanding that at any time makes them ; nor because they are imprinted on the mind from any patterns that are anywhere out of the mind, and existed before : but because, being once made about abstract ideas, so as to be true, they will, whenever they can be supposed to be made again at any time, past or to come, by a mind having those ideas, always actually be true. For names being supposed to stand perpetually for the same ideas, and the same ideas having immutably the same habitudes one to another, propositions concerning any abstract ideas that are once true must needs be *eternal verities*[1].

[1] The eternity and immutability of the relations of our abstract ideas are here rested on their being elaborations of our own understanding, and in this way independent of the powers at work in the universe of which we know so little. Whether any of them constitute *à priori* synthetic judgments, or whether they are all only analytical and explicative, he does not consider.

CHAPTER XII.

OF THE IMPROVEMENT OF OUR KNOWLEDGE[1].

BOOK IV.

CHAP. XII.

Know-
ledge is
not got
from
Maxims.

1. IT having been the common received opinion amongst men of letters, that *maxims* were the foundation of all knowledge ; and that the sciences were each of them built upon certain *praecognita*, from whence the understanding was to take its rise, and by which it was to conduct itself in its inquiries into the matters belonging to that science, the beaten road of the Schools has been, to lay down in the beginning one or more *general propositions*, as foundations whereon to build the knowledge that was to be had of that subject. These doctrines, thus laid down for foundations of any science, were called *principles*, as the beginnings from which we must set out, and look no further backwards in our inquiries[1], as we have already observed[2].

2. One thing which might probably give an occasion to this way of proceeding in other sciences, was (as I suppose) the good success it seemed to have in *mathematics*, wherein men, being observed to attain a great certainty of knowledge, these sciences came by pre-eminence to be called Μαθήματα, and Μάθησις, learning, or things learned, thoroughly learned, as having of all others the greatest certainty, clearness, and evidence in them.

---

[1] It is as obstructions to free inquiry and criticism that Locke warns against *received* maxims or axioms. This is not expressly to assert that experience is interpretable without presupposing more than is presented in its contingent data. Scientific verification itself presupposes the 'maxim,' that rational order is immanent in nature; for if the universe were a chaos, verification would be impossible. Empiricism is full of unconscious assumptions of its own.

[2] Ch. vii.

BOOK IV.

—◆—

CHAP. XII.

But from
comparing
clear and
distinct
Ideas.

3. But if any one will consider, he will (I guess) find, that the great advancement and certainty of real knowledge which men arrived to in these sciences, was not owing to the influence of these principles, nor derived from any peculiar advantage they received from two or three general maxims, laid down in the beginning; but from the clear, distinct, complete ideas their thoughts were employed about, and the relation of equality and excess so clear between some of them, that they had an intuitive knowledge, and by *that* a way to discover it in others; and this without the help of those maxims. For I ask, Is it not possible for a young lad to know that his whole body is bigger than his little finger, but by virtue of this axiom, that *the whole is bigger than a part*; nor be assured of it, till he has learned that maxim? Or cannot a country wench know that, having received a shilling from one that owes her three, and a shilling also from another that owes her three, the remaining debts in each of their hands are equal? Cannot she know this, I say, unless she fetch the certainty of it from this maxim, that *if you take equals from equals, the remainder will be equals*, a maxim which possibly she never heard or thought of? I desire any one to consider, from what has been elsewhere said, which is known first and clearest by most people, the particular instance, or the general rule; and which it is that gives life and birth to the other[1]. These general rules are but the comparing our more general and abstract ideas, which are the workmanship of the mind[2], made, and names given to them for the easier dispatch in its reasonings, and drawing into comprehensive terms and short rules its various and multiplied observations. But knowledge began in

---

[1] Unless universality is implied, the 'particular instance' teaches nothing, except perhaps its own momentary presentation. But the implied universal, in abstraction from all particular instances, need not be present in consciousness, and doubtless is not in most cases. It is left to the philosopher to recognise its immanence. It is the particular instance that first quickens it into intellectual life, and in that way may be said to be its 'origin' in the history of perception, when perception is regarded as an event.

[2] They are 'the workmanship of the mind,' inasmuch as, without intellectual activity in the individual, there can be no *conscious* recognition of a maxim, or self-evident principle, in its abstract form. Moreover the errors into which we fall, in accepting and applying abstract principles, show us that they are the 'workmanship' of a fallible human understanding.

the mind, and was founded on particulars[1]; though afterwards, perhaps, no notice was taken thereof: it being natural for the mind (forward still to enlarge its knowledge) most attentively to lay up those general notions, and make the proper use of them, which is to disburden the memory of the cumbersome load of particulars. For I desire it may be considered, what more certainty there is to a child, or any one, that his body, little finger, and all, is bigger than his little finger alone, after you have given to his body the name *whole*, and to his little finger the name *part*, than he could have had before; or what new knowledge concerning his body can these two relative terms give him, which he could not have without them? Could he not know that his body was bigger than his little finger, if his language were yet so imperfect that he had no such relative terms as whole and part? I ask, further, when he has got these names, how is he more certain that his body is a whole, and his little finger a part, than he was or might be certain before he learnt those terms, that his body was bigger than his little finger? Any one may as reasonably doubt or deny that his little finger is a part of his body, as that it is less than his body. And he that can doubt whether it be less, will as certainly doubt whether it be a part[2]. So that the maxim, the whole is bigger than a part, can never be made use of to prove the little finger less than the body, but when it is useless, by being brought to convince one of a truth which he knows already. For he that does not certainly know that any parcel of matter, with another parcel of matter joined to it, is bigger than either of them alone, will never be able to know it by the help of these two relative terms, whole and part, make of them what maxim you please.

---

[1] Without 'particulars' there can be no actual human knowledge, and yet knowledge implies more than is presented in the sensuous particulars that we know.

[2] But the mind that sees the universal principle that is embodied in the particular example has gained a philosophic insight that is wanting in 'the child.' One may see the truth of a particular proposition without seeing the universal principle which is presupposed in its truth; but that principle cannot be denied without inducing paralysis of the particular proposition. In all this, Locke's reluctance to let us leave the concrete, and his disposition to regard what is not obviously practical as unworthy of regard, is apparent, as well as his horror of what seemed to him logomachy.

BOOK IV.
CHAP. XII.
Dangerous
to build
upon
precarious
Principles.

4. But be it in the mathematics as it will, whether it be clearer, that, taking an inch from a black line of two inches, and an inch from a red line of two inches, the remaining parts of the two lines will be equal, or that *if you take equals from equals, the remainder will be equals* : which, I say, of these two is the clearer and first known[1], I leave to any one to determine, it not being material to my present occasion. That which I have here to do, is to inquire, whether, if it be the readiest way to knowledge to begin with general maxims, and build upon them, it be yet a safe way to take the *principles* which are laid down in any other science as unquestionable truths ; and so receive them without examination[2], and adhere to them, without suffering them to be doubted of, because mathematicians have been so happy, or so fair, to use none but self-evident and undeniable. If this be so, I know not what may not pass for truth in morality, what may not be introduced and proved in natural philosophy.

Let that principle of some of the old philosophers, That all is Matter, and that there is nothing else, be received for certain and indubitable, and it will be easy to be seen by the writings of some that have revived it again in our days, what consequences it will lead us into[3]. Let any one, with Polemo[4], take the world ; or with the Stoics[5], the aether, or the sun; or with Anaximenes[6], the air, to be God ; and what a divinity, religion, and worship must we needs have ! Nothing can be so dangerous as *principles* thus *taken up without questioning or*

[1] The 'clearer and first known' truths are not therefore the philosophical truths.

[2] 'without examination.' What he here pleads against is, dogmatic assumption of uncriticised maxims; which often turn out on critical examination not to be self-evident principles, but individual prejudices. Hence his suspicion of abstract principles, which are more apt to mislead in this way than particular facts and tentative generalizations.

[3] What do those who presuppose this 'principle' in all their reasonings mean by 'matter'?

[4] A disciple of Plato, and one of the masters of Zeno the Stoic.

[5] The Stoical deity is conceived (by analogy) as Ether, and as fire, under the influence of which it is assumed that all things grow and then dissolve,—out of which they are gradually evolved, and into which they are gradually refunded in a perpetual process—Platonic speculation being superseded by the Stoical dogmatism to which Locke here refers.

[6] 'air' — dogmatically adopted by Anaximenes, 'as the ultimate principle, universal substance, or deity, out of which the universe issued.'

examination; especially if they be such as concern morality, which influence men's lives, and give a bias to all their actions. Who might not justly expect another kind of life in Aristippus, who placed happiness in bodily pleasure ; and in Antisthenes, who made virtue sufficient to felicity ? And he who, with Plato, shall place beatitude in the knowledge of God, will have his thoughts raised to other contemplations than those who look not beyond this spot of earth, and those perishing things which are to be had in it[1]. He that, with Archelaus[2], shall lay it down as a principle, that right and wrong, honest and dishonest, are defined only by laws, and not by nature, will have other measures of moral rectitude and pravity, than those who take it for granted[3] that we are under obligations antecedent to all human constitutions.

5. If, therefore, those that pass for *principles* are *not certain*, To do so (which we must have some way to know, that we may be able is no certain to distinguish them from those that are doubtful[4],) but are Way to only made so to us by our blind assent, we are liable to be Truth. misled by them ; and instead of being guided into truth, we shall, by principles, be only confirmed in mistake and error.

6. But since the knowledge of the certainty of principles, as But to compare

---

[1] Note this rare expression of sympathy with Platonic thought, as opposed to the merely secular utilities to which Locke is so apt to appeal.

[2] A pupil of Anaxagoras. Locke's account of these ancients is crude and uncritical.

[3] As Locke himself does.

[4] ‘ It is a question of some moment, whether the differences among men about first principles can be brought to any issue. When in disputes one man maintains that to be a first principle which another denies, commonly both parties appeal to common sense, and so the matter rests. Now is there no way of discussing this appeal ? Is there no mark or criterion whereby first principles that are truly such may be distinguished from those that assume the character without a just title ? ’ (Reid's *Essays*, VI. ch. iv.) Reid grants

that it is contrary to the nature of first principles to admit of direct or apodictical proof. But may we not so exhibit them as that, from the constitution of the reason that is immanent in human nature and in the universe, the rationality of those that are genuine, or really implied in reason, may be made obvious ? Indeed, in the long run, those that are genuine ‘ support themselves, and gain rather than lose ground among mankind.’ But one way of testing them philosophically is, critical analysis of what is implied in a progressive intelligible experience, although it must be remembered that this very analysis proceeds upon presuppositions. Genuine first principles *are* reason ; and reason cannot be proved to be rational without begging the question.

BOOK IV.

CHAP. XII.

clear, complete Ideas, under steady Names.

well as of all other truths, depends only upon the perception we have of the agreement or disagreement of our ideas, the way to improve our knowledge is not, I am sure, blindly, and with an implicit faith, to receive and swallow principles [1]; but is, I think, to get and fix in our minds clear, distinct, and complete ideas, as far as they are to be had, and annex to them proper and constant names. And thus, perhaps, without any other principles, but *barely considering those perfect ideas*, and by *comparing them one with another*, finding their agreement and disagreement, and their several relations and habitudes; we shall get more true and clear knowledge by the conduct of this one rule, than by taking up principles, and thereby putting our minds into the disposal of others [2].

The true Method of advancing Knowledge is by considering our abstract Ideas.

7. We must, therefore, if we will proceed as reason advises, adapt our methods of inquiry to *the nature of the ideas we examine*, and the truth we search after. General and certain truths are only founded in the habitudes and relations of *abstract ideas* [3]. A sagacious and methodical application of our thoughts, for the finding out these relations, is the only way to discover all that can be put with truth and certainty concerning them into general propositions. By what steps we are to proceed in these, is to be learned in the schools of the mathematicians, who, from very plain and easy beginnings, by gentle degrees, and a continued chain of reasonings, proceed to the discovery and demonstration of truths that appear at first sight beyond human capacity. The art of finding proofs, and the admirable methods they have invented for the singling out and laying in order those intermediate ideas that demonstratively show the equality or inequality of unapplicable

---

[1] Cf. Bk. I. ch. iii. § 24.

[2] Locke's reaction against 'first principles' means with him reaction against blind authority, although it looks like rejection of the ultimate authority of self-evidencing reason—'the candle of the Lord' of Whichcote and Culverwell. But it is only abstract science that is got by this method of contemplating abstract ideas. It is otherwise with inquiries about concrete substances. Cf. § 9.

[3] Except the existence of the Supreme Mind, our own existence as actually manifested in consciousness, and the existence of other finite beings manifested to our senses—all human certainties are, according to Locke, confined to relations of abstract ideas, which are their own archetypes, and are thus independent of our imperfect knowledge of the changing concrete universe.

quantities, is that which has carried them so far, and produced such wonderful and unexpected discoveries: but whether something like this, in respect of other ideas, as well as those of magnitude, may not in time be found out, I will not determine. This, I think, I may say, that if other ideas that are the real as well as nominal essences of their species, were pursued in the way familiar to mathematicians, they would carry our thoughts further, and with greater evidence and clearness than possibly we are apt to imagine[1].

8. This gave me the confidence to advance that conjecture, which I suggest, (chap. iii.) viz. that *morality* is capable of demonstration as well as mathematics[2]. For the ideas that ethics are conversant about, being all real essences[3], and such as I imagine have a discoverable connexion and agreement one with another; so far as we can find their habitudes and relations, so far we shall be possessed of certain, real, and general truths; and I doubt not but, if a right method were taken, a great part of morality might be made out with that clearness, that could leave, to a considering man, no more reason to doubt, than he could have to doubt of the truth of propositions in mathematics, which have been demonstrated to him.

By which Morality also may be made clearer.

9. In our search after the knowledge of *substances*[4], our want of ideas that are suitable to such a way of proceeding obliges us to a quite different method. We advance not here, as in the other, (where our abstract ideas are real as well as nominal essences,) by contemplating our ideas[5], and considering

Our Knowledge of Substances is to be improved,

---

[1] In the seventeenth century mathematics was the ideal and objective example of scientific certainty, up to which it was sought to raise other departments of inquiry. We see this in Descartes and Spinoza, also in Hobbes.

[2] That is, pure or abstract morality. Cf. Bk. III. ch. xi. §§ 16–18; IV. ch. iii. §§ 18–19.

[3] The 'real essence' being identical with the 'nominal essence' in all abstract ideas.

[4] 'substances,' i. e. the particular

things and persons of which the actual universe consists, and whose customary modes of behaviour we want to find out.

[5] The relations of our own abstract ideas are discovered by bare contemplation of the ideas. Not so in our inquiries about 'substances' and their modes of behaviour, which are manifested in our sense-perceptions and self-consciousness, independently of our will: they suggest as their archetypes 'real essences,' beyond the grasp of human perception.

BOOK IV.

—•◦•—

CHAP. XII.

not by contempla-tion of abstract ideas, but only by Experi-ence.

their relations and correspondences; that helps us very little, for the reasons, that in another place we have at large set down[1]. By which I think it is evident, that substances afford matter of very little *general* knowledge; and the bare con-templation of their abstract ideas[2] will carry us but a very little way in the search of truth and certainty. What, then, are we to do for the improvement of our knowledge in substantial beings? Here we are to take a quite contrary course: the want of ideas of their real essences sends us from our own thoughts to the things themselves as they exist[3]. *Experience here must teach me what reason*[4] *cannot*: and it is by *trying* alone, that I can *certainly know*, what other qualities co-exist[5] with those of my complex idea, v. g. whether that yellow, heavy, fusible body I call *gold*, be malleable, or no; which experience (which way ever it prove in that particular body I examine) makes me not certain, that it is so in all, or any other yellow, heavy, fusible bodies, but that which I have tried[6]. Because it is no consequence one way or the other from my complex idea: the necessity or inconsistence of malleability hath no visible connexion with the combination of that colour, weight, and fusibility in any body. What I have said here of the nominal essence of gold, supposed to consist of a body of such a determinate colour, weight, and fusibility, will hold true, if malleableness, fixedness, and solubility in *aqua regia* be added to it. Our reasonings from these ideas[7] will carry us but a little way in the certain discovery of the other properties in those masses of matter

---

[1] Bk. II. ch. xxiii; III. ch. vi.

[2] 'their abstract ideas,' i.e. the nominal essences we associate with them, in making them subjects of our common terms.

[3] i.e. 'things' as actually manifested in their sense-ideas or sensible quali-ties, and our own mind as actually manifested to us in its operations.

[4] 'reason,' i.e. abstract reasoning, which cannot demonstrate beyond our own abstract ideas.

[5] 'co-exist,' i.e. at the moment of the 'trial' only, he must mean, for

this is implied in ch. xi. § 9.

[6] Of the distant, and the future, as such, we never have had, and never can have any experience, if by expe-rience is meant nothing more than the direct momentary datum of sense. The inductive *saltus*, which transcends this datum, as well as expectation and hope in every form, thus need faith in order to constitute experience in the wider meaning of that term.

[7] 'those ideas,' i.e. those abstract ideas which make up our nominal essence of gold. Cf. Bk. III. ch. vi.

wherein all these are to be found. Because the *other* properties
of such bodies, depending not on these, but on that unknown
real essence on which these also depend, we cannot by them
discover the rest; we can go no further than the simple ideas
of our nominal essence will carry us, which is very little beyond
themselves; and so afford us but very sparingly any certain,
universal, and useful truths. For, upon trial, having found
that particular piece (and all others of that colour, weight, and
fusibility, that I ever tried) malleable, that also makes now,
perhaps, a part of my complex idea, part of my nominal
essence of gold: whereby though I make my complex idea to
which I affix the name gold, to consist of more simple ideas
than before; yet still, it not containing the real essence of any
species of bodies, it helps me not certainly to know (I say to
know, perhaps it may be to conjecture) the other remaining
properties of that body, further than they have a visible
connexion with some or all of the simple ideas that make up
my nominal essence. For example, I cannot be certain, from
this complex idea, whether gold be fixed or no; because, as
before, there is no *necessary* connexion or inconsistence to be
discovered betwixt *a complex idea of a body yellow, heavy,
fusible, malleable*; betwixt these, I say, and *fixedness*; so that
I may certainly know, that in whatsoever body these are found,
there fixedness is sure to be. Here, again, for assurance,
I must apply myself to experience; as far as that reaches[1],
I may have certain knowledge, but no further.

10. I deny not but a man, accustomed to rational and
regular experiments[2], shall be able to see further into the
nature of bodies, and guess righter[3] at their yet unknown

---

[1] And as 'experience,' properly
speaking, does not in any case exceed
the *immediate* data of sense, or at the
utmost, in addition, past data stored in
memory—our 'certain knowledge' of
the sensible world is limited to those
data, if indeed this experience can be
said to constitute knowledge. All
beyond this to which we give our
assent, he here argues, for the hun-
dredth time, is presumed probability.
The presumption is sustained by our
general trust in the divine reasonableness of the universe. So that what is
called physical *science* is essentially
faith in a physical order that is subordinate to the moral order that alone
is ultimate or supreme.

[2] 'accustomed to rational and regular
experiments,' i. e. who practises scien-
tifically sufficient inductive methods.

[3] 'guess righter.' The hypotheses
under which he reduces his particular
experience are probably true. But

BOOK IV.
———
CHAP. XII.
venience,
not
Science.

properties, than one that is a stranger to them : but yet, as I have said, this is but judgment and opinion, not knowledge and certainty. This way of *getting and improving our knowledge*[1] *in substances only by experience and history*, which is all that the weakness of our faculties in this state of mediocrity[2] which we are in in this world can attain to, makes me suspect that *natural philosophy is not capable of being made a science.* We are able, I imagine, to reach very little general knowledge concerning the species of bodies, and their several properties. Experiments and historical[3] observations we may have, from which we may draw advantages of ease and health, and thereby increase our stock of conveniences for this life ; but beyond this I fear our talents reach not, nor are our faculties, as I guess, able to advance[4].

We are
fitted for
moral
Science,
but only
for pro-
bable inter-
pretations
of external
Nature.

11. From whence it is obvious to conclude, that, since our faculties are not fitted to penetrate into the internal fabric and real essences of bodies ; but yet plainly discover to us the being of a God, and the knowledge of ourselves, enough to lead us into a full and clear discovery of our duty and great concernment; it will become us, as rational creatures, to employ those faculties we have about what they are most adapted to, and follow the direction of nature, where it seems to point us out the way. For it is rational to conclude,

after all, his 'science of nature' is throughout hypothetical, and none of it *à priori* synthetical, while it is elastic, or subject to progressive evolution in our gradually amended 'science.'

[1] Here and elsewhere in the context, he calls this 'knowledge,' inconsistently with his own definition of knowledge. This chapter and the next form a transition from the first part of the Fourth Book, which is concerned with Knowledge, to the second part which deals with Probability.

[2] 'mediocrity'—man is intellectually intermediate between the nescience of the mere animal, and the Omniscience of God.

[3] 'historical,' i. e. in observations of events, or objects presented in succession, as in the 'historical plain method' adopted by Locke, in his inquiry into *what happens* in a human understanding.

[4] May we not say that our faculties, in exercising trust in the intelligible order of the sensible world, therein presuppose *trust in God*, i. e. in the supremacy of Reason, active and perfect; thus interpreting the world of the senses as a revelation (in part) of the Supreme Mind, and not merely as a means for 'increasing our stock of conveniences for this life'? Viewed in its higher relations, the sensible world thus forms a Divine poem, obscure but increasingly understood.

that our proper employment lies in those inquiries, and in that sort of knowledge which is most suited to our natural capacities, and carries in it our greatest interest, i. e. the condition of our eternal estate[1]. Hence I think I may conclude, that *morality* is *the proper science and business of mankind in general,* (who are both concerned and fitted to search out their *summum bonum* ;) as several arts, conversant about several parts of nature, are the lot and private talent of particular men, for the common use of human life, and their own particular subsistence in this world. Of what consequence the discovery of one natural body and its properties may be to human life, the whole great continent of America is a convincing instance : whose ignorance in useful arts, and want of the greatest part of the conveniences of life, in a country that abounded with all sorts of natural plenty, I think may be attributed to their ignorance of what was to be found in a very ordinary, despicable stone, I mean the mineral of *iron.* And whatever we think of our parts or improvements in this part of the world, where knowledge and plenty seem to vie with each other ; yet to any one that will seriously reflect on it, I suppose it will appear past doubt, that, were the use of iron lost among us, we should in a few ages be unavoidably reduced to the wants and ignorance of the ancient savage Americans, whose natural endowments and provisions come no way short of those of the most flourishing and polite nations. So that he who first made known the use of that contemptible mineral, may be truly styled the father of arts, and author of plenty.

12. I would not, therefore, be thought to disesteem or In the study of

---

[1] Locke's conclusion here appears to be the opposite of Kant's, whose *à priori* knowledge of nature, yet nescience in the supernatural sphere, is in contrast to Locke's exclusion of physics from human knowledge, and recognition of Eternal Mind, and our own personality and moral relations to God, as within the range of a human understanding. But it is a 'judgment' that is sufficient for action that Locke has in view, and Kant proposes a moral proof not only of the existence of God, but of the immortality of the human soul.

In the deepest and truest philosophy, the *ego*, the world, and God, are combined in an endless development, under a supreme Divine Purpose, faith in which sustains the sciences of nature, but in constant subordination to faith in a moral and spiritual ideal.

BOOK IV.

—•—

CHAP. XII.

Nature we
must
beware of
Hypo-
theses and
wrong
Principles.

dissuade the study of *nature*[1]. I readily agree the contemplation of his works gives us occasion to admire, revere, and glorify their Author: and, if rightly directed, may be of greater benefit to mankind than the monuments of exemplary charity that have at so great charge been raised by the founders of hospitals and almshouses. He that first invented printing, discovered the use of the compass, or made public the virtue and right use of *kin kina*[2], did more for the propagation of knowledge, for the supply and increase of useful commodities, and saved more from the grave than those who built colleges, workhouses, and hospitals. All that I would say is, that we should not be too forwardly possessed with the opinion or expectation of knowledge, where it is not to be had, or by ways that will not attain to it: that we should not take doubtful systems for complete sciences; nor unintelligible notions for scientifical demonstrations. In the knowledge of bodies, we must be content to glean what we can from particular experiments: since we cannot, from a discovery of their real essences, grasp at a time whole sheaves, and in bundles comprehend the nature and properties of whole species together. Where our inquiry is concerning co-existence, or repugnancy to co-exist, which by contemplation of our ideas we cannot discover; there experience, observation, and natural history, must give us, by our senses and by retail, an insight into corporeal substances. The knowledge of *bodies* we must get by our senses, warily employed in

---

[1] 'nature,' i.e. the world of sensible things, as determined in the chain of physical or phenomenal causality. Cf. Bk. II. ch. xxi, and the relative annotations. Nature is thus contrasted with the spiritual economy, and also with the supernatural or miraculous. But if, as sometimes intended, 'nature' comprehends the spiritual as well as the sensuous universe, and the supreme immanent order to which mechanical causation is subordinate, then there can be nothing supernatural; for this is only to say that there can be nothing ultimately irrational in the constitution of things. 'The only distinct meaning of the word natural,' says Bishop Butler,

'is *stated, fixed, settled*. . . . And from hence it must follow that a person's notion of what is natural will be enlarged, in proportion to his greater knowledge of the works of God. Nor is there any absurdity in supposing, that there may be beings in the universe whose capacities, and knowledge, and views may be so *extensive* as that the whole Christian dispensation may to them appear *natural*, i.e. analogous or conformable to God's dealings with other parts of his creation; as natural as the visible course of things appears to us.' (*Analogy*, Pt. I. ch. i.)

[2] *kin kina*—quinine.

taking notice of their qualities and operations on one an- BOOK IV.
other [1] : and what we hope to know of *separate spirits* [2] in this
world, we must, I think, expect only from revelation. He CHAP. XII.
that shall consider how little general maxims, precarious
principles, and hypotheses laid down at pleasure [3], have promoted true knowledge, or helped to satisfy the inquiries of
rational men after real improvements ; how little, I say, the
setting out at that end [4] has, for many ages together, advanced
men's progress, towards the knowledge of natural philosophy,
will think we have reason to thank those who in this latter
age have taken another course, and have trod out to us,
though not an easier way to learned ignorance, yet a surer
way to profitable knowledge.

13. Not that we may not, to explain any phenomena of The true Use of Hypo-
nature, make use of any probable hypothesis whatsoever :
hypotheses, if they are well made, are at least great helps theses.
to the memory, and often direct us to new discoveries [5]. But
my meaning is, that we should not take up any one too
hastily (which the mind, that would always penetrate into
the causes of things, and have principles to rest on, is very

---

[1] To interpret a sense-idea as the real quality of a substance, or as the immediate manifestation of the power of a substance, implies more than apprehension of transitory sense-phenomena.

[2] 'separate spirits'—angels or devils. Cf. ch. xi. § 12.

[3] He mixes together ' maxims, principles, and hypotheses,' because what are called maxims and first principles are often doubtful hypotheses, or obstinate prejudices. Cf. Bk. I. ch. iii. §§ 22-24, and Bk. IV. ch. vii.

[4] This is that beginning 'at the wrong end '—that 'letting loose our thoughts into the vast ocean of being' at the outset, instead of beginning with the data of experience, and seeking by gradual analysis to find the ultimate interpretation,—which the *Essay* was meant to warn men against. Cf. Introduction, § 7.

[5] On the office of hypothesis in the interpretation of nature, cf. *Novum Organum*, I. 19, and Dr. Fowler's annotation ; also II. 20. The disposition fostered by Locke would prefer hypotheses, suggested in order to be verified by ideas presented in the senses or in reflection, to Kant's *à priori* judgments, to which the objects of experience *must* conform. Locke sees in the former the presuppositions of a progressive and elastic physics, with its tentative generalisations, provisional definitions, and gradually amended nominal essences. He would hold hypothetically, not apodeictically, even to the end, all generalised assertions about the coexistences and sequences in the universe, including even the assertion that there *are* orderly coexistences and sequences, as well as permanent substances in which the ordered coexistence and sequence appears.

BOOK IV.
CHAP. XII.

apt to do,) till we have very well examined particulars, and made several experiments, in that thing which we would explain by our hypothesis, and see whether it will agree to them all ; whether our principles will carry us quite through, and not be as inconsistent with one phenomenon of nature, as they seem to accommodate and explain another. And at least that we take care that the name of *principles* deceive us not, nor impose on us, by making us receive that for an unquestionable truth, which is really at best but a very doubtful conjecture ; such as are most (I had almost said all) of the hypotheses in natural philosophy [1].

Clear and distinct Ideas with settled Names, and the finding of those intermediate ideas which show their Agreement or Disagreement, are the Ways to enlarge our Knowledge.

14. But whether natural philosophy be capable of certainty [2] or no, the ways to enlarge our knowledge, as far as we are capable, seems to me, in short, to be these two :—

First, The first is to get and settle in our minds [3 determined ideas of those things whereof we have general or specific names; at least, so many of them as we would consider and improve our knowledge in, or reason about.] [4And if they be specific ideas of substances, we should endeavour also to make them as complete as we can, whereby I mean, that we should put together as many simple ideas as, being constantly observed to co-exist, may perfectly determine the species ; and each of those simple ideas which are the ingredients of our complex ones, should be clear and distinct in our minds.] For it being evident that our knowledge cannot exceed our ideas ; [5 as far as] they are either imperfect, confused, or obscure, we cannot expect to have certain, perfect, or clear knowledge [6].

---

[1] Cf. Bk. I. ch. iii. §§ 23, 24 ; ch. vii. It is against those spurious axioms, or dogmatic (as distinguished from suggestive) hypotheses, that he contends throughout his controversy with ' innate ideas and principles '—not against self-evident truths of reason, which, even in their most abstract form, may help at least to 'silence wranglers.'

[2] 'capable of certainty,' i.e. of rising into the certainty of ' knowledge,' as distinct from presumption that rests on the custom of experience.

[3] In first edition—'as far as we can, clear, distinct, and constant ideas of those things we would consider and know.'

[4] Added in fourth edition.

[5] ' where '—in first three editions.

[6] This sentence was quoted by Stillingfleet, to show that Locke's theory of knowledge is inconsistent with recognition of mysteries in religion. Locke replied that he did not place certainty in *perfect* clearness of idea : he only held that there could not be

Secondly, The other is the art of finding out those inter- BOOK IV.
mediate ideas, which may show us the agreement or repugnancy ——•——
of other ideas, which cannot be immediately compared. CHAP. XII.

15. That these two (and not the relying on maxims, and Mathe-
drawing consequences from some general propositions) are matics an
instance
the right methods of improving our knowledge in the ideas of this.
of other modes besides those of quantity, the consideration
of mathematical knowledge will easily inform us. Where
first we shall find that he that has not a perfect and clear
idea of those angles or figures of which he desires to know
anything, is utterly thereby incapable of any knowledge
about them. Suppose but a man not to have a perfect exact
idea of a right angle, a scalenum, or trapezium, and there is
nothing more certain than that he will in vain seek any
demonstration about them. Further, it is evident, that it
was not the influence of those maxims which are taken for
principles in mathematics, that hath led the masters of that
science into those wonderful discoveries they have made.
Let a man of good parts know all the maxims generally
made use of in mathematics ever so perfectly, and contemplate
their extent and consequences as much as he pleases, he will,
by their assistance, I suppose, scarce ever come to know that
the square of the hypothenuse in a right-angled triangle is
equal to the squares of the two other sides. The knowledge
that 'the whole is equal to all its parts,' and 'if you take
equals from equals, the remainder will be equal,' &c., helped
him not, I presume, to this demonstration : and a man may,
I think, pore long enough on those axioms, without ever
seeing one jot the more of mathematical truths. They have
been discovered by the thoughts otherwise applied : the mind
had other objects, other views before it, far different from
those maxims, when it first got the knowledge of such truths
in mathematics, which men, well enough acquainted with
those received axioms, but ignorant of their method who
first made these demonstrations, can never sufficiently admire.
And who knows what methods to enlarge our knowledge

knowledge of those relations of an idea   of its relations. Hence the additions
that are obscure ; but an obscure idea   and modifications in the text of this
might be clear and cognizable in some   section.

BOOK IV.

CHAP. XII.

in other parts of science may hereafter be invented, answering that of algebra in mathematics, which so readily finds out the ideas of quantities to measure others by; whose equality or proportion we could otherwise very hardly, or, perhaps, never come to know [1]?

[1] It is our intuitive and demonstrative knowledge of abstractions, not our concrete judgments of presumed probabilities, that Locke has in view in this and the preceding section.

CHAPTER XIII.

SOME FURTHER CONSIDERATIONS CONCERNING OUR KNOWLEDGE.

BOOK IV.

CHAP.
XIII.

Our
Know-
ledge
partly
necessary,
partly
voluntary.

1. OUR knowledge, as in other things, so in this, has so great a conformity with our sight, that it is neither wholly necessary, nor wholly voluntary[1]. If our knowledge were altogether necessary, all men's knowledge would not only be alike, but every man would know all that is knowable; and if it were wholly voluntary, some men so little regard or value it, that they would have extreme little, or none at all. Men that have senses cannot choose but receive some ideas by them; and if they have memory, they cannot but retain some of them; and if they have any distinguishing faculty, cannot but perceive the agreement or disagreement of some of them one with another; as he that has eyes, if he will open them by day, cannot but see some objects, and perceive a difference in them. But though a man with his eyes open in the light, cannot but see, yet there be certain objects which he may choose whether he will turn his eyes to; there may be in his reach a book containing pictures and discourses, capable to delight or instruct him, which yet he may never have the will to open, never take the pains to look into.

---

[1] Absolute certainty is determined by necessity of reason. But although we are thus *obliged* to perceive it, when the relations which it involves are consciously realised by us, we are not in like manner obliged consciously to realise those relations. It is not necessary for each man actually to perceive all that, when perceived, must be seen by him to be intellectually necessary. Accordingly universal *conscious* assent is no proper test of knowledge ; for much that is potentially certain is not seen by all men to be certain, because the insight demands a corresponding development of the individual mind that can thus respond.

BOOK IV.

CHAP.
XIII.

The appli-
cation
of our
Faculties
voluntary ;
but, they
being
employed,
we know
as things
are, not as
we please.

2. There is also another thing in a man's power, and that is, though he turns his eyes sometimes towards an object, yet he may choose whether he will curiously survey it, and with an intent application endeavour to observe accurately all that is visible in it. But yet, what he does see, he cannot see otherwise than he does. It depends not on his will to see that black which appears yellow ; nor to persuade himself, that what actually scalds him, feels cold. The earth will not appear painted with flowers, nor the fields covered with verdure, whenever he has a mind to it : in the cold winter, he cannot help seeing it white and hoary, if he will look abroad. Just thus is it with our understanding : all that is voluntary in our knowledge is, the employing or withholding any of our *faculties* from this or that sort of objects, and a more or less accurate survey of them : but, *they being employed*[1]*, our will hath no power to determine the knowledge of the mind one way or another* ; that is done only by the objects themselves, as far as they are clearly discovered. And therefore, as far as men's senses are conversant about external objects, the mind cannot but receive those ideas which are presented by them, and be informed of the existence of things without : and so far as men's thoughts converse with their own determined ideas, they cannot but in some measure observe the agreement or disagreement that is to be found amongst some of them, which is so far knowledge : and if they have names for those ideas which they have thus considered, they must needs be assured of the truth of those propositions which express that agreement or disagreement they perceive in them, and be undoubtedly convinced of those truths. For what a man sees, he cannot but see ; and what he perceives, he cannot but know that he perceives.

3. Thus he that has got the ideas of numbers, and hath taken the pains to compare one, two, and three, to six, cannot choose but know that they are equal : he that hath got

---

[1] He does not intend to say that what we are intellectually necessitated to know, and are thus under obligation to know, implies a purely passive perception of what is thus known. Our intellect must be actively employed in the perception of the necessity.

the idea of a triangle, and found the ways to measure its
angles and their magnitudes, is certain that its three angles
are equal to two right ones ; and can as little doubt of that,
as of this truth, that, It is impossible for the same thing to be,
and not to be.

4. He also that hath the idea of an intelligent, but frail
and weak being, made by and depending on another, who is
eternal, omnipotent, perfectly wise and good, will as certainly
know that man is to honour, fear, and obey God, as that the
sun shines when he sees it. For if he hath but the ideas of
two such beings in his mind, and will turn his thoughts that
way, and consider them, he will as certainly find that the
inferior, finite, and dependent, is under an obligation to obey
the supreme and infinite, as he is certain to find that three,
four, and seven are less than fifteen ; if he will consider and
compute those numbers : nor can he be surer in a clear
morning that the sun is risen ; if he will but open his eyes,
and turn them that way. But yet these truths, being ever so
certain, ever so clear, he may be ignorant of either, or all of
them, who will never take the pains to employ his faculties,
as he should, to inform himself about them [1].

---

[1] 'The touchstone of science is the universal validity of its results for all normally constituted and duly instructed minds.' (Pearson's *Grammar of Science*, p. 30.) The touchstone of metaphysical or theological truth in like manner presupposes due instruction, and individual development of spiritual elements potentially present in all, but awakened into full consciousness in comparatively few

CHAPTER XIV.

OF JUDGMENT[1].

Our Know-ledge being short, we want something else.

1. THE understanding faculties being given to man, not barely for speculation, but also for the conduct of his life, man would be at a great loss if he had nothing to direct him but what has the certainty of true *knowledge*. For that being very short and scanty, as we have seen, he would be often utterly in the dark, and in most of the actions of his life, perfectly at a stand, had he nothing to guide him in the absence of clear and certain knowledge. He that will not eat till he has demonstration that it will nourish him ; he that will not stir till he infallibly knows the business he goes about will succeed, will have little else to do but to sit still and perish.

What Use to be made of this twilight State.

2. Therefore, as God has set some things in broad daylight; as he has given us some certain knowledge, though limited to a few things in comparison, probably as a taste of what intellectual creatures are capable of to excite in us a desire and endeavour after a better state : so, in the greatest part of our concernments, he has afforded us only the twilight, as I may so say, of probability ; suitable, I presume, to that state of mediocrity and probationership he has been pleased to place us in here ; wherein, to check our over-confidence and presumption, we might, by every day's experience, be made

---

[1] Locke's restricted application of the term 'judgment,' which he opposes to 'knowledge,' has been already noted. In the more usual meaning of judg-ment, every affirmation and negation, certain or probable, is so named. Locke limits 'judgment' to (more or less) probable assertions in contrast to the self-evident and demonstrated ones which constitute knowledge proper, or absolute certainty.

sensible of our short-sightedness and liableness to error; the
sense whereof might be a constant admonition to us, to spend
the days of this our pilgrimage with industry and care, in the
search and following of that way which might lead us to
a state of greater perfection [1]. It being highly rational to
think, even were revelation silent in the case, that, as men
employ those talents God has given them here, they shall
accordingly receive their rewards at the close of the day,
when their sun shall set, and night shall put an end to their
labours.

3. The faculty which God has given man to supply the Judgment,
want of clear and certain knowledge, in cases where that or assent
to Proba-
cannot be had, is *judgment*: whereby the mind takes its bility,
supplies
ideas to agree or disagree; or, which is the same, any propo- our want
sition to be true or false, without perceiving a demonstrative of Know-
ledge.
evidence in the proofs. The mind sometimes exercises this
judgment out of necessity, where demonstrative proofs and
certain knowledge are not to be had; and sometimes out of
laziness, unskilfulness, or haste, even where demonstrative and
certain proofs are to be had [2]. Men often stay not warily to
examine the agreement or disagreement of two ideas, which
they are desirous or concerned to know; but, either incapable
of such attention as is requisite in a long train of gradations,
or impatient of delay, lightly cast their eyes on, or wholly
pass by the proofs; and so, without making out the
demonstration, determine of the agreement or disagreement
of two ideas, as it were by a view of them as they are at a
distance, and take it to be the one or the other, as seems most
likely to them upon such a loose survey. This faculty of the
mind, when it is exercised immediately about things, is called
judgment; when about truths delivered in words, is most
commonly called *assent* or *dissent*: which being the most

---

[1] Probable evidence is relative to
a finite intelligence of the universe.
Men must more or less rest in faith on
probability, in lack of omniscience.
The application of this faith, in a due
response to moral evidence, is a better
test of moral and spiritual character
than either intuitive or demonstrative
knowledge of matters which admit of
absolute certainty.

[2] As when a conclusion in mathematics is accepted by a man on the
authority of a mathematical expert,
without his personal perception of its
demonstrable truth.

Judgment is the presuming Things to be so, without perceiving it.

usual way, wherein the mind has occasion to employ this faculty, I shall, under these terms, treat of it, as least liable in our language to equivocation.

4. Thus the mind has two faculties conversant about truth and falsehood :—

First, *KNOWLEDGE*[1], whereby it certainly *perceives*, and is undoubtedly satisfied of the agreement or disagreement[2] of any ideas.

Secondly, *JUDGMENT*, which is the putting ideas together, or separating them from one another in the mind, when their certain agreement or disagreement[2] is not perceived, but *presumed* to be so ; which is, as the word imports, taken to be so before it certainly appears[3]. And if it so unites or separates them as in reality things are, it is right judgment[3].

---

[1] 'Knowledge' is properly a product, and not a 'faculty' which produces. Locke's knowledge-faculty is what he elsewhere calls intellectual perception—manifested in self-evidence, in demonstration, and in sense-perception.

[2] 'agreement or disagreement,' i. e. truth or falsehood.

[3] So that in all judgments of probability, risk of error must be faced. Human life turns upon judgments which must be so far intellectual 'leaps in the dark,'—the sunshine of perceived certainty being therein withdrawn from the finite intelligence.

CHAPTER XV.

OF PROBABILITY.

BOOK IV.

CHAP. XV.

Probability
is the
appear-
ance of
Agree-
ment upon
fallible
Proofs.

1. As *demonstration* is the showing the agreement or disagreement of two ideas, by the intervention of one or more
proofs, which have a constant, immutable, and visible
connexion one with another ; so *probability* is nothing but the
appearance of such an agreement or disagreement, by the
intervention of proofs, whose connexion is not constant and
immutable, or at least is not perceived to be so, but is, or
appears for the most part to be so, and is enough to induce
the mind to judge the proposition to be true or false, rather
than the contrary[1]. For example : in the demonstration of
it a man perceives the certain, immutable connexion there
is of equality between the three angles of a triangle, and
those intermediate ones which are made use of to show their
equality to two right ones ; and so, by an intuitive knowledge
of the agreement or disagreement of the intermediate ideas in
each step of the progress, the whole series is continued with
an evidence, which clearly shows the agreement or disagreement of those three angles in equality to two right ones : and
thus he has certain knowledge that it is so. But another
man, who never took the pains to observe the demonstration,

---

[1] A perceived intellectual necessity is the synthesis of our ideas in *know-ledge*. On the other hand, *judgments of probability* are states of mind which, by the laws of nature or of spirit, spontaneously follow the pre-sentation of the probable evidence,— the sequence depending in each case on the education, previous experience, and circumstances of the judge. Judg-ments of probability are induced through contingent data of experience ; certainties are perceived through data and presuppositions of pure reason. In a 'human understanding' of the universe these two elements are mixed in various proportions.

BOOK IV.
CHAP. XV.

hearing a mathematician, a man of credit, affirm the three angles of a triangle to be equal to two right ones, assents to it, i. e. receives it for true : in which case the foundation of his assent is the probability of the thing ; the proof being such as for the most part carries truth with it : the man on whose testimony he receives it, not being wont to affirm anything contrary to or besides his knowledge, especially in matters of this kind : so that that which causes his assent[1] to this proposition, that the three angles of a triangle are equal to two right ones, that which makes him take these ideas to agree, without knowing them to do so, is the wonted veracity of the speaker in other cases, or his supposed veracity in this.

It is to supply our Want of Knowledge.

2. Our knowledge, as has been shown, being very narrow, and we not happy enough to find certain truth in everything which we have occasion to consider ; most of the propositions we think, reason, discourse—nay, act upon, are such as we cannot have undoubted knowledge of their truth : yet some of them border so near upon certainty, that we make no doubt at all about them ; but assent to them as firmly, and act, according to that assent, as resolutely as if they were infallibly demonstrated, and that our knowledge of them was perfect and certain[2]. But there being degrees herein, from the very neighbourhood of certainty and demonstration, quite

---

[1] 'Assent' to what is presumed to be probable is regarded as 'caused,' rather than concluded—as the natural effect of a natural cause ; and probabilities lie within the sphere of change, or physical causation, within which unconditional certainty is unattainable by man, or by any other than omniscient intelligence : man is therein *made* to take ideas to agree without *knowing* them to do so. 'Whence it proceeds,' says Bishop Butler, 'that *likeness* should *beget* that presumption, opinion, and full conviction, which the human mind is formed to receive from it, and which it does necessarily produce in every one . . . belongs to the subject of logic, and is a part of that subject which has not yet been

thoroughly considered. . . . But this does not hinder but that we may be, as we unquestionably are, assured that analogy is of weight towards determining our judgment and our practice. . . . This general way of arguing is evidently natural. For there is no man can make a question, that the sun will rise to-morrow ; and be seen, where it is seen at all, in the figure of a circle, and not in that of a square.' (*Analogy*, Introd.)

[2] This we do, not under the intellectual necessity of which we are conscious in dealing with abstract conceptions, but, by a spiritual law, which induces faith, in our state of partial intellectual blindness.

down to improbability and unlikeness, even to the confines of BOOK IV.
impossibility; and also degrees of assent from full assurance
and confidence, quite down to conjecture, doubt, and distrust : CHAP. XV.
I shall come now, (having, as I think, found out *the bounds of
human knowledge and certainty*[1],) in the next place, to consider
*the several degrees and grounds of probability, and assent or
faith*[2].

3. Probability is likeliness to be true, the very notation of Being that
the word signifying such a proposition, for which there be which
arguments or proofs to make it pass, or be received for true. presume
The entertainment the mind gives this sort of propositions be true,
is called *belief, assent,* or *opinion,* which is the admitting or before
receiving any proposition for true, upon arguments or proofs them to
that are found to persuade us to receive it as true, without be so.
certain knowledge that it is so. And herein lies the difference
between *probability* and *certainty, faith,* and *knowledge,* that
in all the parts of knowledge there is intuition; each
immediate idea, each step has its visible and certain
connexion: in belief, not so. That which makes me believe,
is something extraneous to the thing I believe; something
not evidently joined on both sides to, and so not manifestly
showing the agreement or disagreement of those ideas that
are under consideration.

4. Probability then, being to supply the defect of our The
knowledge, and to guide us where that fails, is always Grounds
conversant about propositions whereof we have no certainty, bility are
but only some inducements to receive them for true. The formity
grounds of it are, in short, these two following :— with our
    First, The conformity[3] of anything with our own knowledge, perience,
observation, and experience. or the
    Secondly, The testimony of others, vouching their observa- of others.

---

[1] See ch. i–xi.
[2] Cf. Introd. § 3.
[3] 'conformity.'— Analogy or likeness to what each man has already
had experience of—the *custom* of
his previous experience—is taken as
the basis of what appears probable to
him. And as in these respects men

differ indefinitely, what appears probable to one may seem the reverse to
another, whose analogies of personal
experience, and the reports he has
received from others, have formed a
different criterion of likelihood in his
mind.

tion and experience[1]. In the testimony of others, is to be considered : 1. The number. 2. The integrity. 3. The skill of the witnesses. 4. The design of the author, where it is a testimony out of a book cited. 5. The consistency of the parts, and circumstances of the relation. 6. Contrary testimonies[2].

In this,
all the
Argu-
ments pro
and con
ought to be
examined,
before we
come to a
Judgment.
5. Probability wanting that intuitive evidence which infallibly determines the understanding and produces certain knowledge, the mind, if it *will proceed rationally*, ought to examine all the grounds of probability, and see how they make more or less for or against any proposition, before it assents to or dissents from it ; and, upon a due balancing the whole, reject or receive it, with a more or less firm assent, proportionably to the preponderancy of the greater grounds of probability on one side or the other[3]. For example :—

If I myself see a man walk on the ice, it is past probability ; it is knowledge[4]. But if another tells me he saw a man in England, in the midst of a sharp winter, walk upon water hardened with cold, this has so great conformity with what is usually observed to happen, that I am disposed by the nature of the thing itself to assent to it ; unless some manifest

---

[1] This is called by some 'foreign,' in contrast to personal experience—founded by the witnesses in like manner on the custom of *their* experience, and 'conformity' with its analogies.

[2] This section suggests the consideration of testimony in its wide meaning, including historical criticism and credibility ; also the weight due to the evidence of authority in disputed questions of science, and of philosophical and religious thought.

[3] In questions which have to be determined by presumptions of probability, there are reasons on both sides, and objections to every conceivable conclusion. Yet unless we resolve to remain in suspense, which is itself a negative judgment, we are bound in reason to seek for the conclusion that is least open to objection, and most in analogy with our previous experience : this, when recognised, we are naturally

induced to assent to. As human life turns upon judgments of probability, this 'balancing' of reasons and objections, in the light of the analogies of personal and foreign experience, is the chief intellectual employment of mankind. The different judgments they are led to form depend upon differences in the history and spiritual experience of the individual judges.

[4] ' Seeing ' is ' knowing,' according to ch. xi, only when the body that is seen is present. In the supposed instance, the ' man,' so far forth as his *visible* qualities go, is present ; but, as visible qualities *alone* do not constitute the nominal essence of man, I cannot, on Locke's teaching, *know* that a *man* is walking on ice, only by what I see. The sight involves a 'judgment' of probability about absent coexisting qualities in the thing seen.

suspicion attend the relation of that matter of fact. But if
the same thing be told to one born between the tropics, who never saw nor heard of any such thing before[1], there the whole probability relies on testimony[2]: and as the relators are more in number, and of more credit, and have no interest to speak contrary to the truth, so that matter of fact is like to find more or less belief. Though to a man whose experience has always been quite contrary, and who has never heard of anything like it, the most untainted credit of a witness will scarce be able to find belief[3]. As it happened to a Dutch ambassador, who entertaining the king of Siam with the particularities of Holland, which he was inquisitive after, amongst other things told him, that the water in his country would sometimes, in cold weather, be so hard, that men walked upon it, and that it would bear an elephant, if he were there. To which the king replied, *Hitherto I have believed the strange things you have told me, because I look upon you as a sober fair man, but now I am sure you lie*[4].

The king of Siam.

6. Upon these grounds depends the probability of any proposition: and as the conformity of our knowledge, as the certainty of observations, as the frequency and constancy of experience, and the number and credibility of testimonies do more or less agree or disagree with it, so is any proposition in itself more or less probable[5]. There is another, I confess,

Probable arguments capable of great Variety.

---

[1] So that it has no 'conformity' with the analogies of *his* experience.

[2] That is, on the analogy between the intellectual and moral qualities of the individual witness and one's own standard of trustworthy testimony.

[3] Because it more accords with the analogies of his personal experience to find testimony (intentionally or unintentionally) in error, than to suppose the truth of what is wholly out of analogy with all that *he* has ever experienced. He is thus induced to reject the testimony—his own experience being for him the ultimate standard of probability. This is Hume's reason for rejecting *à priori* all testimony to miracles. It was probably

suggested by this sentence. The case of the king of Siam in what follows is mentioned by Hume. The force of the argument in each case depends on the custom and analogies of personal experience. This explains the incredulity of the *king of Siam*, in forming a judgment that with our experience *we* can reject as erroneous. Cf. ch. xvi. § 13.

[4] Locke may have heard this story during his stay in Holland, when the *Essay* was in preparation.

[5] Judgments of probability are therefore so far *subjective*, because dependent on the amount and kind of experience of which each judge has been the subject; his sagacity in interpreting

which, though by itself it be no true ground of probability, yet is often made use of for one, by which men most commonly regulate their assent, and upon which they pin their faith more than anything else, and that is, *the opinion of others*; though there cannot be a more dangerous thing to rely on, nor more likely to mislead one ; since there is much more falsehood and error among men, than truth and knowledge. And if the opinions and persuasions of others, whom we know and think well of, be a ground of assent, men have reason to be Heathens in Japan, Mahometans in Turkey, Papists in Spain, Protestants in England, and Lutherans in Sweden. But of this wrong ground of assent I shall have occasion to speak more at large in another place [1].

that experience; and the degree to which the spiritual reason immanent in man has, in him, been evolved out of latent into conscious intelligence.

[1] See chh. xvii. § 19; xx. §§ 17, 18. The individualism of Locke, characteristic of his age, reacts against submission to *human authority* in matters of science and opinion. Yet we cannot dispense with the authority of *experts* and, in many cases, dependence on men of higher intelligence and larger experience than our own is the most reasonable means we can use for the attainment of truth.

CHAPTER XVI.

OF THE DEGREES OF ASSENT.

BOOK IV.

Снар.
XVI.

Our
Assent
ought to
be regu-
lated by
the
Grounds
of Prob-
ability.

1. THE grounds of probability we have laid down in the foregoing chapter: as they are the foundations on which our *assent* is built, so are they also the measure whereby its several degrees are, or ought to be regulated: only we are to take notice, that, whatever grounds of probability there may be, they yet operate no further on the mind which searches after truth, and endeavours to judge right, than they appear; at least, in the first judgment or search that the mind makes. I confess, in the opinions men have, and firmly stick to in the world, their assent is not always from an actual view of the reasons that at first prevailed with them: it being in many cases almost impossible, and in most, very hard, even for those who have very admirable memories, to retain all the proofs which, upon a due examination, made them embrace that side of the question. It suffices that they have once with care and fairness sifted the matter as far as they could ; and that they have searched into all the particulars, that they could imagine to give any light to the question ; and, with the best of their skill, cast up the account upon the whole evidence : and thus, having once found on which side the probability appeared to *them*[1], after as full and exact an inquiry as they can make,

[1] Assent on ground of probability is a better test of the man by whom it is given than intellectual perception of what is intuitively or demonstratively certain ; for what is considered probable by each man depends upon the extent and variety of his physical and spiritual experience ; also upon the degree of development of his higher faculties, under the laws by which they are conditioned. Unless everything can be known about everything that exists, probability must determine the judgment in all that admits of being questioned ; and in such matters right judgment implies more true humanity and goodness than do logical conclusions about abstract certainties.

they lay up the conclusion in their memories, as a truth they have discovered ; and for the future they remain satisfied with the testimony of their memories, that this is the opinion that, by the proofs they have once seen of it, deserves such a degree of their assent as they afford it.

These cannot always be actually in View; and then we must content ourselves with the remembrance that we once saw ground for such a Degree of Assent.

2. This is all that the greatest part of men are capable of doing, in regulating their opinions and judgments ; unless a man will exact of them, either to retain distinctly in their memories all the proofs concerning any probable truth, and that too, in the same order, and regular deduction of consequences in which they have formerly placed or seen them ; which sometimes is enough to fill a large volume on one single question : or else they must require a man, for every opinion that he embraces, every day to examine the proofs : both which are impossible. It is unavoidable, therefore, that the *memory* be relied on in the case, and that men be persuaded of several opinions, whereof the proofs are not actually in their thoughts ; nay, which perhaps they are not able actually to recall. Without this, the greatest part of men must be either very sceptics ; or change every moment, and yield themselves up to whoever, having lately studied the question, offers them arguments, which, for want of memory, they are not able presently to answer [1].

The ill consequence of this, if our former Judgments were not rightly made.

3. I cannot but own, that men's sticking to their past judgment, and adhering firmly to conclusions formerly made, is often the cause of great obstinacy in error and mistake. But the fault is not that they rely on their memories for what they have before well judged, but because they judged before they had well examined [2]. May we not find a great number (not to say the greatest part) of men that think they have formed right judgments of several matters ; and that for no other reason, but because they never thought otherwise ? that

---

[1] This is virtually faith in myself, as to judgments formerly reached by me, in which I regard *myself* as having been sufficiently an expert to make them now worthy of acceptance by me as true.

[2] In other words, one often exaggerates his own claim to be treated as an expert, in regard to any of his past judgments, even to the extent of taking the mere fact that he has *long* so judged as a sufficient reason for continuing so to judge.

imagine themselves to have judged right, only because they
never questioned, never examined, their own opinions? Which is indeed to think they judged right, because they never judged at all. And yet these, of all men, hold their opinions with the greatest stiffness; those being generally the most fierce and firm in their tenets, who have least examined them. What we once *know*, we are certain is so: and we may be secure, that there are no latent proofs undiscovered, which may overturn our knowledge, or bring it in doubt. But, in matters of *probability*, it is not in every case we can be sure that we have all the particulars before us, that any way concern the question; and that there is no evidence behind, and yet unseen, which may cast the probability on the other side, and outweigh all that at present seems to preponderate with us. Who almost is there that hath the leisure, patience, and means to collect together all the proofs concerning most of the opinions he has, so as safely to conclude that he hath a clear and full view; and that there is no more to be alleged for his better information? And yet we are forced to determine ourselves on the one side or other. The conduct of our lives, and the management of our great concerns, will not bear delay: for those depend, for the most part, on the determination of our judgment in points wherein we are not capable of certain and demonstrative knowledge, and wherein it is necessary for us to embrace the one side or the other [1].

4. Since, therefore, it is unavoidable to the greatest part of men, if not all, to have several *opinions*, without certain and indubitable proofs of their truth [2]; and it carries too great an imputation of ignorance, lightness, or folly for men to quit *The right Use of it, mutual Charity and Forbearance,*

---

[1] Even the most overwhelming probability, with its practical certainty, is different in kind from what Locke means by *knowledge*. Its reasonableness depends, not on our insight of intellectual necessity, but on the analogies of each man's personal experience, including his indirect experience, through testimony, of foreign experiences. But in the 'minor affairs of life,' which will not bear delay, men must act on judgments that are determined by uncertain balances; and those who have to act are often of narrow experience, and ill able to discern those deeper analogies of things, which determine a spiritual interpretation of reality, as distinguished from the interpretations of agnostic materialism.

[2] 'Truth and error,' says Cudworth, 'are usually to be found on both sides of a great question.'

BOOK IV.
Chap.
XVI.

in a
necessary
diversity of
opinions.

and renounce their former tenets presently upon the offer of
an argument which they cannot immediately answer, and show
the insufficiency of: it would, methinks, become all men to
maintain peace, and the common offices of humanity, and
friendship, in the diversity of opinions; since we cannot
reasonably expect that any one should readily and obsequiously
quit his own opinion, and embrace ours, with a blind resigna-
tion to an authority which the understanding of man acknowledges not[1]. For however it may often mistake, it can own
no other guide but reason, nor blindly submit to the will and
dictates of another. If he you would bring over to your
sentiments be one that examines before he assents, you must
give him leave at his leisure to go over the account again.
and, recalling what is out of his mind, examine all the
particulars, to see on which side the advantage lies: and if he
will not think our arguments of weight enough to engage him
anew in so much pains, it is but what we often do ourselves
in the like case; and we should take it amiss if others should
prescribe to us what points we should study. And if he be
one who takes his opinions upon trust, how can we imagine
that he should renounce those tenets which time and custom
have so settled in his mind, that he thinks them self-evident,
and of an unquestionable certainty; or which he takes to be
impressions he has received from God himself, or from men
sent by him[2]? How can we expect, I say, that opinions thus
settled should be given up to the arguments or authority of
a stranger or adversary, especially if there be any suspicion
of interest or design, as there never fails to be, where men
find themselves ill treated? We should do well to commiserate

[1] As long as men, in forming their
judgments of probability, have to
appeal to different personal experiences, with correspondingly different
analogies, and with powers of interpreting the same which differ, alike by
education and by the original constitution of the interpreter, it is inevitable
that their judgments should differ. But
a store of overwhelming probabilities
is the ground on which the received

physical science is gradually increasing
—although Locke refuses to call it
'science,' because it is not susceptible
of demonstration, like relations of
abstract ideas.

[2] It is to counteract this condition
of mind that Locke argues against
what he calls 'innate' ideas and
principles, and warns against 'commonly received maxims or axioms.'
Cf. Bk. I. ch. iii. §§ 22-24; Bk. IV. ch. vii.

our mutual ignorance, and endeavour to remove it in all the gentle and fair ways of information ; and not instantly treat others ill, as obstinate and perverse, because they will not renounce their own, and receive our opinions, or at least those we would force upon them, when it is more than probable that we are no less obstinate in not embracing some of theirs. For where is the man that has incontestable evidence of the truth of all that he holds, or of the falsehood of all he condemns; or can say that he has examined to the bottom all his own, or other men's opinions[1]? The necessity of believing without knowledge, nay often upon very slight grounds, in this fleeting state of action and blindness we are in[2], should make us more busy and careful to inform ourselves than constrain others.

---

[1] This is what Locke elsewhere calls *bottoming*. 'It is necessary in any question proposed to examine and find out upon what it bottoms. Most of the difficulties that come in our way, when well considered and traced, lead to some proposition which, known to be true, clears the doubt, and gives an easy solution of the question; whilst topical and superficial arguments, of which there is store to be found on both sides, filling the head with variety of thoughts, and the mouth with copious discourse, serve only to amuse the understanding, and entertain company without coming to the bottom of the question,—the only place of rest and stability for an inquisitive mind, whose tendency is only to truth and knowledge.' (*Conduct of the Understanding*, § 44.) Locke's 'bottoming' is simply philosophising, or going in quest of those necessary maxims or axioms which stop wrangling—innate principles which may remain latent or unconscious till thus quickened into conscious exercise.

[2] With Locke, all our expectations of events, and our inductive interpretations of the changing universe, can be only presumed probabilities, matters of assent or belief, not of knowledge. In his view, the infinite region of the real—beyond each person's consciousness of his own personal existence, the existence of Supreme Spirit or God, and present or the remembered objects of sense-perception—form the sphere of probable presumptions, in their degrees from absolute practical certainty down to doubtful opinion and ignorance. It is thus unphilosophical for a man to assert absolute certainty in any *general* propositions other than abstract mathematical, moral, and verbal ones ; and in *particular* propositions, of more than one's own existence, as far back as his memory is capable of going ; the existence of Eternal Mind ; and the existence of finite beings, other than himself, that are or were perceived by his senses. For all the rest he must be satisfied to exercise judgments of faith and probability, which depend upon his mental development and experience, tests of his individual character, and enough for all the purposes of a human life before and after physical death. All further intellectual intercourse with the changing world of things and persons, to which we are introduced by sense-perception and self-consciousness, must therefore be more or less tentative and hypothetical.

BOOK IV.
CHAP.
XVI.

At least, those who have not thoroughly examined to the bottom all their own tenets, must confess they are unfit to prescribe to others; and are unreasonable in imposing that as truth on other men's belief, which they themselves have not searched into, nor weighed the arguments of probability, on which they should receive or reject it. Those who have fairly and truly examined, and are thereby got past doubt in all the doctrines they profess and govern themselves by, would have a juster pretence to require others to follow them: but these are so few in number, and find so little reason to be magisterial in their opinions, that nothing insolent and imperious is to be expected from them: and there is reason to think, that, if men were better instructed themselves, they would be less imposing on others[1].

Proba-
bility is
either of
sensible
Matter of
Fact,
capable of
human
testimony,
or of what

5. But to return to the grounds of assent, and the several degrees of it, we are to take notice, that the propositions we receive upon inducements of *probability* are of *two sorts*: either concerning some particular existence, or, as it is usually termed, matter of fact, which, falling under observation, is capable of human testimony; or else concerning things, which,

---

[1] This section presents part of Locke's argument in his famous *Letters on Toleration.* In the seventeenth century freedom of individual judgment from legal and social restraint was argued for upon various grounds. Chillingworth, Jeremy Taylor, Glanvill, and other divines of the Church of England, pleaded for toleration of the inevitable differences in opinion, as Locke here does, on the ground of the necessary limits and weakness of the profoundest understanding of the universe that man is capable of, especially in the region of religious thought. The 'toleration' for which Locke argued, and which was one of his leading ideas, implied a revolution in the medieval conception of human life. It expressed the revolt from dogmatic authority, in favour of a critical treatment of beliefs, that was becoming a characteristic of the modern spirit. This was represented by Protestantism in religion, and by Montaigne and Descartes, Campanella and Bacon in philosophy, as well as by the rise of experimental inquiry in physics. In religion it implied a protest against those who in theology assume absolute certainty in questions which must be determined by balanced probabilities, and by the moral evidence that appeals to faith. The enforcement of a general toleration, amidst increasing religious differences, with its liberation of the understanding from everything except the reasonable restraints of personal and foreign experience, is the most important practical application of Locke's answer in the *Essay* to his own memorable question, about the nature and extent of a human understanding of the universe and of God.

being beyond the discovery of our senses, are not capable of any such testimony.

6. Concerning the *first* of these, viz. *particular matter of fact.*

I. Where any particular thing, consonant[1] to the constant observation of ourselves and others in the like case, comes attested by the concurrent reports of all that mention it, we receive it as easily, and build as firmly upon it, as if it were certain knowledge ; and we reason and act thereupon with as little doubt as if it were perfect demonstration. Thus, if all Englishmen, who have occasion to mention it, should affirm that it froze in England the last winter, or that there were swallows seen there in the summer, I think a man could almost as little doubt of it as that seven and four are eleven. The first, therefore, and *highest degree of probability*, is, when the general consent of all men, in all ages, as far as it can be known, concurs with a man's constant and never-failing experience in like cases, to confirm the truth of any particular matter of fact attested by fair witnesses : such are all the stated constitutions and properties of bodies, and the regular proceedings of causes and effects in the ordinary course of nature. This we call an argument from the nature of things themselves[2]. For what our own and other men's *constant observation* has found always to be after the same manner, that we with reason conclude to be the effect of steady and regular causes ; though they come not within the reach of our knowledge[3]. Thus, That fire warmed a man, made lead fluid, and changed the colour or consistency in wood or charcoal ; that iron sunk in water, and swam in quicksilver : these and the like propositions about particular facts, being agreeable to our constant experi-

---

[1] 'consonant,' that is to say, to a human experience of the actual analogies presented by the phenomena and events in which the universe reveals itself to man.

[2] Rather from the reason or order that is immanent in their nature, without which they would be absolutely incomprehensible.

[3] Even in this class of cases we do not have the absolute certainty of *knowledge*, only sufficient presumption of *probability*. The methods and philosophy of a sufficient induction, here touched by Locke, are nowhere expressly treated in the *Essay*—only here and there by implication.

ence, as often as we have to do with these matters ; and being generally spoke of (when mentioned by others) as things found constantly to be so, and therefore not so much as controverted by anybody—we are put past doubt that a relation affirming any such thing to have been, or any predication that it will happen again in the same manner, is very true. These *probabilities* rise so near to *certainty*, that they govern our thoughts as absolutely, and influence all our actions as fully, as the most evident demonstration ; and in what concerns us we make little or no difference between them and certain knowledge. Our belief, thus grounded, rises to *assurance.*

II. Unquestionable Testimony, and our own Experience that a thing is for the most part so, produce Confidence.

7. II. The *next degree of probability* is, when I find by my own experience, and the agreement of all others that mention it, a thing to be for the most part so, and that the particular instance of it is attested by many and undoubted witnesses : v.g. history giving us such an account of men in all ages, and my own experience, as far as I had an opportunity to observe, confirming it, that most men prefer their private advantage to the public : if all historians that write of Tiberius, say that Tiberius did so, it is extremely probable. And in this case, our assent has a sufficient foundation to raise itself to a degree which we may call *confidence.*

III. Fair Testimony, and the Nature of the Thing indifferent, produce unavoidable Assent.

8. III. In things that happen indifferently, as that a bird should fly this or that way ; that it should thunder on a man's right or left hand, &c., when any particular matter of fact is vouched by the concurrent testimony of unsuspected witnesses, there our assent is also *unavoidable.* Thus : that there is such a city in Italy as Rome : that about one thousand seven hundred years ago, there lived in it a man, called Julius Cæsar ; that he was a general, and that he won a battle against another, called Pompey. This, though in the nature of the thing there be nothing for nor against it, yet being related by historians of credit, and contradicted by no one writer, a man cannot avoid believing it, and can as little doubt of it as he does of the being and actions of his own acquaintance, whereof he himself is a witness.

Experience and Testimonies

9. Thus far the matter goes easy enough. Probability upon such grounds carries so much evidence with it, that it naturally determines the judgment, and leaves us as little

liberty to believe or disbelieve, as a demonstration does, whether we will know, or be ignorant. The difficulty is, when testimonies contradict common experience, and the reports of history and witnesses clash with the ordinary course of nature, or with one another; there it is, where diligence, attention, and exactness are required, to form a right judgment, and to proportion the assent to the different evidence and probability of the thing: which rises and falls, according as those two foundations of credibility, viz. *common observation in like cases,* and *particular testimonies in that particular instance,* favour or contradict it. These are liable to so great variety of contrary observations, circumstances, reports, different qualifications, tempers, designs, oversights, &c., of the reporters, that it is impossible to reduce to precise rules the various degrees wherein men give their assent. This only may be said in general, That as the arguments and proofs *pro* and *con,* upon due examination, nicely weighing every particular circumstance, shall to any one appear, upon the whole matter, in a greater or less degree to preponderate on either side; so they are fitted to produce in the mind such different entertainments, as we call *belief, conjecture, guess, doubt, wavering, distrust, disbelief,* &c.

10. This is what concerns assent in matters wherein testimony is made use of: concerning which, I think, it may not be amiss to take notice of a rule observed in the law of England; which is, That though the attested copy of a record be good proof, yet the copy of a copy, ever so well attested, and by ever so credible witnesses, will not be admitted as a proof in judicature. This is so generally approved as reasonable, and suited to the wisdom and caution to be used in our inquiry after material truths, that I never yet heard of any one that blamed it. This practice, if it be allowable in the decisions of right and wrong, carries this observation along with it, viz. *That any testimony, the further off it is from the original truth, the less force and proof it has.* The being and existence of the thing itself, is what I call the original truth. A credible man vouching his knowledge of it is a good proof; but if another equally credible do witness it from his report, the testimony is weaker: and a third that

BOOK IV.

CHAP.
XVI.

attests the hearsay of an hearsay is yet less considerable. So that in traditional truths, each remove weakens the force of the proof: and the more hands the tradition has successively passed through, the less strength and evidence does it receive from them[1]. This I thought necessary to be taken notice of: because I find amongst some men the quite contrary commonly practised, who look on opinions to gain force by growing older; and what a thousand years since would not, to a rational man contemporary with the first voucher, have appeared at all probable, is now urged as certain beyond all question, only because several have since, from him, said it one after another. Upon this ground propositions, evidently false or doubtful enough in their first beginning, come, by an inverted rule of probability, to pass for authentic truths; and those which found or deserved little credit from the mouths of their first authors, are thought to grow venerable by age, are urged as undeniable.

Yet History is of great Use.

11. I would not be thought here to lessen the credit and use of *history*: it is all the light we have in many cases, and we receive from it a great part of the useful truths we have, with a convincing evidence. I think nothing more valuable than the records of antiquity: I wish we had more of them, and more uncorrupted. But this truth itself forces me to say, That no probability can rise higher than its first original. What has no other evidence than the single testimony of one only witness must stand or fall by his only testimony, whether good, bad, or indifferent; and though cited afterwards by hundreds of others, one after another, is so far from receiving any strength thereby, that it is only the weaker[2]. Passion, interest, inadvertency, mistake of his meaning, and a thousand odd reasons, or capricios[3], men's minds are acted

---

[1] 'To speak truly, says Bacon, *'Antiquitas saeculi juventus mundi.* These times are the ancient times, when the world is ancient, and not those which we account ancient, *ordine retrogrado,* by a computation backward from ourselves.' (*Advancement of Learning,* Bk. I, S. and E., vol. iii. p. 291. See the context.)

[2] Must the testimony of history then at last die out? Cf. Hume's *Treatise,* Pt. iii. sect. xiii, with its reference to Craig's *Theologiae Christianae Principia Mathematica* (1699), which seeks to demonstrate that thus historical Christianity must cease to be credible in 1454 years from the date of his book.

[3] 'capricios'—caprices, from *caper,* a goat—the waywardness of a goat.

by, (impossible to be discovered,) may make one man quote another man's words or meaning wrong. He that has but ever so little examined the citations of writers, cannot doubt how little credit the quotations deserve, where the originals are wanting; and consequently how much less quotations of quotations can be relied on. This is certain, that what in one age was affirmed upon slight grounds, can never after come to be more valid in future ages by being often repeated. But the further still it is from the original, the less valid it is, and has always less force in the mouth or writing of him that last made use of it than in his from whom he received it.

12. [*Secondly*], The probabilities we have hitherto mentioned are only such as concern matter of fact, and such things as are capable of observation and testimony. There remains that other sort, concerning which men entertain opinions with variety of assent, though *the things be such, that falling not under the reach of our senses, they are not capable of testimony.* Such are, 1. The existence, nature and operations of finite immaterial beings without us; as spirits, angels, devils, &c. Or the existence of material beings which, either for their smallness in themselves or remoteness from us, our senses cannot take notice of—as, whether there be any plants, animals, and intelligent inhabitants in the planets, and other mansions of the vast universe. 2. Concerning the manner of operation in most parts of the works of nature: wherein, though we see the sensible effects, yet their causes are unknown, and we perceive not the ways and manner how they are produced. We see animals are generated, nourished, and move; the loadstone draws iron; and the parts of a candle, successively melting, turn into flame, and give us both light and heat. These and the like effects we see and know: but the causes that operate, and the manner they are produced in, we can only guess and probably conjecture. For these and the like, coming not within the scrutiny of human senses, cannot be examined by them, or be attested by anybody; and therefore can appear more or less probable, only as they more or less agree to truths that are established in our minds, and as they hold proportion

to other parts of our knowledge and observation. *Analogy* in these matters is the only help we have, and it is from that alone we draw all our grounds of probability[1]. Thus, observing that the bare rubbing of two bodies violently one upon another, produces heat, and very often fire itself, we have reason to think, that what we call *heat* and *fire* consists in a violent agitation of the imperceptible minute parts of the burning matter. Observing likewise that the different refractions of pellucid bodies produce in our eyes the different appearances of several colours ; and also, that the different ranging and laying the superficial parts of several bodies, as of velvet, watered silk, &c., does the like, we think it probable that the *colour* and shining of bodies is in them nothing but the different arrangement and refraction of their minute and insensible parts. Thus, finding in all parts of the creation, that fall under human observation, that there is *a gradual connexion of one with another, without any great or discernible gaps between, in all that great variety of things we see in the world*, which are so closely linked together, that, in the several ranks of beings, it is not easy to discover the bounds betwixt them ; we have reason to be persuaded that, *by such gentle steps*, things ascend upwards in degrees of perfection[2].

[1] The other sort of propositions, received upon ' inducements of probability,' also find the ground of their acceptance in their supposed analogy with the order that is presupposed in nature. ' There is a certain *analogy*, constancy, and uniformity, in the phenomena or appearance of nature, which are a foundation for general rules : and these are a grammar for the understanding of nature, or that series of effects in the visible world, whereby we are enabled to *foresee* what will come to pass in the natural course of things. . . . So far forth as analogy obtains in the universe, there may be vaticination.' (*Siris*, § 252.)

[2] Locke here touches a more comprehensive speculation than is usual with him. This idea of graduated ascent in the order of ' creation ' is older than Aristotle, who, in the *De Anima*, distinguishes in the ψυχή, or principle of life, the vegetative, the animal, and the rational stage ; each gradation in the evolution being represented as a unity which secures its own end and also contains potentially the elements of the next succeeding stage in an ascending process. At the merely vegetative stage, the potential vitality is so oppressed by inorganic matter that we have only the blind, insentient growth of the plant. Disengaged in some measure from this pressure, on the next stage sensation and motive force are developed, as in the lower animals, with their automatic or mechanically necessitated and instinctive life. At a still higher stage, the ψυχή, further disengaged, reveals itself as the self-conscious, calculating, free

BOOK IV.
CHAP.
XVI.

It is a hard matter to say where sensible and rational begin, and where insensible and irrational end : and who is there quick-sighted enough to determine precisely which is the lowest species of living things, and which the first of those which have no life ?   Things, as far as we can observe, lessen and augment, as the quantity does in a regular cone ; where, though there be a manifest odds betwixt the bigness of the diameter at a remote distance, yet the difference between the upper and under, where they touch one another, is hardly discernible.   The difference is exceeding great between some men and some animals : but if we will compare the understanding and abilities of some men and some brutes, we shall find so little difference, that it will be hard to say, that that of the man is either clearer or larger.   Observing, I say, such gradual and gentle descents downwards in those parts of the creation that are beneath man, the rule of analogy may make it probable, that it is so also in things above us and our observation ; and that there are several ranks of intelligent beings, excelling us in several degrees of perfection, ascend‑ing upwards towards the infinite perfection of the Creator, by gentle steps and differences, that are every one at no great

---

agency of man, and the vital agent unfolds the latent elements of reason and responsibility.   Supreme active Reason pervades and consummates the whole.   Or, as Bacon puts it from another point of view :—'It is an assured truth, and a conclusion of experience, that a little, or superficial knowledge of philosophy may incline the mind of man to atheism, but a further proceeding therein doth bring the mind back again to religion ; for in the entrance to philosophy, when the second causes, which are next unto the senses, do offer themselves to the mind of man, if it dwell and stay there, it may induce some oblivion of the highest cause ; but when a man passeth on further, and seeth the dependence of causes, and the works of Provi‑dence ; then, according to the allegory of the poets, he will easily believe that the highest link of nature's chain must needs be tied to the foot of Jupiter's chair.' (*Advancement of Learning*, First Book.)   'Iamblicus teacheth, what is also a received notion of the Pytha‑goreans and Platonists, that there is no chasm in nature, but a *chain* or *scale* of beings, rising by gentle uninter‑rupted graduations from the lowest to the highest, each nature being informed and perfected by the participation of a higher.' (Berkeley, *Siris*, § 274.)   The conception of a chain (σειρά) connecting the phenomena presented in nature, in a continuous evolution, with one another, and with the all-pervading immanent yet transcendent Reason, forming a Cosmos in which things are thus linked with things, is the govern‑ing thought in *Siris*.   And of Leibniz's system the principle of continuity is of course the essence.

BOOK IV. distance from the next to it.   This sort of probability, which
CHAP. is the best conduct of rational experiments, and the rise of
XVI. hypothesis, has also its use and influence; and a wary
reasoning from analogy leads us often into the discovery of
truths and useful productions, which would otherwise lie
concealed.

One Case   13. Though the common experience and the ordinary
where
contrary course of things have justly a mighty influence on the minds
Experi- of men, to make them give or refuse credit to anything
ence
lessens proposed to their belief; yet there is one case, wherein the
not the strangeness of the fact lessens not the assent to a fair
Testi-
mony. testimony given of it.   For where such supernatural [1] events
are suitable to ends aimed at by Him who has the power to
change the course of nature, there, *under such circumstances,*
that may be the fitter to procure belief, by how much the
more they are beyond or contrary to ordinary observation.
This is the proper case of *miracles,* which, well attested, do
not only find credit themselves, but give it also to other
truths, which need such confirmation [2].

---

[1] 'We may pass after death,' says Bishop Butler, 'into a new state just as *naturally* as we came into the present. . . . And though one were to allow any confused, undetermined sense which people please to put on the word *natural,* it would be a shortness of thought scarce credible to imagine, that no system or course of things can be so, but only what we see at present.' (*Analogy,* p. 37.) A higher life for man in the future must be incredible to one whose analogies are all found within the ordinary mechanism of the nature that is presented to the senses, so that his faith is confined to this narrow sphere, in distrust of the larger reason, and the higher analogies of the spiritual life. An agnostic materialism or naturalism is all that this limited faith can admit, inadequate as it is to a true human interpretation of the universal system to which we belong.

[2] 'A miracle' (says Locke, in his *Discourse on Miracles,* written in 1702), 'I take to be a sensible operation, which being above the comprehension of the spectator, and in *his* opinion contrary to the established course of nature, is taken by him to be divine.' An event is thus regarded as miraculous or not, according as it is or is not referable to a law which the individual can formulate; and as it cannot be mechanically tested, our belief, in each case of alleged miracle, must be determined by the *analogies of moral purpose in the universe.* A miracle is not an event which violates or supersedes all law. This would imply temporary insanity in the universe, instead of that rationality or order without which man himself could not exercise rational life.   It is an event determined by *higher laws than the spectator can discover*; or it may be than are discoverable by the faculties and experience of *any human being:* although its place in the supreme natural order may be within the intel-

14. Besides those we have hitherto mentioned, there is one sort of propositions that challenge the highest degree of our assent, upon bare testimony, whether the thing proposed agree or disagree with common experience, and the ordinary course of things, or no. The reason whereof is, because the testimony is of such an one as cannot deceive nor be deceived : and that is of God himself. This carries with it an assurance beyond doubt, evidence beyond exception. This is called by a peculiar name, *revelation* [1], and our assent to it, *faith* [2], which [3 as absolutely determines our minds, and as perfectly excludes all wavering,] as our knowledge itself ; and we may as well doubt of our own being, as we can whether any revelation from God be true. So that faith is a settled and sure principle of assent and assurance, and leaves no manner of room for doubt or hesitation. *Only we must be sure that it be a divine revelation, and that we understand it right* : else we shall expose ourselves to all the extravagancy of enthusiasm, and all the error of wrong principles, if we have faith and assurance in what is not *divine* revelation. And therefore, in those cases, our assent can be rationally no higher than the evidence of its being a revelation, and that this is the meaning of the expressions it is delivered in. If the evidence of its being a revelation, or that this is its true sense, be only on probable proofs, our assent can reach no higher than an assurance or diffidence, arising from the more or less apparent probability of the proofs. But of *faith*, and the precedency it ought to have before other arguments of

lectual reach of a more comprehensive intelligence and experience than man's. What is a miracle to a man, thus would not be a miracle to a higher intelligence. And to Omniscience no event could be miraculous.

[1] 'revelation.' The whole evolution of the universe—in us as well as around us, including its spiritual facts, and also those physical events which men regard as miraculous, while they must really be in harmony with supreme reason—constitutes our *revelation* of God, in the full meaning of the term revelation. For they are uninterpretable, save on the presupposition that we are living and having our being in God.

[2] Locke usually means by *faith*, 'assent to a proposition as coming from God, in some extraordinary way of communication' (cf. ch. xviii. § 2). Occasionally he uses it as a synonym for belief or assent, in contrast to knowledge—hardly ever for the trust which is at the root of our intelligence and our lives.

[3] In first four editions—'has as much certainty as.'

BOOK IV.

CHAP. XVI.

persuasion, I shall speak more hereafter [1] ; where I treat of it as it is ordinarily placed, in contradistinction to reason ; though in truth it be nothing else but *an assent founded on the highest reason* [2].

[1] Ch. xviii.

[2] 'Christian faith,' says Coleridge, 'is the perfection of human intelligence.' That reason, in its highest form, becomes faith, in the sense of assent founded on the spiritual constitution of man, is true in a deeper meaning of faith than that contemplated by Locke.

CHAPTER XVII.

OF REASON.

1. THE word *reason* in the English language has different
significations[1] : sometimes it is taken for true and clear

[1] *Reason*, among the most ambiguous of philosophical terms, here and elsewhere with Locke, as with many of his English contemporaries, signifies the inferential faculty, or power of drawing conclusions, either demonstratively, by deduction from self-evident principles, or inductively, on grounds of probability. It is thus synonymous with *reasoning*, to the exclusion, or at least in disregard, of the common rational sense on which all reasoning depends. It means discursive as distinguished from intuitive intelligence. So too Reid, in his *Inquiry* : 'Philosophers pitying the credulity of the vulgar resolve to have no faith but what is founded upon reason [reasoning]. They apply to philosophy to furnish them with reasons for the belief of those things which all mankind have believed without being able to give any reason for it.' (Introd. 3.) 'First principles fall not within the province of reason, but of common sense.' (ch. ii. 6.) But in his *Essays* (vi. 2) he ascribes to reason ' two offices, or two degrees. The first is, to judge of things self-evident; the second, to draw conclusions that are not self-evident from those that are. The first of these is the province and sole province of common sense; and therefore it coincides with reason in its whole extent, and is only another name for one branch or one degree of reason.' In later and contemporary philosophical nomenclature, reason is confined to this second meaning, and is thus contrasted with the understanding, with its empirical generalisations, and tentative conclusions, or reason in Locke's meaning. But deeper analysis shows that discursive understanding, thus exercised, depends for the rationality of its results on what is higher than itself, or intuitively evident. Reason in its highest meaning is, as Coleridge has it, ' the power of universal and necessary convictions ; the source and substance of truths above sense, having their evidence in themselves.' Its presence is always marked by the intellectual necessity of the position affirmed : this necessity being conditional, when a truth of reason is applied to facts of experience, or to the rules and maxims of the understanding ; but absolute, when the subject matter is the growth or offspring of reason. The use of ' reason,' to signify discursive intelligence only, in Locke and by eighteenth-century philosophers, and to signify intuitive or noetic intelligence only, in the nineteenth, as previously in the seventeenth century, is a signal example of a far-reaching revolution in modern English philosophic thought in the interval.

BOOK IV.

CHAP. XVII.

Various Significations of the word Reason.

principles: sometimes for clear and fair deductions from those principles: and sometimes for the cause, and particularly the final cause [1]. But the consideration I shall have of it here is in a signification different from all these; and that is, as it stands for a faculty in man, that faculty whereby man is supposed to be distinguished from beasts, and wherein it is evident he much surpasses them [2].

Wherein Reasoning consists.

2. If general knowledge [3], as has been shown [4], consists in a perception of the agreement or disagreement of our own ideas, and the knowledge of the existence of all things without us [5] (except only of a God [6], whose existence every man may certainly know and demonstrate to himself [7] from his own existence), be had only by our senses, what room is there for the exercise of any other faculty, but *outward sense* and *inward perception*? What need is there of *reason* [8]? Very

[1] Thus a spark is in part the reason in things, or the explanation, of an explosion of gunpowder; seeing is the reason, or final cause, of our visual organism. So too we speak of reason, not merely as a human faculty, but as immanent in, and constitutive of, the nature of things. The ultimate premises in a train of reasonings are also called the reason of the final conclusion.

[2] 'Reason' is applicable to the abstracting, as distinguished from the merely sensuous or animal, activity of man. Cf. Bk. II. ch. xi. § 10.

[3] 'general knowledge,' i. e. intuitive certainty of the truth of any general abstract proposition.

[4] Ch. i. § 2; ch. vi.

[5] What of the intuitive knowledge we were said to have of 'our own existence' (ch. ix. § 3), and through reflection of the operations of our own minds (Bk. II, ch. i. § 4)? This seems here to be covered by 'perception'— afterwards called 'inward.'

[6] Here again we have the deistical conception which puts God at a distance 'without us.'

[7] This power to 'demonstrate' God's existence implies reason, in the sense

of reasoning, in addition to 'outward sense and inward perception.'

[8] 'Outward sense' gives us, according to ch. xi, that imperfect knowledge of things, outside our organisms, which is called sense-perception; and 'inward perception,' including 'reflection,' gives us knowledge of our own existence, and of the relations of our abstract ideas, along with a demonstrative proof of the existence of God. But 'demonstration' presupposes discursive faculty, and in itself shows the need of 'reason' [i. e. reasoning], as does all our 'general knowledge' of the relations of our abstract ideas in mathematics and morality. This chapter concentrates attention upon discursive activity, which carries us from the intuited data of outward sense and inward perception to the completer conceptions of the phenomena and laws of the universe, which are the issue of attempts to grasp intellectually what is dimly apprehended in sense. This chapter contains Locke's account of discursive, as supplementary to intuitive and sensuous, activity of mind, in the way both of increasing the number of

much : both for the enlargement of our knowledge, and
regulating our assent. For it hath to do both in knowledge
and opinion, and is necessary and assisting to all our other
intellectual faculties, and indeed contains two of them, viz.
sagacity and *illation.* By the one, it finds out ; and by the
other, it so orders the intermediate ideas [1] as to discover what
connexion there is in each link of the chain, whereby the
extremes are held together ; and thereby, as it were, to draw
into view the truth sought for, which is that which we call
illation or *inference*, and consists in nothing but the perception
of the connexion there is between the ideas, in each step of
the deduction ; whereby the mind comes to see, either the
certain agreement or disagreement of any two ideas, as in
demonstration, in which it arrives at *knowledge* ; or their
probable connexion, on which it gives or withholds its assent,
as in *opinion* [2]. Sense and intuition reach but a very little
way [3]. The greatest part of our knowledge depends upon
deductions and intermediate ideas : and in those cases where
we are fain to substitute assent instead of knowledge, and
take propositions for true, without being certain they are so,
we have need to find out, examine, and compare the grounds
of their probability. In both these cases, the faculty which
finds out the means, and rightly applies them, to discover
certainty in the one, and probability in the other, is that
which we call *reason.* For, as reason perceives the necessary
and indubitable connexion of all the ideas or proofs one to
another, in each step of any demonstration that produces
knowledge ; so it likewise perceives the probable connexion
of all the ideas or proofs one to another, in every step of
a discourse, to which it will think assent due [4]. This is the

our certainties, and of determining
when and why assent is due to
reason, in questions which admit only
of probable solutions.

[1] 'intermediate ideas,' i. e. middle
terms, and implied principles of probation in a reasoning or syllogism.

[2] The former in demonstrated and
abstract knowledge ; the latter in
matter-of-fact inferences.

[3] Our sphere of self-evidence and

immediate sense-presentation is narrow.

[4] ' Reason ' is thus with Locke the
faculty in the exercise of which we
extend our intellectual view, beyond
the immediate data of external and
internal ' perception '; whether to add
to our knowledge by demonstration,
or to our belief by reasonable presumptions of probability.

BOOK IV.

———

CHAP.
XVII.

lowest degree of that which can be truly called reason. For where the mind does not perceive[1] this probable connexion, where it does not discern whether there be any such connexion or no ; there men's opinions are not the product of judgment, or the consequence of reason, but the effects of chance and hazard, of a mind floating at all adventures, without choice and without direction[2].

Reason in its four degrees.

3. So that we may in *reason* consider these *four degrees* : the first and highest is the discovering and finding out of truths ; the second, the regular and methodical disposition of them, and laying them in a clear and fit order, to make their connexion and force be plainly and easily perceived ; the third is the perceiving their connexion ; and the fourth, a making a right conclusion. These several degrees may be observed in any mathematical demonstration ; it being one thing to perceive the connexion of each part, as the demonstration is made by another ; another to perceive the dependence of the conclusion on all the parts ; a third, to make out a demonstration clearly and neatly one's self ; and something different from all these, to have first found out these intermediate ideas or proofs by which it is made[3].

Whether Syllogism is the great Instrument of Reason : First Cause to doubt this.

4. There is one thing more which I shall desire to be considered concerning reason ; and that is, whether *syllogism*, as is generally thought, be the proper instrument of it, and the usefullest way of exercising this faculty[4]. The causes I have to doubt are these :—

First, Because syllogism serves our reason but in one only of the forementioned parts of it ; and that is, to show the

---

[1] 'perceive' probable connection, instead of, as elsewhere, 'presume' probable connection, might imply that to determine what is, and what is not probable is itself knowledge, and not mere presumption—that probability presupposes a basis of certainty, in order that any judgment of what is probable may be formed *reasonably*. Could we reach even probability, if nothing that is absolutely certain could be

'perceived' by us ?

[2] Fancy has then taken the place of reasonableness.

[3] The illustration given follows the inverse order of gradation to that in which the principles which it illustrates were presented, beginning with the *minimum* and ending with the *maximum* of ratiocinative power implied.

[4] In all or any of its four degrees.

connexion of the proofs in any one instance, and no more[1];
but in this it is of no great use, since the mind can perceive
such connexion, where it really is, as easily, nay, perhaps
better, without it.

If we will observe the actings of our own minds, we shall
find that we reason best and clearest, when we only observe
the connexion of the proof, without reducing our thoughts to
any rule of syllogism[2]. And therefore we may take notice, that
there are many men that reason exceeding clear and rightly,
who know not how to make a syllogism. He that will look
into many parts of Asia and America, will find men reason
there perhaps as acutely as himself, who yet never heard of
a syllogism, nor can reduce any one argument to those forms[3]:
[4 and I believe scarce any one makes syllogisms in reasoning
within himself.] Indeed syllogism is made use of, on occasion,
to discover a fallacy[5] hid in a rhetorical flourish, or cunningly
wrapt up in a smooth period ; and, stripping an absurdity of
the cover of wit and good language, show it in its naked
deformity. [6 But the weakness or fallacy of such a loose

---

[1] The third of the above-mentioned 'degrees in reason.'

[2] This supposes that it has been 'generally thought' that men *consciously* syllogise in every instance of their employment of the illative conjunctions ; whereas what is alleged is that they syllogise by implication, and for the most part unconsciously. The discovery that the issues of the spontaneous 'actings of our own minds' in reasoning admit of being presented in syllogistic forms, and of having their verbal consistency by this means tested, is due to reflective analysis of what is latent in the inferential product.

[3] On the contrary, it is only *after* men have *spontaneously* produced inferences, valid and invalid, that they are able *reflectively* to recognise, that what is produced may be formulated in syllogism, and that syllogism is the formal unit of a chain of reasonings.

[4] Added in the fourth edition. We are of course usually unconscious of the syllogisms into which our solitary reasonings may nevertheless be analysed by the logician. We can draw conclusions in ignorance of logic, just as we can use ultimate principles when we are strangers to metaphysics and to epistemological philosophy.

[5] Locke here recognises the reflective use of syllogism, for the detection of fallacies, which otherwise might remain hidden in our concrete reasonings.

[6] What follows, within brackets, in this and the next paragraph, was introduced in the fourth edition, instead of the following sentence :—'But the mind is not taught to reason by these rules; it has a native faculty to perceive the coherence or incoherence of its ideas, and can range them right without any such perplexing repetitions.' This misrepresentation of the proper office of syllogism is expounded and insisted upon in the present text.

BOOK IV.
CHAP.
XVII.

discourse it shows, by the artificial form it is put into, only to those who have thoroughly studied *mode* and *figure*, and have so examined the many ways that three propositions may be put together, as to know which of them does certainly conclude right, and which not, and upon what grounds it is that they do so. All who have so far considered *syllogism*, as to see the reason why in three propositions laid together in one form, the conclusion will be certainly right, but in another not certainly so, I grant are certain of the conclusion they draw from the premises in the allowed *modes* and *figures*. But they who have not so far looked into those forms, are not sure by virtue of syllogism, that the conclusion certainly follows from the premises; they only take it to be so by an implicit faith in their teachers and a confidence in those forms of argumentation; but this is still but believing, not being certain [1]. Now, if, of all mankind those who can make syllogisms are extremely few in comparison of those who cannot; and if, of those few who have been taught logic, there is but a very small number who do any more than believe that syllogisms, in the allowed *modes* and *figures* do conclude right, without knowing certainly that they do so: if syllogisms must be taken for the only proper instrument of reason and means of knowledge, it will follow, that, before Aristotle, there was not one man that did or could know anything by reason; and that, since the invention of syllogisms [2], there is not one of ten thousand that doth.

[1] Most persons accept conclusions of mathematical demonstrations, in like manner, on the authority of mathematical experts. This does not discredit mathematics as an abstract and applied science. Nor need an analogous fact with regard to the reflective demonstrations of scientific logic, which enable the logician to evolve the abstract syllogistic forms, discredit those forms, or their occasional application in helping him to discover fallacies.

[2] 'invention of syllogisms.' In its earlier meaning, to 'invent' is not to contrive artificially, feign, or fashion, but to *discover*—to remove that which hides anything. Aristotle is the 'inventor' of syllogisms, inasmuch as he discovered that each link in a chain of inferences is necessarily capable of expression in syllogistic form. But the invention or discovery presupposes performance of the ratiocinative process, in unconsciousness of its syllogistic implications. 'Il faut avouer,' says Leibniz, 'que la forme scolastique des syllogismes est peu employée dans le monde . . . cependant l'invention de la forme des syllogismes est une des plus belles de l'esprit humain, et même des plus considérables. C'est

But God has not been so sparing to men to make them BOOK IV.
barely two-legged creatures, and left it to Aristotle to make CHAP.
them rational, i.e. those few of them that he could get so XVII.
to examine the grounds of syllogisms, as to see that, in above Aristotle.
three score ways that three propositions may be laid together,
there are but about fourteen wherein one may be sure that the
conclusion is right; and upon what grounds it is, that, in these
few, the conclusion is certain, and in the other not. God has
been more bountiful to mankind than so. He has given them
a mind that can reason, without being instructed in methods
of syllogizing: the understanding is not taught to reason by
these rules; it has a native faculty to perceive the coherence
or incoherence of its ideas, and can range them right, without
any such perplexing repetitions [1]. I say not this any way to
lessen Aristotle, whom I look on as one of the greatest men
amongst the ancients; whose large views, acuteness, and
penetration of thought and strength of judgment, few have
equalled [2]; and who, in this very invention of forms of
argumentation, wherein the conclusion may be shown to be
rightly inferred, did great service against those who were not
ashamed to deny anything. And I readily own, that all right
reasoning may be reduced to his forms of syllogism [3]. But
yet I think, without any diminution to him, I may truly say,

une espèce de *mathematique universelle* dont l'importance n'est pas assez connue : et l'on peut dire qu'un *art d'infallibilité* y est contenu.' (*Nouveaux Essais.*)

[1] 'All this is not less absurd than if any one, on being told of the discoveries of modern chemists respecting caloric, and on hearing described the process by which it is conducted through a boiler into the water, which it converts into a gas of sufficient elasticity to overcome the pressure of the atmosphere, should reply—"If all this were so, it would follow that before the time of these chemists no one ever did or could make any liquor boil." ' (Whately, *Logic*, p. 6.)

[2] Coming from Locke, a leader in the reaction of modern free thought

against scholasticism and antiquity, this is strong language; also when compared even with Reid, according to whom Aristotle ' seems to have had a greater passion for fame than for truth, and to have wanted rather to be admired as the prince of philosophers than to be useful ; so that it is dubious whether there be in his character most of the philosopher or of the sophist.' (*Brief Account of Aristotle's Logic*, ch. i. § 1.)

[3] Cf. Bk. III. ch. x. §§ 11–13, with the annotations. In granting that all right reasoning may be exhibited in syllogistic form, and that latent fallacies may be thereby effectively exposed, Locke acknowledges the chief intellectual service rendered by syllogism.

that they are not the only nor the best way of reasoning, for the leading of those into truth who are willing to find it, and desire to make the best use they may of their reason, for the attainment of knowledge[1]. And he himself, it is plain, found out some forms to be conclusive, and others not, not by the forms themselves, but by the original way of knowledge, i.e. by the visible agreement of ideas.] Tell a country gentlewoman that the wind is south-west, and the weather lowering, and like to rain, and she will easily understand it is not safe for her to go abroad thin clad in such a day, after a fever: she clearly sees the probable connexion of all these, viz. south-west wind, and clouds, rain, wetting, taking cold, relapse, and danger of death, without tying them together in those artificial and cumbersome fetters of several syllogisms, that clog and hinder the mind, which proceeds from one part to another quicker and clearer without them: and the probability which she easily perceives in things thus in their native state would be quite lost, if this argument were managed learnedly, and proposed in *mode* and *figure*[2]. For it very often confounds the connexion; and, I think, every one will perceive in mathematical demonstrations, that the knowledge gained thereby comes shortest and clearest without syllogism.

[[3]Inference is looked on as the great act of the rational

---

[1] To test the verbal consistency of our reasonings, as the syllogistic forms do, is not to test the actual truth of their conclusions. Syllogism is only the logic of the formal understanding. The critical logic of premises, and of the ultimate ideas and principles of noetic reason, properly called metaphysic. is the philosophical method that has in view ' the leading of those into *truth* who are willing to find it, and desire to make the best use they may of their reason for the attainment of knowledge.' It is only indirectly that the exhibition of our concrete reasonings as syllogisms can contribute to this. When by this means we become fully conscious of what they imply, we may be more apt to observe not only their verbal inconsistencies, but also their unwarranted premises.

[2] This illustration of a probable or empirical, not demonstrative, inference, suggests an inquiry into the function of syllogism in experimental investigation of truth, including its relation to so-called inductive and analogical inferences, as followed out, for instance, in J. S. Mill's *Logic*, Bk. II. ch. iii.

[3] What follows, in the nine following paragraphs within brackets (pp. 392-400), was introduced in the fourth edition, in room of the following :—

' Secondly, Because though syllogism serves to show the force or fallacy of an argument, made use of in the usual way of discoursing, *by supplying the absent proposition*, and so faculty, and so it is when it is rightly made : but the mind, either very desirous to enlarge its knowledge, or very apt to favour the sentiments it has once imbibed, is very forward to make inferences ; and therefore often makes too much haste, before it perceives the connexion of the ideas that must hold the extremes together.

To infer, is nothing but by virtue of one proposition laid down as true, to *draw in* another as true, i. e. to see or suppose such a connexion of the two ideas of the inferred proposition. V. g. Let this be the proposition laid down, 'Men shall be punished in another world,' and from thence be inferred this other, 'Then men can determine themselves.' The question now is, to know whether the mind has made this inference right or no : if it has made it by finding out the intermediate ideas, and taking a view of the connexion of them, placed in a due order, it has proceeded rationally, and made a right inference : if it has done it without such a view, it has not so much made an inference that will hold, or an inference of right reason, as shown a willingness to have it be, or be taken for such. But in neither case is it syllogism that discovered those ideas, or showed the connexion of them ; for they must be both found out, and the connexion everywhere perceived, before they can rationally be made use of in syllogism : unless it can be said, that any idea, without considering what connexion it hath with the two other, whose agreement should be shown by it, will do well enough in a syllogism, and may be taken at a venture for the *medius terminus*, to prove any conclusion. But this nobody will say ; because it is by virtue of the perceived agreement of the intermediate idea with the extremes, that the extremes are concluded to agree ; and therefore each intermediate idea must be such as in the whole chain hath a visible connexion with those two it has been placed between, or else thereby the conclusion cannot be inferred or drawn in : for wherever

setting it before the view in a clear light ; yet it no less engages the mind in the perplexity of obscure, equivocal, and fallacious terms, wherewith this artificial way of reasoning always abounds : it being adapted more to the attaining of victory in dispute than the discovery and confirmation of truth in fair enquiries.'

BOOK IV.
—•+•—
CHAP.
XVII.

any link of the chain is loose and without connexion, there the whole strength of it is lost, and it hath no force to infer or draw in anything. In the instance above mentioned, what is it shows the force of the inference, and consequently the reasonableness of it, but a view of the connexion of all the intermediate ideas that draw in the conclusion, or proposition inferred? V.g. 'Men shall be punished;' 'God the punisher;' 'Just punishment;' 'The punished guilty;' 'Could have done otherwise;' 'Freedom;' 'Self-determination;' by which chain of ideas thus visibly linked together in train, i.e. each intermediate idea agreeing on each side with those two it is immediately placed between, the ideas of *men* and *self-determination* appear to be connected, i.e. this proposition 'men can determine themselves' is drawn in or inferred from this, 'that they shall be punished in the other world.' For here the mind, seeing the connexion there is between the *idea of men's punishment in the other world* and the *idea of God punishing*; between *God punishing* and *the justice of the punishment*; between *justice of punishment* and *guilt*; between *guilt* and a *power to do otherwise*; between a *power to do otherwise* and *freedom*; and between *freedom* and *self-determination*, sees the connexion between *men* and *self-determination*.

The connexion must be discovered before it can be put into Syllogism.

Now I ask, whether the connexion of the extremes be not more clearly seen in this simple and natural disposition, than in the perplexed repetitions, and jumble of five or six syllogisms. I must beg pardon for calling it jumble, till somebody shall put these ideas into so many syllogisms, and then say that they are less jumbled, and their connexion more visible, when they are transposed and repeated, and spun out to a greater length in artificial forms, than in that short and natural plain order they are laid down in here, wherein everyone may see it, and wherein they must be seen before they can be put into a train of syllogisms. For the *natural* order of the connecting ideas must direct the order of the syllogisms, and a man must see the connexion of each intermediate idea with those that it connects, before he can with reason[1] make use of it in a syllogism. And when all those

---

[1] 'with reason,' i.e. with due regard to the reason that is latent in the nature of things, as to which the exhibition of our inferences in syllo-

syllogisms are made, neither those that are nor those that are BOOK IV.
not logicians will see the force of the argumentation, i.e., the
connexion of the extremes, one jot the better. [¹ For those
that are not men of art, not knowing the true forms of
syllogism, nor the reasons of them, cannot know whether
they are made in right and conclusive modes and figures
or no, and so are not at all helped by the forms they are
put into ; though by them the natural order, wherein the mind
could judge of their respective connexion, being disturbed,
renders the illation much more uncertain than without them.]
And as for the logicians themselves, they see the connexion
of each intermediate idea with those it stands between, (on
which the force of the inference depends,) as well before as
after the syllogism is made, or else they do not see it at all.
For a syllogism neither shows nor strengthens the connexion²
of any two ideas immediately put together, but only by the
connexion seen in them shows what connexion the extremes
have one with another. But what connexion the intermediate has with either of the extremes in the syllogism, that
no syllogism does or can show. That the mind only doth or
can perceive as they stand there in that juxta-position only
by its own view, to which the syllogistical form it happens
to be in gives no help or light at all : it only shows that *if*
the intermediate idea agrees with those it is on both sides
immediately applied to ; then those two remote ones, or, as
they are called, *extremes*, do certainly agree ³ ; and therefore

gistic form gives us no direct information. But this it may do indirectly,
by bringing the latent propositions in
the ratiocination which it formulates
into the full view of the mind, in the
exercise of the faculties by which
certain knowledge and probability are
determined. As Chillingworth puts it
to an argumentative antagonist :—' I
beseech you, when you write again,
do us the favour to write nothing but
in syllogisms. For I find it still an extreme trouble to find out the concealed
propositions which are to connect the
parts of your enthymemes.'
¹ This sentence is bracketed by
Locke in the original.

² ' connexion,' i. e. the natural connexion.
³ Syllogism leaves all its conclusions
only hypothetically true, because dependent upon the hypothesis that the
premises are true. Syllogistic logic
supplies in its forms criteria of verbal
consistency only, but no guarantee
either of certain knowledge or of probability, in the conclusions which it
formulates. It is the logic of the self-
consistency that truth presupposes ;
but there may be verbal self-consistency
in error. Locke is naturally impatient
with an organon of inference which
does not go further than this.

the immediate connexion of each idea to that which it is applied to on each side, on which the force of the reasoning depends, is as well seen before as after the syllogism is made, or else he that makes the syllogism could never see it at all. This, as has been already observed, is seen only by the eye, or the perceptive faculty, of the mind, taking a view of them laid together, in a juxta-position; which view of any two it has equally, whenever they are laid together in any proposition, whether that proposition be placed as a *major* or a *minor*, in a *syllogism* or no.

Of what use, then, are syllogisms?   I answer, their chief and main use is in the Schools, where men are allowed without shame to deny the agreement of ideas that do manifestly agree; or out of the Schools, to those who from thence have learned without shame to deny the connexion of ideas, which even to themselves is visible.   But to an ingenuous searcher after truth, who has no other aim but to find *it*, there is no need of any such form to force the allowing of the inference: the truth and reasonableness of it is better seen in ranging of the ideas in a simple and plain order: and hence it is that men, in their own inquiries after truth, never use syllogisms to convince themselves [¹or in teaching others to instruct willing learners].   Because, before they can put them into a syllogism, they must see the connexion that is between the intermediate idea and the two other ideas it is set between and applied to, to show their agreement; and when they see that, they see whether the inference be good or no; and so *syllogism* comes too late to settle it. For to make use again of the former instance, I ask whether the mind, considering the idea of justice, placed as an intermediate idea between the punishment of men and the guilt of the punished, (and till it does so consider it, the mind cannot make use of it as a *medius terminus*,) does not as plainly see the force and strength of the inference as when it is formed into a syllogism.   To show it in a very plain and easy example; let *animal* be the intermediate idea or *medius terminus* that the mind makes use of to show the

---

¹ Added in the posthumous editions.

connexion of *homo* and *vivens* ; I ask whether the mind
does not more readily and plainly see that connexion in the
simple and proper position of the connecting idea in the
middle thus :

Homo—Animal—Vivens,

than in this perplexed one,

Animal— Vivens—Homo—Animal :

which is the position these ideas have in a syllogism, to show
the connexion between *homo* and *vivens* by the intervention
of *animal.*

Indeed syllogism is thought to be of *necessary* use, even to Not the
the lovers of truth, to show them the fallacies that are often only way
to detect
concealed in florid, witty, or involved discourses. But that Fallacies.
this is a mistake will appear, if we consider, that the reason
why sometimes men who sincerely aim at truth are imposed
upon by such loose, and, as they are called, rhetorical
discourses, is, that their fancies being struck with some lively
metaphorical representations, they neglect to observe, or
do not easily perceive, what are the *true* ideas upon which
the inference depends. Now, to show such men the weakness
of such an argumentation, there needs no more but to strip
it of the superfluous ideas, which, blended and confounded
with those on which the inference depends, seem to show
a connexion where there is none; or at least to hinder the
discovery of the want of it ; and then to lay the naked ideas
on which the force of the argumentation depends in their due
order ; in which position the mind, taking a view of them,
sees what connexion they have, and so is able to judge of
the inference without any need of a syllogism at all.

I grant that mode and figure is commonly made use of in
such cases, as if the detection of the incoherence of such
loose discourses were wholly owing to the syllogistical form ;
and so I myself formerly thought, till, upon a stricter
examination, I now find[1], that laying the intermediate ideas

---

[1] Locke vacillates in his judgment
of the function and intellectual utility
of syllogism. In his *Second Vindication
of the Reasonableness of Christianity,*
published in 1697 (more than two
years before this passage was introduced into the *Essay*), he calls syllogism 'the true touchstone of right

naked in their due order, shows the incoherence of the argumentation better than syllogism ; not only as subjecting each link of the chain to the immediate view of the mind in its proper place, whereby its connexion is best observed ; but also because syllogism shows the incoherence only to those (who are not one of ten thousand) who perfectly understand mode and figure, and the reason upon which those forms are established ; whereas a due and orderly placing of the ideas upon which the inference is made, makes every one, whether logician or not logician, who understands the terms, and hath the faculty to perceive the agreement or disagreement of such ideas, (without which, in or out of syllogism, he cannot perceive the strength or weakness, coherence or incoherence of the discourse) see the want of connexion in the argumentation, and the absurdity of the inference.

And thus I have known a man unskilful in syllogism, who at first hearing could perceive the weakness and inconclusiveness of a long artificial and plausible discourse, wherewith others better skilled in syllogism have been misled : and I believe there are few of my readers who do not know such. And indeed, if it were not so, the debates of most princes' councils, and the business of assemblies, would be in danger to be mismanaged, since those who are relied upon, and have usually a great stroke in them, are not always such who have the good luck to be perfectly knowing in the forms of syllogism, or expert in *mode* and *figure*. And if syllogism were the only, or so much as the surest way to detect the fallacies of artificial discourses ; I do not think that all mankind, even princes in matters that concern their crowns and dignities, are so much in love with falsehood and

arguing,' and proposes to test the incoherence of his adversary by this means. ' If he [Mr. Edwards] can but find arguments to prove his propositions that will bear the test of setting down in form, and will so publish them, I will allow myself to be mistaken. Nay, which is more, if he or anybody, in the 112 pages of his *Socinianism Unmasked,* can find but ten arguments that will bear the test of syllogism—the true touchstone of right arguing—I will grant that that treatise deserves all those recommendations he has bestowed upon it.' This is to use syllogistic form as a means for bringing wranglers, who argue for victory, to the true issue. But see also Locke's *Thoughts concerning Education,* §§ 188, 189.

mistake, that they would everywhere have neglected to BOOK IV.
bring syllogism into the debates of moment; or thought it
ridiculous so much as to offer them in affairs of consequence; CHAP. XVII.
a plain evidence to me, that men of parts and penetration,
who were not idly to dispute at their ease, but were to act
according to the result of their debates, and often pay for
their mistakes with their heads or fortunes, found those
scholastic forms were of little use to discover truth or fallacy,
whilst both the one and the other might be shown, and
better shown without them, to those who would not refuse
to see what was visibly shown them[1].

Secondly, Another reason that makes me doubt whether
syllogism be the only proper instrument of reason, in the
discovery of truth, is, that of whatever use *mode* and *figure*
is pretended to be in the laying open of fallacy, (which has
been above considered,) *those scholastic forms of discourse
are not less liable to fallacies than the plainer ways of argumentation*; and for this I appeal to common observation,
which has always found these artificial methods of reasoning
more adapted to catch and entangle the mind, than to
instruct and inform the understanding. And hence it is
that men, even when they are baffled and silenced in this
scholastic way, are seldom or never convinced, and so brought
over to the conquering side: they perhaps acknowledge
their adversary to be the more skilful disputant, but rest
nevertheless persuaded of the truth on their side, and go
away, worsted as they are, with the same opinion they
brought with them: which they could not do if this way of
argumentation carried light and conviction with it, and
made men see where the truth lay[2]; and therefore syllogism
has been thought more proper for the attaining victory in
dispute, than for the discovery or confirmation of truth in

Another cause to doubt whether Syllogism be the only proper instrument of Reason, in the discovery of truth.

---

[1] This is as if syllogism were offered as an artificial method of reasoning, and not as the reflex analysis of what is implied in each verbally consistent and conclusive unit of inference.

[2] Which, as already remarked, syllo-gism can secure only indirectly; for a knowledge of its forms does not supply the want of other knowledge, and can only help us to formulate to advantage what we already know, or suppose that we know.

fair inquiries. And if it be certain, that fallacies can be couched in syllogism[1], as it cannot be denied; it must be something else, and not syllogism, that must discover them[2].

I have had experience how ready some men are, when all the use which they have been wont to ascribe to anything is not allowed, to cry out, that I am for laying it wholly aside. But to prevent such unjust and groundless imputations, I tell them, that I am not for taking away any helps to the understanding in the attainment of knowledge. And if men skilled in and used to syllogisms, find them assisting to their reason in the discovery of truth, I think they ought to make use of them. All that I aim at, is, that they should not ascribe more to these forms than belongs to them, and think that men have no use, or not so full an use, of their reasoning faculties without them. Some eyes want spectacles to see things clearly and distinctly; but let not those that use them therefore say nobody can see clearly without them: those who do so will be thought, in favour of art (which, perhaps, they are beholden to,) a little too much to depress and discredit nature. Reason, by its own penetration, where it is strong and exercised, usually sees quicker and clearer without syllogism[3]. If use of those spectacles has so dimmed its sight, that it cannot without them see consequences or inconsequences in argumentation, I am not so unreasonable as to be against the using them. Every one knows what best fits his own sight; but let him not thence conclude all in the dark, who use not just the same helps that he finds a need of.]

---

[1] I. e. those fallacies which logicians call *material*, in which the premises are irrelevant or unwarranted, while their conclusions are necessitated, so far as the abstract principles of identity and contradiction (not in their Hegelian meaning and application) are concerned.

[2] Cf. Bacon on Syllogism, *Novum Organum*, I. 11–14, where he alleges that the received logic serves rather to consolidate error than to assist the search for truth, and complains that syllogism is not applied to the ultimate, and is applied in vain to the intermediate, axioms of science, being no match for the subtlety of nature, in that it commands assent to the conclusion, but does not take hold of the thing. 'Assensum itaque constringit, non res,' Bacon says.

[3] Locke's point seems to be, that insight of the truth of their premises cannot be promoted by syllogising our reasonings, but that syllogistic analysis of reasonings may help to expose a wrangling antagonist, and thus cut wrangling short.

5. But however it be in knowledge, I think I may truly say, it is *of far less, or no use at all in probabilities.* For the assent there being to be determined by the preponderancy, after due weighing of all the proofs, with all circumstances on both sides, nothing is so unfit to assist the mind in that as syllogism; which running away with one assumed probability, or one topical argument, pursues that till it has led the mind quite out of sight of the thing under consideration; and, forcing it upon some remote difficulty, holds it fast there; entangled perhaps, and, as it were, manacled, in the chain of syllogisms, without allowing it the liberty, much less affording it the helps, requisite to show on which side, all things considered, is the greater probability[1].

6. But let it help us (as perhaps may be said) in convincing men of their errors and mistakes: (and yet I would fain see the man that was forced out of his opinion by dint of syllogism,) yet still it fails our reason in that part, which, if not its highest perfection, is yet certainly its hardest task, and that which we most need its help in; and that is *the finding out of proofs, and making new discoveries*[2]. The rules of syllogism serve not to furnish the mind with those intermediate ideas that may show the connexion of remote ones[3]. This way of reasoning discovers no new proofs, but is the art of marshalling and ranging the old ones we have already. The forty-seventh proposition of the first book of Euclid is very true; but the discovery of it, I think,

BOOK IV.
CHAP.
XVII.

Syllogism helps little in Demonstration,

less in Probability.

Serves not to increase our Knowledge, but to fence with the Knowledge we suppose we have.

---

[1] This is to say, that syllogism, while it may serve a purpose in formulating reasonings that are concerned with matter that admits of demonstration, is worse than useless in its application to inductive, analogical, or experimental inferences. For these are concerned with matters of fact, contingent in relation to a human understanding, and which man has to determine by the balance of probabilities. That balance varies, in the estimates of individual judges, according as material or spiritual categories have preponderating significance.

[2] It constitutes, in short, a logic of consistency, not a logic of experimental proof, or calculated induction. It is the organ of the critical understanding, not of the genius of discovery in its victories over our original ignorance of the real universe into which we are born.

[3] They do not necessarily provide us with the appropriate middle terms in our concrete inferences. If they did, syllogistic science would virtually supersede all other intellectual inquiry than that directed to itself.

not owing to any rules of common logic. A man knows first, and then he is able to prove syllogistically. So that syllogism comes after knowledge, and then a man has little or no need of it [1]. But it is chiefly by the finding out those ideas that show the connexion of distant ones, that our stock of knowledge is increased, and that useful arts and sciences are advanced [2]. Syllogism, at best, is but the art of fencing with the little knowledge we have [3], without making any addition to it. And if a man should employ his reason all this way, he will not do much otherwise than he who, having got some iron out of the bowels of the earth, should have it beaten up all into swords, and put it into his servants' hands to fence with and bang one another. Had the King of Spain employed the hands of his people, and his Spanish iron so, he had brought to light but little of that treasure that lay so long hid in the dark entrails of America. And I am apt to think, that he who shall employ all the force of his reason only in brandishing of syllogisms, will discover very little of that mass of knowledge which lies yet concealed in the secret recesses of nature; and which, I am apt to think, native rustic reason (as it formerly has done) is likelier to open a way to, and add to the common stock of mankind [4], rather than any scholastic proceeding by the strict rules of *mode* and *figure*.

Other Helps to reason than Syllogism should be sought.

7. I doubt not, nevertheless, but there are ways to be found to assist our reason in this most useful part; and this the judicious Hooker [5] encourages me to say, who in his Eccl. Pol. 1. i. § 6, speaks thus: 'If there might be added the right helps of true art and learning, (which helps, I must plainly

---

[1] Rather, by implication, it precedes all other knowledge, in logical, although not in chronological, order; for no knowledge can be self-contradictory. On the other hand, an aggregate of reasonings may be verbally consistent, and so satisfy the syllogistic test, without being real knowledge. Conclusions warranted by syllogism alone, are only hypothetically true.

[2] Here the help of a logic of principles is needed, if attainable, for regu-

lating our interpretation of the ideas or phenomena that are presented by the real world, in the senses and reflectively.

[3] Or that we suppose we have.

[4] 'add to.' Syllogism is analytic of concrete reasonings, in quest of their form; not an organ of intellectual or experiential synthesis.

[5] Hooker is one of Locke's favourite authors, to whom even he refers occasionally as an authority.

confess, this age of the world, carrying the name of a learned BOOK IV.
age, doth neither much know nor generally regard,) there
would undoubtedly be almost as much difference in maturity CHAP.
of judgment between men therewith inured, and that which XVII.
men now are, as between men that are now, and innocents[1].'
I do not pretend to have found or discovered here any of
those 'right helps of art,' this great man of deep thought
mentions: but that is plain, that syllogism, and the logic now
in use[2], which were as well known in his days, can be none
of those he means. It is sufficient for me, if by a Discourse,
perhaps something out of the way, I am sure, as to me,
wholly new and unborrowed, I shall have given occasion
to others to cast about for new discoveries, and to seek
in their own thoughts for those right helps of art[3], which will
scarce be found, I fear, by those who servilely confine
themselves to the rules and dictates of others[4]. For beaten
tracks lead this sort of cattle[5], (as an observing Roman calls
them,) whose thoughts reach only to imitation, *Non quo
eundum est, sed quo itur.* But I can be bold to say, that this
age is adorned with some men of that strength of judgment
and largeness of comprehension, that, if they would employ
their thoughts on this subject, could open new and undiscovered ways to the advancement of knowledge.

8. Having here had occasion to speak of syllogism in

[1] So Bacon, on the levelling consequences of the adoption of his
method.

[2] Aristotle's.

[3] ' Few books have contributed more
to rectify prejudice—to undermine
established errors—to diffuse a just
mode of thinking—to excite a fearless
spirit of inquiry—and yet to contain
it within the boundaries which nature
has prescribed to the human understanding. An amendment of the
general habits of thought is, in most
parts of knowledge, an object as important as even the discovery of new
truths, though it is not so palpable,
nor in its nature so capable of being
estimated by superficial observers. In

the mental and moral world, which
scarcely admits of anything which can
be called discovery, the correction of
the intellectual habits is probably the
greatest service which can be rendered
to science. In this respect the merit
of Locke is unrivalled. If Locke made
few discoveries, Socrates made none.
Yet both did more for the improvement of the understanding than the
authors of the most brilliant discoveries. (Sir James Mackintosh on
Locke's Essay.)

[4] Hence Locke's dread of ' innate '
ideas and principles, in which he saw
the germ of unreasoning deference to
authority.

[5] 'cattle'—cattel in the early editions.

BOOK IV.

CHAP.
XVII.

We can reason about Particulars; and the immediate object of all our reasonings is nothing but particular ideas.

general, and the use of it in reasoning, and the improvement of our knowledge, it is fit, before I leave this subject, to take notice of one manifest mistake in the rules of syllogism: viz. that no syllogistical reasoning can be right and conclusive, but what has at least one *general* proposition in it. As if we could not reason, and have knowledge about particulars: whereas, in truth, the matter rightly considered, the immediate object of all our reasoning and knowledge, is nothing but particulars. Every man's reasoning and knowledge is only about the ideas existing in his own mind; which are truly, every one of them, particular existences: and our knowledge and reason about other things, is only as they correspond with those our particular ideas. So that the perception of the agreement or disagreement of our particular ideas, is the whole and utmost of all our knowledge. Universality is but accidental to it, and consists only in this, that the particular ideas about which it is are such as more than one particular thing can correspond with and be represented by [1]. But the perception of the agreement or disagreement of [2 any two ideas,] and consequently our knowledge, is equally clear and certain, whether either, or both, or neither of those ideas, be capable of representing more real beings than one, or no. [3 One thing more I crave leave to offer about syllogism, before I leave it, viz. May one not upon just ground inquire whether the form syllogism now has, is that which in reason it ought to have? For the *medius terminus* being to join the extremes, i. e. the intermediate ideas, by its intervention, to show the agreement or disagreement of the two in question, would not the position of the *medius terminus* be more natural, and show

---

[1] Thus with Locke all our ideas are *particular,* whether they happen to be complex or are recognised in their simplicity; and 'the whole and utmost of all our knowledge' is perception of the agreement or disagreement of particular ideas of things, which only by accident, or contingently, resemble the ideas in which other particular things manifest themselves. Locke fails to distinguish between ideas as sense-phenomena, and ideas as concepts or meanings. And how can any inference be made if particulars *per se* are our sole original data? To infer is to transcend such data, and this presupposes an immanent rational universality in the data, without which they could not be reasoned about.

[2] 'any two ideas'—' our particular ideas,' in first three editions.

[3] Added in fourth edition.

the agreement or disagreement of the extremes clearer and
better, if it were placed in the middle between them? Which
might be easily done by transposing the propositions, and
making the *medius terminus* the predicate of the first, and the
subject of the second [1]. As thus:

> *Omnis homo est animal.*
> *Omne animal est vivens.*
> *Ergo, omnis homo est vivens.*

> *Omne corpus est extensum et solidum.*
> *Nullum extensum et solidum est pura extensio.*
> *Ergo, corpus non est pura extensio.*

I need not trouble my reader with instances in syllogisms
whose conclusions are particular. The same reason holds for
the same form in them, as well as in the general.]

9. *Reason*, though it penetrates into the depths of the sea Our
and earth, elevates our thoughts as high as the stars, and leads Reason
often fails
us through the vast spaces and large rooms of this mighty us.
fabric, yet it comes far short of the real extent of even
corporeal being. And there are many instances wherein it
fails us: as,

I. It perfectly fails us, where our ideas fail [2]. It neither First,
does nor can extend itself further than they do. And there- In cases
when we
fore, wherever we have no ideas, our reasoning stops, and we have no
are at an end of our reckoning: and if at any time we reason Ideas.
about words which do not stand for any ideas, it is only about
those sounds, and nothing else.

10. II. Our reason is often puzzled and at a loss, because Secondly,
of the obscurity, confusion, or imperfection of the ideas it is Because
our Ideas
employed about; and there we are involved in difficulties and are often
contradictions. Thus, not having any perfect idea of the obscure
or im-
least extension of matter, nor of *infinity*, we are at a loss perfect.
about the divisibility of matter [3]; but having perfect, clear,

---

[1] The form of the syllogism, according to the intensive as contrasted with
the extensive interpretation of its
terms, i. e. the intensive syllogism.

[2] Cf. ch. iii. § 1.
[3] Cf. Bk. II. ch. xxiii. §§ 30, 31.
[4] 'No priestly dogmas, invented on purpose to tame and subdue the rebellious

BOOK IV.

CHAP. XVII.

and distinct ideas of *number*, our reason meets with none of those inextricable difficulties in numbers, nor finds itself involved in any contradictions about them. Thus, we having but imperfect ideas of the operations of our minds, and of the beginning of motion, or thought how the mind produces either of them in us, and much imperfecter yet of the operation of God, run into great difficulties about *free created agents*, which reason cannot well extricate itself out of[1].

Thirdly, Because we perceive not intermediate Ideas to show conclusions.

11. III. Our reason is often at a stand, because it perceives not those ideas, which could serve to show the certain or probable agreement or disagreement of any other two ideas : and in this some men's faculties far outgo others. Till algebra, that great instrument and instance of human sagacity, was discovered, men with amazement looked on several of the demonstrations of ancient mathematicians, and could scarce forbear to think the finding several of those proofs to be something more than human.

Fourthly, Because we often proceed upon wrong Principles.

12. IV. The mind, by proceeding upon false principles, is often engaged in absurdities and difficulties, brought into straits and contradictions, without knowing how to free itself : and in that case it is in vain to implore the help of reason, unless it be to discover the falsehood and reject the influence of those wrong principles[2]. Reason is so far from clearing the difficulties which the building upon false foundations brings a man into, that if he will pursue it, it entangles him the more, and engages him deeper in perplexities.

Fifthly, Because we often

13. V. As obscure and imperfect ideas often involve our reason, so, upon the same ground, do dubious words and

---

reason of mankind, ever shocked common sense more than the doctrine of the infinite divisibility of extension, with its consequences.' (Hume, *Inquiry H. U.* sect. xii. p. 1.)

[1] Cf. Bk. II. ch. xxi. §§ 8–55. Locke, in controversy with Stillingfleet, repeatedly repudiates the allegation that he held ' *clear* and *distinct* ' ideas to be necessary to certainty. ' My notion of certainty by ideas is, that certainty consists in the perception of the agreement or disagreement of [our par-

ticular] ideas, such as we have, whether they be in all their parts perfectly clear or no : nor have I any notions of certainty more than this one.' (*First Letter*, p. 50.) He thus repudiates rejection of what is mysterious, or imperfectly known, e. g. the fact of created free agency in coexistence with the omniscience and omnipotence of God.

[2] Cf. Bk. I. chh. i. ii. iii ; IV. ch. vii.

uncertain signs, often, in discourses and arguings, when not BOOK IV.
warily attended to, puzzle men's reason, and bring them to
a nonplus[1]. But these two latter are our fault, and not the CHAP. XVII.
fault of reason[2]. But yet the consequences of them are employ
nevertheless obvious; and the perplexities or errors they fill doubtful Terms.
men's minds with are everywhere observable.

14. Some of the ideas that are in the mind, are so there, Our
that they can be by themselves immediately compared one highest Degree of
with another: and in these the mind is able to perceive that Know-
they agree or disagree as clearly as that it has them. Thus ledge is intuitive,
the mind perceives, that an arch of a circle is less than the without Reason-
whole circle, as clearly as it does the idea of a circle: and ing.
this, therefore, as has been said, I call *intuitive knowledge*[3];
which is certain, beyond all doubt, and needs no probation,
nor can have any; this being the highest of all human
certainty. In this consists the evidence of all those *maxims*
which nobody has any doubt about, but every man (does not,
as is said, only assent to, but) *knows* to be true, as soon as
ever they are proposed to his understanding. In the discovery
of and assent to these truths, there is no use of the discursive
faculty, *no need of reasoning*, but they are known by a superior
and higher degree of evidence. And such, if I may guess at
things unknown, I am apt to think that angels have now, and
the spirits of just men made perfect shall have, in a future
state, of thousands of things which now either wholly escape
our apprehensions, or which our short-sighted reason having
got some faint glimpse of, we, in the dark, grope after.

15. But though we have, here and there, a little of this clear The next
light, some sparks of bright knowledge, yet the greatest part is got by Reason-
of our ideas are such, that we cannot discern their agreement ing.

---

[1] Cf. Bk. III.

[2] We cannot help the limitation of
our (particular) ideas to the data of
external and internal sense, nor the
frequent obscurity of those ideas that is
due to the finitude of our experience,
nor the absence in many cases of all
media of proof; so that many problems
must remain for ever insoluble by man.
But the fallacy of undue assumption of
premises, as well as fallacies due to the

ambiguous use of language, are faults
which the human reasoner might
have avoided.

[3] Cf. ch. ii. § 1; iii. § 3; also Locke's
Elements of Natural Philosophy, ch. xii.
Locke throughout makes *intuition of
what is self-evident* the foundation and
highest degree of knowledge, in the
discovery of which 'there is no need
of the discursive faculty or reasoning.'

or disagreement by an immediate comparing them. And in all these we have *need of reasoning*, and must, by discourse and inference, make our discoveries. Now of these there are two sorts, which I shall take the liberty to mention here again:—

First, through Reasonings that are Demonstrative.

First, Those whose agreement or disagreement, though it cannot be seen by an immediate putting them together, yet may be examined by the intervention of other ideas which can be compared with them. In this case, when the agreement or disagreement of the intermediate idea, on both sides, with those which we would compare, is *plainly discerned*: there it amounts to *demonstration*[1] whereby knowledge is produced, which, though it be certain, yet it is not so easy, nor altogether so clear as intuitive knowledge. Because in that there is barely one simple intuition, wherein there is no room for any the least mistake or doubt: the truth is seen all perfectly at once. In demonstration, it is true, there is intuition too, but not altogether at once; for there must be a remembrance of the intuition of the agreement of the medium, or intermediate idea, with that we compared it with before, when we compare it with the other: and where there be many mediums, there the danger of the mistake is the greater. For each agreement or disagreement of the ideas must be observed and seen in each step of the whole train, and retained in the memory, just as it is; and the mind must be sure that no part of what is necessary to make up the demonstration is omitted or overlooked. This makes some demonstrations long and perplexed, and too hard for those who have not strength of parts distinctly to perceive, and exactly carry so many particulars orderly in their heads. And even those who are able to master such intricate speculations, are fain sometimes to go over them again, and there is need of more than one review before they can arrive at certainty. But yet where the mind clearly retains the intuition it had of the agreement of any idea with another, and that with a third, and that with a fourth, &c., there the agreement of the first and the fourth is a demonstration,

[1] Cf. chh. ii. §§ 2–13; iii. §§ 18–20; x.; xi. § 10; *Elements of Nat. Philos.* ch. xii.

and produces certain knowledge ; which may be called *rational*[1] *knowledge*, as the other is intuitive.

16. Secondly, There are other ideas, whose agreement or disagreement can no otherwise be judged of but by the intervention of others which have not a certain agreement with the extremes, but an *usual* or *likely* one : and in these it is that the *judgment* is properly exercised ; which is the acquiescing of the mind, that any ideas do agree, by comparing them with such probable mediums. This, though it never amounts to knowledge, no, not to that which is the lowest degree of it[2] ; yet sometimes the intermediate ideas tie the extremes so firmly together, and the probability is so clear and strong, that *assent* as necessarily follows it, as *knowledge* does demonstration. The great excellency and use of the judgment is to observe right, and take a true estimate of the force and weight of each probability ; and then casting them up all right together, choose that side which has the overbalance.

17. *Intuitive knowledge* is the perception of the *certain* agreement or disagreement of two ideas immediately compared together.

Rational knowledge is the perception of the *certain* agreement or disagreement of any two ideas, by the intervention of one or more other ideas.

Judgment is the thinking or taking two ideas to agree or disagree, by the intervention of one or more ideas, whose certain agreement or disagreement with them it does not perceive, but hath observed to be *frequent* and *usual*.

18. Though the deducing one proposition from another, or making inferences in *words*, be a great part of reason, and that which it is usually employed about ; yet the principal act of ratiocination is *the finding the agreement or disagreement of two ideas one with another, by the intervention of a third.* As a man, by a yard, finds two houses to be of the same length,

---

[1] Cf. chh. xiv. xv. xvi ; *Elements of Nat. Philos.* ch. xii.

[2] 'lowest degree of it,' i. e. 'sensible knowledge,' or sense-perception, of which in this chapter he takes no particular account. Cf. chh. ii. § 14 ; iii. § 15 ; xi. §§ 8, 9 ; *Elements of Nat. Philos.* ch. xii.

BOOK IV.

CHAP.
XVII.

which could not be brought together to measure their equality by juxta-position. Words have their consequences, as the signs of such ideas: and things agree or disagree, as really they are; but we observe it only by our ideas [1].

Four sorts of Arguments.

19. Before we quit this subject, it may be worth our while a little to reflect on *four sorts of arguments*, that men, in their reasonings with others, do ordinarily make use of to prevail on their assent; or at least so to awe them as to silence their opposition.

First, *Argumentum ad verecundiam.*

I. The first is, to allege the opinions of men, whose parts, learning, eminency, power, or some other cause has gained a name, and settled their reputation in the common esteem with some kind of authority. When men are established in any kind of dignity, it is thought a breach of modesty for others to derogate any way from it, and question the authority of men who are in possession of it. This is apt to be censured, as carrying with it too much pride, when a man does not readily yield to the determination of approved authors, which is wont to be received with respect and submission by others: and it is looked upon as insolence, for a man to set up and adhere to his own opinion against the current stream of antiquity; or to put it in the balance against that of some learned doctor, or otherwise approved writer. Whoever backs his tenets with such authorities, thinks he ought thereby to carry the cause, and is ready to style it impudence in any one who shall stand out against them. This I think may be called *argumentum ad verecundiam* [2].

Secondly, *Argumentum ad Ignorantiam.*

20. II. Secondly, Another way that men ordinarily use to drive others, and force them to submit their judgments, and receive the opinion in debate, is to require the adversary to

---

[1] He here once more advises us to individualise our abstract notions, and thus verify the presence of meaning in our words. 'As long as I confine my thoughts to my own ideas, *divested of words*, I do not see how I can easily be mistaken. The objects I consider, I clearly and adequately know. I cannot be deceived in thinking I have an idea which I have not. It is not possible for me to imagine that any of my own ideas are like or unlike that are not truly so.' (Berkeley, *Principles*, Introd. § 22.)

[2] Locke is always chary of appeals to human authority, which in medieval reasonings had so much taken the place of a purely intellectual appeal. Yet, in many cases, one's judgment of the trustworthiness of the judgment of another person is the only available foundation in reason for an opinion of one's own.

admit what they allege as a proof, or to assign a better. And this I call *argumentum ad ignorantiam*[1].

21. III. Thirdly, A third way is to press a man with consequences drawn from his own principles or concessions. This is already known under the name of *argumentum ad hominem*[2].

22. IV. The fourth is the using of proofs drawn from any of the foundations of knowledge or probability. This I call *argumentum ad judicium*. This alone, of all the four, brings true instruction with it, and advances us in our way to knowledge. For, 1. It argues not another man's opinion to be right, because I, out of respect, or any other consideration but that of conviction, will not contradict him. 2. It proves not another man to be in the right way, nor that I ought to take the same with him, because I know not a better. 3. Nor does it follow that another man is in the right way, because he has shown me that I am in the wrong. I may be modest, and therefore not oppose another man's persuasion : I may be ignorant, and not be able to produce a better : I may be in an error, and another may show me that I am so. This may dispose me, perhaps, for the reception of truth, but helps me not to it: that must come from proofs and arguments, and light arising from

---

[1] We are not bound in reason to accept our adversary's conclusion as proved, because we cannot offer better proof of another conclusion. For the question may be one which transcends man's experience and intelligence, intermediate between mere sense and Omniscience. ' Malebranche having enumerated and showed the difficulties of the other ways whereby he thinks human understanding may be attempted to be explained, and how insufficient they are to give a satisfactory account of the ideas we have, treats this of " seeing all things in God " on that account as the true, *because it is impossible to find a better.* Which argument, so far being only *argumentum ad ignorantiam*, loses all its force as soon as we consider the weakness of our minds, and

the narrowness of our capacities, and have but humility enough to allow that there may be many things which we cannot fully comprehend, and that God is not bound in all he does to subject his ways of operation to the scrutiny of our thoughts, and confine himself to do nothing but what we must comprehend.' (Locke's *Examination of Malebranche*, § 2.)

[2] This argument is legitimate when the question in dispute is not the truth of a proposition but the self-consistency of the person who proposes it. It becomes irrelevant, and therefore fallacious, when used as an *argumentum ad rem*. This and the two preceding arguments, when fallacious, may be regarded as modes of the fallacy of irrelevant reasoning.

BOOK IV.

CHAP.
XVII.

Above,
contrary,
and
according
to Reason.

the nature of things themselves, and not from my shame-facedness, ignorance, or error [1].

23. By what has been before said of reason, we may be able to make some guess at the distinction of things, into those that are according to, above, and contrary to reason [2]. 1. *According to reason* are such propositions whose truth we can discover by examining and tracing those ideas we have from sensation and reflection; and by natural deduction find to be true or probable. 2. *Above reason* are such propositions whose truth or probability we cannot by reason derive from those principles [3]. 3. *Contrary to reason* are such propositions as are inconsistent with or irreconcilable to our clear and distinct ideas. Thus

---

[1] The *argumentum ad judicium* suggests the reference to the limits and ultimate foundations of reason in man contained in the following section.

[2] See Leibniz. The distinction of things according to ' above' and ' contrary to' reason is characteristic of that incomplete knowledge and experience, or merely finite intelligence of the universe, which all *reasoning* implies. It is inconsistent with Omniscience. As Locke elsewhere remarks, ' I think we cannot say God reasons at all; for He has at once a view of all things. But reason [reasoning] is very far from such an intuition ; it is a laborious and gradual progress in the knowledge of things, by comparing one idea with a second, and a second with a third, and that with a fourth, to find the relation between the first and last in this train ; and in search for such intermediate ideas as may show us the relation we desire to know, which sometimes we find, and sometimes not. This way therefore of finding truth, so painful, uncertain, and limited, is proper only to men of finite understandings, but can by no means be supposed in God.' (*Exam. of Malebranche*, § 52.) ' Dieu seul,' says Leibniz, ' a l'avantage de n'avoir que des connaissances intuitives.' (*Nouveaux Essais.*)

[3] ' Il me semble que de la manière que cette définition est couchée, elle va trop loin d'un côte et pas assez loin de l'autre ; et si nous la suivons, tout ce que nous ignorons et que nous ne sommes pas en pouvoir de connaître dans notre présent état serait au-dessus de la raison : par exemple, qu'une telle étoile fixe est plus ou moins grande que le soleil ; item que le Vésuve jettera du feu dans une telle année : ce sont des faits dont la connaissance nous surpasse, non pas parce qu'ils sont au-dessus des sens, car nous pourrions fort bien juger de cela, si nous avions des organes plus parfaits, et plus d'information des circonstances. Il y a aussi des difficultés qui sont au-dessus de notre présente faculté, mais non pas au-dessus de toute la raison ; par exemple, il n'y a point d'astronome ici-bas qui puisse calculer le détail d'une éclipse dans l'espace d'un *Pater*, et sans mettre la plume à la main, cependant il y a peut-être des génies à qui cela ne serait qu'un jeu.' (*Nouveaux Essais.*) And when it is suggested that ' above reason' may mean not only above *our* reason, conditioned by sensation and reflection, but above reason in any finite intelligence, this, he argues, only shifts the difficulty.

the existence of one God is according to reason ; the existence BOOK IV.

of more than one God, contrary to reason ; the resurrection of

the dead, above reason. *Above reason* also may be taken in

a double sense, viz. either as signifying above probability[1], or
above certainty[2] : and in that large sense also, *contrary to
reason*, is, I suppose, sometimes taken.

24. There is another use of the word *reason*, wherein it is
opposed to faith : which, though it be in itself a very improper
way of speaking, yet common use has so authorized it, that it
would be folly either to oppose or hope to remedy it. Only
I think it may not be amiss to take notice, that, however faith
be opposed to reason, faith is nothing but a firm assent of the
mind: which, if it be regulated, as is our duty, cannot be
afforded to anything but upon good reason ; and so cannot be
opposite to it[3]. He that believes without having any reason[4]
for believing, may be in love with his own fancies ; but neither
seeks truth as he ought, nor pays the obedience due to his
Maker, who would have him use those discerning faculties he
has given him, to keep him out of mistake and error. He
that does not this to the best of his power, however he sometimes lights on truth, is in the right but by chance ; and
I know not whether the luckiness of the accident will excuse
the irregularity of his proceeding. This at least is certain,
that he must be accountable for whatever mistakes he runs
into: whereas he that makes use of the light and faculties God
has given him, and seeks sincerely to discover truth by those
helps and abilities he has, may have this satisfaction in doing
his duty as a rational creature, that, though he should miss
truth, he will not miss the reward of it. For he governs his
assent right, and places it as he should, who, in any case or
matter whatsoever, believes or disbelieves according as reason

Reason
and Faith
not
opposite,
for Faith
must be
regulated
by Reason.

---

[1] 'above probability.' Probable propositions are those the truth or falsehood of which cannot be determined (by
man) except by presumptions, founded
on the analogies of experience, in ourselves or in others.

[2] 'above certainty,' i.e. propositions
which, while men can determine them,
as more or less probable, on relative

grounds of probability, transcend the
limits within which man's (absolutely certain) knowledge is confined.

[3] We must always be regulated in
the last resort by reasonableness—in
its large meaning.

[4] 'reason,' i.e. without seeing the
reasonableness of having faith in the
particular authority that we trust in.

BOOK IV.
—•••—
CHAP.
XVII.

directs him. He that doth otherwise, transgresses against his own light, and misuses those faculties which were given him to no other end, but to search and follow the clearer evidence and greater probability[1]. But since reason and faith are by some men opposed[2], we will so consider them in the following chapter.

[1] All the certainty and evidence of *knowledge* depends at last, according to the *Essay*, on the light of rational intuition; and the rational measure of *probability* is conformity to the analogies of experience, in that wide sense which includes spiritual as well as sensuous experience, and the experience of others as well as our own.

[2] Reason and blind submission to authority are opposed; but not reason (either discursive or intuitive) and faith: reason, in a human consciousness, presupposes faith, which Omniscience alone can dispense with.

CHAPTER XVIII.

OF FAITH AND REASON, AND THEIR DISTINCT PROVINCES.

1. IT has been above[1] shown, 1. That we are of necessity ignorant, and want knowledge of all sorts, where we want ideas[2]. 2. That we are ignorant, and want rational knowledge, where we want proofs. 3. That we want certain knowledge and certainty, as far as we want clear and determined specific ideas. 4. That we want probability to direct our assent in matters where we have neither knowledge[3] of our own nor testimony of other men to bottom[4] our reason upon.

From these things thus premised, I think we may come to lay down *the measures and boundaries between faith and reason* : the want whereof may possibly have been the cause, if not of great disorders, yet at least of great disputes, and perhaps mistakes in the world. For till it be resolved how far we are to be guided by reason, and how far by faith, we shall in vain dispute, and endeavour to convince one another in matters of religion.

2. I find every sect, as far as reason will help them, make use of it gladly : and where it fails them, they cry out, It is matter of faith, and above reason. And I do not see how they can argue with any one, or ever convince a gainsayer

---

[1] Cf. chh. iii. xvii. §§ 9-11; also Locke's *Thoughts concerning Reading and Study for a Gentleman.*

[2] 'all sorts,' i. e. intuitive, demonstrative or rational, and sensitive.

[3] 'knowledge' seems here to be taken widely, so as to include judgments of probability, as well as the absolute certainties to which Locke's own definition limits 'knowledge.'

[4] Cf. *Conduct of the Understanding,* § 44. What Locke calls ' bottoming ' is seeking for ultimate truths, a process in which he habitually stops short, through his aversion to forsake the concrete, or to draw off from individual substances.

who makes use of the same plea, without setting down strict boundaries between faith and reason; which ought to be the first point established in all questions where faith has anything to do.

Reason, therefore, here, as contradistinguished to *faith*, I take to be the discovery of the certainty[1] or probability[2] of such propositions or truths, which the mind arrives at by deduction made from such ideas, which it has got by the use of its natural faculties; viz. by sensation or reflection[3].

Faith, on the other side, is the assent to any proposition, not thus made out by the deductions of reason, but upon the credit of the proposer, as coming from God, in some extraordinary way of communication. This way of discovering truths to men, we call *revelation*[4].

First,
No new
simple
Idea

3. *First*, Then I say, that *no man inspired by God can by any revelation communicate to others any new simple ideas which they had not before from sensation or reflection*[5]. For,

---

[1] By demonstrative reasoning.

[2] Through analogical or inductive presumptions in probable inference.

[3] That is, from the phenomena presented in external and internal sense, of which our inferences are attempted interpretations. The interpretations differ in depth and comprehension according to the experience (personal or foreign) and faculty of the reasoner, and in all cases fall short of the perfect interpretation, or rather intuition, which is competent only to Omniscience. Locke's 'reason,' which mainly means reasoning or inference, presupposes intuitive reason, as the (conscious or unconscious) condition of its operation.

[4] This is revelation in the narrower meaning, for in its wider the whole evolution of the universe, in nature and spirit, is revelation of God. A miraculous revelation of God, the object of Locke's '*faith*,' could not, in a divinely or rationally constituted universe, be *anomic*, which would involve insanity in the universe—suspension of the supremacy of mind and purpose in its history. But its original appearance in the minds of 'inspired' men might be determined by laws of the supreme economy that transcend human understanding and ordinary natural law. Hence its contents could not be got by deductions of reason, as in ordinary scientific interpretations of nature.

[5] Without the quickening of external or internal data of experience, the words which signify either the contingent phenomena of sense, or the spiritual ideas of reason and will must remain meaningless. 'This,' as Locke says, 'is true of what Malebranche calls sentiment [sensations], and as true of what he calls ideas [perceptions of reason]. Show me one who has never got by experience, i. e. by seeing or feeling, the idea of space or motion, and I will as soon *by words* make one *who never felt what heat is* have a conception of heat, as he that has not *by his senses perceived* what space or motion is, can, *by words*, be made to conceive either of them.' (*Exam. of Malebranche*, § 49.)

whatsoever impressions he himself may have from the immediate hand of God, this revelation, if it be of new simple
ideas, cannot be conveyed to another, either by words or any
other signs. Because words, by their immediate operation
on us, cause no other ideas but of their natural sounds : and
it is by the custom of using them for signs, that they excite
and revive in our minds latent ideas ; but yet only such
ideas as were there before. For words, seen or heard, recal
to our thoughts those ideas only which to us they have been
wont to be signs of, but cannot introduce any perfectly new,
and formerly unknown simple ideas. The same holds in all
other signs ; which cannot signify to us things of which we
have before never had any idea at all.

Thus whatever things were discovered to St. Paul, when
he was rapt up into the third heaven; whatever new ideas
his mind there received, all the description he can make to
others of that place, is only this, That there are such things,
'as eye hath not seen, nor ear heard, nor hath it entered
into the heart of man to conceive.' And supposing God
should discover to any one, supernaturally, a species of
creatures inhabiting, for example, Jupiter or Saturn, (for that
it is possible there may be such, nobody can deny,) which had
six senses ; and imprint on his mind the ideas conveyed to
theirs by that sixth sense : he could no more, by words,
produce in the minds of other men those ideas imprinted by
that sixth sense, than one of us could convey the idea of any
colour, by the sound of words, into a man who, having the
other four senses perfect, had always totally wanted the fifth,
of seeing. For our simple ideas, then, which are the foundation, and sole matter of all our notions and knowledge, we
must depend wholly on our reason, I mean our natural
faculties [1] ; and can by no means receive them, or any of them,
from traditional revelation. I say, *traditional revelation*, in
distinction to *original revelation*. By the one, I mean that
first impression which is made immediately by God on the
mind of any man, to which we cannot set any bounds [2] ; and

---

[1] Here 'reason' means the intelligent nature of man in general,
and not merely either his inferential

faculty *per se,* or his share of intuitive
reason *per se.*

[2] Men might have had a hundred or

BOOK IV.

CHAP. XVIII.

Secondly, Traditional Revelation may make us know Propositions knowable also by Reason, but not with the same Certainty that Reason doth.

by the other, those impressions delivered over to others in words, and the ordinary ways of conveying our conceptions one to another[1].

4. *Secondly,* I say that *the same truths may be discovered, and conveyed down from revelation, which are discoverable to us by reason, and by those ideas we naturally may have.* So God might, by revelation, discover the truth of any proposition in Euclid ; as well as men, by the natural use of their faculties, come to make the discovery themselves. In all things of this kind there is little need or use of revelation, God having furnished us with natural and surer means to arrive at the knowledge of them. For whatsoever truth we come to the clear discovery of, from the knowledge and contemplation of our own ideas, will always be certainer to us than those which are conveyed to us by *traditional revelation*[2]. For the knowledge we have that this revelation came

a thousand senses, with corresponding simple ideas of *sense* for which man can have no names, because he can have no corresponding ideas ; and we can set no bounds to the ideas of *reflection* of which spiritual beings might be the recipients. External and internal perception, exercised by each man, may be called ' original ' revelations ; what they have revealed to one man, when communicated in words to another, is in its way an example of ' traditional' revelation—both ' natural' because capable of being tested by us in terms of ordinary natural law.

[1] Unless ' revelation ' is essentially a development of spiritual principles and ideas that are *latent* in all men, and *evoked* in the consciousness of inspired persons, on occasion of ' extraordinary ' events, and under laws undiscoverable by physical understanding. Any way, revelation presupposes spiritual experience of which the mind is somehow capable, not spoken or written words alone, apart from data in the experience of the recipient. Without this basis in the spiritual constitution of those to whom it comes,

a ' traditional revelation ' would be a revelation of empty words ; as incapable of conveying ideas as a verbal revelation of colours to one born blind. The 'external revelation,' whether in natural science, morality, or religion, must find a *response*, due to what was originally latent in the recipient.

[2] The revelation of God accepted in Christendom, as presented, at special periods in history, under conditions which are called ' supernatural '—because incapable of being resolved by us into the commonly experienced course of events—is called ' traditional,'—as conveyed, according to Catholics, by a living supernatural society, the Church; according to Protestants, through a collection of inspired books. But neither Church nor Bible can be *blindly* assumed as *ultimate* authority in religion. In neither can the ' bottom of the question ' be thus reached, that ' only place of rest and stability for the inquisitive mind.' Each must at last make good the reasonableness of its claim. But this does not mean reason operating within the presupposition, that the

at first from God, can never be so sure as the knowledge we
have from the clear and distinct perception of the agreement
or disagreement of our own ideas: v. g. if it were revealed
some ages since, that the three angles of a triangle were equal
to two right ones, I might assent to the truth of that proposition, upon the credit of the tradition, that it was revealed :
but that would never amount to so great a certainty as the
knowledge of it, upon the comparing and measuring my own
ideas of two right angles, and the three angles of a triangle[1].
The like holds in matter of fact knowable by our senses[2];
v. g. the history of the deluge is conveyed to us by writings
which had their original from revelation : and yet nobody,
I think, will say he has as certain and clear a knowledge of
the flood as Noah, that saw it ; or that he himself would
have had, had he then been alive and seen it[3]. For he has
no greater an assurance than that of his senses, that it is
writ in the book supposed writ by Moses inspired : but he
has not so great an assurance that Moses wrote that book as
if he had seen Moses write it. So that the assurance of its
being a revelation is less still than the assurance of his
senses.

ordinary course of events must supply
all its ultimate premises ; and that
what is to man supernatural or miraculous would be really anomic, purposeless, and inexplicable, even to
an intelligence that could see all
in the light of the moral and spiritual
economy. The Church, or the Bible,
or both, may present the ' supernatural' occasion of awakening in
response that spiritual intuition of
what God is, which is the essence of
the revelation, Christian religion being
the highest form of human feeling and
action.

[1] This traditional revelation of
'mathematical truth' is not properly
spoken of as a 'revelation' till it
becomes a rational one in the mind of
the recipient, in whom those mathematical truths were latent; but the
'tradition' may be the occasion on
which one in whose mind the truth

that the three angles of a triangle are
equal to two right angles had not
been awakened, comes to see this truth.
The tradition has called it into consciousness.

[2] Revelation may be either the education—evolution—of our latent insight of God, or information as to events
otherwise inaccessible to us.

[3] This is revelation of extraordinary facts or events in sense-
experience, as distinguished from a
revelation of spiritual principles. But
there must be something that responds
to and assimilates the revelations, in
the persons to whom they are presented. Locke would make revelation
too external or mechanical—dogmatically assertive — independent of the
divine that is immanent or latent in
man, although naturally overborne by
his animal constitution.

BOOK IV.

CHAP.
XVIII.

Even Original Revelation cannot be admitted against the clear Evidence of Reason.

5. In propositions, then, whose certainty is built upon the clear perception of the agreement or disagreement of our ideas, attained either by immediate intuition, as in self-evident propositions, or by evident deductions of reason in demonstrations we need not the assistance of revelation, as necessary to gain our assent, and introduce them into our minds. Because the natural ways of knowledge could settle them there, or had done it already; which is the greatest assurance we can possibly have of anything, unless where God immediately reveals it to us: and there too our assurance can be no greater than our knowledge is, that it *is* a revelation from God. But yet nothing, I think, can, under that title, shake or overrule plain knowledge; or rationally prevail with any man to admit it for true, in a direct contradiction to the clear evidence of his own understanding[1]. For, since no evidence of our faculties, by which we receive such revelations, can exceed, if equal, the certainty of our intuitive knowledge, we can never receive for a truth anything that is directly contrary to our clear and distinct knowledge; v. g. the ideas of one body and one place do so clearly agree, and the mind has so evident a perception of their agreement, that we can never assent to a proposition that affirms the same body to be in two distant places at once[1], however it should pretend to the authority of a divine revelation: since the evidence, first, that we deceive not ourselves, in ascribing it to God; secondly, that we understand it right; can never be so great as the evidence of our own intuitive knowledge, whereby we discern it impossible for the same body to be in two places at once[2]. And therefore *no propo-*

[1] The sceptical idea, that theological truth may be philosophical error, and *vice versa*, is discountenanced by Locke, who professedly rejects the unreasonable, alike in inspired theology and philosophy, thus bridging over the chasm left by Bacon between ' Human Learning ' and ' inspired Divinity, the Sabaoth and port of all man's labours and peregrinations.'

[2] As he seems to imply that the Catholic doctrine of transubstantiation does, under which the natural sense impressions of bread and wine continue to be presented by the transubstantiated elements in the Eucharist. Its philosophical defenders (e. g. Leibniz) argue for the rational possibility of the real essence of body existing at once in a plurality of places, presenting different qualities in each place ; and against Locke's supposition that we have intuitive knowledge that this is ' impossible.'

sition can be received for divine revelation, or obtain the assent due to all such, if it be contradictory to our clear intuitive knowledge. Because this would be to subvert the principles and foundations of all knowledge, evidence, and assent whatsoever: and there would be left no difference between truth and falsehood, no measures of credible and incredible in the world, if doubtful propositions shall take place before self-evident[1]; and what we certainly know give way to what we may possibly be mistaken in. In propositions therefore contrary to the clear perception of the agreement or disagreement of any of our ideas, it will be in vain to urge them as matters of faith. They cannot move our assent under that or any other title whatsoever. For faith can never convince us of anything that contradicts our knowledge. Because, though faith be founded on the testimony of God (who cannot lie) revealing any proposition to us: yet we cannot have an assurance of the truth of its being a divine revelation greater than our own knowledge. Since the whole strength of the certainty depends upon our knowledge that God revealed it; which, in this case, where the proposition supposed revealed contradicts our knowledge or reason, will always have this objection hanging to it, viz. that we cannot tell how to conceive that to come from God, the bountiful Author of our being, which, if received for true, must overturn all the principles and foundations of knowledge he has given us; render all our faculties useless; wholly destroy the most excellent part of his workmanship, our understandings; and put a man in a condition wherein he will have less light, less conduct than the beast that perisheth. For if the mind of man can never have a clearer (and perhaps not so clear) evidence of anything to be a divine revelation, as it has of the principles of its own reason, it can never have a ground to quit the clear evidence of its reason, to give a place to a proposition, whose revelation has not a greater evidence than those principles have[2].

---

[1] 'self-evident propositions' being with Locke 'necessary to certainty, and that on which all certainty is founded,' whether they come into the individual mind earlier or later.

[2] Faith cannot respond to any authoritative assertion which implies that the universe in its ultimate consti-

BOOK IV.
—◆—
CHAP.
XVIII.

Tradi-
tional
Revelation
much less.

6. Thus far a man has use of reason, and ought to hearken to it, even in immediate and original revelation[1], where it is supposed to be made to himself. But to all those who pretend not to immediate revelation, but are required to pay obedience, and to receive the truths revealed to others, which, by the tradition of writings, or word of mouth, are conveyed down to them, reason has a great deal more to do, and is that only which can induce us to receive them. For matter of faith being only divine revelation, and nothing else, faith, as we use the word, (called commonly *divine faith*[2]), has to do with no propositions, but those which are supposed to be divinely revealed. So that I do not see how those who make revelation alone the sole object of faith can say, That it is a matter of faith, and not of reason, to believe that such or such a proposition, to be found in such or such a book, is of divine inspiration ; unless it be revealed that that proposition, or all in that book, was communicated by divine inspiration. Without such a revelation, the believing, or not believing, that proposition, or book, to be of divine authority, can never be matter of faith, but matter of reason ; and such as I must come to an assent to only by the use of my reason, which can never require or enable me to believe that which is contrary to itself : it being impossible for reason ever to procure any assent to that which to itself appears unreasonable[3].

In all things, therefore, where we have clear evidence from

tuition is *anomic* — irregular, chaotic, independent of all law or reason ; although its order may transcend physical laws that are measurable by the custom of human sense.

[1] ' immediate revelation,' through the inspiration, or extraordinary spiritual insight, of those who are the subjects of the inspiration. This is the ' original,' from which the 'traditional revelation ' issues ; subject to the risks of conveyance through and to human minds, and of misunderstanding, under the conditions of human language, in dealing with all which reason has much to do.

[2] This is faith in its theological meaning,—to be distinguished from philosophical faith, and also from faith either as trust in a man, or as synonymous with belief generally. In all real faith there is correspondence between its object and the moral and practical reason—the latter responding to the former.

[3] But that often ' appears unreasonable,' at the point of view of the understanding judging according to sense, which is not unreasonable when reason is taken in its larger meaning as intuitive, and including the moral and spiritual constitution of man.

our ideas, and those principles of knowledge I have above BOOK IV.
mentioned, reason is the proper judge; and revelation, though
it may, in consenting with it, confirm its dictates, yet cannot
in such cases invalidate its decrees: nor can we be obliged,
where we have the clear and evident sentence of reason, to
quit it for the contrary opinion, under a pretence that it is
matter of faith : [¹which can have no authority against the
plain and clear dictates of reason].

7. But, *Thirdly*, There being many things wherein we have
very imperfect notions, or none at all ; and other things, of
whose past, present, or future existence, by the natural use
of our faculties, we can have no knowledge at all ; these, as
being beyond the discovery of our natural faculties, and
above reason, are, when revealed, *the proper matter of faith.*
Thus, that part of the angels rebelled against God, and
thereby lost their first happy state : and that [²the dead shall
rise, and live again] : these and the like, being beyond the
discovery of reason, are purely matters of faith, with which
reason has directly nothing to do.

Thirdly, Things above Reason are, when revealed, the proper matter of faith.

8. But since God, in giving us the light of reason, has not
thereby tied up his own hands from affording us, when he
thinks fit, the light of revelation in any of those matters
wherein our natural faculties are able to give a probable
determination ; *revelation*, where God has been pleased to
give it, *must carry it against the probable conjectures of reason.*
Because the mind not being certain of the truth of that it
does not evidently know³, but only yielding to the proba-

Or not contrary to Reason, if revealed, are Matter of Faith ; and must carry it against probable conjectures of Reason.

---

¹ Added in second edition.

² In first three editions—'the *bodies* of men shall rise and live again,' changed to 'the dead' in the fourth edition, after controversy with Stillingfleet, for the reason thus explained :— 'I must not part with this article of the resurrection without returning my thanks to your lordship for making me take notice of a fault in my *Essay*. When I writ that book, I took it for granted that the Scripture had mentioned in express terms the resurrection of the *body*. But upon the occasion your lordship has given me to look more narrowly into what revelation has declared concerning the resurrection, and finding no such express words in the Scripture as that "the body shall rise," or "be raised," I shall, in the next edition of it, change these words of my book—"the dead *bodies* of men shall rise," into these of the Scripture—"the *dead* shall rise." ' (*Reply to Second Letter*, pp. 209-10. Cf. pp. 165-211.)

³ This is another of the expressions quoted by Stillingfleet to prove that Locke makes *clear* ideas indispensable to certainty, and thus rejects what is

bility that appears in it, is bound to give up its assent to such a testimony which, it is satisfied, comes from one who cannot err, and will not deceive. But yet, it still belongs to reason to judge of the truth of its being a revelation, and of the signification of the words wherein it is delivered. Indeed, if anything shall be thought revelation which is contrary to the plain principles of reason, and the evident knowledge the mind has of its own clear and distinct ideas; there reason must be hearkened to, as to a matter within its province. Since a man can never have so certain a knowledge, that a proposition which contradicts the clear principles and evidence of his own knowledge was divinely revealed, or that he understands the words rightly wherein it is delivered, as he has that the contrary is true, and so is bound to consider and judge of it as a matter of reason, and not swallow it, without examination, as a matter of faith.

9. First, Whatever proposition is revealed, of whose truth our mind, by its natural faculties and notions, cannot judge, that is purely matter of faith, and above reason.

Secondly, All propositions whereof the mind, by the use of its natural faculties, can come to determine and judge, from naturally acquired ideas, are matter of reason; with this difference still, that, in those concerning which it has but an uncertain evidence, and so is persuaded of their truth only upon probable grounds, which still admit a possibility of the contrary to be true, without doing violence to the certain evidence of its own knowledge, and overturning the principles of all reason; in such probable propositions, I say, an evident revelation ought to determine our assent, even against probability. For where the principles of reason have not evidenced a proposition to be certainly true or false, there clear revelation, as another principle of truth and ground of assent, may determine; and so it may be matter of faith, and be also above reason. Because reason, in that particular matter, being able to reach no higher than pro-

mysterious as unfit to be believed. As to which Locke explains his position to be, 'that certainty consists in the perception of the agreement or disagreement of ideas *such as we have,* whether they be in all their parts and relations perfectly clear and distinct or no.'

bability, faith gave the determination where reason came
short; and revelation discovered on which side the truth lay[1].
10. Thus far the dominion of faith reaches, and that
without any violence or hindrance to reason; which is not
injured or disturbed, but assisted and improved by new
discoveries of truth, coming from the eternal fountain of all
knowledge. Whatever God hath revealed is certainly true:
no doubt can be made of it. This is the proper object of
faith: but whether it be a *divine* revelation or no, reason
must judge; which can never permit the mind to reject
a greater evidence to embrace what is less evident, nor allow
it to entertain probability in opposition to knowledge and
certainty. There can be no evidence that any traditional
revelation is of divine original, in the words we receive it,
and in the sense we understand it, so clear and so certain as
that of the principles of reason[2]: and therefore *Nothing that*

BOOK IV.

CHAP.
XVIII.

In Matters
where
Reason
can afford
certain
Know-
ledge, that
is to be
hearkened
to.

[1] Faith, in short, is the sole organ
for the reception and assimilation of
truths that are 'above reason' (e. g.
that the dead shall rise); and may be
an organ for the certain determination
of propositions which otherwise could
be only probable to a human mind.
It is thus a harmonious supplement to
a merely natural understanding of the
universe. This section is so far a
summary of §§ 4-8.

[2] Here Locke seems to confine all
'traditional revelation' within the
sphere of probability, excluding certainty. On which Halyburton, a Scotch
divine, thus comments, in an *Essay concerning the Reason of Faith* (1714):—
'We say and shall prove, that the Scriptures do *evidence themselves to be from
God*, which we hope may effectually
repel the force of what Mr. Locke
has urged, and show that there is no
reason for ranking all the truths therein
delivered amongst those conjectural
things that lean only on probabilities
and reasonings from them, which
Mr. Locke evidently does; when he
sinks traditional revelation to the point
of certainty below intuitive, rational,

and sensible knowledge, and banishes
all faith properly so called, leaving no
room for it, and putting in its place an
act of reason proceeding upon probabilities, i.e. on historical proofs; which
he reckons only among probabilities,
for which I blame him not.' (p. 134.)
Leibniz, too, thus comments on this
chapter:—'Si vous ne prenez la *foi*
que pour ce qui est fondée dans des
motifs de crédibilité (comme on les
appelle), et la detachez de la grâce
interne, qui y détermine l'esprit immédiatement, tout ce que vous dites,
monsieur, est incontestable. Il faut
avouer qu'il y a bien des jugements
plus évidents que ceux qui dependent
de ces motifs. Les uns y sont plus
avancés que les autres, et même il y a
quantité de personnes qui ne les ont
jamais connus et encore moins pesés,
et qui, par conséquent, n'ont pas
même ce qui pourrait passer pour un
motif de probabilité. Mais la grâce
interne du Saint-Esprit y supplée
immédiatement d'une manière surnaturelle, et c'est ce qui fait ce que les
théologiens appellent proprement une
foi divine. Il est vrai que Dieu ne la

BOOK IV.
CHAP.
XVIII.

is contrary to, and inconsistent with, the clear and self-evident dictates of reason, has a right to be urged or assented to as a matter of faith, wherein reason hath nothing to do [1]. What-soever is divine revelation, ought to overrule all our opinions, prejudices, and interest, and hath a right to be received with full assent. Such a submission as this, of our reason to faith, takes not away the landmarks of knowledge : this shakes not the foundations of reason, but leaves us that use of our faculties for which they were given us.

If the Boundaries be not set between Faith and Reason, no Enthusiasm or Extravagancy in Religion can be contradicted.

11. If the provinces of faith and reason are not kept distinct by these boundaries, there will, in matters of religion, be no room for reason at all ; and those extravagant opinions and ceremonies that are to be found in the several religions of the world will not deserve to be blamed. For, to this crying up of faith in *opposition* to reason, we may, I think, in good measure ascribe those absurdities that fill almost all the religions which possess and divide mankind. For men having been principled with an opinion, that they must not consult reason in the things of religion, however apparently contradictory to common sense and the very principles of all their knowledge, have let loose their fancies and natural superstition ; and have been by them led into so strange opinions, and extravagant practices in religion, that a considerate man cannot but stand amazed at their follies, and judge them so far from being acceptable to the great and wise God, that he cannot avoid thinking them ridiculous and offensive to a sober good man. So that, in effect, religion, which should most distinguish us from beasts, and ought most peculiarly to elevate us, as rational creatures, above

donne jamais que lorsque ce qu'il fait croire est fondé en raison ; autrement il detruirait les moyens de connaître la verité, et ouvrirait la porte à l'enthousiasme ; mais il n'est point nécessaire que tous ceux qui ont cette foi divine connaissent ces raisons, et encore moins qu'il les aient toujours devant les yeux. Autrement les simples et idiots n'auraient jamais la vrai foi, et les plus éclaires ne l'auraient pas quand ils pourraient en avoir le plus de besoin, car ils ne peuvent pas se souvenir toujours des raisons de croire. (*Nouveaux Essais.*)

[1] What can be shown to be absolutely unreasonable, or 'contrary to reason,' must be rejected by all who are endowed with reason, as the alternative to a universal doubt. See Stillingfleet's first *Answer*, pp. 45–47, and Toland's *Christianity not Mysterious*, *passim.*

brutes, is that wherein men often appear most irrational, and
more senseless than beasts themselves. *Credo, quia im-*
possibile est: I believe, because it is impossible, might, in
a good man, pass for a sally of zeal; but would prove a very
ill rule for men to choose their opinions or religion by [1].

[1] It must be remembered, however, that 'reason,' in Locke's narrow meaning of inferential understanding, judging according to sense, is an inadequate test of possibility in things spiritual, which appeal to the entire constitution of man, with its latent powers of response to a deeper conception of life and the universe than the merely physical.

CHAPTER XIX.

[¹ OF ENTHUSIASM.]

BOOK IV.

Chap.
XIX.

Love of
Truth
necessary.

[1. He that would seriously set upon the search of truth, ought in the first place to prepare his mind with a love of it ². For he that loves it not, will not take much pains to get it; nor be much concerned when he misses it. There is nobody in the commonwealth of learning who does not profess himself a lover of truth: and there is not a rational creature that would not take it amiss to be thought otherwise

¹ This chapter was added in the fourth edition. 'What I shall add concerning Enthusiasm,' Locke writes to Molyneux (Oates, April 6, 1695), 'I guess will very much agree with your thoughts, since yours jump so right with mine about the place where it is to come in; I having designed it for ch. xviii. lib. iv, as a false principle of reasoning, often made use of. But to give an historical account of the various ravings men have embraced for religion, would, I fear, be beside my purpose, and enough to make a huge volume.' The influence of enthusiasm in withdrawing men from the genuine pursuit of truth, by substituting sensuous emotion for genuine spiritual insight, is the subject suggested by this chapter.

² 'Truth,' says Bacon, 'which only doth judge itself, teacheth that the inquiry of truth, which is the love-making or wooing of it; the knowledge of truth, which is the presence of it; and the belief of truth, which is

the enjoying of it—is the sovereign good of human nature.' (*Essay* I.) The love of truth was Locke's ruling passion. It finds expression in many parts of his books and correspondence, along with praise of that 'indifferency,' or freedom from bias, which he represents as its characteristic. He sees in the adoption of enthusiastic sentiment for the direction of our judgments, neglect of natural understanding, if not of supernatural reason, as their ultimate criterion; and want of that love of truth which seeks to see things as they really are, because they are what they are, to which this chapter recalls mere enthusiasts. But Locke's exaggerated regard for the empirical understanding of things leads him to disparage imagination, emotion, and reason in that highest meaning which implies philosophical faith—as factors in a human interpretation of the universe.

of. And yet, for all this, one may truly say, that there are very few lovers of truth, for truth's sake, even amongst those who persuade themselves that they are so. How a man may know whether he be so in earnest, is worth inquiry: and I think there is one unerring mark of it, viz. The not entertaining any proposition with greater assurance than the proofs it is built upon will warrant. Whoever goes beyond this measure of assent, it is plain receives not the truth in the love of it; loves not truth for truth's sake, but for some other bye-end. For the evidence that any proposition is true (except such as are self-evident) lying only in the proofs a man has of it, whatsoever degrees of assent he affords it beyond the degrees of that evidence, it is plain that all the surplusage of assurance is owing to some other affection, and not to the love of truth: it being as impossible that the love of truth should carry my assent above the evidence there is to me, that it is true, as that the love of truth should make me assent to any proposition for the sake of that evidence which it has not, that it is true: which is in effect to love it as a truth, because it is possible or probable that it may not be true. In any truth that gets not possession of our minds by the irresistible light of self-evidence[1], or by the force of demonstration[2], the arguments that gain it assent[3] are the vouchers and gage of its probability to us[4]; and we can receive it for no other than such as they deliver it to our understandings. Whatsoever credit or authority we give to any proposition more than it receives from the principles and proofs[5] it supports itself upon, is owing to our inclinations that way, and is so far a derogation from the love of truth as such: which, as it can receive no

---

[1] Cf. chh. ii. § 1; xvii. § 14.

[2] Cf. chh. ii. §§ 2-13: xvii. § 15.

[3] Cf. chh. xiv-xvii.

[4] 'to us' — suggests the relative character of probability, as dependent upon the spiritual development and experience of the persons whose 'assent' is given.

[5] But we must not limit our available 'principles and proofs,' for determining judgment by 'evidence,' to those supplied by the empirical understanding, judging according to the custom of sense; or suppose that we can thus reach our best and truest attainable conceptions of the law, order, or meaning that is immanent in the universe. All that is highest within us must be in response to all that is highest without us, in order to a final interpretation of the realities amidst which we live.

BOOK IV.

CHAP.
XIX.

A Forwardness
to dictate
another's
beliefs,
from
whence.

evidence from our passions or interests[1], so it should receive no tincture from them.

2. The assuming an authority of dictating to others, and a forwardness to prescribe to their opinions, is a constant concomitant of this bias and corruption of our judgments. For how almost can it be otherwise, but that he should be ready to impose on another's belief, who has already imposed on his own? Who can reasonably expect arguments and conviction from him in dealing with others, whose understanding is not accustomed to them in his dealing with himself? Who does violence to his own faculties, tyrannizes over his own mind, and usurps the prerogative that belongs to truth alone, which is to command assent by only its own authority, i. e. by and in proportion to that evidence which it carries with it.

Force of
Enthusiasm,
in which
reason is
taken
away.

3. Upon this occasion I shall take the liberty to consider *a third ground of assent*[2], which with some men has the same authority, and is as confidently relied on as either faith or reason; I mean *enthusiasm*: which, laying by reason, would set up revelation without it. Whereby in effect it takes away both reason and revelation, and substitutes in the room of them the ungrounded fancies of a man's own brain, and assumes them for a foundation both of opinion and conduct[3].

---

[1] ' our passions and interests '—especially our sensuous passions and selfish interests.

[2] Locke's other two grounds of 'assent' are reason or inference and faith.

[3] *Reason,* or inferential thought, and *faith* in a miraculous divine revelation are both to be tested by the objective evidence that evokes a response from the reason that is in us—practical as well as speculative. Faith, while it accepts all the scientific discoveries of the empirical understanding, moves on a higher plane, and interprets them all in harmony with the supremacy of spiritual law and moral purpose.

Nothing in ' science,' the product of reason in its narrower meaning, can contradict philosophical or divine faith; for a lower law cannot contradict a higher, although it may be explained by it.

While reasoning and faith must be reasonable, Locke's ' enthusiasm,' determined by sensuous emotion, incited by fancy, supersedes proof and contradicts reason. Genuine faith is reasonable; this sort of enthusiasm is blind. But emotion and imagination are motive forces indispensable to the discoveries of science and the insight of faith, both which imply possession by an ideal.

4. *Reason* is *natural revelation*, whereby the eternal Father
of light and fountain of all knowledge, communicates to
mankind that portion of truth which he has laid within
the reach of their natural faculties : *revelation* is *natural*
reason enlarged by a new set of discoveries communicated
by God immediately; which reason vouches the truth of,
by the testimony and proofs it gives that they come from
God. So that he that takes away reason to make way for
revelation, puts out the light of both, and does muchwhat
the same as if he would persuade a man to put out his eyes,
the better to receive the remote light of an invisible star
by a telescope[1].

5. Immediate revelation being a much easier way for men
to establish their opinions and regulate their conduct, than the
tedious and not always successful labour of strict reasoning,
it is no wonder that some have been very apt to pretend to
revelation, and to persuade themselves that they are under
the peculiar guidance of heaven in their actions and opinions,
especially in those of them which they cannot account for
by the ordinary methods of knowledge and principles of
reason. Hence we see, that, in all ages, men in whom
melancholy has mixed with devotion, or whose conceit of
themselves has raised them into an opinion of a greater
familiarity with God, and a nearer admittance to his favour
than is afforded to others, have often flattered themselves
with a persuasion of an immediate intercourse with the
Deity, and frequent communications from the Divine Spirit.
God, I own, cannot be denied to be able to enlighten the
understanding by a ray darted into the mind immediately
from the fountain of light: this they understand he has
promised to do, and who then has so good a title to expect
it as those who are his peculiar people, chosen by him, and
depending on him[2]?

---

[1] Locke's rigid separation between religion revealed and natural religion became (partly through the *Essay*) characteristic of theology in the eighteenth century, with its mechanically external 'evidence,' and oversight of the 'ground of assent' that is found in the harmony between both the natural and the supernatural revelation and the divine reason latent in man, for the recognition and interpretation of what is revealed.

[2] The extravagance of the sects under the Commonwealth, which

BOOK IV.
CHAP.
XIX.

Enthusiastic impulse.

6. Their minds being thus prepared, whatever groundless opinion comes to settle itself strongly upon their fancies, is an illumination from the Spirit of God, and presently of divine authority: and whatsoever odd action they find in themselves a strong inclination to do, that impulse is concluded to be a call or direction from heaven, and must be obeyed: it is a commission from above, and they cannot err in executing it.

What is meant by Enthusiasm.

7. This I take to be properly *enthusiasm* [1], which, though founded neither on reason nor divine revelation, but rising from the conceits of a warmed or overweening brain, works yet, where it once gets footing, more powerfully on the persuasions and actions of men than either of those two, or both together: men being most forwardly obedient to the impulses

vexed and disturbed his early years, may have been in Locke's view in this chapter.

[1] 'L'enthousiasme,' says Leibniz, 'était au commencement un bon nom, et comme le sophisme marque proprement un exercice de la sagesse, l'enthousiasme signifie qu'il y a une divinité en nous : *Est Deus in nobis* . . . Mais les hommes ayant consacré leurs passions, leurs fantaisies, leurs songes, et jusqu'à leur fureur pour quelque chose de divin, l'enthousiasme commença à signifier un déréglement d'esprit, attribué à la force de quelque divinité . . . Depuis on l'attribue à ceux qui croient *sans fondement* que leurs mouvements viennent de Dieu.' (*Nouveaux Essais*.) The nature, causes, kinds, and cure of enthusiasm were treated of by Henry More, in his *Enthusiasmus Triumphatus*, which appeared in 1662, nearly thirty years before the *Essay*. 'Enthusiasm,' says More, 'is nothing else but a misconceit of being inspired. Now to be inspired is to be moved, in an extraordinary manner, by the power or spirit of God, to act, speak, or think what is holy, just and true. From hence it will be easily understood what enthusiasm is, viz. a full but false persuasion in a man

that he is inspired' (p. 2). 'The enthusiastic spirit,' says Glanvill, 'brings reason into disgrace, denying the use thereof in the affairs of faith and religion' (*Essays*, p. 20). Enthusiasm, thus understood, was satirised by Butler and Swift, in Locke's time, and afterwards by Warburton and Lavington among the bishops, as well as in a host of eighteenth-century polemical tracts, e. g. *A Letter concerning Enthusiasm to my Lord* — (1708); *Reflections upon a Letter concerning Enthusiasm* (1709); *Nature and Consequences of Enthusiasm*, by a Protestant Dissenter (1719); *Enthusiasm explained: with rules to preserve the Mind from being tainted by it* (1739); *A Discourse proving that the Apostles were no Enthusiasts* (1730), by Archibald Campbell, S.T.P., author of *Enquiry into Moral Virtue*; *Christian Piety freed from the many delusions of Modern Enthusiasts* (1755); *Letters on Enthusiasm* (1772); *Essays on Enthusiasm* (1780), by William Green, &c. Enthusiasm, in its favourable meaning, as intellect and will charged with corresponding emotion, is not to be confounded with this 'misconceit of being inspired,' against which Locke and More warn us.

they receive from themselves ; and the whole man is sure
to act more vigorously where the whole man is carried by
a natural motion. For strong conceit, like a new principle,
carries all easily with it, when got above common sense, and
freed from all restraint of reason and check of reflection, it is
heightened into a divine authority, in concurrence with our
own temper and inclination.

8. Though the odd opinions and extravagant actions Enthu-
enthusiasm has run men into were enough to warn them siasm
accepts its
against this wrong principle, so apt to misguide them both in supposed
their belief and conduct: yet the love of something extraor- illumina-
tion with-
dinary, the ease and glory it is to be inspired, and be above out search
and proof.
the common and natural ways of knowledge, so flatters many
men's laziness, ignorance, and vanity, that, when once they
are got into this way of immediate revelation, of illumination
without search, and of certainty without proof and without
examination, it is a hard matter to get them out of it.
Reason is lost upon them, they are above it : they see the
light infused into their understandings, and cannot be mistaken ; it is clear and visible there, like the light of bright
sunshine; shows itself, and needs no other proof but its own
evidence : they feel the hand of God moving them within,
and the impulses of the Spirit, and cannot be mistaken in
what they feel. Thus they support themselves, and are sure
reasoning hath nothing to do with what they see and feel in
themselves : what they have a sensible experience of admits
no doubt, needs no probation. Would he not be ridiculous,
who should require to have it proved to him that the light
shines, and that he sees it? It is its own proof, and can
have no other. When the Spirit brings light into our minds,
it dispels darkness. We see it as we do that of the sun at
noon, and need not the twilight of reason to show it us.
This light from heaven is strong, clear, and pure ; carries its
own demonstration with it : and we may as naturally take
a glow-worm to assist us to discover the sun, as to examine
the celestial ray by our dim candle, reason [1].

---

[1] Cf. ch. ii. § 1. Locke's intuition, 'the candle of the Lord,' or that 'inspiration of the Almighty' which gives man understanding, may be contrasted with the ungrounded conceit of inspiration, here called enthusiasm.

BOOK IV.

CHAP.
XIX.

Enthu-
siasm how
to be dis-
covered.

9. This is the way of talking of these men: they are sure, because they are sure: and their persuasions are right, because they are strong in them. For, when what they say is stripped of the metaphor of seeing and feeling, this is all it amounts to: and yet these similes so impose on them, that they serve them for certainty in themselves, and demonstration to others.

The
supposed
internal
Light
examined.

10. But to examine a little soberly this internal light, and this feeling on which they build so much. These men have, they say, clear light, and they see; they have awakened sense, and they feel: this cannot, they are sure, be disputed them. For when a man says he sees or feels, nobody can deny him that he does so. But here let me ask: This seeing, is it the perception of the truth of the proposition, or of this, that it is a revelation from God? This feeling, is it a perception of an inclination or fancy to do something, or of the Spirit of God moving that inclination? These are two very different perceptions, and must be carefully distinguished, if we would not impose upon ourselves. I may perceive the truth of a proposition, and yet not perceive that it is an immediate revelation from God [1]. I may perceive the truth of a proposition in Euclid, without its being, or my perceiving it to be, a revelation [2]: nay, I may perceive I came not by this knowledge in a natural way, and so may conclude it revealed, without perceiving that it is a revelation of God. Because there be spirits which, without being divinely commissioned, may excite those ideas in me, and lay them in such order before my mind, that I may perceive their connexion. So that the knowledge of any proposition coming into my mind, I know not how, is not a perception that it is from God. Much less is a strong persuasion that it is true, a perception that it is from God, or so much as true [3]. But however it be called light and seeing, I suppose it is at most

---

[1] Except so far as all 'intuitive knowledge' is 'an immediate revelation from God,' who is therein manifested as immanent in our spirits and in the universe.

[2] I.e. a 'supernatural' revelation, and thus inexplicable by *us*, under the customary laws of nature.

[3] For in those cases it would be destitute of the criteria of divine origin that we seek for in the genuine presuppositions of reason, and also in a really miraculous revelation.

but belief and assurance: and the proposition taken for a revelation, is not such as they *know* to be true, but *take* to be true. For where a proposition is known to be true, revelation is needless: and it is hard to conceive how there can be a revelation to any one of what he knows already. If therefore it be a proposition which they are persuaded, but do not know, to be true, whatever they may call it, it is not seeing, but believing. For these are two ways whereby truth comes into the mind, wholly distinct, so that one is not the other. What I see, I know to be so, by the evidence of the thing itself: what I believe, I take to be so upon the testimony of another. But this testimony I must know to be given, or else what ground have I of believing? I must see that it is God that reveals this to me, or else I see nothing [1]. The question then here is: How do I know that God is the revealer of this to me; that this impression is made upon my mind by his Holy Spirit; and that therefore I ought to obey it? If I know not this, how great soever the assurance [2] is that I am possessed with, it is groundless; whatever light I pretend to, it is but *enthusiasm*. For, whether the proposition supposed to be revealed be in itself evidently true, or visibly probable, or, by the natural ways of knowledge, uncertain, the proposition that must be well grounded and manifested to be true, is this, That God is the revealer of it, and that what I take to be a revelation is certainly put into my mind by Him, and is not an illusion dropped in by some other spirit, or raised by my own fancy. For, if I mistake not, these men receive it for true, because they presume God revealed it. Does it not, then, stand them upon to examine upon what grounds they presume it to be a revelation from God? or else all their confidence is mere presumption [3] : and this light they are so

---

[1] But may not what rests only on presumption of probability serve to awaken in one the perception of a latent truth, which, when thus awakened, is *infallibly* discerned to be true?

[2] Yet he says (ch. iv. § 18) that ' wherever we are *sure* that our ideas agree with the reality of things, there is certain real knowledge,' but without adequately noting the marks by which this assurance is distinguished from the 'assurance' of the enthusiast.

[3] 'presumption,' i.e. presumption of probability, not certain or infallible knowledge, may be here used ironically.

BOOK IV.

CHAP.
XIX.

Enthu-
siasm
fails of
Evidence,
that the
Proposi-
tion is
from God.

dazzled with is nothing but an *ignis fatuus*, that leads them constantly round in this circle ; *It is a revelation, because they firmly believe it* ; and *they believe it, because it is a revelation.*

11. In all that is of divine revelation, there is need of no other proof but that it is an inspiration from God : for he can neither deceive nor be deceived. But how shall it be known that any proposition in our minds is a truth infused by God ; a truth that is revealed to us by him, which he declares to us, and therefore we ought to believe? Here it is that enthusiasm fails of the evidence it pretends to. For men thus possessed, boast of a light whereby they say they are enlightened, and brought into the knowledge of this or that truth. But if they know it to be a truth, they must know it to be so, either by its own self-evidence to natural reason, or by the rational proofs that make it out to be so. If they see and know it to be a truth, either of these two ways they in vain suppose it to be a revelation [1]. For they know it to be true the same way that any other man naturally may know that it is so, without the help of revelation. For thus, all the truths, of what kind soever, that men uninspired are enlightened with, came into their minds, and are established there. If they say they know it to be true, because it is a revelation from God, the reason is good : but then it will be demanded how they know it to be a revelation from God. If they say, by the light it brings with it, which shines bright in their minds, and they cannot resist: I beseech them to consider whether this be any more than what we have taken notice of already, viz. that it is a revelation, because they strongly believe it to be true. For all the light they speak of is but a strong, though ungrounded [2] persuasion of their own minds, that it is a truth. For rational grounds from proofs that it is a truth, they must acknowledge to have none; for then it is not received as a revelation, but upon the ordinary grounds that other truths are received : and if they believe it to be true because it is a revelation, and have no other reason for its being a revela-

---

[1] It is a natural revelation either of sense or of reason; not a revelation that is naturally inexplicable by those to whom it appeals. Locke leaves a chasm between the two.

[2] 'ungrounded,' i.e. in intuitive perception.

tion, but because they are fully persuaded, without any other
reason, that it is true, then they believe it to be a revelation
only because they strongly believe it to be a revelation;
which is a very unsafe ground to proceed on, either in our
tenets or actions. And what readier way can there be to run
ourselves into the most extravagant errors and miscarriages,
than thus to set up fancy[1] for our supreme and sole guide,
and to believe any proposition to be true, any action to be
right, only because we believe it to be so? The strength of
our persuasions is no evidence at all of their own rectitude :
crooked things may be as stiff and inflexible as straight : and
men may be as positive and peremptory in error as in truth.
How come else the untractable zealots in different and
opposite parties? For if the light, which every one thinks
he has in his mind, which in this case is nothing but the
strength of his own persuasion, be an evidence that it is from
God, contrary opinions have the same title to be inspirations ;
and God will be not only the Father of lights, but of opposite
and contradictory lights, leading men contrary ways; and
contradictory propositions will be divine truths, if an ungrounded strength of assurance be an evidence that any
proposition is a Divine Revelation.

12. This cannot be otherwise, whilst firmness of persuasion *Firmness*
is made the cause of believing[2], and confidence of being in *of Per-*
suasion no
the right is made an argument of truth. St. Paul himself *Proof that*
any Pro-
believed he did well, and that he had a call to it, when he *position is*
persecuted the Christians, whom he confidently thought in *from God.*
the wrong: but yet it was he, and not they, who were
mistaken. Good men are men still liable to mistakes, and
are sometimes warmly engaged in errors, which they take
for divine truths, shining in their minds with the clearest
light.

13. Light, true light, in the mind is, or can be, nothing else *Light in*
but the evidence of the truth of any proposition ; and if it be *the Mind,*
what.
not a self-evident proposition, all the light it has, or can have,

---

[1] 'fancy'—'phancy' in the early   put in place of a ground in reason for
editions.   so believing.

[2] 'made the cause of believing,' i. e.

BOOK IV.
Chap.
XIX.

is from the clearness and validity of those proofs upon which it is received. To talk of any other light in the understanding is to put ourselves in the dark, or in the power of the Prince of Darkness, and, by our own consent, to give ourselves up to delusion to believe a lie. For, if strength of persuasion be the light which must guide us; I ask how shall any one distinguish between the delusions of Satan, and the inspirations of the Holy Ghost? He can transform himself into an angel of light. And they who are led by this Son of the Morning are as fully satisfied of the illumination, i. e. are as strongly persuaded that they are enlightened by the Spirit of God as any one who is so: they acquiesce and rejoice in it, are actuated by it: and nobody can be more sure, nor more in the right (if their own strong belief may be judge) than they [1].

Revelation must be judged of by Reason.

14. He, therefore, that will not give himself up to all the extravagances of delusion and error must bring this guide of his *light within* to the trial. God when he makes the prophet does not unmake the man. He leaves all his faculties in the natural state, to enable him to judge of his inspirations, whether they be of *divine* original or no [2]. When he illuminates the mind with supernatural light, he does not extinguish that which is natural. If he would have us assent to the truth of any proposition, he either evidences that truth by the usual methods of natural reason, or else makes it known to be a truth which he would have us assent to by his authority, and convinces us that it is from him, by some marks which reason cannot be mistaken in. *Reason must be our last judge and guide in everything* [3]. I do not mean that we must consult reason, and examine whether a proposition revealed

---

[1] Locke's enthusiast substitutes sensuous feeling where spiritual or rational insight is needed. In enthusiastic pretensions to the supernatural, the supposed revelation is approached through sensuous feeling, although, as supersensual, revelation cannot be identified with sensation, however intense.

[2] Is the *test* of the 'divinity' of the 'inspirations' to be found in the inspirations themselves, or in something external to them, e.g. physical miracles, as Locke assumes in the following section?

[3] This sentence might be taken for a motto to the *Essay*, and may be accepted when 'reason' means intelligence based upon the entire constitution of man,—spiritual as well as sensuous. Our judgments and acts must all be determined by what is reasonable, in the large meaning of 'reason.'

from God can be made out by natural principles[1], and if it
cannot, that then we may reject it : but consult it we must,
and by it examine whether it be a revelation from God or
no : and if reason finds it to be revealed from God, reason
then declares for it as much as for any other truth, and makes
it one of her dictates. Every conceit that thoroughly warms
our fancies must pass for an inspiration, if there be nothing
but the strength of our persuasions, whereby to judge of our
persuasions : if reason must not examine their truth by something extrinsical to the persuasions themselves, inspirations
and delusions, truth and falsehood, will have the same
measure, and will not be possible to be distinguished.

15. If this internal light, or any proposition which under
that title we take for inspired, be conformable to the principles
of reason, or to the word of God, which is attested revelation,
reason warrants it, and we may safely receive it for true, and
be guided by it in our belief and actions : if it receive no
testimony nor evidence from either of these rules, we cannot
take it for a revelation, or so much as for true, till we have
some other mark that it is a revelation, besides our believing
that it is so. Thus we see the holy men of old, who had
revelations from God, had something else besides that internal
light of assurance in their own minds, to testify to them that
it was from God. They were not left to their own persuasions
alone, that those persuasions were from God, but had *outward
signs* to convince them of the Author of those revelations.
And when they were to convince others, they had a power
given them to justify the truth of their commission from
heaven, and by visible signs to assert the divine authority of
a message they were sent with. Moses saw the bush burn
without being consumed, and heard a voice out of it : this was
something besides finding an impulse upon his mind to go to

BOOK IV.

CHAP.
XIX.

Belief no
Proof of
Revela-
tion.

---

[1] 'Revelations' may be reasonable
in themselves, and man may be required
by his share of reason to accept them
as divine, although they cannot be discovered by human reason, judging
according to the custom of nature, and
presuppose the application of higher
laws than any that are within the
sphere of the scientific interpreter of
the sensible world. They exemplify
a sphere of law or order in the universe of reality that cannot be fully
'made out' by human understanding.

Pharaoh, that he might bring his brethren out of Egypt: and yet he thought not this enough to authorize him to go with that message, till God, by another miracle of his rod turned into a serpent, had assured him of a power to testify his mission, by the same miracle repeated before them whom he was sent to. Gideon was sent by an angel to deliver Israel from the Midianites, and yet he desired a sign to convince him that this commission was from God. These, and several the like instances to be found among the prophets of old, are enough to show that they thought not an inward seeing or persuasion of their own minds, without any other proof, a sufficient evidence that it was from God; though the Scripture does not everywhere mention their demanding or having such proofs.

Criteria
of a
Divine
Revela-
tion.

16. In what I have said I am far from denying, that God can, or doth sometimes enlighten men's minds in the apprehending of certain truths or excite them to good actions, by the immediate influence and assistance of the Holy Spirit, *without any extraordinary signs accompanying it.* But in such cases too we have reason and Scripture; unerring rules to know whether it be from God or no. Where the truth embraced is consonant to the revelation in the written word of God, or the action conformable to the dictates of right reason or holy writ, we may be assured that we run no risk in entertaining it as such: because, though perhaps it be not an immediate revelation from God, extraordinarily operating on our minds, yet we are sure it is warranted by that revelation which he has given us of truth. But it is not the strength of our private persuasion within ourselves, that can warrant it to be a light or motion from heaven: nothing can do that but the written Word of God without us, or that standard of reason which is common to us with all men[1]. Where reason or Scripture is express for any opinion or action, we may receive it as of divine authority: but it is not the strength of our own persuasions which can by itself give it that stamp. The bent

---

[1] An appeal to 'reason,' whether as determined by the ordinary custom of nature, or as cognizant in faith of supernatural law and purpose, *is,* according to Locke, equally an appeal to this ultimate standard. Cf. Locke's *Discourse of Miracles.*

of our own minds may favour it as much as we please: that BOOK IV.
may show it to be a fondling of our own, but will by
no means prove it to be an offspring of heaven, and of divine CHAP.
original [1].] XIX.

[1] Locke at one time meant to introduce, in this part of the *Essay*, the substance of his posthumous treatise on *The Conduct of the Understanding*. He thus mentions his design to Molyneux:—'I have lately got a little leisure to think of some additions to my book against the next [fourth] edition, and within these few days have fallen upon a subject that I know not how far it will lead me. I have written several passages of it; but the matter the further I go opens the more upon me, and I cannot yet get sight of any end of it. The title of the chapters will be " Of the Conduct of the Understanding," which, if I shall pursue as far as I imagine it will reach, and as it deserves, will, I conclude, make the largest chapter of my *Essay*. It is well for you you are not near me; I should be always pestering you with my notions and papers and reveries.

It would be a great happiness to have a man of thought to lay them before, and a friend that would deal candidly and freely.' (*Locke to Molyneux*, April 10, 1697.) On which Molyneux comments in his reply (May 15). The causes and cure of error are expanded in this posthumous treatise into a code of intellectual ethics, adapted to an understanding that has to form its judgments in the way in which, according to the *Essay*, all human judgments about things must be formed, i. e. in constant dependence on data of experience. The treatise is thus a protest against man's tendency to prejudge, in the absence of sufficient evidence; or, in the presence of evidence, but with inadequate criteria of its sufficiency, which make professed inquiry illusory. The following chapter is in the same strain.

CHAPTER XX.

OF WRONG ASSENT, OR ERROR [1].

BOOK IV.

CHAP. XX.

Causes of Error, or how men come to give assent contrary to probability.

1. KNOWLEDGE being to be had only of visible and certain truth, *error* [1] is not a fault of our knowledge, but a mistake of our judgment giving assent to that which is not true.

But if assent be grounded on likelihood, if the proper object and motive of our assent be probability, and that probability consists in what is laid down in the foregoing chapters, it will be demanded *how men come to give their assents contrary to probability.* For there is nothing more common than contrariety of opinions [2]; nothing more obvious than that one man wholly disbelieves what another only doubts of, and a third stedfastly believes and firmly adheres to [3].

The reasons whereof, though they may be very various, yet, I suppose may all be reduced to these four:

    I. *Want of proofs.*

    II. *Want of ability to use them.*

    III. *Want of will to see them.*

    IV. *Wrong measures of probability.*

---

[1] 'error'—'Errour,' in the early editions. 'L'erreur,' says Malebranche, ' est la cause de la misère des hommes ; c'est le mauvais principe qui a produit le mal dans le monde ; c'est elle qui a fait naître et qui entretient dans notre âme tous les maux qui nous affligent, et nous ne devons point espérer de bonheur solide et véritable qu'en travaillant sérieusement à l'éviter.' (*Recherche de la Vérité,* I. I.) The *Recherche,* with which Locke must have been familiar, is virtually a treatise on the nature and causes of error, in analogy too with the four causes of

error signalised by Locke in this chapter, which may be compared with the *Recherche,* as also with the first book of the *Novum Organum.*

[2] ' contrariety of opinions ' implies error, for they cannot be all adequately true. Yet opinions that are contrary may be one-sided truths, and steps towards the fuller discernment of truth in a higher unity.

[3] Error, according to Locke, is wrong judgment in things which, at man's point of view, admit of doubt. It is thus confined to the presumptions of probability by which, in defect of

2. *First*, By *want of proofs*, I do not mean only the want of those proofs which are nowhere extant, and so are nowhere to be had ; but the want even of those proofs which are in being, or might be procured. And thus men want proofs, who have not the convenience or opportunity to make experi- ments and observations themselves, tending to the proof of any proposition ; nor likewise the convenience to inquire into and collect the testimonies of others : and in this state are the greatest part of mankind, who are given up to labour, and enslaved to the necessity of their mean condition, whose lives are worn out only in the provisions for living[1]. These men's opportunities of knowledge and inquiry are commonly as narrow as their fortunes ; and their understandings are but little instructed, when all their whole time and pains is laid out to still the croaking of their own bellies, or the cries of their children. It is not to be expected that a man who drudges on all his life in a laborious trade, should be more knowing in the variety of things done in the world than a packhorse, who is driven constantly forwards and backwards in a narrow lane and dirty road, only to market, should be skilled in the geography of the country. Nor is it at all more possible, that he who wants leisure, books, and languages, and the opportunity of conversing with variety of men, should be in a condition to collect those testimonies and observations which are in being, and are necessary to make out many, nay most, of the propositions that, in the societies of men, are judged of the greatest moment ; or to find out grounds of assurance so great as the belief of the points he would build on them is thought necessary. So that a great part of mankind are, by the natural and unalterable state of things in this world, and the constitution of human affairs, unavoidably given over to invincible ignorance of those proofs on which others build, and which are necessary to establish those

Omniscience, human life is guided, and by which the experience and moral condition of the person who ‘ assents ’ is tested to a degree that it cannot be by his intuitions of certainties. Locke's four causes of error might be resolved into his first and last.

[1] The idea of intellectually educating every member of the community has originated and gained currency since this was written.

BOOK IV.

CHAP. XX.

opinions : the greatest part of men, having much to do to get the means of living, are not in a condition to look after those of learned and laborious inquiries [1].

Objection, What shall become of those who want Proofs? Answered.

3. What shall we say, then? Are the greatest part of mankind, by the necessity of their condition, subjected to unavoidable ignorance, in those things which are of greatest importance to them? (for of those it is obvious to inquire.) Have the bulk of mankind no other guide but accident and blind chance to conduct them to their happiness or misery? Are the current opinions, and licensed guides of every country sufficient evidence and security to every man to venture his great concernments on; nay, his everlasting happiness or misery? Or can those be the certain and infallible oracles and standards of truth, which teach one thing in Christendom and another in Turkey? Or shall a poor countryman be eternally happy, for having the chance to be born in Italy ; or a day-labourer be unavoidably lost, because he had the ill-luck to be born in England? How ready some men may be to say some of these things, I will not here examine : but this I am sure, that men must allow one or other of these to be true, (let them choose which they please,) or else grant that God has furnished men with faculties sufficient to direct them in the way they should take [2], if they will but seriously employ them that way, when their ordinary vocations allow them the leisure. No man is so wholly taken up with the attendance on the means of living, as to have no spare time at all to think of his soul, and inform himself in matters of religion. Were men as intent upon this as they are on things of lower concernment, there are none so enslaved to the necessities of life who might not find many vacancies that might be husbanded to this advantage of their knowledge.

People hindered

4. Besides those whose improvements and informations are straitened by the narrowness of their fortunes, there are others

---

[1] The large dependence of individuals upon experts, and the authority of other persons, in the formation of their opinions, is implied in this state of affairs. Experts, too, become mere specialists more and more, as the mass of human experience increases and thus becomes more incapable of assimilation by each man.

[2] Here as elsewhere Locke shows an unphilosophic indifference to merely speculative truth and its elevating influence upon the intellect and character.

whose largeness of fortune would plentifully enough supply
books, and other requisites for clearing of doubts, and discovering of truth: but they are cooped in close, by the laws
of their countries, and the strict guards of those whose interest
it is to keep them ignorant, lest, knowing more, they should
believe the less in them. These are as far, nay further, from
the liberty and opportunities of a fair inquiry, than these poor
and wretched labourers we before spoke of: and however they
may seem high and great, are confined to narrowness of
thought, and enslaved in that which should be the freest part
of man, their understandings. This is generally the case of all
those who live in places where care is taken to propagate truth
without knowledge ; where men are forced, at a venture, to be
of the religion of the country ; and must therefore swallow
down opinions, as silly people do empiric's pills, without
knowing what they are made of, or how they will work, and
having nothing to do but believe that they will do the cure :
but in this are much more miserable than they, in that they
are not at liberty to refuse swallowing what perhaps they had
rather let alone ; or to choose the physician, to whose conduct
they would trust themselves [1].

5. *Secondly,* Those who *want skill to use those evidences*
they have of probabilities ; who cannot carry a train of consequences in their heads ; nor weigh exactly the preponderancy
of contrary proofs and testimonies, making every circumstance
its due allowance ; may be easily misled to assent to positions
that are not probable. There are some men of one, some but
of two syllogisms, and no more ; and others that can but
advance one step further. These cannot always discern that
side on which the strongest proofs lie ; cannot constantly
follow that which in itself is the more probable opinion. Now
that there is such a difference between men, in respect of their
understandings, I think nobody, who has had any conversation
with his neighbours, will question : though he never was at
Westminster-Hall or the Exchange on the one hand, nor at
Alms-houses or Bedlam on the other. Which great difference

---

[1] The preceding may be compared with Bacon's *idola specus.*

BOOK IV.

CHAP. XX.

in men's intellectuals, whether it rises from any defect in the organs of the body, particularly adapted to thinking; or in the dulness or untractableness of those faculties for want of use; or, as some think, in the natural differences of men's souls themselves; or some, or all of these together; it matters not here to examine: only this is evident, that there is a difference of degrees in men's understandings, apprehensions, and reasonings, to so great a latitude, that one may, without doing injury to mankind, affirm, that there is a greater distance between some men and others in this respect, than between some men and some beasts[1]. But how this comes about is a speculation, though of great consequence, yet not necessary to our present purpose[2].

Third cause of Error, Want of Will to use them.

6. *Thirdly,* There are another sort of people that want proofs, not because they are out of their reach, but *because they will 'not use them*: who, though they have riches and leisure enough, and want neither parts nor [[3] other helps, are yet never the better for them. Their hot pursuit of pleasure, or constant drudgery in business, engages some men's thoughts elsewhere: laziness and oscitancy[4] in general, or a particular aversion for books, study, and meditation, keep others from any serious thoughts at all; and some out of fear that an impartial inquiry would not favour those opinions which best suit their prejudices, lives, and designs, content themselves, without examination, to take upon trust what they find convenient and in fashion. Thus, most men, even of those

---

[1] The individual inequality of men, intellectual and other, is a natural law, with which some modern democratic maxims are in open collision. This second cause of error is virtually a modification of Locke's fourth cause.

[2] 'Quant à ceux qui manquent de capacité, il y en a peut-être moins qu'on ne pense; je crois que le bon sens avec l'application peuvent suffire à tout ce qui ne demande pas la promptitude. . . . Quelque différence originale qu'il y ait entre nos âmes (comme je crois en effet qu'il y en a) il est toujours sûr que l'une pourrait aller aussi loin que l'autre (mais non pas peut-être si vite) si elle était menée comme il faut.' (*Nouveaux Essais.*)

[3] In first edition—'learning, may yet, through their hot pursuit of pleasure, or business, or else out of laziness, or fear that the doctrines whose truth they would inquire into would not suit well with their opinions, lives, or designs, may never come to the knowledge of, nor give their assent to, those probabilities which.'

[4] 'oscitancy'—gaping idleness, ab *ore ciendo.* Cf. *Conduct of the Understanding,* § 37.

that might do otherwise, pass their lives without an acquaintance with, much less a rational assent to, probabilities they are concerned to know, though they] lie so much within their view, that, to be convinced of them, they need but turn their eyes that way. We know some men will not read a letter which is supposed to bring ill news ; and many men forbear to cast up their accounts, or so much as think upon their estates, who have reason to fear their affairs are in no very good posture. How men, whose plentiful fortunes allow them leisure to improve their understandings, can satisfy themselves with a lazy ignorance, I cannot tell : but methinks they have a low opinion of their souls, who lay out all their incomes in provisions for the body, and employ none of it to procure the means and helps of knowledge ; who take great care to appear always in a neat and splendid outside, and would think themselves miserable in coarse clothes, or a patched coat, and yet contentedly suffer their minds to appear abroad in a piebald livery of coarse patches and borrowed shreds, such as it has pleased chance, or their country tailor (I mean the common opinion of those they have conversed with) to clothe them in. I will not here mention how unreasonable this is for men that ever think of a future state, and their concernment in it, which no rational man can avoid to do sometimes : nor shall I take notice what a shame and confusion it is to the greatest contemners of knowledge, to be found ignorant in things they are concerned to know[1]. But this at least is worth the consideration of those who call themselves gentlemen, That, however they may think credit, respect, power, and authority the concomitants of their birth and fortune, yet they will find all these still carried away from them by men of lower condition, who surpass them in knowledge. They who are blind will always be led by those that see, or else fall into the ditch : and he is certainly the most subjected, the most enslaved, who is so in his understanding[2].

---

[1] This misleading influence might come under Locke's first cause of error, in so far as 'want of proofs' is due to want of will. Cf. Malebranche, *Recherche*, Liv. V.

[2] 'Pour ce qui se rapporte à la foi, plusieurs regardent la pensée qui les pourrait porter à la discussion comme une tentation du démon, qu'ils ne croient pouvoir mieux surmonter qu'en

BOOK IV.
—•—
CHAP. XX.

In the foregoing instances some of the causes have been shown of wrong assent, and how it comes to pass, that probable doctrines are not always received with an assent proportionable to the reasons which are to be had for their probability: but hitherto we have considered only such probabilities whose proofs do exist, but do not appear to him who embraces the error.

Fourth cause of Error, Wrong Measures of Probability: which are—

7. *Fourthly,* There remains yet the last sort, who, even where the real probabilities appear, and are plainly laid before them, do not admit of the conviction, nor yield unto manifest reasons, but do either ἐπέχειν, suspend their assent [1], or give it to the less probable opinion. And to this danger are those exposed who have taken up *wrong measures of probability,* which are:

   I. *Propositions that are not in themselves certain and evident, but doubtful and false, taken up for principles* [2].

   II. *Received hypotheses.*

   III. *Predominant passions or inclinations.*

   IV. *Authority.*

I. Doubtful Propositions taken for Principles.

8. I. The first and firmest ground of probability is the conformity anything has to our own knowledge; especially that part of our knowledge which we have embraced, and continue to look on as *principles.* These have so great an influence upon our opinions, that it is usually by them we judge of truth, and measure probability; to that degree, that what is inconsistent with our principles, is so far from passing for probable with us, that it will not be allowed possible. The reverence borne to these principles is so great,

---

tournant l'esprit à toute autre chose. (*Nouveaux Essais.*)

[1] This ἐποχή, or suspense of judgment on all possible questions, was the profession of the Pyrrhonists and other Greek sceptics, adopted as means towards the ἀταραξία, or peace of mind, which this philosophy promised to its disciples.

[2] Cf. Bk. I. ch. iii. § 24 ; also Bk. IV.

ch. vii. It was against this 'wrong measure of probability' that, under the form of assault on 'innate principles,' the *Essay* was originally directed. Locke always prefers the reasoning that is made to turn on facts and events, to that which proceeds upon the absolute validity of abstract maxims.

and their authority so paramount to all other, that the testimony, not only of other men, but the evidence of our own
senses are often rejected, when they offer to vouch anything
contrary to these established rules. How much the doctrine
of *innate principles*, and that principles are not to be proved or
questioned, has contributed to this, I will not here examine [1].
This I readily grant, that one truth cannot contradict another :
but withal I take leave also to say, that every one ought very
carefully to beware what he admits for a principle, to examine
it strictly, and see whether he certainly knows it to be true
of itself, by its own evidence, or whether he does only with
assurance believe it to be so, upon the authority of others.
For he hath a strong bias put into his understanding, which
will unavoidably misguide his assent, who hath imbibed *wrong
principles*, and has blindly given himself up to the authority
of any opinion in itself not evidently true.

9. There is nothing more ordinary than children's receiving Instilled
into their minds propositions (especially about matters of in child-
religion) from their parents, nurses, or those about them : hood.
which being insinuated into their unwary as well as unbiassed
understandings, and fastened by degrees, are at last (equally
whether true or false) riveted there by long custom and
education, beyond all possibility of being pulled out again.
For men, when they are grown up, reflecting upon their
opinions, and finding those of this sort to be as ancient in their
minds as their very memories, not having observed their early
insinuation, nor by what means they got them [1], they are apt
to reverence them as sacred things, and not to suffer them to
be profaned, touched, or questioned : they look on them as
the Urim and Thummim set up in their minds immediately
by God himself, to be the great and unerring deciders of truth
and falsehood, and the judges to which they are to appeal in
all manner of controversies [2].

[1] Hence the practical importance, in
Locke's view, of his inquiry into the
conditions on which man's ideas,
intuitions, and beliefs depend.

[2] 'We thus mistake the infusions of
education for the principles of universal
nature. . . . Like the hermit, we think
the sun shines nowhere but in our
cell, and all the world to be in darkness but ourselves.' (Glanvill, *Scepsis*,
pp. 95, 97.)

BOOK IV.
CHAP. XX.
Of irresistible efficacy.

10. This opinion of his principles (let them be what they will) being once established in any one's mind, it is easy to be imagined what reception any proposition shall find, how clearly soever proved, that shall invalidate their authority, or at all thwart with these internal oracles; whereas the grossest absurdities and improbabilities, being but agreeable to such principles, go down glibly, and are easily digested. The great obstinacy that is to be found in men firmly believing quite contrary opinions, though many times equally absurd, in the various religions of mankind, are as evident a proof as they are an unavoidable consequence of this way of reasoning from received traditional principles. So that men will disbelieve their own eyes, renounce the evidence of their senses, and give their own experience the lie, rather than admit of anything disagreeing with these sacred tenets. Take an intelligent Romanist [1] that, from the first dawning of any notions in his understanding, hath had this principle constantly inculcated, viz. that he must believe as the church (i.e. those of his communion) believes, or that the pope is infallible [2], and this he never so much as heard questioned, till at forty or fifty years old he met with one of other principles: how is he prepared easily to swallow, not only against all probability, but even the clear evidence of his senses, the doctrine of *transubstantiation*? This principle has such an influence on his mind, that he will believe that to be flesh which he sees to be bread [3]. And what way will you take to

---

[1] 'an intelligent Romanist'—'un Luthérien de bon sens,' in the French version.

[2] 'or that the pope is infallible'— omitted in the French version.

[3] The necessary irrationality of 'transubstantiation' would not be granted by the philosophical Romanist, nor of consubstantiation by a philosophical Lutheran. 'Il paraît bien, monsieur,' says Leibniz, commenting on this passage, 'que vous n'êtes pas assez instruit des sentiments des évangéliques qui admettent la *présence réelle* du corps de notre Seigneur dans l'eucharistie. Ils se sont expliqués mille fois qu'ils ne veulent point de *consubstantiation* du pain et du vin, avec la chair et le sang de Jésus-Christ, et encore moins qu'une même chose soit chair et pain ensemble. Ils enseignent seulement qu'en recevant les symboles visibles on reçoit d'une manière invisible et surnaturelle le corps du Sauveur sans qu'il soit enfermé dans le pain. Et la présence qu'ils entendent n'est point locale ou spatiale pour ainsi dire, c'est-à-dire déterminée par les dimensions du corps présent, de sorte que tout ce que les sens y peuvent opposer ne les regarde point. Et pour faire voire que les inconvénients qu'on

convince a man of any improbable opinion he holds, who, BOOK IV.
with some philosophers, hath laid down this as a foundation CHAP. XX.
of reasoning, That he must believe his reason (for so men improperly call arguments drawn from their principles) against
his senses? Let an enthusiast be principled that he or his
teacher is inspired, and acted by an immediate communication of the Divine Spirit, and you in vain bring the
evidence of clear reasons against his doctrine. Whoever,
therefore, have imbibed wrong principles, are not, in things
inconsistent with these principles, to be moved by the most
apparent and convincing probabilities, till they are so candid
and ingenuous to themselves, as to be persuaded to examine
even those very principles, which many never suffer themselves to do.

11. II. Next to these are men whose understandings are II. Re-
cast into a mould, and fashioned just to the size of a received ceived
hypothesis[1]. The difference between these and the former, is, theses.
that they will admit of matter of fact, and agree with dissenters
in that; but differ only in assigning of reasons and explaining
the manner of operation. These are not at that open defiance
with their senses, with the former: they can endure to hearken
to their information a little more patiently; but will by no
means admit of their reports in the explanation of things;

---

pourrait tirer de la raison ne les
touchent point non plus, ils dé-
clarent que ce qu'ils entendent par la
substance du corps ne consiste point
dans l'entendue ou dimension; et ils ne
font point difficulté d'admettre que le
corps glorieux de Jésus-Christ garde
une certaine présence ordinaire et
locale, mais convenable à son état,
dans le lieu sublime où il se trouve
tout différent de cette présence sacra-
mentale dont il s'agit ici, ou de sa présence miraculeuse avec laquelle il
gouverne l'Église. . . . Pour montrer
l'absurdité de leur doctrine, il faudrait
démontrer que toute l'essence du corps
ne consiste que dans l'étendue et de
ce qui est uniquement mesuré par là.'
(*Nouveaux Essais.*) This comment,

confined to the Lutheran consubstantiation, suggests that Leibniz used the
French version of Locke's *Essay* instead
of the original.

[1] Cf. Bacon on the abuse of hypothesis, in the first Book of the *Novum
Organum*, and Spinoza on adequate
and inadequate ideas, and on *intellectus*
and *imaginatio*, in his *De Intellectus
Emendatione*, vii–x. Unwarranted
'principles' are the wrong measure of
probability that is apt to beset deductive
reasonings; unverified hypothesis is
the besetting sin of inductive inquiry,
which is so ready to adapt nature,
with its infinite complexities, to our
thoughts, instead of bringing them
more nearly into harmony with the
ideas that are latent in Nature.

nor be prevailed on by probabilities, which would convince them that things are not brought about just after the same manner that they have decreed within themselves that they are. Would it not be an insufferable thing for a learned professor, and that which his scarlet would blush at, to have his authority of forty years standing, wrought out of hard rock, Greek and Latin, with no small expense of time and candle, and confirmed by general tradition and a reverend beard, in an instant overturned by an upstart novelist? Can any one expect that he should be made to confess, that what he taught his scholars thirty years ago was all error and mistake; and that he sold them hard words and ignorance at a very dear rate. What probabilities, I say, are sufficient to prevail in such a case? And who ever, by the most cogent arguments, will be prevailed with to disrobe himself at once of all his old opinions, and pretences to knowledge and learning, which with hard study he hath all this time been labouring for; and turn himself out stark naked, in quest afresh of new notions [1]? All the arguments that can be used will be as little able to prevail, as the wind did with the traveller to part with his cloak, which he held only the faster. To this of wrong hypothesis may be reduced the errors that may be occasioned by a true hypothesis, or right principles, but not rightly understood [2]. There is nothing more familiar than this. The instances of men contending for different opinions, which they all derive from the infallible

---

[1] As Descartes tried to do. 'Those persons' (says Glanvill), 'who have always lived at home, and have never seen any other country than their native one, are apt confidently to persuade themselves that their own is the best, because it is their own; whereas they that have travelled and observed other places speak more candidly of their native soil. So those confined understandings, that never looked beyond the opinions in which they were bred, are exceedingly assured of the truth and comparative excellence of their own tenants; whereas the larger minds, that have traversed the divers climates of opinions, and considered the various sentiments of inquiring men, are more cautious in their conclusions and more sparing in their affirmations.' (Glanvill, *Essays.*) The first step in philosophical intelligence of the universe is consciousness of our ignorance of it, and the last is little more than the discovery of why we are thus ignorant. The profoundest searchers after truth are those who have through life added to their real knowledge by diminishing its apparent bulk.' (*Essays.*)

[2] Cf. *Novum Organum*, I. 19.

truth of the Scripture, are an undeniable proof of it.   All that
call themselves Christians, allow the text that says, μετανοεῖτε,
to carry in it the obligation to a very weighty duty.   But yet
how very erroneous will one of their practices be, who, understanding nothing but the French, take this rule with one
translation to be, *Repentez-vous*, repent; or with the other,
Fatiez pénitence, do penance.

12. III. Probabilities which cross men's appetites and prevail- III. Pre-
ing passions run the same fate [1].   Let ever so much probability dominant
Passions.
hang on one side of a covetous man's reasoning, and money
on the other; it is easy to foresee which will outweigh.   Earthly
minds, like mud walls, resist the strongest batteries: and
though, perhaps, sometimes the force of a clear argument may
make some impression, yet they nevertheless stand firm, and
keep out the enemy, truth, that would captivate or disturb
them.   Tell a man passionately in love, that he is jilted; bring
a score of witnesses of the falsehood of his mistress, it is ten
to one but three kind words of hers shall invalidate all their
testimonies.   *Quod volumus, facile credimus*; what suits our
wishes, is forwardly believed, is, I suppose, what every one
hath more than once experimented: and though men cannot
always openly gainsay or resist the force of manifest probabilities that make against them, yet yield they not to the
argument.   Not but that it is the nature of the understanding
constantly to close with the more probable side; but yet
a man hath a power to suspend and restrain its inquiries, and
not permit a full and satisfactory examination, as far as the
matter in question is capable, and will bear it to be made.
Until that be done, there will be always these two ways left
of evading the most apparent probabilities:

13. First, That the arguments being (as for the most part Two
they are) brought in words, *there may be a fallacy latent in them*: Means of
evading
and the consequences being, perhaps, many in train, they may Proba-
be some of them incoherent.   There are very few discourses bilities:
I. Sup-

---

[1] 'Intellectus humanus luminis sicci   also Spinoza's 2nd letter to Oldenburg,
non est; sed recipit infusionem a   in which this aphorism of Bacon's is
voluntate et affectibus, id quod generat   referred to.   But the *lumen siccum* of
ad quod vult scientias: quod enim   the understanding, measured only by
mavult homo verum esse, potius   sense, is not the atmosphere in which
credit.' (*Novum Organum*, I. 49.) See   to judge of spiritual realities.

BOOK IV.
CHAP. XX.
posed
Fallacy
latent in
the words
employed.

so short, clear, and consistent, to which most men may not, with satisfaction enough to themselves, raise this doubt ; and from whose conviction they may not, without reproach of disingenuity or unreasonableness, set themselves free with the old reply, *Non persuadebis, etiamsi persuaseris* ; though I cannot answer, I will not yield.

Supposed
unknown
Arguments
for the
contrary.

14. Secondly, Manifest probabilities may be evaded, and the assent withheld, upon this suggestion, That *I know not yet all that may be said on the contrary side.* And therefore, though I be beaten, it is not necessary I should yield, not knowing what forces there are in reserve behind. This is a refuge against conviction so open and so wide, that it is hard to determine when a man is quite out of the verge of it.

What Probabilities
naturally
determine
the Assent.

15. But yet there is some end of it ; and a man having carefully inquired into all the grounds of probability and unlikeliness ; done his utmost to inform himself in all particulars fairly, and cast up the sum total on both sides ; may, in most cases, come to acknowledge, upon the whole matter, on which side the probability rests : wherein some proofs in matter of reason, being suppositions upon universal experience, are so cogent and clear, and some testimonies in matter of fact so universal, that he cannot refuse his assent. So that I think we may conclude, that, in propositions, where though the proofs in view are of most moment, yet there are sufficient grounds to suspect that there is either fallacy in words, or certain proofs as considerable to be produced on the contrary side ; there assent, suspense, or dissent, are often voluntary actions. But where the proofs are such as make it highly probable, and there is not sufficient ground to suspect that there is either fallacy of words (which sober and serious consideration may discover) nor equally valid proofs yet undiscovered, latent on the other side (which also the nature of the thing may, in some cases, make plain to a considerate man ;) there, I think, a man who has weighed them can scarce refuse his assent to the side on which the greater probability appears. Whether it be probable that a promiscuous jumble of printing letters should often fall into a method and order, which should stamp on paper a coherent discourse [1] ; or that

[1] So Cicero, *De Natura Deorum*, II. 37.

a blind fortuitous concourse of atoms, not guided by an under- BOOK IV.
standing agent, should frequently constitute the bodies of any CHAP. XX.
species of animals: in these and the like cases, I think, nobody
that considers them can be one jot at a stand which side
to take, nor at all waver in his assent. Lastly, when there
can be no supposition (the thing in its own nature indifferent,
and wholly depending upon the testimony of witnesses) that
there is as fair testimony against, as for the matter of fact
attested; which by inquiry is to be learned, v. g. whether
there was one thousand seven hundred years ago such a man
at Rome as Julius Cæsar: in all such cases, I say, I think it
is not in any rational man's power to refuse his assent; but
that it necessarily follows, and closes with such probabilities.
In other less clear cases, I think it is in man's power to suspend
his assent; and perhaps content himself with the proofs he
has, if they favour the opinion that suits with his inclination
or interest, and so stop from further search. But that a man
should afford his assent to that side on which the less probability appears to him, seems to me utterly impracticable, and
as impossible as it is to believe the same thing probable and
improbable at the same time.

16. As knowledge is no more arbitrary than perception; Where it
so, I think, assent is no more in our power than knowledge. is in our
When the agreement of any two ideas appears to our minds, suspend
whether immediately or by the assistance of reason, I can no our Judg-
more refuse to perceive, no more avoid knowing it, than I can ment.
avoid seeing those objects which I turn my eyes to, and look
on in daylight; and what upon full examination I find the
most probable, I cannot deny my assent to. But, though we
cannot hinder our knowledge, where the agreement is once
perceived; nor our assent, where the probability manifestly
appears upon due consideration of all the measures of it: yet
we can hinder both *knowledge* and *assent, by stopping our
inquiry*, and not employing our faculties in the search of any
truth. If it were not so, ignorance, error, or infidelity, could
not in any case be a fault. Thus, in some cases we can prevent
or suspend our assent: but can a man versed in modern or
ancient history doubt whether there is such a place as Rome,
or whether there was such a man as Julius Cæsar? Indeed,

BOOK IV.
CHAP XX.

there are millions of truths that a man is not, or may not think himself concerned to know; as whether our king Richard the Third was crooked or no; or whether Roger Bacon was a mathematician or a magician. In these and such like cases, where the assent one way or other is of no importance to the interest of any one; no action, no concernment of his following or depending thereon, there it is not strange that the mind should give itself up to the common opinion, or render itself to the first comer. These and the like opinions are of so little weight and moment, that, like motes in the sun, their tendencies are very rarely taken notice of. They are there, as it were, by chance, and the mind lets them float at liberty. But where the mind judges that the proposition has concernment in it: where the assent or not assenting is thought to draw consequences of moment after it, and good and evil to depend on choosing or refusing the right side, and the mind sets itself seriously to inquire and examine the probability: there I think it is not in our choice to take which side we please, if manifest odds appear on either. The greater probability, I think, in that case will determine the assent: and a man can no more avoid assenting, or taking it to be true, where he perceives the greater probability, than he can avoid knowing it to be true, where he perceives the agreement or disagreement of any two ideas.

If this be so, the foundation of error will lie in wrong measures of probability[1]; as the foundation of vice in wrong measures of good.

IV. Authority.

17. IV. The fourth and last wrong measure of probability I shall take notice of, and which keeps in ignorance or error more people than all the other together, is that which I have mentioned in the foregoing chapter: I mean the giving up

---

[1] But Locke guards against Bacon's sanguine anticipation of the levelling consequences of the adoption of right methods of induction and 'measures of probability,' and the Baconian ideal of the knowledge of nature that is thus attainable by man. 'Nostra vero inveniendi scientias,' says Bacon, 'ea est ratio, ut non multum ingeniorum acumini et robori relinquatur; sed quae ingenia et in- tellectus fere exaequet.' (*Nov. Org.* I. 61.) 'Nostra via inveniendi scientias exaequat fere ingenia, et non multum excellentiae eorum relinquit: cum omnia per certissimas regulas et demonstrationes transigat.' (122.) Locke, on the contrary, enlarges upon the infinite subtlety of the universe which we try to interpret, and the inevitable differences of faculty on the part of its human interpreters.

our assent to the common received opinions[1], either of our BOOK IV.
friends or party, neighbourhood or country. How many men CHAP. XX.
have no other ground for their tenets, than the supposed
honesty, or learning, or number of those of the same profession? As if honest or bookish men could not err; or
truth were to be established by the vote of the multitude:
yet this with most men serves the turn. The tenet has had
the attestation of reverend antiquity; it comes to me with
the passport of former ages, and therefore I am secure in the
reception I give it: other men have been and are of the same
opinion, (for that is all is said,) and therefore it is reasonable
for me to embrace it. A man may more justifiably throw
up cross and pile for his opinions, than take them up by such
measures. All men are liable to error, and most men are
in many points, by passion or interest, under temptation to it.
If we could but see the secret motives that influenced the
men of name and learning in the world, and the leaders of
parties, we should not always find that it was the embracing
of truth for its own sake, that made them espouse the
doctrines they owned and maintained. This at least is
certain, there is not an opinion so absurd, which a man may
not receive upon this ground. There is no error to be named,
which has not had its professors: and a man shall never want
crooked paths to walk in, if he thinks that he is in the right
way, wherever he has the footsteps of others to follow[2].

[1] 'Quant aux opinions reçues, elles ont pour elles quelque chose d'approchant à ce qui donne ce qu'on appelle *présomption* chez les jurisconsultes; et quoiqu'on ne soit point obligé de les suivre toujours sans preuves, on n'est pas autorisé non plus à les détruire dans l'esprit d'autrui sans avoir des preuves contraires. C'est qu'il n'est point permis de rien changer sans raison. On a fort disputé sur l'*argument tiré du grand nombre des approbateurs d'un sentiment*, depuis que feu M. Nicole publia son livre sur l'Église; mais tout ce qu'on peut tirer de cet argument, lorsqu'il s'agit d'approuver une raison, et non pas attester un fait, ne peut être reduit qu'à ce que je viens de dire. Et comme cent chevaux ne courent pas plus vite qu'un cheval, quoiqu'ils puissent tirer davantage, il en est de même de cent hommes comparés à un seul; ils ne sauraient aller plus droit, mais travailleront plus efficacement; ils ne sauraient mieux juger, mais ils seront capables de fournir plus de matière où le jugement puisse être exercé. C'est ce que porte le proverbe: *Plus vident oculi quam oculus.*' (*Nouveaux Essais.*)

[2] Authority *as such* cannot be the ultimate criterion of truth. The ground of the authority claimed by experts and

BOOK IV.
CHAP. XX.
Not so
many men
in Errors
as is
commonly
supposed.

18. But, notwithstanding the great noise is made in the world about errors and opinions, I must do mankind that right as to say, *There are not so many men in errors and wrong opinions as is commonly supposed.* Not that I think they embrace the truth ; but indeed, because concerning those doctrines they keep such a stir about, they have no thought, no opinion at all. For if any one should a little catechise the greatest part of the partizans of most of the sects in the world, he would not find, concerning those matters they are so zealous for, that they have any opinions of their own : much less would he have reason to think that they took them upon the examination of arguments and appearance of probability. They are resolved to stick to a party that education or interest has engaged them in ; and there, like the common soldiers of an army, show their courage and warmth as their leaders direct, without ever examining, or so much as knowing, the cause they contend for. If a man's life shows that he has no serious regard for religion ; for what reason should we think that he beats his head about the opinions of his church, and troubles himself to examine the grounds of this or that doctrine ? It is enough for him to obey his leaders, to have his hand and his tongue ready for the support of the common cause, and thereby approve himself to those who can give him credit, preferment, or protection in that society[1]. Thus men become professors

by books or churches must at last be tested by reason. We are justified in accepting an authority as infallible only on grounds that can be ultimately justified as reasonable. But reason must not be limited to understanding determined by sense alone, and exclusively under categories of sense.

[1] Perhaps Locke makes too much of self-interest as the motive which induces the mass of mankind to surrender their judgments to others, and to act blindly under foreign influence, without being aware how empty of meaning, for their own minds at least, are the watchwords of faith which they thus verbally adopt. ' The justice you would herein do to men,' says Leibniz, com-

menting on this of Locke, ' does not after all redound much to their credit ; for people are to be excused more for following erroneous opinions sincerely than selfishly. Perhaps, however, there is among men more sincerity than you seem to allow, and that without understanding fully the cause which they support, men submit themselves with an implicit trust, often blindly, but still in good faith, to the judgment of those whose authority they have once recognised.' Moreover, the elements of truth usually mixed with errors that have long and widely prevailed, must not be forgotten in explaining and excusing apparent surrender to error.

of, and combatants for, those opinions they were never
convinced of nor proselytes to ; no, nor ever had so much
as floating in their heads : and though one cannot say there
are fewer improbable or erroneous opinions in the world
than there are, yet this is certain ; there are fewer that
actually assent to them, and mistake them for truths, than
is imagined.

CHAPTER XXI.

OF THE DIVISION OF THE SCIENCES[1].

BOOK IV.
—•—
CHAP.
XXI.
Science
may be
divided
into three
sorts.

1. ALL that can fall within the compass of human understanding[2], being either, *First*, the nature of things, as they are in themselves[3], their relations[4], and their manner of operation[5]: or, *Secondly*, that which man himself ought to do, as a rational and voluntary agent, for the attainment of any end, especially happiness[6]: or, *Thirdly*, the ways and means whereby the knowledge of both the one and the other of these is attained and communicated[7] ; I think science may be divided properly into these three sorts :—

[1] 'science,' here and throughout this chapter, is used in a wider meaning than in preceding parts of the *Essay*, where it is confined to what is either intuitively, demonstratively, or sensuously certain, i. e. to *knowledge* in the strict Lockian meaning of that term. Accordingly, concrete sciences of particular substances, bodies or spirits, are held by Locke to transcend human understanding, which must be satisfied with nominal, in defect of real, essences, and is unable to interpret the secondary qualities and passive powers of bodies in the light of their primary or essential qualities. Cf. Bk. II. ch. viii; III. ch. vi; IV. ch. iii. § 26. Yet here probable judgments about things, about human actions, and about the signs of both, are included in 'science' or 'knowledge'—another example of Locke's vacillating use of words.

[2] What is here proposed is, accordingly, a 'division' of 'all that can fall within the compass of human understanding.' It ought to be a corollary from the outcome of the *Essay* regarding the origin, and especially the limits, of human knowledge and belief. One expects here a philosophical organisation, upon this basis, of the intellectual possessions and prospects of mankind, in which the facts and arguments of the *Essay* might appropriately culminate, instead of a 'division of the sciences,' analogous to that attributed to the Stoics (adopted also by Gassendi), without logical consistency or adequate philosophical basis.

[3] 'things, as they are in themselves,' i. e. as particular substances, bodies or spirits, of which we can form complex ideas that may be more or less in harmony with their real essences.

[4] 'their relations,' e. g. of sameness or difference, extent and duration, causality, &c.

[5] 'their manner of operation,' i. e. the 'modes,' simple or mixed, which may be referred to them, and which have been abstracted from them.

[6] The free actions of human agents, viewed in relation to Locke's ideal of happiness. Cf. Bk. II. chh. xxi, xxvii.

[7] The methods for finding what is, and what we ought to be.

2. *First,* The knowledge of things, as they are in their own BOOK IV.
proper beings, then constitution, properties, and operations;
CHAP.
whereby I mean not only matter and body, but spirits also, XXI.
which have their proper natures, constitutions, and operations, First,
as well as bodies. This, in a little more enlarged sense Physica.
of the word, I call Φυσική, or *natural philosophy.* The end
of this is bare speculative truth: and whatsoever can afford
the mind of man any such, falls under this branch, whether
it be God himself, angels, spirits, bodies; or any of their
affections[1], as number, and figure, &c.

3. *Secondly,* Πρακτική, The skill of right applying our own Secondly,
powers and actions, for the attainment of things good and Practica.
useful. The most considerable under this head is *ethics*[2],
which is the seeking out those rules and measures of human
actions, which lead to happiness, and the means to practise
them. The end of this is not bare speculation and the
knowledge of truth; but right, and a conduct suitable to it.

4. *Thirdly,* the third branch may be called Σημειωτική, Thirdly,
or *the doctrine of signs*; the most usual whereof being Σημειωτική.
words, it is aptly enough termed also Λογική, *logic*: the
business whereof is to consider the nature of signs, the mind
makes use of for the understanding of things, or conveying
its knowledge to others. For, since the things the mind
contemplates are none of them, besides itself[3], present to
the understanding, it is necessary that something else, as
a sign or representation of the thing it considers, should be

---

[1] 'affections'—which give rise to 'modes—simple and mixed.'

[2] 'ethics'—'Ethicks' in the early editions, here and elsewhere. The 'demonstrable' nature of abstract ethics, and its consequent claim to become 'science,' i. e. 'knowledge, in Locke's stricter meaning, repeatedly suggested in the *Essay,* scarcely holds good of the applied science here partly in view.

[3] 'besides itself.' This qualification cannot mean that one can discover even what his own mind is, when regarded as a particular spiritual substance, otherwise than through ideas of reflection upon its operations, i. e. through the ideas or phenomena in which our mind reveals to us what it is. The *Essay* throughout makes ideas, presented in 'reflection,' the indispensable source of our knowledge of ourselves; even as ideas or phenomena of sensation are the necessary condition of our cognitions of what our own bodies and the bodies around us are. The *intellectus ipse* indeed may be said to be not 'present to the understanding,' in the same way of ideas as the transitory operations of our minds are, but this could hardly be what Locke intends.

BOOK IV.
CHAP.
XXI.

present to it : and these are *ideas*[1]. And because the scene of ideas that makes one man's thoughts cannot be laid open to the immediate view of another[2], nor laid up anywhere but in the memory, a no very sure repository[3] : therefore to communicate our thoughts to one another, as well as record them for our own use, signs of our ideas are also necessary : those which men have found most convenient, and therefore generally make use of, are *articulate sounds*. The consideration, then, of *ideas* and *words* as the great instruments of knowledge, makes no despicable part of their contemplation who would take a view of human knowledge in the whole extent of it[4]. And perhaps if they were distinctly weighed, and duly considered, they would afford us another sort of logic and critic, than what we have been hitherto acquainted with[5].

This is the first and most general Division of the Objects of our Understanding.

5. This seems to me the first and most general, as well as natural division of the objects of our understanding. For a man can employ his thoughts about nothing, but either, the contemplation of *things* themselves, for the discovery of truth ; or about the things in his own power, which are his own *actions*, for the attainment of his own ends ; or the *signs* the mind makes use of both in the one and the other, and the right ordering of them, for its clearer information. All which three, viz. *things*, as they are in themselves knowable[6] ; *actions* as they depend on us, in order to happiness ; and the right use of *signs* in order to knowledge, being *toto coelo*

[1] To know what particular things or actions really are without having *ideas* of them, would, according to Locke's use of language, be to know the things or actions without knowing them. To be known they must be *signified* in and through their qualities, phenomena, or simple ideas.

[2] This is now disputed.

[3] Cf. Bk. II. ch. x. §§ 4, 5, 8, 9.

[4] *Semeiotica*, which might be called the instrumental part of ' the sciences,' in contrast to the other two divisions, the speculative and the practical, is that under which the *Essay concerning Human Understanding* itself might be placed, especially its second and third books, about *ideas* and *words*. These are our primary and secondary 'signs' of what things really are, and of what our actions ought to be.

[5] He has in view the scholastic logic, which is adapted to evolve the consequences of abstract ' maxims,' not to criticise maxims or principles themselves, in the light of experience and actual intuition. Cf. Bk. I. ch. iii. § 25. So Bacon, *Novum Organum*, I. 11-19.

[6] It is a division of knowable ' objects,' rather than of special sciences in a philosophical system, that Locke proposes.

different, they seemed to me to be the three great provinces BOOK IV.
of the intellectual world, wholly separate and distinct one CHAP.
from another[1]. XXI.

[1] Some of the defects of this ' division of the sciences,' especially how one member of the division may virtually absorb the other two, are thus exposed by Leibniz :—' Cette division a déjà été célébre chez les Anciens, car sous la logique ils comprenaient encore, comme vous faites, tout ce qu'on rapporte aux paroles, et à l'explication de nos pensées, *artes dicendi*. Cependant il y a de la difficulté là-dedans; car la science de raisonner, de juger, d'inventer, paraît bien différente de la connaissance des étymologies des mots et de l'usage des langues, qui est quelque chose d'indéfini et d'arbitraire. De plus, en expliquant les mots on est obligé de faire une course dans les sciences mêmes, comme il paraît par les dictionnaires; et de l'autre côté on ne saurait traiter la science sans donner en même temps les définitions des termes. Mais la principale difficulté qui se trouve en cette division des sciences est que chaque partie paraît engloutir le tout ; premièrement la *morale* et la *logique* tomberont dans la *physique*, prise aussi généralement qu'on vient de la dire ; car en parlant des esprits, c'est-à-dire des substances qui ont de l'entendement et de la volonté, et en expliquant cet entendement à fond, vous y ferez entrer toute la logique ; et en expliquant dans la doctrine des esprits ce qui appartient à la volonté, il faudrait parler du bien et du mal, de la félicité et de la misère, et il ne tiendra qu'à vous de pousser assez cette doctrine pour y faire entrer toute la philosophie pratique. En échange, tout pourrait entrer dans la philosophie pratique comme servant à notre félicité . . . Et en traitant toutes les matières par dictionnaires, suivant l'ordre et l'alphabet, la doctrine des langues (que vous mettez dans la *logique* avec les Anciens, c'est-à-dire dans la discursive) s'emparera à son tour du territoire des deux autres. Voilà donc vos trois grandes provinces de l'Encyclopédie en guerre continuelle, puisque l'une entreprend toujours sur les droits des autres.' (*Nouveaux Essais*.)

Before Locke, English philosophy had produced divisions of human knowledge superior to that of Locke in logical consistency and philosophic depth—in particular those of Bacon and Hobbes. The Baconian well-known map of the Intellectual World, presented in the second book of his *Advancement of Learning*—afterwards adopted with modifications by D'Alembert, in the French *Encyclopédie*—presents three great provinces, History, Poesy, and Philosophy, emanating severally from Memory, Imagination, and Reason, and comprehends an elaborate scheme of divisions and subdivisions under each of these heads. While in many ways open to criticism, it is a magnificent example of the architectonic genius of its author. An elaborate classification of ' the several subjects of knowledge' is given by Hobbes, in the 9th chapter of the First Part of the *Leviathan*, in which the cardinal principle is the distinction between History, natural or civil, or observation of facts, and Science, or knowledge derived by inference—subdivided into natural and political philosophy.

Hegel and Comte have made us familiar with attempts to organise human knowledge that have cast into the shade this crude and superficial scheme of Locke, as well as the more laboured ones of his great English predecessors.

INDICES

(A)

INDEX TO
THE TEXT OF LOCKE'S ESSAY[1]

—+—

A.

Abstraction, i. 206-7 ; puts a perfect distance betwixt men and brutes, 207-8; what, ii. 18-9; an act of the mind, i. 213-4.

Abstract ideas, why made, i. 516-7.

Abstract terms cannot be affirmed one of another, ii. 101.

Accident, i. 391.

Actions, the best evidence of men's principles, i. 71 ;. but two sorts of actions, i. 311-12, 388 ; unpleasant may be made pleasant, and how, i. 362-3; cannot be the same in different places, i. 441 ; considered as modes, or as moral, i. 481-2.

Adequate ideas, i. 502 ff.; we have not, of any species of substances, ii. 217-8.

Affirmations are only in concrete, ii. 101.

Agreement and disagreement of our ideas fourfold, ii. 168-71.

Algebra, ii. 356.

Alteration, i. 435.

Analogy useful in natural philosophy, ii. 379-82.

Anger, i. 306.

Antipathy and sympathy, whence, i. 530-1.

Arguments of four sorts, ii. 410-1 ; (1) ad verecundiam, ib.; (2) ad ignorantiam, ib.; (3) ad homi-

nem, ib.; (4) ad judicium, ib. this alone right, ib.

Aristotle, i. 115, ii. 391-2.

Arithmetic, the use of ciphers in, ii. 210.

Artificial things, are most of them collective ideas, i. 425 ; why we are less liable to confusion about artificial things than about natural, ii. 89-90; have distinct species, 90.

Assent to maxims, i. 43-4; upon hearing and understanding the terms, i. 51-4; a mark of self-evidence, ib.; not a mark of innate, ib., i. 109.

Assent to probability, ii. 365 ; ought to be proportioned to the proofs, ii. 366, 369, 429, 442 ff.

Association of ideas, i. 527 ff.; this association how made, 529-30; its ill influence as to errors and intellectual habits, 530-4; and this especially in sects of philosophy and religion, 534-5.

Assurance, ii. 375-6.

Atheism in the world, and so idea of God not innate, i. 96-7.

Atom, what, i. 442.

Attention, i. 194, 299-300.

Authority: relying on others' opinions, one great cause of error, ii. 456-7.

Axioms, not the foundation of sciences, ii. 273. (See Maxims.)

[1] This Index is the one appended to the early editions of the *Essay*, with a few corrections.

IDEAS (*continued*).

stances, are not perfect ἔκτυπα, 512 ; of modes, are perfect archetypes, 512–13.

True or False, i. 514 ff. ; when false, 523–4 ; as bare appearances in the mind, neither true nor false, 514–5, 523, 525; as referred to other men's ideas, or to real existence, or to real essences, may be true or false, 515–16 ; reason of such reference, 516 ; simple ideas referred to other men's ideas, least apt to be false, 517 ; complex ones in this respect more apt to be false, especially those of mixed modes, 518–9 ; simple ideas, referred to existence, are all true, 519–21 ; though they should be different in different men, 520; complex ideas of modes are all true, 521 ; of substances, when false, 522–3 ; ideas, when right or wrong, 525–6.

Extent of our Ideas : ideas that we are incapable of, ii. 213–14 ; that we cannot attain, because of their remoteness, 215–16 ; because of their minuteness, 216–17.

Ideas and Terms : simple ideas and modes have all abstract as well as concrete names, ii. 102 ; of substances, we have scarcely any abstract names, 102–3.

Identical propositions teach nothing, ii. 292–5.

Identity, not an innate idea, i. 93–4 ; and diversity, i. 439 ff. ; of a plant, wherein it consists, 443 ; of animals, 443–4 ; of a man, 444 ff. ; unity of substance does not always make the same identity, 445 ; personal identity, 448 ff. ; depends on the same consciousness, 450–1, 458–9, 464–5; continued existence makes identity, 469–70 ; and diversity in ideas, the first perception of the mind, ii. 169.

Idiots and madmen, i. 209–10.

Ignorance : our ignorance infinitely exceeds our knowledge, ii. 212–13 ; causes of ignorance, 213 ; (1) for want of ideas, 213–20 ; (2) for the want of a discoverable connexion between the ideas we have, 220–3 ; (3) for want of tracing the ideas we have, 223–4.

Illation, what, ii. 387.

Immensity, i. 220 ; how this idea is got, 277–8.

Immoralities of whole nations, i. 72–5.

Immortality, not annexed to any shape, ii. 239–40.

Impenetrability, i. 151–2.

Imposition of opinions unreasonable, ii. 371–4.

Impossibile est idem esse et non esse, not the first thing known, i. 59.

Impossibility, not an innate idea, i. 93.

Impression on the mind, what, i. 40–2.

Inadequate ideas, i. 502 ff.

Incompatibility, how far knowable, ii. 204.

Individuationis principium, is existence, i. 441–2.

Infallible judge of controversies, i. 102.

Inference, what, ii. 387, 393–4.

Infinite : why the idea of infinite not applicable to other ideas as well as those of quantity, since they can be as often repeated, i. 279–81 ; the idea of infinity of space or number, and of space or number infinite, must be distinguished, 281–3 ; our idea of infinite very obscure, 282 ; number furnishes us with the clearest ideas of infinite, 283 ; the idea of infinite a growing idea, 285 ; we have no positive idea of infinite, 285–6 ; our idea of infinite partly positive, partly comparative, partly negative, 286–8 ; why some men think they have an idea of infinite duration, but not of infinite space, 290–2 ; why disputes about infinity are usually perplexed, 292 ; our idea of infinity has its original in sensation and reflection, 293.

Infinity, why more commonly allowed to duration than to expansion, i. 259–61 ; how applied to God by us, 276–7 ; how we get this idea, 277–8 ; the infinity of number, duration, and space, different ways considered, 283–4.

Innate principles, to no purpose, if men can be ignorant or doubtful of them, 76–8 ; principles of my lord Herbert examined, 80 ff. ; moral

rules innate to no purpose, if efface-
able, or alterable, 85-6; innate
propositions, to be distinguished
from other propositions by their
clearness and usefulness, 111-12;
the doctrine of innate principles of
ill consequence, and how, 116-17.
Innate truths, must be the first
that are consciously known, i. 60.
Instant, what, i. 243; and continual
change, 244-5.
Intuitive knowledge, ii. 176-8; our
highest certainty, 407.
Invention, wherein it consists, i. 199.
Iron, of what advantage to mankind,
ii. 351.

J.

Joy, i. 305.
Judgment: wrong judgments in
reference to good and evil, i. 354 ff.;
wherein judgment consists, ii. 361-
2; one cause of wrong judgment,
361; judgment distinguished from
knowledge, 362.

K.

KNOWLEDGE.
Has a great connexion with
words, ii. 143, 251; how it
differs from probability, 364-5;
what, 167-8; how much our
knowledge depends on our senses,
160-1; actual, 172; habitual,
ib.; habitual, twofold, 172-5; intuitive, 176-8; intuitive the clearest,
177; intuitive irresistible, *ib.*; demonstrative, 178-85; of general
truths, is all either intuitive or
demonstrative, 185; of particular
outward existences, is sensitive,
185-8; of our own existence, intuitive, 304-5; of a God, demonstrative, 306; clear ideas do not
always produce clear knowledge,
188-9; knowledge partly necessary, partly voluntary, 357-9;
why some, and yet so little, *ib.*;
how increased by testimony, 375.
Its beginning and progress,
i. 48-51, 211-2; begins in particulars, ii. 274; it is given us in the
faculties we have to attain to it, i.
102; men's knowledge according to
the employment of their faculties,

112-14; to be got only by the application of our own thought to the
contemplation of things, 115-16.
Its Extent, ii. 190 ff.; our
knowledge goes not beyond our
ideas, 190; nor beyond the perception of their agreement and
disagreement, *ib.*; reaches not to
all connexions of our ideas, 190-2;
much less to the whole reality of
things, 191; yet very improvable if
right ways are taken, 192; of co-
existence of ideas in substances
very narrow, 199 ff.; and therefore
our knowledge of substances very
narrow, *ib.*; what required to any
tolerable knowledge of substances,
264-5; of other relations inde-
terminable, 207; of existence, 212;
certain and universal, where to
be had, 221-2; ill use of words
a great hindrance to knowledge,
223-4; general, where to be got,
224-5; lies only in our thoughts,
263-4, 266; what kind of knowledge we have of nature, 205, 352-3.
Its Reality, ii. 226 ff.; knowledge of mathematical truths, how
real, 231-2; of morality, real, 232;
of substances, how far real, 235-7;
what makes our knowledge real,
228.
Self-evident knowledge, ii.
268 ff.; of identity and diversity, as
large as our ideas, 269-71; of
co-existence, very scanty, 271-2;
of relations of modes, not so scanty,
272; of real existence, properly
none but of our own existence and
of God, 272.
Improvement of knowledge,
ii. 341 ff.; not improved by maxims,
341; why so thought, *ib.*; improved
only by perfecting and comparing
ideas, 342-3, 345-6, 354-5; and
finding their relations, 346; by intermediate ideas, 355; in substances, how to be improved, 347-9;
considering things, and not names,
the way to knowledge, 237.

L.

Language, why it changes, i. 384;
wherein it consists, ii. 3-4; its use,
47; its imperfections, 104 ff.; double

298 ; concerning substances, generally either trifling or uncertain, 299–300 ; merely verbal, how to be known, 301–2 ; abstract terms, predicated one of another, produce merely verbal propositions, *ib.* ; or part of a complex idea predicated of the whole, 302 ; more propositions merely verbal than is suspected, *ib.*; universal propositions concern not existence, 303 ; what propositions concern existence, *ib.* ; certain propositions concerning existence are particular, concerning abstract ideas may be general, 338–40 ; mental and verbal, 244 ff.; mental, hard to be treated, 245–6.

Punishment, what, i. 474 ; and reward, follow consciousness, 459–60, 467–8 ; an unconscious drunkard why punished, 462–3.

Q.

QUALITIES.
Of substances, depend on remote causes, ii. 260–2 ; leading qualities of substances known by showing, not by descriptions, 159–60 ; qualities in bodies, and ideas in the mind, i. 168–9 ; distinctions in qualities of bodies, 177–8.

Primary Qualities, what, i. 169–70 ; ideas of, how produced in us, 171–2.

Secondary Qualities, what, 170–1 ; ideas of, how produced in us, 172–3 ; depend on the primary, 173.

Primary and Secondary contrasted : ideas of primary qualities are resemblances, of secondary not, 173–4; division of qualities of bodies threefold, 178–9 ; the secondary being either (*a*) immediately, or (*b*) mediately perceivable, 181–2 ; how far the three sorts of qualities are and are thought to be resemblances, 179–80 ; the ideas of the primary alone really exist, 174; the secondary exist in things only as modes of, and conditioned by, the primary, 175–7 ; why they are ordinarily taken for real, 180–1 ; in what sense they are real, 498; they would be quite other if we could discern the real constitution of the

QUALITIES (*continued*).
parts or atoms on which they depend, 401.

Connexion between primary and secondary qualities of substances, indemonstrable, ii. 183–5 ; and for the most part quite unknown, ii. 199–204, 220–3, 255 ff.

Quotations, how little to be relied on, ii. 378–9.

R.

Real ideas, i. 497 ff.

Reason, its various significations, ii. 385–6 ; what, 386–8 ; is natural revelation, 431 ; it must judge of revelation, 438–9; it must be our last guide in everything, *ib.* ; four parts of reason, 388 ; where reason fails us, 405–7 ; necessary in all but intuition, 407–8 ; as contradistinguished to faith, what, 415–6 ; helps us not to the knowledge of innate truths, i. 42 ff.; general ideas, general terms, and reason usually grow together, 49.

Recollection, i. 298.

Reflection, i. 123–4.

Related, i. 427.

Relations, i. 426 ff., 471 ff.; proportional, 471 ; natural, 471–2 ; instituted, 472–3 ; moral, 473 ff.; are innumerable, 482–3 ; terminate in simple ideas, 483–4 ; our clear ideas of relation, 484–5 ; names of relations doubtful, 485 ; without correlative terms not so easily observed, 427–8 ; different from the things related, 428 ; change without any change in the subject, 428–9; always between two, 429; all things capable of relation, *ib.* ; the idea of the relation often clearer than of the things related, 430–1 ; all terminate in simple ideas of sensation and reflection, 431–2.

Relative, i. 427 ; some relative terms taken for external denominations, 428 ; some for absolute, *ib.*; how to be known, 431–2 ; many words, though seeming absolute, are relatives, 438.

Religion, all men have time to inquire into, ii. 444 ; but in many

INDEX TO THE

PROLEGOMENA AND ANNOTATIONS

—+•+—

Abbreviation : X = contrasted with.

—+•+—

THE END.

CATALOGUE OF DOVER BOOKS

Teach Yourself

These British books are the most effective series of home study books on the market! With no outside help they will teach you as much as is necessary to have a good background in each subject, in many cases offering as much material as a similar high school or college course. They are carefully planned, written by foremost British educators, and amply provided with test questions and problems for you to check your progress; the mathematics books are especially rich in examples and problems. Do not confuse them with skimpy outlines or ordinary school texts or vague generalized popularizations; each book is complete in itself, full without being overdetailed, and designed to give you an easily-acquired branch of knowledge.

TEACH YOURSELF ALGEBRA, P. Abbott. The equivalent of a thorough high school course, up through logarithms. 52 illus. 307pp. 4¼ x 7.　　　　　　　　　　　T680 Clothbound **$2.00**

TEACH YOURSELF GEOMETRY, P. Abbott. Plane and solid geometry, covering about a year of plane and six months of solid. 268 illus. 344pp. 4½ x 7.　　　　T681 Clothbound **$2.00**

TEACH YOURSELF TRIGONOMETRY, P. Abbott. Background of algebra and geometry will enable you to get equivalent of elementary college course. Tables. 102 illus. 204pp. 4½ x 7.
T682 Clothbound **$2.00**

TEACH YOURSELF THE CALCULUS, P. Abbott. With algebra and trigonometry you will be able to acquire a good working knowledge of elementary integral calculus and differential calculus. Excellent supplement to any course textbook. 380pp. 4¼ x 7.　　　T683 Clothbound **$2.00**

TEACH YOURSELF THE SLIDE RULE, B. Snodgrass. Basic principles clearly explained, with many applications in engineering, business, general figuring, will enable you to pick up very useful skill. 10 illus. 207pp. 4¼ x 7.　　　　　　　　　　　T684 Clothbound **$2.00**

TEACH YOURSELF MECHANICS, P. Abbott. Equivalent of part course on elementary college level, with lever, parallelogram of force, friction, laws of motion, gases, etc. Fine introduction before more advanced course. 163 illus. 271pp. 4½ x 7.　　T685 Clothbound **$2.00**

TEACH YOURSELF ELECTRICITY, C. W. Wilman. Current, resistance, voltage, Ohm's law, circuits, generators, motors, transformers, etc. Non-mathematical as much as possible. 115 illus. 184pp. 4¼ x 7.　　　　　　　　　　　　　　　　　　　　　T230 Clothbound **$2.00**

TEACH YOURSELF HEAT ENGINES E. DeVille. Steam and internal combustion engines; non-mathematical introduction for student, for layman wishing background, refresher for advanced student. 76 illus. 217pp. 4¼ x 7.　　　　　　　　　T237 Clothbound **$2.00**

TEACH YOURSELF TO PLAY THE PIANO, King Palmer. Companion and supplement to lessons or self study. Handy reference, too. Nature of instrument, elementary musical theory, technique of playing, interpretation, etc. 60 illus. 144pp. 4¼ x 7.　　T959 Clothbound **$2.00**

TEACH YOURSELF HERALDRY AND GENEALOGY, L. G. Pine. Modern work, avoiding romantic and overpopular misconceptions. Editor of new Burke presents detailed information and commentary down to present. Best general survey. 50 illus. glossary; 129pp. 4¼ x 7.
T962 Clothbound **$2.00**

TEACH YOURSELF HANDWRITING, John L. Dumpleton. Basic Chancery cursive style is popular and easy to learn. Many diagrams. 114 illus. 192pp. 4¼ x 7.　　T960 Clothbound **$2.00**

TEACH YOURSELF CARD GAMES FOR TWO, Kenneth Konstam. Many first-rate games, including old favorites like cribbage and gin and canasta as well as new lesser-known games. Extremely interesting for cards enthusiast. 60 illus. 150pp. 4¼ x 7.　　T963 Clothbound **$2.00**

TEACH YOURSELF GUIDEBOOK TO THE DRAMA, Luis Vargas. Clear, rapid survey of changing fashions and forms from Aeschylus to Tennessee Williams, in all major European traditions. Plot summaries, critical comments, etc. Equivalent of a college drama course; fine cultural background 224pp. 4¼ x 7.　　　　　　　　　　　　　　T961 Clothbound **$2.00**

TEACH YOURSELF THE ORGAN, Francis Routh. Excellent compendium of background material for everyone interested in organ music, whether as listener or player. 27 musical illus. 158pp. 4¼ x 7.　　　　　　　　　　　　　　　　　T977 Clothbound **$2.00**

TEACH YOURSELF TO STUDY SCULPTURE, William Gaunt. Noted British cultural historian surveys culture from Greeks, primitive world, to moderns. Equivalent of college survey course. 23 figures, 40 photos. 158pp. 4¼ x 7.　　　　　　　　T976 Clothbound **$2.00**

New Books

101 PATCHWORK PATTERNS, Ruby Short McKim. With no more ability than the fundamentals of ordinary sewing, you will learn to make over 100 beautiful quilts: flowers, rainbows, Irish chains, fish and bird designs, leaf designs, unusual geometric patterns, many others. Cutting designs carefully diagrammed and described, suggestions for materials, yardage estimates, step-by-step instructions, plus entertaining stories of origins of quilt names, other folklore. Revised 1962. 101 full-sized patterns. 140 illustrations. Index. 128pp. 7⅞ x 10¾.
T773 Paperbound **$1.85**

ESSENTIAL GRAMMAR SERIES
By concentrating on the essential core of material that constitutes the semantically most important forms and areas of a language and by stressing explanation (often bringing parallel English forms into the discussion) rather than rote memory, this new series of grammar books is among the handiest language aids ever devised. Designed by linguists and teachers for adults with limited learning objectives and learning time, these books omit nothing important, yet they teach more usable language material and do it more quickly and permanently than any other self-study material. Clear and rigidly economical, they concentrate upon immediately usable language material, logically organized so that related material is always presented together. Any reader of typical capability can use them to refresh his grasp of language, to supplement self-study language records or conventional grammars used in schools, or to begin language study on his own. Now available:

ESSENTIAL GERMAN GRAMMAR, Dr. Guy Stern & E. F. Bleiler. Index. Glossary of terms. 128pp. 5⅜ x 8.
T422 Paperbound **$1.00**

ESSENTIAL FRENCH GRAMMAR, Dr. Seymour Resnick. Index. Cognate list. Glossary. 159pp. 5⅜ x 8.
T419 Paperbound **$1.00**

ESSENTIAL ITALIAN GRAMMAR, Dr. Olga Ragusa. Index. Glossary. 111pp. 5⅜ x 8.
T779 Paperbound **$1.00**

ESSENTIAL SPANISH GRAMMAR, Dr. Seymour Resnick. Index. 50-page cognate list. Glossary. 138pp. 5⅜ x 8.
T780 Paperbound **$1.00**

PHILOSOPHIES OF MUSIC HISTORY: A Study of General Histories of Music, 1600-1960, Warren D. Allen. Unquestionably one of the most significant documents yet to appear in musicology, this thorough survey covers the entire field of historical research in music. An influential masterpiece of scholarship, it includes early music histories; theories on the ethos of music; lexicons, dictionaries and encyclopedias of music; musical historiography through the centuries; philosophies of music history; scores of related topics. Copiously documented. New preface brings work up to 1960. Index. 317-item bibliography. 9 illustrations; 3 full-page plates. 5⅜ x 8½. xxxiv + 382pp.
T282 Paperbound **$2.00**

MR. DOOLEY ON IVRYTHING AND IVRYBODY, Finley Peter Dunne. The largest collection in print of hilarious utterances by the irrepressible Irishman of Archey Street, one of the most vital characters in American fiction. Gathered from the half dozen books that appeared during the height of Mr. Dooley's popularity, these 102 pieces are all unaltered and uncut, and they are all remarkably fresh and pertinent even today. Selected and edited by Robert Hutchinson. 5⅜ x 8½. xii + 244p.
T626 Paperbound **$1.00**

TREATISE ON PHYSIOLOGICAL OPTICS, Hermann von Helmholtz. Despite new investigations, this important work will probably remain preeminent. Contains everything known about physiological optics up to 1925, covering scores of topics under the general headings of dioptrics of the eye, sensations of vision, and perceptions of vision. Von Helmholtz's voluminous data are all included, as are extensive supplementary matter incorporated into the third German edition, new material prepared for 1925 English edition, and copious textual annotations by J. P. C. Southall. The most exhaustive treatise ever prepared on the subject, it has behind it a list of contributors that will never again be duplicated. Translated and edited by J. P. C. Southall. Bibliography. Indexes. 312 illustrations. 3 volumes bound as 2. Total of 1749pp. 5⅜ x 8.
S15-16 Two volume set, Clothbound **$15.00**

THE ARTISTIC ANATOMY OF TREES, Rex Vicat Cole. Even the novice with but an elementary knowledge of drawing and none of the structure of trees can learn to draw, paint trees from this systematic, lucid instruction book. Copiously illustrated with the author's own sketches, diagrams, and 50 paintings from the early Renaissance to today, it covers composition; structure of twigs, boughs, buds, branch systems; outline forms of major species; how leaf is set on twig; flowers and fruit and their arrangement; etc. 500 illustrations. Bibliography. Indexes. 347pp. 5⅜ x 8.
T1016 Clothbound **$4.50**

HOW PLANTS GET THEIR NAMES, L. H. Bailey. In this basic introduction to botanical nomenclature, a famed expert on plants and plant life reveals the confusion that can result from misleading common names of plants and points out the fun and advantage of using a sound, scientific approach. Covers every aspect of the subject, including an historical survey beginning before Linnaeus systematized nomenclature, the literal meaning of scores of Latin names, their English equivalents, etc. Enthusiastically written and easy to follow, this handbook for gardeners, amateur horticulturalists, and beginning botany students is knowledgeable, accurate and useful. 11 illustrations. Lists of Latin, English botanical names. 192pp. 5⅜ x 8½.
T796 Paperbound **$1.15**

PIERRE CURIE, Marie Curie. Nobel Prize winner creates a memorable portrait of her equally famous husband in a fine scientific biography. Recounting his childhood, his haphazard education, and his experimental research (with his brother) in the physics of crystals, Mme. Curie brings to life the strong, determined personality of a great scientist at work and discusses, in clear, straightforward terms, her husband's and her own work with radium and radioactivity. A great book about two very great founders of modern science. Includes Mme. Curie's autobiographical notes. Translated by Charlotte and Vernon Kellogg. viii + 120pp. 5⅜ x 8½.
T199 Paperbound **$1.00**

STYLES IN PAINTING: A Comparative Study, Paul Zucker. Professor of Art History at Cooper Union presents an important work of art-understanding that will guide you to a fuller, deeper appreciation of masterpieces of art and at the same time add to your understanding of how they fit into the evolution of style from the earliest times to this century. Discusses general principles of historical method and aesthetics, history of styles, then illustrates with more than 230 great paintings organized by subject matter so you can see at a glance how styles have changed through the centuries. 236 beautiful halftones. xiv + 338pp. 5⅝ x 8½.
T760 Paperbound **$2.00**

NEW VARIORUM EDITION OF SHAKESPEARE
One of the monumental feats of Shakespeare scholarship is the famous New Variorum edition, containing full texts of the plays together with an entire reference library worth of historical and critical information: all the variant readings that appear in the quartos and folios; annotations by leading scholars from the earliest days of Shakespeare criticism to the date of publication; essays on meaning, background, productions by Johnson, Addison, Fielding, Lessing, Hazlitt, Coleridge, Ulrici, Swinburne, and other major Shakespeare critics; original sources of Shakespeare's inspiration. For the first time, this definitive edition of Shakespeare's plays, each printed in a separate volume, will be available in inexpensive editions to scholars, to teachers and students, and to every lover of Shakespeare and fine literature. Now ready:

KING LEAR, edited by Horace Howard Furness. Bibliography. List of editions collated in notes. viii + 503pp. 5⅜ x 8½.
T1000 Paperbound **$2.25**

MACBETH, edited by Horace Howard Furness Jr. Bibliography. List of editions collated in notes. xvi + 562pp. 5⅜ x 8½.
T1001 Paperbound **$2.25**

ROMEO AND JULIET, edited by Horace Howard Furness. Bibliography. List of editions collated in notes. xxvi + 480pp. 5⅜ x 8½.
T1002 Paperbound **$2.25**

OTHELLO, edited by Horace Howard Furness. Bibliography. List of editions collated in notes. x + 471pp. 5⅜ x 8½.
T1003 Paperbound **$2.25**

HAMLET, edited by Horace Howard Furness. Bibliography. List of editions collated in notes. Total of 926pp. 5⅜ x 8½.
T1004-1005 Two volume set, Paperbound **$4.50**

THE GARDENER'S YEAR, Karel Capek. The author of this refreshingly funny book is probably best known in U. S. as the author of "R. U. R.," a biting satire on the machine age. Here, his satiric genius finds expression in a wholly different vein: a warm, witty chronicle of the joys and trials of the amateur gardener as he watches over his plants, his soil and the weather from January to December. 59 drawings by Joseph Capek add an important second dimension to the fun. "Mr. Capek writes with sympathy, understanding and humor," NEW YORK TIMES. "Will delight the amateur gardener, and indeed everyone else," SATURDAY REVIEW. Translated by M. and R. Weatherall. 59 illustrations. 159pp. 4½ x 6½.
T1014 Paperbound **$1.00**

THE ADVANCE OF THE FUNGI, E. C. Large. The dramatic story of the battle against fungi, from the year the potato blight hit Europe (1845) to 1940, and of men who fought and won it: Pasteur, Anton de Bary, Tulasne, Berkeley, Woronin, Jensen, many others. Combines remarkable grasp of facts and their significance with skill to write dramatic, exciting prose. "Philosophically witty, fundamentally thoughtful, always mature," NEW YORK HERALD TRIBUNE. "Highly entertaining, intelligent, penetrating," NEW YORKER. Bibliography. 64 illustrations. 6 full-page plates. 488pp. 5⅜ x 8½.
T437 Paperbound **$2.25**

THE PAINTER'S METHODS AND MATERIALS, A. P. Laurie. Adviser to the British Royal Academy discusses the ills that paint is heir to and the methods most likely to counteract them. Examining 48 masterpieces by Fra Lippo Lippi, Millais, Boucher, Rembrandt, Romney, Van Eyck, Velazquez, Michaelangelo, Botticelli, Frans Hals, Turner, and others, he tries to discover how special and unique effects were achieved. Not conjectural information, but certain and authoritative. Beautiful, sharp reproductions, plus textual illustrations of apparatus and the results of experiments with pigments and media. 63 illustrations and diagrams. Index. 250pp. 5⅜ x 8.
T1019 Clothbound **$3.75**

CHANCE, LUCK AND STATISTICS, H. C. Levinson. The theory of chance, or probability, and the science of statistics presented in simple, non-technical language. Covers fundamentals by analyzing games of chance, then applies those fundamentals to immigration and birth rates, operations research, stock speculation, insurance rates, advertising, and other fields. Excellent course supplement and a delightful introduction for non-mathematicians. Formerly "The Science of Chance." Index. xiv + 356pp. 5⅜ x 8. **T1007 Paperbound $1.85**

THROUGH THE ALIMENTARY CANAL WITH GUN AND CAMERA: A Fascinating Trip to the Interior, George S. Chappell. An intrepid explorer, better known as a major American humorist, accompanied by imaginary camera-man and botanist, conducts this unforgettably hilarious journey to the human interior. Wildly imaginative, his account satirizes academic pomposity, parodies cliché-ridden travel literature, and cleverly uses facts of physiology for comic purposes. All the original line drawings by Otto Soglow are included to add to the merriment. Preface by Robert Benchley. 17 illustrations. xii + 116pp. 5⅜ x 8½. **T376 Paperbound $1.00**

TALKS TO TEACHERS ON PSYCHOLOGY and to Students on Some of Life's Ideals, William James. America's greatest psychologist .invests these lectures with immense personal charm, invaluable insights, and superb literary style. 15 Harvard lectures, 3 lectures delivered to students in New England touch upon psychology and the teaching of art, stream of consciousness, the child as a behaving organism, education and behavior, association of ideas, the gospel of relaxation, what makes life significant, and other related topics. Interesting, and still vital pedagogy. x + 146pp. 5⅜ x 8½. **T261 Paperbound $1.00**

A WHIMSEY ANTHOLOGY, collected by Carolyn Wells. Delightful verse on the lighter side: logical whimsies, poems shaped like decanters and flagons, lipograms and acrostics, alliterative verse, enigmas and charades, anagrams, linguistic and dialectic verse, tongue twisters, limericks, travesties, and just about very other kind of whimsical poetry ever written. Works by Edward Lear, Gelett Burgess, Poe, Lewis Carroll, Henley, Robert Herrick, Christina Rossetti, scores of other poets will entertain and amuse you for hours. Index. xiv + 221pp. 5⅜ x 8½. **T1020 Paperbound $1.25**

LANDSCAPE PAINTING, R. O. Dunlop. A distinguished modern artist is a perfect guide to the aspiring landscape painter. This practical book imparts to even the uninitiated valuable methods and techniques. Useful advice is interwoven throughout a fascinating illustrated history of landscape painting, from Ma Yüan to Picasso. 60 half-tone reproductions of works by Giotto, Giovanni Bellini, Piero della Francesca, Tintoretto, Giorgione, Raphael, Van Ruisdael, Poussin, Gainsborough, Monet, Cezanne, Seurat, Picasso, many others. Total of 71 illustrations, 4 in color. Index. 192pp. 7⅜ x 10. **T1018 Clothbound $6.00**

PRACTICAL LANDSCAPE PAINTING, Adrian Stokes. A complete course in landscape painting that trains the senses to perceive as well as the hand to apply the principles underlying the pictorial aspect of nature. Author fully explains tools, value and nature of various colors, and instructs beginners in clear, simple terms how to apply them. Places strong emphasis on drawing and composition, foundations often neglected in painting texts. Includes pictorial-textual survey of the art from Ancient China to the present, with helpful critical comments and numerous diagrams illustrating every stage. 93 illustrations. Index. 256pp. 5⅜ x 8. **T1017 Clothbound $3.75**

PELLUCIDAR, THREE NOVELS: AT THE EARTH'S CORE, PELLUCIDAR, TANAR OF PELLUCIDAR, Edgar Rice Burroughs. The first three novels of adventure in the thrill-filled world within the hollow interior of the earth. David Innes's mechanical mole drills through the outer crust and precipitates him into an astonishing world. Among Burroughs's most popular work. Illustrations by J. Allan St. John. 5⅜ x 8½. **T1051 Paperbound $2.00** / **T1050 Clothbound $3.75**

JOE MILLER'S JESTS OR, THE WITS VADE-MECUM. Facsimile of the first edition of famous 18th century collection of repartees, bons mots, puns and jokes, the father of the humor anthology. A first-hand look at the taste of fashionable London in the Age of Pope. 247 entertaining anecdotes, many involving well-known personages such as Colley Cibber, Sir Thomas More, Rabelais, rich in humor, historic interest. New introduction contains biographical information on Joe Miller, fascinating history of his enduring collection, bibliographical information on collections of comic material. Introduction by Robert Hutchinson. 96pp. 5⅜ x 8½. **Paperbound $1.00**

THE HUMOROUS WORLD OF JEROME K. JEROME. Complete essays and extensive passages from nine out-of-print books ("Three Men on Wheels," "Novel Notes," "Told After Supper," "Sketches in Lavender, Blue and Green," "American Wives and Others," 4 more) by a highly original humorist, author of the novel "Three Men in a Boat." Human nature is JKJ's subject: the problems of husbands, of wives, of tourists, of the human animal trapped in the drawing room. His sympathetic acceptance of the shortcomings of his race and his ability to see humor in almost any situation make this a treasure for those who know his work and a pleasant surprise for those who don't. Edited and with an introduction by Robert Hutchinson. xii + 260pp. 5⅜ x 8½. **T58 Paperbound $1.00**

Miscellaneous

THE COMPLETE KANO JIU-JITSU (JUDO), H. I. Hancock and K. Higashi. Most comprehensive guide to judo, referred to as outstanding work by Encyclopaedia Britannica. Complete authentic Japanese system of 160 holds and throws, including the most spectacular, fully illustrated with 487 photos. Full text explains leverage, weight centers, pressure points, special tricks, etc.; shows how to protect yourself from almost any manner of attack though your attacker may have the initial advantage of strength and surprise. This authentic Kano system should not be confused with the many American imitations. xii + 500pp. 5⅜ x 8.

T639 Paperbound **$2.00**

THE MEMOIRS OF JACQUES CASANOVA. Splendid self-revelation by history's most engaging scoundrel—utterly dishonest with women and money, yet highly intelligent and observant. Here are all the famous duels, scandals, amours, banishments, thefts, treacheries, and imprisonments all over Europe: a life lived to the fullest and recounted with gusto in one of the greatest autobiographies of all time. What is more, these Memoirs are also one of the most trustworthy and valuable documents we have on the society and culture of the extravagant 18th century. Here are Voltaire, Louis XV, Catherine the Great, cardinals, castrati, pimps, and pawnbrokers—an entire glittering civilization unfolding before you with an unparalleled sense of actuality. Translated by Arthur Machen. Edited by F. A. Blossom. Introduction by Arthur Symons. Illustrated by Rockwell Kent. Total of xlviii + 2216pp. 5⅜ x 8.

T338 Vol I Paperbound **$2.00**
T339 Vol II Paperbound **$2.00**
T340 Vol III Paperbound **$2.00**
The set **$6.00**

BARNUM'S OWN STORY, P. T. Barnum. The astonishingly frank and gratifyingly well-written autobiography of the master showman and pioneer publicity man reveals the truth about his early career, his famous hoaxes (such as the Fejee Mermaid and the Woolly Horse), his amazing commercial ventures, his fling in politics, his feuds and friendships, his failures and surprising comebacks. A vast panorama of 19th century America's mores, amusements, and vitality. 66 new illustrations in this edition. xii + 500pp. 5⅜ x 8.

T764 Paperbound **$1.65**

THE STORY OF THE TITANIC AS TOLD BY ITS SURVIVORS, ed. by Jack Winocour. Most significant accounts of most overpowering naval disaster of modern times: all 4 authors were survivors. Includes 2 full-length, unabridged books: "The Loss of the S.S. Titanic," by Laurence Beesley, "The Truth about the Titanic," by Col. Archibald Gracie, 6 pertinent chapters from "Titanic and Other Ships," autobiography of only officer to survive, Second Officer Charles Lightoller; and a short, dramatic account by the Titanic's wireless operator, Harold Bride. 26 illus. 368pp. 5⅜ x 8.

T610 Paperbound **$1.50**

THE PHYSIOLOGY OF TASTE, Jean Anthelme Brillat-Savarin. Humorous, satirical, witty, and personal classic on joys of food and drink by 18th century French politician, litterateur. Treats the science of gastronomy, erotic value of truffles, Parisian restaurants, drinking contests; gives recipes for tunny omelette, pheasant, Swiss fondue, etc. Only modern translation of original French edition. Introduction. 41 illus. 346pp. 5⅝ x 8⅜.

T591 Paperbound **$1.50**

THE ART OF THE STORY-TELLER, M. L. Shedlock. This classic in the field of effective story-telling is regarded by librarians, story-tellers, and educators as the finest and most lucid book on the subject. The author considers the nature of the story, the difficulties of communicating stories to children, the artifices used in story-telling, how to obtain and maintain the effect of the story, and, of extreme importance, the elements to seek and those to avoid in selecting material. A 99-page selection of Miss Shedlock's most effective stories and an extensive bibliography of further material by Eulalie Steinmetz enhance the book's usefulness. xxi + 320pp. 5⅜ x 8.

T635 Paperbound **$1.50**

CREATIVE POWER: THE EDUCATION OF YOUTH IN THE CREATIVE ARTS, Hughes Mearns. In first printing considered revolutionary in its dynamic, progressive approach to teaching the creative arts; now accepted as one of the most effective and valuable approaches yet formulated. Based on the belief that every child has something to contribute, it provides in a stimulating manner invaluable and inspired teaching insights, to stimulate children's latent powers of creative expression in drama, poetry, music, writing, etc. Mearns's methods were developed in his famous experimental classes in creative education at the Lincoln School of Teachers College, Columbia Univ. Named one of the 20 foremost books on education in recent times by National Education Association. New enlarged revised 2nd edition. Introduction. 272pp. 5⅜ x 8.

T490 Paperbound **$1.75**

FREE AND INEXPENSIVE EDUCATIONAL AIDS, T. J. Pepe, Superintendent of Schools, Southbury, Connecticut. An up-to-date listing of over 1500 booklets, films, charts, etc. 5% costs less than 25¢; 1% costs more; 94% is yours for the asking. Use this material privately, or in schools from elementary to college, for discussion, vocational guidance, projects. 59 categories include health, trucking, textiles, language, weather, the blood, office practice, wild life, atomic energy, other important topics. Each item described according to contents, number of pages or running time, level. All material is educationally sound, and without political or company bias. 1st publication. Second, revised edition. Index. 244pp. 5⅜ x 8.

T663 Paperbound **$1.50**

THE ROMANCE OF WORDS, E. Weekley. An entertaining collection of unusual word-histories that tracks down for the general reader the origins of more than 2000 common words and phrases in English (including British and American slang): discoveries often surprising, often humorous, that help trace vast chains of commerce in products and ideas. There are Arabic trade words, cowboy words, origins of family names, phonetic accidents, curious wanderings, folk-etymologies, etc. Index. xiii + 210pp. 5⅜ x 8.   T710 Paperbound **$1.25**

PHRASE AND WORD ORIGINS: A STUDY OF FAMILIAR EXPRESSIONS, A. H. Holt. One of the most entertaining books on the unexpected origins and colorful histories of words and phrases, based on sound scholarship, but written primarily for the layman. Over 1200 phrases and 1000 separate words are covered, with many quotations, and the results of the most modern linguistic and historical researches. "A right jolly book Mr. Holt has made," N. Y. Times. v + 254pp. 5⅜ x 8.   T758 Paperbound **$1.35**

AMATEUR WINE MAKING, S. M. Tritton. Now, with only modest equipment and no prior knowledge, you can make your own fine table wines. A practical handbook, this covers every type of grape wine, as well as fruit, flower, herb, vegetable, and cereal wines, and many kinds of mead, cider, and beer. Every question you might have is answered, and there is a valuable discussion of what can go wrong at various stages along the way. Special supplement of yeasts and American sources of supply. 13 tables. 32 illustrations. Glossary. Index. 239pp. 5½ x 8½.   T514 Clothbound **$4.00**

SAILING ALONE AROUND THE WORLD. Captain Joshua Slocum. A great modern classic in a convenient inexpensive edition. Captain Slocum's account of his single-handed voyage around the world in a 34 foot boat which he rebuilt himself. A nearly unparalleled feat of seamanship told with vigor, wit, imagination, and great descriptive power. "A nautical equivalent of Thoreau's account," Van Wyck Brooks. 67 illustrations. 308pp. 5⅜ x 8.   T326 Paperbound **$1.00**

FARES, PLEASE! by J. A. Miller. Authoritative, comprehensive, and entertaining history of local public transit from its inception to its most recent developments: trolleys, horsecars, streetcars, buses, elevateds, subways, along with monorails, "road-railers," and a host of other extraordinary vehicles. Here are all the flamboyant personalities involved, the vehement arguments, the unusual information, and all the nostalgia. "Interesting facts brought into especially vivid life," N. Y. Times. New preface. 152 illustrations, 4 new. Bibliography. xix + 204pp. 5⅜ x 8.   T671 Paperbound **$1.50**

HOAXES, C. D. MacDougall. Shows how art, science, history, journalism can be perverted for private purposes. Hours of delightful entertainment and a work of scholarly value, this often shocking book tells of the deliberate creation of nonsense news, the Cardiff giant, Shakespeare forgeries, the Loch Ness monster, Biblical frauds, political schemes, literary hoaxers like Chatterton, Ossian, the disumbrationist school of painting, the lady in black at Valentino's tomb, and over 250 others. It will probably reveal the truth about a few things you've believed, and help you spot more readily the editorial "gander" and planted publicity release. "A stupendous collection . . . and shrewd analysis." New Yorker. New revised edition. 54 photographs. Index. 320pp. 5⅜ x 8.   T465 Paperbound **$2.00**

A HISTORY OF THE WARFARE OF SCIENCE WITH THEOLOGY IN CHRISTENDOM, A. D. White. Most thorough account ever written of the great religious-scientific battles shows gradual victory of science over ignorant, harmful beliefs. Attacks on theory of evolution; attacks on Galileo; great medieval plagues caused by belief in devil-origin of disease; attacks on Franklin's experiments with electricity; the witches of Salem; scores more that will amaze you. Author, co-founder and first president of Cornell U., writes with vast scholarly background, but in clear, readable prose. Acclaimed as classic effort in America to do away with superstition. Index. Total of 928pp. 5⅜ x 8.   T608 Vol I Paperbound **$2.00**
                    T609 Vol II Paperbound **$2.00**

THE SHIP OF FOOLS, Sebastian Brant. First printed in 1494 in Basel, this amusing book swept Europe, was translated into almost every important language, and was a best-seller for centuries. That it is still living and vital is shown by recent developments in publishing. This is the only English translation of this work, and it recaptures in lively, modern verse all the wit and insights of the original, in satirizations of foibles and vices: greed, adultery, envy, hatred, sloth, profiteering, etc. This will long remain the definitive English edition, for Professor Zeydel has provided biography of Brant, bibliography, publishing history, influences, etc. Complete reprint of 1944 edition. Translated by Professor E. Zeydel, University of Cincinnati. All 114 original woodcut illustrations. viii + 399pp. 5½ x 8⅝.   T266 Paperbound **$2.00**

ERASMUS, A STUDY OF HIS LIFE, IDEALS AND PLACE IN HISTORY, Preserved Smith. This is the standard English biography and evaluation of the great Netherlands humanist Desiderius Erasmus. Written by one of the foremost American historians it covers all aspects of Erasmus's life, his influence in the religious quarrels of the Reformation, his overwhelming role in the field of letters, and his importance in the emergence of the new world view of the Northern Renaissance. This is not only a work of great scholarship, it is also an extremely interesting, vital portrait of a great man. 8 illustrations. xiv + 479pp. 5⅜ x 8½.   T331 Paperbound **$2.00**

CATALOGUE OF DOVER BOOKS

CHRONICLES OF THE HOUSE OF BORGIA, Frederick Baron Corvo (Frederick W. Rolfe). In the opinion of many this is the major work of that strange Edwardian literary figure, "Baron Corvo." It was Corvo's intention to investigate the notorious Borgias, from their first emergence in Spain to the Borgia saint in the 16th century and discover their true nature, disregarding both their apologists and their enemies. How well Corvo succeeded is questionable in a historical sense, but as a literary achievement and as a stylistic triumph the "Chronicles" has been a treasured favorite for generations. All the fabulous intrigues and devious currents and countercurrents of the Renaissance come vividly to life in Corvo's work, which is peopled with the notorious and notable personages of Italy and packed with fascinating lore. This is the first complete reprinting of this work, with all the appendices and illustrations. xxi + 375pp. 5⅝ x 8½.
T275 Paperbound $2.00

ERROR AND ECCENTRICITY IN HUMAN BELIEF, Joseph Jastrow. A thoroughly enjoyable exposé, by a noted psychologist, of the ineradicable gullibility of man. Episodes throughout history —180 A.D. to 1930—that will shock and amuse by revelations of our tendency to fashion belief from desire not reason: the case of "Patience Worth," Ozark woman taking down novels from dictation of 17th-century girl from Devon; "Taxil," perhaps greatest hoaxer of all time; the odic force of Baron Reichenbach; Charles Richet, Nobel Laureate, accepting brazen trickeries of Eusapia Palladino; dozens of other lunacies, crank theories, public tricksters and frauds. For anyone who likes to read about the aberrations of his race. Formerly "Wish and Wisdom." 58 illustrations; 22 full-page plates. Index. xiv + 394pp. 5⅜ x 8½.
T986 Paperbound $1.85

FADS AND FALLACIES IN THE NAME OF SCIENCE, Martin Gardner. Formerly entitled IN THE NAME OF SCIENCE, this is the standard account of various cults, quack systems, and delusions which have masqueraded as science: hollow earth fanatics, Reich and orgone sex energy, dianetics, Atlantis, multiple moons, Forteanism, flying saucers, medical fallacies like iridiagnosis, zone therapy, etc. A new chapter has been added on Bridey Murphy, psionics, and other recent manifestations in this field. This is a fair, reasoned appraisal of eccentric theory which provides excellent inoculation against cleverly masked nonsense. "Should be read by everyone, scientist and non-scientist alike," R. T. Birge, Prof. Emeritus of Physics, Univ. of California; Former President, American Physical Society. Index. x + 365pp. 5⅜ x 8.
T394 Paperbound $1.75

MONEY CONVERTER AND TIPPING GUIDE FOR EUROPEAN TRAVEL, C. Vomacka. A small, convenient handbook crammed with information on currency regulations and tipping for every European country including the Iron Curtain countries, plus Israel, Egypt, and Turkey. Currency conversion tables for every country from U.S. to foreign and vice versa. The only source of such information as phone rates, postal rates, clothing sizes, what and when to tip, duty-free imports, and dozens of other valuable topics. Always kept up to date. 128 pp. 3½ x 5¼.
T260 Paperbound 75¢

HOW ADVERTISING IS WRITTEN—AND WHY, Aesop Glim. The best material from the famous "Aesop Glim" column in Printer's Ink. Specific, practical, constructive comments and criticisms on such matters as the aims of advertising, importance of copy, art of the headline, adjusting "tone of voice," creating conviction, etc. Timely, effective, useful. Written for the person interested in advertising profession, yet it has few equals as a manual for effective writing of any kind. Revised edition. 150pp. 5⅜ x 8.
T782 Paperbound $1.25

THE WORLD'S GREAT SPEECHES, edited by Lewis Copeland and Lawrence Lamm. 255 speeches ranging over scores of topics and moods (including a special section of "Informal Speeches" and a fine collection of historically important speeches of the U.S.A. and other western hemisphere countries), present the greatest speakers of all time from Pericles of Athens to Churchill, Roosevelt, and Dylan Thomas. Invaluable as a guide to speakers, fascinating as history both past and contemporary, much material here is available elsewhere only with great difficulty. 3 indices: Topic, Author, Nation. xx + 745pp. 5⅜ x 8. T468 Paperbound $3.00

Pets

CARE AND FEEDING OF BUDGIES (SHELL PARRAKEETS), C. H. Rogers. Sources of information and supply. Index. 40 illustrations. 93pp. 5 x 7¼.
T937 Paperbound 65¢

THE CARE AND BREEDING OF GOLDFISH, Anthony Evans. Hundreds of important details about indoor and outdoor pools and aquariums; the history, physical features and varieties of goldfish; selection, care, feeding, health and breeding—with a special appendix that shows you how to build your own goldfish pond. Enlarged edition, newly revised. Bibliography. 22 full-page plates; 4 figures. 129pp. 5 x 7¼.
T935 Paperbound 75¢

OBEDIENCE TRAINING FOR YOUR DOG, C. Wimhurst. You can teach your dog to heel, retrieve, sit, jump, track, climb, refuse food, etc. Covers house training, developing a watchdog, obedience tests, working trials, police dogs. "Proud to recommend this book to every dog owner who is attempting to train his dog," says Blanche Saunders, noted American trainer, in her Introduction. Index. 34 photographs. 122pp. 5 x 7¼. T938 Paperbound $1.00

History, Political Science

THE POLITICAL THOUGHT OF PLATO AND ARISTOTLE, E. Barker. One of the clearest and most accurate expositions of the corpus of Greek political thought. This standard source contains exhaustive analyses of the "Republic" and other Platonic dialogues and Aristotle's "Politics" and "Ethics," and discusses the origin of these ideas in Greece, contributions of other Greek theorists, and modifications of Greek ideas by thinkers from Aquinas to Hegel. "Must" reading for anyone interested in the history of Western thought. Index. Chronological Table of Events. 2 Appendixes. xxiv + 560pp. 5⅜ x 8. T521 Paperbound **$2.50**

THE IDEA OF PROGRESS, J. B. Bury. Practically unknown before the Reformation, the idea of progress has since become one of the central concepts of western civilization. Prof. Bury analyzes its evolution in the thought of Greece, Rome, the Middle Ages, the Renaissance, to its flowering in all branches of science, religion, philosophy, industry, art, and literature, during and following the 16th century. Introduction by Charles Beard. Index. xl + 357pp. 5⅜ x 8. T40 Paperbound **$2.00**

THE ANCIENT GREEK HISTORIANS, J. B. Bury. This well known, easily read work covers the entire field of classical historians from the early writers to Herodotus, Thucydides, Xenophon, through Poseidonius and such Romans as Tacitus, Cato, Caesar, Livy. Scores of writers are studied biographically, in style, sources, accuracy, structure, historical concepts, and influences. Recent discoveries such as the Oxyrhinchus papyri are referred to, as well as such great scholars as Nissen, Gomperz, Cornford, etc. "Totally unblemished by pedantry." Outlook. "The best account in English," Dutcher, A Guide to Historical Lit. Bibliography, Index. x + 281pp. 5⅜ x 8. T397 Paperbound **$1.65**

HISTORY OF THE LATER ROMAN EMPIRE, J. B. Bury. This standard work by the leading Byzantine scholar of our time discusses the later Roman and early Byzantine empires from 395 A.D. through the death of Justinian in 565, in their political, social, cultural, theological, and military aspects. Contemporary documents are quoted in full, making this the most complete reconstruction of the period and a fit successor to Gibbon's "Decline and Fall." "Most unlikely that it will ever be superseded," Glanville Downey, Dumbarton Oaks Research Lib. Geneological tables. 5 maps. Bibliography. Index. 2 volumes total of 965pp. 5⅜ x 8. T398, 399 Two volume set, Paperbound **$4.50**

A HISTORY OF ANCIENT GEOGRAPHY, E. H. Bunbury. Standard study, in English, of ancient geography; never equalled for scope, detail. First full account of history of geography from Greeks' first world picture based on mariners, through Ptolemy. Discusses every important map, discovery, figure, travel expedition, war, conjecture, narrative, bearing on subject. Chapters on Homeric geography, Herodotus, Alexander expedition, Strabo, Pliny, Ptolemy, would stand alone as exhaustive monographs. Includes minor geographers, men not usually regarded in this context: Hecataeus, Pytheas, Hipparchus, Artemidorus, Marinus of Tyre, etc. Uses information gleaned from military campaigns such as Punic Wars, Hannibal's passage of Alps, campaigns of Lucullus, Pompey, Caesar's wars, the Trojan War. New introduction by W. H. Stahl, Brooklyn College. Bibliography. Index. 20 maps. 1426pp. 5⅜ x 8. T570-1, clothbound, 2-volume set **$12.50**

POLITICAL PARTIES, Robert Michels. Classic of social science, reference point for all later work, deals with nature of leadership in social organization on government and trade union levels. Probing tendency of oligarchy to replace democracy, it studies need for leadership, desire for organization, psychological motivations, vested interests, hero worship, reaction of leaders to power, press relations, many other aspects. Trans. by E. & C. Paul. Introduction. 447pp. 5⅜ x 8. T569 Paperbound **$2.00**

A HISTORY OF HISTORICAL WRITING, Harry Elmer Barnes. Virtually the only adequate survey of the whole course of historical writing in a single volume. Surveys developments from the beginnings of historiographies in the ancient Near East and the Classical World, up through the Cold War. Covers major historians in detail, shows interrelationship with cultural background, makes clear individual contributions, evaluates and estimates importance; also enormously rich upon minor authors and thinkers who are usually passed over. Packed with scholarship and learning, clear, easily written. Indispensable to every student of history. Revised and enlarged up to 1961. Index and bibliography. xv + 442pp. 5⅜ x 8½. T104 Paperbound **$2.25**

Prices subject to change without notice.

Dover publishes books on art, music, philosophy, literature, languages, history, social sciences, psychology, handcrafts, orientalia, puzzles and entertainments, chess, pets and gardens, books explaining science, intermediate and higher mathematics, mathematical physics, engineering, biological sciences, earth sciences, classics of science, etc. Write to:

Dept. catrr.
Dover Publications, Inc.
180 Varick Street, N. Y. 14, N. Y.